Oxford Resources for IB
Diploma Programme

2023 EDITION

BIOLOGY

Andrew Allott

STUDY GUIDE

OXFORD
UNIVERSITY PRESS

Great Clarendon Street, Oxford, OX2 6DP, United Kingdom

Oxford University Press is a department of the University of Oxford.
It furthers the University's objective of excellence in research, scholarship, and education by publishing worldwide. Oxford is a registered trade mark of Oxford University Press in the UK and in certain other countries.

First published in 2023

British Library Cataloguing in Publication Data
Data available

9781382016438

9781382016445 (ebook)

10 9 8 7 6 5 4 3 2 1

Paper used in the production of this book is a natural, recyclable product made from wood grown in sustainable forests.

The manufacturing process conforms to the environmental regulations of the country of origin.

Printed in China by Golden Cup.

Acknowledgements

The publisher and authors would like to thank the following for permission to use photographs and other copyright material:

Cover: Jasius/Getty Images.

Photos: p2(l): Voices in the Sea; p2(r): L. Shyamal / Wikimedia Commons (CC BY SA 2.5); p5: Jerome Walker / Wikimedia Commons; p8(t): Andrew Allott; p8(b): NASA; p15(t): Glow Images / Getty Images; 15(b): Andrew Allott; p17(t): Science Photo Library / Alamy Stock Photo; p17(m): Volodymyr Dvornyk / Shutterstock; p17(b): nobeastsofierce / Shutterstock; p25: Yikrazuul / Wikimedia Commons; p60(t): Eye of Science / Science Photo Library; p60(b): Wellcome Collection (CC BY 4.0); p61: Toyoshi Fujimoto, Research Institute for Diseases of Old Age; p64(t): Science Photo Library / Alamy Stock Photo; p64(b): Science History Images / Alamy Stock Photo; p65(tl): Louisa Howard; p65(tr): agefotostock / Alamy Stock Photo; p65(ml): Microscape / Science Photo Library; p65(bl): Science History Images / Alamy Stock Photo; p65(br): Louisa Howard; p69(tr): Science Pictures Ltd / Science Photo Library; p69(bl): M.I. Walker / Science Photo Library; p77: BioMedical / Shutterstock; p78: Science History Images / Alamy Stock Photo; p96(P): Rattiya Thongdumhyu/Shutterstock; p96(A): Jose Luis Calvo / Shutterstock; p96(M): Dimarion / Shutterstock; p96(I): staticd / Wikimedia Commons (CC BY-SA 3.0); p98: Josef Reischig / Wikimedia Commons (CC BY-SA 3.0); p104: M.I. Walker / Science Photo Library; p105: Rudmer Zwerver / Shutterstock; p106: PR Philippe Vago, ISM / Science Photo Library; p109: Zita / Shutterstock; p110: The History Collection / Alamy Stock Photo; p111(l): sudarat wilairat / Alamy Stock Photo; p111(r): Peter R. Crane, Pollyanna von Knorring; p117: Choksawatdikorn / Shutterstock; p118(t): Emilio Ereza / Alamy Stock Photo; p118(b): Al Carrera / Shutterstock; p121: blickwinkel / Alamy Stock Photo; p129: © The Royal Society for the Protection of Birds; p130: Mediscan / Alamy Stock Photo; p133(tl): Jon Houseman and Matthew Ford / Wikimedia Commons (CC BY-SA 4.0); p133(mr): Nuance Communications, Inc.; p133(bl): Biophoto Associates / Science Photo Library; p135: M.R.W.HH / Wikimedia Commons; p144: Susumu Nishinaga / Science Photo Library; p145: Choksawatdikorn / Shutterstock; p147: NIBSC / Science Photo Library; p148: Oxford University Press; p159: Josie Elias / Alamy Stock Photo; p160(l): joanna wnuk / Shutterstock; p160(m): Kiorio / Shutterstock; p160(r): agefotostock / Alamy Stock Photo; p178: Freepik Company; p179(t): umbrellahead56 / Wikimedia Commons (CC BY 2.0); p179(b): Public Domain; p180(l): Andrew Allott; p180(r): The History Collection / Alamy Stock Photo; p181: uzuri / Shutterstock; p182(l): Nature Picture Library / Alamy Stock Photo; p182(r): Reading Room 2020 / Alamy Stock Photo; p183(m): Manor Photography / Alamy Stock Photo; p183(b): Ondrej Prosicky / Alamy Stock Photo; p184(t): DrimaFilm / Shutterstock; p184(b): The Book Worm / Alamy Stock Photo; p185(t): First Collection / Alamy Stock Photo; p185(bl): Public Domain; p185(br): Iakov Filimonov / Shutterstock; p186: NASA Image Collection / Alamy Stock Photo; p188(t): Mike Prince / Flicker (CC BY 2.0); p188(b) bilwissedition Ltd. & Co. KG / Alamy Stock Photo; p194(tr): nattanan726 / Shutterstock; p190(t): imageBROKER / Alamy Stock Photo; p190(b): Sekar B / Shutterstock; p191: BCC Bioscience Image Library; p193(l): Frank Vincentz / Wikimedia Commons; p193(r): Fir Mamat / Alamy Stock Photo; p194(tl): Jeff Dean (CC BY-SA 2.5); p194(br): Erni / Shutterstock; p196: mauritius images GmbH / Alamy Stock Photo; p197(tl): Natural History Museum, London / Science Photo Library; p197(tm): Peter Brown; p197(tr): Peter Brown; p197(bl): Didier Descouens / Wikimedia Commons (CC BY-SA 4.0); p197(br): Atudu / Wikimedia Commons; p198: Melanie Hobson / Shutterstock; p199(l): Wellcome Collection; p199(r): Gregory F. Maxwell / Wikimedia Commons (GFDL-1.2 only); p201: Andrew Thomson / Alamy Stock Photo; p203(t): Kevin Thiele; p203(b): Andrew Allott; p204(l): Maria Azzurra Mugnai / Wikimedia Commons (CC BY-SA 3.0); p204(r): Doug Allan / Photodisc / Getty Images; p205: Craig Lovell / Eagle Visions Photography / Alamy Stock Photo; p207(t): Chronicle / Alamy Stock Photo; p207(b): Public Domain; p211: Andriy Blokhin / Shutterstock; p215: GL Archive / Alamy Stock Photo; p216(l): Interior Department / Alamy Stock Photo; p216(r): Neil Bowman / Alamy Stock Photo; p221(t): agefotostock / Alamy Stock Photo; p221(b): Bazzano Photography / Alamy Stock Photo; p222: agefotostock / Alamy Stock Photo; p227: Gizem Gecim / Alamy Stock Photo; p229: Mark Baldwin-Smith / Wikimedia Commons (CC BY-SA 3.0); p230: Hylke E. Beck.

Artwork by Q2A Media, Six Red Marbles, Aptara Inc., International Baccalaureate, George Gilchrist, Alison Allott, and Oxford University Press.

Every effort has been made to contact copyright holders of material reproduced in this book. Any omissions will be rectified in subsequent printings if notice is given to the publisher.

Contents

Answers: www.oxfordsecondary.com/ib-science-support

Themes in IB Biology

Biology is the study of life. Biologists have identified characteristics that are encountered at all levels of organization (molecule, cell, organism and ecosystem) and in all forms of life, throughout the world. Four pairs of these recurring themes feature in IB Biology.

Theme A: Unity and diversity

Unity is oneness and is characterized by similarities rather than differences. There are striking similarities between living organisms. Some are due to convergence, with different groups finding the same solution to a problem, so becoming similar in certain ways. More commonly unity is due to shared ancestry. Even if differences develop, species retain many of the characteristics that their common ancestor held, so they are fundamentally similar. Some characteristics such as the genetic code are shared by all organisms, showing the unity of all life as it has evolved from a universal common ancestor.

Diversity is variety, so is characterized by differences. The rich biodiversity of life has developed by evolution. By developing differences, living organisms avoid competition and can thrive in the widely different habitats on Earth.

Theme B: Form and function

Form is the three-dimensional structure of something. Living organisms develop intricate and recognizable forms at every level of organization from molecule to ecosystem.

Function is the role of something. By performing its functions, each part of a system helps the whole system. If something in a cell, organism, species or ecosystem does not function effectively, the chances of survival are decreased. There is therefore powerful natural selection for efficient performance of function.

There is a very close relationship between form and function. To perform a function effectively, appropriate form is required. This is known in biology as adaptation. Form is often superbly adapted to function, not through design, but by evolution over many generations and across immensities of time.

Theme C: Interaction and interdependence

In an interaction, each entity has an effect on the other entity—the effects are reciprocal rather than unidirectional. There are interactions in living systems, at every level, from molecules to the whole biosphere.

Effects can be helpful or harmful. In parasitism, for example, the parasite benefits and the host is harmed. There is a trend for evolution of interactions which help rather than harm. A relationship between two species in which each helps the other is a mutualism.

Interdependence is a relationship in which each entity is reliant on the other. The interactions between them are essential.

Systems are based on interactions and interdependence of components. Systems result in emergence of new properties at each level of biological organization.

Theme D: Continuity and change

Continuity is continuing without gaps or interruptions. Change is something becoming different. Matter and energy show both continuity and change. The carbon atoms recycled by living organisms have existed since they were produced in stars billions of years ago, but chemical reactions change how they are bonded to other atoms. Energy cannot be created or destroyed but can be changed from one form to another.

Life continues in an individual as long as equilibrium is maintained in the body and external threats are countered. Harmful changes tend to happen and need to be reversed. Continuity in a species requires reproduction, because no individual lives for ever. It also requires evolutionary change in response to environmental change. Continuity in ecosystems depends on recycling of elements and a supply of energy.

Themes are tested in IB Biology exams. There will be one question based on each Theme in Paper 1, and some questions in Section B of Paper 2 will also be based on a Theme.

Levels of organization in IB Biology

Level 1: Molecules	Level 2: Cells
A molecule is a group of atoms joined together by covalent bonds. The simplest molecules consist of two atoms joined by a single bond, for example hydrogen. Organisms make a huge range of molecules, based on carbon. Macromolecules made by organisms, such as proteins and DNA, are very large. Molecular biologists aim to explain all life processes in terms of the structure and activities of molecules made by cells.	A cell is the smallest unit of self-sustaining life. New cells can only be formed by division of existing cells. Cells have cytoplasm with enzymes that catalyse the chemical reactions of metabolism. Cells are all bounded by a plasma membrane, separating them from the external environment so internal chemical concentrations can be controlled. A highly ordered state is maintained in the cell using instructions in the genes and a supply of energy.

Level 3: Organisms	Level 4: Ecosystems
An organism is an individual living being. It may consist of one cell or many genetically identical cells. New organisms can only be formed by reproduction of existing organisms. A species is a group of organisms that can reproduce with each other, passing on genes which determine the characteristics of each organism and the species. An organism's survival depends on its interdependent parts continuing to perform their functions.	An ecosystem is a part of the biosphere, such as a lake or forest. In an ecosystem there are many relationships between the living organisms and between the organisms and the non-living environment. An ecosystem therefore includes all organisms plus the environment. Relationships within an ecosystem help regulate it and allow persistence over long periods of time, but if external influences break key relationships, there can be rapid collapse.

Levels of organization are tested in IB Biology exams. Multiple-choice questions in Paper 1 are organized according to Levels, starting with Molecules and ending with Ecosystems. In Section B of Paper 2, some questions will be based on one Level.

Assessment in IB Biology

Twenty per cent of marks that decide biology grades are for the Internal Assessment, a scientific investigation assessed by the teacher; 80% of marks are awarded for written exams. The exams are in three parts for both SL and HL biology students. Papers 1A and 1B are taken in the same session (morning or afternoon). Paper 2 is taken in a separate session.

Standard level (SL)	Higher level (HL)
Paper 1A (45 minutes) • 30 multiple–choice questions, testing knowledge and understanding of the whole syllabus.	**Paper 1A (60 minutes)** • 40 multiple–choice questions, testing knowledge and understanding of the whole syllabus.
Paper 1B (45 minutes) • Four questions testing data-analysis and syllabus knowledge, with a total of 25 marks. • Data used in these questions is in a variety of forms such as graphs, photographs, diagrams and micrographs. • The syllabus includes many items titled *application of skills*, which are tested in these questions. About half of the 25 marks are for skills in biological science, such as the design of experiments including controls. • The other half of the marks are for knowledge and understanding of the syllabus. • One question will be based on each of the four Themes in the syllabus (Themes A, B, C and D). • Each question is worth between 5 and 8 marks, and is divided into parts (a, b, c). At least one question has a 3-mark part, but most parts of the questions are shorter.	**Paper 1B (60 minutes)** • Four questions testing data-analysis and syllabus knowledge, with a total of 35 marks. • Data used in these questions is in a variety of forms such as graphs, photographs, diagrams and micrographs. • The syllabus includes many items titled *application of skills*, which are tested in these questions. About half of the 35 marks are for skills in biological science, such as the design of experiments including controls. • The other half of the marks are for knowledge and understanding of the syllabus. • One question will be based on each of the four Themes in the syllabus (Themes A, B, C and D). • Each question is worth between 7 and 10 marks, and is divided into parts (a, b, c). In each of the four questions there is at least one 3-mark or 4-mark part, but most parts are shorter.
Paper 2 (1 hour and 30 minutes) **Section A** • Section A has 34 marks, with between 10 and 12 marks for Question 1 (the data-analysis question). • Question 1 is based on scientific research and tests data-analysis skills and general biological understanding, rather than knowledge of specific parts of the syllabus. The data can be in a variety of forms such as tables, graphs and charts. The skills tested are also varied, for example calculating percentages, comparing results, identifying trends, correlations and other relationships, and evaluating evidence. • The remainder of Section A is short–answer questions (usually 5 or 6) that test knowledge and understanding of the syllabus. All the four Levels of Organization will be tested (Molecules, Cells, Organisms and Ecosystems) . **Section B** • Section B has a choice of two extended–response questions, one of which is answered. • Each question has three parts (a, b and c), with a mark total of 16. • One of the three parts of each question is longer, with 7 or 8 marks. • For the Section B question answered, one mark is for overall quality. To earn this mark, answers must stick to the question, be concise and understood easily without re-reading.	**Paper 2 (2 hours and 30 minutes)** **Section A** • Section A has 48 marks, with between 12 and 15 marks for Question 1 (the data-analysis question) . • Question 1 is based on scientific research and tests data-analysis skills and general biological understanding, rather than knowledge of specific parts of the syllabus. The data can be in a variety of forms such as tables, graphs and charts. The skills tested are also varied, for example calculating percentages, comparing results, identifying trends, correlations and other relationships, and evaluating evidence. • The remainder of Section A is short–answer questions (usually 7 or 8) that test knowledge and understanding of the syllabus. All the four Levels of Organization will be tested (Molecules, Cells, Organisms and Ecosystems). **Section B** • Section B has a choice of three extended–response questions, two of which are answered. • Each question has three parts (a, b and c), with a mark total of 16. • One of the three parts of each question is longer, with 7 or 8 marks. • For both Section B questions answered, one mark is for overall quality. To earn this mark, answers must stick to the question, be concise and understood easily without re-reading.

1 Molecules

A1.1 Water

1. Water is essential for life

Water with substances dissolved in it is an aqueous solution. The first living cells originated in aqueous solutions, sometimes called "primeval soup".

A medium is something in which processes can occur. The eight processes of life happen in water, so after more than three billion years of evolution, water is still the medium for life.

Metabolism: because aqueous solutions are liquid, both the water and solutes dissolved in it are free to move and, in some cases, react chemically. Reactants and products of most chemical reactions in living organisms (= metabolism) are dissolved in water.

Nutrition: the reactions of both photosynthesis and digestion take place in aqueous solution.

Growth: cytoplasm is an aqueous solution, so cells must absorb water by osmosis to increase in size.

Reproduction: sperm swim to the egg through water; mammalian foetuses are supported by water in the uterus.

Movement: aquatic organisms swim through water or drift in currents; pumping of blood and sap transports substances dissolved in water.

Response to stimuli: nerve impulses are movements of dissolved Na^+ and K^+ ions; hormone transport is in blood.

Excretion: urine is an aqueous solution of waste products; excretion of waste gases (for example, CO_2) requires a moist surface.

Homeostasis: blood plasma and tissue fluid are aqueous solutions that are regulated to form a stable and ideal internal environment for cells.

2. Hydrogen bonds

A **molecule** is two or more atoms joined together by one or more covalent bonds. A covalent bond is formed when two atoms share a pair of electrons. In some cases, the nucleus of one of the atoms is more attractive to the electrons than the other, so the electrons are not shared equally. The consequence of this is that the covalent bond is polar, with one of the atoms having a slight positive charge and the other a slight negative charge. Molecules with polar covalent bonds have **polarity**.

Water molecules are polar. A hydrogen nucleus is less attractive to electrons than an oxygen nucleus, so in a water molecule the two hydrogen atoms have a slight positive charge and the oxygen atom has a slight negative charge.

▸ *Water molecule with delta plus and delta minus poles*

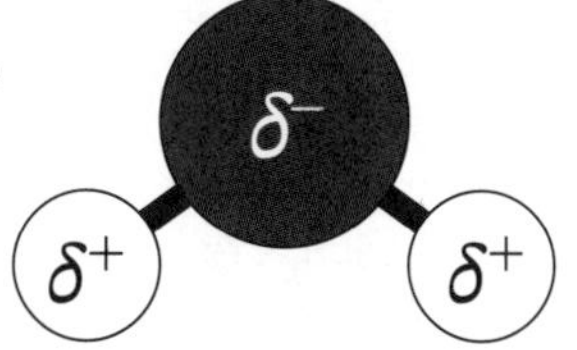

The two bonds between oxygen and hydrogen atoms in a water molecular are **intramolecular**. An **intermolecular** bond can form between the positive pole of one water molecule and the negative pole of another water molecule. This is called a **hydrogen bond**.

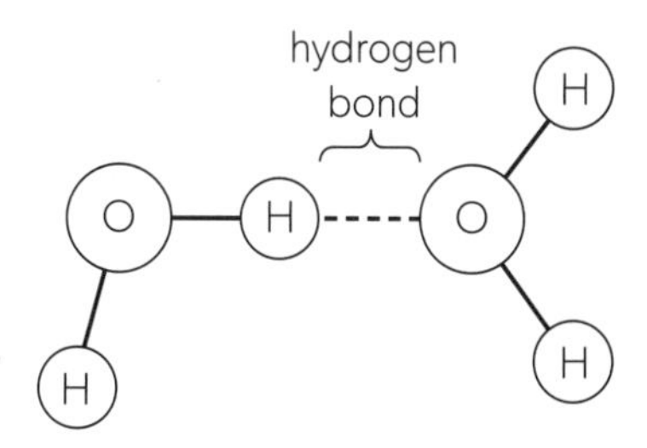

Individual hydrogen bonds are weak, but water molecules are small so relatively large numbers of the bonds form in a volume of water. Collectively, these bonds influence the properties of water markedly.

3. Cohesion

Water molecules stick to each other (cohere) because of the hydrogen bonds that form between them.

- Strong pulling forces (tensions) are exerted to suck water up to the tops of the tallest trees in tubular xylem vessels. Because of the cohesion resulting from hydrogen bonds, the columns of water molecules in these vessels rarely break despite powerful suction forces.
- The surface of water on ponds is used as a habitat by some animals, even though they are denser than water (e.g. the insect *Gerris lacustris* pictured right).

To break through the water surface, hydrogen bonds would have to be broken, which requires more energy than is available. This effect of water surfaces forming a cohesive structure that resists breakage is called surface tension.

4. Adhesion

Whereas cohesion is water molecules sticking to each other, adhesion is water sticking to another substance. Adhesion happens if the other substance is hydrophilic.

Hydrophilic substances are attractive to water because they can make intermolecular bonds with the water molecules.

Polar and charged materials are hydrophilic.

- Polar substances such as cellulose in plant cell walls form hydrogen bonds with water. Cell walls therefore tend to remain saturated with water and draw more water from the nearest supply if they have become unsaturated due to evaporation, for example when a leaf transpires.
- Capillary action is water being drawn through narrow spaces because it adheres to the surfaces of the spaces. Water moves through pores in dry soils by this process because the solids in the soil—humus (dead organic matter) and particles of sand, silt and clay—are hydrophilic. The water can move upwards.

5. Water is a solvent

A wide range of hydrophilic molecules and ions dissolve in water. Polar molecules dissolve by forming hydrogen bonds with water. Ions with positive charges form electrostatic interactions with the δ^- poles of water molecules and negative ions with the δ^+ poles. For example, sodium chloride dissolves in water like so:

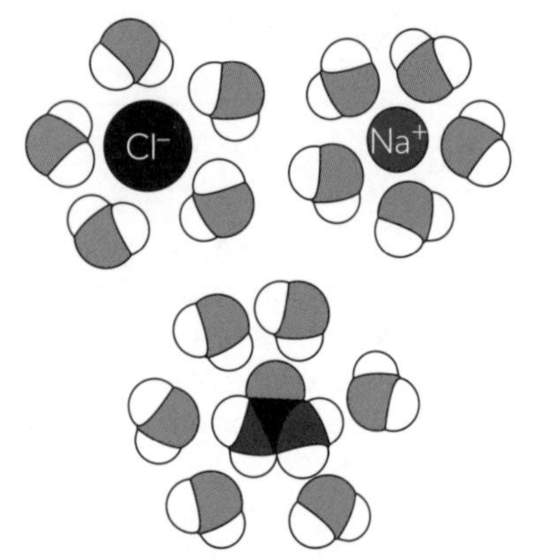

Urea molecules are polar and dissolve with hydrogen bonds between positive and negative poles of the urea and water molecules.

Most chemical reactions in cells are catalysed by enzymes and take place in aqueous solution, which allows both enzymes and substrates to move, so substrate–active site collisions can occur.

Transport systems in plants and animals rely on the solvent properties. Blood plasma, xylem sap and phloem sap are all aqueous solutions that are pumped to transfer the solutes from one part of the plant or animal to another.

If a substance is not hydrophilic it is said to be **hydrophobic**. This does not mean that it is repelled by water, but that water molecules are more strongly attracted to each other than to the non-polar molecules of hydrophobic substances. Hydrophobic substances are therefore insoluble in water. They can also form a barrier to water and hydrophilic substances. The wax on leaf surfaces and oils on human skin are hydrophobic and prevent dehydration. Hydrocarbon tails in the centre of cell membranes form a barrier that allows cells to regulate the movement of hydrophilic substances across the membrane.

6. Physical properties of water

Air and water have markedly different physical properties, with consequences for animals that swim in water or fly in the air. This can be illustrated with black-throated loons (birds that dive in water to feed and also fly) and the ringed seal (a mammal that only comes out of the water to breed).

Buoyancy—solids float in fluids if their density is lower. Consider the densities in the table. The seal's density is close to that of seawater so it can float easily. The loon's density is far higher than that of air so it beats its wings to remain airborne.

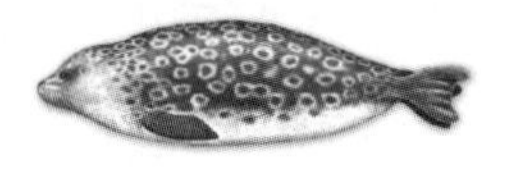

	Density (mg per cm^3)
Pure water	1,000
Seawater	1,025
Air	1.225
Loon	700–850
Seal	1,025–1,045

Viscosity—resistance to flow of a fluid due to cohesion between the molecules. Water has high viscosity due to hydrogen bonding. Air's viscosity is more than 50 times less. The seal has to overcome much more resistance when it swims through water than the loon when it flies in air.

Thermal conductivity—the ability of a material to transfer heat. Water's thermal conductivity is more than 20 times that of air. The seal is therefore more vulnerable to hypothermia in the cold northerly habitats of these species.

Specific heat capacity—the quantity of heat needed to raise the temperature of a gram of a material by one degree. It takes 3,500 times as much heat to raise the temperature of a given volume of water by a degree than air because water is much denser. Water therefore heats up and cools down much more slowly than air; marine and freshwater habitats are much more thermally stable than terrestrial habitats.

AHL

7. Extraplanetary origin of water on Earth

The Earth was formed from gas and dust about 4.5 billion years ago. Initially any water would have boiled and been lost, so the 1.4 billion cubic kilometres of water now on Earth must have arrived later, when the Earth had cooled down, so the water could remain liquid and be retained.

The leading hypothesis is that the water was brought when asteroids containing ice collided with the early Earth. The ice would have melted, adding to the volume of liquid water in the growing oceans.

Two factors promote the retention of water in a liquid state on Earth:

- strong gravitational pull due to Earth's size
- intensity of sunlight due to distance from the Sun keeps the Earth below 100°C and mostly above 0°C.

8. Extra-terrestrial life and water

Water is a unifying feature in biology—it is the medium of life for all species on Earth. We may reasonably expect life only to be found on planets in the universe that have liquid water. When we are searching for extra-terrestrial life, we need not look on dry planets!

To retain liquid water, a planet must be large enough for gravity to be strong and temperatures must be warm enough for ice to melt, but not so hot that water boils. The planet must be in the "Goldilocks zone" which is the range of distances from a star that keep temperatures between 0 and 100°C.

Planet	Distance from Sun (km)	Average temperature (°C)
Venus	108×10^6	+462
Earth	149×10^6	+14
Mars	216×10^6	−60

Meanings of terms

Acid—a substance that can donate one or more protons and so become negatively charged, for example deoxyribonucleic acid (DNA).

Atom—a unit of matter with positively charged protons grouped in the nucleus and negatively charged electrons in orbitals around the nucleus; atoms have no net charge because the number of protons and electrons is equal.

Base—a substance that can accept one or more protons (H^+) and so become positively charged, for example adenine and other bases in DNA.

Catalyst—a substance that increases the rate of a reaction but is itself unchanged at the end of the reaction.

Concentration—the amount of substance per unit volume.

Condensation—a reaction in which two molecules are combined into one molecule and water is eliminated.

Covalent bond—a region of high electron density between two atoms due to the sharing of a pair of electrons, which attracts the nuclei of both atoms, holding them together.

Hydrogen bond—an attraction between an electronegative atom (such as oxygen) and a hydrogen atom bonded to another electronegative atom.

Hydrolysis—the separation of one molecule into two using hydrogen (H) and hydroxyl groups (OH) released by splitting a water molecule.

Hydrophilic—having an affinity (attraction) for water.

Hydrophobic—having a low affinity for water and more affinity for non-polar molecules.

Intermolecular force—an attraction between molecules.

Intramolecular force—a bond between atoms within a molecule.

Ion—an atom or molecule that has become positively charged by losing one or more electrons or negatively charged by gaining one or more electrons.

Ionic bond—a bond formed by attraction between positively- charged and negatively charged ions or between positively- charged and negatively charged groups on molecules.

Isotope—one of the two or more alternative forms of an element, with the same number of protons and electrons per atom as other forms, but a different number of neutrons.

Macromolecule—a molecule with a molecular mass of more than 10,000

Molecule—two or more atoms joined together by one or more covalent bonds.

Oxidation—a reaction in which hydrogen is removed, electrons are removed, or oxygen is added.

Pigment—a substance that absorbs wavelengths of visible light and so appears coloured.

Polymer—a molecule consisting of a series of many subunits linked by covalent bonds; an oligomer has fewer than 10 subunits.

Radioactive—a type of isotope with an unstable nucleus which can emit radiation (α, β or γ rays).

Reduction—a reaction in which hydrogen is added, electrons are added, or oxygen is removed.

Solute—a dissolved substance in a solution.

Solvent—a liquid that can dissolve other substances to make a solution.

Synthesis—the production of more complex molecules from simpler substances by one or more chemical reactions.

A1.2 Nucleic acids

1. DNA is the universal genetic material

Living organisms are constructed out of molecules. Genes are the instructions for doing this and are themselves constructed out of molecules.

A key feature in the unity of life is that the molecule used as genetic material in all living organisms is DNA (deoxyribonucleic acid).

Some viruses, including coronaviruses (such as Covid) use RNA instead of DNA as genetic material, but viruses are not usually considered to be living. Also, DNA and RNA are very similar—they are the two types of nucleic acid.

2. Nucleotides

The subunits in both DNA and RNA are nucleotides.

Each nucleotide consists of three parts:

- a pentose sugar, with five carbon atoms and a five-atom "ring"
- a phosphate
- a base, whose molecules contain nitrogen and have either one or two rings.

In diagrams of nucleotides, these parts are usually shown as pentagons, circles and rectangles, respectively. The figure shows how the sugar, the phosphate and the base are linked up in a nucleotide.

3. Sugar–phosphate "backbone" of DNA and RNA

The nucleotides in a strand of DNA or RNA are linked together by covalent bonds between the pentose sugar of one nucleotide and the phosphate of the next one.

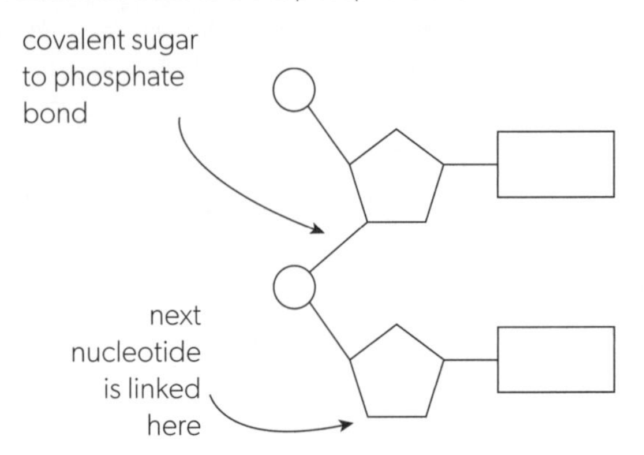

However many nucleotides have been linked up, another can always be added to the end of the chain where a pentose sugar can make a bond with the phosphate of a free nucleotide.

Sugars and phosphates alternate in RNA and DNA molecules, with an unbroken chain of covalently bonded atoms in the sequence $[-O-P-O-C-C-C-]_n$ where n is the number of nucleotides. Because this chain of atoms is covalently bonded, it gives strength to DNA and RNA molecules, helping them to store information reliably for long periods.

4. Nitrogenous bases

There are four different bases in both DNA and RNA, three of which are the same. These bases can be arranged in any sequence along a strand of nucleotides. The sequence forms the basis of the genetic code that all organisms use to store information.

Nucleic acid	One-ring bases (pyrimidines)		Two-ring bases (purines)	
DNA	C	Cytosine	A	Adenine
	T	Thymine	G	Guanine
RNA	C	Cytosine	A	Adenine
	U	Uracil	G	Guanine

5. Formation of RNA

The pentose sugar in RNA is ribose. There is a single strand of nucleotides, linked by covalent sugar–phosphate bonds.

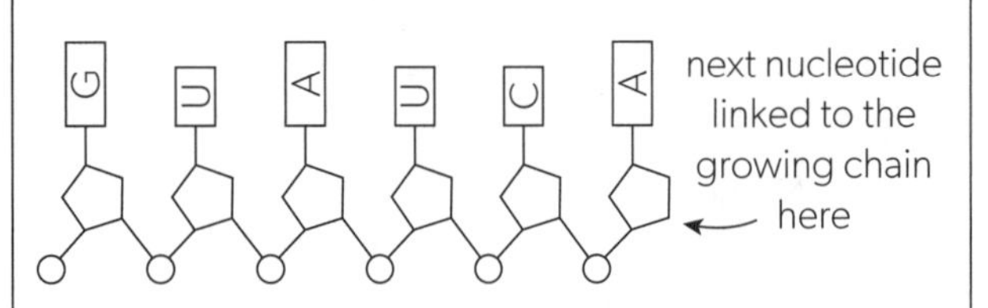

Water is produced by bonding sugar to phosphate, so it is a condensation reaction.

RNA is an example of a polymer—a molecule composed of repeating subunits (monomers) linked together by covalent bonds (see *Topics B1.1* and *B1.2* for more examples of polymers).

6. DNA as a double helix

There are two strands of nucleotides in DNA, which are linked by hydrogen bonding between their bases.

Each base will only form hydrogen bonds with one other base, so two base pairs only are possible: adenine with thymine and cytosine with guanine (A-T and C-G). They are known as complementary base pairs.

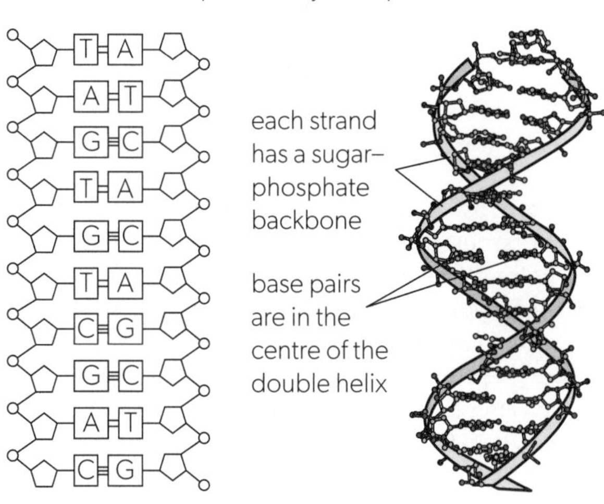

The two strands are antiparallel—they run alongside each other but in opposite directions.

The strands are wound together to form a double helix, which is the overall shape of a DNA molecule.

7. Comparing DNA and RNA

There are three differences between DNA and RNA.

1. The pentose is ribose in RNA but deoxyribose in DNA.
2. DNA has the base thymine but RNA has uracil instead.
3. RNA usually has one strand of nucleotides whereas DNA usually has two.

8. Complementary base pairing

Complementary base pairing has three roles in cells:

DNA replication—sequences of bases in DNA can be copied accurately, so the genetic information of a cell can be passed on to daughter cells.

Transcription—RNA can be made with the same base sequence as one of the two strands of a DNA molecule. Messenger RNA (mRNA) carries the base sequence of a protein-coding gene to the ribosome.

Translation—a base sequence can be used to determine the amino acid sequence in a polypeptide. Messenger RNA carries a series of three-base codons. Each transfer RNA molecule (tRNA) has one three-base anticodon and it carries one amino acid. Ribosomes link codons to anticodons by complementary base pairing, allowing the base sequence of every codon to be translated into a specific amino acid in a polypeptide (see *Topic D1.2*).

9. Diversity of DNA base sequences

Bases can be arranged in any sequence in DNA. Because any of the four bases could occupy each position along a DNA strand, the number of possible sequences is 4^n, where n is the number of bases. Even with just 10 bases there are over a million possible sequences. A typical gene has over a thousand bases and whole genomes have billions of bases. The number of possible sequences and therefore DNA's capacity to store information is effectively limitless.

10. Conservation of the genetic code

Each of the 64 codons of the genetic code indicates either one of the 20 amino acids or the end of the polypeptide. There are 1.5101095×10^{84} ways of assigning meanings to the 64 codons, but all organisms use the same meanings, with only minor variations. This universality of the genetic code suggests strongly that all life evolved from the same original ancestor, with minor differences added since then.

11. 3′ and 5′ ends of RNA and DNA

AHL

The two ends of a strand of nucleotides in DNA or RNA are different. They are known as the 3′ and 5′ ends (3 prime and 5 prime). The 3′ end has a pentose sugar (ribose or deoxyribose) to which the phosphate of another nucleotide can be linked. The phosphate would bond with the –OH group on the C3 of the deoxyribose. The 5′ end has a phosphate, attached to the C5 of a pentose.

When a new strand of DNA or RNA is being constructed, each extra nucleotide is added to the pentose at the 3′ end of the growing strand. This is done by bonding the phosphate of a free nucleotide, which is the nucleotide's 5′ end. Nucleotides are therefore added in a 5′ to 3′ direction.

The two strands in a DNA molecule are antiparallel because they run in opposite directions. Each end of a DNA double helix therefore has one strand with a 3′ end and one with a 5′ end.

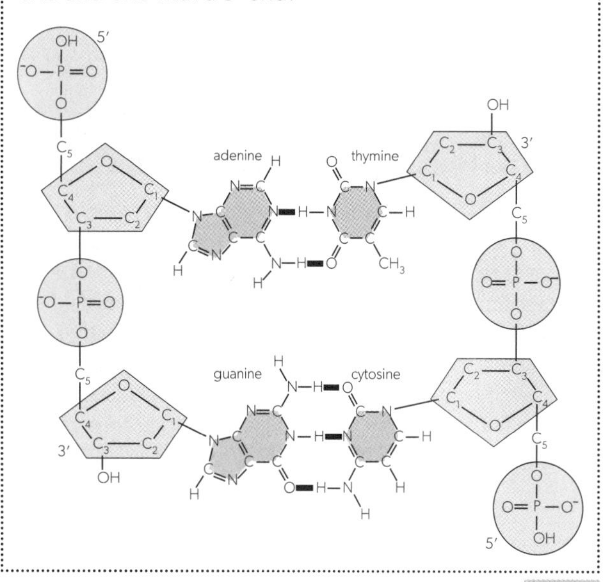

AHL

12. Purines bond with pyrimidines

The nitrogenous bases in DNA are in two chemical groups:

- adenine and guanine are purine bases with two rings of atoms
- cytosine and thymine are pyrimidine bases with one ring.

Each base pair in DNA therefore has one purine and one pyrimidine. As a consequence, the two base pairs are of equal width and require the same distance between the two sugar–phosphate backbones in the double helix. This helps to make the structure of DNA stable and allows any sequence of bases in genes to fit in a DNA molecule.

13. Nucleosomes

Nucleosomes are disc-like structures, used by eukaryotes to package DNA into condensed chromosomes and also to help control replication and transcription.

Each nucleosome has a core of eight histone proteins with a DNA wound round twice and one more histone securing the structure. There is some linker DNA between adjacent nucleosomes. Eukaryotic DNA looks like a string of beads in electron micrographs because of nucleosomes.

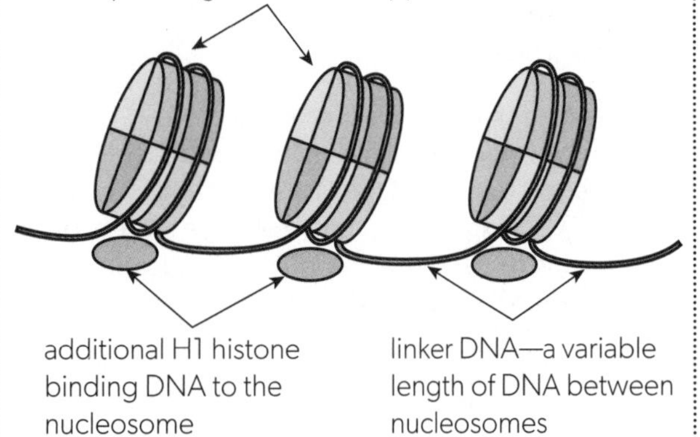

Adapted from Bunnik, E.M., Le Roch, K.G. (2013). Nucleosome. In: Hommel, M., Kremsner, P. (eds) Encyclopedia of Malaria. Springer, New York, NY. https://doi.org/10.1007/978-1-4614-8757-9_31-1

14. The Hershey–Chase experiment

In the early 1950s it was still unclear whether genes were made of DNA or protein. Hershey and Chase used the T2 virus to investigate this. T2 infects *E. coli*, which is a bacterium. Proteins of T2 start being produced inside *E. coli* soon after the virus comes into contact with it. This can only happen if genes of the virus are inside *E. coli*. To identify the genetic material, Hershey and Chase had to find out which part of the virus had entered the bacterium.

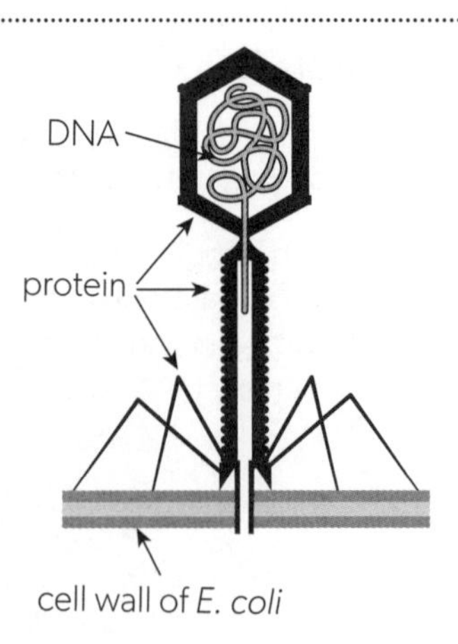

Viruses such as T2 consist only of DNA and protein, so their genes must be made of one of these materials. DNA contains the element P (phosphorus) but not S (sulfur), and protein contains S but not P. Hershey and Chase prepared one strain of T2 with its DNA labelled with the radioactive isotope ^{32}P and another with its protein radioactively labelled with ^{35}S. These two strains of T2 were mixed separately with *E. coli*. After leaving enough time for the bacteria to be infected, the mixture was agitated in a high-speed mixer and then centrifuged at 10,000 rpm to separate a solid pellet containing the bacteria from a liquid supernatant containing viruses. A Geiger counter was used to locate the radioactivity. The results are shown in the diagram.

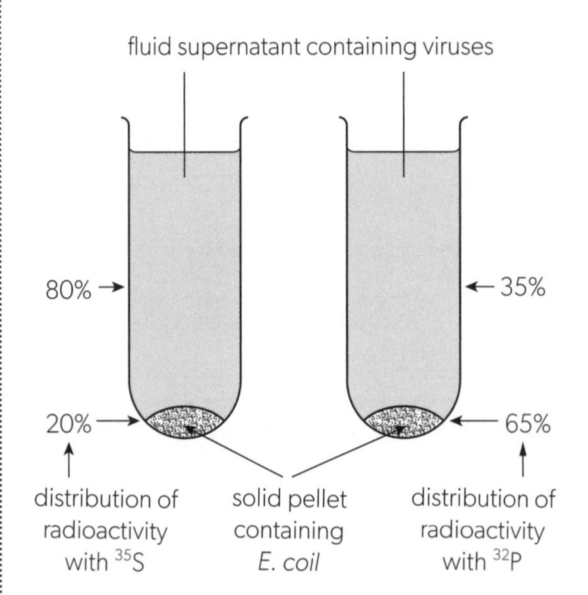

Analysis of results

With ^{32}P most of the radioactivity is in the pellet, showing that much of the viral DNA is inside the bacteria. With ^{35}S most of the radioactivity is in the supernatant, showing the protein coats of the viruses remained outside the bacteria and were shaken off by the mixer. The small proportion of radioactivity in the pellet with ^{35}S can be explained by some protein coats remaining attached to the bacteria and by the presence of some fluid containing protein coats in the pellet. This and other experiments carried out by Hershey and Chase gave strong evidence for genetic material (genes) being composed of DNA rather than protein.

AHL

15. Chargaff's data

Before the structure of DNA had been discovered, the amounts of each of the four bases were measured.

- The amounts of each base were not equal—not 25%.
- The percentages were the same in different tissues from one species, for example spleen and thymus tissue from cattle, but there were differences between species.

Erwin Chargaff drew attention to other trends in the numbers of bases that applied to the DNA of all the species investigated, including eukaryotes and prokaryotes:

adenine = thymine and guanine = cytosine

purines (A + G) = 50% and pyrimidines (T + C) = 50%

The table gives a sample of Chargaff's data:

Source of DNA	Purines		Pyrimidines	
	% A	% G	% C	% T
Mycobacterium tuberculosis—bacteria	15.1	34.9	35.4	14.6
Human—a mammal	29.3	20.0	20.7	30.0
Octopus—a mollusc	33.2	17.6	17.6	31.6
Corn (maize)—a plant	26.8	23.2	22.8	27.2

Crick and Watson discovered the reason for these trends:

- DNA contains complementary pairs of bases
- a purine base always pairs with a pyrimidine
- adenine pairs with thymine, and cytosine with guanine.

NOS

Progress in science often follows technological developments that allow new experimental techniques

The isotopes of an element have the same chemical properties but there are physical differences that allow them to be distinguished in experiments. Radioisotopes can be detected by the radiation that they emit. When radioisotopes were made available to scientists as research tools from the 1940s onwards, experiments such as that of Hershey and Chase became possible.

NOS

Scientists can use evidence to falsify a claim formulated as a hypothesis, theory or model

DNA was discovered in the 19th century. The tetranucleotide hypothesis was proposed in the early 20th century. This suggested that DNA molecules are a chain of alternating sugar and phosphate groups, with a base attached to each sugar and a repeating sequence of the four bases. A prediction based on the tetranucleotide hypothesis is that there must be equal numbers of the four bases A, C, G and T.

Chargaff's data showed that the numbers are not equal, so the tetranucleotide hypothesis must be false. The base sequence of DNA might therefore be variable, so it could be the genetic material. This realization started the race to discover the structure of DNA.

A well-designed experiment has two possible outcomes:

- results that fit the hypothesis, which could therefore be true
- results that prove the hypothesis to be false.

Even if many experiments provide support for a hypothesis, it is still possible that a future experiment will falsify it, because scientists can never do every possible experiment. This is called the problem of induction. It is a strength of science, not a weakness—scientists must keep an open mind: "Think it possible that you might be mistaken".

NOS

Introducing nature of science

Science is an academic discipline, with different methods and different fields of study from other disciplines such as history. The scientific method is a very powerful tool for making discoveries about the natural world. In IB Group 4 sciences, the elements of scientific investigation are known as the *nature of science*.

The biology programme includes selected contexts through which a general understanding of the nature of science can be developed, for example the formulation and testing of hypotheses. These are indicated by the NOS tab in this Study Guide.

General understanding of the nature of science will help with some questions in IB Biology exams, but definitions of nature of science terms or concepts do not need to be memorized.

End of topic questions—A1 Questions

A1.1 Water

1. The diagram shows water molecules.
   a. State how many intermolecular bonds and intramolecular bonds are shown in the diagram. (2)
   b. Distinguish between the two types of bond shown in the diagram. (3)

$H^{\delta+}$ $H^{\delta+}$
$\delta+$ $\delta-$ $\delta+$ $\delta-$
$H - O \cdots\cdots H - O$

   c. The photo shows drops of water on the upper and lower surfaces of a glass block. The drop on the upper surface is wider and shallower. Explain the shapes of the drops, using the concepts of cohesion and adhesion. (3)

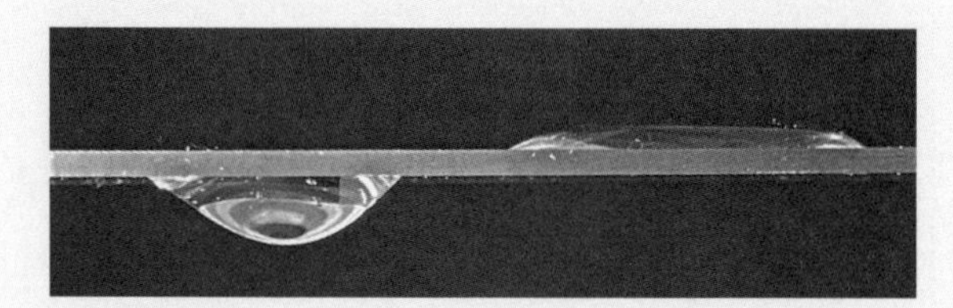

2. Identify what is defined by each of these statements:
   a. a unit of matter with one or more positively charged protons in a nucleus and an equal number of negatively charged electrons in orbitals around the nucleus (1)
   b. two or more atoms joined together by one or more covalent bonds (1)
   c. an atom or molecule that has become positively charged by losing one or more electrons, or negatively charged by gaining one or more electrons. (1)

3. (HL only) About two-thirds of the mass of the planet Neptune is water.

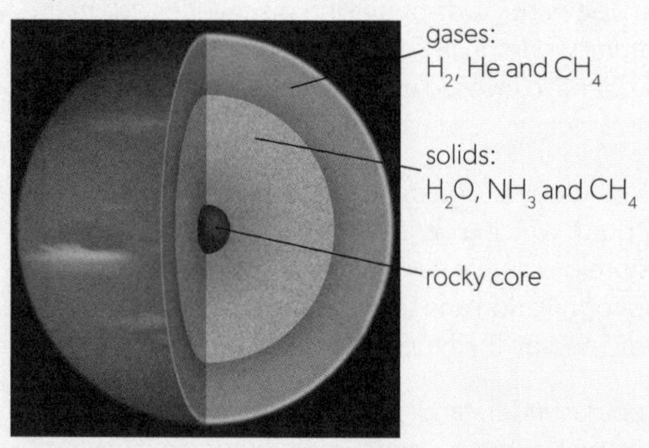

   a. Discuss which of the eight processes of life are dependent on H_2O. (7)
   b. Outline features that make Neptune unsuitable for life. (3)
   c. Identify the origin of H_2O on Neptune. (3)

A1.2 Nucleic acids

1. The table shows the base composition of genetic material from different sources.

Source of genetic material	*Base composition (%)*				
	A	C	G	T	U
Cattle thymus gland	28.2	22.5	21.5	27.8	0.0
Cattle spleen	27.9	22.1	22.7	27.3	0.0
Cattle sperm	28.7	22.0	22.2	27.2	0.0
Salmon	29.7	20.4	20.8	29.1	0.0
Wheat	27.3	22.8	22.7	27.1	0.0
Yeast	31.3	17.1	18.7	32.9	0.0
E. coli (bacteria)	26.0	25.2	24.9	23.9	0.0
Human sperm	31.0	18.4	19.1	31.5	0.0
Influenza virus	23.0	24.5	20.0	0.0	32.5

   a. Deduce the type of genetic material used by:
      i. cattle (1)
      ii. *E. coli* (1)
      iii. influenza viruses. (1)
   b. Suggest a reason for the difference between cattle thymus gland, spleen and sperm in measurements of base composition. (1)
   c. i. Explain why the total amount of adenine plus guanine is close to 50% in the genetic material of many of the species in the table. (3)
      ii. Identify two other trends in the base composition of the species that have 50% adenine plus guanine. (2)
   d. i. Identify a species in the table that does not follow the trends described in **c**. (1)
      ii. Explain the reasons for the base composition of this species being different. (2)
2. a. Draw a diagram to show the structure of DNA. Include a total of six nucleotides in your diagram. (9)
   b. Describe **three** features of DNA that make it ideal as a genetic material. (6)
3. a. (HL only) Distinguish between:
      i. 3′ and 5′ ends of an RNA molecule (2)
      ii. ribose and deoxyribose (2)
      iii. purines and pyrimidines (2)
      iv. nucleotides and nucleosomes. (2)
   b. State what an isotope is.(3)
   c. Distinguish between radioactive and non-radioactive isotopes. (3)
   d. Describe how Hershey and Chase used isotopes to distinguish between protein and DNA in their experiments. (4)

B1.1 Carbohydrates and lipids

1. Bonding of carbon atoms

Carbon atoms consist of six electrons orbiting a nucleus of six protons and six, seven or eight neutrons depending on the isotope. Four of the six electrons are in the outer shell, so carbon atoms can form four covalent bonds. Carbon atoms can bond covalently with other carbon atoms or other types of atom.

In a methane molecule (shown right) there are single covalent bonds between a carbon atom and four hydrogen atoms (so the formula is CH_4). In a carbon dioxide molecule, a carbon atom has two double covalent bonds with oxygen atoms (so the formula is CO_2).

Carbon can bond covalently to other non-metals, with hydrogen, oxygen, nitrogen and phosphorus all occurring commonly in carbon compounds made by living organisms.

Carbon's ability to link to four other atoms allows complex molecular structures to be formed, which can include rings or chains of atoms. The rings can be single or multiple and the chains can extend to any number of atoms and may be branched or unbranched.

All these possibilities result in a diverse range of carbon compounds, which form the basis of life in all organisms.

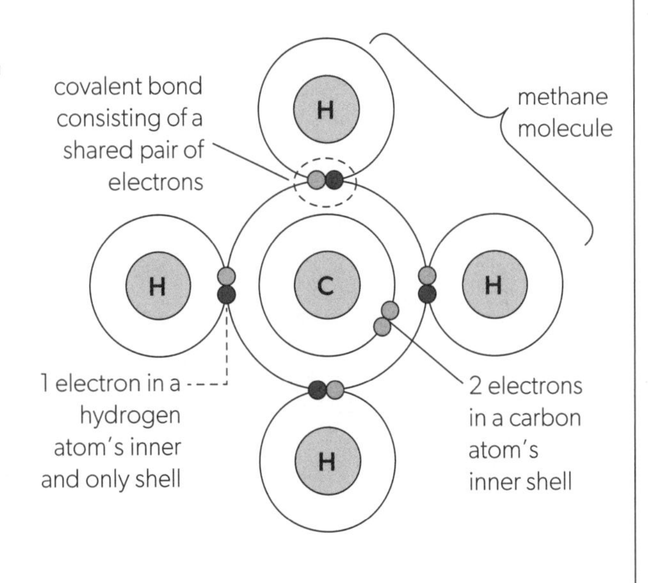

2. Condensation reactions

Living organisms produce macromolecules (very large molecules) from subunits that are linked up using covalent bonds. The subunits are monomers and a chain of 10 or more monomers is a polymer. For example, a polypeptide is a polymer, consisting of a chain of amino acids, which are linked together by covalent bonds. Nucleic acids (DNA and RNA) are polymers, with nucleotides as the subunits. A polysaccharide is also a polymer with monosaccharides (single sugar units) as subunits.

The covalent bonds that link the monomers in these polymers are made by condensation reactions. In a condensation reaction, two molecules are joined together to form a larger molecule, plus a molecule of water. The water is made by removing an –OH (hydroxyl group) from one of the molecules and a hydrogen from the other. This allows a new covalent bond to be made to link the two molecules.

The diagrams show two glucose molecules being linked by condensation to form a disaccharide (maltose). A polysaccharide is produced by linking on more glucose molecules by condensation.

3. Hydrolysis reactions

Hydrolysis reactions are the reverse of condensation reactions. In a hydrolysis reaction a large molecule is broken down into smaller molecules and water is used up in the process. Water molecules are split into –H and –OH groups, hence the name hydrolysis (lysis = splitting). The –H and –OH are needed to make new bonds after a bond in the large molecule has been broken. Hydrolysis reactions are used to digest food.

Examples of hydrolysis reactions used to digest polymers:

polypeptide + water ⟶ amino acids

polysaccharide + water ⟶ monosaccharides

glyceride + water ⟶ fatty acids + glycerol

The diagrams show the bond that links two nucleotides being broken by hydrolysis.

OH + H

H_2O

- C–O bond is broken
- OH from water bonds to the C
- H from water bonds to the O

NOS

Agreed conventions and common terminology facilitate unambiguous communication

A carbon atom has a diameter of 0.15 nanometres. All scientists should understand this, because nanometres are part of the International System of Units (SI)—a universally agreed convention for measurement in science. There are seven base units with other units derived from them. Multipliers can be added as prefixes to any of the units:

kilo	= ×1,000
mega	= ×1,000,000
tera	= ×1,000,000,000

milli	= ÷1,000
micro	= ÷1,000,000
nano	= ÷1,000,000,000

4. Recognizing monosaccharides

Monosaccharides are sugars that cannot be split into simpler sugars, so they are monomers. Most monosaccharides used by living organisms contain three, five or six carbon atoms (trioses, pentoses and hexoses). They contain only atoms of carbon, hydrogen and oxygen, in the ratio 1:2:1, so pentoses have the formula $C_5H_{10}O_5$ and hexoses $C_6H_{12}O_6$.

- One of the oxygen atoms in monosaccharides is bonded only to carbon, either by a double bond to one carbon, or more usually by two single bonds to different carbon atoms, in a ring of atoms. The other oxygens are part of OH groups. Molecules of pentose and hexose usually exist in a ring form and can be recognized by their shared features:

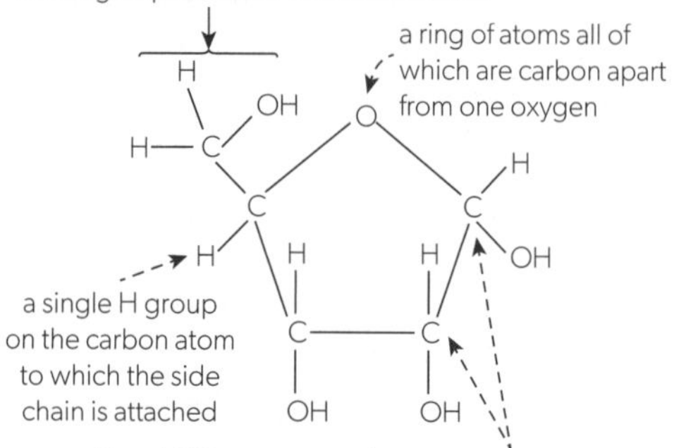

The molecule shown in the diagram above is D-ribose. The D indicates that this is the right-handed form. Left-handed forms of ribose and glucose can exist but living organisms do not use them. D-glucose can exist in two forms, alpha and beta. A numbering system is used so the carbon atoms can be referred to directly. The alpha and beta forms of glucose differ in whether the OH groups on C❶ and C❹ face in the same direction or opposite directions:

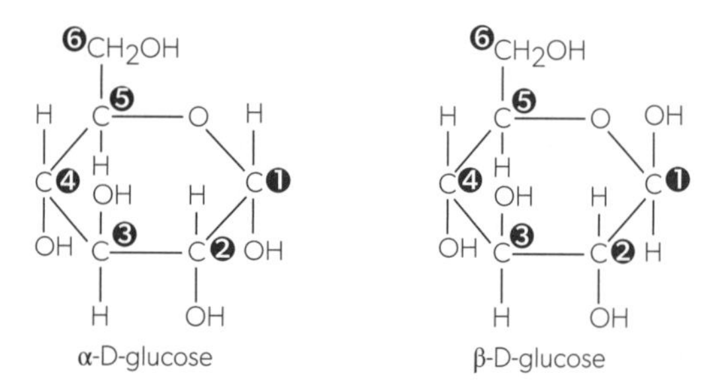

α-D-glucose β-D-glucose

There are clear links between the properties of glucose and how living organisms use this monosaccharide:

Property	Function of glucose
Soluble in water	Transport of carbohydrate in blood, where glucose is dissolved in the plasma
Can be oxidized	Source of energy, released when glucose is used as a substrate in cell respiration
Chemically stable	Energy storage, usually after conversion to a polysaccharide

5. Polysaccharides

Plants use starch as an energy store. Mammals use glycogen (in liver and muscle). Some fungi and bacteria use glycogen. Both starch and glycogen are composed of alpha glucose. Glucose is linked to these polysaccharides with a glycosidic bond, made by a condensation reaction:

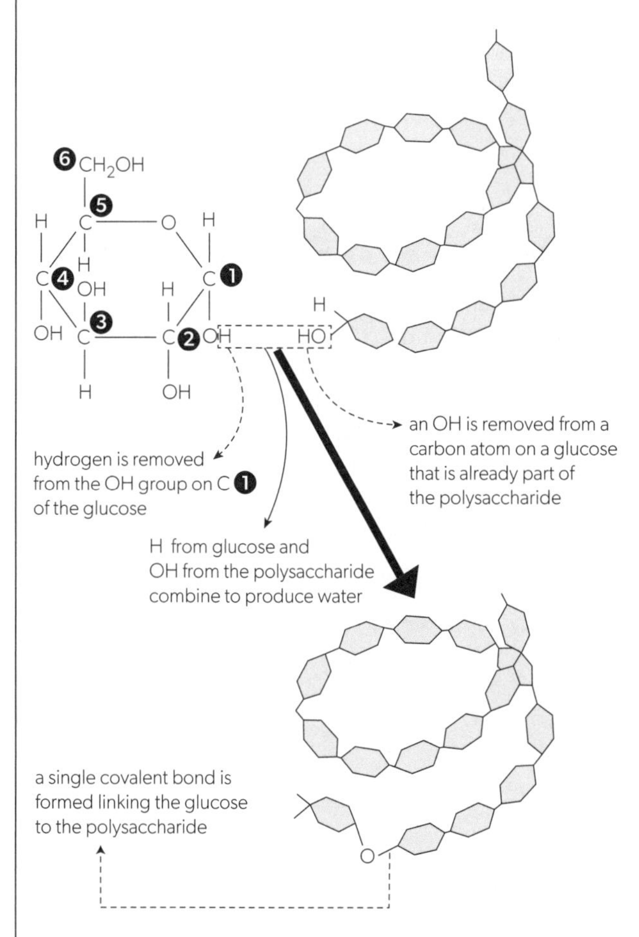

hydrogen is removed from the OH group on C❶ of the glucose
an OH is removed from a carbon atom on a glucose that is already part of the polysaccharide
H from glucose and OH from the polysaccharide combine to produce water
a single covalent bond is formed linking the glucose to the polysaccharide

C❶ of the extra glucose is most frequently linked to C❹ of the terminal glucose in the polysaccharide. This is 1-4 glycosidic bonding.

A chain of alpha glucose monomers linked by 1-4 bonds is helical.

C❶ can also be linked to C❻, making 1-6 glycosidic bonds which give the molecule a branched structure. Approximately 25% of starch molecules have no 1-6 bonds so are unbranched—they are amylose. About 75% of starch molecules have some 1-6 bonds so they are branched—they are amylopectin.

Glycogen molecules are similar to amylopectin, but with twice as much branching. The diagram shows part of a glycogen or amylopectin molecule.

1-6 glycosidic bond

1-4 glycosidic bond

Starch and glycogen function well as energy stores:

- The coiled and branched form of the molecules makes them compact, so they do not take up much space in cells.
- They are relatively insoluble so do not draw an excessive amount of water into cells by osmosis.
- When in surplus, glucose can easily be added and when scarce it can be removed. This can be done at more points in branched chains so addition or removal is more rapid.

6. Structure of cellulose

Cellulose is composed of beta glucose molecules, linked by 1-4 glycosidic bonds. The glucose molecules alternate in their orientation (up-down-up-down). This is due to the OH groups on C❶ and C❹ of beta-glucose facing in opposite directions. The consequence is that whereas amylose made from alpha-glucose is helical, cellulose made from beta-glucose is a straight chain. This allows groups of cellulose molecules to be packed together in parallel, with hydrogen bonds forming cross links. These structures are called cellulose microfibrils. They have enormous tensile strength and are the main component of plant cell walls.

7. Cell–cell recognition

Glycoproteins and glycolipids are components of plasma membranes, with short chains of sugars (oligosaccharides) projecting outwards from the membrane. The carbohydrate is attached either to protein in the membrane (glycoproteins) or to lipid (glycolipids). Interactions between the oligosaccharides and carbohydrate-binding proteins in adjacent cells allow cell–cell recognition.

Oligosaccharides in the membranes of adjacent cells can become linked, binding the cells together into a tissue. Cells in a multicellular organism can recognize foreign cells or infected body cells by the oligosaccharides of their glycoproteins and glycolipids. ABO blood groups in humans are due to a glycoprotein and glycolipid in red blood cells.

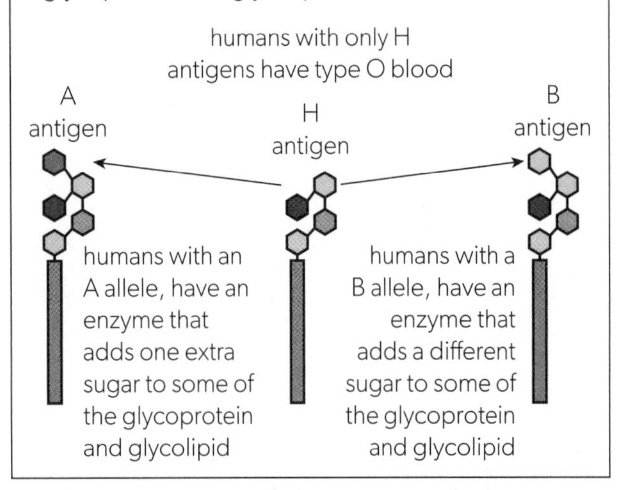

8. Lipids are hydrophobic

Lipids are defined by solubility—they dissolve in non-polar solvents such as toluene but are sparingly soluble or insoluble in water. This is because lipid molecules have few charged groups (+ or −) and few groups that form hydrogen bonds.

They are chemically diverse, with fats, oils, waxes and steroids as the main groups made by organisms. The C:O and H:O ratios are higher than in carbohydrates and other hydrophilic carbon compounds.

The table shows CHO composition of four lipids and glucose for comparison:

Example	Formula	Function
Glucose	$C_6H_{12}O_6$	Sugar in blood plasma
Palmitic acid	$C_{16}H_{32}O_2$	Animal fat component
Linoleic acid	$C_{18}H_{32}O_2$	Plant oil component
Octacosanoic acid	$C_{28}H_{56}O_2$	Wax on leaves (cutin)
Cholesterol	$C_{27}H_{46}O$	Membrane component

9. Formation of triglycerides and phospholipids

Triglycerides (fats and oils) are made by combining fatty acids and glycerol. Fatty acids have a carboxyl group which is acidic. Two ways of representing it are shown.

—COOH or —C(=O)OH

The fatty acids also have an unbranched hydrocarbon chain. The example shown below is stearic acid, a saturated fatty acid.

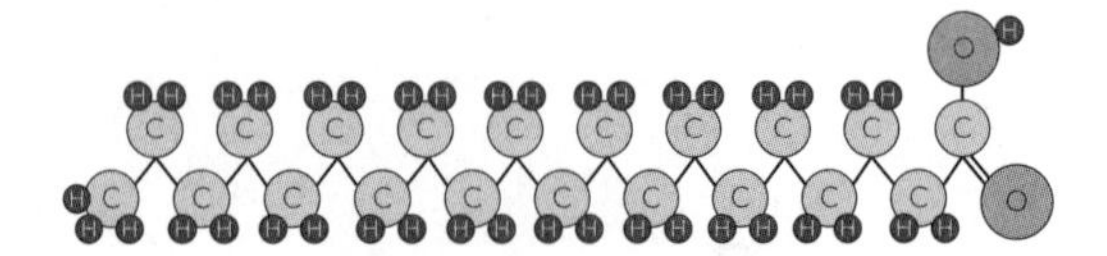

Glycerol is an alcohol with three hydroxyl (OH) groups. A fatty acid is linked to glycerol by a condensation reaction, using the COOH group of the fatty acid and a hydroxyl group of glycerol. The molecule produced is a monoglyceride. Because glycerol has three OH groups, two more fatty acids can be linked to it, producing a triglyceride. The new bonds that link the fatty acids to the glycerol are ester bonds.

3 fatty acids
glycerol
HO—CH_2
HO—CH
HO—CH_2
condensation reaction
triglyceride (a fat or oil)
+ $3H_2O$
hydrocarbon chain of fatty acid
ester bond

Phospholipids are made by combining two fatty acids and one phosphate group with glycerol. As with production of triglycerides, condensation reactions create ester bonds and water is produced.

Because the phosphate is group is hydrophilic and the hydrocarbon chains of the fatty acids are hydrophobic, they are on opposite sides of the molecule:

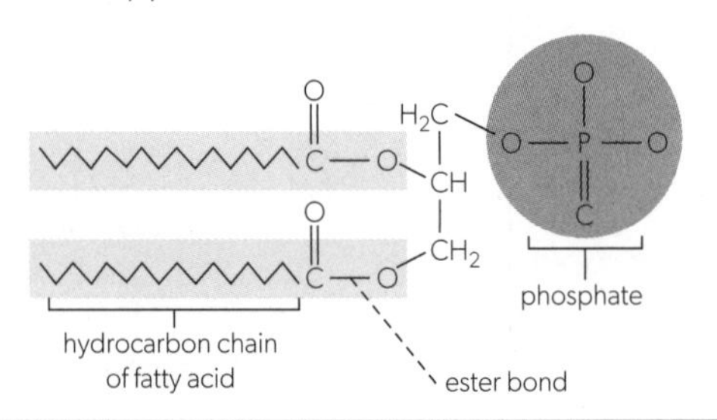

10. Differences between fatty acids

Fatty acids vary in the number of carbon atoms in the hydrocarbon chain and in the bonding of the carbon and hydrogen atoms.

Saturated fatty acids—all the carbon atoms are connected by single covalent bonds so the number of hydrogen atoms bonded to the carbons cannot be increased.

Monounsaturated fatty acids—there is a double bond between two of the carbon atoms and if this was replaced by a single bond, more hydrogen could be incorporated.

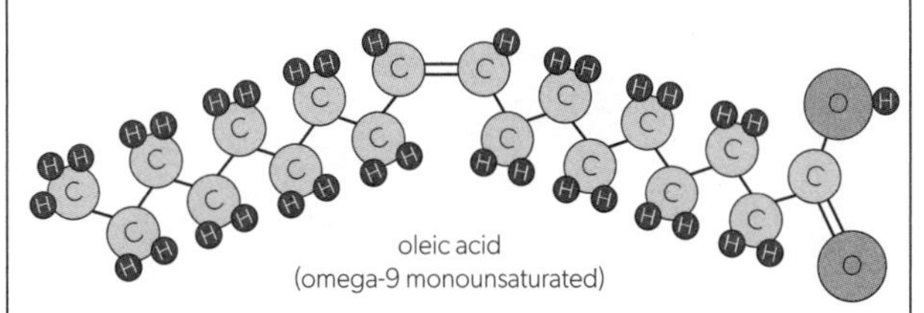

Polyunsaturated fatty acids—there are two or more double bonds. The position of the double bond nearest to the CH_3 terminal is significant. In omega-3 fatty acids, it is the third bond from CH_3 and in omega-6 fatty acids it is the sixth.

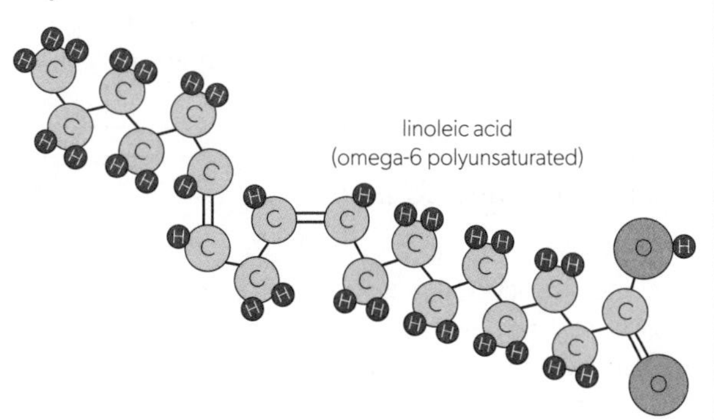

A double bond puts a kink into the hydrocarbon chain. A consequence is that unsaturated fatty acids do not pack together as neatly as saturated fatty acids, so they change from solid to liquid (melt) at a lower temperature.

Fatty acid	C	Double bonds	Melting point (°C)
Stearic acid	18	0	69
Oleic acid	18	1	13
Linoleic acid	18	2	–5

Triglycerides with mostly unsaturated fatty acids are liquid at room temperature (20°C)—they are oils.

Triglycerides with mostly saturated fatty acids are solid at 20°C and liquid at 37°C (body temperature)—they are fats.

Stores of triglyceride must remain liquid, so birds and mammals with constant high body temperatures can store fats. Plants and other organisms must use oils instead as their tissues are sometimes below the melting point of fats.

11. Triglycerides in adipose tissues

Adipose cells can accumulate large amounts of triglyceride. Fats and oils are inert and coalesce into compact droplets, which do not cause osmosis. Fats and oils are very efficient energy stores because they release twice as much energy per gram as carbohydrates when used in cell respiration. Adipose tissue can be used to store energy anywhere in the body, but much of it is positioned next to the skin. This is because fats and oils are poor heat conductors, so they function as thermal insulators and reduce loss of body heat to the environment.

12. Formation of phospholipid bilayers

Phospholipids are the basic component of all biological membranes. Phospholipid molecules are amphipathic. This means that part of the molecule is attracted to water (hydrophilic) and part is not attracted (hydrophobic). The phosphate head is hydrophilic and the two fatty acid tails, which are composed of hydrocarbon chains, are hydrophobic.

When phospholipids are mixed with water they naturally become arranged into bilayers, with the hydrophilic heads facing outwards and making contact with the water and the hydrocarbon tails facing inwards away from the water. This is a very stable structure because hydrophobic tails in the centre of the bilayer are more attracted to each other than to water outside the membrane and the hydrophilic heads of the phospholipids are more attracted to the water.

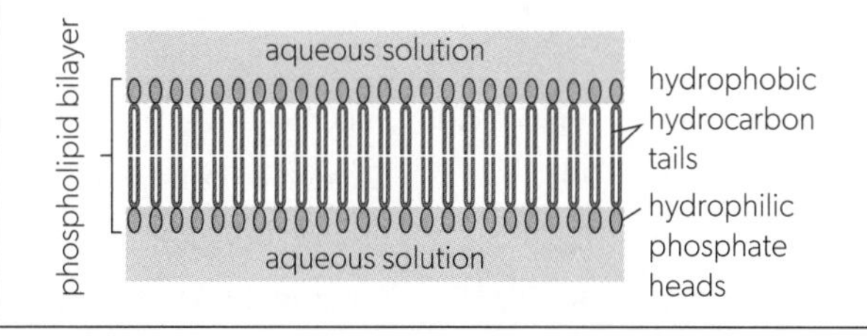

13. Steroids

Steroids are a group of lipids with molecules similar to that of sterol. They have four fused rings of carbon atoms, three with six and one with five carbon atoms.

There are hundreds of different steroids, which differ in the position of C=C double bonds and the functional groups such as –OH that are attached to the four-ring structure. Steroids are mostly hydrocarbon and therefore hydrophobic. This allows them to pass through phospholipid bilayers and therefore enter or leave cells.

testosterone (male sex hormone) — CH_3, OH, CH_3, O

oestradiol (a female sex hormone) — CH_3, OH, HO

B1.2 Proteins

1. Amino acid structure

Amino acids have a central carbon atom with four different atoms or groups linked to it:

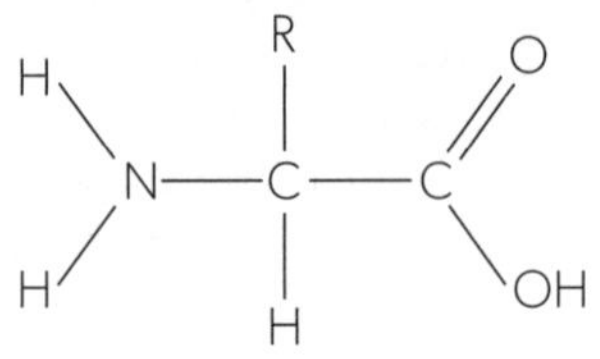

amino acid

- hydrogen atom
- amine group ($-NH_2$)
- carboxyl group ($-COOH$)
- R-group (R).

Each of the 20 amino acids in proteins has a different R-group.

2. Formation of dipeptides

Amino acids are linked together by condensation reactions. The new bond formed between the amine group of one amino acid and the carboxyl group of the next is a peptide bond.

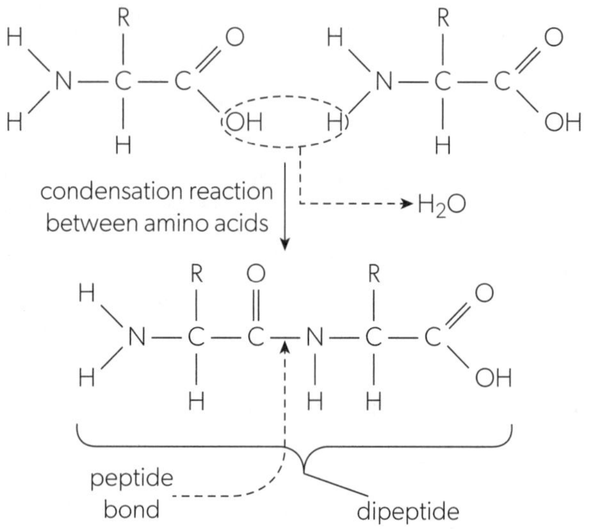

condensation reaction between amino acids

H_2O

peptide bond

dipeptide

A molecule consisting of two amino acids linked together is a dipeptide. Polypeptides consist of many amino acids linked by peptide bonds.

3. Essential amino acids

All of the 20 amino acids that are used to make polypeptides are produced in plants by photosynthesis. These amino acids pass to animals in their food. Animals can use metabolic pathways to convert some amino acids into others—these are the non-essential amino acids. An essential amino acid is one that cannot be synthesized in sufficient quantities by an animal so must be obtained from the diet.

Nine of the 20 amino acids are essential in humans. For example, the amino acid phenylalanine is essential as it cannot be synthesized by the human body but tyrosine is non-essential as it can be made from phenylalanine.

Animal-based foods (fish, meat, milk, eggs) supply amino acids in the proportions needed in the human diet, but some plant-based foods have too little of specific amino acids for human needs. For example, cereals such as wheat have a low lysine content, whereas peas and beans are low in methionine. Both of these amino acids are essential in the human diet.

In a vegan diet attention must therefore be given to ensure that enough of each essential amino acid is consumed. Traditional plant-based diets in successful civilizations have been found to provide such a balance.

4. Variety of peptide chains

- A peptide is an unbranched chain of amino acids. If there are between 2 and 10 amino acids, the chain is an oligopeptide. If there are more than 20 amino acids it is a polypeptide. There can be over 10,000 amino acids in a peptide chain—any number is possible, though most polypeptides have between 50 and 2,000 amino acids.

  The table shows some examples.

Peptide	Amino acids	Function
Glucagon	29	Glucose-release hormone
Myoglobin	153	Oxygen storage in muscle
Titin	27–35,000	Elastic recoil in muscle

- Twenty amino acids are coded for in the genetic code. The first amino acid in a peptide chain (and every subsequent amino acid) can be any of these 20. If we consider a chain of 10 amino acids, the number of possible sequences is 20^{10} which is over 10 trillion. If we add all the possibilities for longer amino acid sequences, the number of possible peptide chains is effectively infinite.
- The amino acid sequence of a polypeptide is coded for by a gene. The sequence of bases in the DNA of the gene determines the sequence of amino acids in the polypeptide.
- Over two million polypeptides have so far been identified in living organisms. This is only a small proportion of the possible sequences. Other sequences are either not useful or the gene for making them has never evolved.

5. Denaturing proteins

Most proteins are delicate and their three-dimensional shape is easily damaged by changes to chemical or physical conditions. This is called denaturation.

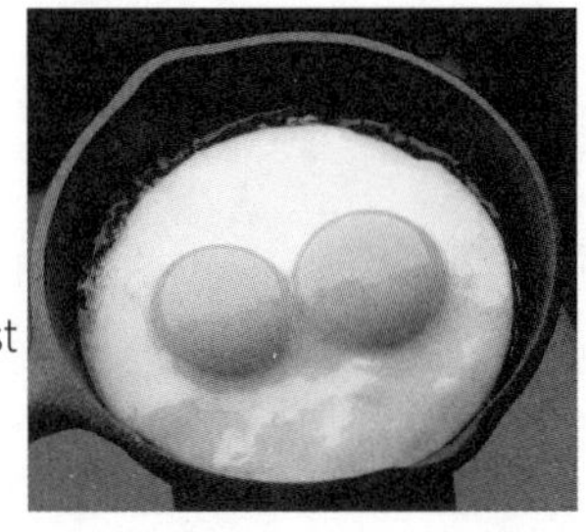

1. Heat causes vibrations within protein molecules that break intramolecular bonds and cause the conformation to change. Heat denaturation is almost always irreversible. This can be demonstrated by heating egg white, which contains dissolved albumin proteins. The albumins are denatured by the heat and in their new conformations are insoluble. This causes the liquid egg white to turn into a white solid.

2. Every protein has an ideal or optimum pH at which its conformation is normal. If the pH is increased by adding alkali or decreased by adding acid, the conformation of the protein may initially stay the same but denaturation occurs when the pH has deviated too far from the optimum. This is because the pH change causes intramolecular bonds to break within the protein molecule. The photograph shows egg white mixed with hydrochloric acid.

AHL

6. R-groups of amino acids

Of the four groups linked to the central carbon of an amino acid, the amine and carboxyl groups are used to form peptide bonds and the hydrogen atom has little influence, so it is the R-groups of the amino acids in peptide chains that largely determine the properties of proteins. They are very diverse in their chemical nature.

- Half of the R-groups are hydrophobic, some with rings of atoms and one (methionine) containing sulfur. These hydrophobic R-groups are more attracted to each other than to the other half of the R-groups which are hydrophilic.
- About a third of the hydrophilic R-groups are polar but do not ionize. They can form hydrogen bonds with other R-groups.
- Another third of the hydrophilic R-groups have an amine group that can accept a proton, so they are basic. The extra proton makes the R-group positively charged.
- The other third of the hydrophilic R-groups can donate a proton, so they are acidic. Loss of a proton makes them negatively charged, so they can also form ionic bonds with positively charged R-groups.
- One R-group is mildly hydrophilic and contains an –SH group. Pairs of these R-groups can form a covalent S–S bond called a disulfide bridge.
- Both hydrophobic and hydrophilic R-groups vary in size, ranging from glycine with just a single hydrogen atom, to tryptophan which is the largest. They also differ in shape, some having unbranched or branched chains of atoms and others having rings.

7. Conformations of proteins

Protein conformations are most easily understood by recognizing four levels of structure, from primary to quaternary. Primary structure is the number and sequence of amino acids in a polypeptide.

The conformation of a molecule is the arrangement of its atoms in space. In carbon compounds there can be changes of conformation due to bond rotation, giving alternative structures for the same compound.

Cells construct proteins with each amino acid in a precise position, so the overall conformation of the protein is predictable and repeatable. Software has been developed (for example, AlphaFold) for predicting these conformations from amino acid sequences but even with powerful computers, predicted conformations are sometimes found to be false.

As a polypeptide is synthesized by a ribosome, from the N-terminal to the C-terminal, it gradually develops its conformation, guided by the chemical properties of each amino acid added. Parts of the chain may coil up to form a helix and, at particular points, folds may form to make the shape globular. Every time a polypeptide with a particular sequence of amino acids is synthesized on a ribosome, its conformation will tend to be precisely the same. It is stabilized by intramolecular bonds between the amino acids brought together by the coiling and folding processes.

The primary structure of beta-endorphin is a sequence of 31 amino acids (right), which determines the distinctive conformation of this small polypeptide, allowing it to bind to opioid receptors and thus act as a neurotransmitter in the brain.

N-terminal
Tyrosine
Glycine
Glycine
Phenylalanine
Methionine
Threonine
Serine
Glutamic acid
Lysine
Serine
Glutamine
Threonine
Proline
Leucine
Valine
Threonine
Leucine
Phenylalanine
Lysine
Asparagine
Alanine
Isoleucine
Isoleucine
Lysine
Asparagine
Alanine
Tyrosine
Lysine
Lysine
Glycine
Glutamic acid
C-terminal

AHL

8. Secondary structure of proteins

When amino acids are linked together by peptide bonds, a repeating sequence of covalently bonded carbon and nitrogen atoms is formed: N–C–C–N–C–C–This forms the strong backbone of the polypeptide.

Each nitrogen atom in the repeating sequence has a hydrogen bonded to it (N–H) and every second carbon atom has an oxygen atom double bonded to it (C=O). Hydrogen bonds can form between the N–H and C=O groups in a polypeptide if they are brought close together. For example, if sections of polypeptide run parallel, hydrogen bonds can form between them. The structure that develops is called a beta-pleated sheet.

If the polypeptide is wound into a right-handed helix, hydrogen bonds can form between adjacent turns of the helix. The structure that develops is called an alpha helix.

Because the groups forming hydrogen bonds are regularly spaced, these helices and sheets always have the same dimensions.

Alpha helices and beta-pleated sheets stabilized by hydrogen bonding are the secondary structure of a polypeptide.

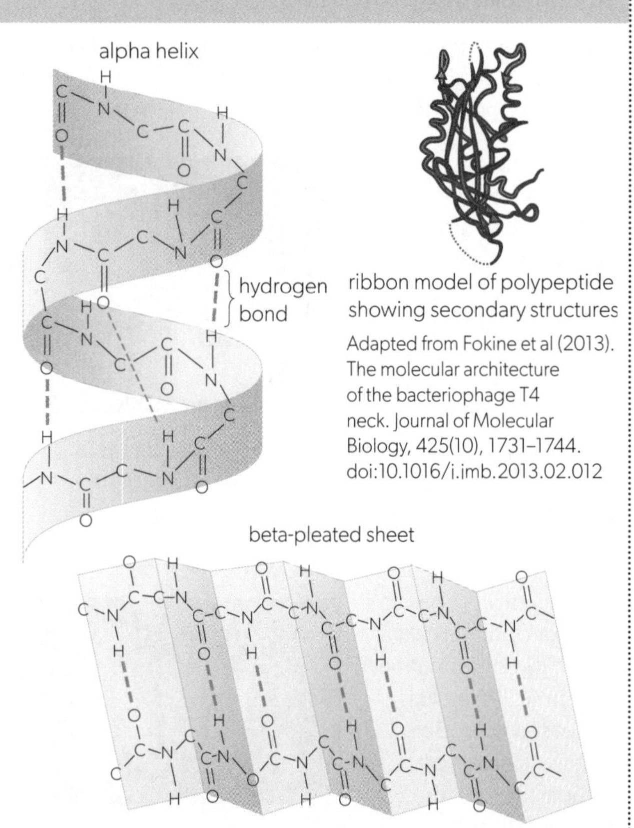

ribbon model of polypeptide showing secondary structures

Adapted from Fokine et al (2013). The molecular architecture of the bacteriophage T4 neck. Journal of Molecular Biology, 425(10), 1731–1744. doi:10.1016/i.imb.2013.02.012

9. Tertiary structures of proteins

Tertiary structure is the three-dimensional conformation of a polypeptide. It is formed when a polypeptide folds up after being produced by translation. The conformation is stabilized by intramolecular bonds and interactions that form between amino acids in the polypeptide, especially between their R-groups. Intramolecular bonds can form between amino acids widely separated in the primary structure but brought together during the folding process.

There are four main types of interaction:

- **hydrogen bonds** where two polar R-groups interact
- **ionic bonds** between NH^+ and COO^- groups
- **disulfide bonds**—sulfur–sulfur covalent bonds which can only form where two cysteines come together
- **hydrophobic interactions**—the weakest type of interaction that forms between two or more non-polar R-groups.

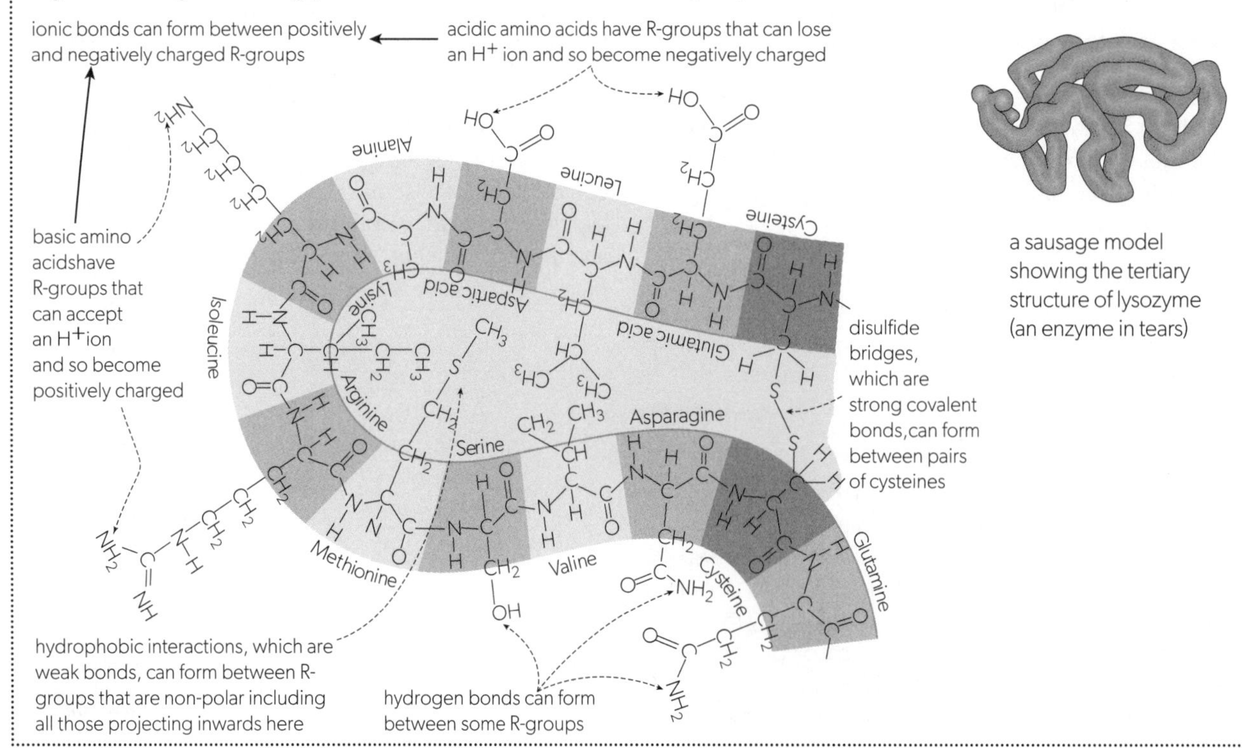

ionic bonds can form between positively and negatively charged R-groups
acidic amino acids have R-groups that can lose an H+ ion and so become negatively charged
basic amino acidshave R-groups that can accept an H+ion and so become positively charged
disulfide bridges, which are strong covalent bonds,can form between pairs of cysteines
hydrophobic interactions, which are weak bonds, can form between R-groups that are non-polar including all those projecting inwards here
hydrogen bonds can form between some R-groups
Alanine
Leucine
Cysteine
Lysine
Aspartic acid
Glutamic acid
Isoleucine
Arginine
Serine
Asparagine
Methionine
Valine
Cysteine
Glutamine
a sausage model showing the tertiary structure of lysozyme (an enzyme in tears)

AHL

10. Effects of amino acid polarity

Proteins with hydrophilic (polar) amino acids on their outer surface tend to dissolve in water. They often have hydrophobic (non-polar) amino acids in their core. This arrangement stabilizes the protein's tertiary structure in aqueous solutions.

Proteins with hydrophobic amino acids on their outer surface are attracted to the non-polar core of membranes, so they become integral membrane proteins. The diagram shows how they can adopt a variety of positions depending on the distribution of polar and non-polar amino acids on their surface.

The distribution of polar and non-polar amino acids determines the tertiary structure of proteins and also where they are located in cells. Many proteins are water-soluble so remain dissolved in the cytoplasm or in aqueous solutions inside organelles. There are also many proteins that are an integral part of membranes.

hydrophobic parts of membrane proteins are embedded in the membrane

hydrophilic parts of membrane proteins protrude

11. Quaternary structure of proteins

Some proteins contain a non-polypeptide structure called a prosthetic group. They are known as conjugated proteins. Haemoglobin is an example as the haem groups are not polypeptides.

Quaternary structure is the linking of two or more polypeptides to form a single protein. The same types of intramolecular bonding are used as in tertiary structure.

Goodsell, D. S. (2004). Carbonic anhydrase. RCSB Protein Data Bank. doi:10.2210/rcsb_pdb/mom_2004_1

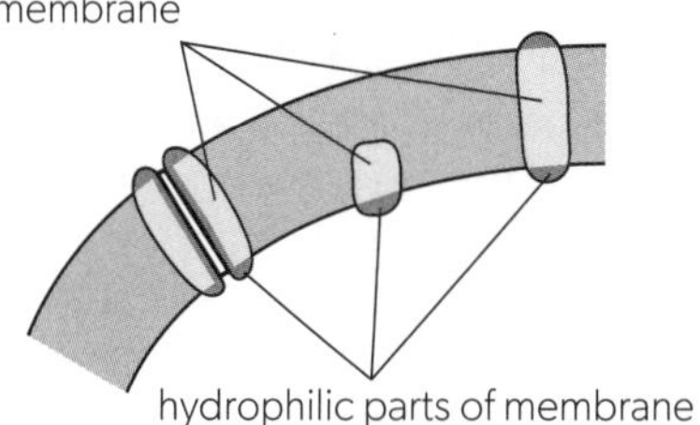

there is a haem group in each haemoglobin polypeptide (two shown here)

12. Globular and fibrous proteins

Form and function are closely related in proteins. Fibrous proteins have unfolded polypeptides, so are narrow and elongated. They have structural roles within and between cells. Globular proteins have folded polypeptides and therefore a rounded shape. Their varied shapes allow them to have many roles in cells.

Collagen is a fibrous protein. Its three polypeptides are more elongated than alpha helices, so they can be wound together into a triple helix. Like a rope, collagen can withstand pulling forces (tensions) by stretching rather than breaking. Collagen is produced by fibroblasts and released into the extracellular matrix of tissues where tensile strength is needed in skin, bones, tendons, and ligaments.

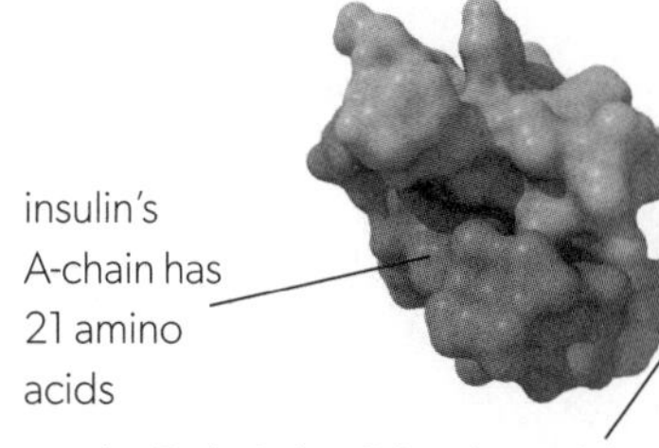

the B-chain has 30 amino acids; the A and B chains are made as a 110-amino acid-long polypeptide which is folded and cross-linked by disulfide bonds; a middle section is then removed

Insulin is a globular protein that functions as a hormone. Small size and a hydrophilic surface allows molecules of insulin to be carried dissolved in blood plasma. Insulin's distinctive shape allows it to bind to a site on a specific receptor protein, located in the plasma membrane of target cells.

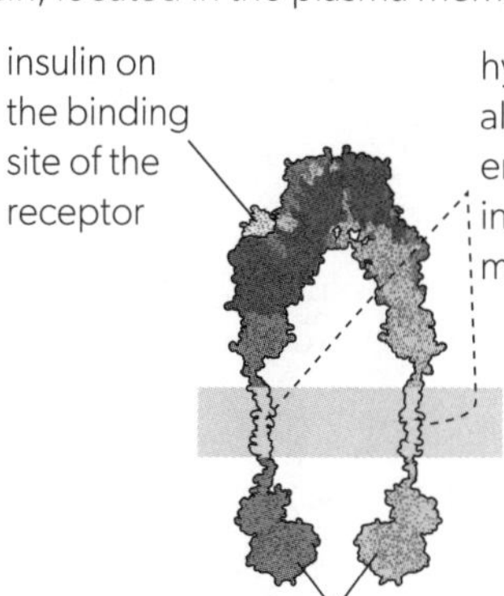

Adapted from RCSB Protein Data Bank

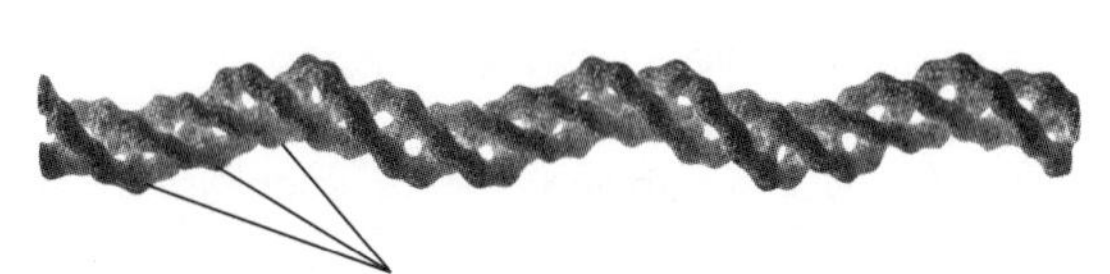

collagen has three polypeptides with an amino acid sequence that prevents formation of alpha helices, so the chains can be wound together into a rope-like conformation

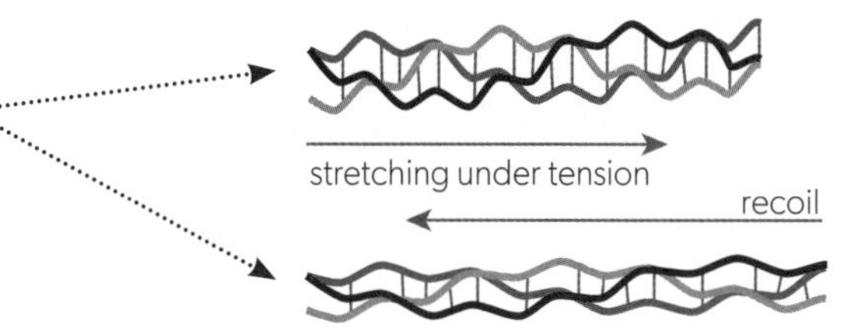

End of topic questions—B1 Questions

B1.1 Carbohydrates and lipids

1. a. List these SI prefixes in size order from smallest to largest: centi, kilo, mega, micro, milli, nano. (4)
   b. State the SI units and their symbols for measuring the following:
      i. length
      ii. mass
      iii. time
      iv. temperature
      v. electric current
      vi. amount of substance. (6)

   The table shows the fatty acid content of four foods.

Food	Fatty acids (grams per 100 g of food)		
	Saturated fatty acids	Mono unsaturated	Poly unsaturated
Lamb	9.9	9.6	1.8
Lettuce	Trace	Trace	0.1
Pecans	5.7	42.5	18.7
Salmon	1.9	5.3	2.4

   c. Calculate the total fatty acid content of each food. (2)
   d. Suggest reasons, based on form and function, for:
      i. differences between pecans and the other three foods in total fatty acid content (2)
      ii. differences between lamb and lettuce in fatty acids (3)
      iii. different proportions of fatty acids in lamb and salmon. (3)
2. a. State the difference between ionic bonds and covalent bonds. (2)
   b. Compare and contrast pentoses and hexoses. (3)
   c. Distinguish between starch and cellulose in form and function. (5)
3. Lipid molecules are non-polar and are therefore hydrophobic.
   a. Explain the reasons for non-polar molecules being hydrophobic. (3)
   b. Suggest how the hydrophobic nature of lipid molecules helps:
      i. triglycerides store energy (2)
      ii. steroid hormones (e.g. testosterone) enter cells. (1)
   c. Explain how the amphipathic nature of phospholipids helps them form biological membranes. (4)

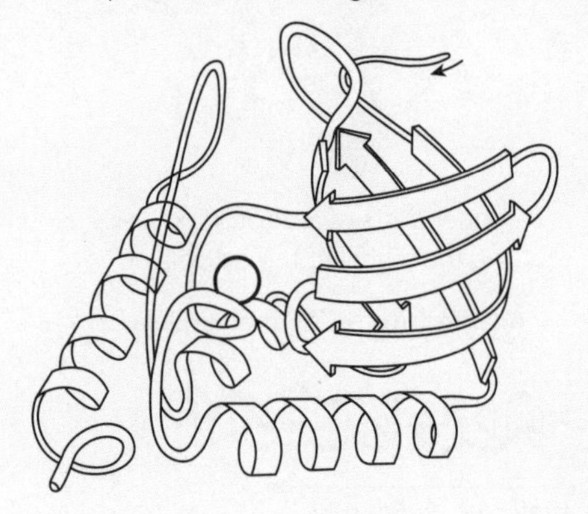

B1.2 Proteins

1. The following table shows the mass of the nine essential amino acids in rice protein and chickpea protein. The table also shows the protein percentage (according to the WHO) if the recommended total daily amount of protein consumed is entirely rice or chickpea protein.
   a. Explain the reasons for some (but not all) amino acids being essential. (2)
   b. i. Deduce from the data whether the WHO recommends that we should eat equal amounts of each amino acid. (2)
      ii. Suggest reasons for needing more of some amino acids in the diet than others. (2)
      iii. Using the data in the table, identify the amino acid needed in the greatest quantity. (1)
   c. Using the data in the table, justify the conclusion that *eating all dietary protein as rice would result in malnutrition*. (1)
   d. Discuss, using the data in the table, whether a vegan diet can supply enough of each essential amino acid. (2)

Amino acid	Rice (grain)		Chickpea (legume)	
	mg per g	% of WHO amount	mg per g	% of WHO amount
Histidine	2.68	176%	2.76	182%
Isoleucine	4.45	146%	4.29	141%
Leucine	8.7	144%	7.13	118%
Lysine	4.01	88%	6.7	147%
Methionine	2.37	156%	1.31	87%
Phenylalanine	5.43	143%	5.37	141%
Threonine	3.85	169%	3.72	163%
Tryptophan	1.34	220%	0.96	158%
Valine	6.17	156%	4.2	106%

2. a. Draw a molecule of the amino acid glycine, which has a single hydrogen atom as its R-group. (2)
   b. i. Draw a dipeptide consisting of two glycine molecules, with the peptide bond between them indicated. (3)
      ii. Calculate the difference in the numbers of hydrogen and oxygen atoms between this dipeptide and two separate glycine molecules. (2)
      iii. Explain the differences in part **ii**. (1)
      iv. Calculate how many hydrogen and oxygen atoms a polypeptide containing 100 glycine molecules would have. (2)
3. (HL only) The diagram (left) shows the structure of a nuclease. The circle represents a calcium ion.
   a. Describe the structure of this nuclease. (7)
   b. Outline its function. (3)
   c. List the types of intramolecular interaction between R-groups that stabilize protein structure. (4)
   d. Explain what determines the pattern of intramolecular interactions within a protein. (3)
   e. Outline the structure and function of collagen. (3)

C1.1 Enzymes and metabolism

1. Enzymes are biological catalysts

Catalysts speed up chemical reactions without being changed themselves. Enzymes are biological catalysts, made by living organisms. They cause very large increases in the rates of chemical reactions in cells. Many reactions that are useful to living organisms would be extremely slow without an enzyme acting as a catalyst. This would slow down life processes such as cell respiration, digestion, photosynthesis and growth. For example, the enzyme carbonic anhydrase can speed up conversion of hydrogen carbonate ions to carbon dioxide by a factor of 10^7.

This reaction must happen in red blood cells during the second or so that it takes them to pass through capillaries of alveoli in the lungs. Without carbonic anhydrase, CO_2 would not be breathed out fast enough.

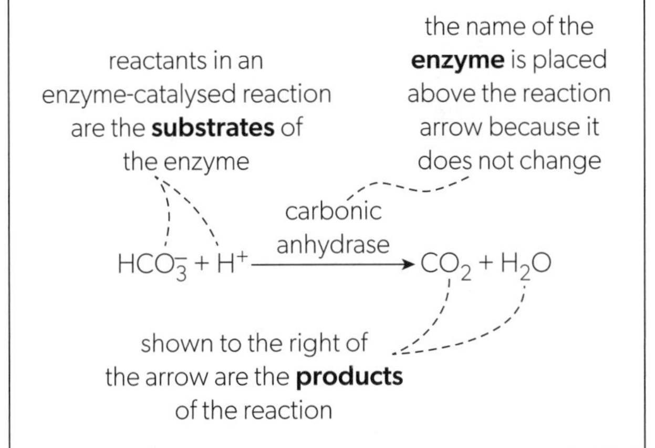
reactants in an enzyme-catalysed reaction are the **substrates** of the enzyme
the name of the **enzyme** is placed above the reaction arrow because it does not change
carbonic anhydrase
$HCO_3^- + H^+ \rightarrow CO_2 + H_2O$
shown to the right of the arrow are the **products** of the reaction

2. Enzymes in metabolism

Enzymes show specificity in their catalytic activity. Each enzyme speeds up one specific reaction or group of reactions. This allows cells to control which reactions happen—enzymes are only produced for reactions that are required in the cell.

Cells produce thousands of different enzymes, because thousands of chemical reactions must occur for a cell to carry out basic "housekeeping" processes and also its specialized functions.

Enzymes typically catalyse small chemical changes. Major chemical conversions happen via a series of reactions, catalysed by different enzymes. The product of one enzyme's reaction is the substrate for the next enzyme. This is an example of interdependence, with the activity of both enzymes restricted if the other is not active enough.

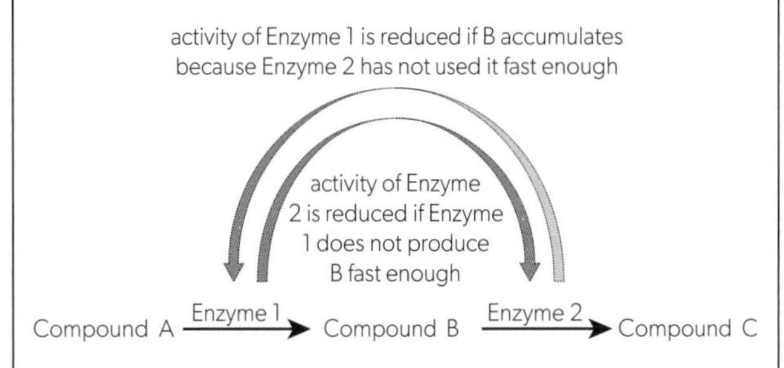
activity of Enzyme 1 is reduced if B accumulates because Enzyme 2 has not used it fast enough
activity of Enzyme 2 is reduced if Enzyme 1 does not produce B fast enough
Compound A
Enzyme 1
Compound B
Enzyme 2
Compound C

Metabolism is the complex network of interdependent and interacting chemical reactions catalysed by enzymes that occur in living organisms. One series of enzyme-catalysed reactions is a metabolic pathway.

3. Anabolism and catabolism

Anabolism is the energy-requiring part of metabolism in which simpler substances are transformed into more complex molecules.

Examples:

- Synthesis of very large molecules (macromolecules) such as proteins and glycogen from smaller single subunits (monomers) by condensation reactions with ATP as the energy source.
- Photosynthesis reactions that produce sugars and other carbon compounds from carbon dioxide and water, with light as the energy source.

Catabolism is the energy-releasing part of metabolism in which complex substances are broken down into smaller molecules.

Examples:

- Digestion of very large molecules (macromolecules) such as proteins, cellulose and starch into monomers by hydrolysis reactions, in which water molecules are split.
- Cell respiration reactions in which glucose or fats are oxidized to release energy, with water and carbon dioxide as waste products.

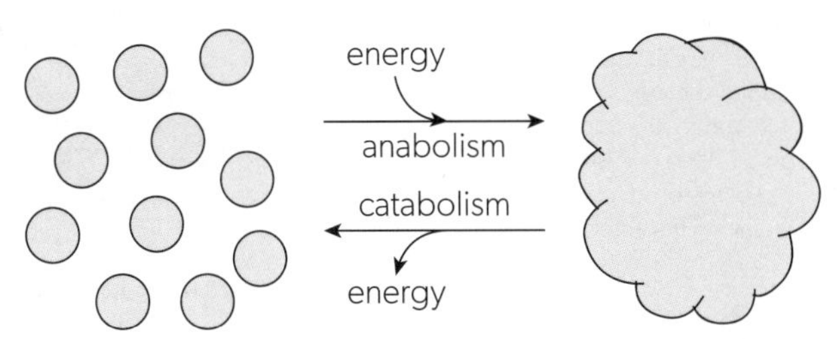
energy
anabolism
catabolism
energy

4. Enzymes as globular proteins

Enzymes are globular proteins. Each enzyme has a site on its surface where catalysis occurs. This is the active site. The substrates of an enzyme bind to its active site and are converted into products. The active site may only consist of a few amino acids, brought together by the folding of the polypeptide chain, but it has the three-dimensional shape and chemical properties that cause the substrates to change extremely rapidly into products. The amino acids at the active site interact with each other to provide the ideal chemical environment for the substrate–product transformation. Some active sites include a non-amino acid component such as a metal ion.

6. Molecular motion and collisions

Molecules in a liquid are in continual random motion. This movement is needed for a substrate molecule and the active site of an enzyme to come together. In some cases, both substrate and enzyme move. In other cases, either the substrate or the enzyme is immobilized and the other must move to it.

Small molecules move more quickly than large molecules. Most enzymes are larger than their substrates, but this is not invariably the case and enzymes used in replication and transcription are smaller than DNA molecules so must move in relation to them.

The meeting of a substrate and active site is often referred to as a collision. The shape and chemical properties of the active site complement those of the substrate, so when close enough and in an appropriate orientation the two are chemically attracted to each other and fit together. A successful collision therefore results in binding of the substrate to the active site.

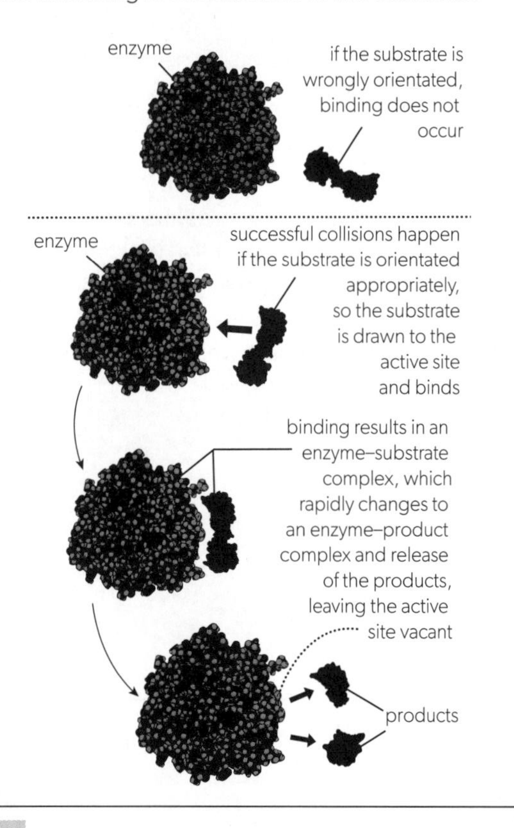
enzyme
if the substrate is wrongly orientated, binding does not occur
enzyme
successful collisions happen if the substrate is orientated appropriately, so the substrate is drawn to the active site and binds
binding results in an enzyme–substrate complex, which rapidly changes to an enzyme–product complex and release of the products, leaving the active site vacant
products

5. Substrate–active site binding

The first stage in enzyme catalysis is binding of the substrate (or substrates) to the active site. The active site and substrate are not rigid unchanging structures like a lock and key. Instead, they interact with each other during the binding process, with both becoming modified to fit the other. The substrate induces reversible changes in the active site and the active site induces changes in the substrate that facilitate its conversion to the product. These changes can affect bond angles, bond lengths and ionization. They tend to weaken bonds within the substrate molecule.

The concept of substrate and active site achieving complementarity through mutually induced changes is known as induced-fit binding.

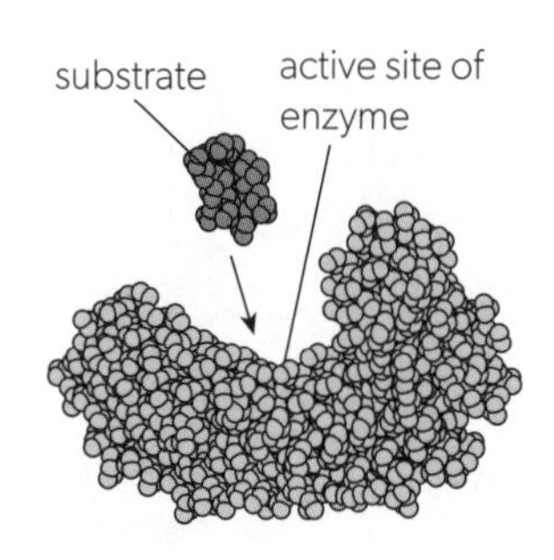
substrate
active site of enzyme

during binding, the conformation of both the active site and the substrate change so they become complementary to each other

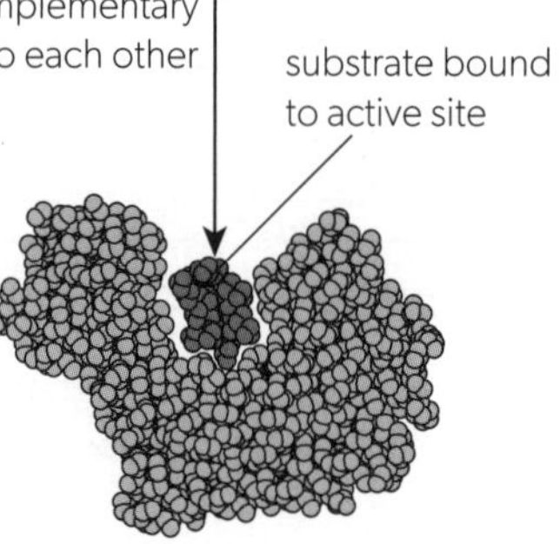
substrate bound to active site

changes in the substrate during binding weaken its bond, making transformation into products faster;
the products dissociate from the active site and the enzyme returns to its original conformation
products

Substances other than the substrate do not usually interact with the active site in a way that results in induced-fit binding or catalysis of a chemical change. This helps to explain enzyme–substrate specificity.

7. Enzyme–substrate specificity and denaturation

The structure of an active site is very precise and distinctive. The structure of the substrate is complementary to it, so binding occurs. Molecules other than the substrate are not attracted to the active site or do not fit it, so do not bind, making enzymes substrate-specific.

Like all proteins, enzymes can be denatured, altering the structure of the active site, so substrates do not bind or binding does not cause the substrates to be changed into products. Denaturation of proteins is covered in *Section B1.2.5*.

The chance of an enzyme molecule becoming denatured increases as temperature rises, but with many enzymes the chance is low until 50°C or more. Enzymes do not all immediately denature if temperature rises above 37°C (human body temperature).

NOS

Sketch graphs

Graphs A to H show the relationship between two variables. If results from an experiment are plotted on a graph, the independent variable should be on the x-axis (across the bottom of the graph). The dependent variable should be on the y-axis (up the side). The distinction between independent and dependent variables is explained in *Section C1.1.9*.

Graphs A to D all show positive correlations. In Graph A, the two variables are directly proportional, but in B to D they are not. Graph B shows an exponential increase.

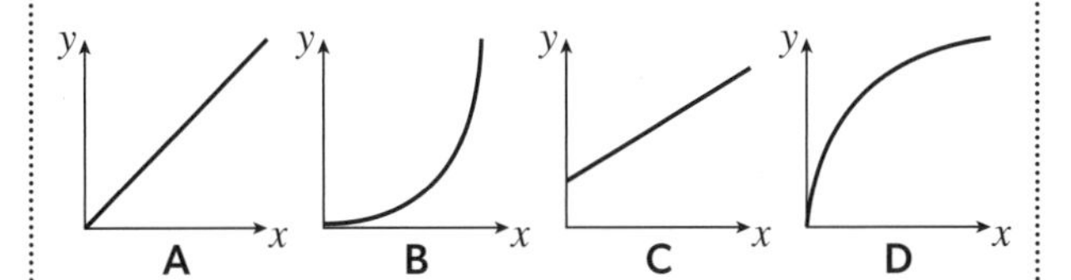

Graphs E to G all show negative correlations. In Graph H, there is a negative correlation at lower values of x but no relationship at higher values. In Graph F, the two variables are inversely proportional, but in E, G and H they are not.

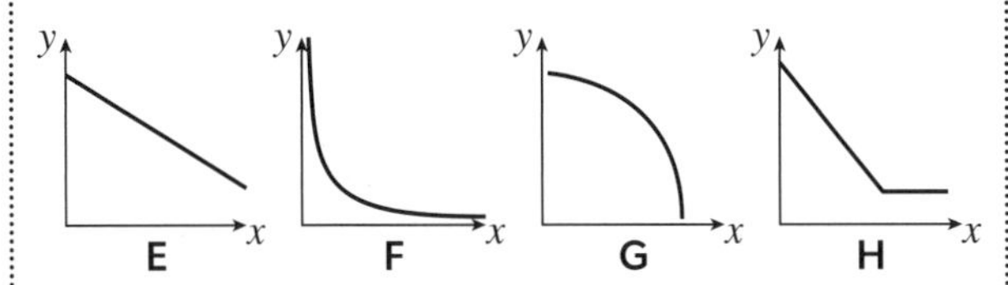

Sometimes biologists draw a sketch graph without any plotted points, to show a predicted relationship or a generalized relationship. That type of sketch graph is an example of a model. The model can be tested by performing a real experiment and seeing if the sketch graph fits the results from the experiment.

8. Factors affecting enzyme activity

Enzyme activity is catalysis of a reaction. The rate of enzyme activity is how frequently the reaction is catalysed. It can be measured by the amount of substrate used up or the amount of product formed per unit time.

Enzyme activity is affected by external factors, such as temperature and pH.

- Temperature affects the rate of molecular movement and therefore the number of substrate–active site collisions per unit time. It can also cause denaturation.

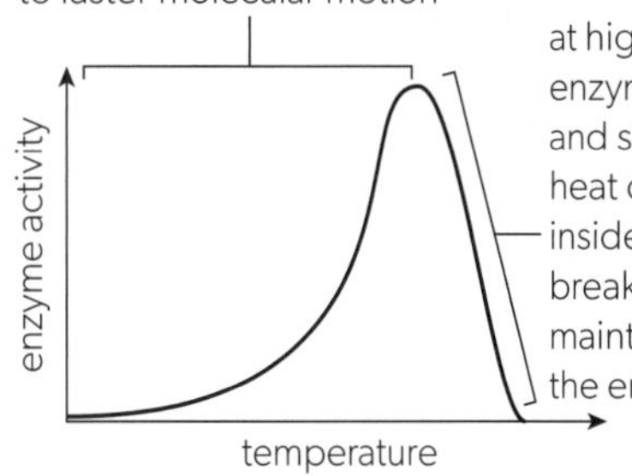

- Substrate concentration affects the number of substrate–active site collisions per unit time.

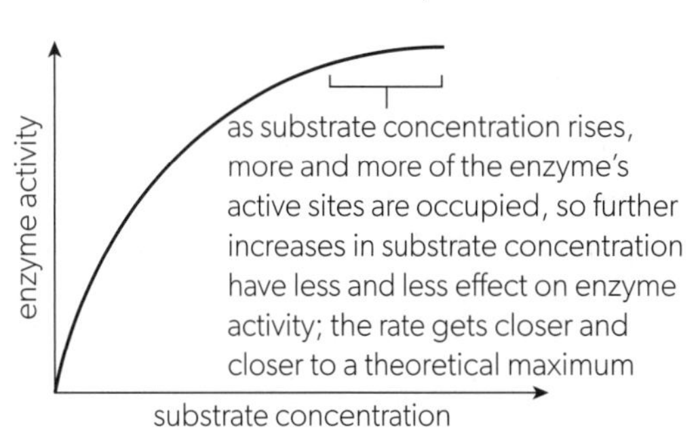

as substrate concentration rises, more and more of the enzyme's active sites are occupied, so further increases in substrate concentration have less and less effect on enzyme activity; the rate gets closer and closer to a theoretical maximum
enzyme activity
substrate concentration

- pH affects the ionization of COOH and NH_2 groups, which alters enzyme conformations and can cause denaturation.

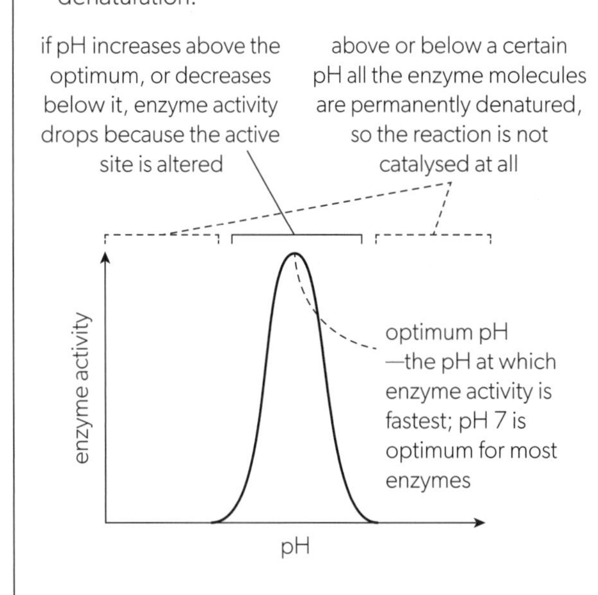

9. Measuring the rate of enzyme-catalysed reactions

The rate of a reaction catalysed by an enzyme can be assessed in experiments by measuring either the quantity of substrate used per unit time, or the quantity of a product formed per unit time. These quantities can be measured as a mass or volume. The units if measuring mass are grams or milligrams per second (g or mg s^{-1}) or for volumes are cubic decimetre or cubic centimetre per second (dm^3 or $cm^3\ s^{-1}$).

Example: Slices of potato were added to 50 cm^3 of hydrogen peroxide. The mass of the mixture was measured every two minutes. The catalase in the potato tissue catalysed the conversion of hydrogen peroxide to water plus oxygen. The oxygen was released into the air, so the mass of the mixture decreased. The tables show the raw results. The mass decreases were calculated by subtracting each mass from the previous one and the rate of mass decrease per second was calculated by dividing the decreases by the time periods in seconds (120 seconds). The results in the table are an example of **secondary data**, because they have been collected by someone else.

The graph shows the rate of mass decrease over time. A slight decrease in rate can be seen during the 12-minute period. This is probably due to a decrease in hydrogen peroxide concentration, as it is used up in the reaction.

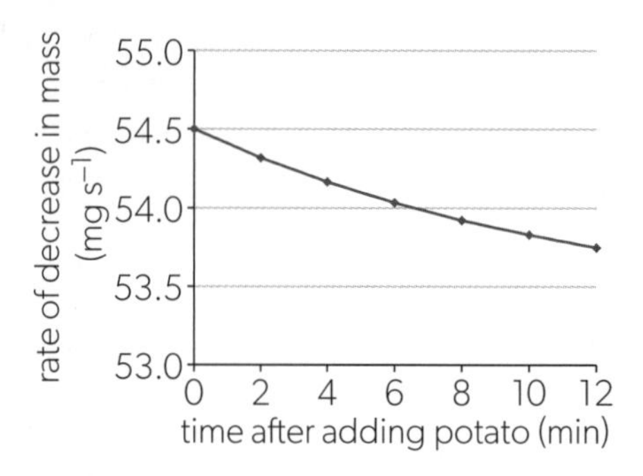

Time after potato added (min)	0	2	4	6	8	10	12
Mass of mixture (g)	54.49	54.31	54.16	54.03	53.92	53.83	53.75

Time interval (min)	0–2	2–4	4–6	6–8	8–10	10–12
Mass decrease (g)	0.18	0.15	0.13	0.11	0.09	0.08
Mass decrease (mg)	180	150	130	110	90	80
Rate of mass decrease (mg s^{-1})	1.50	1.25	1.08	0.92	0.075	0.067

In enzyme experiments and many other biological experiments, there are three types of variable:

Independent variable—this is the factor that you are investigating.

- It is best to investigate only one factor at a time so there is just one independent variable. It is independent because you choose the levels of the variable.
- The range should be wide enough to show all trends. If temperature was the independent variable for example, a range from 0 to 80°C would show both increases due to faster molecular motion and decreases due to denaturation.
- It may be necessary to measure the independent variable to make sure it is at the intended level.

Dependent variable—the level of this variable in an experiment depends on the level of the independent variable—there is a causal link.

- If temperature is the independent variable in an enzyme experiment, the rate of enzyme activity is the dependent variable.
- You might time how long it takes for the substrate to be used up, or measure the quantity of a product formed after a certain time.
- The measurement should be quantitative and as accurate as possible, for example a time to the nearest second. The measurements should be in SI units.

Control variables—these are factors other than the independent variable that could affect the dependent variable.

- They must be kept constant so that they do not affect the results of the experiment.
- For example, if substrate concentration is the independent variable in an enzyme experiment, temperature, pH and enzyme concentration are all control variables.
- Temperature should be kept constant at 20°C or some other suitable temperature, using a water bath or heat block.
- Buffer solutions can be used to keep pH at a specific constant level.

10. Enzymes lower activation energy

Energy is required to break chemical bonds. Energy is released when chemical bonds are made. To convert reactants into products in chemical reactions, bonds must first be broken or weakened in the reactants. Only then can new bonds be formed to generate the products. There is a stage between the breaking and making of bonds when the reactants have changed into a transition state but not yet become products. This is when their energy level is at a maximum. Even if the transition state only lasts for a very short time, it must be passed through.

The amount of energy needed to break bonds within the reactant and reach the transition state is the activation energy of the reaction. In exothermic reactions, more energy is released as the molecules change from the transition state into products than the activation energy. In endothermic reactions less is released.

Enzymes reduce the activation energy of reactions. They do this by weakening bonds in their substrates so an alternative transition state is reached at a lower energy level. Substrates are therefore much more likely to have the activation energy, so reaction rate is greatly increased.

The graph shows energy changes during an exothermic reaction, with and without an enzyme.

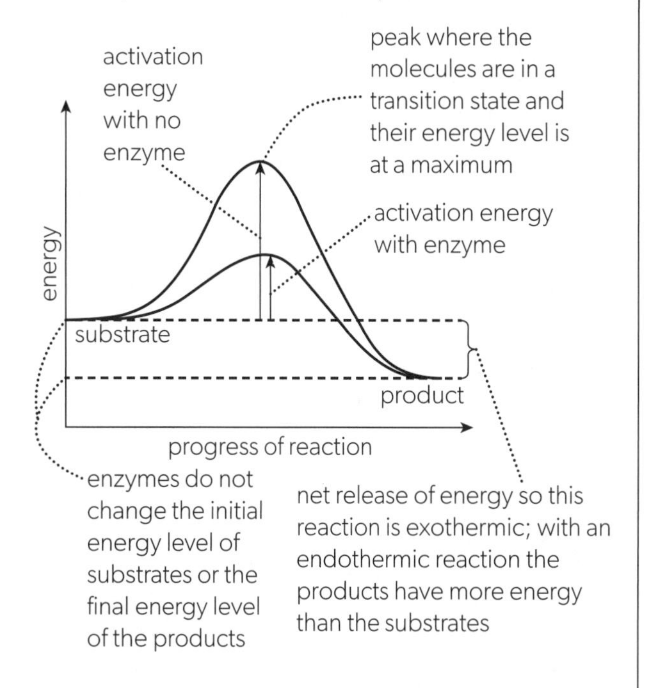

AHL

11. Enzyme-catalysed reactions can be intracellular or extracellular

Most reactions catalysed by enzymes happen inside cells—they are intracellular. Glycolysis and the Krebs cycle are examples of metabolic pathways of reactions that are intracellular.

There are also some enzyme-catalysed reactions that happen outside cells—they are extracellular. The enzymes are synthesized inside cells and are then secreted by exocytosis so they can work outside the cell. Digestion in the human gut is carried out by enzymes working extracellularly.

12. Metabolism and heat energy

Metabolic reactions generate heat. This happens because energy transfers in chemical reactions are not 100% efficient and some chemical energy is inevitably converted to heat.

Heat production is not usually the main function of metabolic reactions, but it is often useful to living organisms as the heat warms up tissues and speeds up enzyme activity.

Mammals, birds and some other animals depend on heat generated by metabolism for maintenance of constant body temperature. They increase the rate of metabolism to avoid hypothermia. Some cells can perform a form of respiration in which all the energy released by oxidizing substrates is converted to heat—this is known as uncoupled respiration.

13. Metabolic pathways can be cyclical or linear

Metabolism is the network of enzyme-catalysed reactions in a cell or organism. Metabolic pathways within this network are either linear or cyclical. Linear pathways are chains of reactions that convert an initial substrate into an end product. Cyclical pathways both use and regenerate a sequence of intermediates. Some reactions are anabolic, with substances fed into the cycle by combining with one of its intermediates. Other reactions are catabolic, with an intermediate splitting to produce a substance that exits.

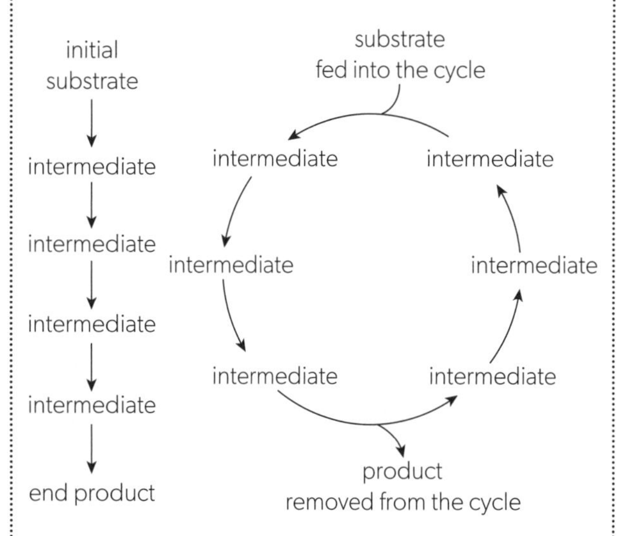

Glycolysis is an example of a linear pathway. The Krebs cycle and Calvin cycle are two of the cyclical pathways in metabolism (see *Topics C1.2* and *C1.3*).

AHL

14. Non-competitive inhibition

All enzymes have an active site on their surface, to which the substrate binds. Many enzymes also have an allosteric site. This has a structure different from that of the active site, so a different substance binds to it. The binding is specific and reversible. In many cases, the substance that binds to the allosteric site is an enzyme inhibitor.

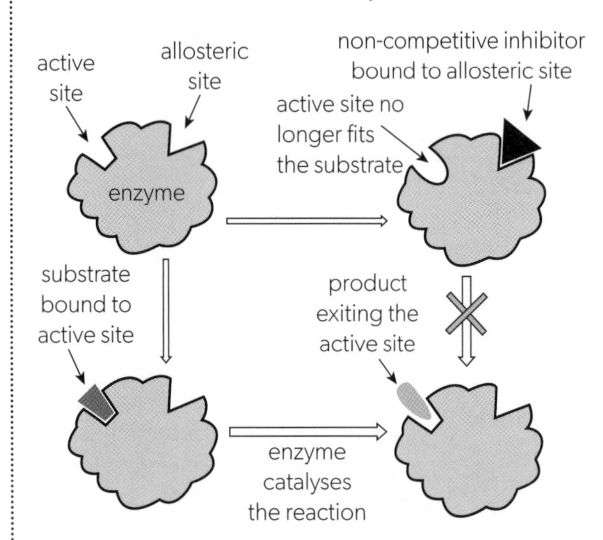

Inhibitors are substances that bind to enzymes and slow down or block enzyme activity. When an inhibitor binds to the allosteric site, it causes interactions within the enzyme that change its conformation. In particular, the chemical properties of the active site are altered. The substrate may still be able to bind, but the active site does not catalyse the reaction, or catalyses it at a slower rate. When the inhibitor dissociates from the active site, the enzyme reverts to its previous conformation and can resume catalysis.

Because of their chemical differences, the inhibitor does not bind to the active site and the substrate does not bind to the allosteric site. They do not therefore compete with each other, so enzyme inhibition using an allosteric site is non-competitive. The substrate cannot prevent binding of the inhibitor, so increases in substrate concentration cannot overcome the inhibition, even at very high substrate concentrations.

The graph shows the effect of a non-competitive inhibitor on enzyme activity. Very high concentrations block enzyme activity completely.

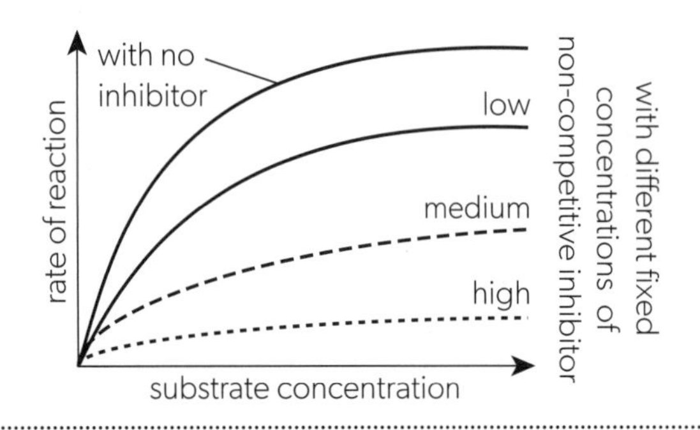

15. Competitive inhibition

The substrate and competitive inhibitor of an enzyme are chemically similar, so both of them can bind to the active site. When the substrate is bound, the inhibitor cannot bind and vice versa. Binding of the inhibitor is reversible, so it eventually dissociates, leaving the active site vacant.

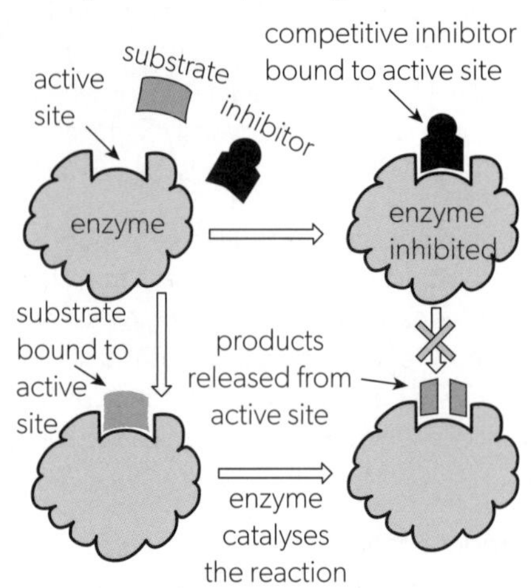

The inhibitor and substrate compete for the active site, with random molecular movements determining which binds when a site becomes vacant. The relative concentrations of the substrate and inhibitor influence the chance of each binding. A fixed low concentration of a competitive inhibitor reduces enzyme activity at low substrate concentrations, but as the substrate concentration rises, a molecule of substrate rather than inhibitor is increasingly likely to bind, so enzyme activity rate is nearly as high as with no inhibitor.

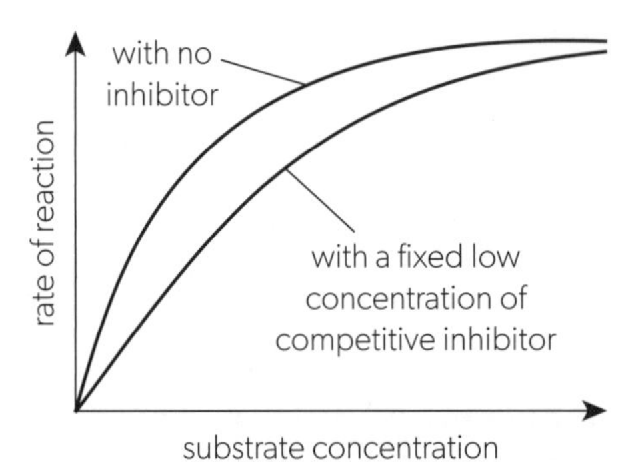

Statins are competitive inhibitors of HMG-CoA reductase. This enzyme catalyses the conversion of HMG-Coenzyme A into mevalonate, which is the rate-limiting step in the metabolic pathway used to synthesize cholesterol in liver cells. All statins have the same structure as HMG-CoA, apart from the Coenzyme A, which is replaced by other groups. Statins bind to the active site of the enzyme, but remain unchanged, preventing binding of the substrate and blocking synthesis of cholesterol. This helps reduce cholesterol levels, reducing the risk of coronary heart disease in some patients.

CH_3 HO COOH H O SCoA — HMG-CoA

HMG-CoA reductase →

CH_3 HO COOH H OH — mevalonate

AHL

16. End-product inhibition

- Metabolic pathways, in most cases, convert an initial substrate to an end product via a series of intermediates.
- Each intermediate is converted into the next by an enzyme-catalysed reaction.
- The end product is useful, but it must be produced at an appropriate rate so it never accumulates or runs out. This can be achieved by end-product inhibition.
- The product of the last reaction in the pathway inhibits the enzyme that catalyses the first reaction.
- The end product binds to an allosteric site on the first enzyme, so it is non-competitive inhibition.
- Binding is reversible and if the end product detaches, the enzyme returns to its original conformation, so the substrate can again bind to the active site.
- The advantage of this method of controlling metabolic pathways is that if there is an excess of the end product the whole pathway is switched off and intermediates do not build up.
- Conversely, as the level of the end product falls, more and more of the enzymes that catalyse the first reaction will start to work and the whole pathway will become activated.
- End-product inhibition is an example of negative feedback.
- The inhibition of threonine deaminase by isoleucine is an example of end-product inhibition. It ensures that supplies of isoleucine are replenished when this amino acid has been used in protein synthesis, but surpluses do not build up.

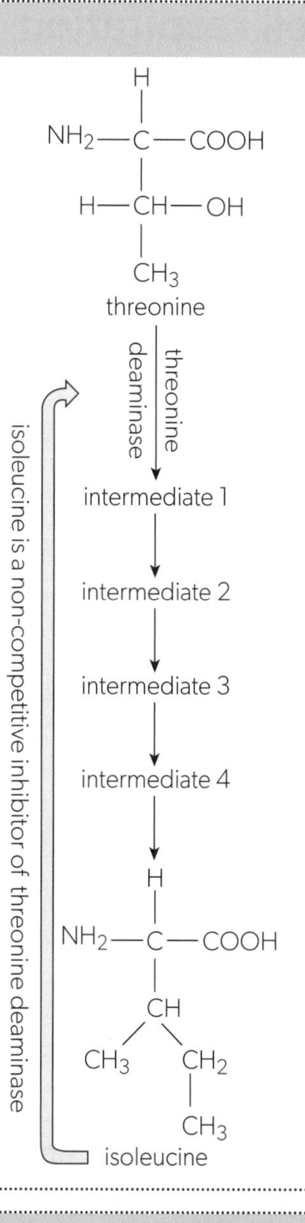

17. Mechanism-based inhibition

Some inhibitors bind irreversibly to the active site of a specific enzyme, by forming a covalent bond. The inhibitor–enzyme complex is stable and can never again function as a catalyst. The reaction between inhibitor and active site is the same every time binding occurs, so is called mechanism-based inhibition. It harms an organism, as each inhibitor molecule permanently inactivates one enzyme molecule.

The antibiotic penicillin, synthesized by *Penicillium* fungi, is an example.

Penicillin (left) bonds covalently with serine in the active site of transpeptidases (the enzymes that cross-link peptidoglycans in the cell wall in Gram-positive bacteria). The wall becomes weak and the bacterial cells burst and die.

Resistance to penicillin is due to base substitution mutations that change the amino acid sequence of transpeptidases. Higher levels of resistance are associated with substitution of threonine with serine at the position adjacent to the penicillin-binding serine in the active site. In combination with other mutations, this prevents penicillin from bonding with serine.

C1.2 Cell respiration

1. Properties of ATP

Every country needs a currency to distribute money. Every cell needs to distribute energy so that a wide range of energy-demanding cellular processes continue. The basic energy currency in all cells is the substance ATP (adenosine triphosphate), a nucleotide with the base adenine, ribose and three phosphate groups.

phosphates
ribose
adenine

ATP has properties that make it ideal as the cellular energy currency:

- Chemically stable at the neutral pH levels typical of cells, so ATP doesn't break down and prematurely release energy.
- Soluble in water so ATP can diffuse freely in cytoplasm, reaching any part of the cell in a fraction of a second.
- Unable to diffuse through the phospholipid bilayers of membranes so ATP's movement within cells can be controlled and there is no leakage out of cells.
- ATP can release a quantity of energy (by removal of the third phosphate group) that is sufficient for a wide range of tasks within the cell, but with a little extra that is wasted by transformation to heat.
- ATP can be easily regenerated by adding a third phosphate group to ADP (adenosine diphosphate).

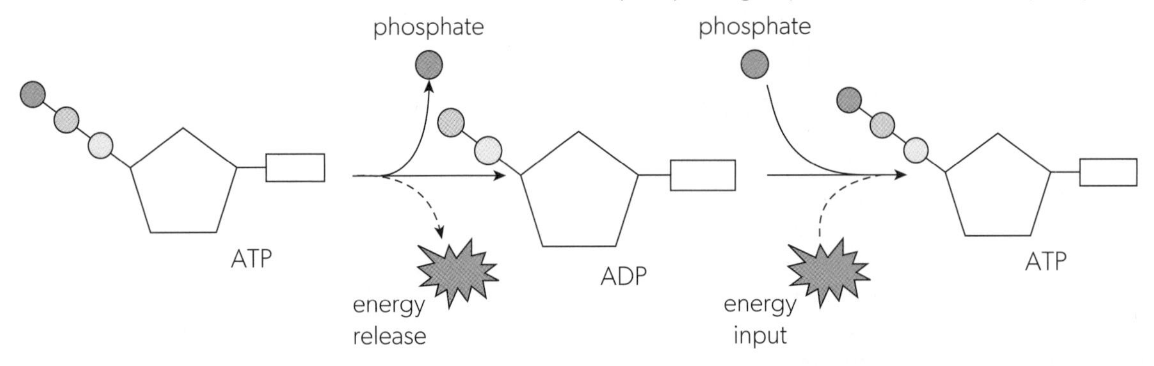

2. Cellular processes requiring ATP

Four examples of processes supplied with energy by ATP:

- Active transport across membranes
- Synthesis of macromolecules (anabolism)
- Movement of cell components such as chromosomes moving during mitosis and meiosis
- Movement of the whole cell (cell motility)

3. Converting between ATP and ADP

ATP and ADP are endlessly interconvertible. Energy is released when ATP is converted to ADP. Energy has to be invested to convert ADP to ATP. This energy can come from a variety of sources including sunlight, oxidation of foods (sugar and fat), and transfer of a phosphate group from other compounds in the cell to ADP.

$$\text{ADP} + \text{phosphate} + \text{energy} \underset{\textit{hydrolysis}}{\overset{\textit{condensation}}{\rightleftharpoons}} \text{ATP} + H_2O$$

Conversion of ADP to ATP is a phosphorylation reaction. It is also a condensation reaction as water is produced, whereas conversion of ATP to ADP requires a water molecule to be split so it is a hydrolysis reaction.

4. Cell respiration as a system for producing ATP

Respiration is the part of metabolism in which carbon compounds are oxidized to release energy in the form of ATP. It happens inside every living cell. Glucose and fatty acids are the principal substrates used in respiration, but a wide range of other carbon compounds can be used, including amino acids.

Cell respiration is different from ventilation and gas exchange:

- Ventilation (breathing) is moving air in and out of the lungs.
- Gas exchange is swapping one gas for another at a surface where a cell or organism is in contact with its environment.

5. Comparing anaerobic and aerobic cell respiration in humans

Cell respiration can be carried out aerobically or anaerobically:

	Aerobic	Anaerobic
Is oxygen used?	Yes	No
What substrates can be used?	Sugars or lipids	Glucose and other sugars
How much ATP is produced per glucose?	30 – 32 (a large yield)	2 (a small yield)
What are the waste products?	Carbon dioxide + H_2O	Lactate (lactic acid)
In a human cell, where do the reactions occur?	Cytoplasm + mitochondria	Cytoplasm only

Simple word equations can be used to show the substrates and end products of respiration in humans using glucose:

Aerobic respiration

glucose + oxygen ⟶ carbon dioxide + water + energy

Anaerobic respiration

glucose ⟶ lactate + energy

6. Investigating the rate of cell respiration

Any device that measures the rate of cell respiration is a respirometer. A sample is put into the apparatus, where it can absorb oxygen from and excrete CO_2 into the air around it. An alkali such as potassium hydroxide absorbs all the CO_2 excreted, so changes in air pressure or volume inside the respirometer are due to oxygen consumption. The decrease in pH of the alkali can be used to deduce the amount of CO_2 produced.

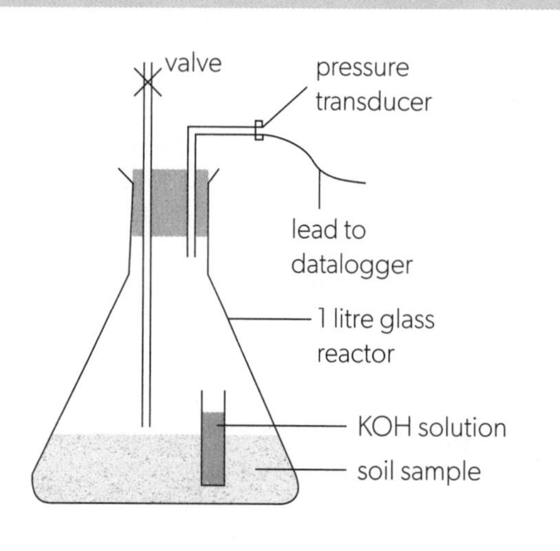

The diagram shows a respirometer used to measure the respiration rate of soil microorganisms. O_2 uptake is calculated from the decrease in air pressure. CO_2 release is calculated from the decrease in pH of the potassium hydroxide solution. Temperature changes affect air pressure so it is essential to prevent the respirometer heating up or cooling down. Respiration rate is O_2 uptake or CO_2 release per unit time.

AHL

7. NAD as a hydrogen carrier in cell respiration

Cell respiration involves many oxidation and reduction reactions. These reactions can occur in different ways:

Oxidation reactions	**Reduction reactions**
A substance is oxidized if:	A substance is reduced if:
• electrons are removed	• electrons are added
• hydrogen is removed	• hydrogen is added
• oxygen is added.	• oxygen is removed.

Oxidation and reduction are opposites and normally happen together, with electrons, hydrogen atoms or oxygen atoms transferred from one substance to another. A reaction in which one substance is oxidized and another is reduced is a redox reaction.

In respiration, pairs of hydrogen atoms are removed from substrates. This is dehydrogenation. It is also oxidation because each hydrogen atom has one electron. Removal of a hydrogen ion (proton) is not oxidation because there is no electron. The hydrogen atoms are accepted by a hydrogen carrier which is therefore reduced. The most commonly used hydrogen carrier is NAD (nicotinamide adenine dinucleotide). It accepts two hydrogen atoms so is reduced.

NAD + 2H ⟶ reduced NAD

In its oxidized state NAD has one positive charge and when it accepts two hydrogen atoms it releases one proton so an alternative version of the equation is this:

$$NAD^+ + 2H \longrightarrow NADH + H^+$$

AHL

8. Glycolysis

Glycolysis is the first part of both aerobic and anaerobic respiration if glucose is the substrate. It happens in the cytoplasm of all cells. There are 10 reactions in this metabolic pathway, each catalysed by a different enzyme. There are four main stages:

1. Phosphorylation

Glucose is phosphorylated twice to form hexose biphosphate. Adding phosphate groups to a molecule is phosphorylation. It raises the energy level of molecules, making them less stable and therefore more reactive. In this case reactions that would not be possible with glucose, happen readily with hexose biphosphate. Two ATPs are used to phosphorylate one molecule of glucose.

2. Lysis

Hexose biphosphate is split to form two molecules of triose phosphate. Lysis is splitting molecules into smaller ones.

3. Oxidation

Two atoms of hydrogen are removed from each triose phosphate molecule. This is oxidation. The end product of glycolysis is pyruvate.

4. ATP formation

Oxidation reactions are usually exothermic. Enough energy is released by oxidizing each triose phosphate molecule to convert two ADP molecules to ATP.

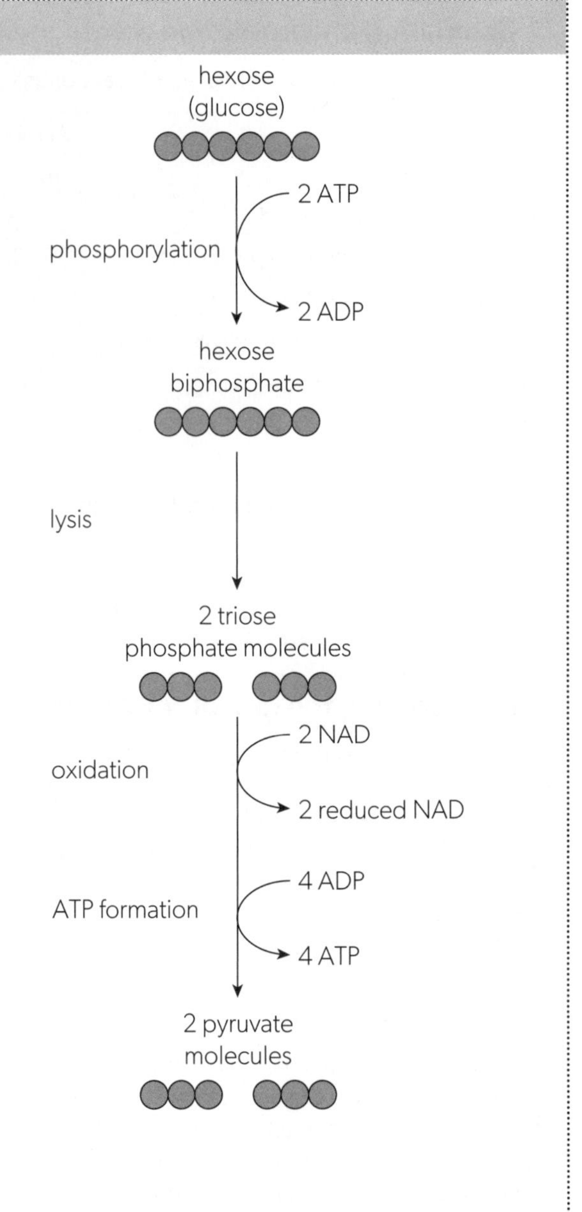

Summary of glycolysis:

- One glucose is converted into two pyruvates.
- Two NADs are converted into two reduced NADs
- Two ATP molecules are used per glucose but four are produced, so there is a net yield of two ATP molecules. This is a small yield of ATP per glucose, but it can be achieved without the use of any oxygen.

9. Regenerating NAD in anaerobic cell respiration

Oxygen is not used in glycolysis, so this pathway can be used for production of ATP by anaerobic respiration.

Glycolysis (and anaerobic cell respiration) can continue in a cell as long as glucose does not run out and both ADP and NAD are regenerated. ADP is regenerated when ATP is used.

In human cells NAD is regenerated by transferring hydrogen atoms from reduced NAD to pyruvate. This oxidizes the reduced NAD to NAD and reduces the pyruvate to lactate.

The net yield of ATP in anaerobic respiration is two per glucose. This is a smaller yield than with aerobic respiration but it can be produced much more rapidly because oxygen does not have to be supplied. It is useful when huge amounts of ATP are needed for a short time, for example in leg muscles during sprinting.

Lactate lowers the pH of cytoplasm and of blood; the lactate is released by cells. Anaerobic respiration is only used for a relatively short time, to prevent blood pH dropping too low.

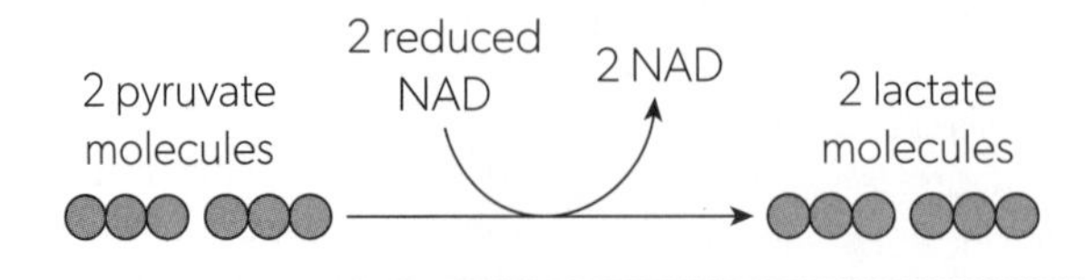

AHL

10. Anaerobic cell respiration in yeast

The metabolic pathway used for anaerobic respiration in yeast is the same as in humans apart from the method used to regenerate NAD. Yeast converts pyruvate to ethanal by removing CO_2 (a decarboxylation reaction). The ethanal is then reduced to ethanol by transferring two hydrogen atoms from reduced NAD, producing NAD. This allows anaerobic respiration to continue as long as glucose is available and ADP is regenerated from ATP.

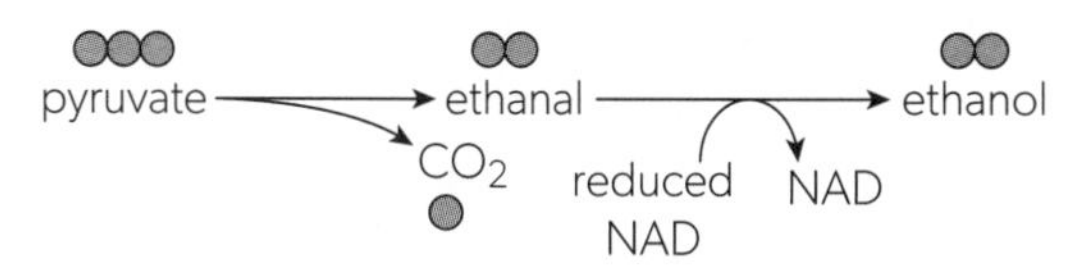

Anaerobic respiration in yeast produces carbon dioxide and ethanol, whereas in humans it produces lactate. Two industries are based on the waste products of anaerobic respiration in yeast—brewing and baking.

1. Carbon dioxide and the baking industry

Yeast is used in baking bread. It is mixed into the dough before baking. The yeast rapidly uses up all oxygen present in the dough and then produces ethanol and carbon dioxide by anaerobic cell respiration. The carbon dioxide forms bubbles making the dough rise—it increases in volume. This makes the dough less dense —it is leavened. When the dough is baked most of the ethanol evaporates and the carbon dioxide bubbles give the bread a light texture, which makes it more appetizing.

Baking

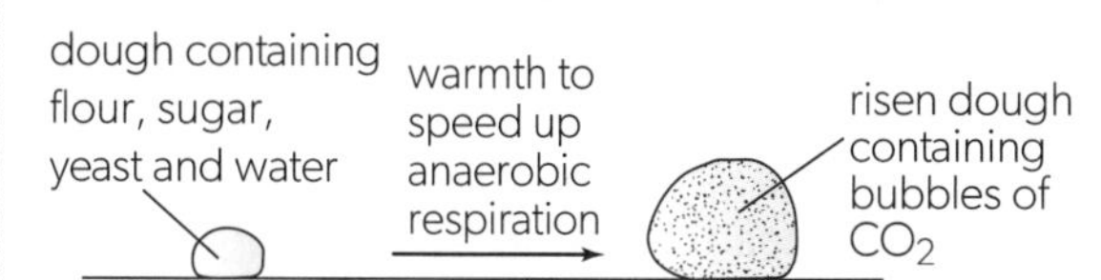

2. Ethanol and the brewing industry

Yeast can be used to produce ethanol by fermentation. The yeast is cultured in a liquid containing sugar (such as grape juice) but not oxygen, so it respires anaerobically. The ethanol concentration of the fluid around the yeast cells can rise to approximately 15% by volume, before it becomes toxic to the yeast and the fermentation ends. Most of the carbon dioxide bubbles out into the atmosphere. Beer, wine and other alcoholic drinks are brewed in this way. Ethanol is also produced by fermentation for use as a fuel.

Brewing

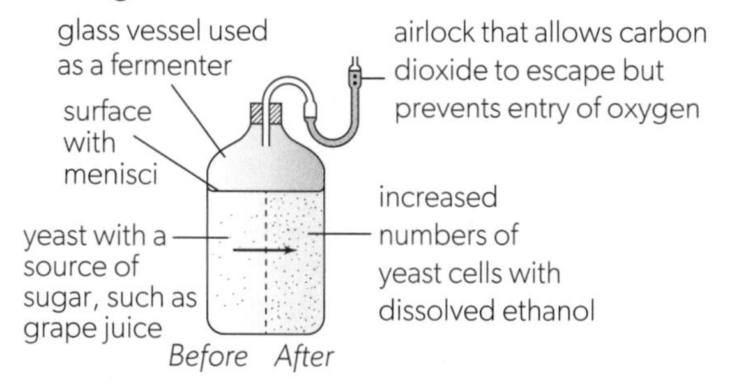

11. The link reaction

If oxygen is available, pyruvate produced in glycolysis can be oxidized further, to release more energy.
A cycle of reactions is used (the Krebs cycle), but pyruvate must first be converted into the acetyl groups (CH_3CO–) that can be fed into the cycle. Conversion of pyruvate produced by glycolysis into acetyl groups needed for the Krebs cycle is known as the link reaction.

Pyruvate is changed in two ways during the link reaction:

1. Decarboxylation—carbon dioxide is removed.
2. Oxidation—a pair of hydrogen atoms is removed.

An acetyl group remains, which is linked to a carrier molecule called CoA (Coenzyme A), to produce acetyl-CoA.

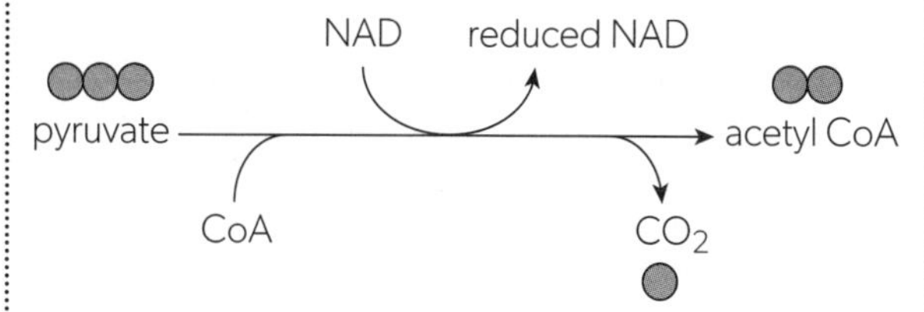

In eukaryotic cells, both the link reaction and the Krebs cycle occur in the matrix of the mitochondrion, where the enzymes needed to catalyse the reactions are.

There are also enzymes in the matrix of the mitochondrion that convert fatty acids into acetyl CoA. Two-carbon fragments are removed from the hydrocarbon chain of a fatty acid and are converted into acetyl groups, which are linked to CoA. The acetyl CoA can then be fed into the Krebs cycle. This is how fatty acids are used as a substrate in aerobic respiration. The membranes of the mitochondrion have transporter proteins for absorbing both pyruvate and fatty acids from the surrounding cytoplasm.

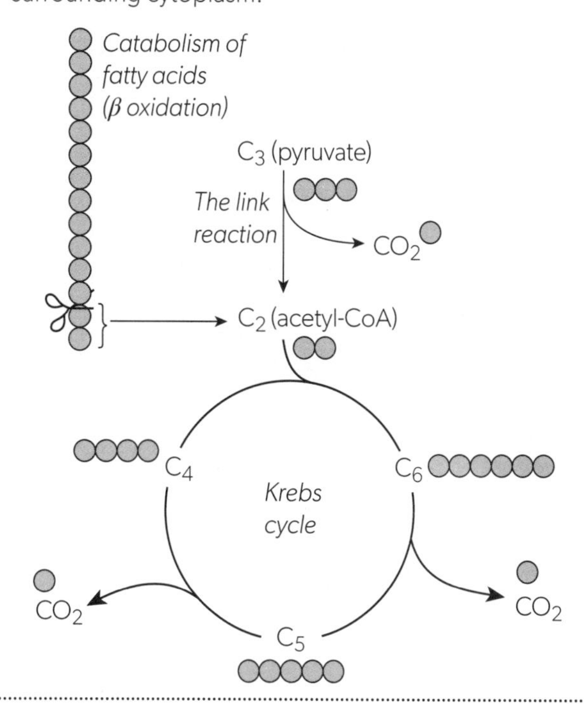

AHL

12. The Krebs cycle

Acetyl groups produced in the link reaction are fed into the Krebs cycle by transfer from acetyl CoA to a four-carbon organic acid (oxaloacetate). This produces a six-carbon organic acid (citrate). Citrate is converted back into oxaloacetate via a series of intermediates. There are in total eight enzyme-catalysed reactions in the cycle, including the initial reaction that converts oxaloacetate to citrate.

Three types of reaction occur:

- Carbon dioxide is removed in two decarboxylation reactions. In most cells the CO_2 is a waste product and is excreted.
- Hydrogen is removed in four reactions. The hydrogen atoms each have an electron, so removal of hydrogen from intermediates is both oxidation and dehydrogenation. The hydrogen is accepted by carriers, which become reduced. In three of the oxidations the hydrogen is accepted by NAD (nicotine adenine dinucleotide). In the other oxidation, the carrier that accepts it is FAD (flavin adenine dinucleotide). These oxidation reactions release energy, much of which is transferred to the carriers when they accept hydrogen. This energy is later released by the electron transport chain and used to make ATP.
- ATP is produced directly in one of the reactions. This reaction is substrate-level phosphorylation.

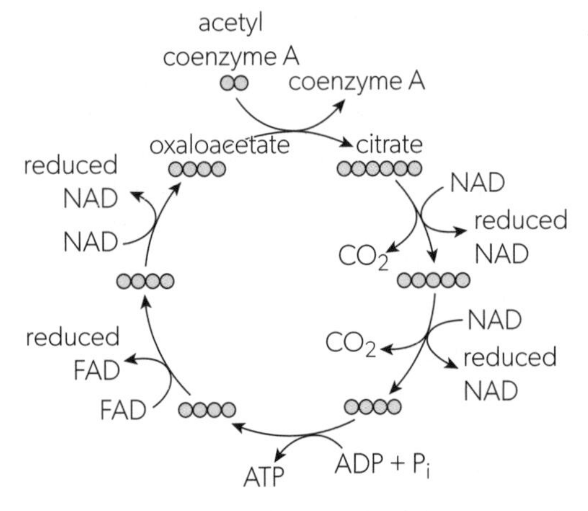

The link reaction and Krebs cycle both happen in the matrix of the mitochondrion (see *Sections A2.2.10* and *B2.2.4*). A simple diagram is shown here.

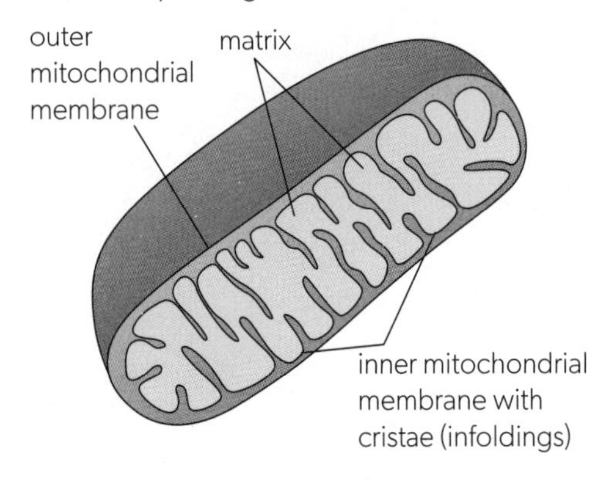

13. The electron transport chain

The electron transport chain is a series of carriers, located in the inner membrane of the mitochondrion. Reduced NAD supplies two electrons to the first carrier in the chain. The electrons (as part of hydrogen atoms) come from oxidation reactions in glycolysis, the link reaction and Krebs cycle. Transfer of electrons from reduced NAD regenerates NAD, which can then accept more hydrogen/electrons from the oxidation of respiratory substrates (carbohydrate or lipid).

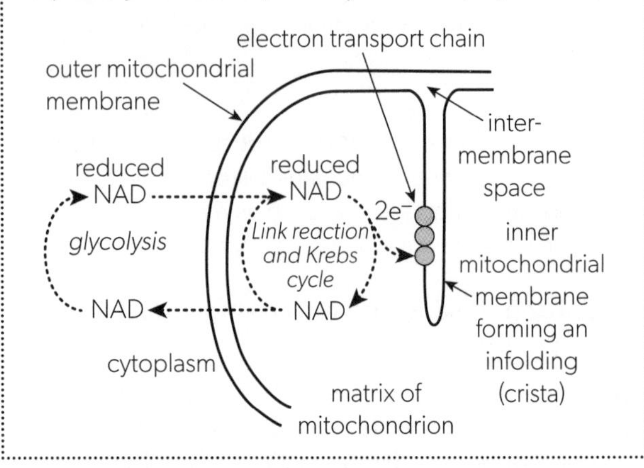

14. Generating a proton gradient

As the electrons pass along the chain from one carrier to the next, they release energy. The electron carriers act as proton pumps and use the energy released by electron flow to pump protons (H^+) from the matrix of the mitochondrion to the intermembrane space. This causes a proton concentration gradient to develop across the inner mitochondrial membrane. The relatively small size of the space between the inner and outer mitochondrial membranes (the intermembrane space) allows a steep gradient to develop rapidly. The difference in proton concentration gives a membrane potential (voltage) of about 150 mV. The membrane is only 5 nm across, so the field strength is an impressive 30 million volts per metre.

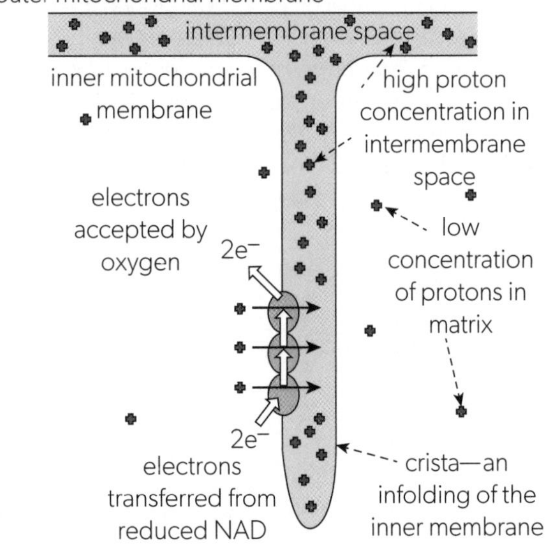

AHL

15. Chemiosmosis

A proton gradient is established across the inner mitochondrial membrane by electron flow through the electron transport chain. This gradient is a store of potential energy, which is used by the enzyme ATP synthase to generate ATP by phosphorylation of ADP. The coupling of the energy-releasing process of electron transport to the energy-requiring process of ATP production is called chemiosmosis.

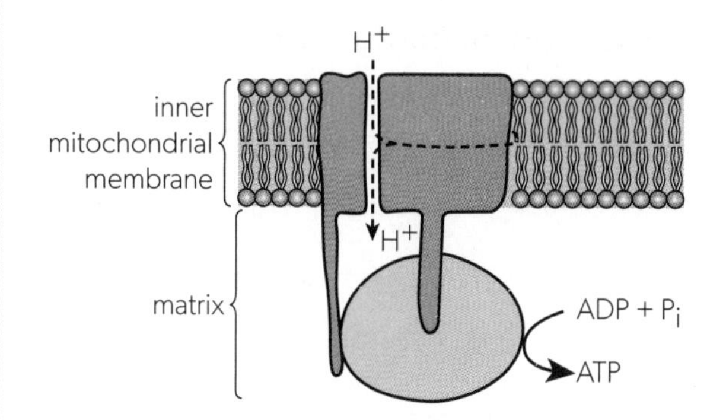

ATP synthase is a large, complex and truly remarkable enzyme. It is one of the triumphs of evolution. ATP synthase has a rotor that can spin on its axis and other parts that are non-rotating. The rotor is embedded in the inner mitochondrial membrane. It allows protons (H^+) to diffuse across the membrane from the intermembrane space to the matrix, down the concentration gradient. The protons do not pass through a pore as they would in a typical channel protein. Instead, ATP synthase has binding sites on the sides of the rotor. Protons from the intermembrane space can bind to these sites, but they can only be released into the matrix when the rotor is in a different position, achieved by rotation. As the protons diffuse from a higher to a lower concentration, they release sufficient energy to cause this rotation. Potential energy from the proton gradient has thus been transformed into kinetic energy of the rotating enzyme.

The rotor has a central stalk that projects out into the matrix. Around this is a globular region of ATP synthase, made up of three subunits. Each of these has an active site where ADP is phosphorylated to ATP. The globular region does not rotate, but rotation of the central stalk within it causes a cycle of conformational changes that allow the active sites to produce ATP:

1. ADP and phosphate bind to different parts of the active site

2. A conformational change to the active site forces ADP and phosphate together, producing ATP

3. The active site returns to its original conformation, so ATP is released and the active site becomes vacant

One 360° turn of the rotor and its central stalk results in the production of three molecules of ATP and requires nine protons to pass through ATP synthase from the intermembrane space to the matrix. Thus, three protons must be pumped into the intermembrane space in order to make one ATP by chemiosmosis.

16. Oxygen is the terminal electron acceptor

Electrons pass from carrier to carrier in the electron transport chain, until the last carrier passes the electrons, now depleted of energy, to oxygen. This happens on the surface of the inner mitochondrial membrane, using oxygen dissolved in the matrix. The oxygen also accepts protons (H^+) from the matrix, to form water. Humans produce about half a litre of water per day in this way.

$$O_2 + 2e^- + 2H^+ \longrightarrow H_2O$$

This reaction removes protons from the matrix and therefore contributes to the proton gradient used in chemiosmosis.

Oxygen's only role in cell respiration is as terminal electron acceptor for the electron transport chain, but if it is not available, electron flow along the electron transport chain stops and reduced NAD cannot be converted back to NAD. Supplies of NAD in the mitochondrion run out and the link reaction and Krebs cycle cannot continue. The only part of cell respiration that can continue is glycolysis, with a relatively small yield of ATP. Oxygen thus greatly increases the ATP yield, per glucose, of cell respiration.

17. Comparing respiratory substrates

Glucose and lipids are both used as respiratory substrates. Both have advantages.

	Lipids (triglycerides)	Carbohydrates
C:H:O ratio	1 : 2 : 0.065 (approximately) so relatively less oxidized, hence a larger yield of energy	1 : 2 : 1 so relatively more oxidized, hence a smaller yield of energy
Energy released	37 kJ per gram	16 kJ per gram
Metabolic pathways used if O_2 available	Beta oxidation to produce acetyl groups, then Krebs cycle and chemiosmosis	Glycolysis + link reaction to produce acetyl groups, then Krebs cycle and chemiosmosis
Type of respiration	Aerobic only	Aerobic or anaerobic

C1.3 Photosynthesis

1. Converting light energy to chemical energy in photosynthesis

There are many different forms of energy, such as chemical energy, heat (thermal energy) and light (a form of radiant energy). Energy can be changed from one form into another. Light energy is transformed into chemical energy in photosynthesis. This happens when light is absorbed by pigments (coloured substances such as chlorophyll) and is changed into chemical energy. The carbon compounds that are produced by photosynthesis contain the chemical energy that previously was light.

2. Carbon dioxide is converted to glucose in photosynthesis

The ratio of atoms in a glucose molecule is 1 carbon : 2 hydrogens : 1 oxygen. The ratio in carbon dioxide molecules is 1 carbon : 2 oxygens. To convert carbon dioxide into glucose, half of the oxygen must therefore be removed and hydrogen must be added.

Hydrogen is obtained by splitting water molecules into hydrogen and oxygen. This can only happen when light is available because energy is required. Twelve water molecules are split for each glucose molecule made:

$$12H_2O \rightarrow 24H + 6O_2$$

Half of the hydrogen atoms become part of a glucose molecule. The other half are used to remove one oxygen atom from carbon dioxide and convert it to water:

$$6CO_2 + 24H \rightarrow C_6H_{12}O_6 + 6H_2O$$

3. Equation for photosynthesis

Synthesis of glucose by photosynthesis can be summed up with a simple equation:

carbon dioxide + water + light → glucose + oxygen

Oxygen is a by-product of splitting water to release hydrogen.

Three groups of organisms carry out photosynthesis: plants, algae and cyanobacteria. These organisms use some of the oxygen that they produce in aerobic cell respiration (for example the roots of plants) but most of it is excreted into the environment.

In organisms that live underwater, the oxygen produced during photosynthesis can sometimes be seen emerging as bubbles, which rise to the water surface. In terrestrial organisms the oxygen diffuses into the atmosphere unseen.

4. Chromatography

1. Tear up a leaf into small pieces

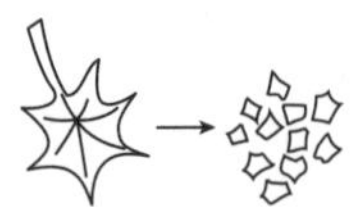

2. Grind the leaf pieces with sharp sand and propanone to extract the leaf pigments

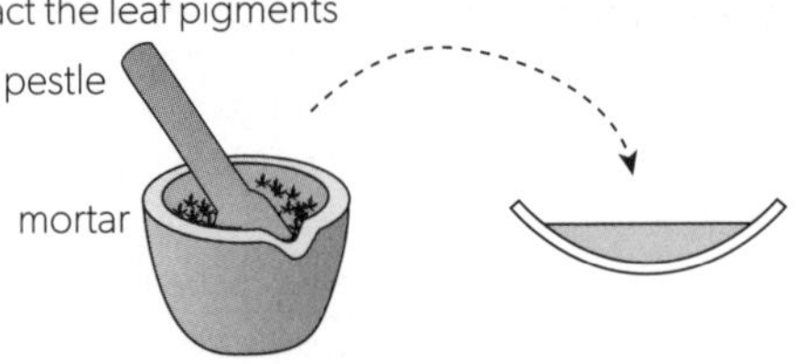

3. Transfer a sample of extract to a watch glass

4. Evaporate to dryness with hot air from a hair-dryer

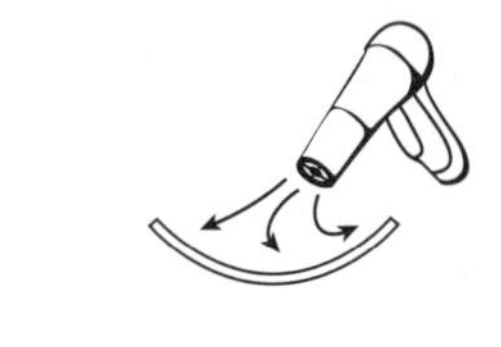

5. Add a few drops of propanone to dissolve the pigments

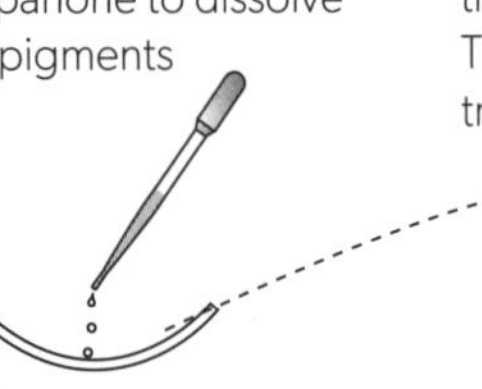

6. Build up a concentrated spot 10 mm from the end of a strip of chromatography paper or TLC strip (thin layer chromatography) by transferring tiny drops of solution

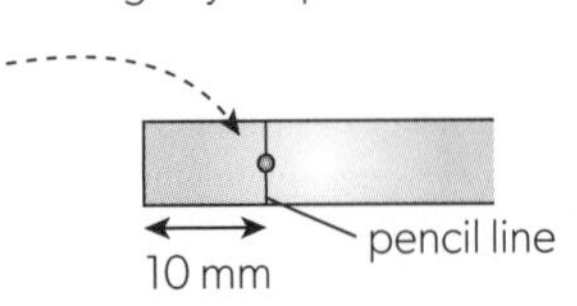

7. Suspend the strip in a tube with the base dipping into running solvent

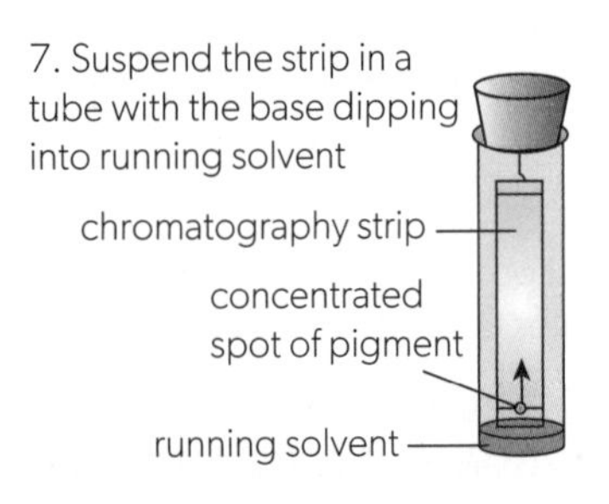

8. Remove the strip from the tube when the running solvent has nearly reached the top. Draw a pencil line to show how far the solvent moved.

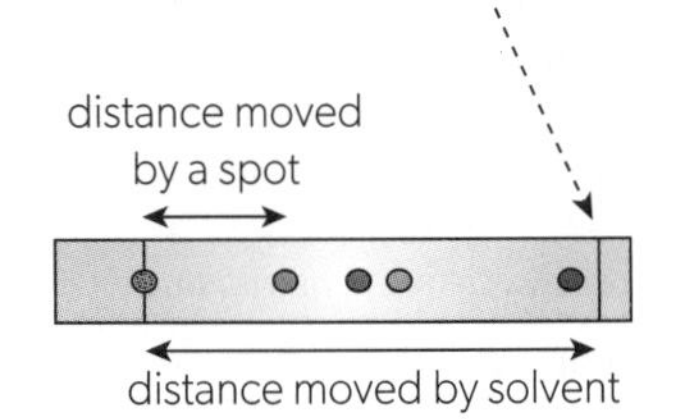

9. The pigment in each spot can be identified from its colour and its R_f value. R_f is the distance moved by a spot, as a proportion of the distance moved by the solvent. Pigments move at different rates. The rate depends on whether a pigment is more attracted to the hydrophobic running solvent or to the hydrophilic chromatography strip. Typical R_f values are shown on the diagram (right).

$$R_f = \frac{\text{distance moved by spot}}{\text{distance moved by solvent}}$$

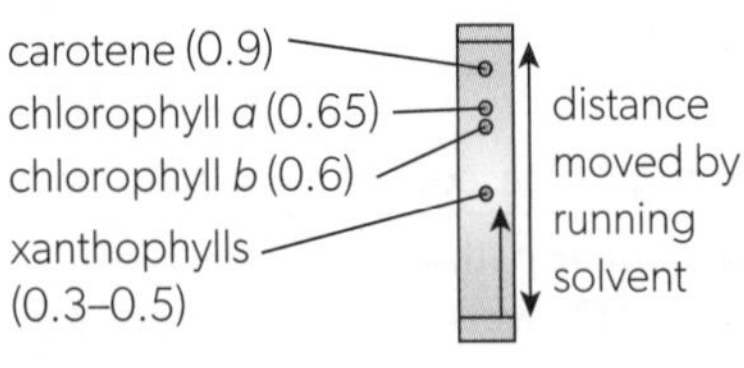

5. Wavelengths of light absorbed in photosynthesis

The Sun emits a wide spectrum of electromagnetic radiation. Particularly large amounts in the range of wavelengths from 400 nm to 700 nm reach the Earth's surface and this range is used both in photosynthesis and human vision. Violet light has the shortest wavelength and red has the longest. The shorter the wavelength, the more energy a photon of light has.

Pigments such as chlorophyll have a structure that allows an electron within the molecule to jump from one energy level up to a higher level, using energy obtained by absorbing a photon of light. This is how solar energy is transformed into chemical energy in photosynthesis. The electron is said to be "excited". Photosynthetic pigments can pass excited electrons on to other molecules. Much of the energy carried by the excited electrons ends up in glucose or other carbon compounds.

For any photosynthetic pigment, only specific wavelengths of light have the amount of energy needed to raise an electron to a higher energy level and only these wavelengths are absorbed. Other wavelengths are reflected. A graph showing which wavelengths are absorbed is an absorption spectrum.

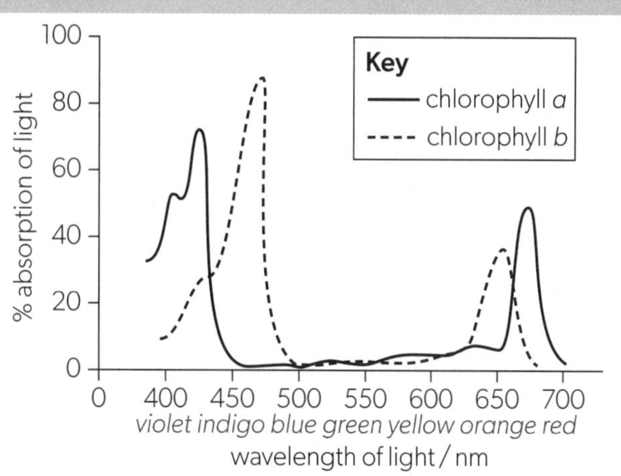

The graph above is the absorption spectrum for the two commonest forms of chlorophyll, *a* and *b*. It shows that chlorophyll absorbs red and blue light most effectively. Very little green light is absorbed but most is reflected, making chlorophyll appear green to us. Although chlorophylls are the main pigments in photosynthesis others are used, including xanthophyll and carotene, which absorb blue and green light but not wavelengths from yellow to red in the spectrum.

6. Comparing absorption and action spectra

A graph showing relative amounts of photosynthesis at different wavelengths of light is an absorption spectrum. The data needed for it is obtained experimentally.

The wavelength of light is the independent variable. It can be varied using LEDs or colour filters.

The dependent variable is a measure of the rate of photosynthesis. This can be the rate of oxygen production or carbon dioxide consumption. Bubbles of oxygen rising from a pondweed can be counted or the rise in pH due to CO_2 consumption can be measured.

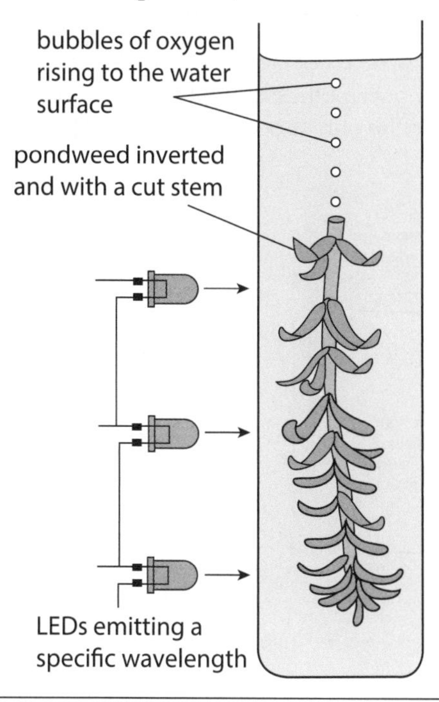

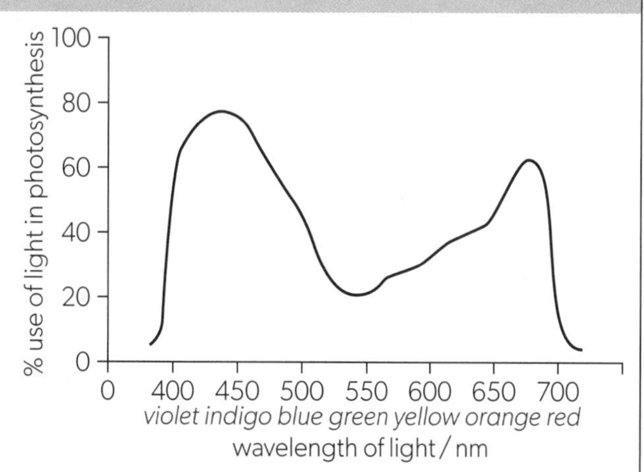

The graph above is a typical action spectrum. It is similar to the absorption spectrum of chlorophyll, with a peak in the blue, a second lower peak in the red and a trough in the green. This is because wavelengths of light absorbed by chlorophyll are used in photosynthesis.

The action spectrum shows that some green light is used in photosynthesis, even though chlorophyll absorbs little. This is due to "accessory" pigments such as xanthophyll and carotene harvesting some wavelengths that chlorophyll does not.

7. Limiting factors on the rate of photosynthesis

Processes such as photosynthesis are affected by various factors, but usually just one of these factors is actually limiting the rate at a particular time. This is the factor that is nearest to its minimum and is called the **limiting factor**. The three possible limiting factors for photosynthesis are **temperature**, **light intensity** and **carbon dioxide concentration**.

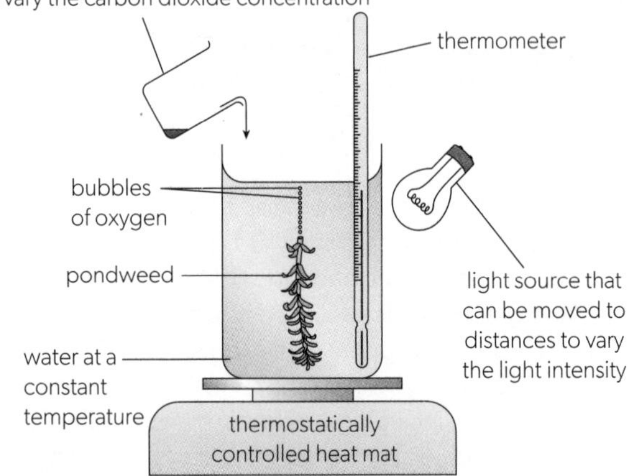

sodium hydrogencarbonate solution added to vary the carbon dioxide concentration
thermometer
bubbles of oxygen
pondweed
light source that can be moved to distances to vary the light intensity
water at a constant temperature
thermostatically controlled heat mat

These principles should be remembered when designing an experiment to investigate the effect of a limiting factor on photosynthesis:

1. Only one limiting factor should be investigated at a time—this is the **independent variable**.

2. A suitable range for the independent variable should be chosen, from the lowest possible level, to a level at which the factor is no longer limiting.

3. An accurate method should be chosen for measuring the rate of photosynthesis. This is the **dependent variable** and is usually a measure of oxygen production per unit time.

4. So the independent variable is the only factor affecting the rate of photosynthesis, all other factors must be kept constant. These are the **control variables**. Of the three factors temperature, light intensity and CO_2 concentration, one will be the independent variable and the other two will be control variables.

Limiting factor	Method of varying the factor	Suggested range	Controlling the factor
Temperature	Place pondweed in water in a thermostatically controlled water bath or on a hot plate to vary the temperature	5°C to 45°C in 5 or 10°C intervals	Set the thermostat at 25°C and keep it there throughout the experiment
Light intensity	Move light source to different distances and measure light intensity with a lux meter [light intensity = 1/distance^2]	4, 5, 7, 10 and 14 cm and no light gives a good range of intensities	Keep the light source at a constant distance, such as 5 cm
Carbon dioxide concentration	Start with boiled, cooled water (no CO_2) then add measured quantities of $NaHCO_3$ to increase the CO_2 concentration	0 to 50 mmol dm^{-3} in 10 mmol dm^{-3} intervals	Add enough $NaHCO_3$ to give a high CO_2 concentration (50 mmol dm^{-3})

NOS

Hypotheses in biological research

Hypotheses are provisional explanations. They require repeated testing. Hypotheses about the effects of three limiting factors on rates of photosynthesis are shown as annotations on the graphs below. You can test them using techniques in the table above.

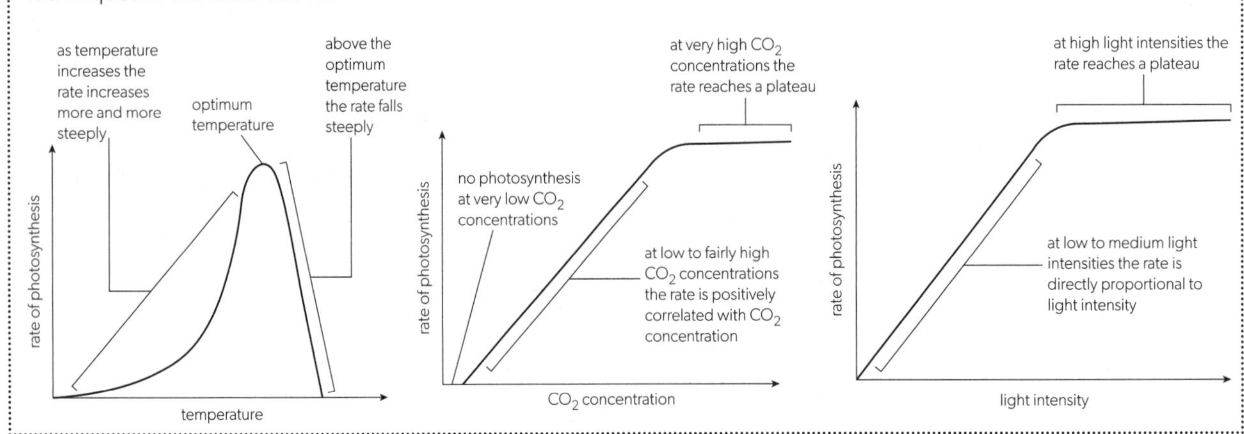

as temperature increases the rate increases more and more steeply
optimum temperature
above the optimum temperature the rate falls steeply
rate of photosynthesis
temperature
at very high CO2 concentrations the rate reaches a plateau
no photosynthesis at very low CO2 concentrations
at low to fairly high CO2 concentrations the rate is positively correlated with CO2 concentration
rate of photosynthesis
CO2 concentration
at high light intensities the rate reaches a plateau
at low to medium light intensities the rate is directly proportional to light intensity
rate of photosynthesis
light intensity

8. Carbon dioxide enrichment experiments

The carbon dioxide concentration of the atmosphere was 270 ppm until the late 18th century. Human activities have since increased it by more than 50%. The CO_2 concentration is forecast during the 21st century to rise to more than double the pre-industrial level. This massive increase will have many effects on the Earth. There is already evidence of faster rates of photosynthesis, because CO_2 concentration commonly is the limiting factor. There is also evidence of increases in growth and accumulation of plant biomass, locking up carbon and helping to lessen the rise in atmospheric CO_2.

Future rates of photosynthesis and plant growth can be predicted from results of experiments in which CO_2 concentration is artificially increased, with other factors unchanged. Experiments in greenhouses have been followed up by free air carbon dioxide enrichment (FACE) experiments where the plants are not in an enclosed space.

In the first series of FACE experiments, plant growth in agricultural crops and young tree plantations was investigated. The second series is being conducted in natural or semi-natural forests around the world. Circles of towers are built from which carbon dioxide can be released. CO_2 concentration is monitored inside the circles and when it drops below 550 ppm, CO_2 is released on the upwind side. Control plots are included, with air rather than carbon dioxide released from the circles of towers. Many variables are monitored in the circular areas from which the consequences of a global rise to 550 ppm CO_2 can be predicted for plants, other organisms and whole ecosystems. In particular, the hypothesis that increased photosynthesis and plant growth will moderate rises in CO_2 concentration can be tested.

AHL

9. Photosystems

Photosystems are molecular arrays of chlorophyll and other accessory pigments with special chlorophylls as the reaction centre, from which pairs of excited electrons are emitted. Photosystems are located in thylakoid membranes. A thylakoid is a sac-like vesicle. In photosynthetic eukaryotes the thylakoids are flattened and arranged in stacks inside chloroplasts. They have two types of photosystem (PS I and PS II) with different structures and functions.

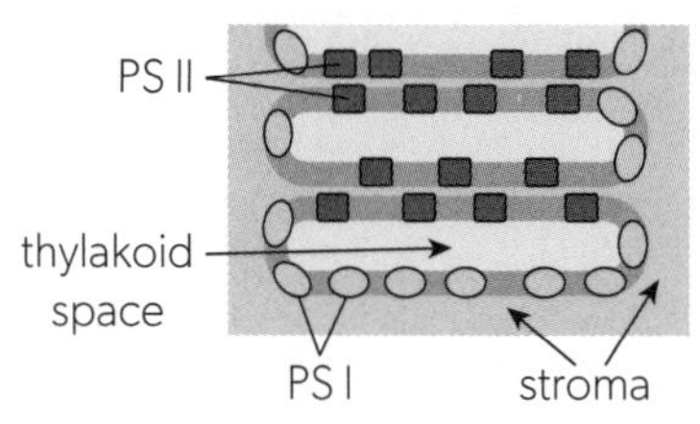

PS I is positioned where the thylakoid membrane is exposed to the surrounding stroma, whereas PS II does not need to be in contact with the stroma. Cyanobacteria also have thylakoids with PS I and II, but they are not located in chloroplasts and the pigments are arranged differently.

10. Pigment molecules in a photosystem

Each photosystem has two types of functional unit: a reaction centre that emits excited electrons and antenna complexes that harvest light energy and funnel it to the reaction centre. Antenna complexes have many pigment molecules, of multiple types, in a precise arrangement. These are the advantages:

- A wider array with a larger number of pigment molecules intercepts more photons of light and therefore supplies energy to the reaction centre at a faster rate.
- Each type of pigment absorbs a narrow range of wavelengths. A wider range of wavelengths can be absorbed and a greater proportion of the energy in sunlight is used because photosystems contain different types of pigment rather than just one.
- Energy is transferred from pigment to pigment by excitation energy transfer. In general, $X^* + Y \rightarrow X + Y^*$, where X and Y are adjacent pigments and the asterisked pigment has excitation energy. The energy passes because Y is at a lower energy level when excited than X. The precisely structured array of pigments in an antenna complex ensures that energy is funnelled to the reaction centre of the photosystem. Part of the array in PS I is shown.

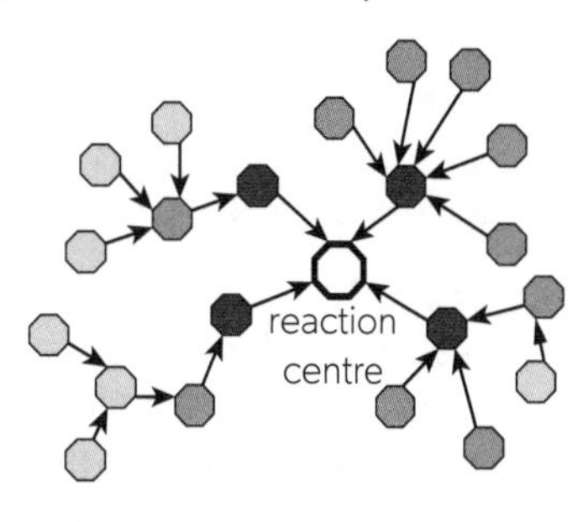

11. Photolysis of water in PS II

Absorption of light allows a special chlorophyll (P680) in the reaction centre of PS II to emit an excited electron. As a consequence, P680 is reduced and remains so until it regains an electron, released when water is split. This happens in the oxygen-evolving complex (OEC) of PS II on the surface of the photosystem facing the space inside the thylakoid. The OEC binds a total of two water molecules and splits them into four electrons, four protons and one molecule of oxygen.

$$2H_2O \rightarrow O_2 + 4H^+ + 4e^-$$

The electrons pass to the P680. The protons are released into the thylakoid space, contributing to a proton gradient across the thylakoid membrane. The oxygen molecules are a waste product and diffuse out of the thylakoids. This splitting of water is called photolysis because it only happens in the light when the P680 chlorophyll has lost electrons.

Evolution of photolysis, billions of years ago, initiated the accumulation of oxygen in the atmosphere, allowing organisms to respire aerobically and causing oxidation of dissolved iron and other minerals in the oceans.

AHL

12. ATP production by chemiosmosis in thylakoids

ATP is one of the two useful products of reactions in the thylakoids—the light-dependent reactions. As in mitochondria, ATP is produced by chemiosmosis (described in *Section C1.2.15*).

ATP synthase is located in thylakoid membranes. A proton gradient is generated by chains of electron carriers in thylakoid membranes. Excited electrons pass along these chains, releasing energy which is used to pump protons from the stroma to the thylakoid space. The electrons can be supplied in two ways:

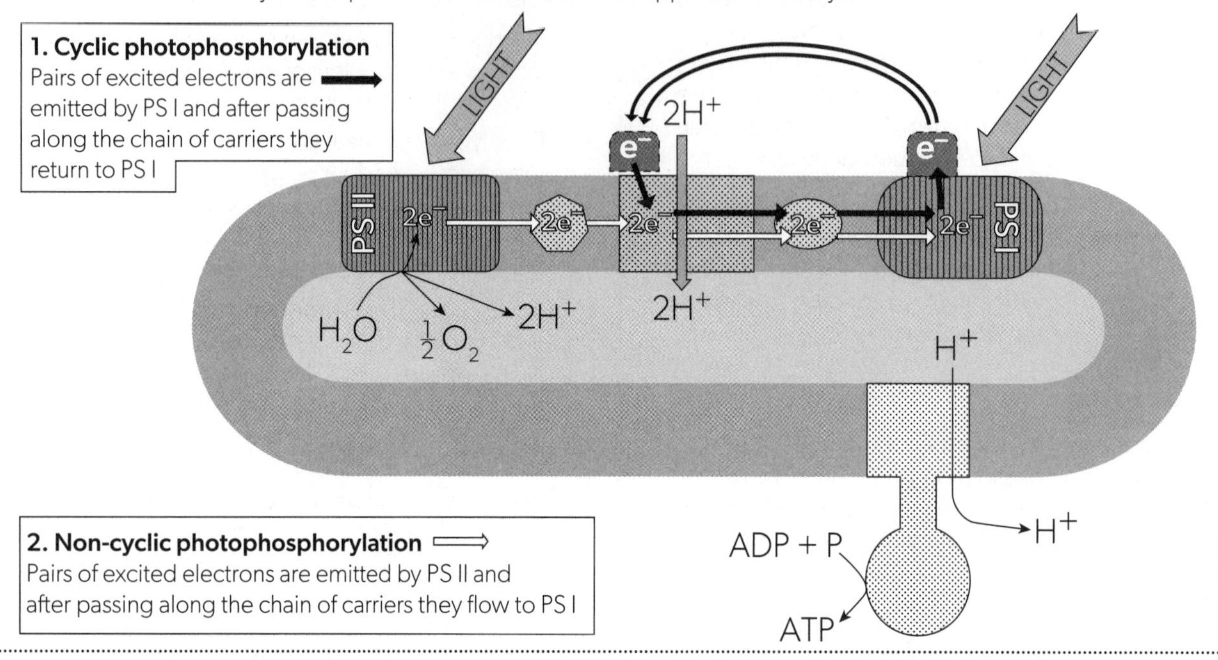

13. NADP is reduced by PS I

Reduced NADP is one of the two useful products of the light-dependent reactions in thylakoids. It is produced using excited electrons emitted by photosystem I. Each electron emitted is accepted by an electron carrier (ferredoxin) on the surface of the thylakoid membrane. The reduced electron carrier binds to an enzyme (NADP reductase) also on the surface of the thylakoid membrane and transfers the electron it is carrying to the enzyme. Two electrons are needed to reduce NADP.

$$\text{NADP} + 2e^- \rightarrow \text{reduced NADP}$$

NADP is dissolved in the stroma. It is reduced when the random molecular motion brings it to the enzyme's active site. Electrons emitted by PS I are replaced by electrons from PS II and passed along the chain of electron carriers. Production of reduced NADP (NADPH) is therefore accompanied by non-cyclic photophosphorylation.

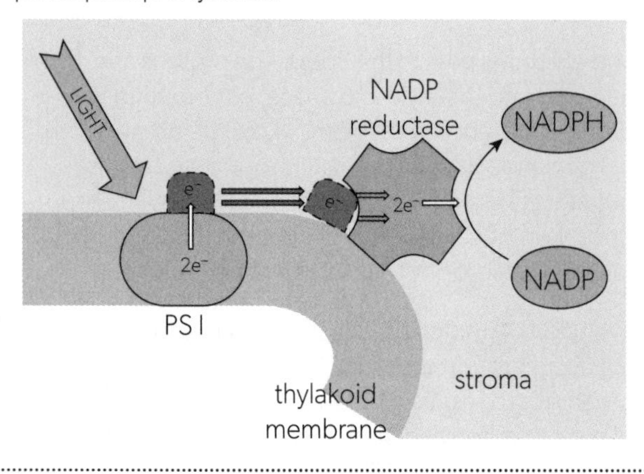

14. Thylakoids

Thylakoids are systems because they consist of interacting and interdependent components.

The thylakoid membrane is the key component:

- Impermeable to protons so a proton gradient can develop
- Encloses a small volume of fluid so a gradient develops rapidly
- Made of phospholipids so can hold photosystems composed of hydrophobic pigment molecules
- Holds other components in the correct relative positions—ATP synthase, electron carriers and NADP reductase.

Each thylakoid component depends on other components:

- PS II supplies excited electrons to the electron carrier chain
- The electron carrier chain supplies energy to proton pumps
- Proton pumps create a proton gradient used by ATP synthase
- PS I supplies excited electrons to NADP reductase
- PS II resupplies PS I with electrons
- Water in the thylakoid space supplies electrons to PS II.

AHL

15. Rubisco

Carbon dioxide diffuses into the stroma of the chloroplast and is then fixed by being converted into a more complex carbon compound. This happens in a carboxylation reaction catalysed by the enzyme Rubisco. Carbon dioxide is combined with ribulose bisphosphate (RuBP), which is a five-carbon sugar. The product of the reaction is an unstable six-carbon compound, which immediately splits to form two molecules of glycerate 3-phosphate.

$$\text{RuBP} + CO_2 \xrightarrow{\text{Rubisco}} 2 \text{ glycerate 3-phosphate}$$

Light energy is not used directly in carbon fixation, so it is a light-independent reaction of photosynthesis.

High concentrations of Rubisco are needed in the stroma of chloroplasts, because it works relatively slowly and is not effective in low carbon dioxide concentrations. Because of this and because of the abundance of photosynthesizing organisms, Rubisco is the most abundant enzyme on Earth.

16. Synthesis of triose phosphate

Glycerate 3-phosphate, formed by carbon fixation, is an organic acid. It is converted into triose phosphate (a three-carbon sugar) by a reduction reaction in the stroma. The hydrogen needed for this is supplied by reduced NADP. Energy is also needed and is supplied by ATP.

$$\text{glycerate 3-phosphate} + \text{reduced NADP} + \text{ATP} \rightarrow \text{triose phosphate} + \text{NADP} + \text{ADP}$$

This reaction is part of the Calvin cycle. All reactions in the Calvin cycle are light-independent because they can happen in the dark, as long as ATP and reduced NADP are available.

17. The Calvin cycle

For the Calvin cycle to continue, every RuBP consumed must be replaced. Triose phosphate is used to regenerate RuBP. Five molecules of triose phosphate are converted by a series of reactions into three molecules of RuBP. This process requires the use of energy in the form of ATP. The reactions are summarized in the diagram below.

For every six molecules of triose phosphate made by the light-independent reactions, five are used to regenerate RuBP and one exits the cycle.

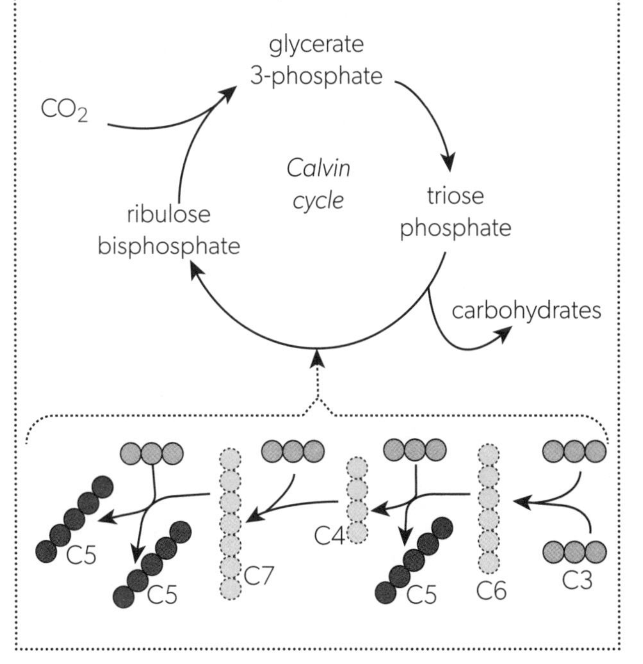

18. Using the products of the Calvin cycle

All of the carbon in compounds in photosynthesizing organisms is fixed in the Calvin cycle. Glucose is produced by linking together two triose phosphates. It can be converted into other carbohydrates such as sucrose for transport, or starch for storage. Pathways for making fatty acids and amino acids start with glycerate 3-phosphate or triose phosphate from the Calvin cycle, or with intermediates from pathways of aerobic respiration.

Mineral nutrients supply all elements other than carbon, hydrogen and oxygen in compounds made by photosynthesizing organisms.

- Nitrogen for making amino acids is supplied by nitrate or ammonium ions.
- Sulfur for amino acids is supplied as sulfate.
- Phosphorus for making phospholipids, ATP and nucleotides for DNA and RNA is supplied as phosphate.

19. Interdependence of photosynthesis reactions

The light-independent reactions cannot happen without a supply of ATP and reduced NADP from the light-dependent reactions. Similarly, the light-dependent reactions require ADP and NADP, which the light-independent reactions produce.

End of topic questions—C1 Questions

C1.1 Enzymes and metabolism

1. In an experiment into the activity of salivary amylase, 5 cm^3 samples of 0.1 mol dm^{-3} starch solution and 0.1 cm^3 samples of undiluted saliva are placed in block heaters at different temperatures, and are mixed when they reach the target temperature. The time taken for each sample of starch to be fully digested is found by repeatedly testing drops of the starch–saliva mixture.
   a. i. State the independent variable. (1)
      ii. State the dependent variable. (1)
   b. The volumes of the starch solution and saliva are control variables. State two other control variables in this experiment. (2)
   c. If 15 samples of starch and saliva are available, discuss whether it would be better to use:
      - five of them at each of 20°C, 30°C and 40°C,
      - three of them at each of 20°C, 30°C, 40°C, 50°C and 60°C or
      - one of them at 5°C intervals from 20 to 90°C. (3)
   d. State the substrate in this experiment. (1)
   e. State the word equation for starch digestion. (2)
   f. Sketch a graph to show the expected relationship between:
      i. temperature and time taken for all starch to be digested in a sample (3)
      ii. temperature and the rate of starch digestion. (2)
2. a. Outline what a catalyst is. (2)
   b. Explain the need for many different enzymes in a cell. (2)
   c. State what collisions occur during enzyme catalysis. (1)
3. Annotate the graph to explain how enzymes change the energy levels during the progress of an exothermic chemical reaction. Include the concept of induced fit in your explanation. (10)

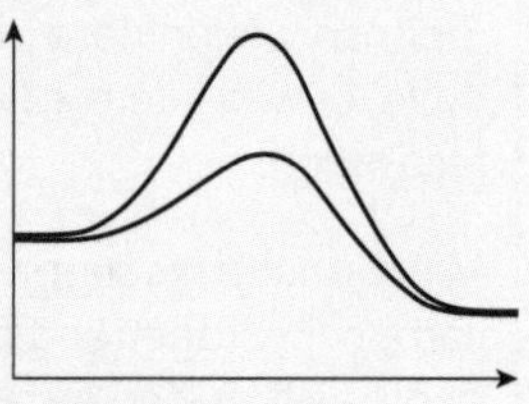

C1.2 Cell respiration

1. The graph shows the results of an experiment in which the respiration rate of yellow-billed magpies was measured at seven temperatures from −10°C to +40°C. Between −10°C and +30°C, the magpies maintained constant body temperature, but above 30°C body temperature increased.

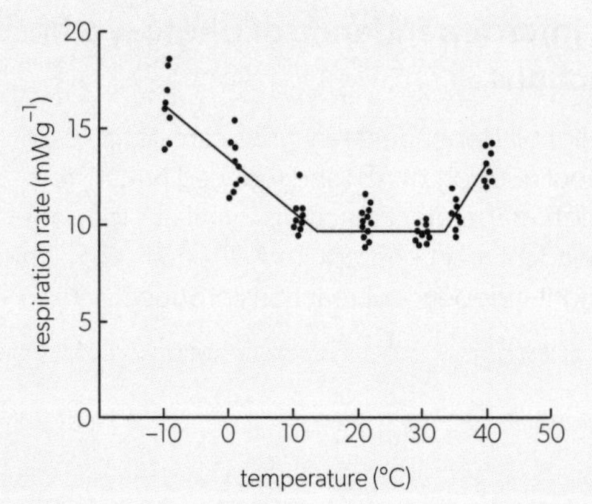

   a. Describe the relationship between external temperature and respiration rate in the magpies. (3)
   b. Explain the change in respiration rate as external temperature drops from +10°C to −10°C. (3)
   c. Suggest a reason for the change as external temperatures increased from +30°C to +40°C. (1)
   d. Suggest two reasons for the variation in respiration rate between the birds at each external temperature. (2)
2. a. Draw a simple diagram of the structure of ATP. (3)
   b. List cell processes that depend on a supply of ATP. (4)
   c. Evaluate whether aerobic or anaerobic cell respiration is a better method of producing ATP. (3)
3. (HL only) The diagram shows parts of a mitochondrion.
   Identify where:
   a. Krebs cycle occurs (1)
   b. electron transport occurs (1)
   c. proton concentration is highest (1)
   d. ATP synthase is located (1)
   e. oxygen accepts electrons. (1)

C1.3 Photosynthesis

1. The graph shows data-logging of three variables in a culture of the alga Chlorella in a fementer.
   a. Explain the causes of rises and fall is in pH. (1)
   b. State the relationship shown in the graph between:
      i. light intensity and CO_2 concentration (1)
      ii. temperature and CO_2 concentration. (1)
   c. From the graph, deduce whether light intensity or temperature has more effect on CO_2 concentration. (2)
2. Predict, giving reasons, future rates of photosynthesis. (5)
3. (HL only) The diagram summarizes the Calvin cycle.

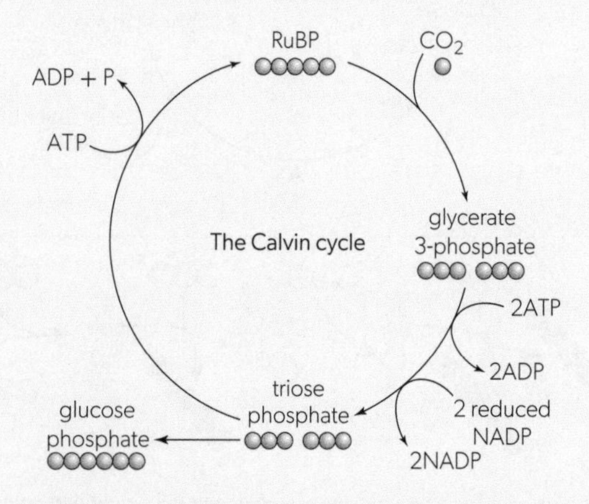

   a. Explain reasons for conversion of five-sixths of triose phosphate into ribulose bisphosphate. (2)
   b. Explain how lack of light prevents the Calvin cycle from producing triose phosphate. (4)
   c. Explain how a lack of CO_2 prevents photosystem II from functioning. (4)

D1.1 DNA replication

1. DNA replication

A replica is an exact copy of something. DNA replication is the synthesis of new strands of DNA with precisely the same base sequence as the original strands.

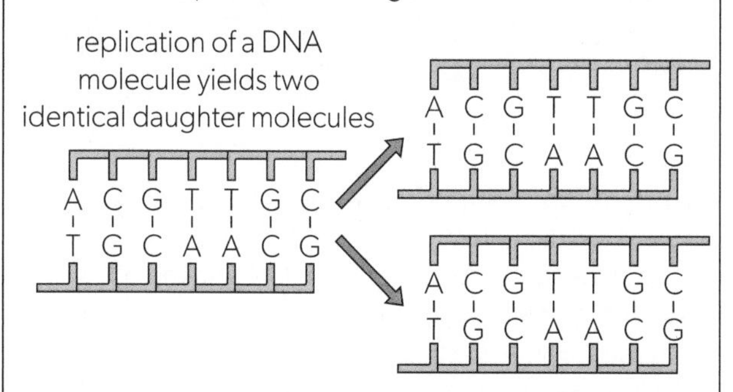

Organisms replicate all their DNA before cell division, so both daughter cells have the entire genome. Unicellular organisms reproduce by cell division. In multicellular organisms, cell division is part of three processes:

- growth, which requires extra body cells to be produced
- replacement of damaged tissues
- reproduction, to provide cells that develop into gametes. DNA replication is thus an example of continuity rather than change. Base sequences pass unchanged from cell to cell in a multicellular organism and from generation to generation by reproduction.

2. DNA replication is semi-conservative

Replication starts with separation of a parent DNA molecule into two single strands, by breaking hydrogen bonds between the bases. Each single strand is then used as a template for the assembly of a new polymer of nucleotides.

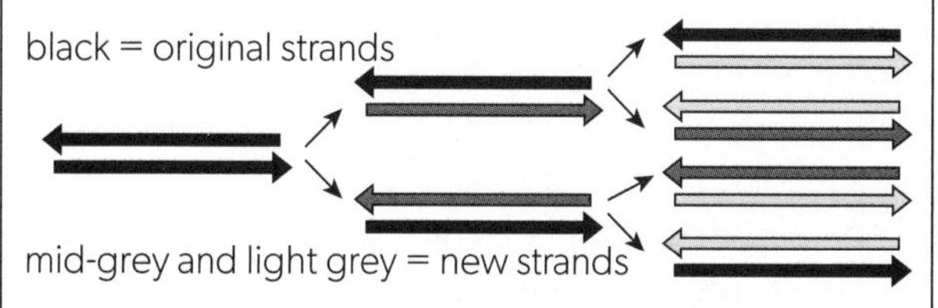

This is called semi-conservative replication because each of the DNA molecules produced has one new strand and one strand conserved from the parent molecule.

The two DNA molecules produced by replication are identical in base sequence to each other and to the original parent molecule. This is due to complementary base pairing. Adenine only pairs with thymine and cytosine only pairs with guanine. The consequence is that each new strand is complementary to the template strand on which it was made and identical to the other template strand. Complementary base pairing ensures a high degree of accuracy in the copying of base sequences—it is very rare for the wrong base to be inserted.

3. Helicase and DNA polymerase

A replication fork is the site where a parent DNA molecule is separated into two single strands, each of which is used as a template for the synthesis of a new strand. The replication fork gradually moves along the parent molecule. The changes that occur at a replication fork are carried out by multiple enzymes working together. The roles of two types of enzyme, helicase and DNA, are shown here.

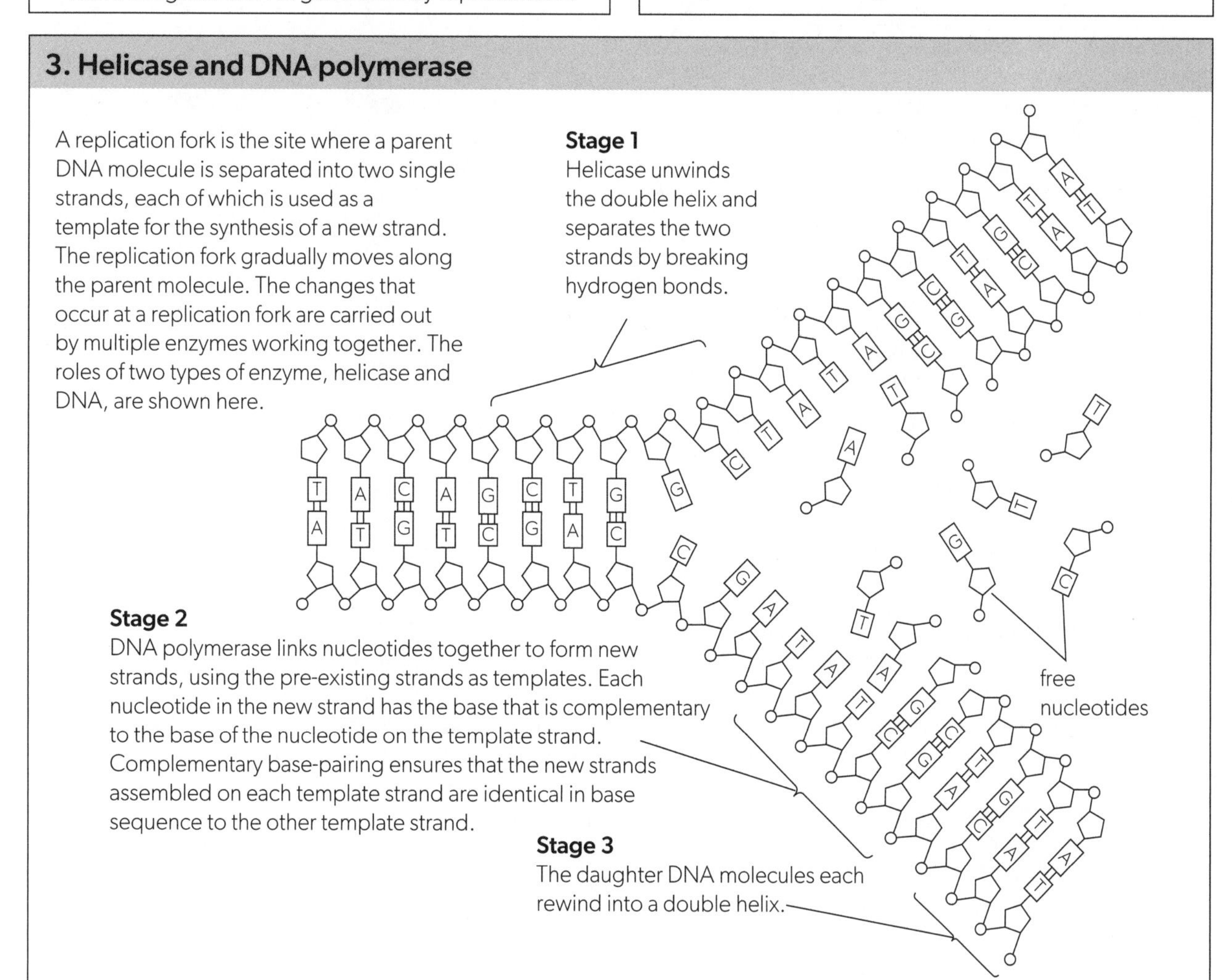

Stage 1
Helicase unwinds the double helix and separates the two strands by breaking hydrogen bonds.
Stage 2
DNA polymerase links nucleotides together to form new strands, using the pre-existing strands as templates. Each nucleotide in the new strand has the base that is complementary to the base of the nucleotide on the template strand. Complementary base-pairing ensures that the new strands assembled on each template strand are identical in base sequence to the other template strand.
Stage 3
The daughter DNA molecules each rewind into a double helix.
free nucleotides

4. PCR and gel electrophoresis

PCR (polymerase chain reaction) is used for copying DNA artificially. It is carried out in small tubes called eppendorfs, which are loaded into a thermocycler (a PCR machine). The eppendorfs contain these things:

- **DNA sample**—this usually contains more DNA than just the length of DNA molecule that is to be copied.
- ***Taq* DNA polymerase**—a special type of heat-stable DNA polymerase. This enzyme is obtained from *Thermus aquaticus*, a bacterium adapted to life in hot springs. It allows high temperatures to be used, speeding up replication.
- **Primers**—short DNA strands that bind to DNA in the sample after it has been split into single strands by heat. Primers are made with the base sequence needed to bind at the point where DNA polymerase should attach to the DNA and start copying. Two primers are needed, one for each of the two single strands formed when the double-stranded DNA in the sample is split.
- **DNA nucleotides**—for assembling the new strands.

PCR happens by a repeated cycle of temperature changes:

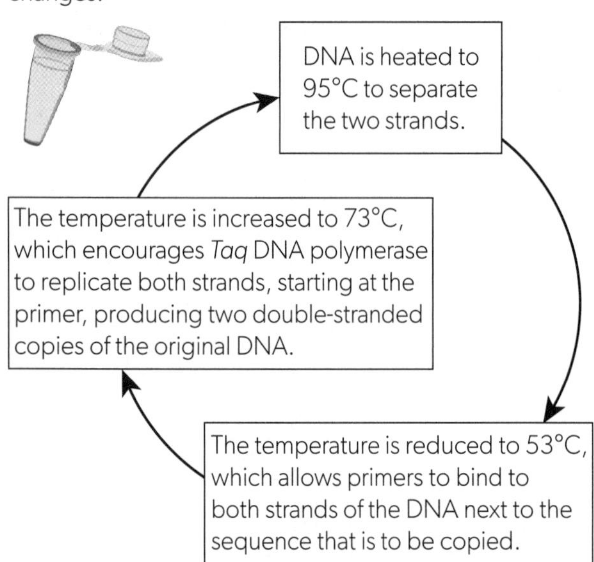

DNA is heated to 95°C to separate the two strands.
The temperature is reduced to 53°C, which allows primers to bind to both strands of the DNA next to the sequence that is to be copied.
The temperature is increased to 73°C, which encourages *Taq* DNA polymerase to replicate both strands, starting at the primer, producing two double-stranded copies of the original DNA.

There are twice as many copies of the desired DNA base sequence after each cycle of replication. This increase is called DNA amplification. By the end of 30–40 rounds of PCR, taking just a few hours, there could be more than a billion copies of a desired sequence in a 0.2 ml eppendorf.

Gel electrophoresis is a method of separating mixtures of positively or negatively charged macromolecules. The mixture is placed in a well near one end of a thin sheet of gel. The gel is a mesh of polymers of an inert material such as agarose, with fluid-filled spaces between the polymers. An electric field is applied to the gel by attaching electrodes at both ends. Charged macromolecules are attracted to one or other of the electrodes. DNA moves towards the positive electrode (the anode) because phosphate groups in DNA molecules are negatively charged. The wells into which DNA is loaded are therefore at the end with the negative electrode.

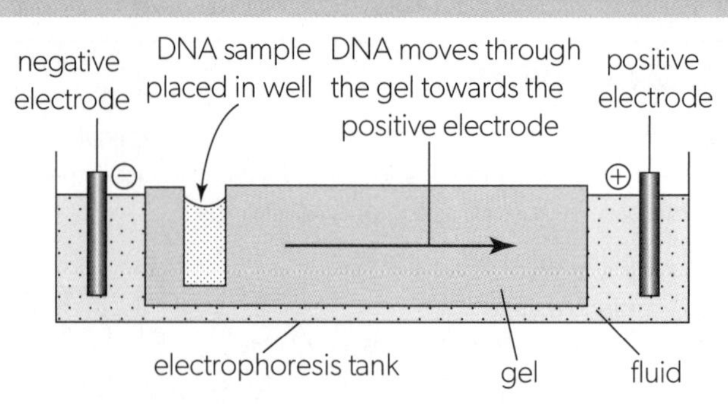

The mesh of polymers in the gel restricts movement, with small molecules moving faster than larger ones. Gel electrophoresis therefore separates DNA on the basis of size of molecule. When the smallest molecules have nearly reached the positive end of the gel, the current is switched off and a stain is used to reveal DNA in the gel. DNA molecules of the same length form a band in the gel. Five or more different samples are run side-by-side in lanes across a gel, starting from separate wells. This allows the pattern of bands to be compared. An example is shown.

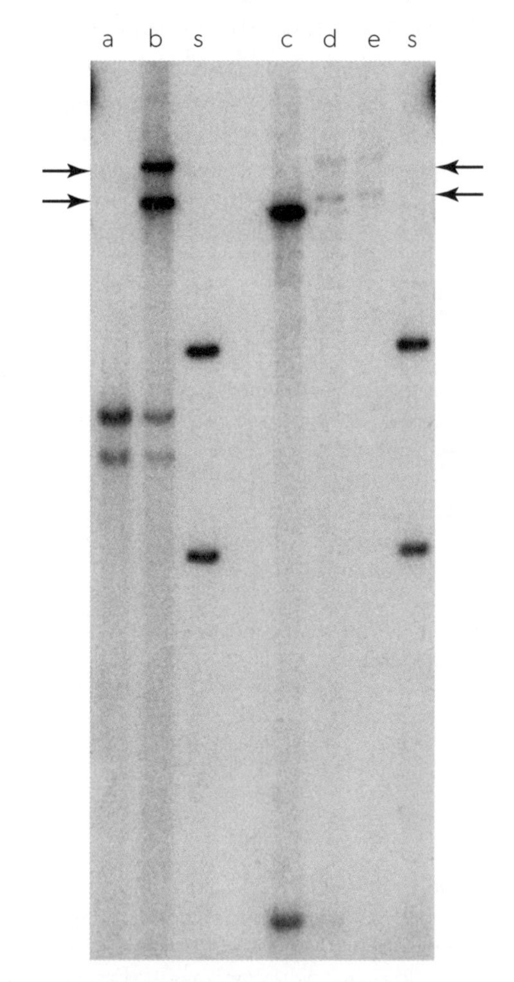

Gel electrophoresis is particularly useful for separating human DNA with short tandem repeats. This DNA occurs at particular positions in the human genome, where short sequences of three to five bases are repeated. The number of repeats is very variable between individuals. For example, at one position on chromosome 7, the sequence GATA is repeated between 6 and 15 times. Each different number of repeats forms a separate band during gel electrophoresis.

5. Applications of PCR and gel electrophoresis

PCR and gel electrophoresis are used together to generate DNA profiles (genetic fingerprints).

1. A DNA sample is taken from a person.
2. Primers are used that promote the simultaneous amplification of about 15 different short tandem repeats (STRs) by the polymerase chain reaction.
3. The amplified STRs are separated by gel electrophoresis, generating a pattern of bands that is very likely to be unique to the individual.

DNA profiling has a range of applications:

Forensic investigations provide evidence for use in court cases. DNA profiling can provide very strong evidence of guilt if a suspect's DNA profile matches that of DNA from the crime scene or from a victim's body. Only tiny quantities of DNA are needed for profiling, which could come from a single human hair or traces of a body fluid.

Paternity tests are used to test whether a man is the father of a child. DNA profiles for the child, their mother and the man are needed. All bands in the child's profile will also be in the profile of the mother or true father. If the child has one or more bands not in the mother's or the man's profile, someone else must be the father.

Example: the Enderby double murder case

The first DNA profiles to be used in a forensic investigation are shown on the image of the electrophoresis gel on page 40.

Key:
a = hair roots from the first victim,
b = mixed semen and vaginal fluids from the first victim,
c = blood of second victim,
d = vaginal swab from second victim,
e = semen stain on second victim,
s = blood of prime suspect.

Two bands in track b indicated by arrows must be from DNA in the culprit's semen but are not present in DNA from the prime suspect, who was not guilty despite having confessed to the murders.

NOS

Reliability of data

Two individuals might have the same number of repeats for one STR, but they are extremely unlikely to have the same number for every type of STR in the genome. However, it is not necessary to include every STR in DNA profiling, because the risk of a false match is already very low with about 10. The profiling system used in the USA uses 13 STR markers and the system used in the UK uses 17 STR markers. This is an example of reliability being enhanced by increasing the number of measurements.

AHL

6. Direction of replication

The directionality of DNA is explained in *Section A1.2.11*. All the nucleotides in a single strand of DNA are oriented in the same way. This is because the strand was assembled by DNA polymerase, which always adds the phosphate of a free nucleotide to the deoxyribose of the nucleotide at the growing end of the chain. The direction of replication is 5′ to 3′, because the phosphate group is the 5′ side of a nucleotide and the deoxyribose is the 3′ end of the chain.

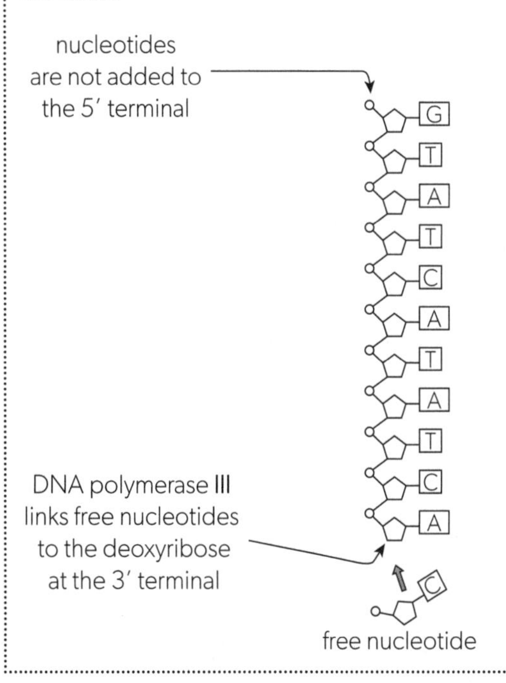

7. Comparing replication on the leading and lagging strand

The two strands of a DNA molecule are antiparallel because they run in opposite directions. The same enzymes are used to assemble chains of DNA nucleotides on the two strands and it always begins with assembly of an RNA primer, but there are also some significant differences. The two strands are known as the leading and lagging strands.

Leading strand

An RNA primer is assembled at the start of the leading strand. As DNA polymerase III moves in the same direction as the replication fork, it can then assemble any length of new strand. Replication is continuous.

Lagging strand

DNA polymerase III moves away from the replication fork, adding nucleotides to the growing chain, but it soon reaches the previous RNA primer, beyond which a new strand of DNA has already been assembled. Replication has to be reinitiated close to the replication fork with another RNA primer. A series of short lengths of DNA strand are assembled on the lagging strand. They are known as Okazaki fragments and are only about 200 nucleotides long in eukaryotes. Replication is therefore discontinuous.

AHL

8. Functions of enzymes in replication

Semi-conservative replication is carried out by a complex system of enzymes. There are differences between prokaryotes and eukaryotes in the mechanism of replication, though the basic principles are the same. The system used in prokaryotes is shown below.

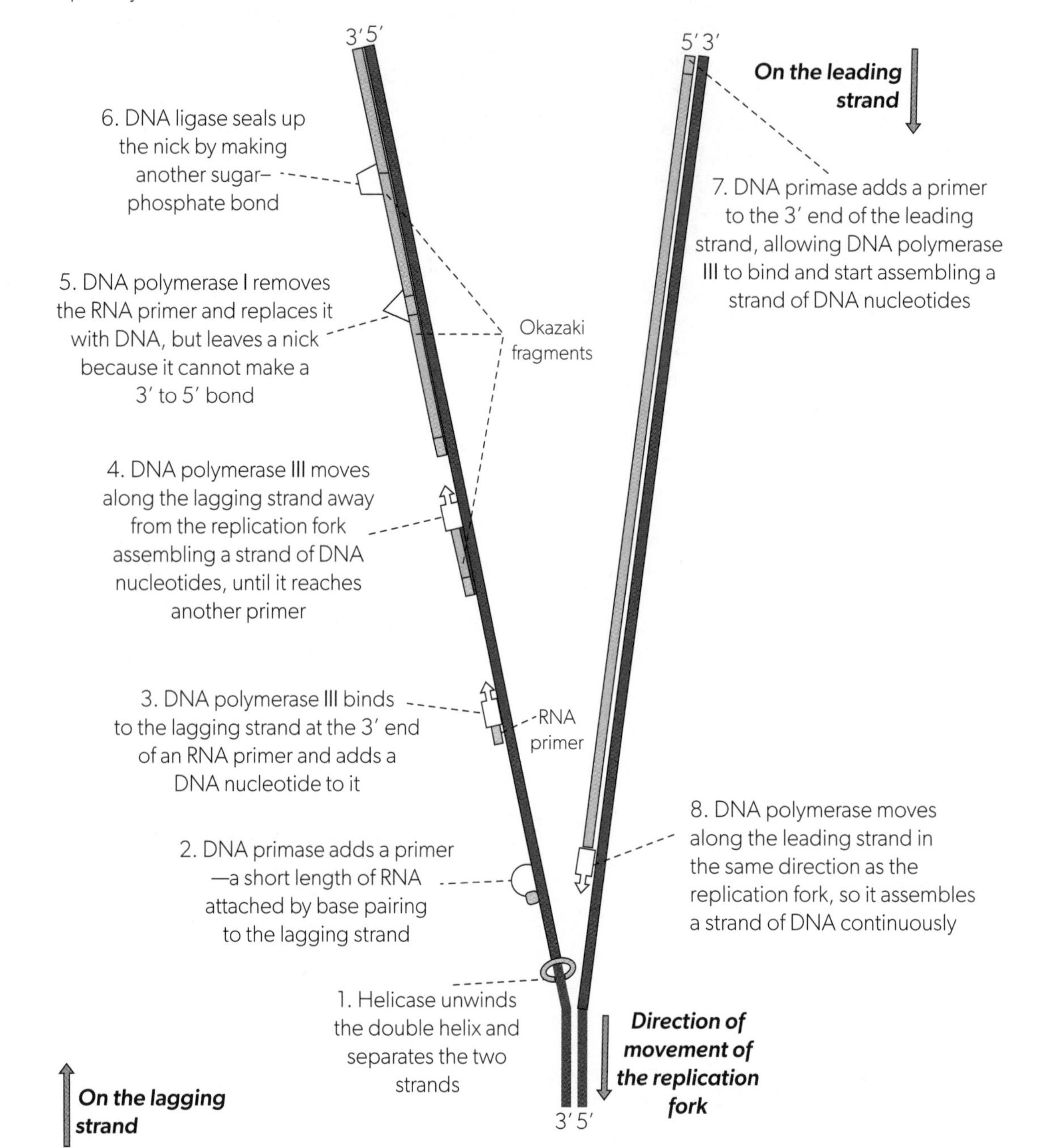

9. Correcting base mismatches

DNA polymerase III usually adds nucleotides correctly according to the rules of complementary base pairing, but occasionally an error is made. For example, a free nucleotide with the base G might be paired with T in the template strand.

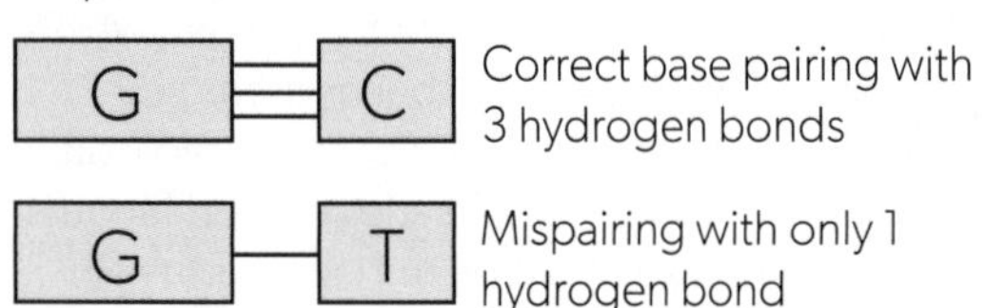

When DNA polymerase III recognizes a base mismatch between the last nucleotide it has added and the base on the template strand, it excises the incorrect nucleotide, moves back along the template strand by one nucleotide and re-inserts a nucleotide with the correct base. This process is known as DNA proofreading. It greatly reduces the frequency of mutation during replication.

D1.2 Protein synthesis

1. Transcription

In transcription, one of the two strands of a DNA molecule is used as a template for synthesizing a molecule of RNA. The process is carried out by the enzyme RNA polymerase. There are some similarities between DNA replication and transcription, but whereas cells replicate entire DNA molecules, they only transcribe part of a DNA molecule—usually just one gene.

RNA polymerase binds to a site on the DNA at the start of the gene and then moves along it, transcribing the gene in a series of stages.

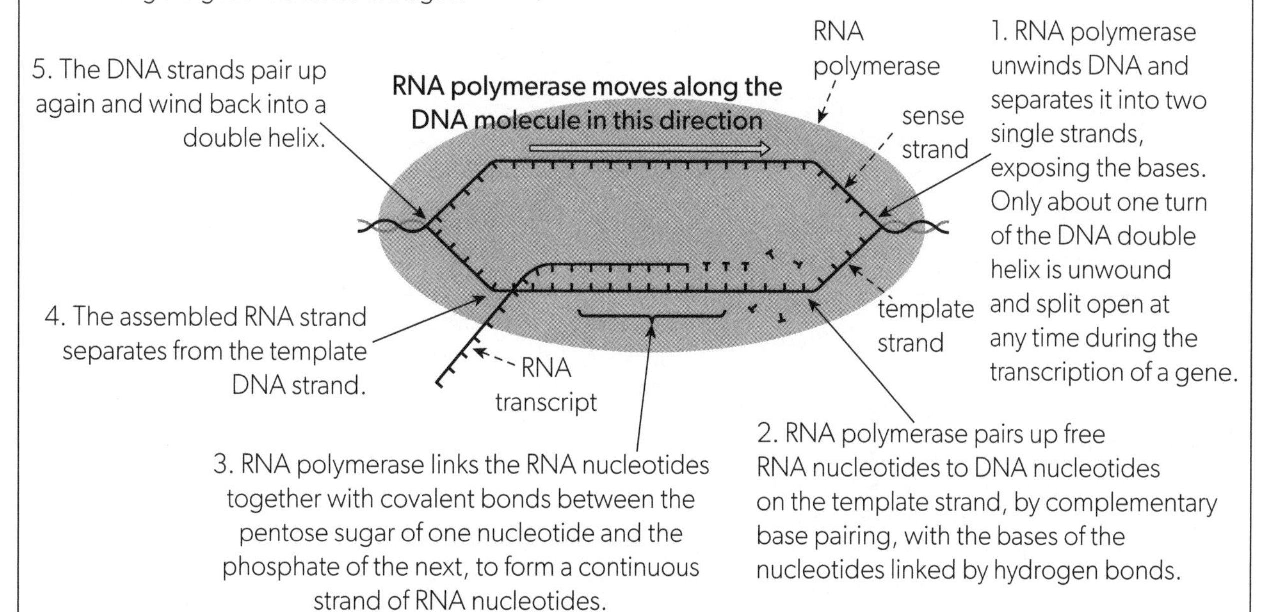

2. Hydrogen bonding in transcription

The same rules of **complementary base pairing** are followed in transcription as in replication (except that uracil pairs with adenine because RNA does not contain thymine).

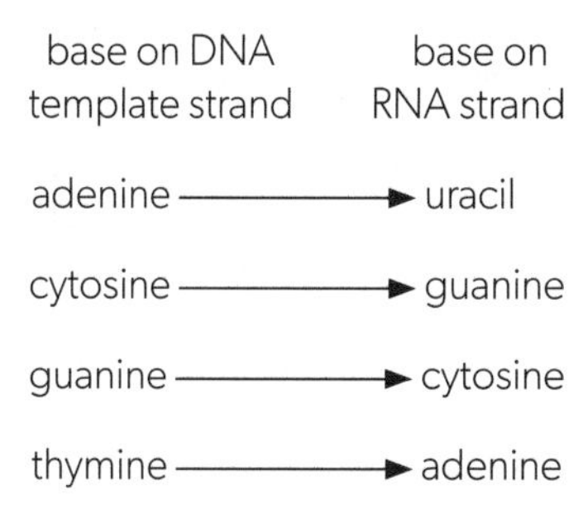

base on DNA template strand
base on RNA strand
adenine → uracil
cytosine → guanine
guanine → cytosine
thymine → adenine

The bases in RNA and DNA pair up by **hydrogen bonding**, which can easily be broken to separate the RNA transcript from the DNA template strand. Hydrogen bonds then form again between bases in the template strand and the other DNA strand (called the sense strand). Logically, the sense strand and RNA transcript must have the same base sequence (apart from the A-T difference) because they both have a sequence complementary to that of the template strand.

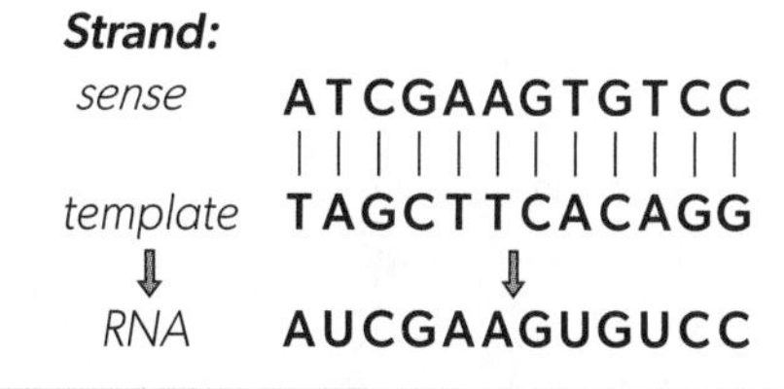

3. Conservation of DNA templates

The components of DNA (phosphate, deoxyribose sugar and the four bases A, C, G and T) are all chemically stable. They are linked together in a strand of DNA by strong covalent bonds. Alternating sugar and phosphate groups form the strong backbone to which sequences of bases are attached. During transcription the DNA is split into single strands, with bases exposed, while a strand of RNA is assembled on the template strand.

The stability of DNA ensures that the base sequence of a gene rarely changes during this process—the structure of DNA promotes continuity rather than change. A gene may be transcribed many times, especially the "housekeeping" genes needed to maintain cells; in some cases, such as brain cells, this is throughout a person's life.

4. Transcription is required for the expression of genes

The sequence of bases in a gene is a store of information. A gene is expressed when the information it holds is used and an observable characteristic is generated within a cell or organism. At any specific time, some genes are being expressed in a cell, but most are not. This is because cells are specialized for particular functions and only develop the characteristics that they need.

The first stage in gene expression is transcription—production of an RNA copy of the base sequence of the sense strand by transcribing the template strand. Transcription of a gene can be switched on or off—this is a key stage in the control of gene expression. The flow chart shows this and subsequent stages in expression of a protein-coding gene—the commonest type.

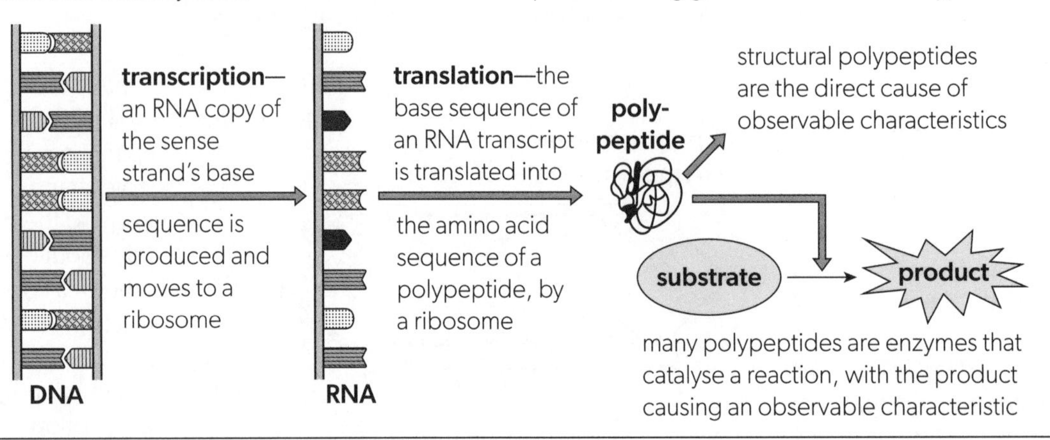

5. Translation

Translation is the synthesis of a polypeptide, with its amino acid sequence determined by the base sequence of an RNA molecule. The RNA molecule is transcribed from a protein-coding gene and is called messenger RNA (mRNA). Each base in the polypeptide is coded for by one codon on the mRNA. A codon is a sequence of three bases.

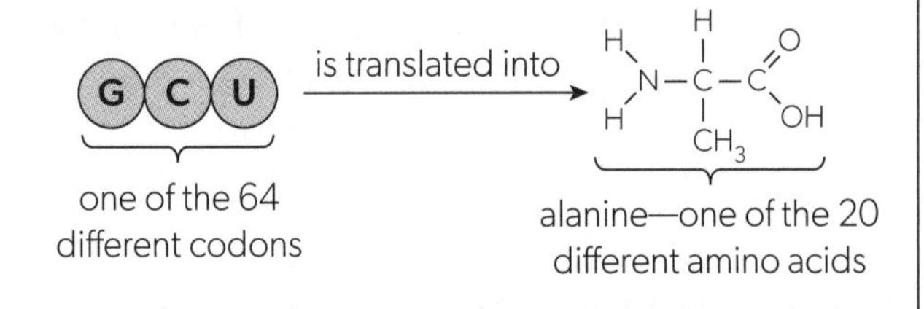

6. Roles of RNA in translation

Ribosomes are the site of translation. They have two subunits (large and small). On the small subunit there is a binding site for mRNA. On the large subunit there are three binding sites for tRNA, with tRNAs attached to at least two of these at all times during translation. The amino acid carried by the most recently arrived tRNA is linked to the growing chain of amino acids held by the previous amino acid to arrive. The linkage is a peptide bond, made at a catalytic site on the surface of the large subunit of the ribosome.

anticodon

large subunit of ribosome

2. Transfer RNA molecules are present around the ribosome in large numbers. Each tRNA has a special triplet of bases called an anticodon and carries the amino acid corresponding to this anticodon.

amino acid

4. The amino acids carried by the tRNA molecules are bonded together by a peptide linkage. A dipeptide is formed, attached to the tRNA on the right. The tRNA on the left detaches. The ribosome moves along the mRNA to the next codon. Another tRNA carrying an amino acid binds. A chain of three amino acids is formed. These stages are repeated until a polypeptide is formed.

direction of movement of ribosome

small subunit of ribosome

1. Messenger RNA binds to a site on the small subunit of the ribosome. The mRNA contains a series of codons consisting of three bases, each of which codes for one amino acid.

3. There are three binding sites for tRNA molecules on the large subunit of the ribosome but only two ever bind at once. A tRNA can only bind if it has the anticodon that is complementary to the codon on the mRNA. The bases on the codon and anticodon link together by forming hydrogen bonds, following the same rules of complementary base pairing as in replication and transcription.

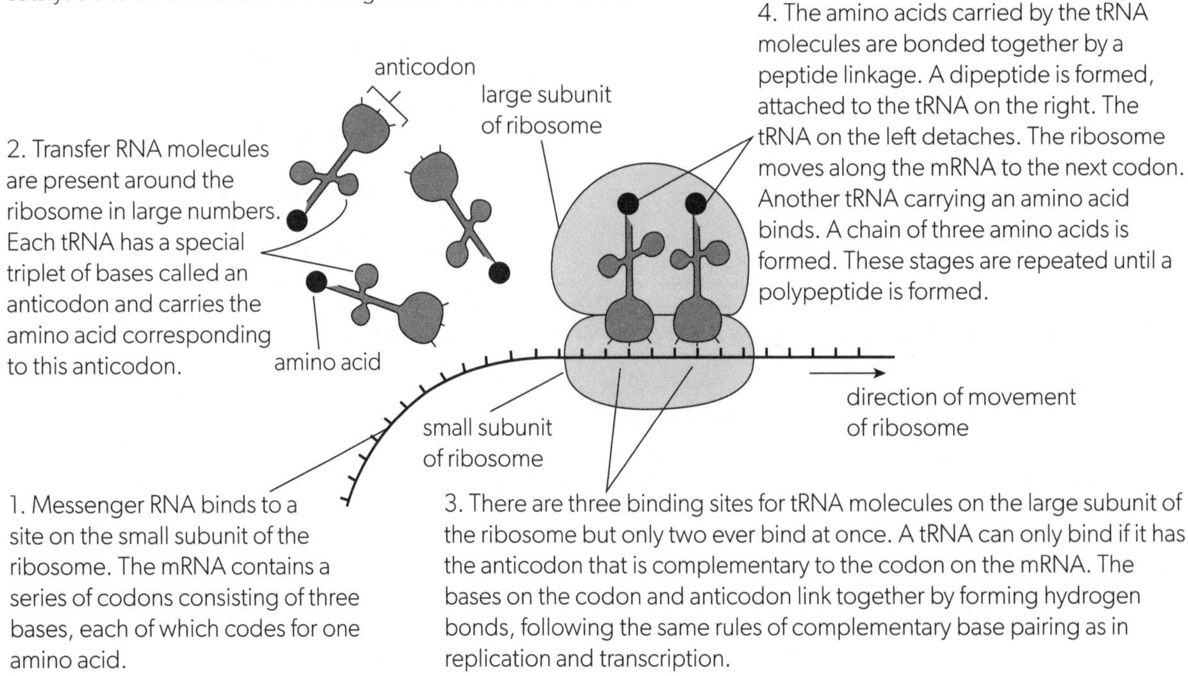

7. Codons pair with anticodons

Translation depends on a group of RNA molecules called transfer RNA (tRNA). Three bases at one end of a tRNA molecule bind to a codon on mRNA during translation, following the rules of complementary base pairing. The three bases are known as the anticodon. At the other end of the tRNA molecule is a site for attaching an amino acid.

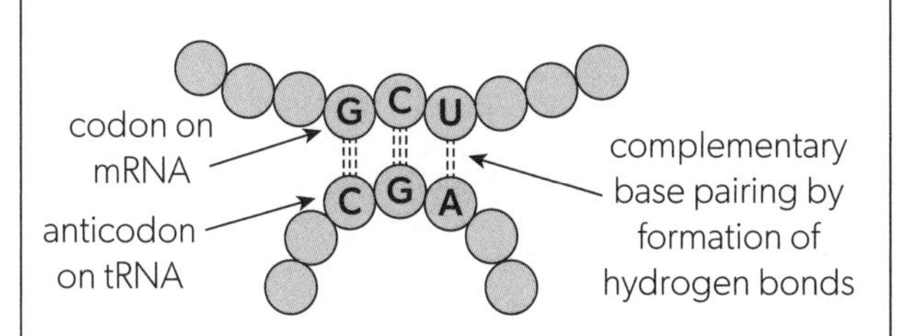

Each type of tRNA has a distinctive three-dimensional shape (like a twisted clover leaf). This is recognized by an enzyme that links on the amino acid corresponding to the anticodon.

8. The genetic code

Triplet

A codon, consisting of three bases, codes for one amino acid, so it is a triplet code. With two bases there would only be 16 codons (4^2)—not enough for the 20 amino acids. With three bases there are 64 different codons (4^3)—more than enough for the 20 amino acids in polypeptides.

Degeneracy

There are more codons than the minimum needed to code for the 20 amino acids. None of the 64 codons are unused and instead there are two or more codons for most amino acids. A code in which more than one symbol is used to represent the same thing is known as a degenerate code.

Universality

The 64 codons of the genetic code have the same meanings in the cells of all organisms, apart from a few minor variations. Universality of the genetic code is strong evidence for all life on Earth having evolved from the same original cells, with the minor coding differences accruing since this common origin.

9. Elongation of the polypeptide chain

The elongation of polypeptides involves a repeated cycle of events.

A peptide bond is made between the amino acid held by the A site tRNA and the amino acid at the end of the polypeptide held by the P site tRNA. This transfers the polypeptide to the A site tRNA. The catalyst for peptide bond formation is ribosomal RNA in the large subunit.

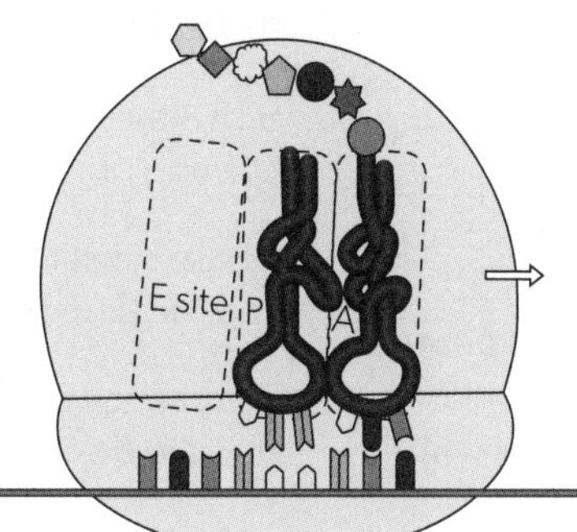

The ribosome moves three bases on along the mRNA towards the 3' end.
This moves the tRNA in the P site to the E site and moves the tRNA carrying the growing polypeptide from the A to the P site, so the A site becomes vacant.

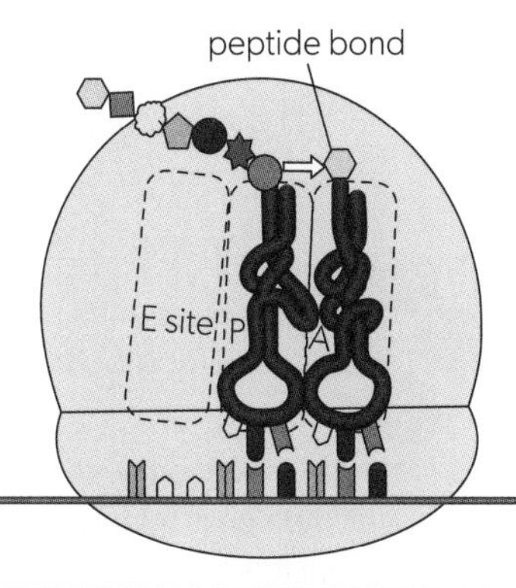

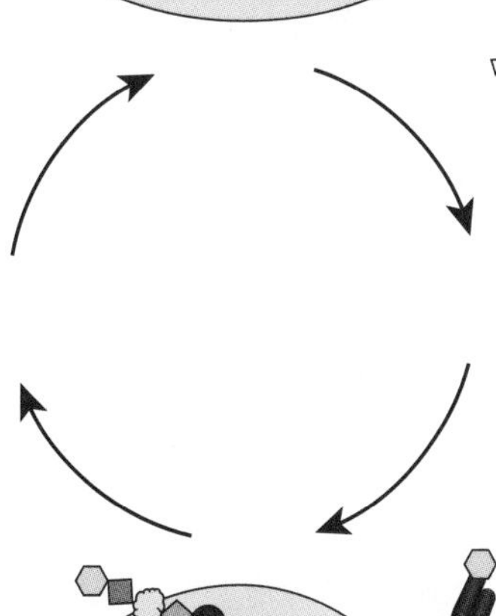

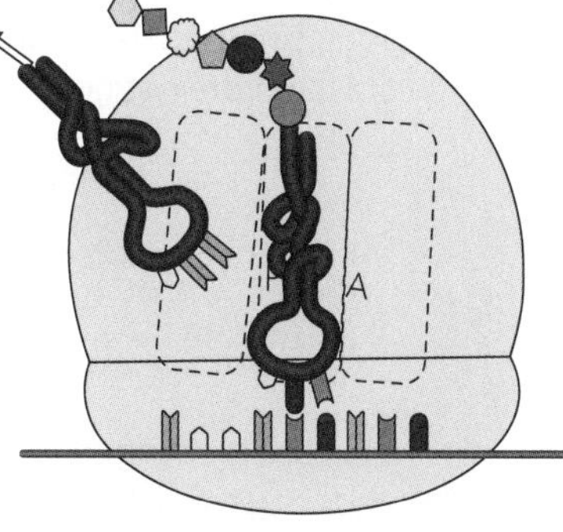

A tRNA with an anticodon complementary to the next codon on the mRNA binds to the A site. The tRNA at the P site is carrying the polypeptide so far assembled and the E site is vacant.

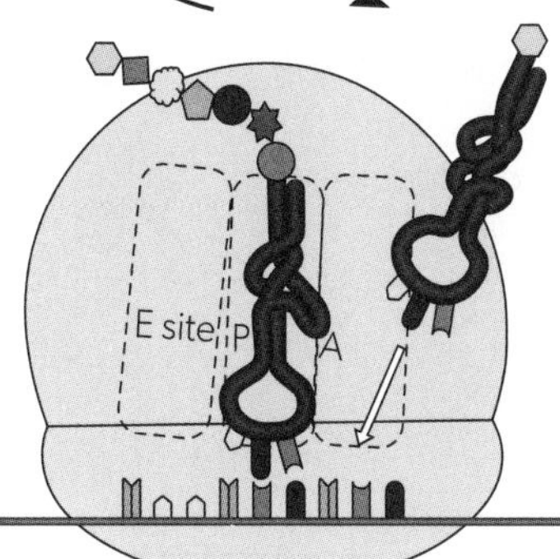

The tRNA in the E site detaches and exits, so this site becomes vacant. The A site is available for binding of a tRNA charged with an amino acid. Any tRNA may approach the site, but unless it has an anticodon that is complementary to the next codon on the mRNA, binding will fail.

10. Using the genetic code

The meaning of each codon in the genetic code is shown in the table. Three codons are **stop** signals that indicate when the synthesis of the polypeptide is complete and translation should end. One codon represents both the start signal and a specific amino acid (methionine).

The table can be used to deduce the sequence of amino acids coded for by an mRNA strand. For example, the sequence CACAGAUGGGUC would be translated into histidine, arginine, tryptophan, valine.

The table could also be used to find possible codons for an amino acid. For example, the amino acid glutamine is coded for either by CAA or CAG.

First base of codon (5′ end)	**Second base of codon on messenger RNA** U	C	A	G	**Third base of codon (3′ end)**
U	Phenylalanine	Serine	Tyrosine	Cysteine	**U**
	Phenylalanine	Serine	Tyrosine	Cysteine	**C**
	Leucine	Serine	STOP	STOP	**A**
	Leucine	Serine	STOP	Tryptophan	**G**
C	Leucine	Proline	Histidine	Arginine	**U**
	Leucine	Proline	Histidine	Arginine	**C**
	Leucine	Proline	Glutamine	Arginine	**A**
	Leucine	Proline	Glutamine	Arginine	**G**
A	Isoleucine	Threonine	Asparagine	Serine	**U**
	Isoleucine	Threonine	Asparagine	Serine	**C**
	Isoleucine	Threonine	Lysine	Arginine	**A**
	Methionine / START	Threonine	Lysine	Arginine	**G**
G	Valine	Alanine	Aspartic acid	Glycine	**U**
	Valine	Alanine	Aspartic acid	Glycine	**C**
	Valine	Alanine	Glutamic acid	Glycine	**A**
	Valine	Alanine	Glutamic acid	Glycine	**G**

11. Mutations can alter protein structure

Protein structure can be changed by a mutation as small as a single base change (a point mutation) in the gene coding for the protein. A single base substitution changes one codon in mRNA transcribed from the gene. In most cases this will change one amino acid in the polypeptide translated from the mRNA. Even a single changed amino acid in a polypeptide can cause radical changes in protein structure, especially if the substitution is between hydrophilic and hydrophobic amino acids. In contrast, some base substitutions have no effect, either because they are same-sense mutations (changing a codon into another codon for the same amino acid), or because the amino acid is chemically similar to the original one and is in a non-critical part of the protein structure.

Example of a point mutation that affects protein structure: the sickle cell mutation

HBB is the gene that codes for the beta polypeptide of haemoglobin, which consists of 146 amino acids.

A base substitution mutation has changed adenine (A) to thymine (T) in the codon for the sixth amino acid.

This changed Hb^A (the original allele of the gene) into Hb^S (the sickle cell allele) with major consequences.

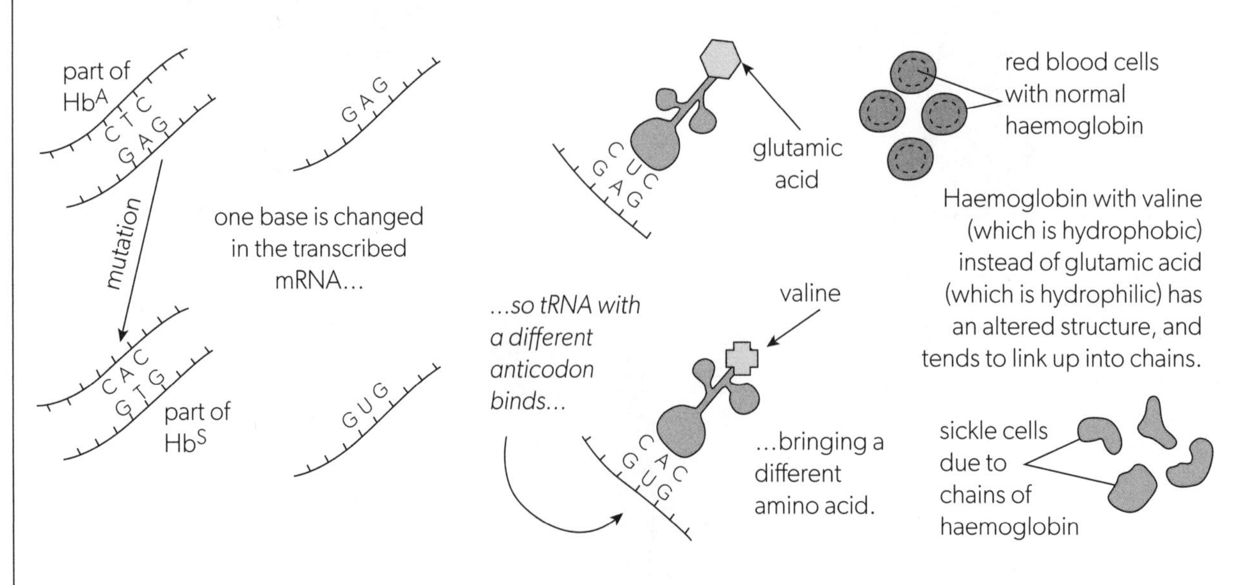

part of Hb^A
CTC
GAG
GAG
mutation
one base is changed in the transcribed mRNA...
CAC
GTG
part of Hb^S
GUG
CUC
GAG
glutamic acid
red blood cells with normal haemoglobin
Haemoglobin with valine (which is hydrophobic) instead of glutamic acid (which is hydrophilic) has an altered structure, and tends to link up into chains.
...so tRNA with a different anticodon binds...
valine
CAC
GUG
...bringing a different amino acid.
sickle cells due to chains of haemoglobin

AHL

12. Direction of transcription and translation

Transcription

RNA polymerase adds the 5' end of the free RNA nucleotide to the 3' end of the growing mRNA molecule, so **transcription occurs in a 5' to 3' direction.**

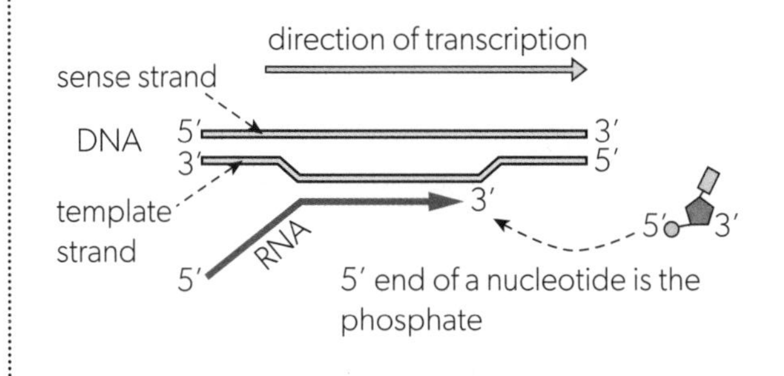

Translation

The ribosome binds to mRNA near its 5' end and moves along it towards the 3' end, translating each codon into an amino acid on the elongating polypeptide, until it reaches a stop codon, so **translation occurs in a 5' to 3' direction.**

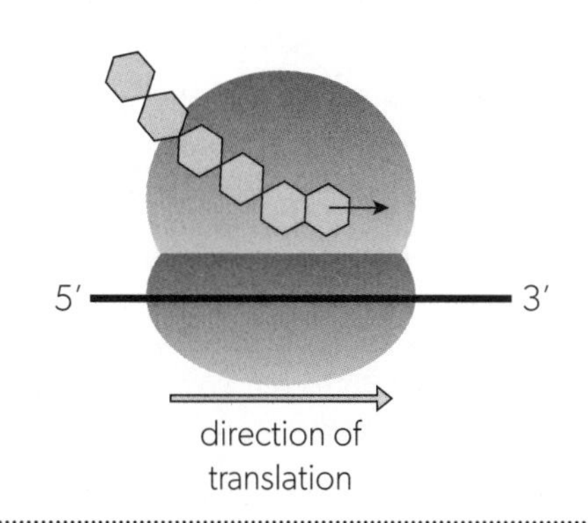

13. Transcription factors

Adjacent to the start of every gene is a section of DNA that is a promoter. It is where transcription of the gene is initiated. The promoter is not itself transcribed and does not code for an amino acid sequence.

RNA polymerase binds directly to the promoter in prokaryotes and then starts transcribing. Repressor proteins can bind to the promoter and prevent transcription.

The control of gene expression is more complicated in eukaryotes. Proteins called **transcription factors** first bind to the promoter or sites close to it, which allows RNA polymerase to bind to the promoter. Several transcription factors are required, some of which may need to be activated by the binding of a hormone or other chemical signal. As in prokaryotes, repressor proteins can bind to the promoter, preventing transcription. There is diversity in the base sequences of promoters and the sites to which transcription factors and repressor proteins bind. A cell can therefore switch on some genes and cause them to be transcribed, while other genes are not being transcribed.

The promoter is "upstream" of the gene, so once transcription has been initiated, RNA polymerase moves along the whole gene, assembling an RNA copy one nucleotide at a time.

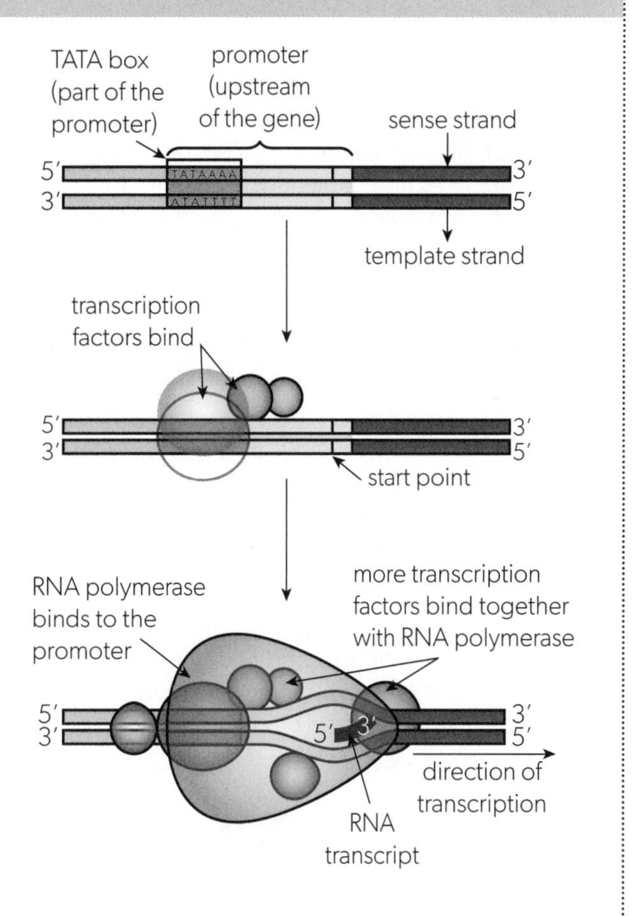

AHL

14. Non-coding sequences in DNA

There are thousands of sequences of bases that code for proteins in the DNA of a species. These coding sequences are transcribed and translated when a cell requires the protein that they code for.

There are also **non-coding sequences**. Some non-coding sequences have important functions.

- **Regulating gene expression**—some base sequences are sites where proteins can bind that either promote or repress the transcription of an adjacent gene.
- **Introns**—in many eukaryote genes the coding sequence is interrupted by one or more non-coding sequences. These introns are removed from mRNA before it is translated. Introns have numerous functions associated with mRNA processing.
- **Telomeres**—these are repetitive base sequences at the ends of chromosomes. When the DNA of a eukaryote chromosome is replicated, the end of the molecule cannot be replicated, so a small section of the base sequence is lost. The presence of the telomere prevents parts of important genes at the ends of the chromosomes from being lost each time DNA is replicated.
- **Genes for tRNA and rRNA**—transcription of these genes produces the transfer RNA used during translation and also the ribosomal RNA that forms much of the structure of the ribosome.

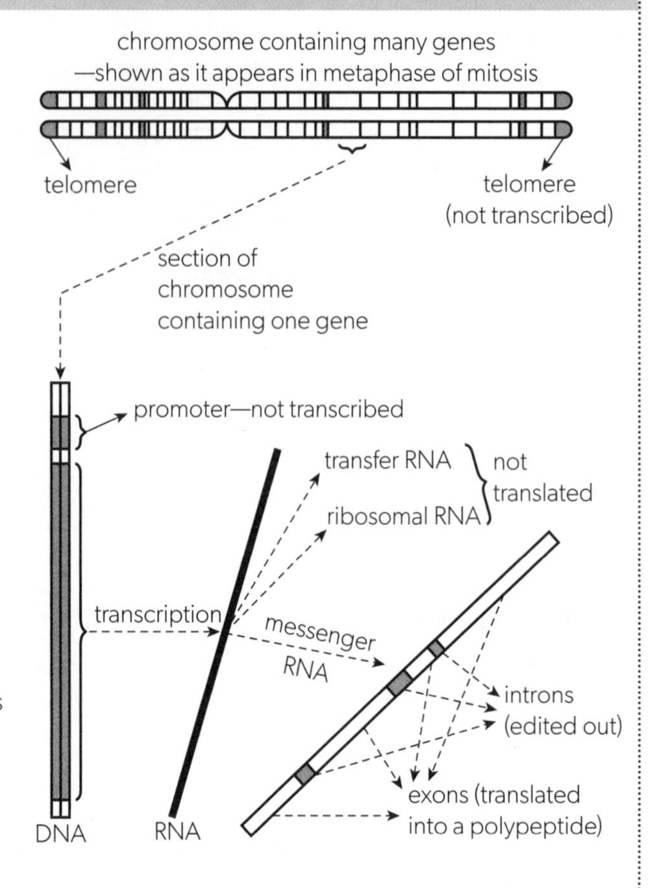

15. Post-transcriptional modification of the RNA transcript

Eukaryotic cells modify mRNA after transcription. This happens before the mRNA exits the nucleus. There are two main types of post-transcriptional modification: removal of nucleotides from within the RNA transcript and addition of nucleotides to the ends of the transcript.

1. The RNA transcript is modified by adding extra nucleotides to give each end of mRNA a special structure:

Five-prime cap—a modified nucleotide is added to the 5' end of the RNA. This nucleotide has three phosphate groups instead of one, so it is similar to ATP. Its base is guanine, with an extra methyl group added.

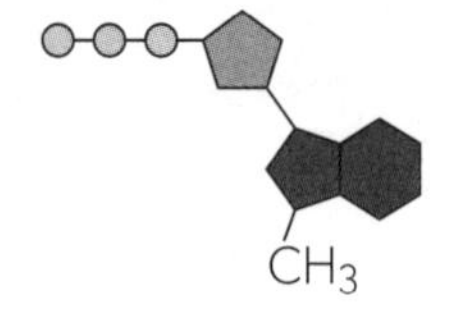

Poly-A tail—between 100 and 200 adenine nucleotides are added to the 3' end of the RNA. Translation stops before the ribosome reaches the poly-A tail.

The 5' cap and the poly-A tail both stabilize the ends of the mRNA by protecting them from digestion by nuclease enzymes.

2. In many eukaryote genes the coding sequence is interrupted by one or more non-coding sequences. These introns are removed from mRNA before it is translated. The remaining parts of the mRNA are **exons**. They are spliced together to form mature mRNA.

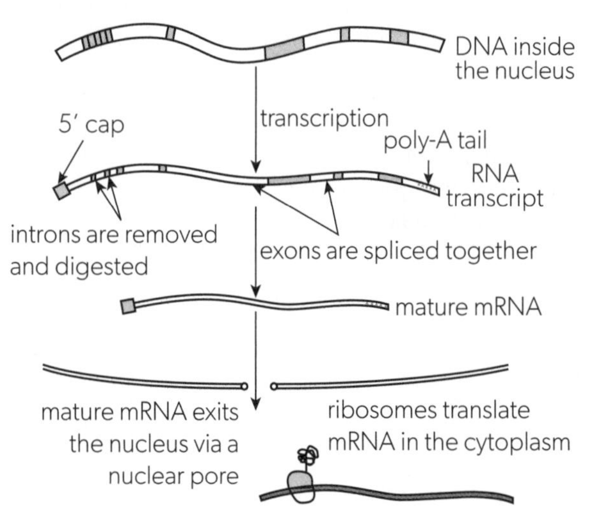

AHL

17. The start of translation

A sequence of events occurs once, to start the process of translation:

1. An **initiator tRNA** with the anticodon AUG binds to the small subunit of the ribosome. The initiator tRNA is carrying the amino acid methionine. In the genetic code, UAC is both the **start codon** and the codon for methionine.

2. The small subunit of the ribosome and initiator tRNA attach to the 5' terminal of mRNA and then move along the mRNA until they reach the start codon.

3. The anticodon of the initiator tRNA and the start codon pair up by formation of hydrogen bonds between the bases.

4. The large subunit of the ribosome binds to the small unit, with the initiator tRNA in the P site. The E and A sites are vacant.

5. A tRNA with an anticodon complementary to the codon adjacent to the start codon binds to the A site. The tRNA is carrying the amino acid that corresponds in the genetic code to the codon.

6. A peptide bond forms between the amino acids held by the tRNAs in the P and A sites. The tRNA at the A site holds the dipeptide that has been formed.

7. The repeated cycle of events then begins that adds amino acids and therefore elongates the polypeptide. The ribosome moves along the mRNA, one codon at a time, causing tRNAs to change position.

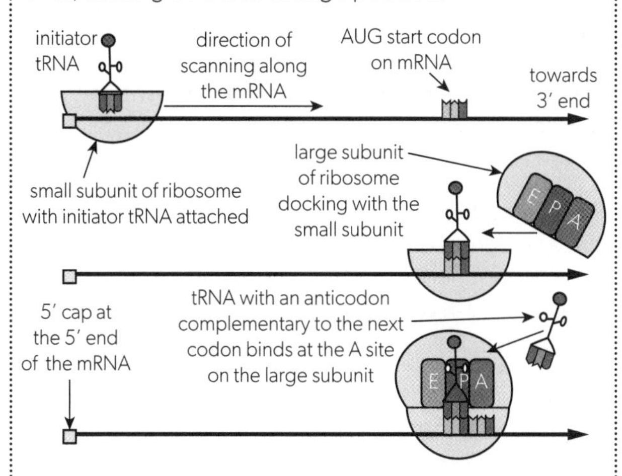

The three tRNA binding sites have different functions and during elongation, every tRNA briefly occupies each site:

A site—for initial binding of a tRNA when it arrives carrying an amino acid (A = amino acyl)

P site—tRNA moves to this site when it is carrying the growing polypeptide; the polypeptide is then transferred to the amino acid held by the tRNA at the A site, by formation of a peptide bond (P = peptidyl)

E site—tRNA moves to this site when it is no longer holding the polypeptide; the tRNA rapidly dissociates from the E site and only returns to the ribosome when an amino acid has been linked to it again (E = exit).

16. Alternative splicing

Some genes have many exons and different combinations of them can be spliced together to produce different proteins. This increases the total number of proteins an organism can produce from its genes.

18. Modification of polypeptides

These are the main types of modification

- Changes to the side chains of amino acids.
- Folding the polypeptide into the tertiary structure.
- Excising part of the polypeptide.
- Combining two or more polypeptides or other components into the quaternary structure of a protein.

The insulin gene is transcribed and the mRNA produced is translated into a 110-amino acid polypeptide, which is preproinsulin. This is converted into proinsulin by a protease in the lumen of the rough ER which removes a 24-amino acid sequence from the N-terminal. The remaining 86 amino acid chain is proinsulin. It is folded and three disulfide bonds are made to stabilize the tertiary structure. Proteases in the Golgi remove a 33-amino acid sequence by breaking peptide bonds between lysine and arginine at two positions. This leaves two chains of 21 and 32 amino acids, held together by the disulfide bonds. Two amino acids are removed from the C-terminal of the B chain to yield mature insulin with a total of 51 amino acids.

19. Amino acids are recycled by proteasomes

Proteasomes are organelles that digest selected proteins. The proteins are tagged with markers called ubiquitin. Tagged proteins are recognized by regulatory subunits at either end of the proteasome. A second subunit then unfolds the polypeptides and feeds them into the central chamber, where the active sites of proteases digest them into short chains of amino acids. These pass out of the proteasome and are digested in the cytoplasm, yielding amino acids that can be used for synthesis of new proteins. Proteasomes digest proteins that are damaged, or have become functionless, or are present in greater quantities than needed in a cell.

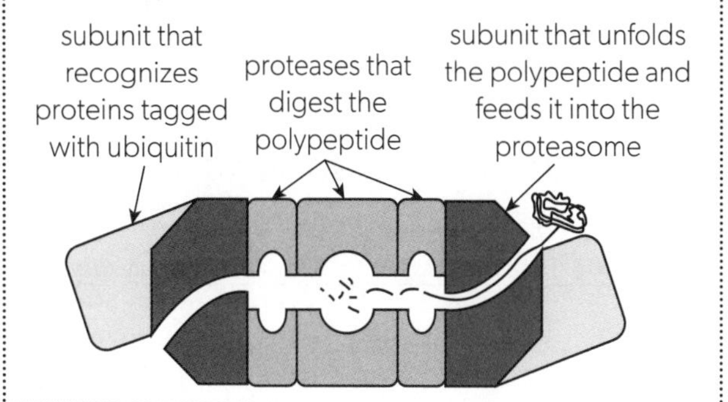

D1.3 Mutation and gene editing

1. Gene mutations

Gene mutations are permanent structural changes to the DNA of a gene.

Many changes to the molecular structure of DNA are possible, but only heritable changes are considered to be mutations. It is the base sequence of DNA that is replicated and therefore inherited, so mutations are changes to the base sequence.

There are three main types of gene mutation: insertions, deletions and substitutions. Insertions and deletions affect one or more nucleotides, whereas substitutions affect a single base in the gene.

Insertions

One or more extra nucleotides are inserted into the DNA of the gene.

Example (with bases grouped in codons):

GGC ACT AGA TTC ACG
↓
GGC AGC TAG ATT CAC G

Deletions

One or more nucleotides are removed from the DNA of the gene.

Example:

GGC ACT AGA TTC ACG
↓
GGC ATA GAT TCA CG

Substitutions

One base is replaced by another base, changing one codon into a different one.

The graphic shows the 12 possible base substitution mutations. Thicker arrows are more common substitutions.

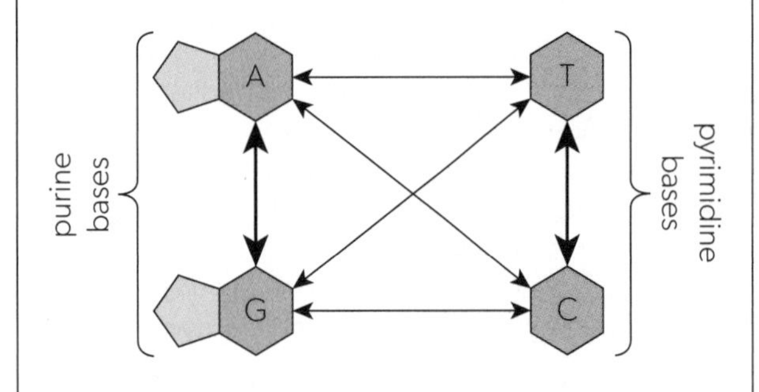

Example:

GGCACTAGATTCACG
↓
GGCAATAGATTCACG

2. Base substitutions

Base substitution mutations can be put into three categories according to their consequences:

- **neutral**—no effects
- **deleterious** (causing harm)—the most harmful mutations are lethal (cause death)
- **beneficial**—these are far rarer than neutral and deleterious mutations.

Base substitutions in the non-coding DNA between genes on chromosomes are unlikely to have any effect, so they are neutral. Only changes to the coding sequences of genes can affect the amino acid sequences of polypeptides.

Same-sense (synonymous) mutations are base substitutions that change one codon for an amino acid into another codon for the same amino acid. They are possible because of the redundancy of the genetic code. For example, a change from AGC to AGT still codes for the amino acid serine. Same-sense mutations do not affect the phenotype, though they may make it possible for a second mutation to change the codon into one for a different amino acid.

Nonsense mutations change a codon for an amino acid into a stop codon (ATT, ATC or ACT). Translation is therefore terminated before a polypeptide has been completed. The resulting protein is unlikely to function properly. The consequences depend on what the protein's function is.

Mis-sense mutations change a codon for one amino acid into a codon for a different amino acid. One amino acid in the polypeptide is therefore different.

This may not have much effect if the new amino acid has a similar structure and chemical properties to the original one (a synonymous substitution) or if it is positioned in part of a protein that is not critical in terms of function.

Mis-sense mutations can also have severe and even lethal effects. Many genetic diseases are due to mis-sense mutations, for example sickle cell disease. A very small proportion of mis-sense mutations have a beneficial effect.

Single nucleotide polymorphisms

If a base substitution mutation spreads by inheritance until 1% or more of the population has it, then it is considered to be a **single nucleotide polymorphism (SNP)**. This only happens if the consequences of the mutation are neutral or beneficial.

3. Insertions and deletions

The consequences of inserting nucleotides to a gene, or removing them from it, depend on whether or not the number of nucleotides is a multiple of 3:

If 3, 6 or any other multiple of 3 nucleotides is inserted (or deleted), there will be extra whole codons (or missing whole codons) in the mRNA transcribed from the gene. The amino acid sequence of the polypeptide translated from the mRNA will therefore be unchanged, apart from one or more extra amino acids (or missing amino acids).

If 1, 2, 4, 5 or any other number of nucleotides that is not a multiple of 3 is inserted or deleted, every codon is changed from the insertion or deletion onwards in the direction of transcription and translation. These insertions and deletions are called frameshift mutations because they change the reading frame for every codon beyond the mutation.

The normal base sequence of the start of exon 18 of the ***BRCA2*** gene is shown with bases inserted or deleted from the start of the second reading frame. Darker grey indicates codons in the mRNA translated from the gene that will be unchanged and paler grey indicates changed codons.

Insertions and deletions of 1 and 2 nucleotides are frameshift mutations.

−3	CTG CCT GTA CAC CTC	one codon fewer
−2	CTG GCC TGT ACA CCT	frameshift
−1	CTG TGC CTG TAC ACC	frameshift
	CTG ATG CCT GTA CAC	original sequence
+1	CTG GAT GCC TGT ACA	frameshift
+2	CTG GCA TGC CTG TAC	frameshift
+3	CTG GCC ATG CCT GTA	one codon extra

Even if a single amino acid is inserted or deleted, the structure of a polypeptide is likely to be radically changed. All insertion or deletion mutations are therefore likely to cause significant change to the structure of a polypeptide and in most cases prevent it functioning properly. This is especially likely with major insertions and deletions and with all frameshift mutations. Frameshift mutations can introduce stop codons, resulting in the earlier ending of translation and production of a truncated polypeptide, almost certainly preventing proper functioning.

4. Mutagens

Mutations can happen at any time, but are particularly likely during DNA replication, when errors in base pairing are sometimes made. There is a low "background" frequency of mutation due to such infrequent but unavoidable changes.

Mutagens are agents that increase the frequency of mutation above the natural background level. Because many mutations are harmful and some are lethal, all mutagens are dangerous. There are two categories:

1. **Chemical mutagens** are substances that cause chemical changes in DNA that result in changes to the base sequence. Many chemical mutagens have been identified including these examples:
- nitrosamines (in cigarettes and other forms of tobacco)
- mustard gas (used in the past as a chemical weapon)
- benzene (a solvent that is widely used in industry).

2. **High energy radiation** breaks bonds in strands of DNA, allowing nucleotides and therefore bases to be inserted or deleted. It can also cause chemical changes in bases, resulting in base substitutions. Many forms of short-wave electromagnetic radiation are mutagenic:
- X-rays (emitted by radioactive elements such as radon)
- beta particles (from radioactive isotopes such as iodine-131 and caesium-137, which were released in the Chernobyl nuclear power plant disaster)
- medium-wave (UVB) and short-wave (UVC) ultraviolet radiation (components of sunlight but mostly absorbed by stratospheric ozone).

Some mutagenic radiation consists of sub-atomic particles:
- gamma rays (from radioactive isotopes such as cobalt-60).

5. Mutations are random

Mutations are random changes that can occur in any gene of any cell. No natural mechanism is known for making a specific change to the base sequence of a particular gene, so living organisms cannot make specific directed mutations to generate beneficial characteristics. The only factor that some organisms can control, to a limited extent, is their overall mutation rate, but which mutations occur is nonetheless random.

Although the process of mutation shows randomness, some base substitutions have a higher probability of occurring than others. Mutations are chemical changes and some chemical changes occur more readily than others. For example, changes between C and T (which are chemically similar with one ring in their molecules) and between A and G (which have two rings) happen more readily than other base substitutions which require the number of rings in the base to change.

Mutation rates are also affected by what the adjacent bases are, so for example adenine between guanine and adenine (GAA) mutates much less frequently than cytosine between adenine and guanine (ACG).

There is also variation in the frequency of mutation according to position of DNA within the genome and its function. For example, protein-coding sequences have a higher average mutation rate than non-coding sequences, presumably because of differences in how these sequences are used within a cell.

6. Germ cell and somatic cell mutations

Gene mutation has different consequences in germ and somatic cells.

Somatic cells are body cells that cannot develop into gametes, so their genes are not inherited by offspring. The consequences of somatic cell mutations are therefore limited. Even a lethal mutation will only kill one somatic cell, which can usually be replaced.

One group of somatic cell mutations have potentially more serious consequences for an individual, because they can cause cancer. These are mutations in genes that control the cell cycle, which can result in uncontrolled cell division and tumour formation. If the tumours spread invasively, they are malignant. Cancer is the growth of malignant tumours. This process is described in *Section D2.1.16*.

Germ cells are either gametes or cells that can develop into gametes. In humans, germ cells are located in the testes and ovaries. If a gene mutates in a germ cell, gametes may be produced carrying the mutation. Through these gametes the mutation can be passed on to offspring.

Initially only the zygote has the mutation, but every cell in a multicellular organism is derived from the zygote by mitosis, so they all carry the mutation. This is what makes it so difficult to carry out gene therapy to change the mutated gene that is causing genetic disease in a person. In the rare but significant cases when a mutation is beneficial, it is useful that all cells in the body inherit it.

The germ line is the continuous chain of cells through which genes are passed from generation to generation.

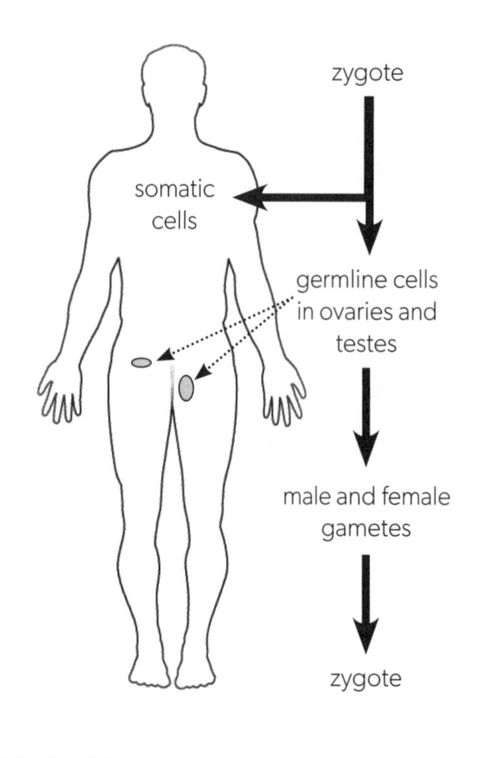

7. Mutation and the origin of genetic variation

Most mutations are harmful, or at best neutral. Even so, the long-term survival of a species would be threatened if no mutation ever occurred.

The environment changes over time and species need to evolve in response. Natural selection and therefore evolution can only occur if there is genetic variation in a population. Mutation is the original source of all genetic variation. New alleles are produced by gene mutation, which enlarges the gene pool of a population and provides more variation on which natural selection can operate.

When environmental change occurs, a few mutations will be beneficial because they make individuals better adapted to the new conditions. So, for the individual organism mutation is usually harmful, but for the species it is, in the long term, vital.

Issues concerned with testing for mutations in humans are discussed in the following nature of science feature (SL/HL).

Commercial genetic tests

NOS

Genetic tests developed by scientists can have social consequences. Many people now pay to have these tests done, to investigate their ancestry or to screen for alleles that cause genetic diseases. A possible unintended consequence is excessive anxiety in those who find they are carrying a mutation that might cause disease. To prevent this, test results must be explained with clarity but also honesty by doctors or scientists.

Genetic testing allows the future health prospects of a person to be assessed. An undesirable consequence of this is that life insurance could then be very expensive for someone with one or more genes that increase the risk of disease and shorten life expectancy.

8. Gene knockout

AHL

The function of some genes is unknown. One approach to determining their function is knockout technology. Individuals are genetically modified so they only have non-functional versions of one specific gene. From the change to the phenotype of the organism, researchers can deduce the gene function.

For example, a strain of knockout mice was produced with non-functioning versions of the leptin gene. These mice became very obese, showing that leptin has a role in regulating fat deposition or energy metabolism.

Several thousand knockout strains of mice have been developed. These are maintained as a living "library" that is available for research. Gene knockout has also been used as a research technique in several other model organisms.

NOS

Ethics of gene editing

Development of techniques such as CRISPR raises the question of whether it is morally right or wrong to edit genes. This question should be answered before a new technique is used.

Many countries have laws to regulate the use of new techniques. International agreement over what should be permitted is needed because harmful consequences could have impacts throughout the world, not just in the country allowing a technique to be used.

There are special ethical concerns over gene editing in humans and particularly over germline editing, which is performed at the embryonic stage or even the gamete stage. Germline editing affects future generations whereas somatic cell editing only affects one individual.

Many countries prohibit germline gene editing but some allow it for research but not reproduction.

Ethical concerns over germline editing:

- Safety—for example, the risk of off-target edits causing damage to other genes.
- Slippery slope arguments—will parents demand editing for enhancement purposes if it is developed for curing genetic diseases?
- Lack of informed consent—permission cannot be obtained from those who will inherit the edited gene.
- Justice—gene editing is likely to remain costly so will only be available to wealthy parents. The consequence could be increased inequity in health and genetic status.

AHL

9. CRISPR-Cas9 in gene editing

Gene editing is deliberate insertion, deletion or substitution of bases to generate a desired sequence. This is a fast-moving field of biology that offers great opportunities, but also some difficult ethical issues. CRISPR-Cas9 is a gene-editing system.

Example of the successful use of CRISPR-Cas9 technology:

Sicilian Rouge High GABA tomatoes were the first example of crop plant editing using CRISPR-Cas9 that has been sold for human consumption. The tomato fruits contain four to five times more GABA than previous varieties. The amino acid GABA is used as a neurotransmitter in the human body. It is claimed to reduce blood pressure and aid relaxation.

GABA is synthesized in tomato fruits as they grow, with a high concentration accumulating. The concentration then rapidly reduces during ripening, due to conversion of GABA to glutamate by the enzyme glutamate decarboxylase. The gene for this enzyme was edited so that the enzyme is inactive and the high concentrations of GABA persist until the ripe tomatoes are eaten.

Cas9 is an endonuclease enzyme that was discovered in bacteria. It cuts DNA at a target sequence, finding this sequence using guide RNA (gRNA). Cas9 is used to destroy viral DNA if it enters the bacterial cells.

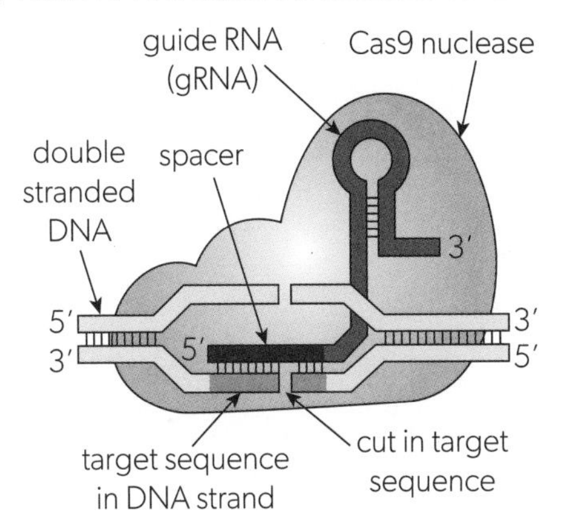

Guide RNA is made by transcribing a "spacer" and a "repeat" from part of the bacterial genome called the CRISPR array. The "spacer" forms a variable 17–20 base sequence at the 5′ end of the gRNA. It is complementary to the target sequence. The "repeat" forms other parts of the gRNA, which are partly double-stranded, generating loops and a distinctive molecular shape that allows it to bind to Cas9.

Cas9 separates the strands of DNA, finds the target sequence using gRNA and then cuts both DNA strands.

A modified version of Cas9 is used for gene editing:

- It makes a nick in one of the DNA strands, not both.
- Reverse transcriptase is attached. This enzyme can make a strand of DNA with a base sequence complementary to an RNA template.

The gRNA is also modified by these additions:

- A template sequence, which is used by reverse transcriptase.
- A primer binding site, with the same base sequence as the DNA adjacent to the target sequence.

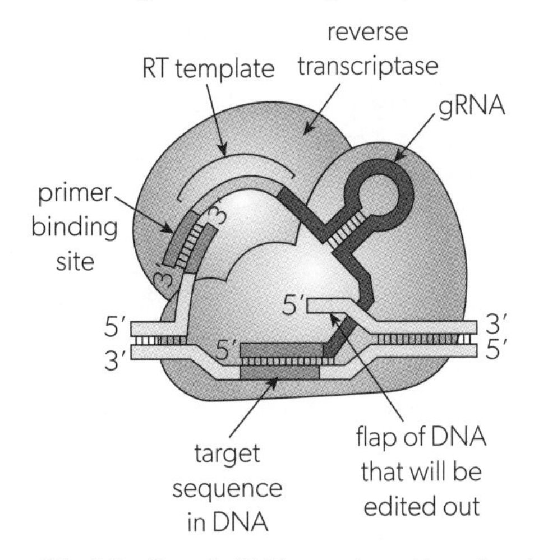

The modified Cas9 and gRNA are placed in cells where gene editing is needed.

AHL

CRISPR-Cas9 in gene editing

Stages in gene editing

1. A molecule of gRNA binds to Cas9. The gRNA has a base sequence complementary to that of the target sequence.

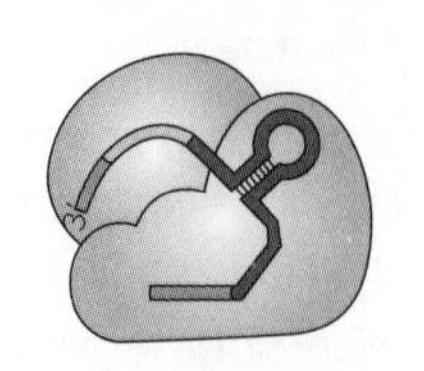

2. Cas9 separates the two DNA strands and moves along the DNA molecule, searching for the target sequence using the "spacer" of the gRNA.

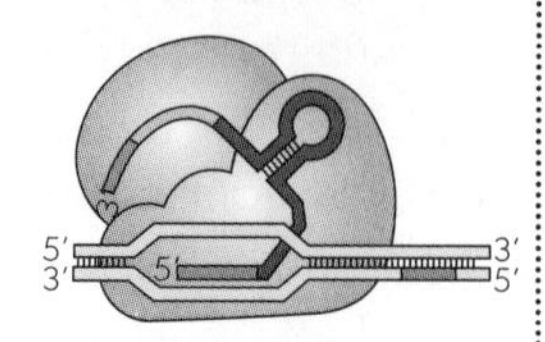

3. The target sequence is recognized by base pairing with the spacer at the end of the gRNA molecule and Cas9 then starts the gene editing process.

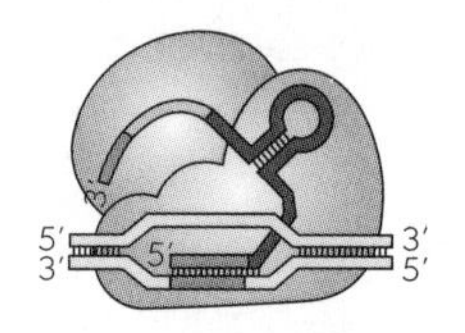

4. With the spacer bound to the target sequence on one DNA strand, Cas9 makes a nick in the other strand, creating 3′ and 5′ ends.

5. The DNA strand on the 3′ side of the nick links to the primer binding site on the gRNA, by complementary base pairing.

6. Reverse transcriptase adds DNA nucleotides to the 3′ end of the DNA strand, using the template sequence in the gRNA to determine the base sequence.

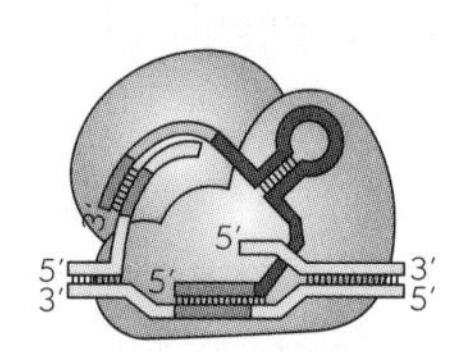

7. gRNA detaches from Cas9 and the two strands of DNA pair up again. The sequence assembled by reverse transcriptase displaces the sequence that was originally paired with the target sequence, which becomes a single-stranded flap.

8. Nucleotides in the flap of single-stranded DNA are removed—this is how the original base sequence is edited out.

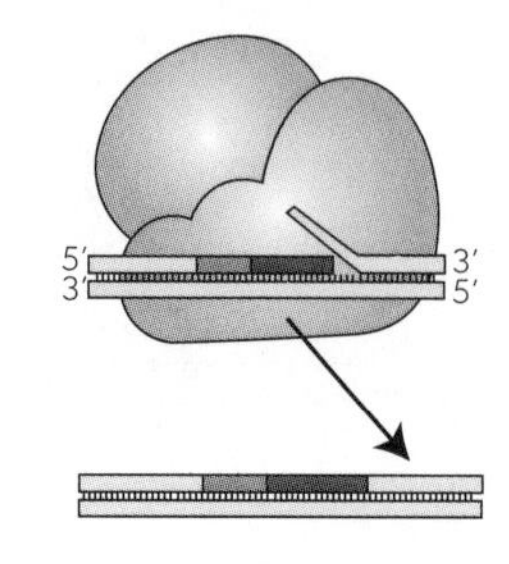

DNA repair enzymes correct any mispairing between the target sequence and the new DNA strand with the desired sequence.

10. Investigating conserved gene sequences

AHL

Conserved sequences are identical or nearly identical across a species or a group of species. Highly conserved sequences are identical or similar over long periods of evolution, so may occur across a wider range of species. There are sequences that are found in all mammals, for example, or even in all vertebrates.

The sequence alignment (below) shows the first 35 bases in exon 9 of the gene for PP13 (placental protein 13) in three mammals. This protein has a role in placenta development. Rhesus monkey and human ancestors diverged about 25 million years ago yet many bases in the sequence are unchanged.

human	CAATGACCCACAGCTGCAGGTGGATTTCTACACT
chimp	CAATGACCCACAGCTGCAGGTGGATTTCTACACT
rhesus	CAATGACCCAGAGCTGCAGGTGGAATTCTACACT

An obvious hypothesis for conserved and highly conserved base sequences is that they have important functions and any mutations that change the sequence are eliminated by natural selection because they prevent the function from being carried out. With protein-coding genes, a polypeptide would fail to function and with genes for ribosomal or transfer RNA, protein synthesis would fail to occur. Some conserved sequences are non-coding parts of the genome, but even though functions of these elements are largely unknown it is likely that they do have functions and this is the reason for them not changing over long periods of evolution.

An alternative hypothesis is based on the finding that mutation rates are not identical for every base in the genome. The conserved non-coding elements might be sequences in regions of the genome where mutation rates are low.

End of topic questions—D1 Questions

D1.1 DNA replication

1. (HL only) *E. coli* were infected with T4 viruses and then started replicating T4 DNA. Unlabelled DNA nucleotides were replaced with radioactively labelled nucleotides for between 2 and 120 s. DNA was extracted, split into single strands, and then separated by centrifugation according to the length of the strands. The shorter the strand of DNA, the closer it was to the top of the centrifuge tube. The graph shows amounts of DNA at each level in the tube measured by the radioactivity.

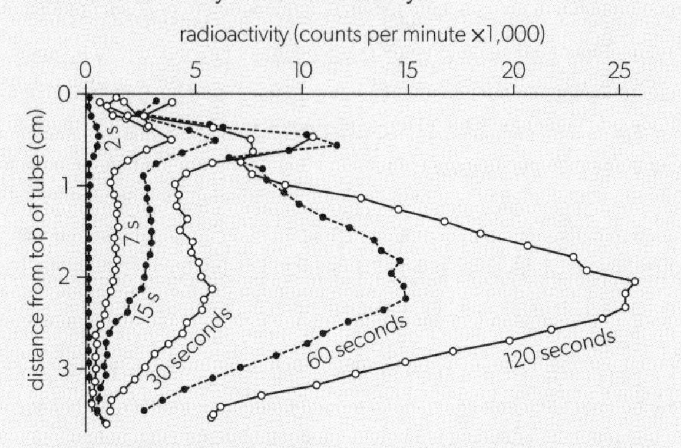

   a. i. State whether the DNA strands at 0.5 cm from the top of the tube were short or long. (1)
      ii. Suggest reasons for short strands of DNA even with increases in replication time. (2)
      iii. Deduce the name for these strands of DNA. (1)
   b. i. Distinguish between the 60 s and 120 s results. (3)
      ii. Explain the differences between these results by the activity of DNA polymerases and ligase. (3)
2. a. Explain the need for separating DNA into single strands during DNA replication. (2)
   b. Outline how DNA is separated into single strands:
      i. when DNA is replicated in a cell nucleus (2)
      ii. during the polymerase chain reaction. (1)
3. The diagram shows the DNA profiles of a child and their parents.
   a. Describe how the paternity of a child can be tested using DNA profiling.(7)
   b. Deduce, giving reasons, which is the profile of the child. (3)

D1.2 Protein synthesis

1. The chart shows variation in numbers of codons per amino acid in the genetic code.
   a. i. Deduce from the chart how many of the 64 codons code for an amino acid. (1)
      ii. State how many codons have another role and what it is. (2)
   b. Calculate the mean number of codons per amino acid. (2)
   c. Calculate the median and mode of the number of codons. (2)
   d. Suggest reasons for most amino acids having an even rather than an odd number of codons. (3)
2. Models of two tRNA molecules are shown below.
   a. Identify, giving reasons, the parts of tRNA labelled with:
      i. a series of three letters. (3)
      ii an arrow. (2)
   b. Outline the relationships between tRNA, translation and transcription. (2)
   c. Explain the importance of both differences and similarities between the structures of the two tRNA molecules. (3)
3. (HL only) Outline the roles of:
   a. promoters (2) c. P sites on a ribosome (2)
   b. poly-A tails (2) d. proteasomes. (2)

D1.3 Mutation and gene editing

1. Amino acid sequences in many SARS-CoV-2 viruses were analysed between 2019 and 2022 to see how many mutations there were. The pie charts show the results a nucleocapsid and a spike protein (N and S).

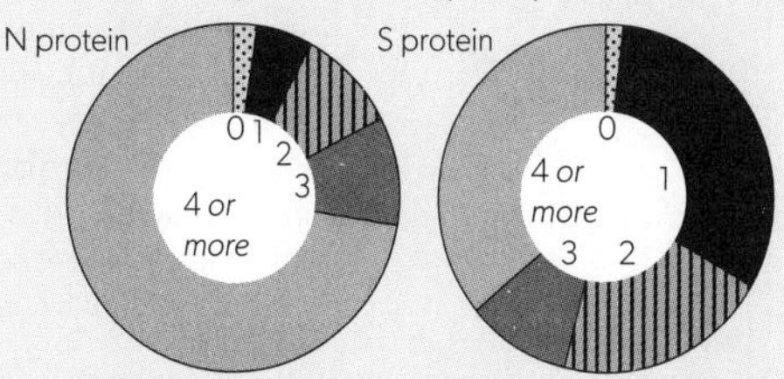

   a. Compare and contrast the data for the proteins. (4)
   b. The N protein is coded by 1,259 bases in the virus genome and the S protein by 3,821 bases. Deduce whether the difference in numbers of mutations between N and S is due to the gene lengths. (2)
   c. Mutation is random, but some base substitutions in the genes for both proteins were common and some were never found. Suggest reasons. (4)
2. a. Outline the possible consequences of a base-substitution mutation for the form and function of proteins. (5)
   b. Discuss the relative effects of base deletion, insertion, and substitution mutations. (5)
3. a. (HL only) Outline how gene knockout is used in biological research. (3)
   b. (HL only) The photo shows developing limb bones in a knockout mouse that lacked two genes: Shh and GL13. Deduce the effect of the lack of these two genes on mouse development. (2)

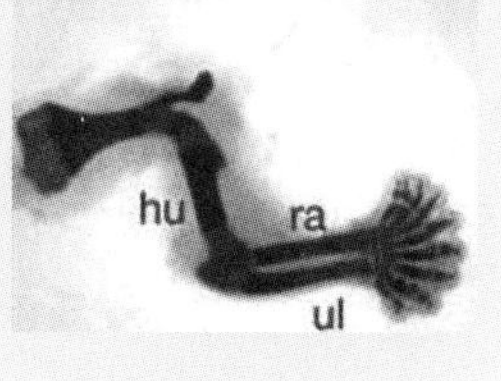

A2.1 Origins of cells

AHL

1. Conditions on early Earth

The Earth was formed about 4.5 billion years ago. Life appeared at some time during the following billion years. Conditions on Earth were very different at that time, compared with those that we experience today.

These were features of the atmosphere:

- little or no oxygen and therefore no stratospheric ozone
- high levels of UV light due to the lack of an ozone layer
- much higher concentrations of CO_2 and methane
- higher temperatures due to these greenhouse gases
- frequent storms with lightning due to high temperatures.

These atmospheric conditions probably caused a variety of carbon compounds to form by chemical reactions that do not now spontaneously occur. The substances produced would have dissolved in water in the atmosphere and been deposited in rainfall, creating a "soup" of carbon compounds in pools, rivers and seas.

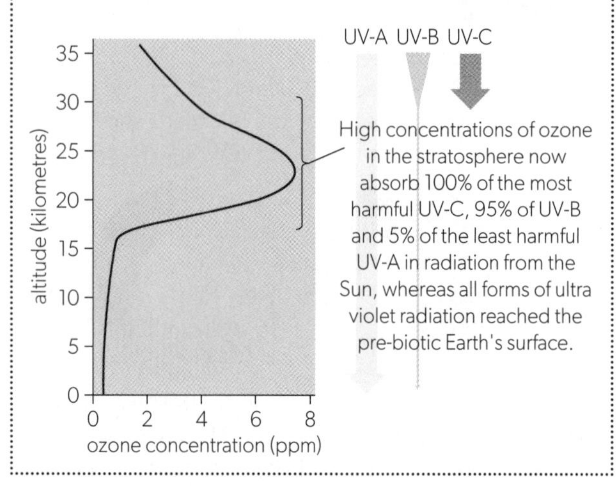
UV-A UV-B UV-C
High concentrations of ozone in the stratosphere now absorb 100% of the most harmful UV-C, 95% of UV-B and 5% of the least harmful UV-A in radiation from the Sun, whereas all forms of ultra violet radiation reached the pre-biotic Earth's surface.
altitude (kilometres)
35
30
25
20
15
10
5
0
0 2 4 6 8
ozone concentration (ppm)

2. Living vs non-living

The difference between living and non-living things has often been debated. Living things are self-sustaining—they maintain themselves in a highly ordered state using energy external sources of energy. Damage must be repaired and there must be periodic regeneration through reproduction. The ability to maintain a highly ordered state must be inherited when a living thing reproduces. Non-living things may have some of these properties, but not all of them.

Individual organisms are obviously alive. Within a multicellular organism, individual cells also have all the properties of life, but subcellular components do not. For that reason, a cell is the smallest unit of self-sustaining life.

3. The spontaneous origin of cells

Until the 19th century some biologists believed that life could develop from non-living material. This was called "spontaneous generation". Cells are highly complex structures and there is no evidence that they can be formed on Earth today, except by division of pre-existing cells.

All the billions of cells in a multicellular organism are formed by repeated cell division, starting with a single cell. This cell was either part of one parent or a fusion of cells from two parents. We can therefore trace the origins of cells back through generations and billions of years of evolution.

Eventually we must reach the first cells (protocells) as life has not always existed on Earth. Before these cells existed, there was only non-living material.

One of the great challenges in biology is to understand how the first living cells evolved from non-living matter and how spontaneous generation could take place then but not now. These are key features of life that must have developed:

catalysis—so selected chemical reactions happened

self-replication of molecules—so there could be inheritance and evolution of useful characteristics

self-assembly—spontaneous building of macromolecules from small subunits

compartmentalization—to separate the ordered interior of the cell from the less ordered environment.

Falsification of hypotheses

NOS

Claims in science, including hypotheses and theories, must be testable, but some are very difficult to test.

Hypotheses about the origins of the first cells are an example. Fossils provide evidence of later stages in evolution, but fossil protocells are unlikely ever to be found. Rocks formed when protocells appeared have probably all been broken down by erosion, or changed by heat and pressure. Also, conditions in that period were not conducive to fossilization and the small size and lack of hard parts make protocells particularly unsuited to fossilization.

It is possible to attempt experimentally to replicate conditions on pre-biotic Earth. However, it is impossible to be certain what the conditions actually were, so results of such experiments must be analysed with caution.

AHL

4. Miller and Urey experiment

The hypothesis that conditions on early Earth allowed the origin of carbon compounds was tested experimentally in the early 1950s by Miller and Urey. They simulated a pre-biotic atmosphere by mixing methane, hydrogen and ammonia in a flask. Water vapour was added by boiling water in another flask. Electrical sparks were used to simulate lightning. The substances produced were condensed and returned to the flask of boiling water.

After the experiment had been running for a week, the condensate was dark red and contained a variety of carbon compounds, including more than 20 amino acids. This shows that carbon compounds could have formed spontaneously before life had evolved, if the conditions on pre-biotic Earth were the same as those in the Miller–Urey apparatus.

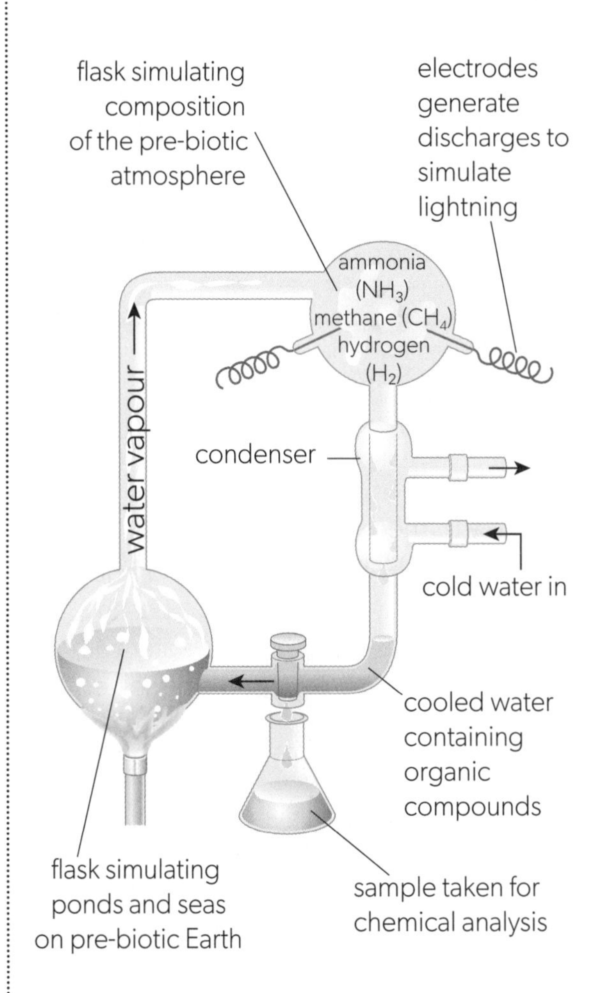

Evaluation of the Miller–Urey experiment:

Strength: repeatable—similar experiments have also shown that a diversity of carbon compounds can form spontaneously in an atmosphere lacking oxygen

Limitation: Miller and Urey probably got some conditions wrong—pre-biotic Earth had more CO_2 and N_2 and less NH_3 and CH_4 and also less lightning.

5. Spontaneous formation of vesicles

Fatty acids have a hydrophobic hydrocarbon chain with a hydrophilic carboxyl group at one end. They naturally form spherical structures in water (micelles) with the hydrophilic part on the outside. Phospholipids have two hydrophobic fatty acid tails and a hydrophilic phosphate head. They naturally form continuous bilayers in water. Small areas of phospholipid bilayer tend to become spherical and are then called vesicles.

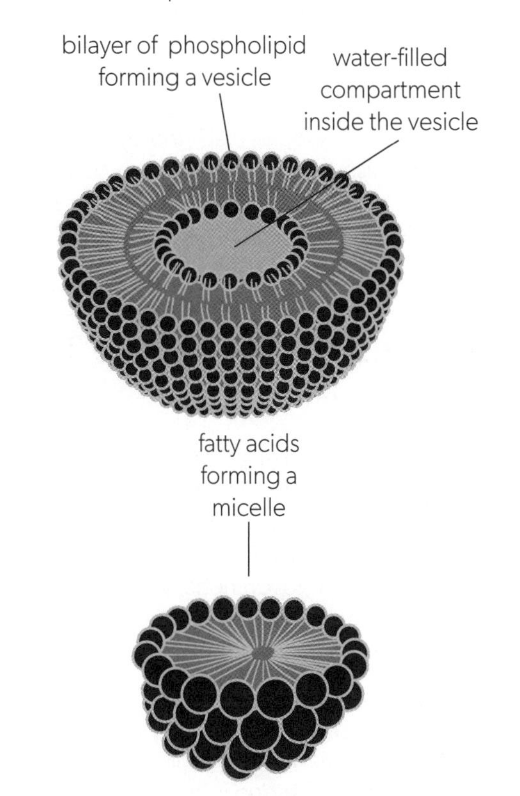

It seems likely that such vesicles would have formed in ponds or seas on pre-biotic Earth, assuming that fatty acids and then phospholipids were spontaneously generated by chemical processes in air and water.

A vesicle is a membrane-bound compartment that allows internal chemistry to become different from that outside the compartment. Spontaneous formation of vesicles was therefore an essential step in the origin of cells.

6. The first genetic material

Whether DNA or enzymes existed first is a "chicken or egg" argument—DNA is needed to make enzymes and enzymes are needed to make DNA. The solution to this conundrum may be that there was a period when RNA was the genetic material and also catalysed reactions inside protocells.

RNA can be copied and passed on to the next generation. Some viruses still use it instead of DNA as genetic material.

Some types of RNA can act as catalysts. Ribozymes in the ribosome are still used to catalyse peptide bond formation during protein synthesis.

AHL

7. Evidence for LUCA

Life may have evolved multiple times on Earth. More than one form may have co-existed for a time, but there is strong evidence that all organisms alive today evolved from one life-form. Other forms presumably became extinct because of competition. All existing organisms on Earth are descendants of the same early ancestors. LUCA is the last universal common ancestor (shared by all).

The strongest evidence for LUCA is genetic. All organisms use a universal genetic code, with only minor variation in the meaning of some of the 64 codons. This is almost certainly due to inheritance from a common ancestor. Also, several hundred genes are found in all organisms, with relatively minor variations. The gene for cytochrome c is an example. These genes give all organisms shared features of their biochemistry that again are evidence for LUCA.

8. Estimating the timeline for early life

1. Fossils

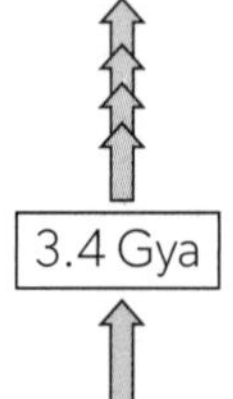

Rocks in Western Australia (the Strelley Pool Formation), contain fossilized stromatolites dating from 3.4 gigayears ago. (A gigayear is a billion years.) Stromatolites are rocky mounds formed by mats of cyanobacteria in shallow seawater which trap sediments and secrete $CaCO_3$.

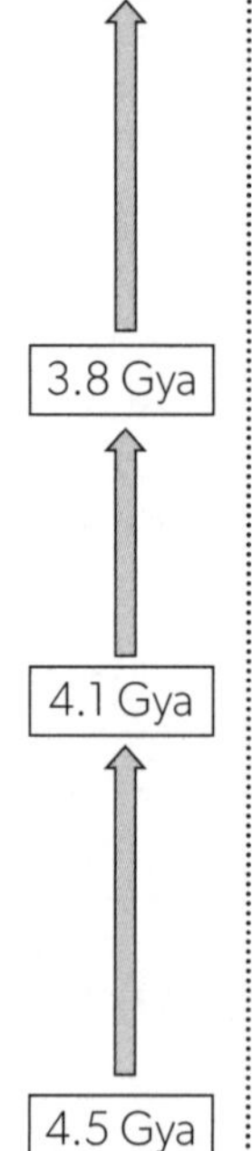

2. Isotope ratios in rock

Carbon originating from living organisms has a low $^{13}C/^{12}C$ ratio. Banded iron rock at Akila in West Greenland dating from 3.8 Gya shows this, suggesting life had evolved by then. Zircon particles found in deposits at Jack Hills in Western Australia also have a low, $^{13}C/^{12}C$ ratio. They were eroded in the past from 4.1 Gya rocks.

3. Genomic information

The number of differences between the genomes of two species is proportional to the time since they diverged from a common ancestor. A recent study using this approach suggested that LUCA and the first living cells existed nearly 4.5 Gya.

9. Evidence for the evolution of LUCA

More than 350 types of protein have been found to occur in a diverse range of bacteria and archaea, suggesting that genes coding for these proteins were in LUCA's genome.

The 350 proteins are needed for anaerobic metabolism and for fixing carbon dioxide and nitrogen. This suggests that LUCA lived in an environment with high concentrations of hydrogen, carbon dioxide and iron. These conditions are found in and around hydrothermal vents in the oceans.

Hydrothermal vents are cracks in the Earth's surface, characterized by gushing hot water carrying reduced (unoxidized) inorganic chemicals such as iron sulfide.

Alkaline hydrothermal vents (white smokers) have a combination of conditions that are needed for the first cells to form. The white "smoke" that emerges (see diagram) is fluid at temperatures of 60°C to 90°C and contains high concentrations of hydrogen, methane, ammonia and sulfides. These chemicals can be used to generate energy anaerobically, which protocells could have used to assemble carbon compounds into polymers. Carbon dioxide, also needed by evolving protocells would have been abundant in the pre-biotic ocean water.

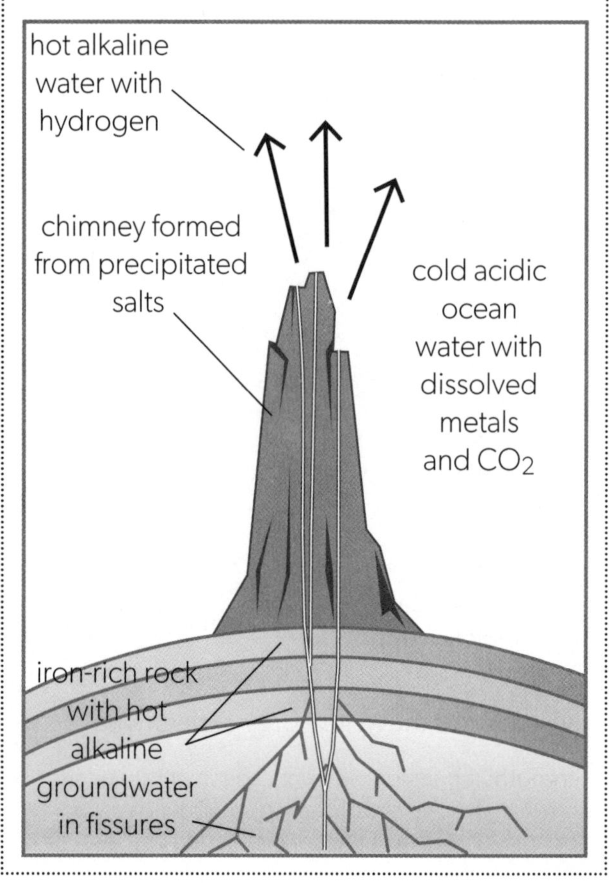

A2.2 Cell structure

1. Cells—basic structural unit of all living organisms

The ancient Greeks debated whether living organisms were composed of an endlessly divisible fluid or of indivisible subunits. The invention of the microscope settled this debate—organisms are made of cells. A cell is the smallest unit of self-sustaining life. Unicellular organisms only have one cell. Multicellular organisms have more than one cell and usually have many.

2. Microscopy skills

Multiple skills are needed to study cells using a microscope:

Skill 1: Making temporary mounts

Put the cells or tissue onto a microscope slide in a drop of water. Lower a cover slip onto the sample carefully to avoid creating air bubbles. Ensure there is only a thin sample on the slide by squeezing out any excess fluid.

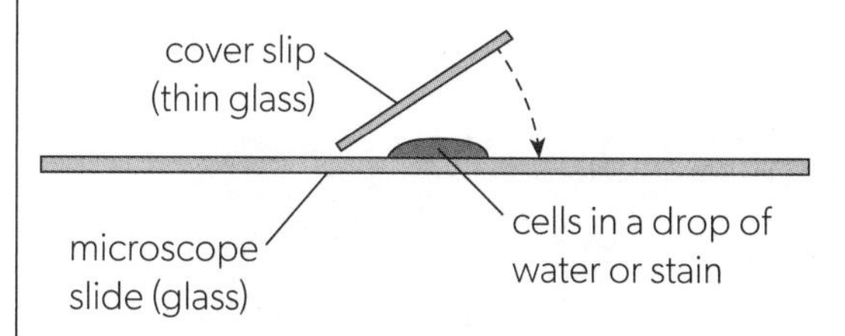

Skill 2: Staining

Colourless or white structures in cells are very hard to see unless they are stained. A stain is a pigment that binds to specific chemicals. For example, methylene blue binds to DNA, so is useful for revealing nuclei in cells. Stains are usually added to cells or tissues on the microscope slide before the cover slip is added.

Skill 3: Measuring sizes using an eyepiece graticule

A graticule is a graduated scale that is placed inside the eyepiece of a microscope. It is used like a ruler to measure the lengths of structures seen with the microscope. The graticule must be calibrated for each objective lens, so the eyepiece units can be converted into micrometres.

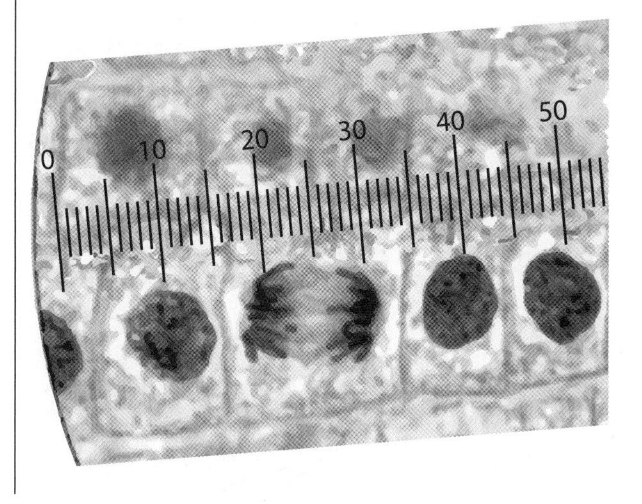

Example

Look at the photograph. Root cells are visible in the microscope field of view. The cell on the left has a diameter of 12 graticule units.

Calibration:

1 graticule unit = 1.5 μm

actual diameter = 12 × 1.5 μm = 18 μm

Skill 4: Focusing with coarse and fine adjustments

Focusing knobs change the distance between the specimen on the microscope slide and the objective lens, which allows the specimen to be brought into focus.

- Start with the specimen and lens as far apart as possible.
- While looking down the microscope, use the coarse focusing knob to move the specimen and objective lens closer together until the specimen comes into focus.
- The fine focusing knob can then be used to get the sharpest possible focus, or to focus on a particular level in the specimen.

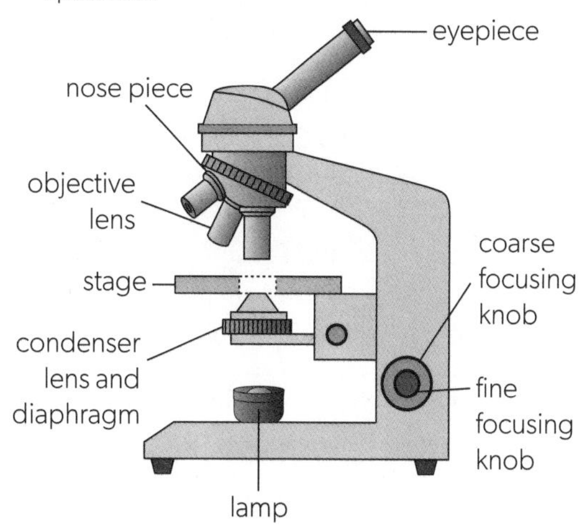

Skill 5: Taking photographs

Microscopes used for research usually have an inbuilt camera that can take photomicrographs of images.

High quality photos can now be taken with any microscope, simply by holding the camera lens of a smartphone close to the eyepiece of the microscope. It may be necessary to adjust the brightness of lighting and the focus to produce the best possible photo.

Skill 6: Calculating actual size and magnification

Only one equation needs to be memorized for calculations:

$$\text{magnification} = \frac{\text{size of image}}{\text{actual size}}$$

Calculating the magnification of an image (which could be a drawing, diagram or photomicrograph):

1. Choose an obvious length, for example the maximum diameter of a cell. Measure it in the image.

2. Measure the same length on the actual specimen.

3. If the units used for the two measurements are different, convert them to the same units. (1 mm = 1,000 μm)

4. Divide the length on the image by the length on the actual specimen. The result is the magnification.

Example

The thickness of the leaf in the electron micrograph below is 32 mm = 32,000 μm. The actual thickness of the leaf in is 80 μm.

$$\textit{Magnification of micrograph} = \frac{32{,}000}{80} = 400$$

Calculating the actual size of a specimen:

1. Rearrange the equation to this:

$$\text{actual size} = \frac{\text{size of image}}{\text{magnification}}$$

2. Divide the size in the image by the magnification.

Example

The diameter of a nucleus in a drawing is 12 mm and the magnification of the drawing is × 1,000.

$$\textit{actual diameter of nucleus} = \frac{12\text{ mm}}{1{,}000} = 0.012\text{ mm} = 12\ \mu\text{m}$$

Skill 7: Adding a scale bar

Scale bars allow sizes of structures in images to be deduced.

1. Rearrange the equation to this:

size of image = actual size × magnification

length of scale bar = length it indicates × magnification

2. Decide what length of scale bar is appropriate, e.g. 10 μm.

3. Multiply this length by the magnification to obtain the length of scale bar that should be added to the image. (Divide by 1,000 to convert μm to mm.)

Example

A scale bar on the drawing from the previous example has a length of 10 μm:

length of scale bar = 10 μm × 1,000

= 10,000 μm = 10 mm

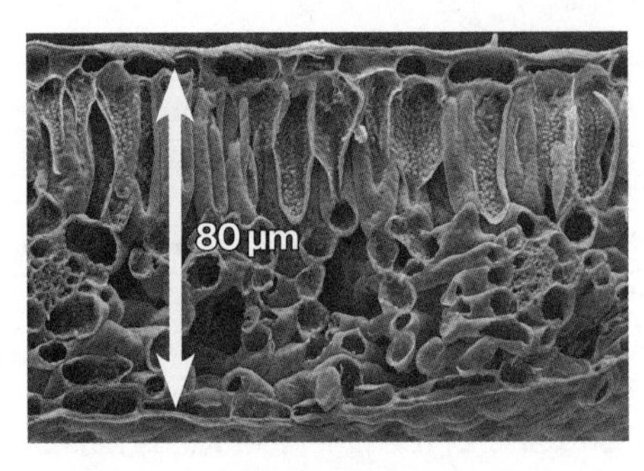

Scanning electron micrograph of a leaf, prepared using the freeze-fracture technique

NOS

Theories

The statement that living organisms are made of cells is an example of a theory, rather than a fact.

Features of theories in science	Cell theory
• Theories are based on observed patterns or on hypotheses that have been tested.	• Robert Hooke and later microscopists observed cells in all organisms that they examined.
• Theories are general explanations that can be applied widely.	• According to cell theory, all organisms are composed of cells.
• Predictions can be generated from theories by deduction.	• Prediction: a newly discovered organism will consist of one or more cells.
• When predictions are tested, a theory is either corroborated, or shown to be false and so rejected.	• Cell theory has been repeatedly corroborated, though some atypical structures have been found.

Observations

Scientists act as observers. Observations can be quantitative or qualitative. A drawing of the structure of a cell is a qualitative observation. A measurement of the diameter of the cell is a quantitative observation. Instruments are required for making quantitative observations. For example, a microscope fitted with an eyepiece graticule is the instrument used to measure diameters of cells.

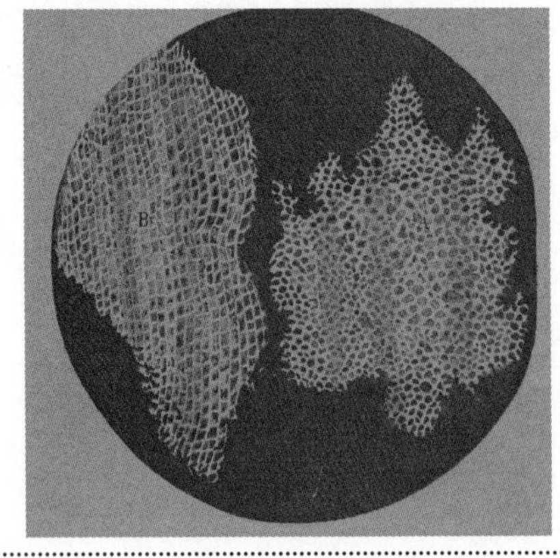

▲ Robert Hooke's drawing of cork cells, from *Micrographia* published in 1665

3. Microscopy developments

Microscopes were first invented in the 17th century. This led to the discovery of cells. Improved light microscopes in the 19th century allowed the discovery of bacteria, chromosomes, mitosis, meiosis, gametes and fertilization. Many developments in microscopy have since been made.

1. Fluorescent stains and immunofluorescence

Fluorescence is absorbance of light and re-emission at a longer wavelength. Fluorescent stains have been used in microscopy for over 100 years and fluorescence microscopes have been developed with intense single-wavelength light sources such as high-power LEDs or lasers. Light re-emitted by a stained sample generates particularly bright images.

Immunofluorescence is a development of fluorescent staining. Antibodies that bind to a specific chemical in the cell are produced. A fluorescent marker is linked to the antibodies. Images produced of cells treated with these antibodies show the cell structure overlain with the bright colour of the fluorescent marker where the specific chemical occurs in the cell. Multicoloured fluorescent images can be produced using multiple types of antibodies with fluorescent markers of different colours.

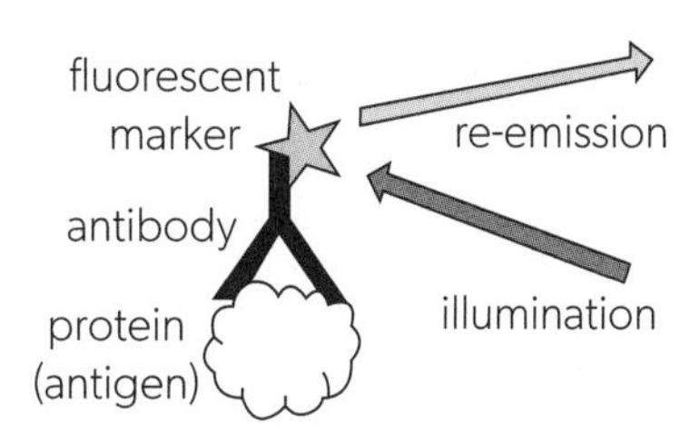

2. Electron microscopes

Magnification can be increased with a microscope until a point beyond which the image can no longer be focused sharply. This is because the resolution of the microscope has been exceeded. Resolution is the ability of a microscope to show two close objects separately in the image. Electron microscopes have better resolution than light microscopes, so they can give much higher magnification and smaller structures can be seen. Electron microscopes have allowed scientists to investigate the detailed structure (ultrastructure) of cells.

Microscope	Resolution	Magnification
Light	0.25 μm	× 500
Electron	0.25 nm	× 500,000

3. Freeze-fracture electron microscopy

This technique is used to produce images of surfaces within cells. A sample is plunged into liquefied propane at −190°C so it rapidly freezes. A steel blade is then used to fracture the frozen sample. The fracture goes through the weakest points of the cells. A vapour of platinum or carbon is fired onto the fracture surface at an angle of about 35° to form a coating. This creates a replica of the fracture surface. The replica is removed from the frozen sample and can be examined using an electron microscope. It is 2 nanometres thick on average but thickness varies because of the angle at which the coating is applied. This gives the impression of a 3D image with shadowing.

The weakest point in cells is usually the middle of membranes, between the two layers of phospholipid. The freeze-fracture process gives a unique image of this part of cells. The image below shows part of a yeast cell.

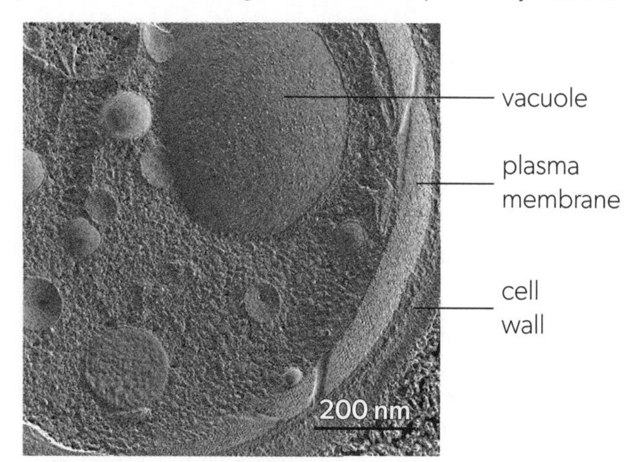

4. Cryogenic electron microscopy

Cryo-EM is used for researching the structure of proteins. A thin layer of a protein solution is applied to a grid and then flash-frozen with liquid ethane at −183°C to create smooth vitreous ice and prevent the formation of water crystals. The grid is placed in an electron microscope and detectors record patterns of electrons transmitted by individual protein molecules. Computer algorithms are used to produce a 3D image of the protein molecules. Cryo-EM can now give resolutions of 0.12 nm so individual atoms in a protein can be located.

Cryo-EM analyses proteins at the instant in time when the water around them froze. This allows scientists to research proteins that change from one form to another as they carry out their function.

4. Cellular structures found in all living organisms

Cell structure is very varied, but there are some key features that all typical cells have:

- **DNA as genetic material**—needed for producing mRNA by transcription, so proteins can be synthesized.
- **Cytoplasm composed mainly of water**—contains enzymes which catalyse many chemical reactions.
- **Plasma membrane composed of lipids**—controls the movement of substances in and out of the cell and allows different chemical conditions to be maintained inside the cell from those outside, such as pH.

5. Structure of prokaryote cells

- In prokaryote cells, there is no nucleus and instead the DNA is in the cytoplasm. There is usually a single chromosome (DNA molecule) which is circular and naked (not associated with proteins). Bacteria are prokaryotes.
- The cell is bounded by both a cell wall and a plasma membrane. The principal component of the cell wall is peptidoglycan.
- The cytoplasm has a high protein content, mostly enzymes. This makes it appear dark in electron micrographs, whereas the region of cytoplasm that holds the DNA is usually paler. There are many ribosomes in the cytoplasm. They are "70S" which indicates a relatively small size. S = svedberg (used to measure how fast something sediments when centrifuged).

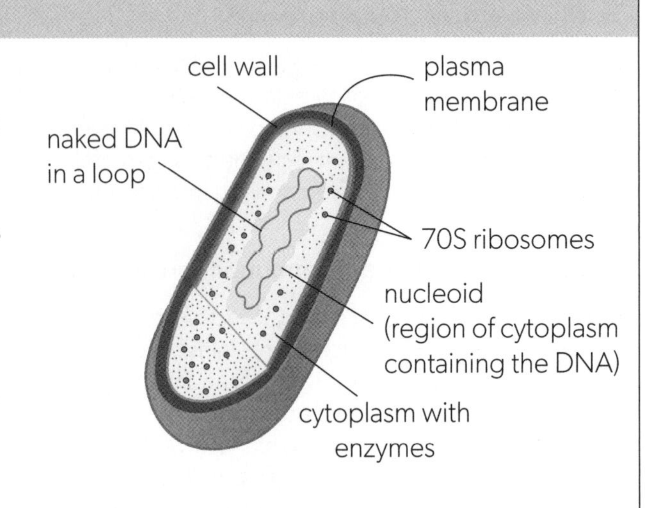

6. Structure of eukaryote cells

In eukaryotic cells there is usually a nucleus and many other organelles. An organelle is a discrete structure that is adapted to perform one or more vital functions within a cell. Organelles in eukaryotes can be classified according to how many membranes surround them:

Number of membranes	Organelles
0	80S ribosomes, microtubules, microfilaments
1	Rough ER, smooth ER, Golgi apparatus, lysosomes, vesicles, vacuoles
2	Nucleus, mitochondria, chloroplasts

The diagram shows the types of organelles that occur in most animal cells. There would be one nucleus only, but many of each of the other organelles, which would be densely packed in the cytoplasm.

Membrane-bound organelles divide the cytoplasm of eukaryotic cells into many small compartments.

Prokaryotic cells are not compartmentalized in this way and the whole cell is a single compartment.

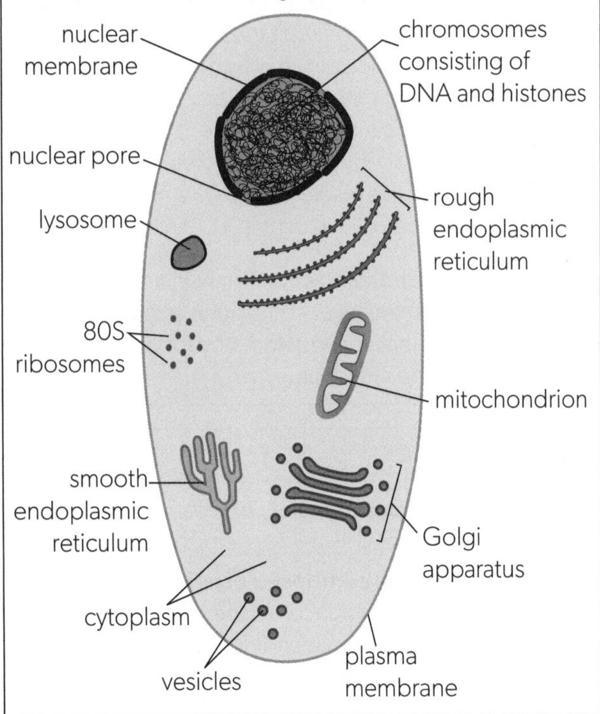

7. Life processes in unicellular organisms

Unicellular organisms consist of only one cell, which carries out all the functions of life. *Amoeba* is an example. It is 0.25–0.75 mm long.

Metabolism—Produces enzymes to catalyse chemical reactions in the cytoplasm.

Nutrition—Feeds on smaller organisms which are engulfed by endocytosis and digested in vesicles.

Growth—Increases in size and dry mass by assimilating digested foods.

Excretion—Metabolic waste products diffuse out of the cell, for example CO_2 from respiration.

Homeostasis—Regulates internal conditions, for example by expelling excess water using contractile vacuoles.

Movement—Draws cytoplasm from one side of the cell and uses it to extend the cell another side—known as ameboid movement.

Response—Reacts to stimuli, for example by moving towards higher concentrations of peptides released by bacteria.

Reproduction—Reproduces asexually using mitosis or sexually using meiosis and gametes.

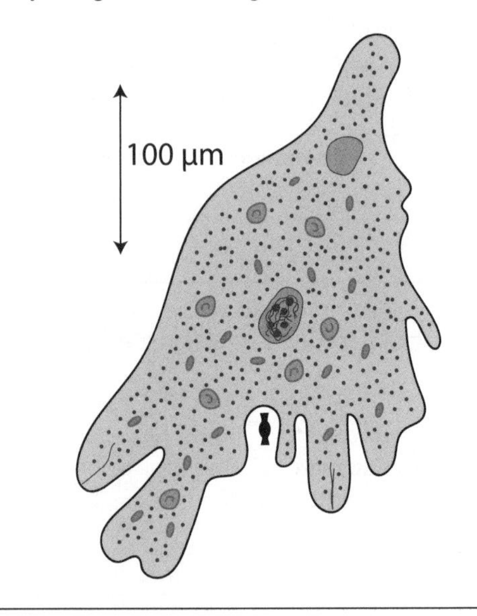

8. Comparing eukaryotic cell structure among animals, fungi and plants

Cell walls are tough layers, outside the plasma membrane. The main component in plant cell walls is cellulose and in fungal cell walls it is chitin. Animal cells do not have walls, which allows them to take in food by endocytosis but makes them vulnerable to bursting if too much water enters by osmosis.

Vacuoles are single-membrane sacs of fluid in the cytoplasm. There is often a large permanent vacuole in cells of fungi and plants, used for storage of substances and pressurizing the cell. Two types of small temporary vacuole occur in some animal cells but not plant or fungus cells: contractile vacuoles that expel excess water by exocytosis and food vacuoles that digest food or pathogens taken in by endocytosis.

Plastids are a family of double-membraned organelles. Plant cells have varied types such as chloroplasts (for photosynthesis) and amyloplasts (to store starch). Animal and fungus cells have no plastids.

Centrioles are organelles composed of a 9+2 arrangement of microtubules. They are used in animal cells to organize assembly of a spindle of microtubules during mitosis and meiosis.

Cilia and **flagella** are whip-like structures with a 9+2 arrangement of microtubules inside and plasma membrane on the outside. They protrude from the cell and generate movement by a beating action. Some types of animal cell have many cilia, which are small and move fluids adjacent to the cell. Male gametes (sperm) in animals have a single flagellum (tail), which is much longer than cilia and causes the sperm to move. Plant and fungus cells have no cilia. Some plants, including ferns and mosses, have motile male gametes with a flagellum, but conifers, flowering plants and almost all fungi do not.

	Animals	Fungi	Plants
Cell wall	×	✓	✓
Vacuoles	Small	Large	Large
Plastids	×	×	✓
Centrioles	✓	×	×
Cilia	Some	×	×
Flagella	Some	Some	Some

9. Atypical cell structure in eukaryotes

Eukaryote cells vary in structure in many ways. Typical cells have one nucleus, but there are atypical cells with a different number.

Some cells are anucleate—they do not have a nucleus, so cannot transcribe DNA to make mRNA and cannot synthesize proteins.

Red blood cells in mammals do not have a nucleus, so there is more space for haemoglobin. Without a source of proteins for repair or other functions they have a limited lifespan—four months at most.

plasma membrane

cytoplasm containing haemoglobin but no nucleus, mitochondria or ribosomes

Phloem sieve tube elements are the subunits of the tubes that transport sugar-containing sap in plants. They initially have a nucleus but it breaks down, so sap can flow more easily. However, they are supplied with proteins by adjacent companion cells, which have a nucleus and rough ER.

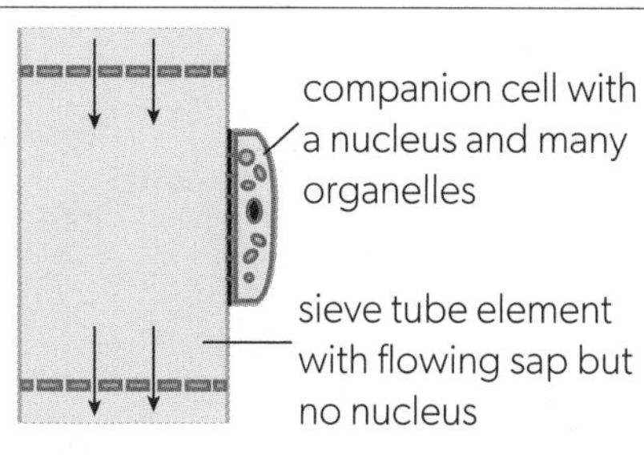

Some cells are multinucleate—they have many nuclei, allowing them to produce more mRNA and therefore more protein.

Skeletal muscle is made up of muscle fibres. Each fibre is enclosed inside a plasma membrane like a cell, but is 300 or more mm long (so much larger) and contains hundreds of nuclei.

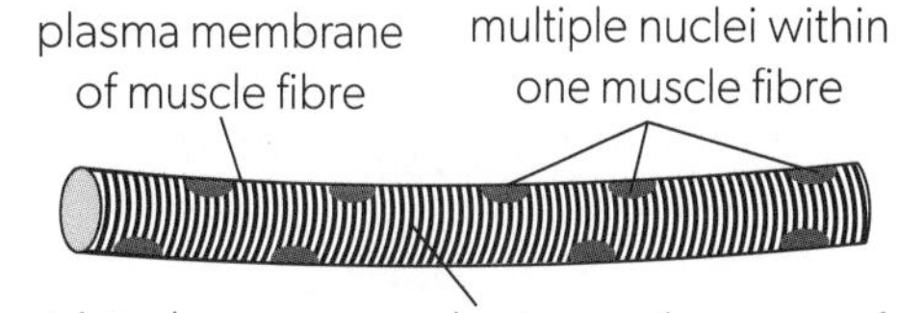

Aseptate fungi consist of thread-like structures called hyphae. These hyphae are not divided up into subunits containing a single nucleus. Instead, there are long undivided sections of hypha which contain many nuclei.

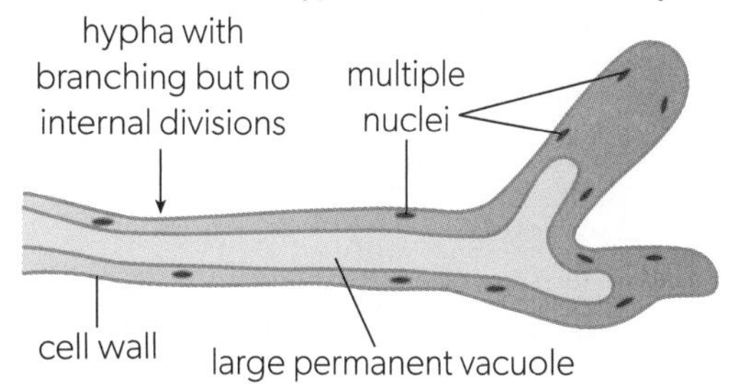

10. Examining cells and their structures in light and electron micrographs

The appearance of cell structures in light and electron micrographs is described in *Section A2.2.11*. Cell types can be identified by the structures that are present. Absence of a structure in one thin section of part of a cell seen in an electron micrograph does not prove that it is absent in the cell.

1. Is a cell prokaryotic or eukaryotic?		2. Is it a plant or animal cell?	
If the cell is part of a multicellular tissue, it must be from a eukaryote because prokaryotes are unicellular or simple chains of cells.		There are differences in structure between plant and animal cells but not all eukaryotes are plants or animals.	
Prokaryotic cells	Eukaryotic cells	Plant cells	Animal cells
• Nucleoid region visible in the cytoplasm • Cytoplasm without membrane-bound organelles	• Nucleus (or chromosomes if the cell is dividing) • Mitochondria or other membrane-bound organelles	• Cell wall always present • Large permanent vacuole often present • Chloroplasts or other plastids present	• Cell wall never present • Only small and temporary vacuoles • Cilia present in some animal cells

11. Creating drawings from electron micrographs

Drawings should be done with a sharp pencil. Structures should be labelled, but it is usually better to annotate (add notes to) drawings with the functions of each structure.

Boundaries of the cell:

Show the **plasma membrane** as a single unbroken line.

If there is a **cell wall** outside the plasma membrane, show it as a double line, as it is far thicker than the cell membrane. Hatching can be used to indicate that the wall is solid. In a healthy plant cell or bacterium, the plasma membrane is pushed up against the cell wall by turgor pressure.

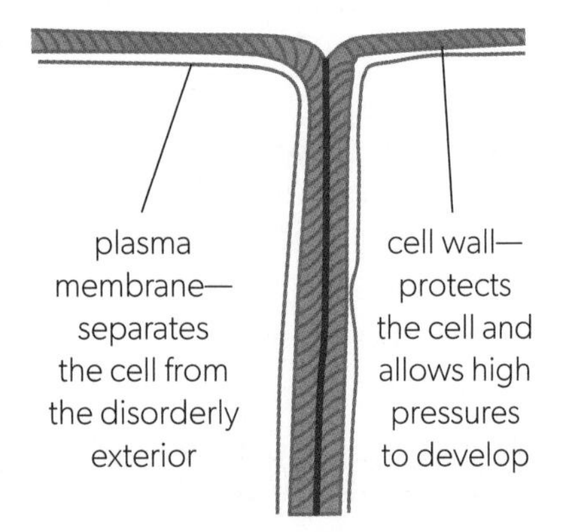

Animal cells do not have a cell wall so their plasma membrane can change shape, with invaginations and protrusions. Some animal cells have **microvilli**—many finger-like protrusions, which increase the surface area for absorption.

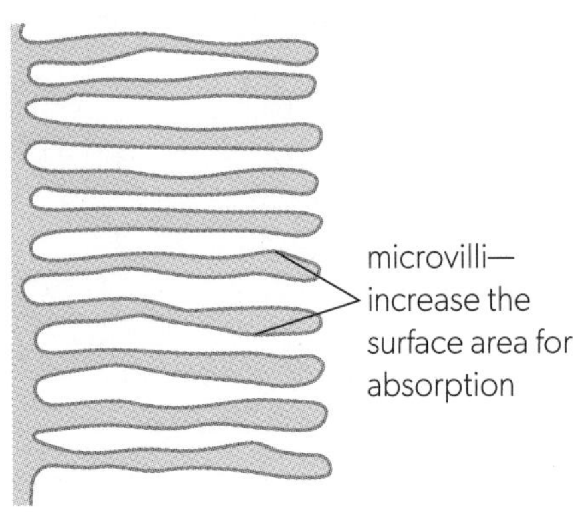

Gene storage in cells:

The **nucleus** of a eukaryotic cell has a double membrane with pores in it. Show it with an unbroken pencil line that doubles back at the pores. The interior of the nucleus has a distinctive grainy appearance. Much of it is lighter euchromatin, with patches of darker heterochromatin often around the edge. Heterochromatin is parts of **chromosomes** that have remained condensed after mitosis. During mitosis the chromosomes all become densely stained heterochromatin. Then the nuclear membrane breaks down, releasing chromosomes into the cytoplasm.

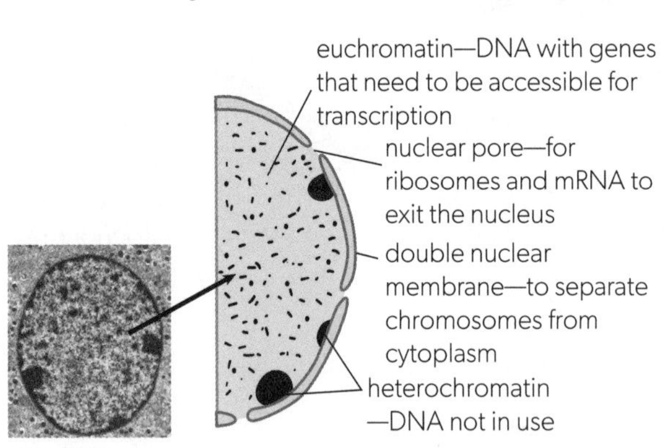

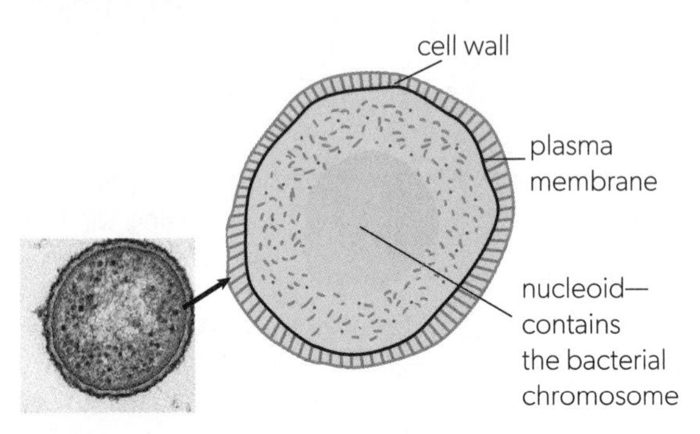

The nucleoid of a prokaryotic cell is a region of less dense staining in the centre of the cell.

Single-membraned organelles:

The large permanent **sap vacuole** of plant and fungus cells appears white or very pale in electron micrographs. The single membranes of vacuoles, vesicles, endoplasmic reticulum and Golgi apparatus should be shown with a single line.

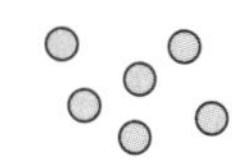

The Golgi apparatus is a stack of flattened membrane-bound sacs, which are usually curved with vesicles at the ends.

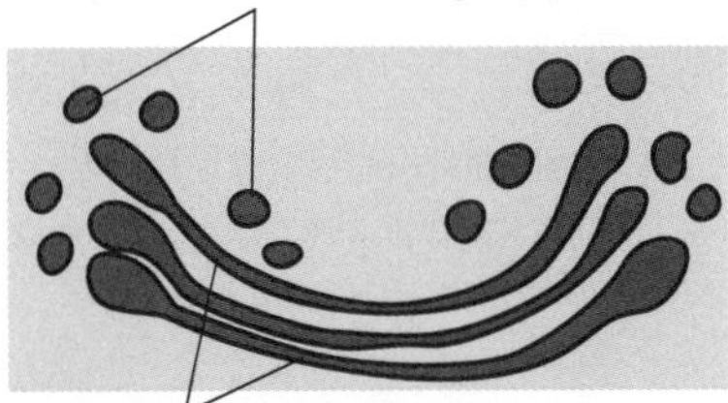

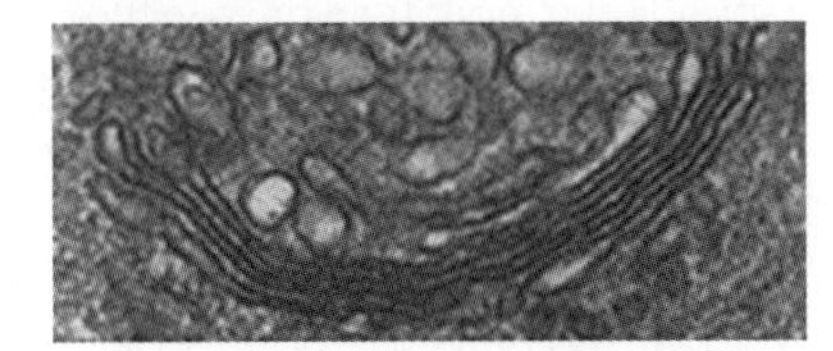

Endoplasmic reticulum is a network of membrane-bound spaces. In **smooth endoplasmic reticulum** they are mostly tubular. In **rough endoplasmic reticulum** they are lamellar (sheet-like). **Ribosomes** appear as densely stained granules with a diameter two to three times the thickness of a cell membrane. Free ribosomes float in the cytoplasm. Rough endoplasmic reticulum (RER) has ribosomes attached to its outer surface.

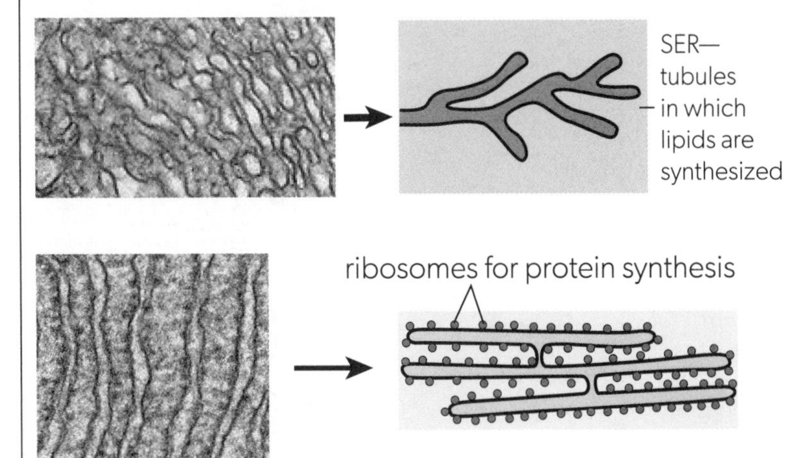

Double-membraned organelles:

Inside the double membrane of a **chloroplast** is an extensive network of thylakoids, which are single-membraned spaces. Most of these are disc-shaped and arranged in stacks (grana). Grains of starch and droplets of oil are sometimes visible.

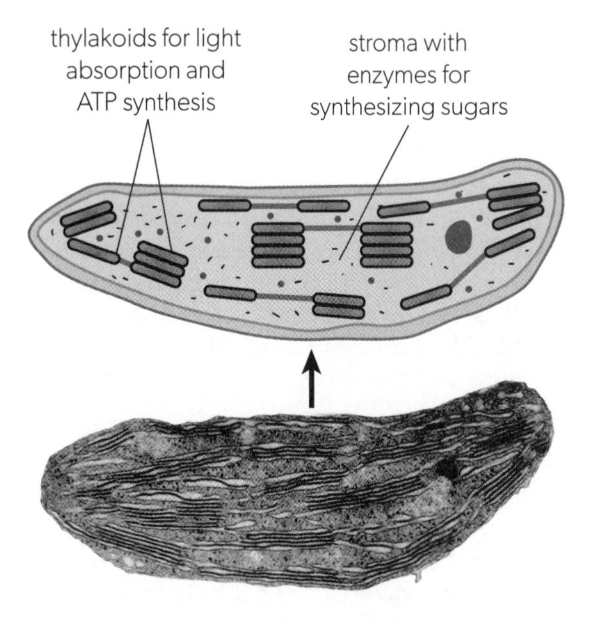

The inner membrane of the **mitochondrion** is infolded, which increases its surface area. Mitochondria appear darker than surrounding cytoplasm due to proteins in the fluid inside them, which stain densely in electron micrographs.

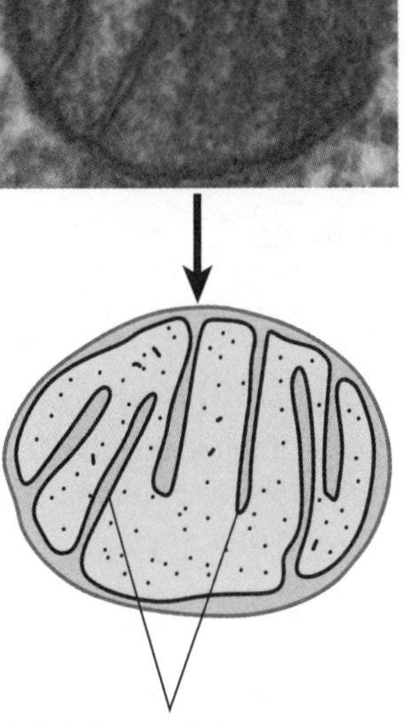

AHL

12. Endosymbiosis

Evidence suggests that all eukaryotes evolved from a unicellular ancestor that had a nucleus and reproduced both sexually by meiosis and fertilization, and asexually by mitosis. This common ancestor respired anaerobically but then it ingested an aerobically respiring bacterium. The bacterium remained alive inside a vacuole in the cytoplasm, giving the common ancestor a supply of ATP produced efficiently by aerobic respiration. The bacterium was provided with food, allowing it to grow and divide and therefore be passed on to daughter cells when the host cell divided. This type of relationship is endosymbiosis because the organisms live together (symbiosis) with one inside the other (endo). It is a mutualistic relationship because they both benefit. This relationship continued when the host cell divided as long as both daughter cells contained at least one aerobic bacterium.

The bacteria continued to grow, divide, pass on genes and evolve inside the host cells. Gradually over many generations the relationship became so close that neither the host cell nor the bacteria inside it could survive without the other and the bacteria evolved into the mitochondria now occurring in all typical eukaryotic cells. Some eukaryotes also ingested photosynthetic bacteria, which developed into the chloroplasts of plants and eukaryotic algae.

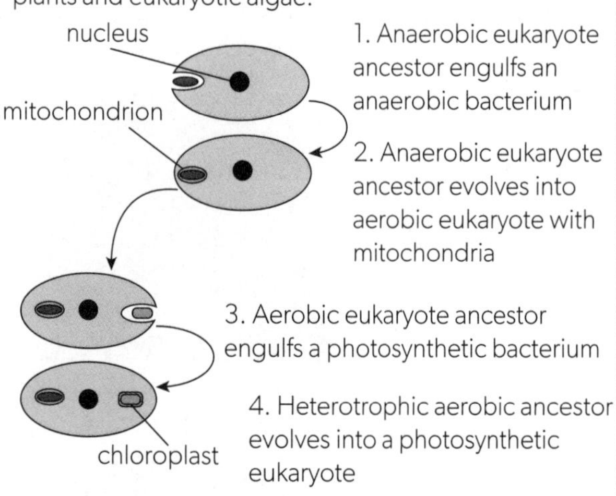

nucleus
mitochondrion
1. Anaerobic eukaryote ancestor engulfs an anaerobic bacterium
2. Anaerobic eukaryote ancestor evolves into aerobic eukaryote with mitochondria
3. Aerobic eukaryote ancestor engulfs a photosynthetic bacterium
4. Heterotrophic aerobic ancestor evolves into a photosynthetic eukaryote
chloroplast

This account of the evolution of eukaryotic cells is known as the endosymbiotic theory. The structure of mitochondria and chloroplasts provides evidence for endosymbiosis. They:

- have a loop of naked DNA, as in bacteria; the DNA contains genes, which are transcribed into RNA
- have 70S ribosomes and make some of their own proteins—suggests they were once independent cells; size of ribosome is the same as in bacteria
- reproduce by splitting in two, as in bacteria
- are double membraned—expected if a bacterium with its own plasma membrane was ingested in a vacuole formed by endocytosis. Originally there would have been a bacterial cell wall between the two membranes, but it had no function so was lost by evolution.

13. Cell differentiation

Cells differentiate in a multicellular organism by developing along different pathways, despite all having the same genome. This is achieved by differences in gene expression between cells. Housekeeping genes are expressed in all living cells, as they are required for basic functions such as respiration. Other genes are only expressed in some cells as they cause the development of specialized structures. For example, genes for synthesis of haemoglobin are only expressed during the development of red blood cells.

Chemical signals in a cell's environment (surroundings) determine which genes are expressed and therefore how a cell differentiates. A tissue develops because a group of cells receive the same signal, so they develop the same structure and carry out the same function. Cells in a tissue interact with each other and (except in blood) they use membrane proteins for the cell-to-cell adhesion that maintains the integrity of the tissue.

The advantage of cell differentiation is that form can match function more specifically. A specialist usually performs a function better than a generalist.

14. Multiple evolutions of multicellularity

All plants and animals are multicellular. Multicellularity evolved independently more than once in the origins of plants, and at least once in animals. Many fungi and eukaryotic algae are multicellular. These are the advantages of being multicellular:

- Lifespan can be longer, because the death of one cell does not prevent the continued survival of an individual.
- Larger body size is possible—useful in animals that are predators, or plants that compete for light.
- Cell differentiation—each cell carries out its function more effectively and more complex body forms can develop.

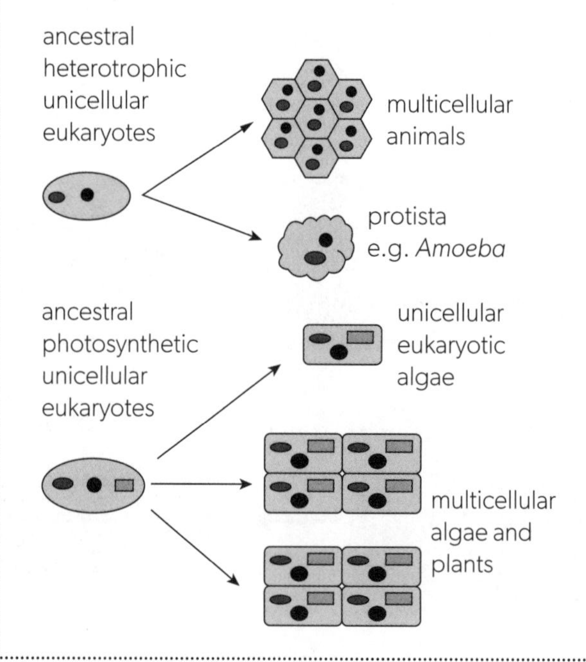

A2.3 Viruses

AHL

1. Shared features of viruses

Viruses are non-cellular. They infect cells and reproduce inside them. Unlike living organisms, which share features because of their common ancestor (LUCA), viruses probably have multiple origins, with any shared features due to convergent evolution.

- **Small size**: most viruses are between 20 and 300 nanometres in diameter. This is smaller than almost all bacteria and much smaller than plant or animal cells. Viruses must be smaller than their host cells so they can enter them. Viruses are also small because they lack cytoplasm and other structural features.
- **Fixed size**: viruses do not grow, so they do not increase in size. A virus is assembled inside a host cell, in a similar way to a car being assembled from components—both a virus and a car are their full size as soon as assembly is completed. Many viruses are composed of a fixed number of components, each with a fixed size, so this determines the overall size.
- **Nucleic acid as genetic material**: all viruses have genes made of DNA or RNA and they use the universal genetic code. This is essential as their proteins are synthesized by the nucleic acid-to-polypeptide translation mechanisms of their host cell.
- **Capsid made of protein**: before viruses are released from their host cell, their genetic material is packed into a protein coat called the capsid. This is made of repeating protein subunits. Self-assembly of the repeating subunits of the capsid gives viruses a symmetrical structure that is strikingly different from the shape of living cells.
- **No cytoplasm and few or no enzymes**: viruses rely on the metabolism of their host. The few enzymes produced by some viruses are required for replication of the virus's genetic material, for infecting host cells, or for lysis (bursting host cells to release the new viruses).

2. Viruses are diverse in structure

The diversity of viruses suggest that they have multiple evolutionary origins.

1. Genetic diversity: no genes occur in all viruses. The genetic material can be DNA or RNA and it can be single- stranded or double-stranded. If DNA, the molecule can be linear or circular. If RNA, the genes can be 'positive-sense' and used directly as mRNA or 'negative sense' and need to be transcribed before translation.

2. Enveloped and non-enveloped viruses: some viruses become enveloped in membrane during lysis, with phospholipids from the plasma membrane of the host cell and proteins, mostly glycoproteins, from the virus itself. The membrane helps the enveloped virus to make contact with a host cell and infect it. Other viruses do not become enclosed in a membrane—they are non-enveloped. Animal viruses are mostly enveloped. Plant viruses and bacteriophages are mostly non-enveloped.

Example	Bacteriophage lambda	COVID-19	HIV
Type	Bacteriophage—DNA viruses that use prokaryotes as hosts	Corona virus—RNA viruses with crown shape and animal hosts	Retrovirus—viruses that convert RNA to DNA after entry to host
Enveloped?	Non-enveloped	Enveloped	Enveloped
Genetic material	1 double-stranded DNA molecule with 32 genes	1 single-stranded positive-sense RNA molecule with 16 genes	2 copies of a single-stranded positive-sense RNA molecule with 9 genes
Features	Can follow either a lytic cycle in which it bursts and kills the host or a lysogenic cycle with its DNA inserted into the host cell DNA, so it is passed on to daughter cells when the host divides	Caused a pandemic starting in 2020 that killed more than 6 million people. The disease was zoonotic because the virus spread to humans from another species, probably a bat	The virus contains reverse transcriptase which makes a double-stranded copy of the viral RNA genome, which is integrated into the host cell's chromosomes
Host	*E. coli*—a gut bacterium	Epithelium cells in the airways and lungs of humans	T-helper cells in the human immune system
Structure	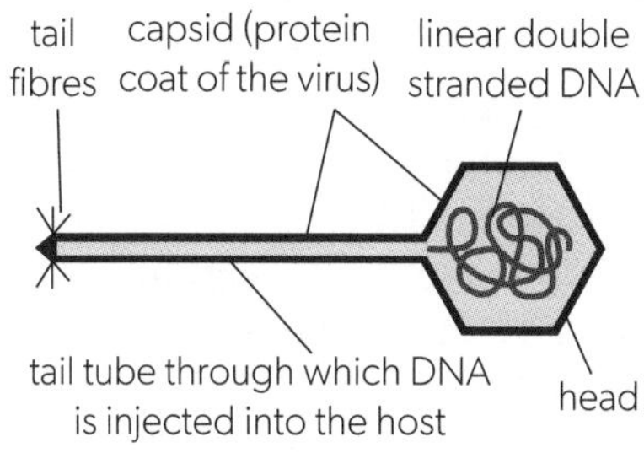 tail fibres; capsid (protein coat of the virus); linear double stranded DNA; tail tube through which DNA is injected into the host; head	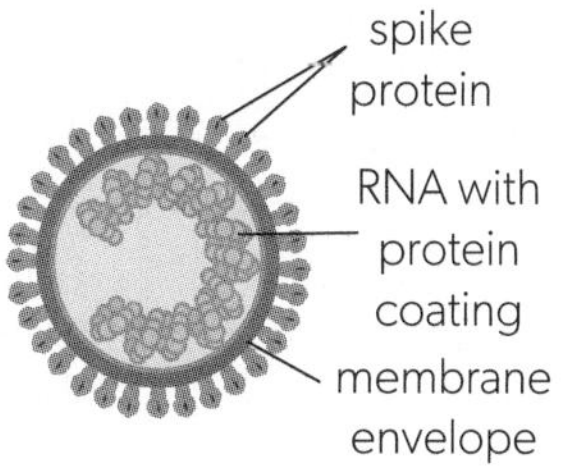 spike protein; RNA with protein coating; membrane envelope	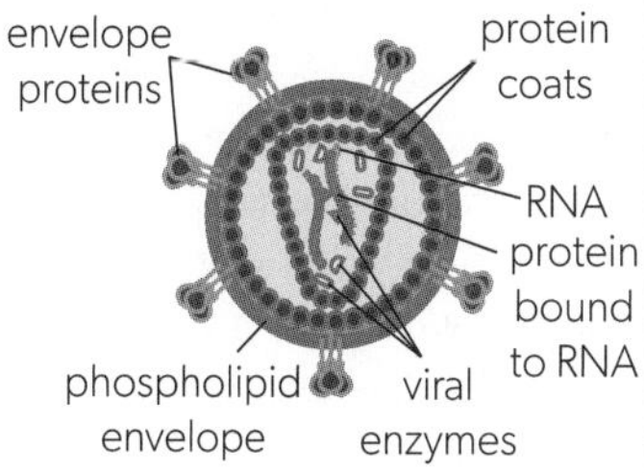 envelope proteins; protein coats; RNA protein bound to RNA; phospholipid envelope; viral enzymes

AHL

3. The lytic cycle

Bacteriophage lambda binds to its host, *Escherichia coli* using proteins at the tip of its tail. It then injects its DNA into the host cell through the tubular tail. The viral DNA has single-stranded ends, which link by base pairing to convert the molecule from a linear to a circular form. Like all viruses, lambda relies on the host cell for almost all life functions including providing energy and nutrition.

If the virus follows the lytic cycle, it reproduces inside the host cell and then bursts it, releasing the new viruses, which can then infect other host cells.

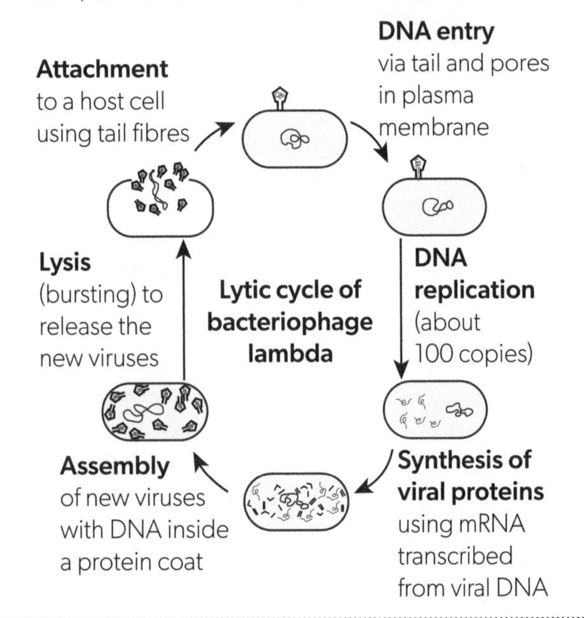
Attachment to a host cell using tail fibres
DNA entry via tail and pores in plasma membrane
DNA replication (about 100 copies)
Synthesis of viral proteins using mRNA transcribed from viral DNA
Assembly of new viruses with DNA inside a protein coat
Lysis (bursting) to release the new viruses
Lytic cycle of bacteriophage lambda

4. The lysogenic cycle

The lysogenic cycle is an alternative to the lytic cycle for bacteriophage lambda and other viruses. The virus attaches to a host cell and injects its DNA (as in the lytic cycle) but instead of replication, the virus's DNA becomes integrated into the host cell's DNA molecule. It stays there undetected and inactive. Each time the host replicates its DNA, prior to cell division, it also replicates the viral DNA, so all daughter cells inherit the viral DNA but do not produce viral proteins.

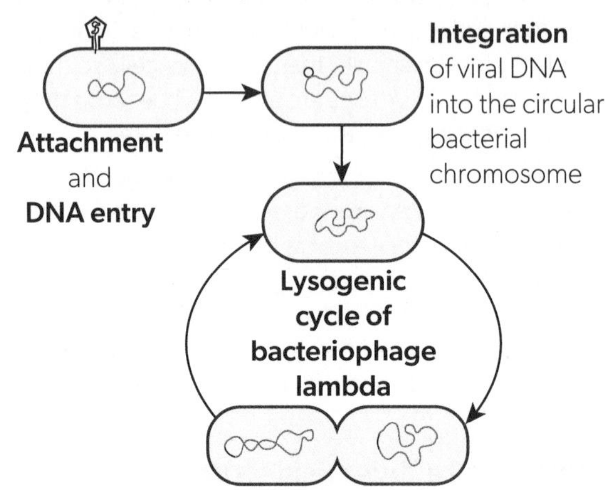
Attachment and **DNA entry**
Integration of viral DNA into the circular bacterial chromosome
Lysogenic cycle of bacteriophage lambda

The viral DNA is known as a prophage while it remains integrated in the bacterial DNA. The virus is **temperate** in this state as it does not kill its host and causes minimal harm. It is lysogenic because it could change to the lytic state and then cause lysis. The stimulus for this can come from inside or outside the bacterial cell.

5. Evidence for several origins of viruses

- Viruses are obligate parasites. They need a host cell in which to replicate. This suggests that cells evolved before viruses.
- Viruses (which are not regarded as truly living) use the same universal genetic code as living organisms. This suggests that viruses evolved from cells.
- Viruses are extremely diverse in structure and genetic constitution. This suggests multiple origins from living cells, rather than all viruses evolving from one common viral ancestor. The similarities between viruses would therefore be due to convergent evolution.
- Viruses could have evolved in a series of steps by taking and modifying cell components. This hypothesis fits with the occurrence of virus-like components in some cells.
- Viruses could have evolved from cells in a series of steps by loss of cell components and of more and more life functions, including respiration and protein synthesis. This fits with the observation that both viruses and bacteria show variation in complexity and self-reliance.

6. Viruses rapidly evolve

Viruses can show extremely rapid rates of evolution. There are three main reasons:

1. Very short generation times of <1 hour in the lytic cycle
2. High mutation rates, especially in RNA viruses
3. Intense natural selection due to host organisms evolving defences such as antibodies for destroying viruses.

Influenza is caused by a rapidly evolving RNA virus. It uses RNA replicase to replicate its genetic material. This enzyme does not proofread or correct errors, leading to a high mutation rate. The flu virus has eight separate RNA molecules. If a host cell is invaded by two different strains of the virus, a new strain can be formed with combination of RNA from the two strains. Transmission of flu between humans and other species also triggers evolution. Because of the rapid evolution of the flu virus, annual vaccinations are needed to give immunity to new strains.

HIV has the highest known mutation rate of any virus. It is a retrovirus that uses reverse transcriptase to convert its single-stranded RNA genome to DNA. This enzyme does not proofread or correct errors. Mutations are also caused by cytidine deaminase, an enzyme made by the host that converts cytosine to uracil. Even within a person infected by one strain of HIV, mutations will produce many genetically different strains, helping the virus to evade the immune system and become resistant to antiretroviral drugs. HIV infection is therefore almost always chronic rather than curable.

End of topic questions—A2 Questions

A2.1 Origins of cells (HL)

1. The table shows estimates for ocean water and fluid emerging from pores in alkaline hydrothermal vents on pre-biotic Earth.

	ocean water	vents
pH	6	11
proton concentration (mol dm^{-3})	10^{-6}	10^{-11}

a. Calculate the ratio between proton concentrations in ocean water and vents. (2)

b. Calculate the same ratio for the Earth as it is now, with pH 8 in the oceans and pH 11 in vents. (2)

c. State where a proton gradient occurs in eukaryotic cells. (1)

2. a. State three types of evidence for the hypothesis that all living organisms share a common ancestor. (3)

b. Explain whether LUCA is most likely to have lived 40 billion, 4 billion or 4 million years ago. (2)

3. a. Define "spontaneous generation of life". (1)

b. Suggest reasons for the hypothesis that *life was generated spontaneously on Earth in the past*. (2)

c. Outline reasons for new cells now only forming by the division of pre-existing cells. (2)

d. Discuss whether cells can survive without:

i. DNA (7) ii. membranes (4) iii. proteins. (4)

A2.2 Cell structure

1. The micrograph shows a transverse section of part of an animal cell.

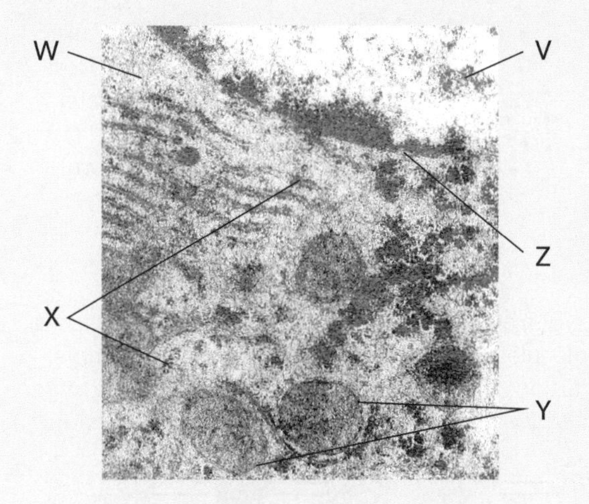

a. Identify the parts labelled **V**, **W**, **X**, **Y** and **Z**. (2)

b. The actual maximum diameter of Y is 2 μm. Calculate the magnification of the electron micrograph. (2)

c. Explain whether the cell is prokaryotic. (2)

d. Deduce two substances that were being synthesized in large quantities by this cell. (2)

e. The dark granules in the cell are glycogen. What conclusions can you draw from this information? (2)

5. a. The electron micrograph was made using freeze fracture. Outline this technique and its advantages. (4)

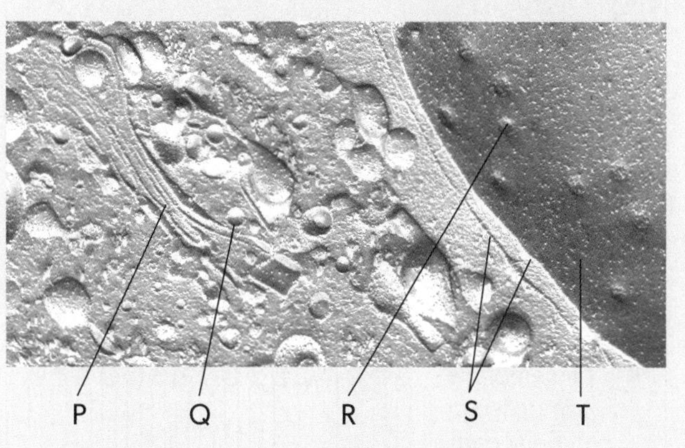

b. Identify structures **P**, **Q**, **R** and **S**. (4)

c. Suggest reasons for the grainy appearance of area **T**. (2)

6. Draw a diagram of the ultrastructure of a plant cell. (10)

7. (HL only) Explain the evidence for the endosymbiotic origin of mitochondria in animal cells. (5)

A2.3 Viruses

1. (HL only) Scientists studied the growth in numbers of a bacteriophage that infects the bacterium *E. coli*, after adding the virus to a culture of the bacteria. The graph shows the results, with five time periods indicated.

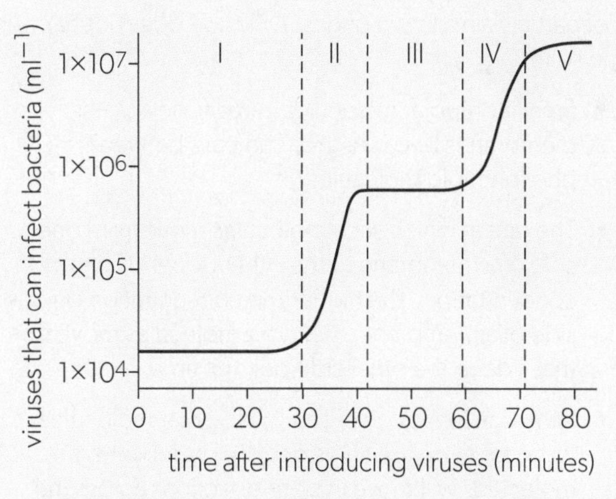

a. Compare and contrast results for the five periods. (2)

b. Deduce what is happening during:

i. phase II (2) ii. phase III. (4)

c. Deduce whether the virus is in a lytic or a lysogenic cycle. (2)

2. a. List the structural features that unite all viruses. (5)

b. Outline the features that differ in viruses. (3)

c. Discuss whether viruses have shared ancestry. (2)

3. (HL only) Explain how viruses exemplify:

a. parasitism (5)

b. convergent evolution (5)

c. generation of variation. (5)

B2.1 Membranes and membrane transport

1. Cell membranes are made from lipid bilayers

Phospholipids naturally form continuous sheet-like bilayers in water. The reasons for this are described in *Section B1.1.12*. Other amphipathic lipids such as cholesterol join with phospholipids to form the bilayers that are the basis of cell membranes—both the plasma membrane that forms the outer boundary of the cell and the membranes of organelles in eukaryote cells.

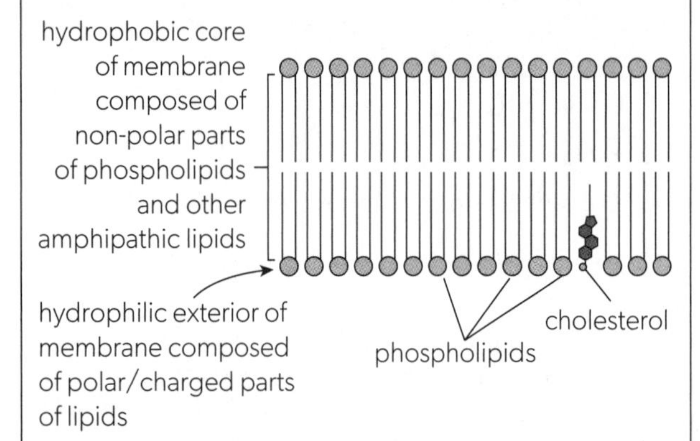

2. Membranes form barriers

Large molecules and hydrophilic particles do not pass easily between the hydrophobic hydrocarbon chains that form the core of a membrane. This gives membranes low permeability to these substances and allows membranes to function as effective barriers between the aqueous solutions.

Low membrane permeability makes it possible to maintain differences in concentration (concentration gradients) across a membrane. The plasma membrane has a particularly important role as it holds useful substances inside the cell and prevents many potentially harmful substances from entering.

Examples of low permeability

Large molecules: proteins, starch, glycogen, cellulose

Polar molecules: glucose, amino acids

Ions: chloride, sodium, potassium, phosphate

3. Simple diffusion across cell membranes

Diffusion is net movement of particles from a region with a higher concentration to a region of lower concentration. Diffusion is passive because it is a natural consequence of the continual random motion of particles in a liquid or gas. Diffusion does not happen in solids.

- Small non-polar molecules can diffuse across membranes because they can pass between phospholipid molecules.
- The rate at which such molecules move from one side of a membrane to the other depends on their concentration. The higher the concentration on one side of a membrane, the more molecules move from that side to the other side per unit time.
- If the concentration of small non-polar molecules is the same on the two sides of a membrane, the molecules will move in both directions across the membrane, but because rates of movement are equal, they cancel out and there is no net movement.
- If there is a higher concentration on one side of a membrane than the other side, the molecules move across in both directions, but more move from the higher to the lower concentration than vice versa. There is therefore a net movement from the higher to the lower concentration. This net movement is simple diffusion, because no special structures are required in the membrane—the molecules move through the phospholipid bilayer.

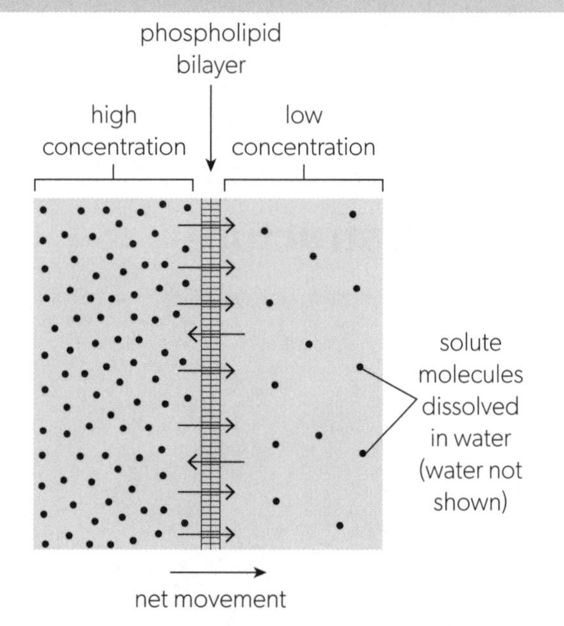

Oxygen and carbon dioxide are both small, non-polar molecules so they can enter or leave cells by simple diffusion. In a respiring animal cell for example, oxygen enters by simple diffusion and carbon dioxide leaves.

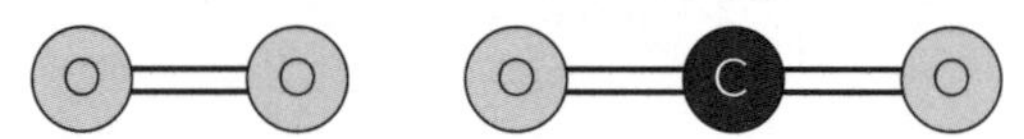

Oxygen is non-polar because the two oxygen atoms share electrons evenly in the double covalent bond between them.

Carbon dioxide has two polar carbon–oxygen bonds, but as the molecule is linear, the polarity is cancelled out, so CO_2 is non-polar.

4. Diversity of membrane proteins

In addition to the basic phospholipid bilayer, the membranes of cells contain proteins. The protein molecules are mostly globular, with a wide range of structures, functions and positions in the membrane.

Integral proteins are embedded in the phospholipid bilayer. **Peripheral proteins** are attached to the surface of the membrane, on one side or the other.

the two sides of most membranes have different functions so the proteins are different

integral proteins have a mostly hydrophobic surface so they are embedded in the bilayer

peripheral proteins are attached to proteins or lipids in the bilayer on one side of the membrane or the other

transmembrane proteins stretch across from one side of the membrane to the other

6. Facilitated diffusion

Ions such as chloride and sodium and polar molecules such as glucose only pass between the phospholipids in a membrane at very slow rates. To allow these substances to diffuse through membranes at the rates required by cells, channel proteins are needed. Inside each channel protein is a pore that allows particles to pass across the membrane in either direction. The diameter of the narrowest part of the pore and charges (+ or −) on the amino acids lining the pore make channel proteins specific—only one substance or group of related substances can pass through. For example, potassium channels only allow potassium ions (K^+) through. No energy from ATP is used.

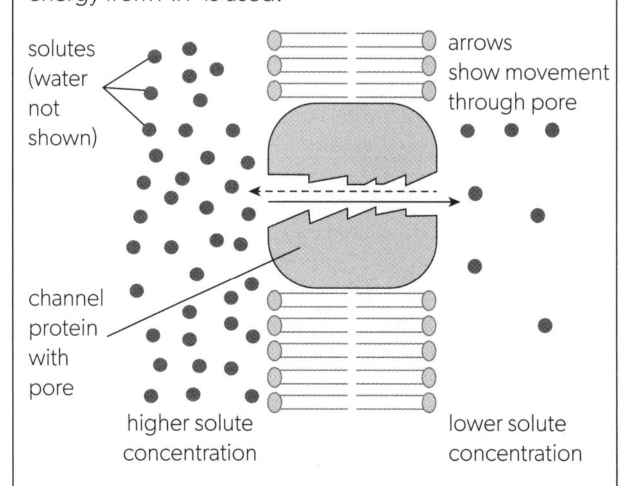

Facilitated diffusion is passive movement of particles across a membrane from a higher concentration to a lower concentration via channel proteins.

Some channel proteins have mechanisms for opening and closing their pores.

5. Osmosis

Water is the solvent, both in the cytoplasm of cells and in the fluids that surround cells. Particles dissolve in water by forming hydrogen bonds or other intermolecular interactions with water molecules.

In aqueous solutions, both the water molecules and solutes are in continual random motion. Membranes are typically very permeable to water but have low permeability to many solutes. For this reason, water moves across membranes far more readily than most solutes. It can move in either direction across a membrane, but because of water's attraction to solutes, there is a net movement from the side with lower solute concentration to the side with higher solute concentration. The direction of net water movement across membranes is thus governed by differences in solute concentration, not water concentration, so it is not typical diffusion and instead is defined as osmosis.

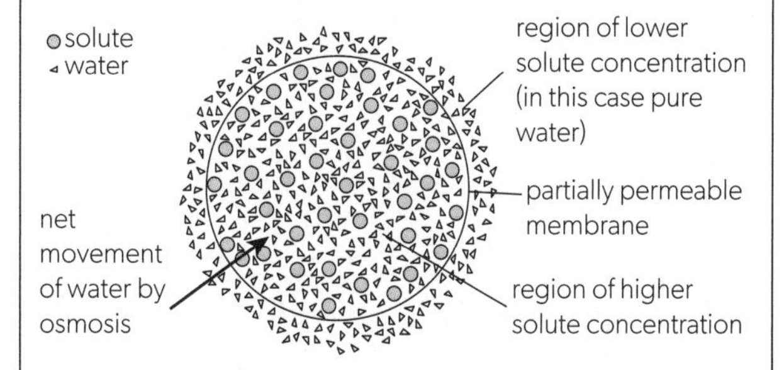

It is the overall concentration of solutes that causes movement of water by osmosis, not concentrations of particular dissolved substances.

Osmosis is the passive movement of water molecules from a region of lower solute concentration to a region of higher solute concentration, across a partially permeable membrane.

Plasma membranes are all permeable to water to some extent, but the permeability can vary. Permeability is increased by placing aquaporins in a membrane. These are transmembrane integral proteins with a pore through which water molecules can pass in either direction. The properties of the pore prevent other particles, such as protons or chloride ions, from passing through.

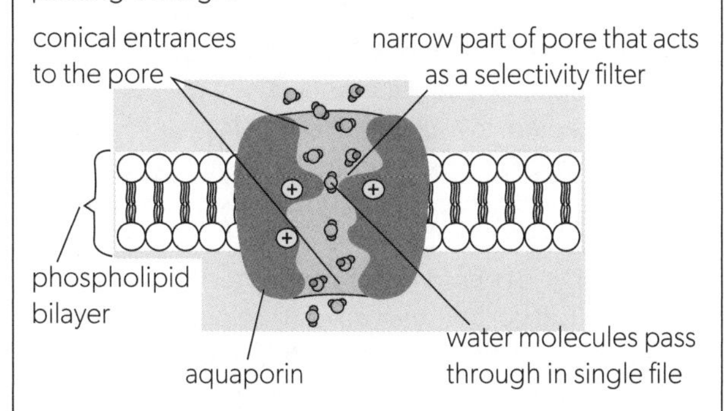

Aquaporins do not use energy to make water move. Water movement across membranes is always passive—water molecules are never pumped.

7. Active transport requires pump proteins

Active transport is the movement of substances across membranes using energy from ATP. Active transport moves substances against the concentration gradient (from a lower to a higher concentration). Protein pumps in the membrane carry out active transport. Pumps work in a specific direction—the substance can only enter the pump on one side and exit on the other side. This is due to the pump alternating between two conformations. ATP causes a change from the more stable to a less stable conformation. The reverse change happens without input of energy.

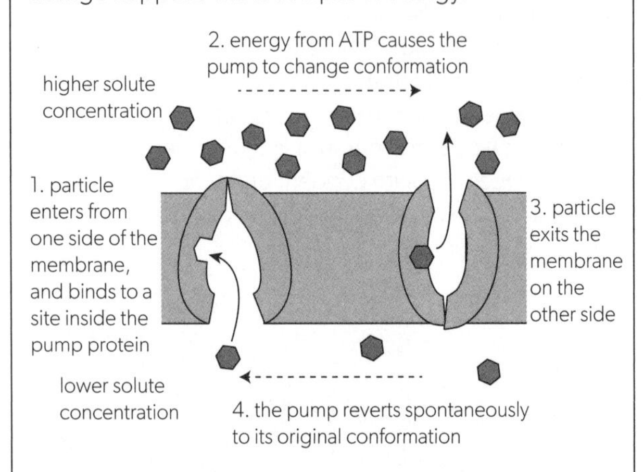

8. Membranes are selectively permeable

Membranes have been described as **semi-permeable** and **partially permeable**, because they allow some substances through, but not others. This fits **simple diffusion** across membranes: particles that are large or hydrophilic cannot pass, but any small and non-polar (hydrophobic) particle can move across, with a net movement down the concentration gradient (from high to low concentration).

Facilitated diffusion and active transport allow cells to exert more control over membrane permeability than this.

- Channel proteins used for **facilitated diffusion** are specific to one type of particle or group of related particles. Cells can select which particles enter or exit, by controlling the types of channel protein placed in their plasma membrane. Also, the pores of some channel proteins can be closed temporarily, preventing movement of particles. Direction of movement cannot be controlled—net movement is always down the concentration gradient.
- Pump proteins used in **active transport** are specific to particular particles and their asymmetrical structure ensures that the particles are only moved in one direction across the membrane. Particles can be moved from the lower to the higher concentration, so active transport can generate concentration gradients. Because of these properties of facilitated diffusion and active transport, the membranes of cells can be described as **selectively permeable**.

9. Glycoproteins and glycolipids

Glycoproteins are polypeptides with carbohydrate attached (ranging from a single sugar up to small polypeptides). They are therefore partly protein and partly carbohydrate. In a similar way, glycolipids are lipids with carbohydrates attached (usually a short chain of up to four glucose subunits). The lipid part usually consists of one or two hydrocarbon chains. Both glycoproteins and glycolipids are components of plasma membranes, with the protein or lipid embedded in the membrane and the hydrophilic carbohydrate part projecting outwards into the extracellular environment. They have two main roles.

Cell adhesion: glycoproteins and glycolipids together form a carbohydrate-rich layer on the outer face of the plasma membrane of animal cells. This layer is the glycocalyx. The glycocalyxes of adjacent cells can fuse, binding the cells together and preventing the tissue from falling apart.

Cell recognition: differences in the types of glycoproteins and glycolipids within plasma membranes allow cells to recognize other cells. This helps in the development of the tissues and organs of multicellular organisms. Cell recognition allows the immune system to distinguish between self and non-self cells, so pathogens and foreign tissue can be recognized and destroyed.

10. Fluid mosaic model

A mosaic is a two-dimensional array of many small and diverse subunits. In the fluid mosaic model of membrane structure, which is widely accepted, the subunits are proteins that float in a lipid bilayer. Hydrophobic parts of the proteins (light grey in the diagram) are embedded in the core of the bilayer and hydrophilic parts (dark grey) are on the surface, or project from the bilayer. The lipids and proteins are mostly free to rotate or move laterally in the membrane because the lipid bilayer is liquid, but they cannot flip over, so differences between the two sides of the membrane can persist.

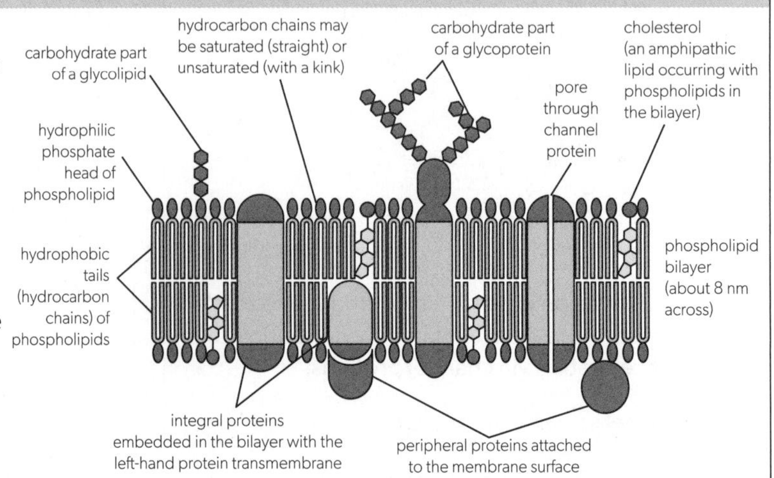

AHL

11. Fluidity of lipid bilayers

Saturated fatty acids have straight chains, so allow phospholipids to pack together tightly in bilayers. This reduces the fluidity of a membrane and therefore its flexibility and permeability by simple diffusion. In contrast, unsaturated fatty acids have one or more kinks in their hydrocarbon chain, so phospholipids pack together more loosely, making a membrane more fluid, flexible and permeable. The diagrams show bilayers with (right) and without (left) unsaturated hydrocarbon chains.

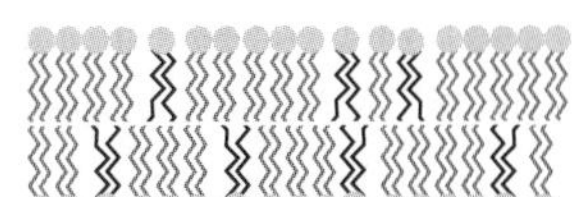

Relative amounts of saturated and unsaturated fatty acids are regulated so that the membranes have the required properties. They must remain fluid but be strong enough to avoid becoming perforated. They must be permeable but not too porous. The ideal ratio of saturated to unsaturated fatty acids depends on the temperatures experienced by a cell. For example, fish from Antarctic waters have more unsaturated fatty acids in their membranes than fish from warmer waters.

12. Cholesterol and membrane fluidity

Cholesterol makes up between 20% and 40% of the lipids in the plasma membranes of eukaryotes. The diagram in *Section B2.1.10* shows the position of cholesterol in membranes.

Cell membranes do not correspond exactly to any of the three states of matter—they are in what is called a liquid-ordered phase. The lipid molecules are packed densely but are still free to move laterally. The fluidity of membranes needs to be carefully controlled.

At high temperatures cholesterol helps to maintain the orderly arrangement of phospholipids. This prevents the membrane from becoming too fluid, so it does not become too porous and remains impermeable to hydrophilic particles such as sodium and hydrogen ions.

At low temperatures cholesterol ensures that saturated fatty acid tails do not solidify, preventing membranes from becoming viscous and inflexible (stiff), which would restrict cell movement and make the cell more likely to burst.

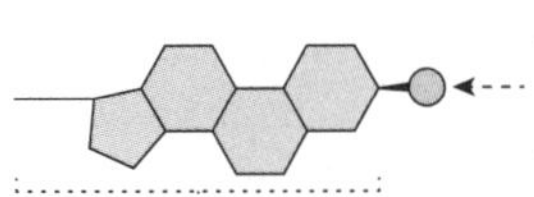
at one end of the molecule is a hydrophilic –OH group which is attracted to hydrophilic heads of phospholipids on the periphery
most of the molecule is hydrophobic so it is attracted to the hydrocarbon tails of phospholipids in the membrane

13. Endocytosis and exocytosis

A vesicle is a small spherical sac of membrane with a droplet of fluid inside. Vesicles are a dynamic feature of most eukaryotic cells, with a continuous cycle of formation, movement and fusion. These changes are possible because of the fluidity of membranes.

Vesicles **move materials** around inside cells.

Examples of intracellular movement using vesicles:

- Proteins synthesized by ribosomes on the rough ER are carried to the Golgi apparatus.
- Proteins processed by the Golgi apparatus are carried to the plasma membrane.
- Phospholipids and cholesterol synthesized by the smooth ER are transported in the vesicle membrane to the plasma membrane of a growing cell to increase its area.

Endocytosis is formation of a vesicle in the cytoplasm by pinching off a piece of plasma membrane. Vesicles made by endocytosis contain water and solutes from outside the cell. They may contain larger molecules needed by the cell that cannot pass through the plasma membrane.

Examples of endocytosis:

- Foetal cells in the placenta absorb proteins from the mother's blood, including antibodies.
- Unicellular organisms including *Amoeba* and *Paramecium* absorb large undigested food particles.
- Phagocytic white blood cells absorb pathogens including bacteria and viruses.

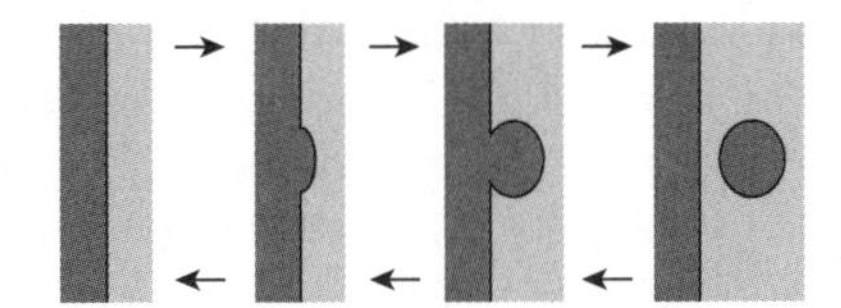

Exocytosis is fusion of a vesicle with the plasma membrane, expelling the contents of the vesicle from a cell.

Examples of exocytosis:

- Gland cells secrete proteins by exocytosis, for example digestive enzymes and protein hormones.
- Neurons secrete neurotransmitter by exocytosis.
- Unicellular organisms such as *Amoeba* and *Paramecium* load excess water into vesicles (sometimes called contractile vacuoles) so it can be expelled by exocytosis.

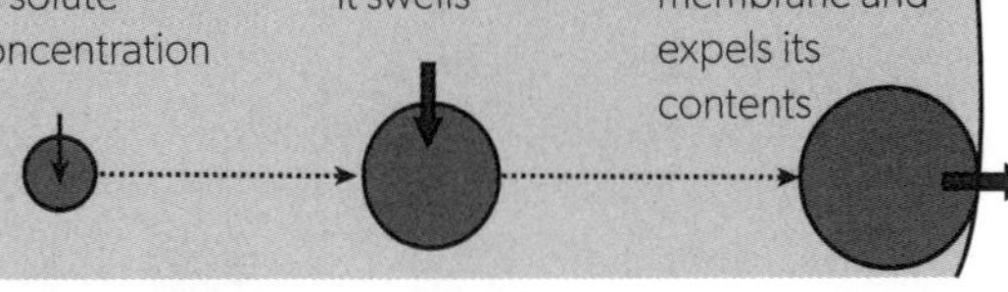
1. Ions are pumped into the contractile vacuole, increasing its solute concentration
2. Water enters the vacuole by osmosis so it swells
3. Contractile vacuole moves to the plasma membrane and expels its contents

In a growing cell, the area of the plasma membrane needs to increase. Phospholipids are synthesized and carried to the plasma membrane in vesicles.

AHL

14. Ion channels in neurons

Gated ion channels open for a fraction of a second to allow a pulse of ions to diffuse through, then close again. They are used in nerve impulses and also in synaptic transmission.

Voltage-gated sodium and potassium channels are used in nerve impulses. They are membrane proteins that can change conformation (shape) in response to changes in the voltage across the membrane. The conformational changes open and close a pore through the channel. Voltages across membranes are due to an imbalance of positive and negative charges. A negative voltage indicates that the overall balance of charges inside the neuron is less positive than outside. The diagrams show how a K^+ channel opens and closes.

1. Closed at −70 mV

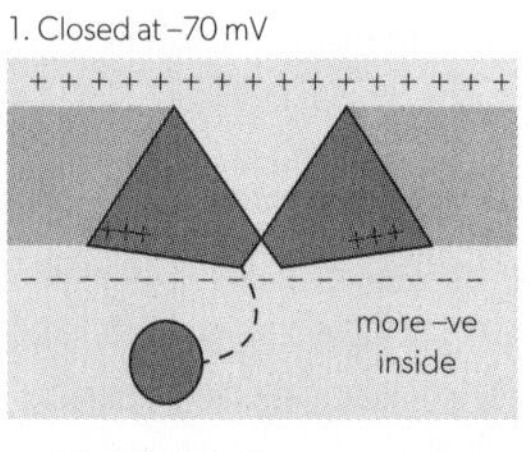

2. Open at +40 mV

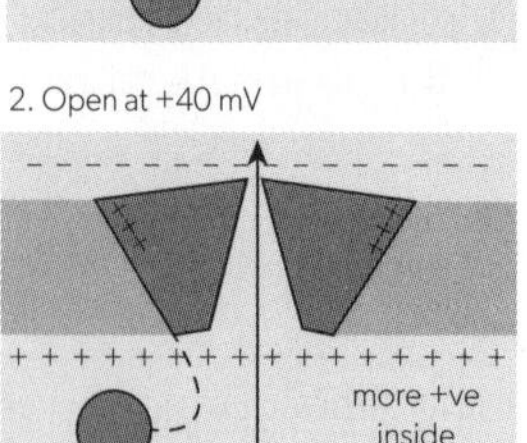

3. Rapidly reclosed at +40 mV

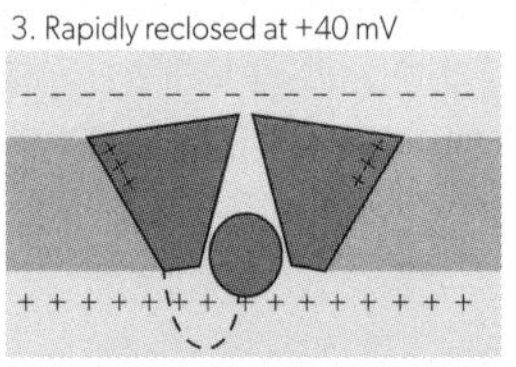

a globular protein "ball" attached by a flexible polypeptide "chain" soon blocks the pore at +40 mV then is ejected at −70 mV

A nerve impulse is a brief movement of sodium ions (Na^+) and then potassium ions (K^+) across the membrane of a neuron. If the voltage is below −50 mV, Na^+ and K^+ channels remain closed. If it rises above −50 mV, Na^+ channels open, allowing sodium ions to diffuse into the neuron. This causes the voltage to rise more. When it reaches +40 mV, K^+ channels open, allowing potassium ions to diffuse out, returning the voltage to its original level of −70 mV.

Nicotinic acetylcholine receptors are used at synapses where acetylcholine is the neurotransmitter. They have proteins in the postsynaptic membrane that are both receptors and channels. They have a site to which both acetylcholine and nicotine can bind.

Binding causes a conformational change, which opens a pore in the protein, through which sodium and other positively charged ions can pass. Sodium diffuses into the postsynaptic neuron, raising its voltage above −50 mV, which initiates a nerve impulse by causing voltage-gated sodium channels to open. Binding of acetylcholine is reversible. When it dissociates from the receptor, the conformational change caused by binding is reversed and the pore in the receptor is closed.

1. Binding sites are vacant so the pore is closed

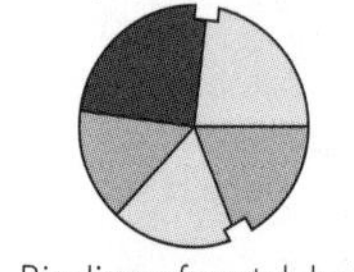

2. Binding of acetylcholine causes the pore to open

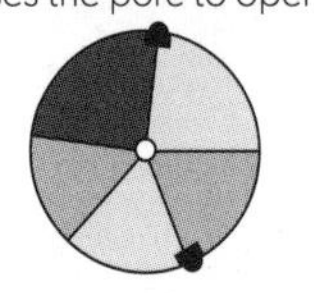

15. Sodium–potassium pumps

Exchange transporters are multi-taskers because they transport different substances in opposite directions across a membrane. Sodium–potassium pumps are an example. Each time a cycle of conformational changes happens, three sodium ions are transported out of the neuron and two potassium ions in. Energy from ATP is needed because both Na^+ and K^+ are pumped from lower to higher concentration, but the amount of energy is reduced by exchanging cations.

The sodium–potassium pump generates concentration gradients of both Na^+ and K^+ across the membrane, which allows a nerve impulse, by facilitated diffusion of these ions through voltage-gated ion channels

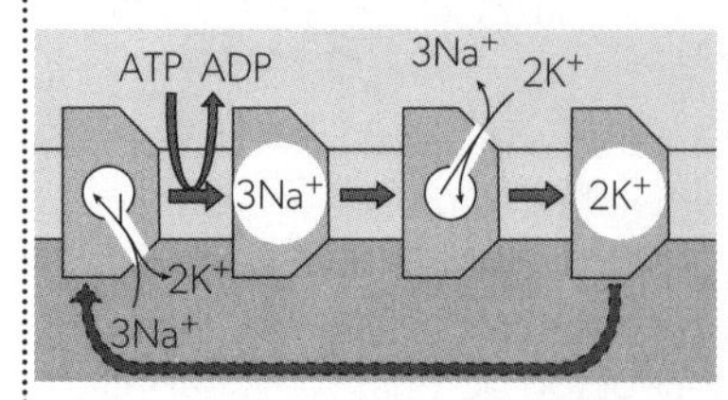

Na^+ concentration already higher on this side

K^+ concentration higher on this side

16. Indirect active transport

Sodium–glucose cotransporters are membrane proteins that move Na^+ and glucose together into a cell. The concentration of Na^+ is lower inside the cell so it moves down its concentration gradient and releases energy. This energy drives the movement of glucose, against the concentration gradient, into the cell. Cotransport of Na^+ and glucose depends on use of ATP to pump Na^+ out of the cell, which maintains the concentration gradient. Movement of glucose into the cell is therefore indirect active transport.

Examples: reabsorption of glucose from filtrate by cells in the wall of the proximal tubule in the kidney and absorption of glucose from digested foods by epithelium cells in the small intestine.

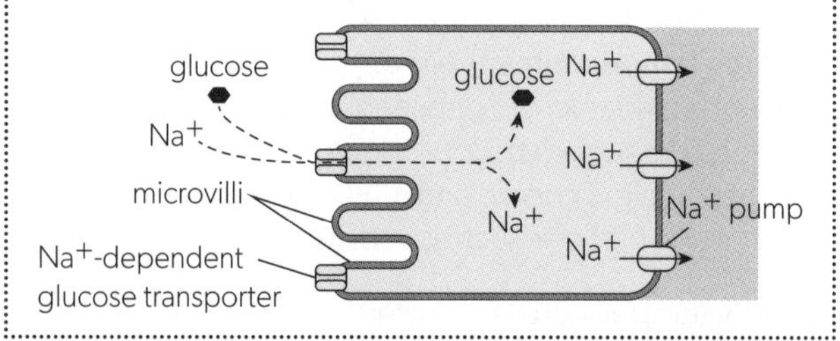

17. Adhesion of cells to form tissues

Cell–cell adhesion molecules (CAMs) link adjacent cells in animals. CAMs are integral membrane proteins that protrude into the extracellular environment. A cell–cell junction is formed by the extracellular parts of CAMs in adjacent cells binding together. Cells of the same type have the same types of CAM which link them up in a tissue. Different cell types have different CAMs, which link cells or tissues to form organs.

extracellular parts of CAMs

membrane

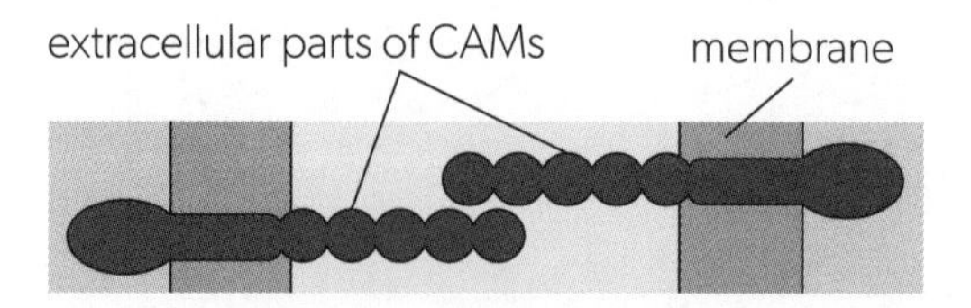

B2.2 Organelles and compartmentalization

1. Organelles

Eukaryote cells contain a variety of organelles (described in *Section A2.2.6*). Each type of organelle is adapted, by its structure, to perform one or more specific functions. The plasma membrane, nucleus, vesicles and ribosomes are all organelles because they have specific functions and their structure is discrete (they are individually distinct).

Some cell structures are not organelles:
- cell wall—outside the plasma membrane so outside the boundary of the cell (extracellular)
- cytoplasm—has diverse rather than specific functions
- cytoskeleton—very extensive structure that extends through the cytoplasm and is not discrete.

NOS

Experiments

Progress in science often follows the development of new techniques. For example, when techniques for separating organelles became available, research into the functions of the various types of organelles was possible.

1. The kitchen blender, with a rotating blade inside a glass container, was invented in the 1920s. It allows tissue to be homogenized, with the cells burst and organelles released.

2. Ultracentrifuges, which can rotate at more than 40,000 revolutions per minute, were invented in the 1920s. They were used for cell fractionation from the 1930s onwards. Organelles in homogenized tissue can be separated into different types because they settle to the base of the centrifuge tube (sediment) at different speeds.

2. Separation of the nucleus and cytoplasm

Eukaryotes modify mRNA before translating it into polypeptides. This happens inside the nucleus, where RNA is produced by transcription. The nuclear membrane ensures that this post-transcriptional modification is completed before mRNA meets the ribosomes that will translate it in the cytoplasm.

In prokaryotes there is no nuclear membrane, so ribosomes can translate mRNA as soon as it is produced and post-transcriptional modification is not possible.

3. Advantages of compartmentalization

The outer membrane of organelles such as lysosomes encloses their contents and creates a compartment that is separated from surrounding cytoplasm.

Advantages:
- The small volume allows enzymes and their substrates to be concentrated, speeding up enzyme activity.
- pH can be kept at the ideal level for the organelle's function.
- Incompatible biochemical processes can be kept separate. For example, lysosomes contain many hydrolytic enzymes that digest proteins and other macromolecules. If not confined within a membrane, they would digest much of the cell. Phagocytic white blood cells digest pathogens and some unicellular organisms digest prey, but not themselves, inside vacuoles, as described in *Section B2.1.13*.

AHL

4. Adaptations of the mitochondrion

Structure and function are closely related in mitochondria. This is an example of adaptation and is due to evolution by natural selection.

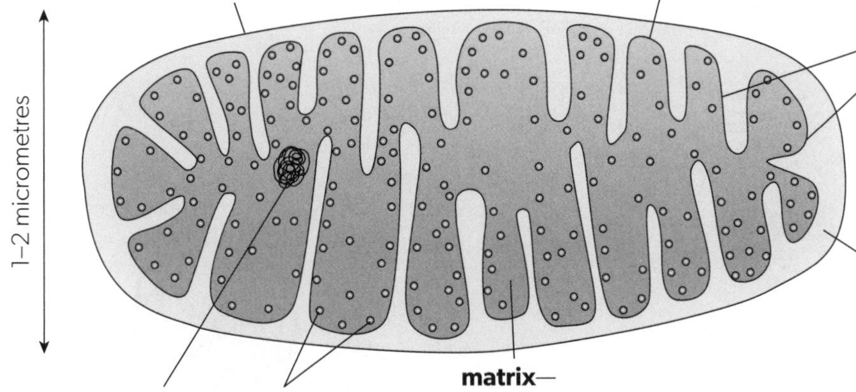

outer mitochondrial membrane—
separates the contents of the mitochondrion from the rest of the cell, creating a compartment with ideal conditions for aerobic respiration

inner mitochondrial membrane—
contains electron transport chains and ATP synthase, which work together to produce ATP by chemiosmosis

cristae—
tubular or shelf-like projections of the inner membrane which increase the surface area available for ATP production

1–2 micrometres

intermembrane space—
the space between the outer and inner membrane is very small, so when protons are pumped into it by electron transport chains, a high proton concentration rapidly develops

naked loop of **DNA** and **70S ribosomes** allow the mitochondrion to synthesize some of its own proteins

matrix—
fluid inside the mitochondrion containing high concentrations of enzymes and substrates for the Krebs cycle and link reaction

AHL

5. Adaptations of the chloroplast

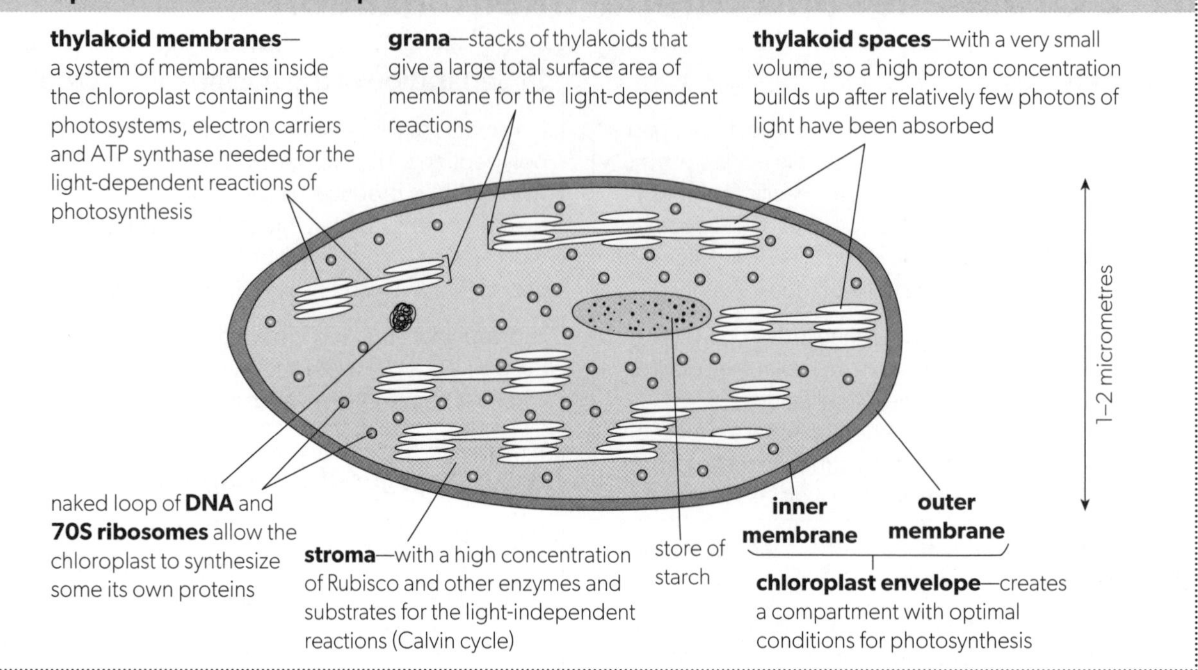

thylakoid membranes—a system of membranes inside the chloroplast containing the photosystems, electron carriers and ATP synthase needed for the light-dependent reactions of photosynthesis
grana—stacks of thylakoids that give a large total surface area of membrane for the light-dependent reactions
thylakoid spaces—with a very small volume, so a high proton concentration builds up after relatively few photons of light have been absorbed
1–2 micrometres
naked loop of **DNA** and **70S ribosomes** allow the chloroplast to synthesize some its own proteins
stroma—with a high concentration of Rubisco and other enzymes and substrates for the light-independent reactions (Calvin cycle)
store of starch
inner membrane
outer membrane
chloroplast envelope—creates a compartment with optimal conditions for photosynthesis

6. Advantages of the double nuclear membrane

A double nuclear membrane has these advantages:

1. Pores can be formed by joining the outer membrane to the inner membrane. Nuclear pores are needed for ribosomes and mRNA to move from the nucleus where they are produced to the cytoplasm where they are used.

2. The nuclear membrane can easily break up into vesicles during mitosis and meiosis, releasing the chromosomes so they can move within the cell. The vesicles move to the poles of the cell where they are later used to construct nuclear membranes around the new daughter nuclei.

8. The Golgi apparatus

The Golgi apparatus is a stack of cisternae (flattened membrane-bound sacs), which is described in *Section A2.2.11*. Polypeptides from the rough ER arrive at the Golgi apparatus in vesicles which fuse with the cisterna on the "cis" side. The polypeptides are trafficked from cisterna to cisterna until they reach the "trans" side. There are enzymes in each cisterna which modify polypeptides by adding non-amino acid structures or cutting and crosslinking. Gradually the final form of a protein is developed. For example, proinsulin is converted to insulin. Vesicles bud off from the cisterna on the trans side and carry the mature proteins either to the plasma membrane for secretion by exocytosis, or to another organelle in the cell.

7. Free ribosomes and the rough ER

Free ribosomes synthesize proteins that are released into the cytoplasm, where they perform their functions. Ribosomes bound to the rough ER make proteins for transport to other membrane-bound organelles in the cell. The proteins enter the lumen of the rough ER and are then transported in vesicles that bud off. Many of the proteins pass to the Golgi apparatus and then on to the plasma membrane for secretion by exocytosis.

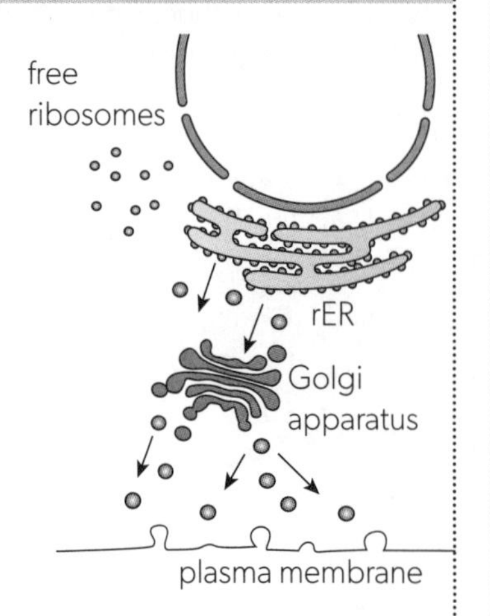

free ribosomes
rER
Golgi apparatus
plasma membrane

9. Clathrin-coated vesicles

Clathrin is a three-legged protein that can be assembled to form a spherical cage.

Clathrin cages are used to pull a patch of membrane inwards from the plasma membrane until a vesicle is formed. Many vesicles remain coated in a framework of clathrin molecules.

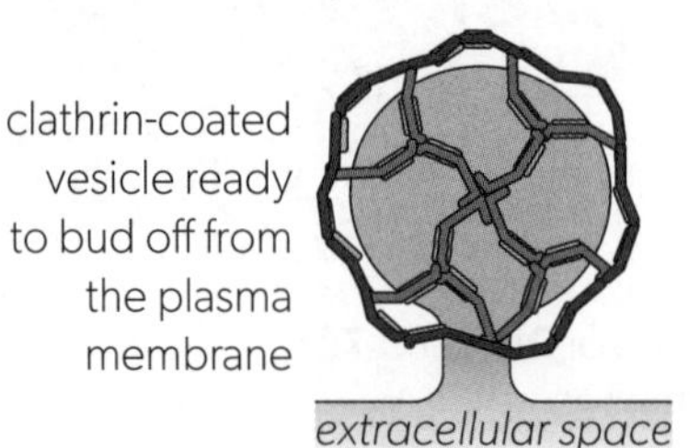

clathrin-coated vesicle ready to bud off from the plasma membrane
extracellular space

The functions of vesicles are described in *Section B2.1.13*.

B2.3 Cell specialization

1. Differentiation in early embryo

Fertilization is fusion of a male and female gamete to produce a **zygote** (single cell). In multicellular organisms this cell divides repeatedly to form an **embryo** with many cells. Mitosis ensures that any cell in the embryo has all the genes in the genome, so it could develop in any way. In an early-stage embryo the cells are all **unspecialized**.

As an embryo grows, the cells develop along different pathways and become **specialized** for specific functions. This is called **differentiation**.

In early-stage embryos, gradients of signalling chemicals known as morphogens become established. Concentrations of morphogens indicate to a cell its position in the embryo and therefore which pathway of differentiation it should follow. For example, there are gradients of morphogens between the anterior (front) and posterior (back) of early-stage embryos. Morphogens are regulators of gene expression—they determine which genes are transcribed to produce mRNA and therefore which proteins are made in each cell.

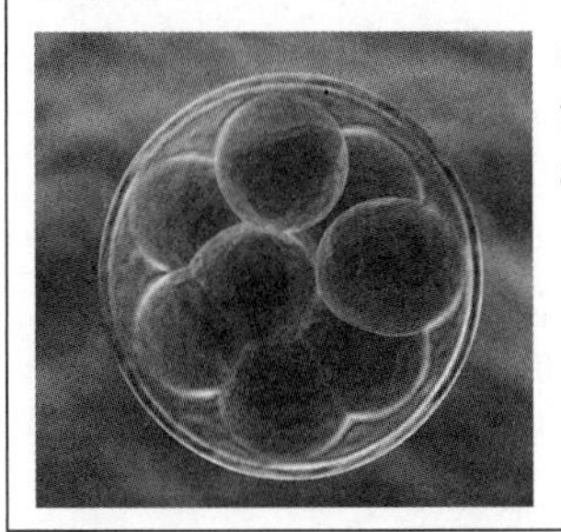

8-cell human embryo—all the cells are unspecialized at this stage

2. Stem cells

Stem cells have two key properties:

- Self-replicating—a stem cell can divide endlessly to produce more stem cells
- Undifferentiated—a stem cell has not developed specialized features that would commit it to one particular role. It retains the capacity to differentiate along different pathways.

4. Types of stem cells

Stem cells can be totipotent, pluripotent or multipotent.

- Stem cells in early-stage animal embryos are **totipotent**—they can differentiate into any cell type. These cells are therefore very useful for use in stem cell therapies.
- During the development of embryos, stem cells soon become **pluripotent**—able to differentiate into many, but not all cell types.
- Stem cells in adult tissue such as bone marrow are **multipotent**—able to differentiate into several cell types.

3. Stem cell niches

All cells in an embryo are stem cells. Most cells produced by division of stem cells become differentiated. Only a small percentage of cells in an adult's body are stem cells, but they are present in many human tissues, giving them considerable powers of regeneration and repair.

The precise location of stem cells within a tissue is called the stem cell niche. It must provide a microenvironment with conditions needed either for the stem cells to remain inactive and undifferentiated over long periods of time or for them to proliferate rapidly and differentiate.

Examples of stem cell niches:

1. **Bone marrow**—the soft, spongy tissue in the middle of the femur, sternum, pelvis and other large bones. Bone marrow contains haematopoietic stem cells that produce huge numbers of red and white blood cells and platelets each day. This is made possible by a generous supply of blood carrying oxygen, amino acids and other nutrients. Bones receive up to 15% of cardiac output, much of which goes to the marrow.

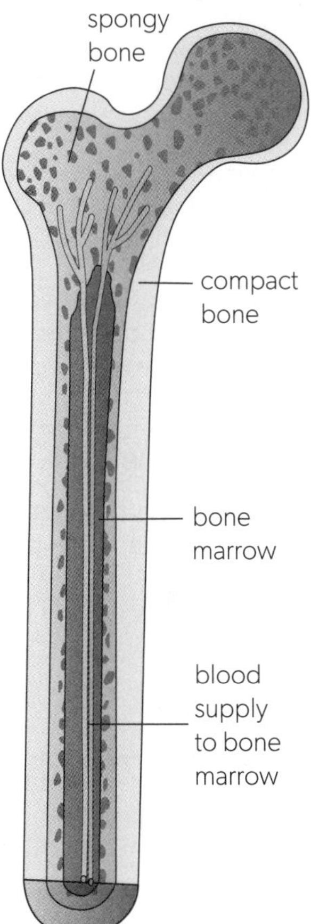

2. **Hair follicles**—pores in the skin that hold hairs. Stem cells at the base of each hair divide repeatedly to generate the many cells needed for hair growth. Human hairs typically grow at a rate of 0.35 mm per day. Blood capillaries supply the necessary nutrients.

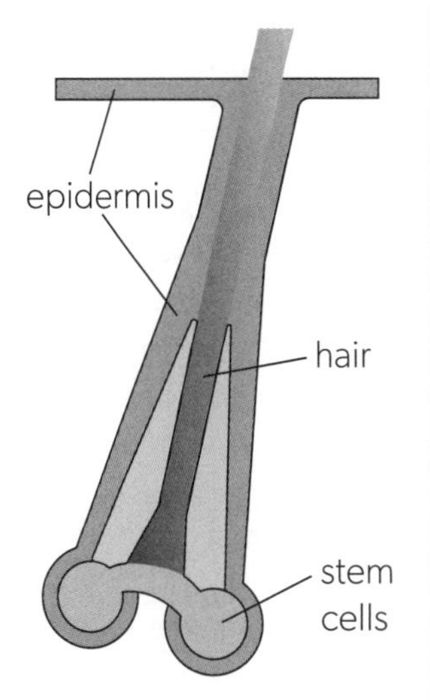

5. Specialization—cell size

For any cell type, there is an ideal size at which the cell's function can be performed most efficiently. These are examples of the wide range of cell size in humans:

male gametes—only 3 µm wide (but 50 µm long), which makes it easier for a sperm to swim to the egg

red blood cells—small in size (7 µm in diameter and 1–2 µm thick) allowing passage through narrow capillaries and giving a large surface area-to-volume ratio so entry and exit of oxygen is rapid

white blood cells—B lymphocytes are 10–12 µm in diameter when inactive, but when activated they grow into 30 µm plasma cells that can produce antibodies in bulk

female gametes—110 µm in diameter, with a very large volume of cytoplasm that contains enough food to sustain the embryo during the early stages of development

neurons—motor neurons have a cell body with diameter 20 µm, but the axon extending out from this can be a metre or more long, allowing signals to be carried this far

striated muscle fibres—very large cells with diameter 20 to 100 µm and lengths that can exceed 100 mm, allowing large and powerful muscle contractions.

6. Limits to cell size

As the size of any object is increased, the ratio between the surface area and the volume decreases.

Consider the surface area-to-volume ratio (SA/V) of cubes of varying size:

Length of sides	1 mm	10 mm	100 mm
Surface area (mm^2)	6	600	60,000
Volume (mm^3)	1	1,000	1,000,000
$\frac{\text{Surface area}}{\text{volume}} \left[\frac{mm^2}{mm^3} = mm^{-1}\right]$	6	0.6	0.06

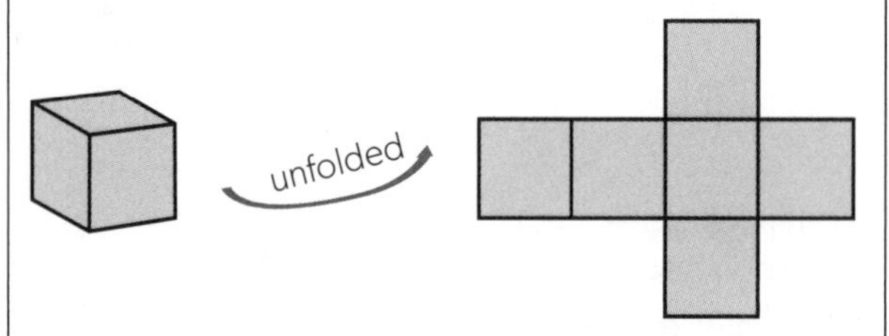

- The surface area-to-volume ratio of cells also decreases as a cell grows larger.
- The rate at which materials enter or leave a cell depends on the surface area of the cell.
- However, the rate at which materials are used or produced depends on the volume.
- A cell that becomes too large may not be able to take in essential materials or excrete waste substances quickly enough. Surface area-to-volume ratios therefore place limits on how large cells can grow before they must divide.

AHL

7. Increasing SA/V ratio

For any volume, a sphere has the smallest surface area-to-volume ratio. Any change in shape to a sphere increases the ratio. Many cell types specialized for an exchange process (absorption or secretion/excretion) have shapes that provide a particularly large area of plasma membrane, across which substances are transferred:

- **flattening**—to make the cell very wide and thin. Red blood cells are flattened discs and type I pneumocytes are an extreme example of flattening
- **microvilli**—finger-like projections on the exposed surface of epithelial cells. Proximal convoluted tubule cells in kidney nephrons (described in *Section D3.3.8*) have many microvilli in their outer membrane which reabsorb glucose and other useful substances from the filtrate flowing past them
- **invagination**—infoldings of the plasma membrane to form tubules, folds or sacs. Proximal convoluted tubule cells have basal channels that increase the surface for pumping of sodium ions out of the cell, to generate the Na^+ concentration gradient that is used for cotransport of glucose.

8. Type I and type II pneumocytes

The alveoli of the lungs (see *Section B3.1.4*) are the air sacs where gas exchange happens. The wall of the alveolus is an epithelium that is one cell thick, but contains two cell types with differences in structure which are adaptations for different functions.

Type I
Type II

Type I pneumocytes: make up 95% of the alveolus wall; adapted to carry out gas exchange; very little cytoplasm so are extremely thin and permeable—gases only have to diffuse a very short distance to pass through them.

Type II pneumocytes:
5% of the area of alveolus wall but are more numerous; have a dense cytoplasm with many vesicles (lamellar bodies)—contain a fluid that is produced and then secreted by exocytosis; fluid keeps the inner surface of the alveolus moist and allows gases to dissolve; contains a natural detergent (surfactant), which reduces surface tension, so preventing the sides of the alveoli from sticking together.

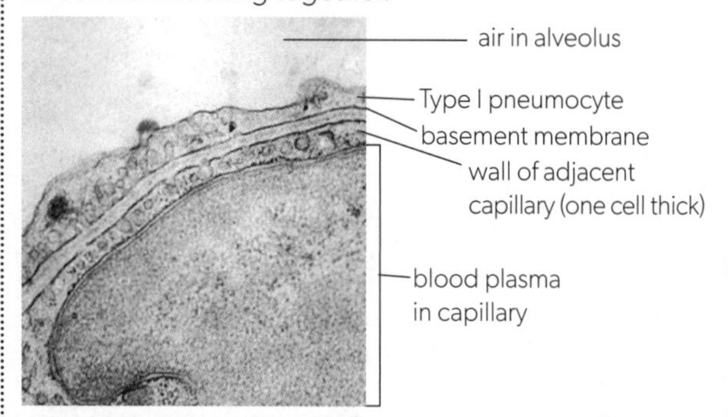

AHL

9. Adaptations of muscles

Muscle tissue exerts pulling forces as it contracts. Cardiac muscle in the wall of the heart pumps blood by contracting. Striated muscle is attached to the skeleton. When it contracts striated muscle exerts force on a bone in order to maintain or change posture (relative position of parts of the body), for locomotion (movement from place to place) or for ventilation of the lungs.

Both cardiac and skeletal striated muscle have contractile myofibrils (see *Topic B3.3*) and large numbers of mitochondria to supply the ATP needed for contractions. Their other adaptations show many differences.

	Cardiac muscle cells	Striated muscle fibres
Branching	Cells are branched so each is connected to several others, allowing electrical stimuli to be propagated rapidly through the tissue.	Unbranched and cylindrical in shape.
Junctions	Cell-to-cell junctions with intercalated discs and connections between plasma membranes and cytoplasm that allow rapid propagation of electrical stimuli from cell to cell.	Blunt ends where fibres meet but no intercalated disc or special connections.
Length	50–100 μm long	30,000 μm long on average
Number of nuclei	One per cell	Many per fibre

It is debatable whether or not a muscle fibre should be classed as a cell. They are enclosed in a plasma membrane, but have many nuclei, rather than just one. They are much larger than most animal cells.

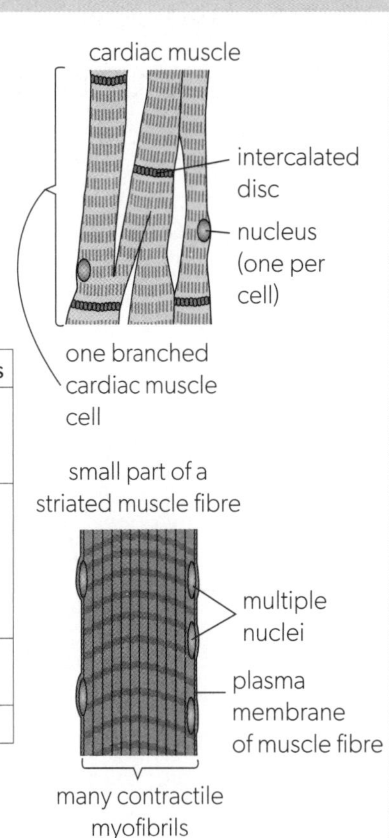

10. Egg cells and sperm—adaptations

Male gametes travel to female gametes and because of this they have very different adaptations. Male gametes in all animals and some plants are motile—they can swim. The faster they swim, the more chance of reaching the egg first and fertilizing it, so small size and an efficient propulsion system are needed. Male gametes are produced in larger numbers than female, to increase the chance of one of them fertilizing an egg.

In humans (and other species) female gametes are much larger as they contain nearly all the food reserves for the early development of the embryo. Because of the large investment of resources, smaller numbers of female than male gametes are produced. Female gametes have a mechanism for allowing one sperm to penetrate but not more.

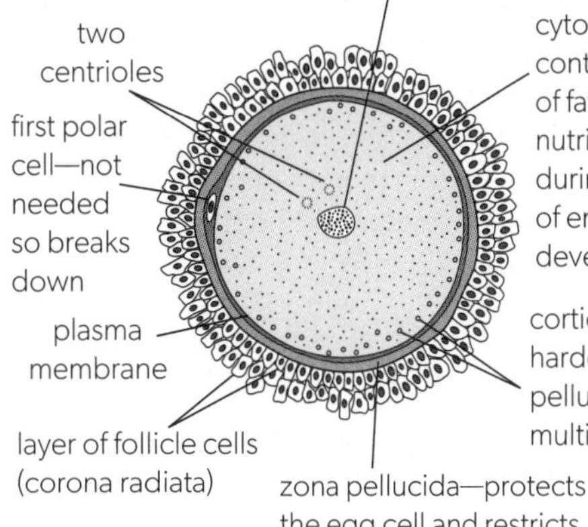

diameter of egg cell = 110 μm

acrosome—contains enzymes that digest the zona pellucida around the egg

haploid nucleus—contains the 23 chromosomes that are passed from father to offspring

tail—provides the propulsion that allows the sperm to swim up the vagina, uterus and oviduct until it reaches the egg

mid-piece (7 μm long)

head (3 μm wide and 4 μm long)

plasma membrane

centriole

helical mitochondria— produce ATP by aerobic respiration to supply energy for swimming and other processes in the sperm

microtubules in a 9 + 2 array—make the sperm tail beat from side to side and generate the forces that propel the sperm

protein fibres—strengthen the tail

B2.1 Membranes and membrane transport

1. Proteins in the plasma membranes can be tagged with fluorescent markers. Mouse cells (with green markers) and human cells (with red markers) were fused together and the mixing of the markers in the membranes was followed at different temperatures.

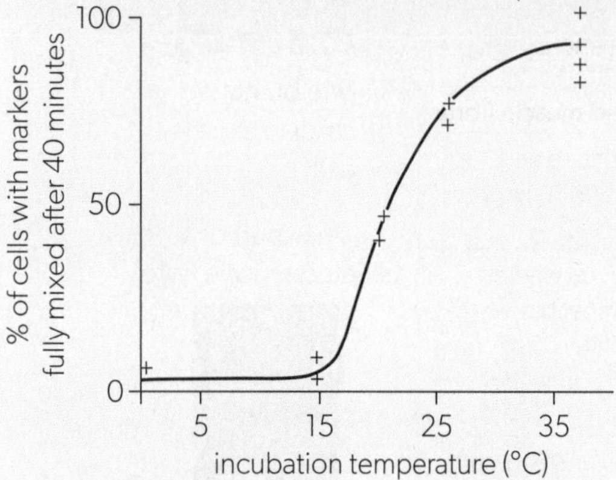

a. Describe the trends shown in the graph for:
   i. temperatures between 15 and 35°C (2)
   ii. temperatures below 15°C. (1)

b. i. Distinguish between fluids and solids. (2)
   ii. Mice and humans maintain body temperatures close to 37°C. Deduce whether their plasma membranes are fluid or solid. (3)

c. Blocking ATP synthesis did not prevent mixing of the markers. Explain the conclusions that can be drawn. (2)

d. i. Predict the results if the experiment was repeated with cells from Arctic fish. (3)
   ii. (HL only) Suggest a difference in composition between the plasma membranes of Arctic fish and tropical fish, that would help them adapt to their habitats. (2)

2. a. Draw a diagram of the structure of cell membranes annotated with functions. (10)

   b. Particles can enter or leave cells by simple diffusion, facilitated diffusion, active transport or osmosis. Identify the method used in these examples.
      i. water entering a root from the soil (1)
      ii. oxygen entering the gill of a salmon (1)
      iii. glucose from digested food entering intestine cells (1)
      iv. Na^+ ions exiting axons during action potentials. (1)

   c. Compare and contrast facilitated diffusion and active transport. (3)

3. (HL only) Cholesterol is the most abundant steroid in the human body.

   a. Outline the chemical nature of steroids. (2)

   b. Explain how cholesterol modulates membrane fluidity. (3)

B2.2 Organelles and compartmentalization

1. The chart shows areas of membrane (μm^2) in a liver cell.

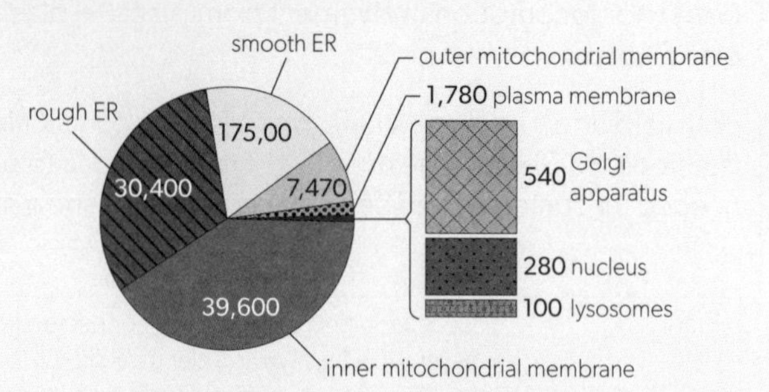

   a. Calculate the liver cell's size, assuming it is cubic. (3)
   b. Explain the difference in area of the inner and outer mitochondrial membranes. (3)
   c. Justify the conclusion that the liver cell was secreting proteins. (2)
   d. Comment on the area of smooth ER in the liver cell. (2)

2. a. Organelles have one membrane, two membranes or none. List three examples of each. (9)
   b. List three structures that are not organelles. (3)

3. a. (HL only) Compare and contrast chloroplasts and mitochondria in
      i. structure (5) ii. function. (5)
   b. Describe the benefits of compartmentalization in cells. (7)
   c. Suggest reasons for the lack of compartmentalization in prokaryotic cells. (3)

B2.3 Cell specialization

1. The table shows percentage composition by volume of three types of liver cell. Cytoplasm volumes do not include membrane-bound organelles, such as ER. Kupffer cells engulf and digest damaged red blood cells. Endothelial cells form the wall of blood capillaries.

Component	Hepatocyte (%)	Endothelial (%)	Kupffer cell (%)
Cytoplasm	57.9	66.9	60.9
Nucleus	9.8	16.4	19.2
Mitochondria	28.32	4.26	4.52
Lysosomes	0.82	6.86	13.57

   a. Suggest reasons for these volume differences:
      i. mitochondria in the three cell types (3)
      ii. lysosomes in the three cell types (3)
      iii. nuclei in hepatocytes and endothelial cells. (2)
   b. The total percentages for each cell type are lower than 100%. Deduce the reason for this. (2)

2. a. Calculate the ratio between the volume of an egg cell (3.5 million μm^3), and a red blood cell (100 μm^3).
   b. Suggest reasons for the difference in volumes. (3)

3. (HL only) Distinguish between the structure of type I pneumocytes in alveoli and striated muscle fibres. (5)

C2.1 Chemical signalling

AHL

1. Receptors and signals

Cells interact with each other by sending and receiving signals. Signals can be chemical or electrical.

Molecules of a chemical signal are produced by one cell and bind to receptors in another cell (the target cell). Receptors are proteins to which signalling chemicals bind at a specific site. They initiate changes in the target cell in response to binding of the chemical signal.

A general term for a molecule that binds selectively to a specific site on another molecule is a ligand. The site on a receptor to which the signalling chemical binds is therefore its ligand-binding site. The selectivity or specificity of binding is similar to enzyme–substrate specificity in enzymes.

1. Ligand approaches binding site

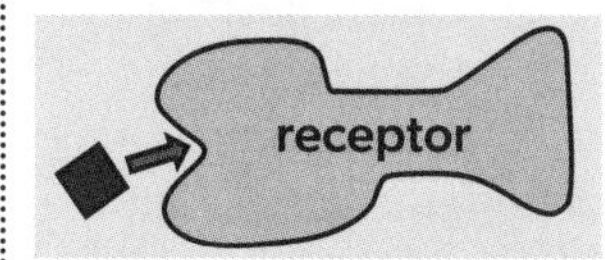

2. Binding causes changes within the receptor

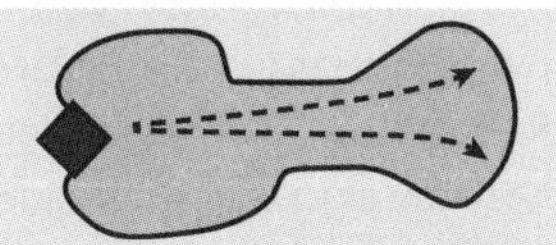

3. Signal is passed on to the cell

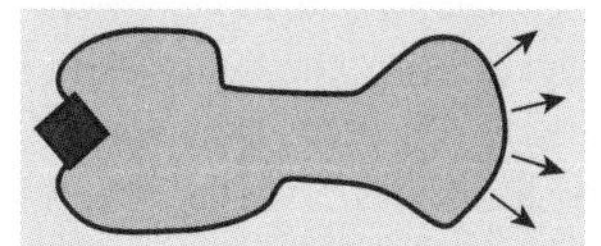

4. Ligand dissociates from the binding site

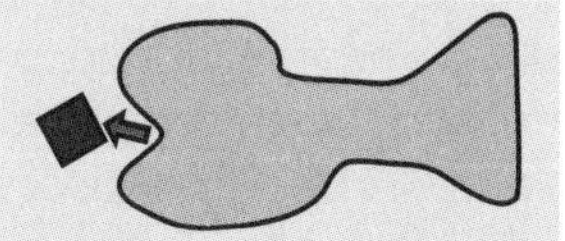

3. Types of signalling chemicals

1. Hormones

- produced by groups of specialized cells in glands
- secreted directly into blood capillaries, so the secreting glands are endocrine and ductless
- transported by blood to all parts of the body, which may take up to a minute
- bind to receptors either inside or on the surface of target cells, triggering changes to the cell's activities, either by promoting or inhibiting specific processes
- persist for minutes or even hours in the body after being secreted, so can have long-lasting effects
- target one or multiple types of target cell, which can be in one or multiple parts of the body, so a single hormone can have complex and widespread effects on the body.

Examples: insulin, thyroxin and testosterone

2. Neurotransmitters

- transmit signals across synapses (junctions between two neurons in the nervous system)
- secreted when a nerve impulse reaches the end of a presynaptic neuron
- diffuse across a narrow gap between the presynaptic and postsynaptic neuron, taking only 0.5 to 1.0 ms
- bind to receptors in the plasma membrane of postsynaptic neurons, which either excites or inhibits transmission of an impulse
- persist for only a fraction of a second before being removed from the synaptic gap, so effects are short-lived
- do not generally diffuse out of the synapse so convey the signal to one specific postsynaptic neuron only.

Examples: acetylcholine, norepinephrine and dopamine

3. Cytokines

- a group of small proteins that act as signalling chemicals
- secreted by a wide range of cells
- one cytokine may be secreted by different cell types
- one cell type may secrete several different cytokines
- some can be secreted by almost any cell type in the body
- do not normally travel as far as hormones and instead act either on the cell that produces them or a nearby cell
- unable to enter cells and instead bind to receptors in the plasma membrane of a target cell
- binding causes cascades of signalling inside the target cell, leading to changes in gene expression and thus cell activity
- one cytokine can bind to several types of receptor and so have multiple effects
- have cell signalling roles in inflammation and other responses of the immune system, in control of cell growth and proliferation and in the development of embryos.

Examples: erythropoietin (EPO), interferon and interleukin

4. Calcium ions

- pumped out of cells by calcium pumps in the plasma membrane, so intracellular concentrations are low
- diffuse into cells through voltage-gated or ligand-gated channels in the plasma membrane
- used for cell signalling in both neurons and muscle
- cause muscle fibres to contract
- cause presynaptic neurons to release neurotransmitter into the synapse.

AHL

2. Quorum sensing

Unicellular organisms can send chemical signals to each other. This can help to adjust activity to population density. A chemical signal is secreted at a low rate by all cells in the population and diffuses freely between cells. Each cell has receptors to which the signalling molecules bind. If the proportion of receptors in a cell with signalling molecules bound to them rises above a threshold, indicating a high population density, changes in the activity of the cell are triggered. This type of control is quorum sensing. Bioluminescence in the bacterium *Vibrio fischeri* is an example.

Vibrio fischeri cells secrete a chemical signal, which acts as an autoinducer. The autoinducer is free to diffuse between cells. It binds to a receptor protein (LuxR) in the cytoplasm. LuxR-autoinducer complexes bind to a specific position in the cell's DNA that induces the transcription of genes coding for the production of luciferase. This enzyme catalyses an oxidation reaction that releases energy in the form of greenish-blue light (bioluminescence). Light is not emitted in a low population density of free-living *Vibrio fischeri* because the concentration of autoinducer is low. The amount of light emitted would be insignificant and energy would be wasted.

Vibrio fischeri forms mutualistic relationships with marine animals such as the bobtail squid. The bacteria live inside the squid's light organ at a high population density, resulting in a high concentration of autoinducer, so bioluminescence is induced. The bright light produced collectively by the bacteria helps to camouflage the squid in moonlight, reducing the risk of predation. Bacteria in the light organ are supplied with sugar and amino acids by the squid. This is an example of **interaction**, because signalling molecules pass from cell to cell and **interdependence** because cells cannot act individually.

4. Chemical categories of hormones and neurotransmitters

Signalling systems using hormones and neurotransmitters have evolved repeatedly and a wide range of chemical substances have become the signalling chemicals. The requirements for a signalling chemical are:

- distinctive in shape and chemical properties so the receptor can distinguish between it and other chemicals
- small and soluble enough to be transported.

The table shows chemical categories of hormones and neurotransmitters.

Hormones		
Amines	**Peptides**	**Steroids**
Melatonin	Insulin	Oestradiol
Thyroxin	Glucagon	Progesterone
Epinephrine	ADH	Testosterone

Neurotransmitters			
Amines	**Gases**	**Amino acids**	**Esters**
Dopamine	Nitrous oxide	Glutamate	Acetylcholine
Norepinephrine		Glycine	

5. Effects of signalling molecules

Signalling molecules vary greatly in how far they are transported and thus how widespread their effects are. Neurotransmitters released by presynaptic neurons may only diffuse 20 to 40 nanometres to reach the postsynaptic neuron and that is the only cell that they signal to, so a neurotransmitter's effects are very localized.

In contrast, hormones are transported long distances in the blood, from the gland that secretes them to target cells in any part of the body. For example, LH is secreted by the pituitary gland adjacent to the brain. Target cells are in the testes of males and in the ovaries of females, so LH's effects are distant from its source.

6. Comparing transmembrane and intracellular receptors

Signalling chemicals either bind to a receptor in the plasma membrane and do not enter the cell, or enter the cell and bind to a receptor in the cytoplasm or nucleus.

Receptors in the plasma membrane are transmembrane proteins with a region protruding into the cytoplasm and a region that is exposed on the outside of the cell. They remain in this position because there are two regions on their surface with hydrophilic amino acids that are attracted to aqueous solutions inside and outside the cell and a band of hydrophobic amino acids between that are attracted to the non-polar tails of phospholipids in the core of the membrane. Intracellular receptors have hydrophilic amino acids on the whole of their surface so they remain dissolved in the aqueous fluids inside the cell.

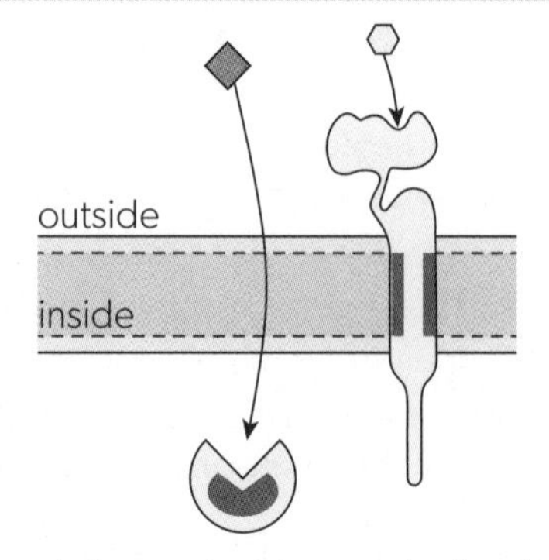

darker and mid grey = hydrophobic
lighter grey = hydrophilic

AHL

7. Signal transduction pathways

Binding of a signalling chemical to a receptor causes a sequence of interactions in the cell, called a signal transduction pathway. These pathways are very varied as they have evolved repeatedly, rather than having a common origin. The main differences are between transduction pathways for transmembrane and intracellular receptors.

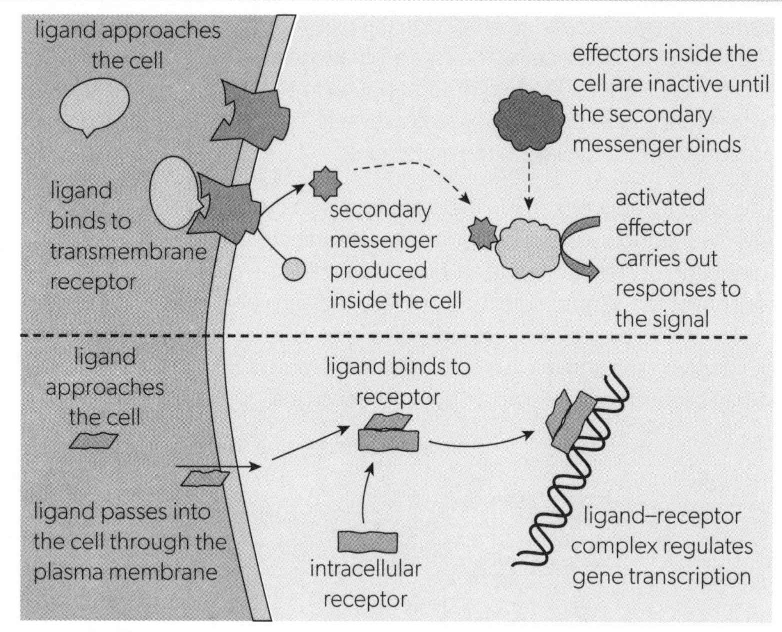

ligand approaches the cell
ligand binds to transmembrane receptor
secondary messenger produced inside the cell
effectors inside the cell are inactive until the secondary messenger binds
activated effector carries out responses to the signal
ligand approaches the cell
ligand passes into the cell through the plasma membrane
ligand binds to receptor
intracellular receptor
ligand–receptor complex regulates gene transcription

1. Transmembrane receptors

Binding of a signalling chemical to the outer side of a transmembrane receptor causes reversible changes to its structure. In particular the inner side that is in contact with the cytoplasm becomes catalytically active and causes production of a secondary messenger within the cell. This conveys the signal to effectors within the cell that carry out responses.

2. Intracellular receptors

Binding of signalling chemicals to intracellular receptors results in the formation of an active ligand–receptor complex. In most cases this then acts as a regulator of gene expression by binding to DNA at specific sites, resulting in the transcription of particular genes being either promoted or inhibited.

8. Transmembrane receptors for neurotransmitters

Receptors for neurotransmitters are located in the plasma membrane of postsynaptic neurons and muscle fibres. Binding of the neurotransmitter results in the opening of membrane channels through which ions can move by facilitated diffusion, changing the membrane potential. This change in potential is a signal that either stimulates or inhibits a nerve impulse in a postsynaptic neuron, or a contraction in a muscle fibre.

Acetylcholine is used as a neurotransmitter in many synapses, including those between neurons and muscle fibres. When acetylcholine binds to the binding site on an acetylcholine receptor, there is a change in the conformation (shape) of the receptor, opening a channel through which sodium ions can pass into the cell. This leads to a local depolarization that triggers an action potential *(see Section C2.2.7)*.

9. G protein-coupled receptors

G protein-coupled receptors (GPCRs) are a large and diverse group of transmembrane receptors. They convey signals into cells using a second protein located in the plasma membrane, called G protein. The three subunits of G protein (α, β and γ) assemble on the surface of the receptor that faces the cytoplasm. A molecule of GDP, bound to the α subunit, maintains the G protein in an inactive state.

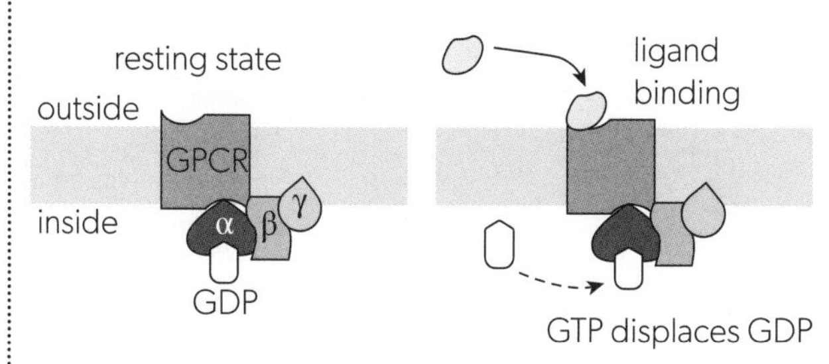

resting state
outside
GPCR
inside
α
β
γ
GDP
ligand binding
GTP displaces GDP

The receptor has a binding site for a ligand on the side facing the extracellular environment. When the ligand binds, conformational changes are triggered in the receptor, which cause changes in the coupled G protein. This results in dissociation of GDP from the α subunit, allowing GTP to bind in its place. Binding of GTP activates the G protein, which separates into its subunits and dissociates from the receptor. The activated G protein subunits cause further interactions within the cell, leading to actions that are the cell's response to the signal brought by the ligand.

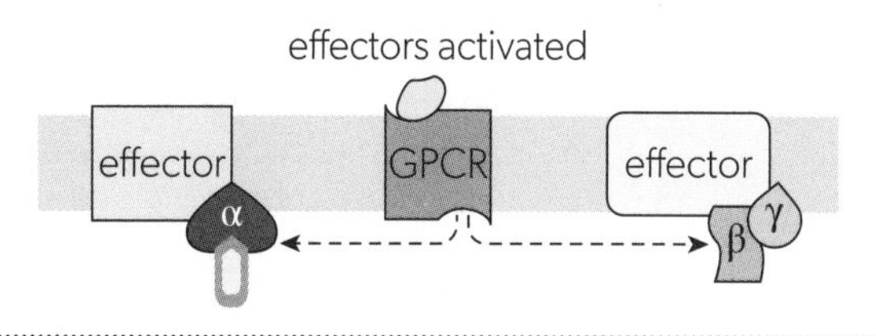

effectors activated
effector
GPCR
effector
α
β
γ

AHL

10. Epinephrine receptors

Epinephrine receptors are located in the plasma membranes of target cells. They are an example of G protein-coupling. Binding of epinephrine to the receptor activates G protein, which activates the enzyme adenylyl cyclase in the membrane.

This enzyme converts ATP in the cytoplasm into cyclic AMP (a secondary messenger). Cyclic AMP initiates a sequence of reactions that amplify the signal, so responses to the binding of epinephrine happen very rapidly inside the cell. For example, liver cells break down glycogen and release glucose into the blood within seconds of receiving an epinephrine signal.

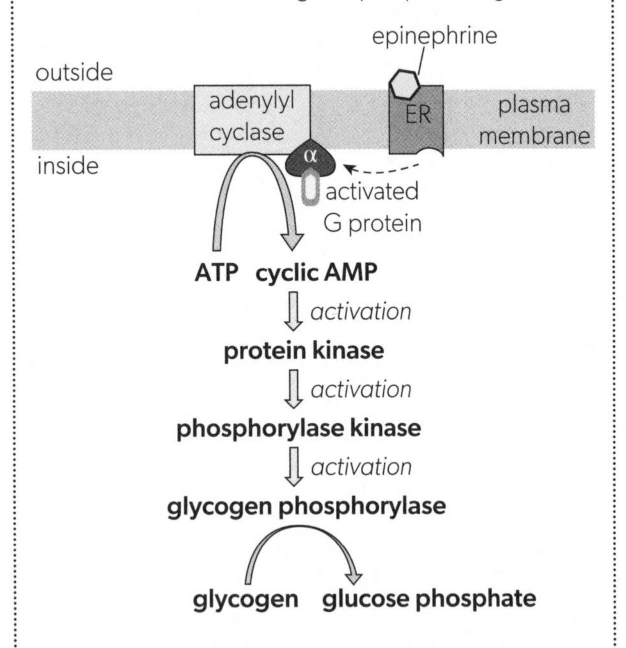

12. Intracellular receptors activate gene expression

Steroid hormones are hydrophobic, making them lipid soluble, so they are able to pass through the plasma membrane. Inside the cell, they bind to receptors in the cytoplasm. The hormone–receptor complex enters the nucleus and attaches to the DNA. This activates the production of a particular polypeptide.

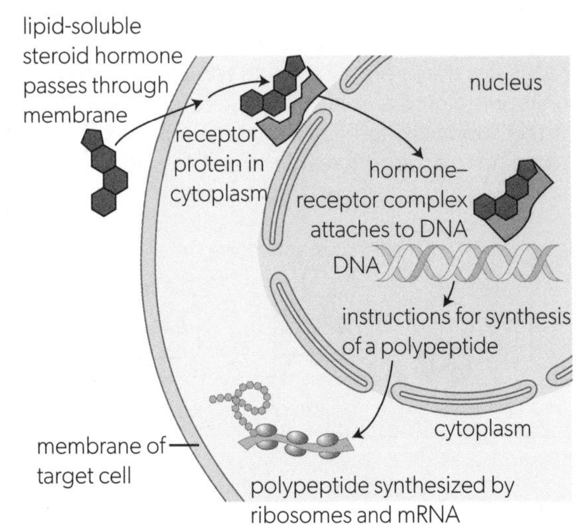

NOS

Science as a shared endeavour

The two names adrenaline and epinephrine were given to the same hormone by different research groups at about the same time. This happened at the end of the 19th or start of the 20th century. Scientists usually agree on a single name but unusually in this case both names have persisted. Adrenaline is used more commonly in Europe, but epinephrine is the commoner name in North America.

Naming conventions are an example of international cooperation in science for mutual benefit. In this case it would have been far better if there had been agreement.

11. Tyrosine kinase activity

Protein kinases are enzymes that transfer phosphate groups from ATP to proteins (phosphorylation). For example, tyrosine kinase transfers phosphate to tyrosine (an amino acid) in specific proteins. Phosphorylation of proteins in many cases activates them and removal of the phosphate makes them inactive again.

Example: insulin receptors

The insulin receptor is a large transmembrane protein with two tails extending into the cytoplasm that are tyrosine kinases. Binding of insulin to a site on the extracellular portion of the protein causes conformational changes that connect the two intracellular tails to form a dimer. Each tail then phosphorylates the other tail. This activates the insulin receptor, which triggers a chain of events inside the cell (signal transduction), that eventually results in vesicles containing glucose transporters to move to the plasma membrane and fuse with it. The transporters thus inserted into the plasma membrane are channel proteins that allow uptake of glucose into the cell by facilitated diffusion. The glucose can then be used as a substrate in cell respiration.

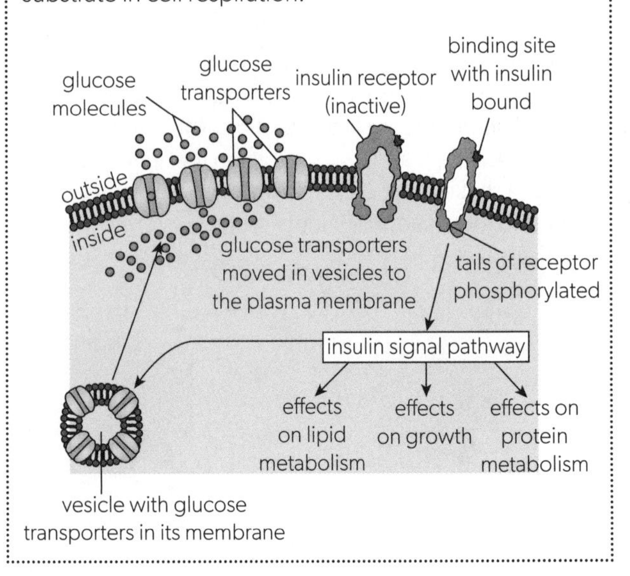

AHL

13. Effects of oestradiol and progesterone

Oestradiol and progesterone are female sex hormones that are secreted by cells in the ovary and by the corpus luteum and placenta during pregnancy. They are both steroid hormones, so diffuse into target cells through the plasma membrane and bind to specific receptors in the cytoplasm.

Oestradiol has a broad range of effects both in the ovary and the uterus. It also affects production and release of gonadotropin-releasing hormone (GnRH) by the hypothalamus (a part of the brain). Just before and during ovulation, oestradiol binds to a receptor in the cytoplasm of cells in the hypothalamus. The resulting oestradiol–receptor complex enters the nucleus where it enhances the transcription of GnRH mRNA. GnRH triggers the secretion of the sex hormones LH and FSH by the anterior pituitary gland adjacent to the hypothalamus.

oestradiol OH HO progesterone O O

Progesterone promotes the development and maintenance of the endometrium (uterus lining) so that it can support a developing foetus. Progesterone binds to a receptor in the cytoplasm of uterus cells. The resulting progesterone–receptor complex enters the nucleus and causes the transcription of specific genes. Through changes to gene expression, progesterone causes cells in the uterus wall to divide repeatedly, leading to thickening of the endometrium.

14. Positive and negative feedback in cell signalling pathways

In both positive and negative feedback systems, amounts of the product of a pathway affect how much more is produced by the pathway. The product usually interacts with an early stage in the pathway.

In **negative feedback**, the product inhibits more of its own production, so more product leads to less production, and less to more.

An example is regulation of thyroxin secretion by the thyroid gland in the neck. Cells in the hypothalamus secrete thyrotropin releasing hormone (TRH) which stimulates cells in the anterior pituitary gland to secrete thyroid stimulating hormone (TSH) which stimulates thyroid gland cells to secrete thyroxin. High levels of thyroxin in the blood inhibit TRH secretion by the hypothalamus and low levels of thyroxin stimulate secretion of TRH. The role of thyroxin in regulation of body temperature is explained in *Section D3.3.5*.

hypothalamus
TRH
pituitary gland
TSH
thyroid gland
thyroxin

hypothalamus
pituitary gland

In **positive feedback**, the product stimulates more of its own production, so more product leads to more production, and less to less.

An example is the LH surge during the ovulatory phase of the menstrual cycle. Oestradiol, secreted by developing follicles in the ovary, stimulates GnRH secretion by the hypothalamus, which stimulates LH secretion by the anterior pituitary gland, which in turn stimulates more secretion of oestradiol by the developing follicles. This feedback loop results in a rapid rise in the concentration of the hormone LH, which causes follicles to become mature and release their eggs on about day 14 of the cycle.

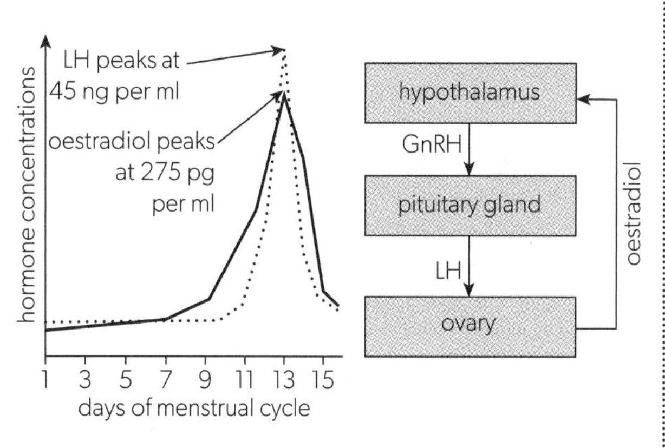

C2.2 Neural signalling

1. Neurons

The nervous system is composed of cells called neurons. There are about 85 billion neurons in a human's nervous system. Neurons help with internal communication by transmitting nerve impulses. A nerve impulse is an electrical signal.

Neurons have a cell body with cytoplasm and a nucleus but they also have narrow outgrowths called nerve fibres along which nerve impulses travel. There are two types of nerve fibre:

- **Dendrites** are short branched nerve fibres, for example those used to transmit impulses between neurons in one part of the brain or spinal cord.

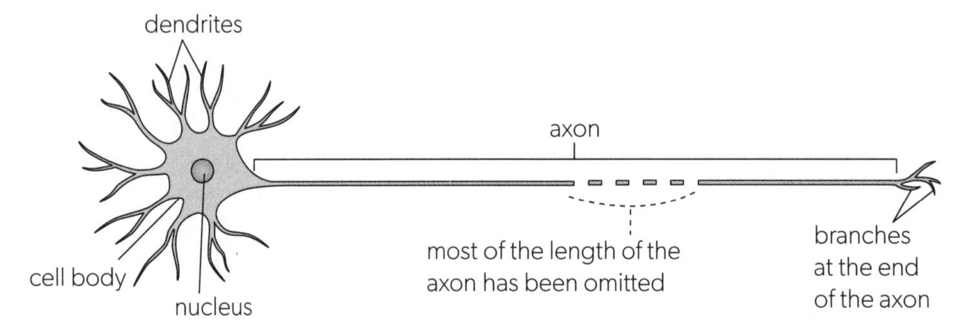

- **Axons** are very elongated nerve fibres, for example those that transmit impulses from the tips of the toes or the fingers to the spinal cord.

3. Nerve impulses as action potentials

Electrical signals can be movements of ions or electrons. Nerve impulses are a type of electrical signal because they are movements of positively charged ions. A nerve impulse is a brief reversal of the normal polarization (resting potential) of a neuron's membrane as a result of facilitated diffusion of Na^+ and K^+ ions. The changes in voltage that happen during a nerve impulse are known as an action potential. There are two stages in an action potential:

I. Depolarization

Sodium channels in the membrane open, allowing Na^+ ions to diffuse into the neuron down the concentration gradient. Entry of Na^+ ions reverses the charge imbalance across the membrane (depolarization), so the inside becomes positive relative to the outside. The potential typically rises from about −70 mV to a positive value of about +40 mV.

II. Repolarization

This happens immediately after depolarization and is due to the closing of the sodium channels and opening of potassium channels. Potassium ions diffuse out of the neuron down their concentration gradient, so the inside of the neuron becomes negative again relative to the outside. The potassium channels remain open until the membrane potential has fallen to −70 or −80 mV.

III. Rebuilding gradients

After an action potential, the sodium–potassium pump soon re-establishes Na^+ and K^+ concentration gradients.

An action potential in one part of the axon triggers an action potential in the next part. This is called the **propagation** of the nerve impulse.

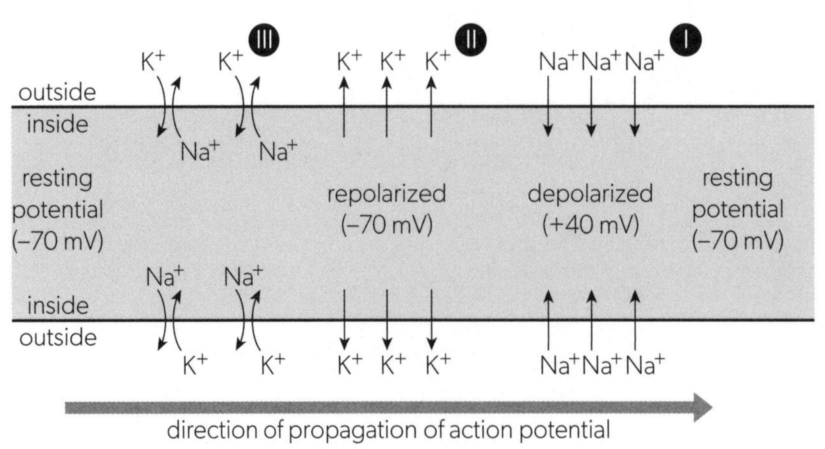

2. Resting potential

The plasma membrane of a cell restricts ion movements, allowing concentration gradients to be maintained between inside and outside.

Differences in the concentrations of positively and negatively charged ions and an overall imbalance in charge cause a potential difference (voltage) across the membrane. Generally, the inside of cells is electrically negative compared with the outside so the membrane potential, measured in millivolts, is a negative value.

Neurons typically have a membrane potential of −70 mV while waiting to transmit an impulse. This is called the resting potential, though energy has to be expended to maintain it.

Sodium–potassium pumps transfer Na^+ ions across the membrane out of the neuron and at the same time transfer K^+ ions in. As this is active transport, it uses energy from ATP and establishes concentration gradients for both ions.

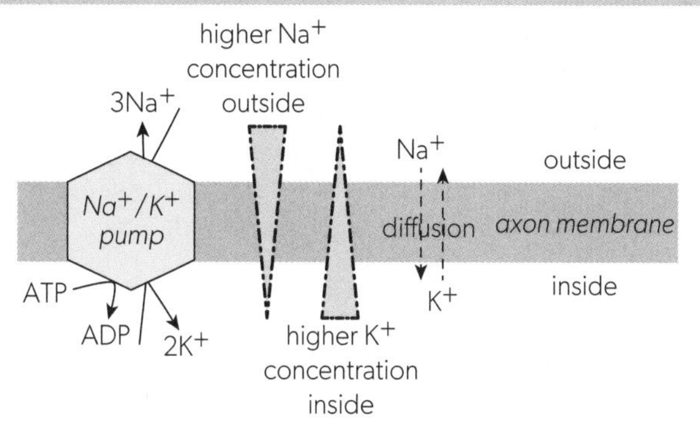

higher Na+ concentration outside
3Na+
Na+/K+ pump
ATP
ADP
2K+
Na+
diffusion
K+
outside
axon membrane
inside
higher K+ concentration inside

The numbers of ions pumped are unequal: when three Na^+ ions are pumped out, only two K^+ ions are pumped in, causing a charge imbalance and resting membrane potential of about −70 mV. (The sodium–potassium pump is described more fully for HL in *Section B2.1.15*.)

Two other factors contribute to the resting potential:

- Na^+ and K^+ ions leak back across the membrane by diffusion. As the membrane is about 50 times more permeable to K^+ than Na^+, leakage of K^+ ions is faster.
- There are negatively charged proteins inside the neuron (organic anions), which also add to the charge imbalance.

5. Synapses

A synapse is a junction between two cells in the nervous system. Synapses are mostly located in the brain and spinal cord. Signals can only be passed in one direction across a synapse. One of the neurons brings the signal in the form of a nerve impulse or action potential. This is the **transmitting neuron** with a **presynaptic membrane**. The other neuron carries the signal away from the synapse, again in the form of a nerve impulse. This is the **receiving neuron** with a **postsynaptic membrane**. Between the two neurons is a narrow fluid-filled gap which is about 20 nm wide. A chemical substance (neurotransmitter) transfers the signal from the presynaptic to the postsynaptic membrane.

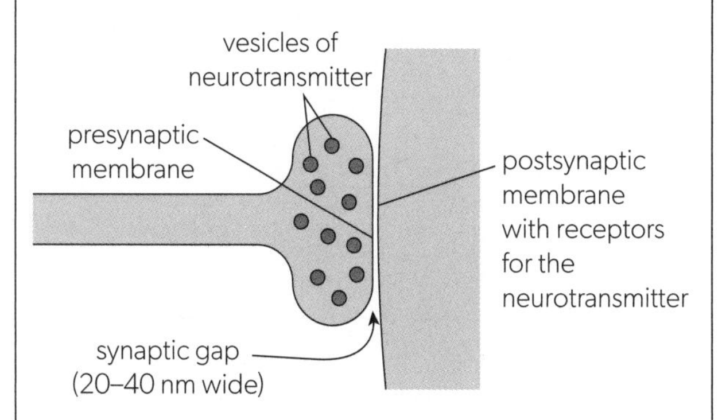

vesicles of neurotransmitter
presynaptic membrane
postsynaptic membrane with receptors for the neurotransmitter
synaptic gap (20–40 nm wide)

There are also synapses between sensory receptor cells and neurons, and between neurons and the effector cells that effect (carry out) responses in the body. The two types of effector cell are muscle fibres and gland cells.

6. Neurotransmission

Synaptic transmission is the sequence of events between the arrival of an impulse at the presynaptic membrane and the initiation of an impulse in the postsynaptic membrane. The first stages of synaptic transmission result in release of neurotransmitter. Arrival of a nerve impulse in the transmitting neuron causes depolarization of the presynaptic membrane. This causes calcium channels to open and as the concentration of Ca^{2+} is higher outside the presynaptic membrane, they diffuse in. Influx of Ca^{2+} causes vesicles containing neurotransmitter to move to the presynaptic membrane and fuse with it, releasing neurotransmitter into the synaptic gap by exocytosis.

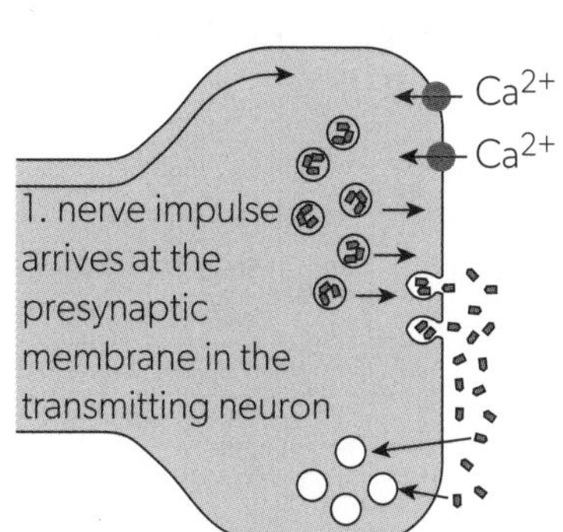

2. depolarization of the presynaptic membrane causes voltage-gated calcium channels to open
3. influx of calcium causes vesicles of neurotransmitter to move to the membrane
Ca2+
Ca2+
1. nerve impulse arrives at the presynaptic membrane in the transmitting neuron
4. neurotransmitter is released into the synaptic gap by exocytosis
5. new vesicles formed and loaded with neurotransmitter pumped back from the synaptic gap

4. Variation in velocity of nerve impulses

Axons are circular in transverse (cross) section with a plasma membrane enclosing cytoplasm. In humans the diameter in most cases is about 1 μm. Nerve impulses travel along axons with this basic structure at a speed of about 1 metre per second (1 m s^{-1}). Two features can increase the speed of nerve impulses considerably:

1. Some animals have axons with larger diameters and impulses are transmitted along wider axons more rapidly, because an increase in diameter reduces resistance. There are giant axons in squid with diameters up to 500 μm that conduct impulses at 25 m s^{-1}. These axons are used to coordinate a rapid jet-propulsion escape response when a squid is in danger. Animals do not have the space or resources for many giant axons, so can only use them to coordinate actions where rapidity is vital. For example, earthworms have just three giant axons that they use for an escape response to predator attacks.

2. Myelination is another modification that increases the speed of nerve impulses. Some axons are coated with many layers of phospholipid bilayer (myelin). Special cells called Schwann cells deposit the myelin by growing round and round the axon to form 20 or more layers of phospholipid bilayer. There are small gaps between adjacent Schwann cells, so the myelin sheath is not continuous. The gaps are called nodes of Ranvier. In myelinated axons the nerve impulse jumps from one node of Ranvier to the next. This is saltatory conduction and is faster than continuous transmission along an axon, so myelinated axons transmit nerve impulses much more rapidly than non-myelinated ones. Speeds can be as much as 100 m s^{-1}.

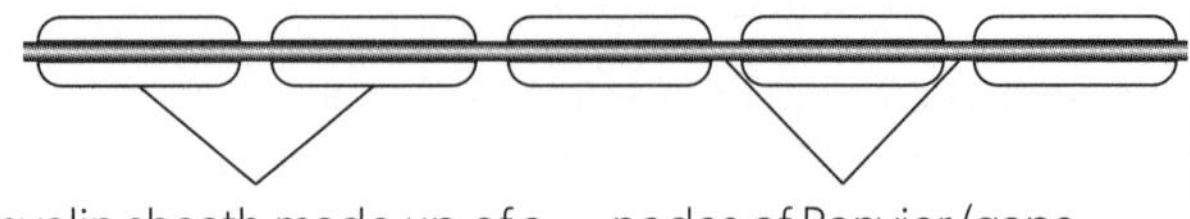

Application of skills: correlation coefficients

Correlation: Two variables are correlated if they vary together and are thus interdependent.

Positive correlation: The variables increase or decrease together.

Negative correlation: Each variable increases when the other variable decreases.

Correlation coefficient, *R*: This is a measure of how strongly associated two variables are. *R* is always between −1 and +1. This range is shown on the scale.

Coefficient of determination, R^2: This is the square of the correlation coefficient and measures the proportion of variation in the dependent variable that can be attributed to the independent variable. For example, if $R = 0.5$ then $R^2 = 0.25$, which indicates that a quarter of the variation in the dependent variable can be attributed to the independent variable. It does not however indicate that there is a causal link: another variable may be causing the correlation by affecting both independent and dependent variables.

Range of the correlation coefficient (*R*) and the coefficient of determination (R^2)

R	R^2	Correlation	Scatter
+1	+1	Perfect positive	All data lies on the regression line
+0.9	+0.81	Large positive	Little scatter in the data
+0.3	+0.09	Small positive	Widely scattered data
0	=0	None	Very widely scattered data
−0.3	+0.09	Small negative	Widely scattered data
−0.9	+0.81	Large negative	Little scatter in the data
−1	+1	Perfect negative	All data lies on the regression line

Data can be plotted on a graph, with a separate data point (dot or cross) for each result in an experiment or individual in a population.

A line of best fit (regression line) can be added to the graph, passing as close to all the data points as possible. With biological data, the dependent variable is usually affected by multiple factors, not just the independent variable. Data points on the graph are therefore scattered to either side of the regression line, so this type of graph is called a scatter graph.

Example of negative correlation: The nerve conduction velocities of nerves in the arm of 37 people were measured. In both nerves, velocity was correlated negatively with the person's height.

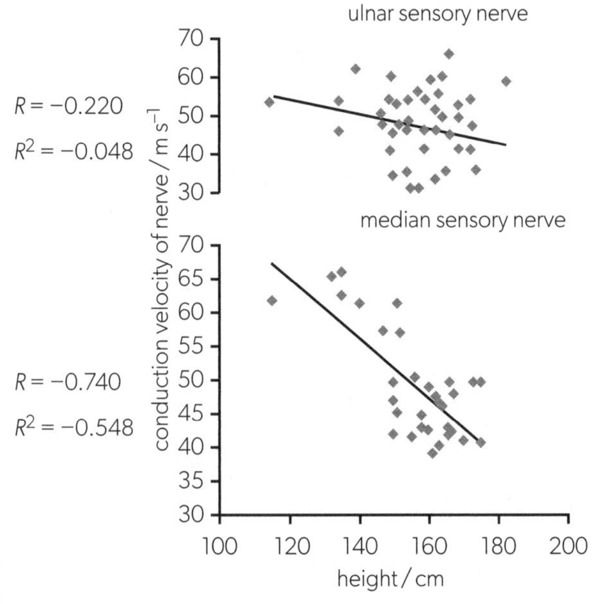

The correlation was stronger for the median sensory nerve than the ulnar sensory nerve. This is shown by the scatter of data points and differences in *R* and R^2.

Example of positive correlation: Axon diameter and conduction are positively correlated.

7. Excitatory postsynaptic potentials

Release of neurotransmitter from the presynaptic membrane triggers the stages of synaptic transmission that culminate in an action potential in the postsynaptic membrane.

- Molecules of neurotransmitter diffuse across the synaptic gap. This happens extremely rapidly because the distance is so short (20 to 40 nanometres).
- The neurotransmitter binds to receptors in the postsynaptic membrane. This binding causes Na^+ channels to open. In many cases the receptor itself acts as the ion channel.
- Na^+ ions diffuse down their concentration gradient across the postsynaptic membrane into the receiving neuron, causing the membrane potential to become less negative.
- If the potential rises from −70 mV to −50 mV, it triggers an action potential in the receiving neuron, which is propagated away from the synapse. A change in potential that is large enough to stimulate an action potential is an **excitatory postsynaptic potential**.

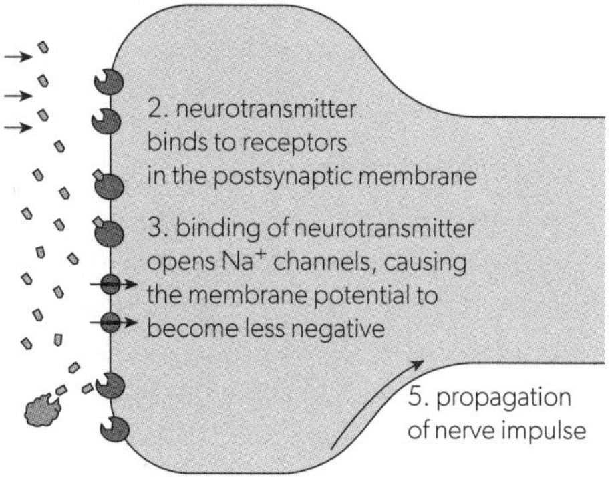

- The neurotransmitter only remains bound to the receptor for a short time and is rapidly removed from the synaptic gap, so only one action potential is initiated in the receiving neuron per action potential arriving in the transmitting neuron.

Acetylcholine is a widely used neurotransmitter at synapses between neurons. It is also used at synapses between neurons and muscle fibres (neuromuscular junctions). Acetylcholine is synthesized from choline and acetyl groups in the transmitting neuron. It binds to a receptor in the postsynaptic membrane which also acts as the channel for Na^+ ions. Acetylcholine is rapidly broken down in the synaptic gap by the enzyme acetylcholinesterase. The diagrams show the acetylcholine receptor with and without the neurotransmitter bound to the binding site.

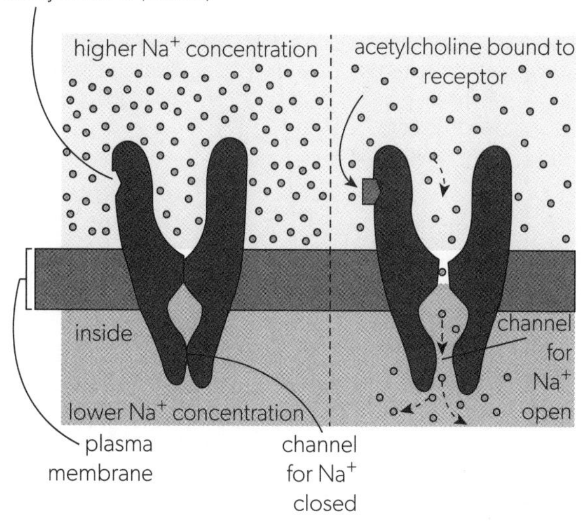

9. Propagation of an action potential

AHL

A nerve impulse is an action potential that travels from one end of an axon to the other. This movement happens because an action potential in one part of an axon triggers an action potential in the next part, which is called the **propagation** of the nerve impulse. It is due to local currents.

Local currents are movements of Na^+ ions by diffusion between one part of an axon that has depolarized and the adjacent part that is still polarized. Depolarization is due to an influx of Na^+ ions, which increases the Na^+ concentration inside the axon and reduces it outside. This causes sodium ions to diffuse along the axon, both inside and outside the membrane. Diffusion inside the axon is from the depolarized to polarized parts and outside the axon it is in the opposite direction.

These local currents make the potential in the region that is still polarized less negative. If the potential across the membrane rises from −70 mV to the threshold potential of −50 mV, voltage-gated sodium channels start to open, triggering an action potential. In the diagram, grey shades indicate relative Na^+ concentrations.

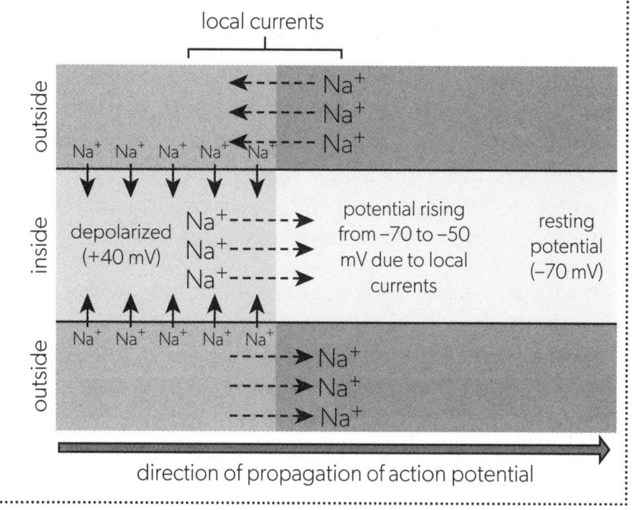

AHL

8. Depolarization and repolarization

Opening of the sodium and potassium channels that cause depolarization and repolarization is a response to changes in voltage across the membrane. This is called voltage-gating. Both channels remain open for only a short time, which helps to make action potentials brief and rapid.

Depolarization (opening of voltage-gated Na^+ channels)

Sodium channels start to open if membrane potential rises from the resting potential of −70 mV to the threshold potential of −50 mV. Sodium ions diffuse into the axon through pores that have opened, raising the membrane potential and causing yet more Na^+ channels to open. This is an example of positive feedback and results in the very rapid rise in membrane potential. Sodium channels only remain open for one to two milliseconds before closing again, but in this time enough Na^+ ions diffuse inwards for the membrane to become depolarized, with the potential typically rising from a negative value of −50 mV to a positive potential of +30 to 40 mV.

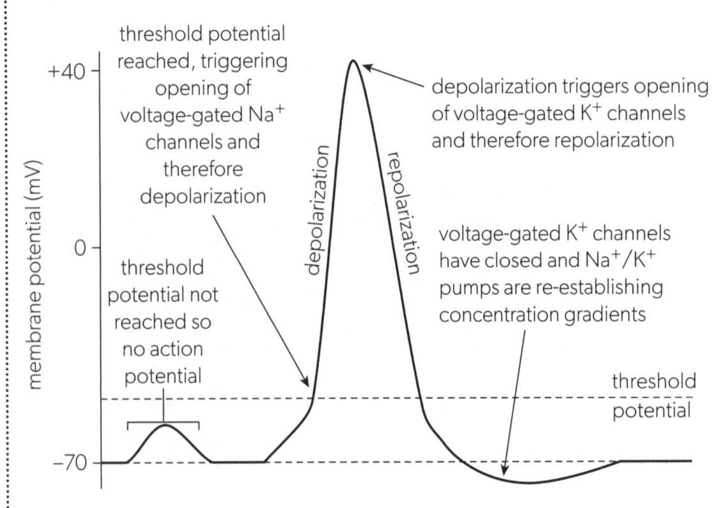

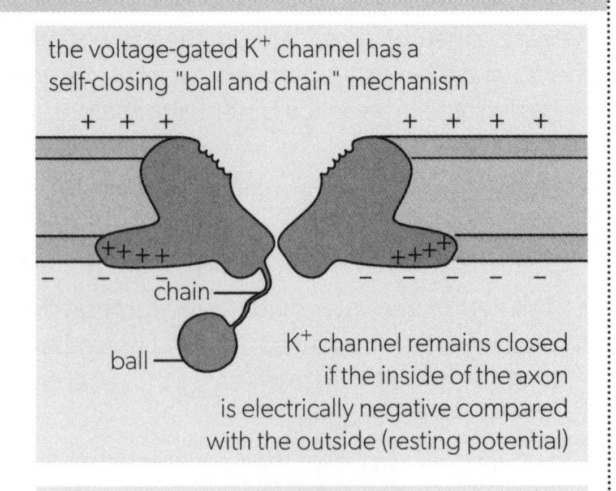

the voltage-gated K⁺ channel has a self-closing "ball and chain" mechanism
chain
ball
K⁺ channel remains closed if the inside of the axon is electrically negative compared with the outside (resting potential)

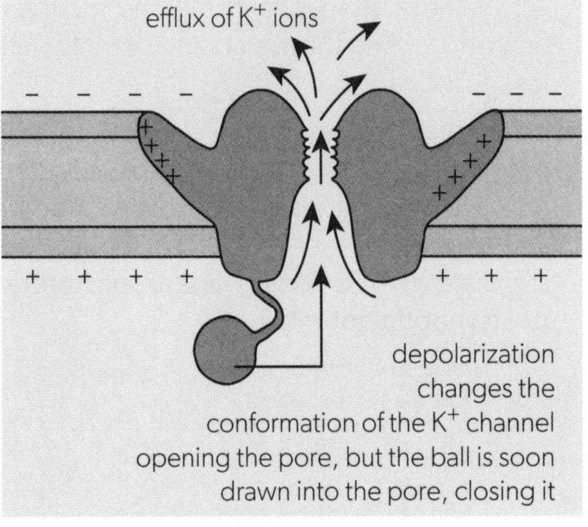

Repolarization (opening of voltage-gated K^+ channels)

The positive membrane potential that develops during depolarization causes voltage-gated potassium channels to open. As with sodium channels, the opening only persists for one to two milliseconds, before the channels close. Even in this short time, enough K^+ ions diffuse out of the axon to repolarize the axon. The membrane potential returns to −70 mV and may briefly overshoot by becoming more negative than this, before the sodium–potassium pump re-establishes concentration gradients.

Threshold potentials

A nerve impulse is "all-or-nothing" because unless the threshold potential is reached, there is no action potential. Smaller rises in potential, for example from −70 to −60 mV, do not trigger opening of sodium channels and instead the sodium–potassium pump re-establishes the resting potential of −70 mV. This is shown in the oscilloscope trace in *Section C2.2.14*.

10. Application of skills: oscilloscope traces

Membrane potential is monitored using microelectrodes placed inside and outside an axon. An oscilloscope displays the results, with time on the *x*-axis and voltage on the *y*-axis. When the axon is at a resting potential (about −70 mV) the trace on the oscilloscope is horizontal. Spikes are action potentials (nerve impulses) with a sudden depolarization followed by a repolarization. The number of spikes in a given time indicates the rate of nerve impulses per second.

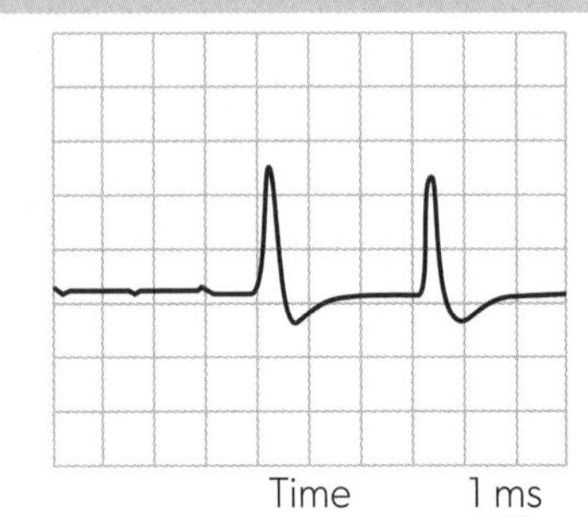

This image of an oscilloscope trace shows the membrane potential of a giant axon in an earthworm. A 10 millisecond period is shown, with the first 4 milliseconds 0.8 seconds at the resting potential of −70 mV. Two action potentials were then stimulated, with an interval between them of 3 milliseconds. If there had been more action potentials with the same intervals between them, the rate would have been 1 impulse per 3 milliseconds = 333 impulses per second.

AHL

11. Saltatory conduction

The structure of myelinated axons is described in *Section C2.2.4*. The myelin sheath prevents movement of Na^+ and K^+ ions across the axon membrane. Both sodium and potassium channels and also sodium–potassium pumps are clustered at nodes of Ranvier, with very few where the axon is coated in myelin.

Action potentials therefore only occur at nodes of Ranvier (gaps between the Schwann cells). Instead of being propagated continuously along the axon, as in unmyelinated axons, the nerve impulse jumps from one node of Ranvier to the next in myelinated nerve fibres.

This is **saltatory conduction**. It speeds up propagation of the nerve impulse greatly, with speeds of up to $100\,m\,s^{-1}$ compared with typical speeds of about $1\,m\,s^{-1}$ in unmyelinated axons.

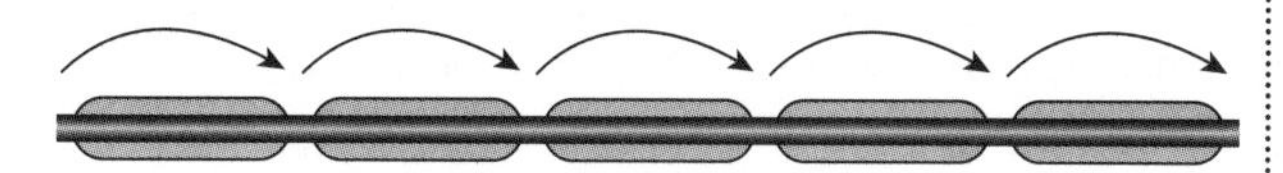

saltatory conduction—impulse jumps from node to node

12. Exogenous chemicals

Exogenous chemicals come from outside the body. They can enter through the skin, the lungs or the gut. They can also be injected. Pesticides and drugs are two groups of exogenous chemicals. In both groups there are chemicals that affect synaptic transmission, either by blocking or promoting it, such as neonicotinoids and cocaine.

Neonicotinoid pesticides are synthetic compounds similar to nicotine. They bind to acetylcholine receptors in cholinergic synapses in the central nervous system of insects, causing the Na^+ channel in the receptor to open. Acetylcholinesterase does not break down neonicotinoids, so the binding is irreversible and the Na^+ ion channel remains open. An excess of Na^+ enters the receiving neuron, overstimulating it and blocking normal synaptic transmission. The consequence in insects is paralysis and death. Neonicotinoids are therefore very effective insecticides, but they can cause harm to bees and other insects with important roles in ecosystems or in agriculture.

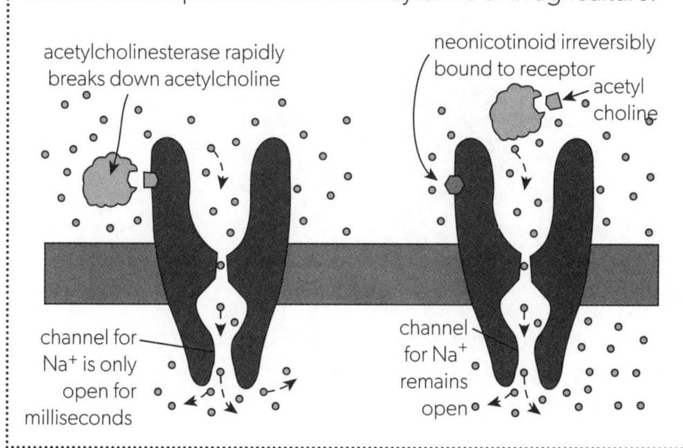

Cocaine acts at synapses that use dopamine as a neurotransmitter. It binds to dopamine reuptake transporters, which are the membrane proteins that pump dopamine back into the presynaptic neuron. Because cocaine blocks these transporters, dopamine builds up in the synaptic cleft and the postsynaptic neuron is continuously excited. Cocaine is therefore an excitatory or stimulant psychoactive drug that gives feelings of euphoria that are unrelated to a reward activity such as eating.

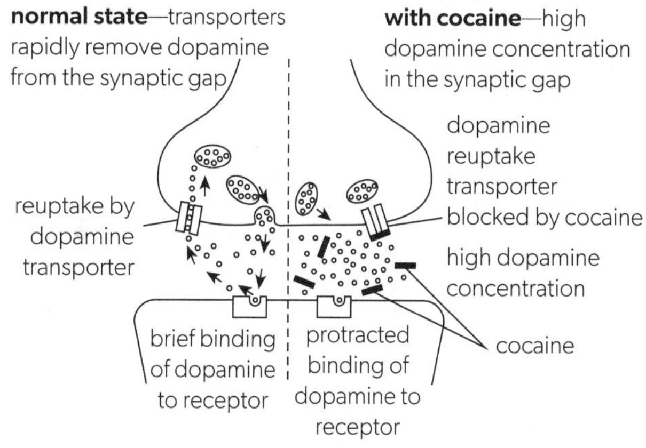

15. Perception of pain

Pain receptors in the skin and other parts of the body detect stimuli such as the chemical substances in a bee's sting, excessive heat or the puncturing of skin by a hypodermic needle. These receptors are the endings of sensory neurons that convey impulses to the central nervous system.

The nerve endings associated with pain receptors have channels for positively charged ions, which open in response to a stimulus such as high temperature, acid, or certain chemicals such as capsaicin in chili peppers. Entry of positively charged ions causes the threshold potential to be reached and nerve impulses then pass through the sensory neuron to the spinal cord. Interneurons in the spinal cord relay the impulse to the cerebral cortex.

When impulses reach sensory areas of the cerebral cortex the sensation of pain is perceived. Signals are transmitted to the prefrontal cortex, allowing us to become fully aware of our pain and evaluate the situation. This will often result in a signal from the brain to the effectors of behaviour that reduces exposure to the stimulus. For example, we may brush off a bee that is stinging us.

AHL

13. Inhibitory neurotransmitters

Many neurotransmitters stimulate action potentials in the postsynaptic membrane, but some have the opposite effect. They make the membrane potential more negative (lower than −70 mV) when they bind to receptors in the postsynaptic membrane. This hyperpolarization makes it more difficult for the postsynaptic neuron to reach the threshold potential, so nerve impulses are inhibited, rather than stimulated. GABA (gamma-amino butyric acid) is an example of an inhibitory neurotransmitter. When it binds to its receptor, a chloride channel opens, causing hyperpolarization of the postsynaptic neuron by an influx of Cl^- ions to the receiving neuron. A transient lowering of membrane potential caused by neurotransmitters such as GABA and acetylcholine is known as an **inhibitory postsynaptic potential**.

Effects of excitatory and inhibitory neurotransmitters

	Excitatory	Inhibitory
Channel opened in postsynaptic membrane	Channel for positively charged ions, usually Na^+	Channel for negatively charged ions, usually Cl^-
Effect on postsynaptic membrane potential	Rises from −70 mV so becomes less negative; may reach threshold potential (−50 mV)	Falls from −70 mV to −80 mV or lower so more negative than the resting potential (hyperpolarization)
Effect on postsynaptic neuron	Excites an impulse if threshold potential reached	Inhibits impulses but does not make them impossible
Example	Acetylcholine	GABA

14. Summation

A single neuron can form synapses with many other neurons. A receiving (postsynaptic) neuron may receive neurotransmitter from many transmitting (presynaptic) neurons. Some neurons in the brain have synapses with hundreds or even thousands of transmitting neurons. The neurotransmitter at each specific synapse is always the same and may be excitatory or inhibitory.

Initiation of an action potential is an "all-or-nothing" event. A single release of excitatory neurotransmitter from one transmitting neuron is often insufficient to trigger an action potential, because a single excitatory postsynaptic potential does not cause the threshold potential to be reached. To reach the threshold, either one transmitting neuron must release neurotransmitter multiple times in a short time or several transmitting neurons must release neurotransmitter more or less simultaneously. Stimulation of an action potential as a result of multiple releases of excitatory neurotransmitter is an example of **summation**.

In the oscilloscope traces below, two excitatory postsynaptic potentials cause an action potential only if close in time.

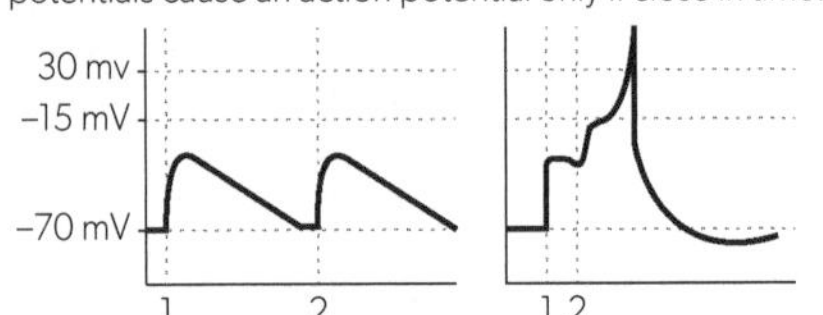

There can also be summation of the effects of inhibitory and excitatory neurotransmitters. Whether or not an action potential is initiated in the receiving neuron depends on the balance between the effects of these two types of neurotransmitters. Inhibitory neurotransmitters counter the effects of excitatory neurotransmitters and prevent the threshold potential from being reached. There is only an action potential with a predominance of excitatory neurotransmitters reaching the postsynaptic membrane, so that the threshold is reached.

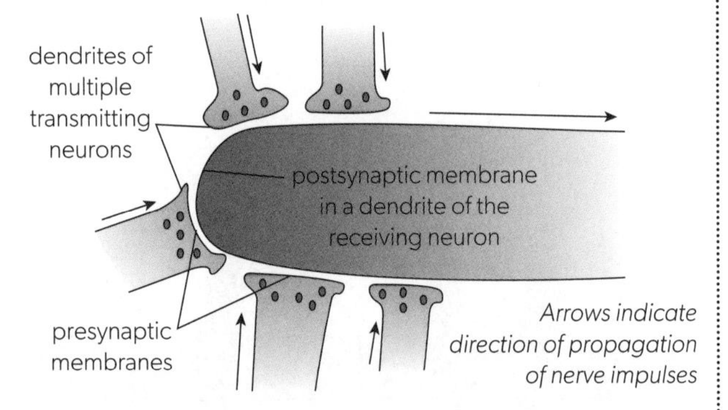

Integration in synapses of signals from many different sources is the basis of decision-making processes in the central nervous system.

16. Consciousness

If we are conscious of something, we are aware of it. We do not have to be actively thinking about something to be aware of it, so we can be simultaneously aware of many things. This state of complex awareness is known as consciousness. There is agreement that it exists, but philosophers and scientists have not reached agreement on how to define it.

Sleep is a state of reduced or partial consciousness. General anaesthetics, used during surgery, make us unconscious, but the mechanisms of action of these drugs are not well understood, so they do not reveal much about the physiological basis of consciousness. Perhaps the most that we can say with certainty is that consciousness is a property that emerges from the interaction of individual neurons in the brain. Consciousness is thus an example of an emergent property.

Emergent properties are the result of interactions between the elements of a system. When we recognize that a system is more than the sum of its parts, we are acknowledging the existence of emergent properties. Two biological examples are the catalytic activity of enzymes and flight in birds.

End of topic questions—C2 Questions

C2.1 Chemical signalling (HL)

1. The graph shows the amount of bioluminescence emitted by a culture of the bacterium *Vibrio fischeri* when given different concentrations of an autoinducer experimentally.

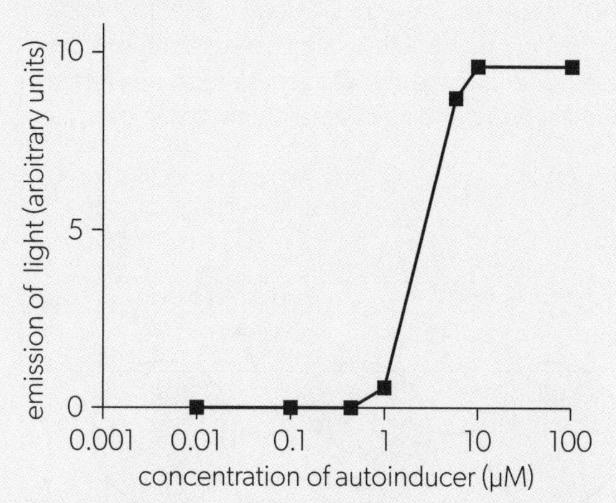

   a. State the type of scale used on the *x*-axis of the graph. (1)

   b. Describe the trend shown by the graph. (3)

   c. Explain what determines the concentration of autoinducer in a natural population of *Vibrio fischeri*. (2)

   d. i. State the name of cell-to-cell communication systems such as the use of an autoinducer in *Vibrio fischeri*. (1)

   ii. Explain how communication using an autoinducer benefits *Vibrio fischeri*. (3)

2. The diagram shows how two types of hormone act on cells.

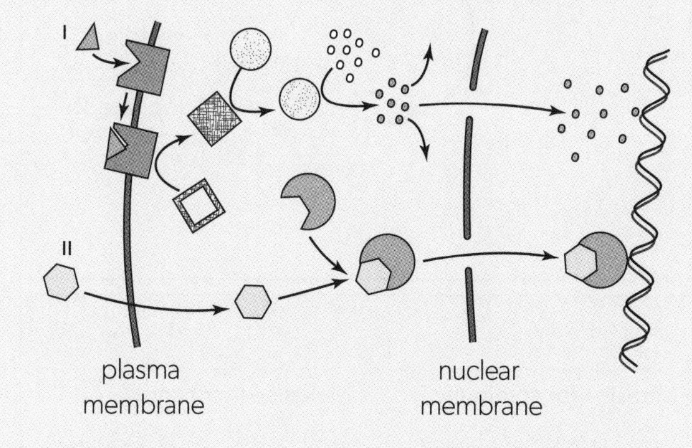

   a. Deduce the two types of hormone, I and II. (2)

   b. Suggest an example of each type of hormone. (2)

   c. Explain all the events shown in the diagram. (6)

3. a. Outline the role of G protein in signalling inside cells. (5)

   b. Outline how binding of insulin to insulin receptors changes the activity of target cells. (5)

C2.2 Neural signalling

1. (HL only) The graph shows an oscilloscope trace for a presynaptic neuron and three traces for the postsynaptic neuron at a synapse in the hippocampus of the brain.

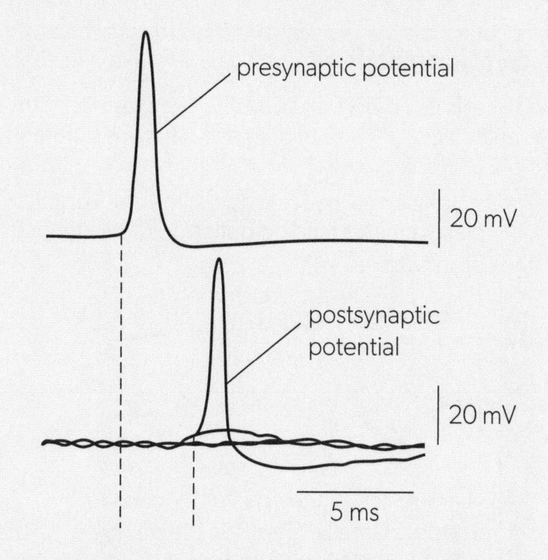

   a. Assuming resting potentials of −60 mV in both neurons, deduce their membrane potential when fully depolarized. (4)

   b. i. Annotate the trace for the presynaptic neuron to show when depolarization and repolarization occurred. (2)

   ii. Estimate the times taken for depolarization and repolarization to occur in the presynaptic neuron. (2)

   c. i. Calculate the delay between the action potentials in the presynaptic and postsynaptic neurons. (2)

   ii. Suggest reasons for this delay. (3)

   d. i. Two of the traces for the postsynaptic neuron show no action potential, despite release of neurotransmitter from the presynaptic neuron, illustrating the "all-or-nothing" principle of action potentials. Deduce the meaning of this principle.

   ii. Suggest two reasons for an action potential not developing in the postsynaptic neuron on two occasions. (2)

2. (HL only) Explain the role of these processes during an action potential:

   a. active transport (5)
   b. facilitated diffusion (5)
   c. simple diffusion (5)
   d. myelin. (5)

3. a. Draw a diagram to show the structure of a neuron. (5)

   b. Annotate the diagram to show the function(s) of each part. (5)

   c. Distinguish between resting and action potentials. (5)

   d. Compare and contrast myelinated and unmyelinated axons in structure and function. (5)

D2.1 Cell and nuclear division

1. Cell division

New cells are produced by division of pre-existing cells. The cell that divides is the mother cell and the two cells produced when it divides are daughter cells.

2. Cytokinesis

Cytokinesis is the division of a cell's cytoplasm to form two cells. It occurs after mitosis and happens differently in plant and animal cells.

- Plants make a new cell wall across the cell's equator, with plasma membrane on both sides. This divides the cell in two.

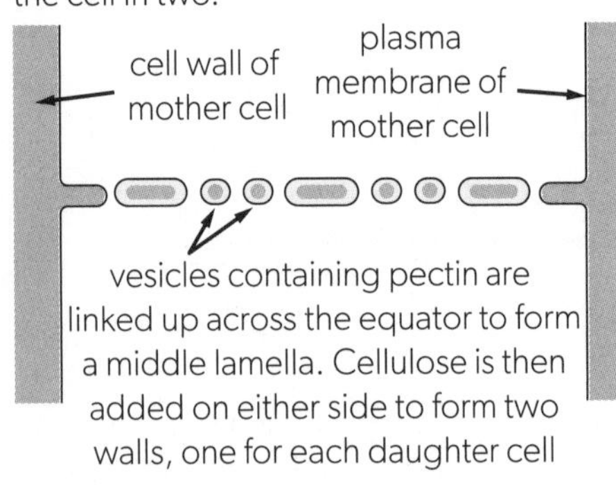
cell wall of mother cell
plasma membrane of mother cell
vesicles containing pectin are linked up across the equator to form a middle lamella. Cellulose is then added on either side to form two walls, one for each daughter cell

- Animals divide the cytoplasm of cells by moving the plasma membrane. Movement is due to actin and myosin proteins adjacent to the membrane. Before cytokinesis they are randomly arranged, but some are reorientated so they run in parallel in a ring around the equator of the cell, where they exert tension to form a cleavage furrow, with the membrane pulled inwards so it eventually splits the cell.

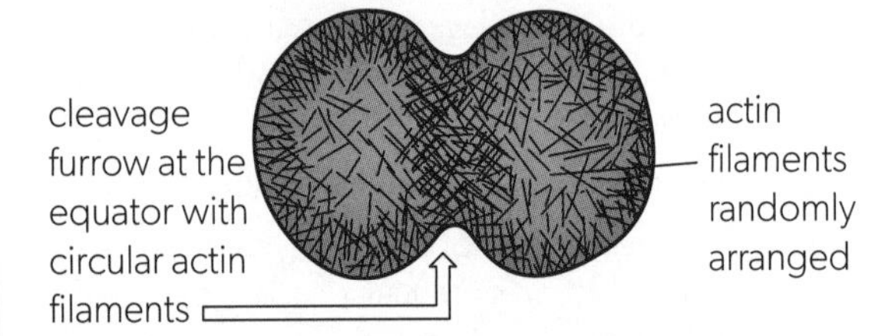
cleavage furrow at the equator with circular actin filaments
actin filaments randomly arranged

Adapted from: Spira, F. et al. (2017). Cytokinesis in vertebrate cells initiates by contraction of an equatorial actomyosin network composed of randomly oriented filaments. eLife, 6. doi:10.7554/elife.30867

3. Cytokinesis can be equal or unequal

In many cases, cytokinesis divides the cytoplasm of the mother cell into equal halves. This happens for example when a human zygote divides to form a two-cell embryo. Cytoplasm is sometimes divided unequally. Small cells produced by unequal division can survive and grow if they receive a nucleus plus at least one mitochondrion and other organelle that cannot be assembled from components in the cell. Oogenesis (egg production) in humans and budding in yeast are two examples.

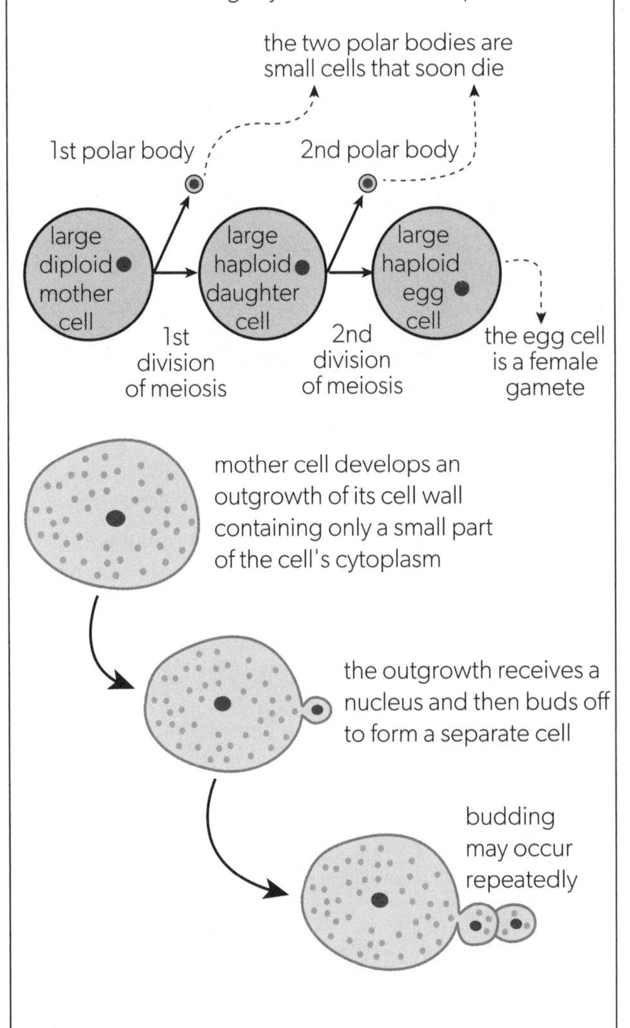
the two polar bodies are small cells that soon die
1st polar body
2nd polar body
large diploid mother cell
large haploid daughter cell
large haploid egg cell
1st division of meiosis
2nd division of meiosis
the egg cell is a female gamete
mother cell develops an outgrowth of its cell wall containing only a small part of the cell's cytoplasm
the outgrowth receives a nucleus and then buds off to form a separate cell
budding may occur repeatedly

4. Mitosis and meiosis

If a mother cell divides before it has divided its nucleus, one daughter cell will receive a nucleus, but the other one will not. Cells without a nucleus cannot synthesize polypeptides, so they do not grow or maintain themselves and have limited lifespans. Red blood cells which are anucleate only survive for about 120 days.

Usually nuclear division does happen before cytokinesis, so each daughter cell can receive a nucleus. There are two types of nuclear division: mitosis or meiosis. They have different roles, so most organisms use both during their life cycle.

Mitosis—for continuity	Meiosis—for change
With mitosis, daughter cells receive all the chromosomes and genes of the mother cell. The chromosome number is unchanged.	In meiosis a diploid nucleus divides into haploid nuclei, halving the chromosome number. This allows haploid gametes to be produced in sexual life cycles.
Mitosis is used in asexual reproduction to produce genetically identical offspring. It is also used in multicellular organisms to produce genetically identical body cells.	Meiosis generates genetic diversity because every haploid cell produced from a diploid mother cell has a different combination of alleles.

5. DNA replication

Cells replicate all their DNA before the start of both mitosis and meiosis.

DNA replication ensures that two daughter cells produced by mitosis will receive the entire genome.

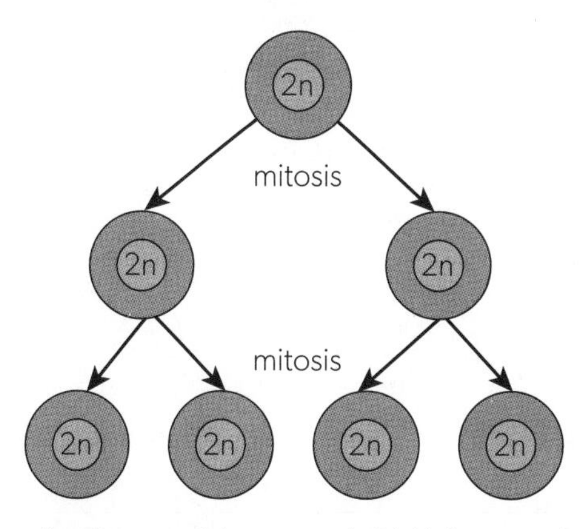

DNA replication provides enough DNA for a mother cell to divide twice in meiosis, producing four haploid cells. It also provides enough DNA for recombination by the process of crossing over.

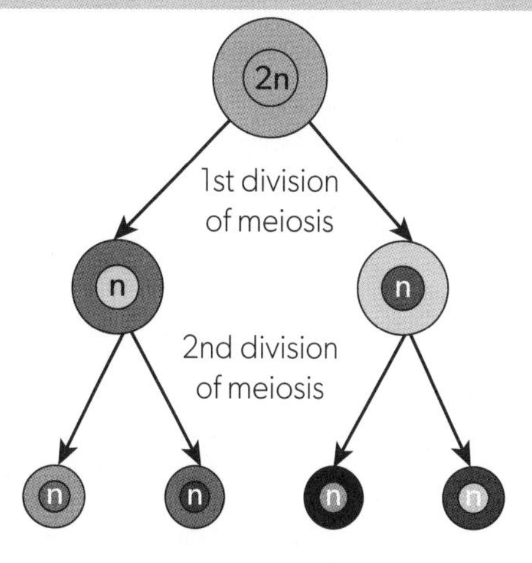

The DNA is in an elongated state when it is replicated and is then packed up tightly (condensed) during the early phases of mitosis or meiosis. Condensation makes the two DNA molecules visible as separate structures. They are called sister chromatids. Throughout the early phases of mitosis and meiosis, each chromosome consists of two sister chromatids. The chromatids only separate in the penultimate phase.

6. Condensation and movement of chromosomes

During mitosis and meiosis, chromatids are separated and moved to opposite ends (poles) of the mother cell. This could not be done if the DNA was still in an elongated state, so it is packed up (condensed) to form much shorter and fatter chromosomes. Initial stages of condensation are carried out by wrapping the double helix of DNA around groups of histone proteins. The structures produced (shown right) are then linked together. Further details of this are given (for HL) in *A1.2.13*.

Later stages of condensation are accomplished by supercoiling, ending up with 10,000 micrometres of DNA packed into each micrometre of chromatid.

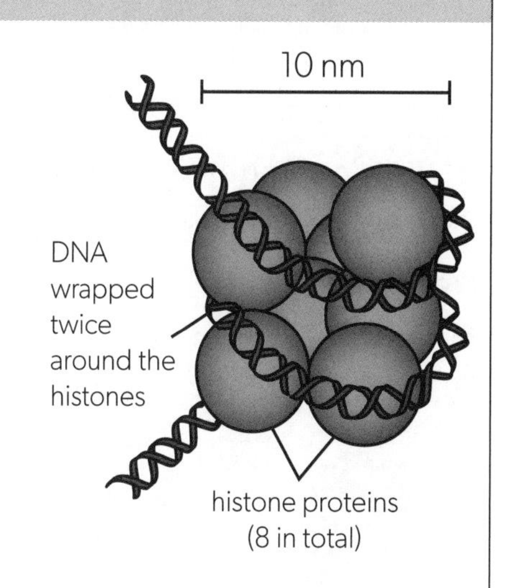

Chromosomes are moved by microtubules and microtubule motors. Microtubules are narrow tubular structures that are assembled from many molecules of tubulin (a globular protein). This happens at the poles of the cell. As more tubulins are added, the microtubules extend further towards the equator of the cell. The microtubules form a spindle shape, tapering at both ends, so are called spindle microtubules.

Microtubule motors cause movement by removing tubulin subunits from the end of microtubules, shortening them. Each chromatid has a microtubule motor, called the kinetochore, which is anchored to the chromatid's centromere. Microtubules that have grown from one of the poles become attached to the kinetochores. During anaphase in mitosis and meiosis, kinetochores remove tubulins from the end of the microtubules, pulling chromosomes to opposite poles.

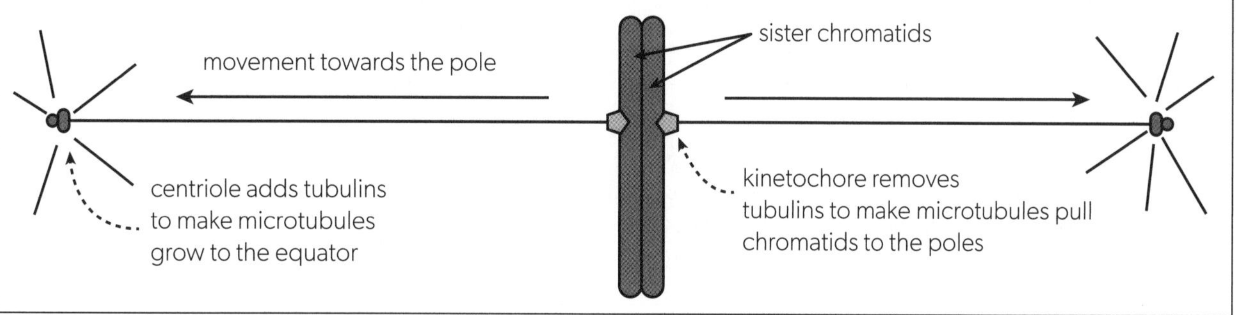

7. Stages of mitosis

① Early prophase

microtubules are growing from the centrioles to form a spindle shape

chromosomes are becoming shorter and fatter by supercoiling (condensation)

② Late prophase

spindle microtubules extend from each pole to the equator

each chromosome consists of two identical sister chromatids formed by DNA replication in interphase, each with a centromere and a kinetochore

③ Metaphase

nuclear membrane has broken down and chromosomes have moved to the equator

spindle microtubules have attached to kinetochores, with sister chromatids attached to opposite poles

④ Anaphase

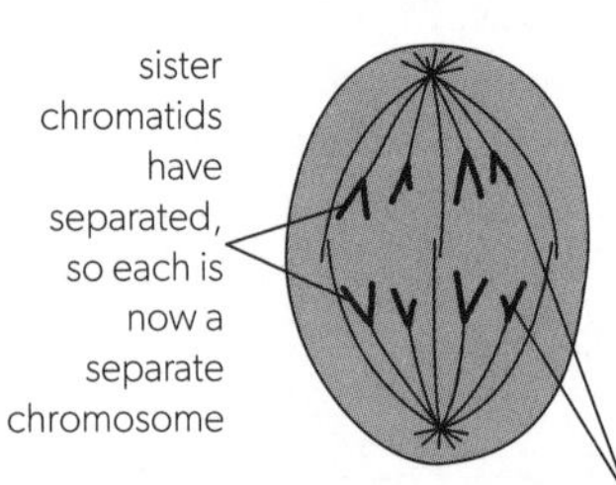
sister chromatids have separated, so each is now a separate chromosome
kinetochores shorten spindle microtubules, pulling genetically identical chromosomes to opposite poles

⑤ Early telophase

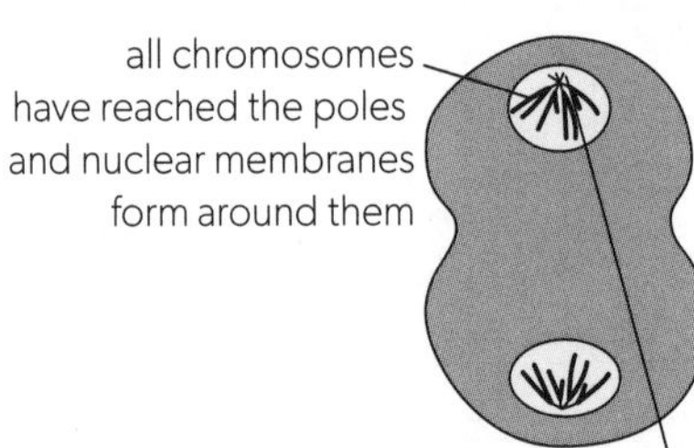
all chromosomes have reached the poles and nuclear membranes form around them
spindle microtubules break down

⑥ Late telophase

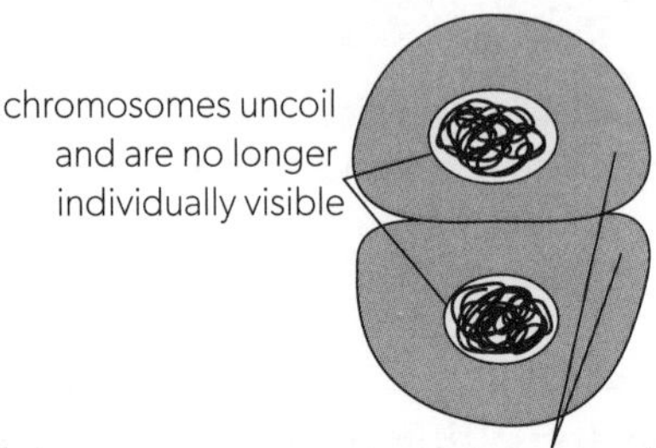
chromosomes uncoil and are no longer individually visible
the cell divides (cytokinesis) to form two cells with genetically identical nuclei

8. Viewing stages of mitosis

Interphase—no sign of condensation

Prophase—condensing inside the nucleus

Metaphase—aligned on the equator

Anaphase—V-shaped and moving to poles

Telophase—decondensing in nuclei at poles

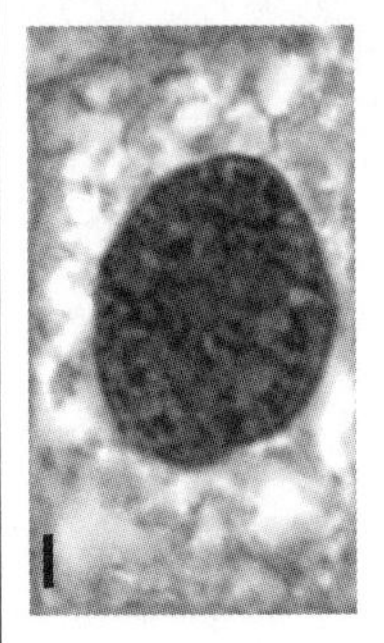
I

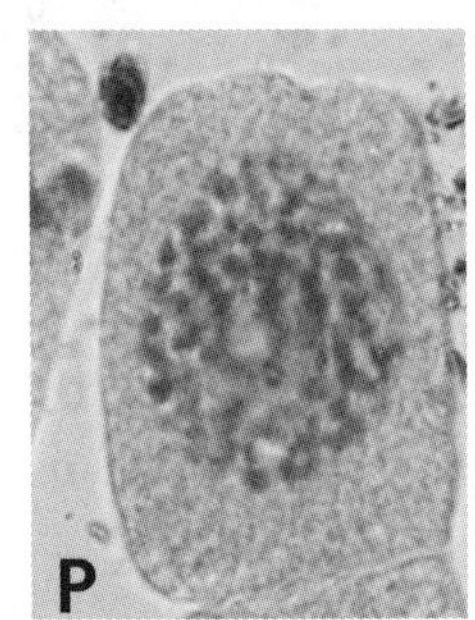
P

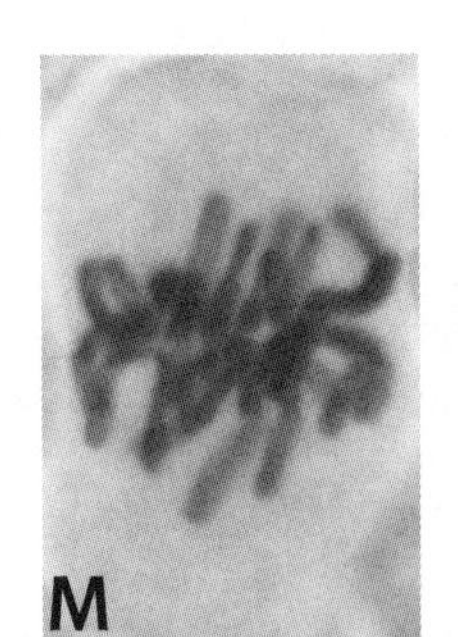
M

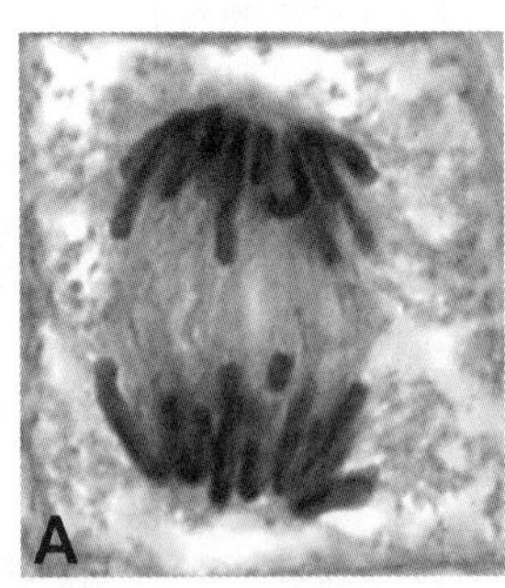
A

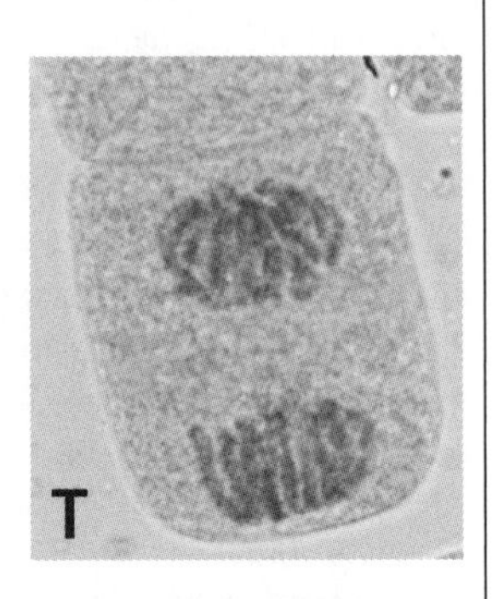
T

AHL

12. Cell proliferation

Cell proliferation is repeated division of cells. It is required for three reasons in plants and animals:

1. **Growth**—to increase the size of the body

Examples: plants have groups of dividing cells (meristems) that are retained throughout the plant's life, to allow growth to continue (indeterminate growth). There are meristems in the apices (tips) of both stems and roots. The root apical meristem lengthens the root. The shoot apical meristem lengthens the stem and produces cells for growing leaves or flowers. All cells in early-stage animal embryos are dividing, so the entire embryo grows rapidly.

2. **Cell replacement**—routine production of cells to replace those with a limited lifespan

Example: a layer of dividing cells in the skin replaces cells that are abraded from the skin surface.

3. **Tissue repair**—healing after loss or damage of tissues

Example: skin cells divide to produce the cells needed to heal a cut or other wound.

9. Meiosis

Meiosis is described as a reduction division because it halves the number of chromosomes. The mother cell that divides has a **diploid** nucleus and the four cells produced all have **haploid** nuclei. A diploid nucleus has two sets of chromosomes, whereas a haploid nucleus has only one set. A diploid nucleus contains pairs of **homologous** chromosomes. Homologous chromosomes carry the same genes, in the same sequence, but they may have different alleles of any of the genes.

The haploid number of chromosomes of a species is represented by the letter *n* so the diploid number is 2*n*. Most body cells in plants and animals are diploid. Gametes such as the sperm and eggs are haploid. Two haploid gametes fuse during fertilization to produce one diploid cell—the zygote. This divides by mitosis to produce more diploid body cells with the same number of chromosomes. If meiosis did not occur at some stage during a sexual life cycle, the chromosome number would double every generation.

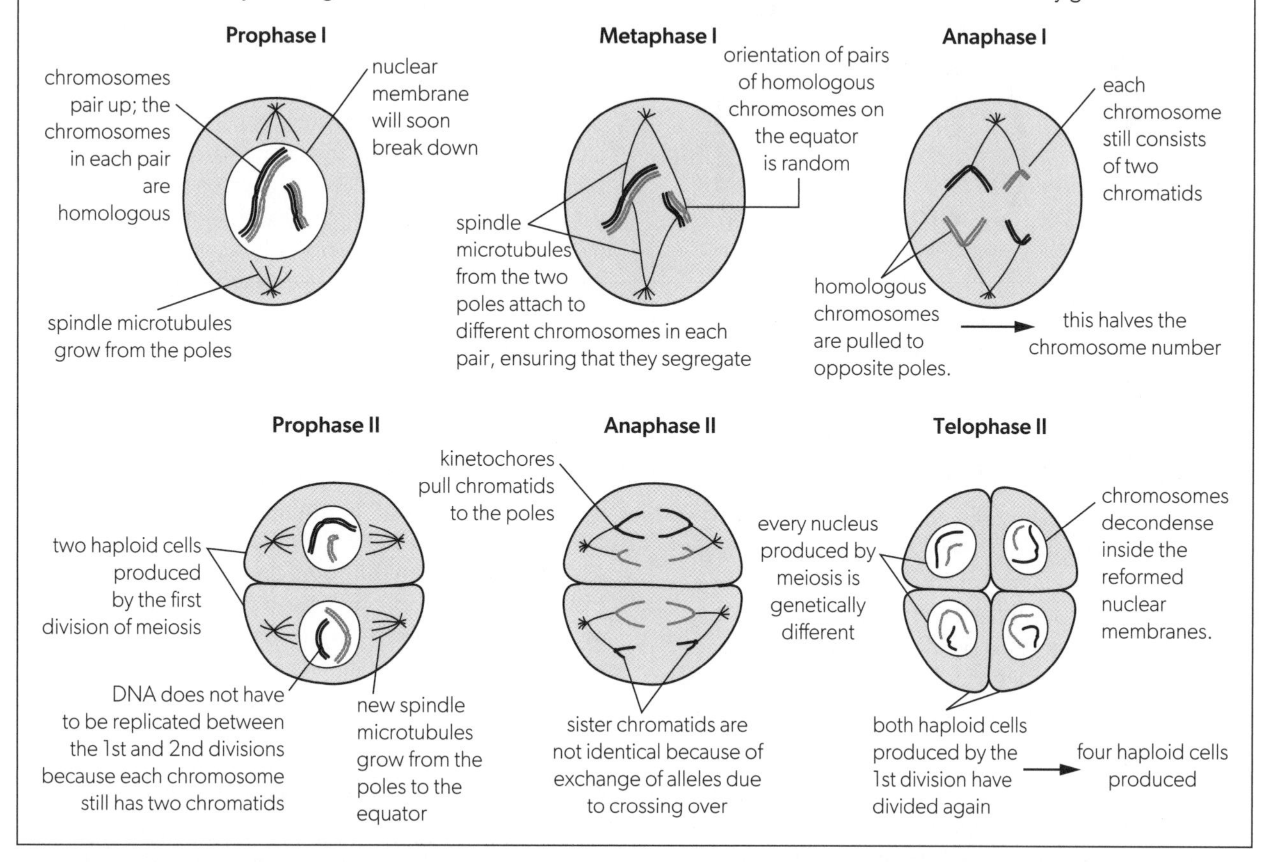

10. Trisomy

Down syndrome is due to an error in meiosis. A pair of homologous chromosomes (pair 21) fails to separate in anaphase 1 (**non-disjunction**) so both move to the same pole. The result is a sperm or egg with two copies of chromosome 21 and a zygote with three copies. A child developing from such a zygote has Down syndrome. Having three chromosomes instead of two is **trisomy**. Most trisomies have more serious consequences and cause death of the gamete or early-stage embryo, for example trisomy of chromosome 1.

11. Meiosis generates variation

Meiosis generates genetic diversity (different combinations of alleles) in two ways:

1. Random orientation of bivalents

A bivalent is a pair of homologous chromosomes, one inherited from the male and one from the female parent. Orientation of each bivalent in metaphase I determines which pole each chromosome moves to. Orientation is random and does not influence other bivalents, so many different combinations can be produced when homologous chromosomes separate in anaphase I. There are 2^n possible combinations—over 8 million in humans where *n* is 23.

2. Crossing over

Homologous chromosomes pair up in the very early stages of meiosis and non-sister chromatids exchange lengths of DNA by "crossing over". This produces chromatids with new combinations of alleles. It is a significant source of genetic variation because where along the length of the chromosomes the exchange occurs is random.

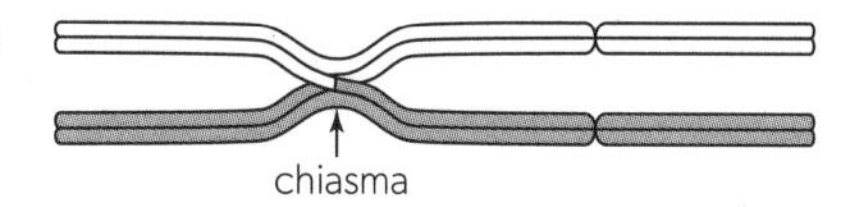

AHL

13. The cell cycle

Cell proliferation is achieved by a repeated sequence of events called the cell cycle. The phases in the cell cycle are shown in the diagram.

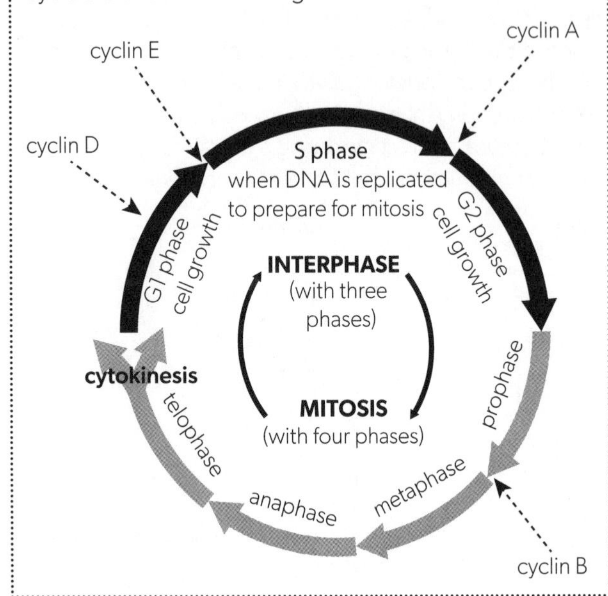

15. Cyclins and control of the cell cycle

There are checkpoints between one phase of the cell cycle and the next. Cyclins are proteins used to control progression though these checkpoints. Their concentrations rise and fall during the cell cycle. At each checkpoint a threshold concentration of one specific cyclin is required for the cell to progress to the next phase. The concentration of that cyclin then falls.

Cyclins bind to kinase enzymes, activating them. The kinases phosphorylate other proteins in the cell, activating them. The phosphorylated proteins perform tasks specific to the phase of the cell cycle that has been entered.

There are four main types of cyclin in human cells. The checkpoints that each cyclin controls are shown in the cell cycle diagram in *Section D2.1.13*.

14. Interphase

Interphase is a very active phase in the life of a cell when many metabolic reactions occur.

Some of these, such as the reactions of cell respiration, also occur during mitosis, but DNA replication in the nucleus and protein synthesis in the cytoplasm only happen during interphase.

During interphase, mitochondria in the cytoplasm grow and divide, so they increase in number. In plant cells chloroplast numbers increase in the same way.

16. Mutations in cell cycle genes

Mutations in two types of gene can change cells in which the cell cycle is under control into tumour cells that divide endlessly:

1. Proto-oncogenes are concerned with control of the cell cycle. Specific mutations change proto-oncogenes into oncogenes, which cause uncontrolled cell division.

2. Tumour suppressor genes normally prevent uncontrolled cell division, but mutations in them can result in a loss of this defence against cancer.

Because cells have multiple barriers to uncontrolled division, multiple genes must have mutated in the same cell for control to be lost. The chance of this is very small but the body contains billions of cells, so the overall risk is significant. Anything that increases the chance of mutations will increase the risk of tumour formation. The causes of gene mutation are explained in *Section D1.3.4*.

17. Tumours

A tumour is a mass of proliferating cells in which normal control of the cell cycle has been lost. A primary tumour is initially formed. **Primary tumours** vary in their rate of growth. **Benign tumours** grow slowly and are not life-threatening so they are not usually regarded as cancer. **Malignant tumours** grow aggressively and may invade neighbouring tissues or spread to form **secondary tumours** in distant parts of the body, so they constitute life-threatening cancers. The spreading of cells to form secondary tumours is **metastasis**.

Application of skills: mitotic index

To calculate the mitotic index, obtain a sample of tissue from a tumour and examine it using a microscope. Count the number of cells in any stage of mitosis, and the total number of cells.

$$\text{mitotic index} = \frac{\text{number of cells in mitosis}}{\text{total number of cells}}$$

The mitotic index is used by doctors to predict how rapidly a tumour will grow and therefore what treatment is needed. A high index indicates a fast-growing tumour.

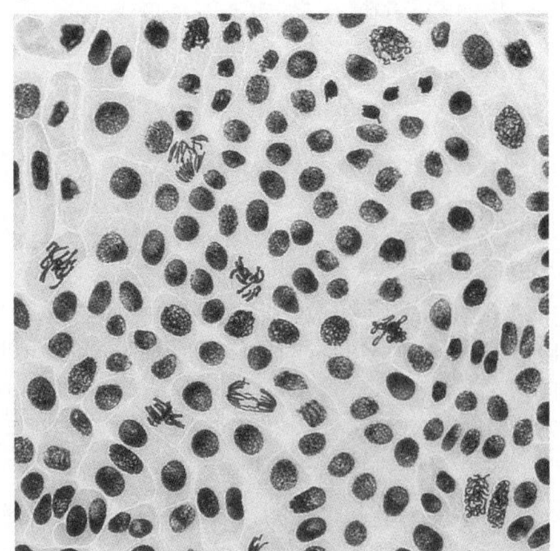

D2.2 Gene expression

AHL

1. Gene expression

The phenotype is all the functional and structural characteristics of an organism. The genotype is all its genetic information. Gene expression is the process of turning the genotype into the phenotype. It happens by transcription to produce mRNA, translation of the mRNA into proteins, and the proteins performing their functions. Many proteins act as enzymes, so have their effect on phenotype by catalysing a reaction.

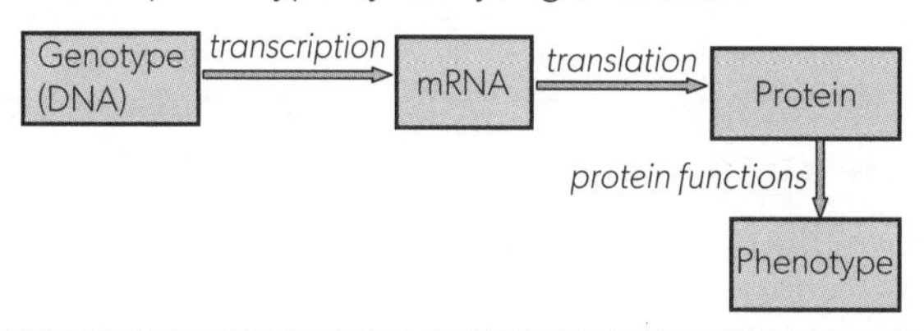

2. Regulation of transcription

Gene expression requires selective transcription of RNA. Promoters, transcription factors and enhancers have roles in this.

Every gene has a **promoter**, located upstream of it (in the 5′ direction). All promoters within the genome of an organism share parts of their base sequence. These consensus sequences are recognized by RNA polymerase which binds to them, ensuring that the enzyme is correctly placed to start transcribing the gene in a 5′ to 3′ direction. RNA polymerase cannot by itself start transcription.

Other DNA-binding proteins are required, known as **transcription factors**. These proteins bind to specific base sequences in the DNA near to the promoter. There are many different types of transcription factor, corresponding to the different base sequences at binding sites. This allows a cell to regulate gene transcription and be selective in which genes are transcribed at all times in the life of the cell. In some cases, genes are regulated individually and in other cases shared transcription factors result in groups of genes being regulated together. Testosterone receptors act as transcription factors. When testosterone has bound to the receptor, the receptor–hormone complex binds to DNA at multiple points, causing transcription by RNA polymerase of a group of genes.

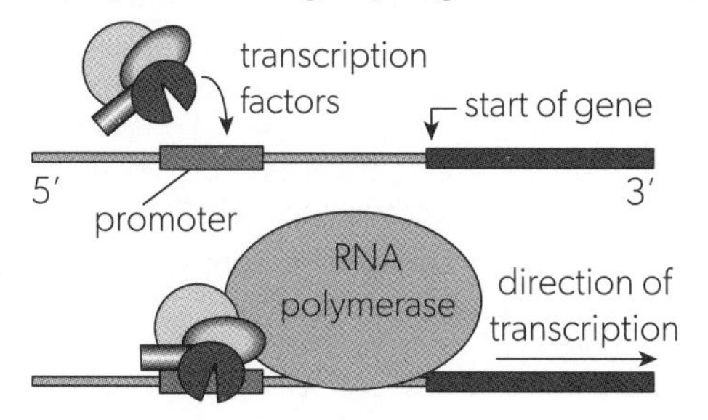

The rate of transcription of genes can be varied by **enhancers**. These are base sequences located either upstream or downstream of a gene. When transcription factors, known as activators, bind to these enhancers, the rate of transcription of the gene is increased.

3. Control of the degradation of mRNA

A molecule of mRNA is translated repeatedly to produce a protein and is then broken down by nucleases. Some proteins are produced briefly in a cell, for example those that control the cell cycle. Others such as the milk protein casein are produced continuously for long periods of time. This is achieved by regulation of mRNA degradation. The poly-A tail has a role in this.

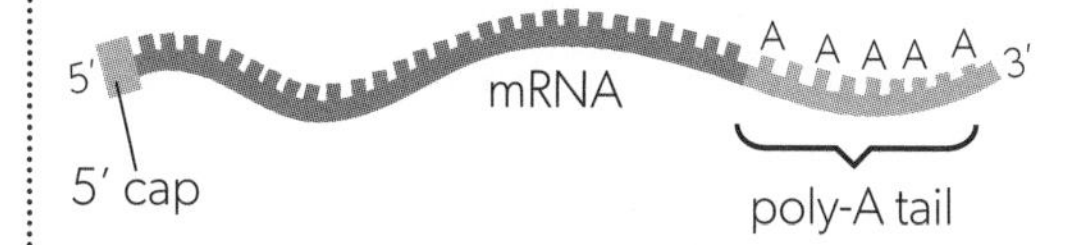

Addition of the poly-A tail to mRNA is described in *Section D1.2.15*. The tail of an mRNA molecule becomes shorter over time. The shorter the poly-A tail, the less likely mRNA is to be translated and the more likely that it will be degraded by nuclease. The rate of shortening varies by a factor of over a thousand. In some types of mRNA, 30 nucleotides are removed per minute; in others, only one or two per hour are removed. Given an average initial tail length of 200 nucleotides in humans, this implies that mRNA molecules might persist and continue to be translated for between 5 minutes and a week.

4. Epigenesis

Epigenesis is the development of a plant or animal from undifferentiated cells. Due to cell differentiation, structures and functions appear that were not present at the start of the organism's life. Differentiation is achieved by activation of some genes and deactivation (silencing) of others. Activation and silencing are carried out by chemical modifications of DNA and the proteins associated with DNA. These modifications are known as **epigenetic tags**. They are reversible and do not alter DNA base sequences so the genotype of the organism is unchanged, but they do alter the phenotype.

5. Comparing the genome, transcriptome and proteome of cells

Genome: the whole of the genetic information of a cell. It includes coding and non-coding sequences.

Transcriptome: the entire set of mRNAs transcribed in a cell. No cell transcribes all its genes at once, so its transcriptome does not include an RNA copy of each protein-coding gene. The transcriptome varies over time within any cell and between cells within an organism.

Proteome: the entire set of proteins produced by a cell. It is based on the transcriptome because proteins are synthesized from the base sequences of mRNA, but the quantities of each protein in a cell are not directly proportional to the quantity of the corresponding mRNAs. The number of molecules of polypeptide translated from each mRNA molecule is regulated as part of the control of gene expression. The pattern of gene expression within a cell determines how that cell differentiates.

6. Methylation

Methylation is replacement of part of a molecule, usually hydrogen, with a methyl group ($-CH_3$). Methyl groups are used as epigenetic tags and have multiple roles in the regulation of gene expression.

1. Methylation of the promoter

Methylation of bases in the promoter prevents binding of some transcription factors, so RNA polymerase does not transcribe the gene downstream of the promoter and it is not expressed. The base that is methylated is usually cytosine (converting it to methylcytosine), but it can also be adenine.

2. Methylation of histones in nucleosomes

The structure of nucleosomes is described in *Section A1.2.13*. Each of the eight histones has its main globular region in the nucleosome core, with a long tail consisting of a chain of amino acids that extends out from the nucleosome. The tails are used to bind adjacent nucleosomes tightly together during condensation of chromosomes, which influences gene expression. Amino acids in the histone tails can have methyl or other groups added. Methylation can cause gene transcription to be activated or repressed depending on which amino acid is the target, because access for transcription factors is increased or decreased.

7. Epigenetic inheritance

Epigenetic tags affect gene expression, so influence phenotypes. Each cell in a multicellular organism has a specific pattern of tags, helping it to produce the proteins needed to perform its functions. The pattern of tags changes during the life of a cell, partly in response to environmental factors. When cells in a tissue divide by mitosis, the pattern of epigenetic tags can be passed on to daughter cells. As a result, the new cells are differentiated for the same functions and changes made to respond to the environment can be conserved.

It had been assumed that all methyl groups and other epigenetic tags would be removed during meiosis and gamete development, so zygotes start life with the "blank canvas" of an undifferentiated cell. There is now evidence that a few epigenetic tags are not removed, so they are passed from parent to offspring and remain in the zygote. This is **transgenerational epigenetic inheritance**. It might allow the environment encountered by one generation to have impacts on gene expression in the next generation. However, epigenetic tags can easily be changed, unlike base sequences which are only altered by random mutations.

8. Environmental effects on gene expression

Air pollution can alter the pattern of epigenetic tags in cells and organisms. Particulates, nitrous oxides, ozone and polyaromatic hydrocarbons in air can decrease DNA methylation across the genome. Expression of genes for proteins that regulate the immune system increases, which may account for increased rates of heart disease, inflammation and asthma.

9. Most epigenetic tags are removed from ovum and sperm

During the production of sperm and eggs in humans, about 99% of epigenetic tags are removed, but some persist into the next generation. This is an example of transgenerational epigenetic inheritance.

Offspring inherit one allele of each autosomal gene from their mother and one from their father. If an individual is heterozygous, with one dominant and one recessive allele, it is the dominant allele which is usually expressed. However, if the dominant allele is silenced by epigenetic tags, the recessive allele will be expressed. As patterns of epigenetic tags can be passed on to daughter cells in mitosis, all cells could then express the recessive allele, despite also having a dominant allele.

Some of the epigenetic tags passed on to the zygote are added during gamete development and there are differences between sperm and eggs in the pattern of these tags. This helps to explain the differences between tigons (♂ tiger × ♀ lion) and ligers (♂ lion × ♀ tiger).

10. Studying twins

Dizygotic (fraternal) twins are formed by release of two eggs during ovulation, with each fertilized by a different sperm. Dizygotic twins share 50% of their genome on average. Monozygotic (identical) twins are formed by splitting of an early-stage embryo to form two parts, each of which develops into a separate individual. Apart from any mutations that may occur, monozygotic twins share all their genes. Any differences in their phenotypes are due to environment, not genotype. They are therefore very useful in research into impacts of the environment on phenotype.

11. External factors that impact gene expression

There are many examples of gene expression being affected by factors external to the cell.

1. Lactase production in the bacterium *E. coli*

A group of genes in *E. coli* codes for proteins needed to absorb and digest lactose, including the gene for lactase. In the absence of lactose, a repressor protein binds to the promoter for this group of genes so they are not expressed. If lactose is present, it enters the cell where it binds to the repressor protein, preventing the repressor from binding to the promoter. This allows RNA polymerase to transcribe the genes, so the cell can utilize lactose in its environment.

Lactose
Lactase
Glucose
Galactose

2. Testosterone—a hormone affecting gene expression

Testosterone secretion and sperm production are described in *Topic D3.1*. Leydig cells in the testes secrete testosterone from puberty onwards. The high testosterone concentrations generated in the testes affect gene expression in cells responsible for sperm production, especially Sertoli (nurse) cells.

Testosterone is a steroid, so it can diffuse into these cells and bind to androgen receptor proteins in the cytoplasm. The testosterone–receptor complexes formed move to the nucleus where they bind to specific DNA base sequences (androgen response elements). This allows other transcription factors to bind to some promoters, resulting in expression of downstream genes. At many other promoters, binding of transcription factors is prevented, so presence of testosterone inhibits expression of genes.

D2.3 Water potential

1. Solvation

Solvents are liquids that can dissolve other substances to make solutions.

Solutes are dissolved substances in solutions.

Solvation is the process of dissolving. Water dissolves many different types of molecules by forming hydrogen bonds with them. It also dissolves many types of ions, because the poles of water molecules are attracted to both positive and negative charges of ions. The solvent properties of water are described in *Section A1.1.5*.

2. Hypertonic, hypotonic and isotonic solutions

Hypertonic—a higher solute concentration

Hypotonic—a lower solute concentration

Isotonic—the same solute concentration.

Water is attracted to the solutes in a solution. Because of this, where water molecules are free to move between two solutions with different solute concentrations, more move from the hypotonic solution to the hypertonic solution than from the hypertonic to the hypotonic. There is therefore a net movement of water up the solute concentration gradient, from the lower to the higher solute concentration.

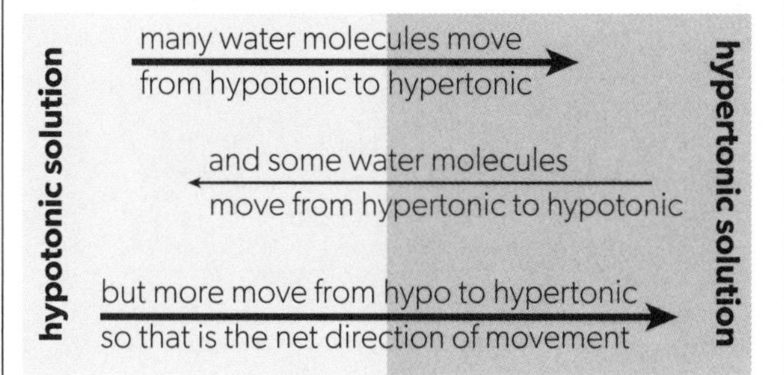

3. Water movement by osmosis

The process of osmosis is described in *Section B2.1.5*. The direction of water movement between cells and their environment can be predicted if the relative solute concentrations are known. The diagrams show three possibilities, with arrows showing the net direction of water movement. When the environment of a cell is isotonic, water molecules do not stop moving, but the numbers moving into and out of the cell are equal, so there is no net movement. This is an example of dynamic equilibrium.

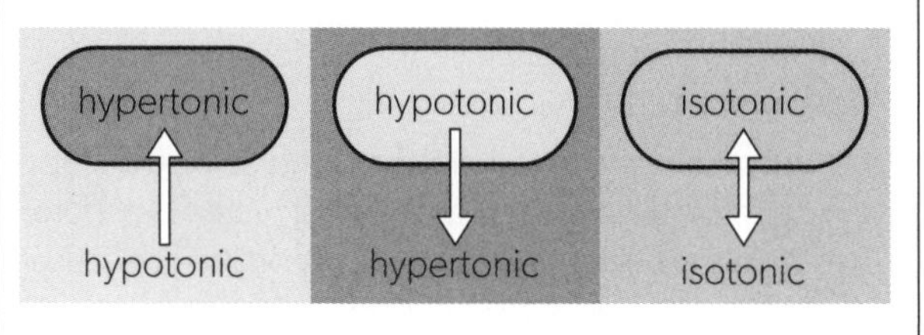

5. Water movement in cells without cell wall

Animal cells and some unicellular organisms have a plasma membrane but no cell wall. If cells without a cell wall are bathed in a hypotonic or hypertonic solution, movement of water by osmosis into or out of the cell can have harmful consequences.

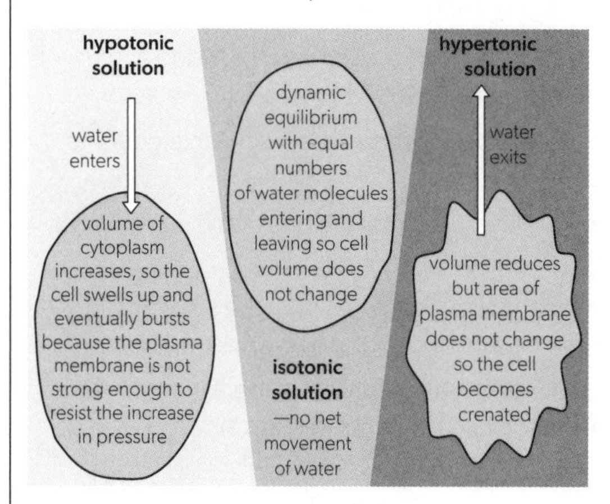

Unicellular organisms that live in freshwater (ponds, lakes and rivers), inevitably take in water by osmosis because their cytoplasm is hypertonic to their environment. To avoid bursting, they must expel water using contractile vacuoles (described in *Section B2.1.13*). Cells inside animals are surrounded by other cells or by extracellular fluids. To prevent swelling or shrinking extracellular fluids must be kept isotonic to cells in the animal. In humans the kidneys are used to regulate the solute concentration of extracellular fluids, including blood plasma.

6. Water movement in cells with a cell wall

Plant cells and some unicellular organisms have both a plasma membrane and a cell wall. The wall protects cells from damage due to hypotonic solutions and allows turgor pressure to develop, but it does not protect against damage from hypertonic solutions. As water moves out of a plant cell into a hypertonic medium, any turgor pressure in the cell is lost and the volume of the cytoplasm decreases. A gap develops between the cell wall and the plasma membrane. A cell in this state is **plasmolysed** and does not usually recover.

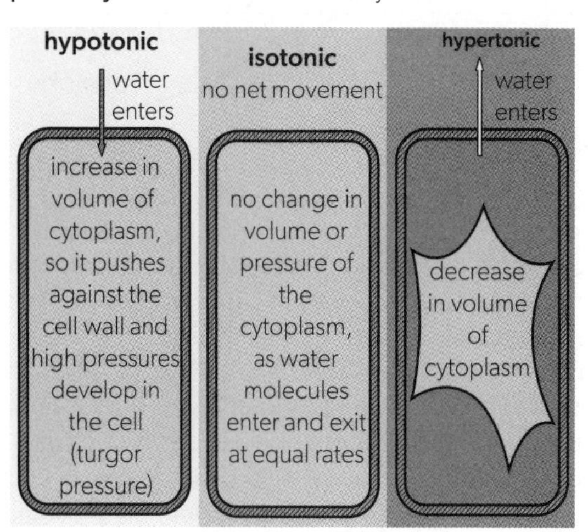

4. Application of skills: deducing isotonic solute concentration for plant tissues

Method

1. Prepare a series of sugar or salt solutions with a range of solute concentrations, from 0.0 mol dm^{-3} upwards. The solute could be glucose, sucrose, sodium chloride or another salt.

2. Cut potato or other plant tissue into samples of equal size and shape, such as cylinders or cuboids.

3. Measure the length of each sample, using a ruler with millimetre graduations.

4. Find the mass of each sample, using an electronic balance.

5. Bathe each tissue sample in one of the solutions for between one and twenty-four hours.

6. Remove the tissue samples from the solutions, dry them and measure their length and mass again.

7. Calculate percentage mass change. Percentage length change can be calculated in a similar way.

$$\% \text{ change} = \frac{(\text{final mass} - \text{initial mass})}{\text{initial mass}} \times 100$$

8. Plot the results for % mass change or % length change on a graph.

9. Read off the solute concentration which would give no mass change due to being isotonic.

The graph shows results for two tissues, pumpkin (*Cucurbita pepo*) and sweet potato (*Ipomoea batatas*).

- The curve for the sweet potato tissue intercepts the *x*-axis at 0.37 mol dm^{-3}, so this is the predicted NaCl concentration at which mass would not change, because there would be no net movement of water. The conclusion is that this concentration of NaCl is isotonic to the sweet potato tissue.
- The curve for pumpkin tissue can be analysed in the same way, with the conclusion that a solution with a concentration of 0.55 mol dm^{-3} NaCl would be isotonic. The pumpkin cells have a higher solute concentration than the sweet potato cells.

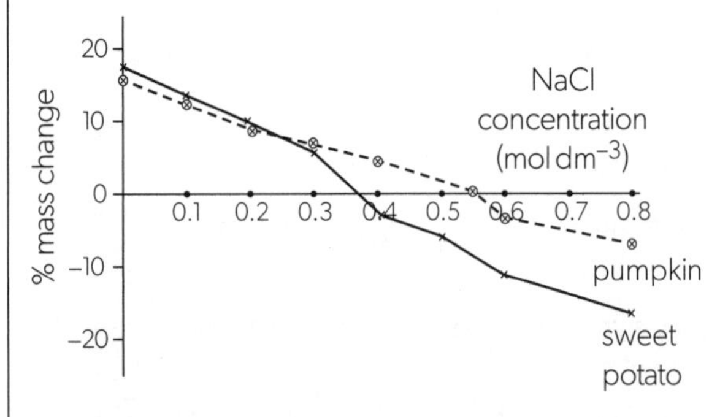

There were no repeats in this experiment—only one sample of tissue was placed in each NaCl concentration. Scientists usually repeat every treatment in their experiments. This helps to avoid drawing conclusions from atypical or anomalous results. It allows the reliability of results to be assessed—the closer together repeats are, the greater the reliability. This can be assessed in an objective and quantitative way, using the statistics **standard deviation** and **standard error of the mean.**

Sample—a sample is a small, representative portion of something. In experiments, the results are a sample of all the results that could possibly have been obtained, so sample size is the number of repeats.

Standard deviation is a measure of variation from the mean. It is almost always calculated using a computer or calculator, so there is no need to learn the formula. Standard deviation is based on calculating the difference between each individual result and the mean result and then squaring the answers. If some results are far from the mean the standard deviation is high, indicating that the data are widely spread.

Standard error is a measure of how reliably the mean of a sample estimates the mean of the whole population. It is found by dividing the sample standard deviation by the square root of the sample size.

Example: Ten samples of carrot tissue were bathed in concentrations of NaCl solution ranging from 0.0 to 0.8 mol dm^{-3}. All the samples were initially 100 mm long and even in thickness. The graph shows mean length after 24 hours, with bars to show mean ± standard error. These error bars show most variation in length at 0.6 and least at 0.2 mol dm^{-3}. A statistical hypothesis test was performed (Student *t*-test).

Analysis

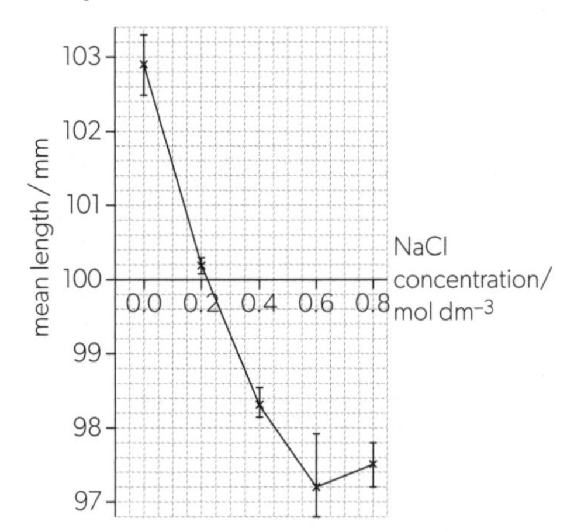

- Differences between the mean length for 0.0 mol dm^{-3} and means for other concentrations were significant at the 1% level.
- The same was true for differences between the mean for 0.2 mol dm^{-3} and means for other concentrations.
- Differences between the mean for 0.4 mol dm^{-3} and both 0.6 and 0.8 were significant at the 5% level.
- No significant difference was found between 0.6 and 0.8 mol dm^{-3}.

Conclusions

- Length increased at 0.2 mol dm^{-3} or less due to water uptake and cells swelling slightly.
- Length decreased at 0.4 mol dm^{-3} and above, due to the cells shrinking slightly as they lost water, but there was no further decrease above 0.6 mol dm^{-3} because plasmolysis had already occurred and the cell walls prevented further decreases in length.

7. Using isotonic solutions in medicine

Osmosis can cause cells in human tissues to either swell and burst, or shrink, due to gain or loss of water. To prevent this, isotonic fluids must be used for some medical procedures.

- Intravenous fluids, injected into veins from a syringe or from an elevated bag, must be close to isotonic to avoid osmotic damage to blood cells.
- Tissues or organs used in medical procedures such as kidney transplants must be bathed in an isotonic solution or isotonic slush (crushed ice) to prevent osmotic damage.

AHL

8. Water potential

Water potential is a measure of the potential energy per unit volume. The symbol for water potential is Ψ (the Greek letter psi) and the units are kilopascals (kPa) or megapascals (MPa). The absolute quantity of potential energy cannot be determined, so all values are relative. Pure water at standard atmospheric pressure and 20°C has been assigned a water potential of zero.

9. Water moves from higher to lower water potential

Water potential allows us to predict the direction of net movement of water molecules. Water moves from a higher to a lower water potential because this minimizes its potential energy. The range of water potentials found in cells is rather unusual—the maximum value is zero. Cells either have a potential of 0 kPa or a negative value, for example −200 kPa in a leaf cell. Lower water potentials are therefore more negative. For example, water moves from a cell with a water potential of −200 kPa to one with −300 kPa.

10. Solute potential and pressure potential

Many factors can influence water potential (Ψ_w) but in living systems only two contributors vary in such a way that they need to be considered:

1. Solute potential (Ψ_s)

Bond formation releases energy. The release of energy during solvation by formation of solute–water bonds reduces the potential energy held by water. This reduction is the solute potential (sometimes called the osmotic potential). With no solutes dissolved in water, solute potential is at its maximum of zero. The more solutes that are dissolved, the more negative it becomes.

2. Pressure potential (Ψ_p)

Rises or falls in hydrostatic pressure change the potential energy of water. The higher the pressure, the more potential energy water has. Atmospheric pressure is defined as having a pressure potential of zero. Pressure potential can be negative or positive because it can be greater or less than atmospheric pressure. Plant cells are usually turgid (above atmospheric pressure) so they have a positive pressure potential, but sap in xylem vessels is usually pulled up to the leaves under tension, so pressure potentials there are negative.

Water potential is the sum of solute potential and pressure potential: $\Psi_w = \Psi_s + \Psi_p$

State	Ψ_w	Explanation	
Fully turgid	zero	Ψ_p is positive but is cancelled out by the negative Ψ_s	$-\Psi_s = \Psi_p$
Partially turgid	−ve	Ψ_p is positive but Ψ_s is more negative, so Ψ_w is negative	$-\Psi_s > \Psi_p$
Flaccid	−ve	Ψ_p is zero, so as Ψ_s and Ψ_w are equal. Ψ_s is very negative, so Ψ_w is also very negative	$\Psi_w = \Psi_s$
Xylem vessel	−ve	If xylem sap is under tension, Ψ_p and Ψ_s are negative so Ψ_w is extremely negative	

11. Water potential in plant tissue

Water movement in plant tissue is always passive, with direction of net movement determined by differences in water potential.

1. Plant tissue bathed in pure water

In pure water, $\Psi_w = 0$.

Water moves into the plant cells until they are fully turgid so $\Psi_w = 0$.

2. Plant tissue in a hypotonic solution

Ψ_s is more negative in the plant tissue than in the solution, so we expect water to move from the solution to the tissue. However, if the plant tissue is initially fully turgid ($\Psi_w = 0$), some water may move from the tissue to the solution until their water potentials are equal.

3. Plant tissue bathed in hypertonic solution

Ψ_s is more negative in the solution than in the plant tissue, so water moves from the tissue to the solution. As water leaves the cells, their pressure potential decreases. If it reaches zero (atmospheric pressure), the cells become flaccid (limp). If water continues to move from cell to solution, the volume of cytoplasm becomes less than the space inside the cell wall and the plasma membrane is pulled away from the cell wall (plasmolysis). However, this may not happen because loss of water concentrates the cytoplasm, so a dynamic equilibrium may be reached between the cytoplasm and the solution before plasmolysis occurs.

4. Adjacent cells with different water potentials

Water moves by osmosis from the cell with higher water potential to the cell with the lower water potential. The net movement continues until the water potential of the two cells is equal. For example, in the leaf sucrose is pumped into phloem cells, making Ψ_s more negative and therefore lowering Ψ_w, so water moves from adjacent cells into the phloem cells.

End of topic questions—D2 Questions

D2.1 Cell and nuclear division

1. The micrograph shows cells in a root tip.

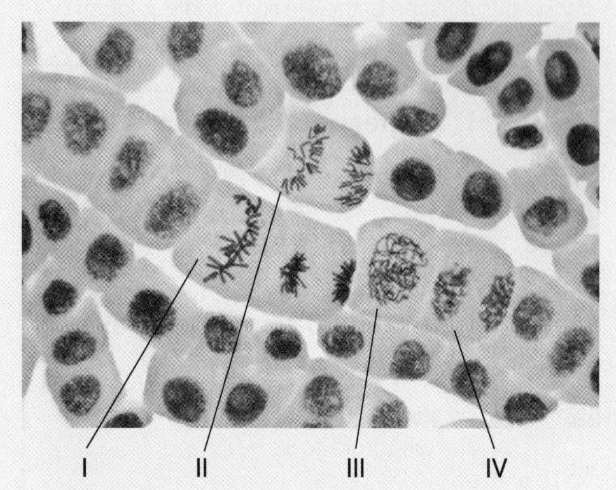

a. Identify the stage of mitosis in cells **I–IV**. (4)

b. State two processes that must occur in a plant cell before mitosis starts. (2)

c. (HL only) Calculate the mitotic index.

2. The micrograph below shows a pair of homologous chromosomes in a cell carrying out meiosis in the grasshopper *Chorthippus parallelus*.

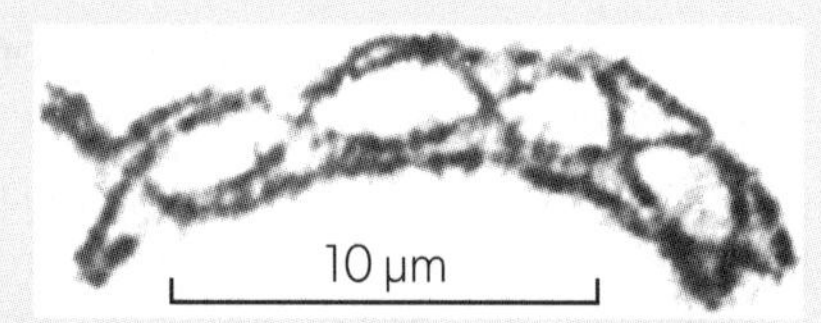

a. Identify the stage of meiosis of the cell that contained the pair of chromosomes. (2)

b. State how many chromatids are visible. (1)

c. Cross-shaped structures (chiasmata) are visible.

i. State how many chiasmata are present. (1)

ii. Explain how the chiasmata were formed. (3)

3. (HL only) Describe the factors that determine whether a tumour is life-threatening of not. (5)

D2.2 Gene expression (HL)

1. The table shows the percentage of twins that share six traits (H = Height, A = Autism, BD = Bipolar disease, D = Diabetes, BC = Breast cancer, S = Stroke).

Type of twins	H	A	BD	D	BC	S
Monozygotic (%)	89	58	38	28	19	17
Dizygotic (%)	58	21	7	2	11	4

a. Explain the reasons for monozygotic twins being more similar in these traits than dizygotic twins. (3)

b. Explain the reasons for monozygotic twins not being identical in their traits. (3)

c. Discuss differences between monozygotic twins in epigenetic tags and whether they are heritable. (3)

d. Suggest a trait shared by 100% of monozygotic twins. (1)

2. a. Explain how testosterone affects gene expression. (5)

b. Outline how gene expression is preventable at these three stages:

i. transcription (3) ii. translation (3)

iii. functioning of a protein. (4)

3. Explain how environmental variation can promote diversity by:

a. differentiation of cells in early-stage embryos (3)

b. phenotypic plasticity in organisms (3)

c. divergence of reproductively isolated populations. (4)

D2.3 Water potential

1. The table gives the results of an experiment in which samples taken from a potato tuber were bathed in solutions with different sucrose concentrations.

Concentration of sucrose (mol dm^{-3})	0.0	0.2	0.4	0.6
Initial mass (g)	22.5	21.8	23.7	22.2
Final mass (g)	25.9	22.9	22.8	18.7
Mass change (g)	+3.4			–3.5
% mass change				–16%

a. Complete the table. (3)

b. Draw a graph to display the percentage mass changes. (4)

c. Estimate the sucrose concentration that would be isotonic with the potato tissue. Explain your reasoning. (3)

2. Water molecules pass in and out of cells via the plasma membrane. Discuss how this is affected by:

a. solute concentrations inside and outside the cell (3)

b. aquaporins (4)

c. (AHL only) pressure potentials inside and outside the cell. (3)

3. (HL) ψ_w (water potential) in soil is 0.1–1.0 MPa whereas ψ_w in air is 10–200 MPa. Explain what causes water in a transpiring plant to move from:

a. soil to cortex cells in the root (3)

b. cortex cells in the root to xylem vessels (3)

c. xylem vessels to spongy mesophyll cells in the leaf (2)

d. spongy mesophyll cells to the air. (2)

4. Organisms differ in how they regulate water movement.

a. Explain how freshwater unicellular organisms regulate their water content. (4)

b. (AHL only) Explain how plants generate root pressure. (4)

A3.1 Diversity of organisms

1. Variation between organisms

An **organism** is an individual plant, animal, bacterium or any other living thing. Variation is one of the key features of living organisms. The patterns of variation are complex and are the basis for naming and classifying organisms.

- There is variation between members of a single species. No two individuals are identical in all their traits.
- There is more variation between members of different species. If the traits of two closely related species are compared, for example humans and chimpanzees, relatively few differences are found. If two distantly related species are compared, such as humans and redwood trees, or *E. coli* bacteria, major differences are observed.

2. Defining a species

From the 17th century onwards, biologists used the term "species" for a group of organisms with shared traits. Biologists have been naming and classifying species ever since. Carl Linnaeus was a pioneer of this research in the 18th century. Linnaeus described the morphology of species—the outward form and inner structure. The idea of a species as a group of organisms with a characteristic outward form and inner structure is the **morphological concept** of a species. For example, *Apodemus sylvaticus* is a species of mouse with characteristic morphology that occurs across much of Europe from Ukraine to France. Mice with similar traits live on many islands including Iceland. They are considered to be part of the same species, despite being unable to breed with populations in mainland Europe.

3. Binomial naming system

When species are discovered, they are given scientific names using the **binomial system**. This system is universal among biologists and has been agreed and developed at a series of international congresses. It avoids the confusion that would result from using the many different local names that can exist for a species. The binomial system is a very good example of cooperation and collaboration between groups of scientists.

The binomial system has these features:

- The first name is the genus name. A genus is a group of closely related species.
- The genus name is given an upper case first letter.
- The second name is the species name.
- The species name is given a lower case first letter.
- Italics are used when a binomial appears in a printed or typed document.

Examples of binomials:

- Animals: *Homo sapiens*—humans
- Plants: *Scrophularia landroveri*—a plant discovered by an expedition that travelled in a Land Rover
- Fungi: *Candida auris*—a yeast that can cause severe infections in humans
- Bacteria: *Yersinia pestis*—the microorganism that causes bubonic plague (Black Death).

Viruses are not given binomials as they are not considered to be living organisms.

4. Defining the biological species concept

The morphological species concept was based on an expectation of clear differences in structure between all species. The concept works well in some groups of organisms, but not in other groups. An alternative species concept was developed, based on the understanding that interbreeding continuing generation after generation prevents members of a species from diverging. This is the biological species concept: **a species is a group of organisms that can successfully interbreed and produce fertile offspring**. By interbreeding, members of a species share the genes in a gene pool, so share many traits. By not interbreeding, different species can diverge and develop more and more differences.

The biological species concept works well with some groups of organisms. For example, the genus *Allium* contains hundreds of species, including onion and garlic, but few interspecific hybrids have been reported in natural habitats and these hybrids are usually sterile.

The biological species concept is very difficult to apply in other groups of plants and animals. Fertile offspring may be produced by hybridization between individuals that are clearly members of different species in terms of morphology, such as lions and tigers. Other challenges to the biological species concept are explained in *Section A3.1.12*. Many other species definitions have been proposed. This is a part of biology where consensus has not yet been achieved.

5. Speciation

Species sometimes become separated into populations that cannot breed with each other. Populations that do not interbreed and live in different environments tend to diverge over time in their traits. Changes may be very gradual and take place over thousands of years or even longer, but eventually the populations become so different that they would not be able to interbreed, even if by migration they encountered each other again. The populations have therefore become separate species. This is speciation—the splitting of one species into two (see *Topic A4.1*).

When taxonomists try to classify living organisms into species, there is often much argument about whether populations in different geographical areas are part of the same species or belong to different species. This is because of the gradual accumulation of differences between populations over time. The rate at which this occurs varies from negligible to rapid. There is no instant in time when one species becomes two, and the decision whether two populations are regarded as the same or different species is somewhat arbitrary.

6. Chromosome number differs among plant and animal species

The number of chromosomes is a characteristic feature of members of a species.

It varies considerably—some species have fewer large chromosomes and others have a greater number of small chromosomes.

The chromosome number that is given for each species is the diploid number, so it is even rather than odd.

Canis familiaris (dog) 78
***Homo sapiens* (humans) 46**
***Pan troglodytes* (chimpanzee) 48**
Oryza sativa (rice) 24
Cricotopus sylvestris (a midge) 4

7. Application of skills: karyotyping and karyograms

Karyotype is the number and type of chromosomes present in a cell or organism.

Karyograms are photographs or diagrams in which the chromosomes of an organism are shown in homologous pairs of decreasing length. Karyograms are prepared so that the karyotype of an individual can be studied. They also provide evidence of speciation history of species.

To prepare a karyogram, cells in metaphase of mitosis are examined microscopically. A cell where none of the chromosomes are overlapping is photographed. The image is processed digitally so the chromosomes can be classified into homologous pairs. Three features help with this:

- Some stains give chromosomes distinctive banding patterns, with different banding in each type of homologous chromosome.
- Chromosomes vary in size. In humans, the largest (chromosome 1) is more than five times longer than the shortest (chromosome 21).
- Each chromosome has a centromere, where there is a constriction in the chromatids. The position of the centromere is fixed for each chromosome type and can be anywhere from close to one end, to exactly central.

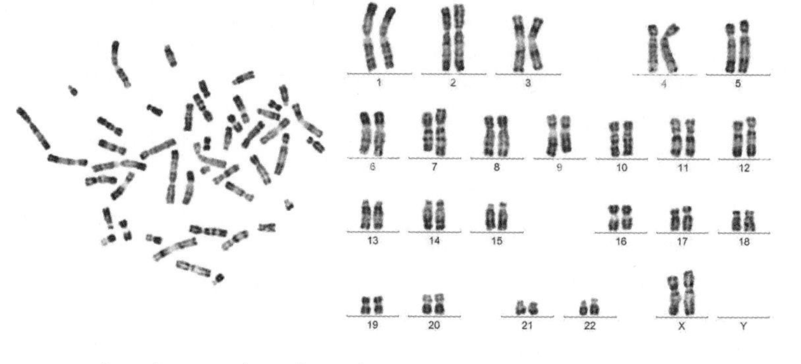

A metaphase spread of human chromosomes is shown above, with the karyogram prepared from them.

Humans have 46 chromosomes whereas our closest relatives (chimpanzees, gorillas and orangutans) all have 48. A reasonable hypothesis to explain the difference is that our ancestors, millions of years ago, had 48 chromosomes but at some point during human evolution, two of them became fused together.

Evidence for this hypothesis comes from chromosome banding patterns. The banding pattern of human chromosome 2 is very similar to the banding of chromosomes 12 and 13 in chimpanzees. Chromosomes normally have one telomere at each end and one centromere. In addition to these structures, human chromosome 2 has a region in the centre with base sequences of telomeres and also an extra vestigial centromere.

human chromosome 2

chimp chromosome 13

chimp chromosome 12

The banding patterns and remnants of extra telomeres and an extra centromere are strong evidence for the hypothesis, which is widely accepted by scientists. No other hypotheses are currently being considered for humans having fewer chromosomes than chimpanzees and other primates.

NOS

Falsification of hypotheses

The hypothesis that human chromosome 2 was formed by fusion of two chromosomes in an ancestor cannot ultimately be proved with certainty, but this is not expected by scientists. The evidence for the hypothesis is strong enough for there to be widespread agreement. For a hypothesis to be scientific, it must be testable, either experimentally or using observations, so hypotheses can be shown to be false and therefore replaced. The hypothesis about the origins of chromosome 2 is certainly testable—evidence could be obtained showing it to be false, so it is scientific.

8. Genomes in a species show unity and diversity

A genome is all of the genetic information of one individual organism or group of organisms. It is the entire base sequence of each of the DNA molecules (chromosomes). A genome contains functional units called genes. A gene is a length of DNA carrying a sequence of hundreds or even thousands of bases. Typically, the members of a species have the same genes, in the same sequence, along each of their chromosomes. This allows parts of the chromosomes to be exchanged during meiosis, promoting genetic diversity in a species without any genes being omitted or duplicated. The genome of a species and the arrangement of genes on the chromosomes is therefore an illustration of the unity in living organisms.

Diversity in the genomes of a species is largely due to variation in individual genes. Alternative forms of a gene, called alleles, often exist within a species. The alleles of a gene differ from each other in base sequence. Usually only one or a very small number of bases are different—for example, one allele might have adenine at a certain base position while another allele might have cytosine in that position. Sometimes larger sections of a gene become altered, but this usually results in loss of gene function.

Positions in a gene where alternative bases may be present are called single nucleotide polymorphisms, abbreviated to SNPs and pronounced "snips". Millions of individual human genomes have been sequenced, allowing researchers to assess the frequency of SNPs. More than 100 million different SNPs have been discovered so far in human genomes. This seems a huge number but remember there are over three billion base pairs in our genome. Most bases are therefore the same in all humans—another illustration of unity.

Within one individual, there are typically about 4,000–5,000 SNPs, so only about 1 base in 650,000 is different from that commonly occurring in humans. This may seem a low level of diversity but these SNPs are the main factor in making humans different from each other, unless we have an identical twin.

These positions are regarded as single nucleotide polymorphisms (SNPs) because at least 1% of individuals have a different base from the others.

These bases vary in fewer than 1% of individuals. If a different base is present, it is regarded as a mutation rather than an SNP.

paternal allele AACTGGACTT**G**AAGCATCTACGTT**A**TCCATGAAG

maternal allele AACTGGACTT**G**AAGCATCTACGTT**C**TCCTGAAGA

The child is homozygous for this SNP because the alleles inherited from their parents have the same base.

The child is heterozygous for this SNP because the alleles inherited from the mother and father have a different base.

9. Variation in genomes between species

There is much more variation in genomes **between** species than **within** species. There are two aspects to the variation between species.

1. Variation in genome size

Genome size is the total amount of DNA in a species. There is immense variation in eukaryotes. Genes can be added to genomes or removed and sections of chromosome can be duplicated or deleted. The chromosome number can increase or decrease. Addition of whole sets of chromosomes (polyploidy) is described for HL in *Section A4.1.11*. Genomes vary considerably in the amount of non-coding DNA, described for HL in *Section D1.2.14*.

2. Variation in base sequence

Two populations of a species will differ at certain positions in their base sequences. If these populations diverge to form separate species, more differences will accumulate over time. Over hundreds of millions of years, immense diversity has developed in the base sequences of the millions of species that have evolved from the last common ancestor of all organisms (described for HL in *Section A2.1.7*). However, in some genes there are few base sequence differences, even between distantly related species. These are genes with a vital function, such as the gene for cytochrome c—a protein all organisms use in respiration.

10. Application of skills: using databases to compare genome size

Genome size varies considerably and is correlated with organism complexity, but is not directly proportional, with some unexpectedly large genomes.

DNA content data for many species of microbe are available from these four independent databases:

- cvalues.science.kew.org
- www.genomesize.com
- www.zbi.ee/fungal-genomesize
- www.ncbi.nlm.nih.gov/genome/microbes

In eukaryotes, genome sizes are given as nuclear DNA contents of a haploid cell such as a gamete (C-values). In prokaryotes, they are given as the DNA content of a typical cell. Measurements are either in mass (usually picograms; 1 pg = 10^{-12} grams) or in number of base pairs or megabase pairs (1 Mbp = 10^6 base pairs).

11. Uses of whole genome sequencing

Whole genome sequencing is determining the entire base sequence of an organism's DNA. It was first done in the 1990s with prokaryotes, which have small genomes, but can now be done for any organism. The speed of sequencing is increasing rapidly and the cost is decreasing. Growth in the number of species with one or more sequences completed is exponential. The Earth BioGenome Project aims to sequence the genomes of all known species. Comparisons between genomes reveal relationships between species and **evolutionary origins** from common ancestors.

Over one million individual human genomes have been sequenced, increasing understanding of human origins and migrations throughout the world and providing more data than ever about genetic diseases and genes that affect human health. In future, it may be possible to sequence the genome of every person. This could lead to **personalized medicine**. If the SNPs and other genetic features in a person's genome are known, it will be easier to predict health problems and prescribe appropriate drugs and other treatments.

AHL

12. Asexual reproduction and horizontal gene transfer defy the biological species concept

The biological species concept works well with many groups of species, but not with species that reproduce asexually or have methods of horizontal gene transfer.

Asexually reproducing species

If members of a species interbreed by sexual reproduction, their traits are remixed every generation. Many species reproduce both sexually and asexually, but as long as there is some interbreeding in a species, divergence between individuals is prevented and the biological species concept can be applied. Some species only reproduce asexually so all offspring are clones of their single parent. As the clones do not interbreed with each other, each is a separate species according to the biological species concept. Mutations cause clones to split, so there are increasing numbers of different clones. Blackberries (*Rubus fruticosus*) are an example of this (despite them producing flowers suggesting sexual reproduction). Hundreds of blackberry clones have been named as separate species but only a few experts can identify these "microspecies". A better policy is to accept organisms that abandon sexual reproduction are no longer species according to the biological species concept.

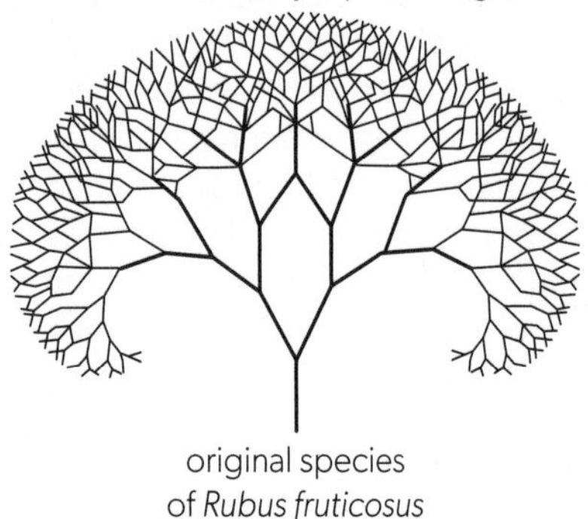

Bacteria with horizontal gene transfer

The evolution of life is often thought to resemble a tree, starting with a single trunk and repeated branches leading to individual species. Once formed, a branch remains separate and does not re-join other branches, because species do not interbreed with other species, so their genes remain separate. Genome sequencing has revealed that between bacteria this separation is not absolute. Genes are sometimes transferred from one species to another and even between distantly related species. This process is called horizontal gene transfer, in contrast with the usual vertical transfer from parent to offspring. Horizontal gene transfer is frequent among bacteria. For example, it is how antibiotic resistance genes can move from one species to another. In fact, there is so much gene transfer between bacteria that it is debatable whether the biological species concept (or any other species concept) can work with prokaryotes.

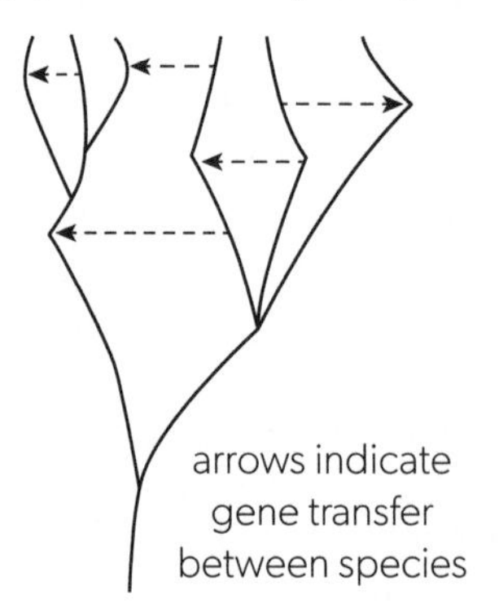

AHL

13. Importance of chromosome number for producing fertile offspring

If two organisms with different chromosome numbers mated and produced offspring, the offspring would almost certainly have problems in carrying out meiosis. Some chromosomes would not be homologous to any other chromosome, so they would not be able to pair during metaphase 1, and segregation of chromosomes into two haploid groups in anaphase 1 would fail. The cells produced by meiosis would not be viable, so gametes could not be produced. This is why offspring of parents with different chromosome numbers are usually infertile. It is the reason for members of a species usually having the same number of chromosomes as each other (see *Section A3.1.6*). Halving of the chromosome number in meiosis and doubling in fertilization is described in *Section D2.1.9*.

14. Application of skills: using and constructing dichotomous keys

Dichotomous keys are used to identify species that are not immediately recognized.

They have these features:

- The key consists of a series of numbered stages.
- Each stage consists of a pair of alternative characteristics.
- Some alternatives state which numbered stage of the key to go to next.
- Some alternatives state the name of the species.

Example: Key for identifying aquarium pondweed:

1. Simple undivided leaves .... *Elodea*
   Leaves forked or divided into segments .... go to 2
2. Leaves forked once or twice into 2–4 segments ..... *Ceratophyllum*
   Leaves divided into more than 4 segments .... go to 3
3. Leaves divided into many flattened segments ....*Cabomba*
   Leaves divided into many filamentous segments .....*Myriophyllum*

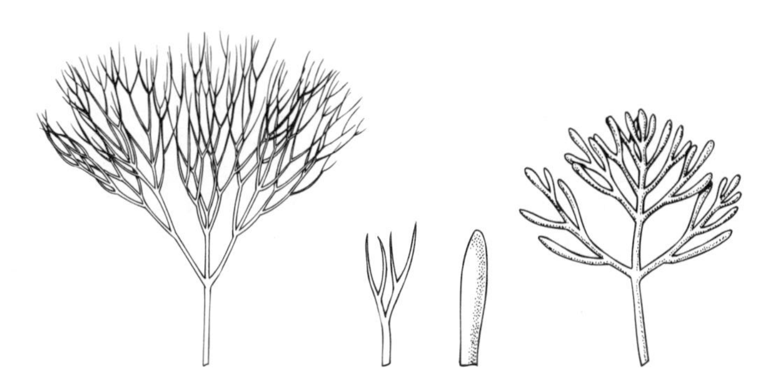

leaves of aquarium plants

Study specimens of a group of plants or animals from your local area and construct a dichotomous key for identifying them. The number of stages in the key should be the same as the number of species, minus one.

The five animals shown below are found in beehives. It would be useful to construct a dichotomous key to allow a beekeeper to identify them, as some of them are very harmful and others are harmless to honey bees.

The most useful keys use characteristics that are easy to observe and are reliable, because they are present in every member of the species.

Galleria mellonella is a species of moth and has three pairs of legs.

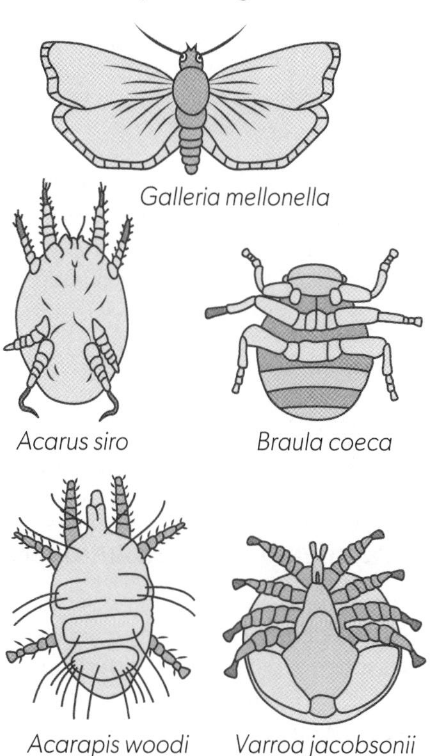

15. Identifying species using barcodes and environmental DNA

DNA barcodes are short sections of DNA from one gene, or at most several genes, that are distinctive enough to identify a species. **Environmental DNA** is obtained from samples of water, soil or any other part of the abiotic environment. Typically, there is DNA from a wide diversity of organisms that have interacted with the sampled environment. DNA barcoding allows scientists to identify these organisms. This advance in technology is allowing the biodiversity of habitats to be investigated rapidly. In a recent case, samples taken from waterholes in northern Australia were analysed using DNA barcodes. This analysis showed that Gouldian finches (*Chloebia gouldiae*), an increasingly rare bird species, had visited the waterholes.

A3.2 Classification and cladistics

AHL

1. Classification systems

A classification system is needed for these reasons:

- **Information storage and retrieval**

  Millions of species have been named and described. More are discovered every day. Biologists have accumulated huge amounts of knowledge about these species. Classification makes it easier to store and retrieve this information.

- **Identification—finding an organism's species name**

  Biologists often need to identify organisms that they do not immediately recognize. It is usually obvious which large group an organism belongs to, for example if it has flowers it is an angiosperm (flowering plant). The organism can then be assigned to one of the sub-groups in the larger group and so on into successively smaller and smaller groups, until the genus and species of the unrecognized organism are identified so its scientific name (binomial) is known. (Use of dichotomous keys in identification is described in *Section A3.1.14.*)

- **Predictive value**

  Species in a classificatory group share many traits, so the characteristics of a species can be predicted from its group.

- **Researching evolutionary origins**

  The classification system groups species that share traits. Species share traits if they evolved from a common ancestor. The classification system can therefore be used to generate hypotheses about evolutionary origins of species.

2. Disadvantages of the traditional hierarchy of taxa

Taxa are groups used to classify organisms, for example phyla, classes and orders.

One taxonomic group is a **taxon**.

Taxonomy is assigning organisms to taxonomic groups.

In the traditional hierarchy of taxa, a genus contains species, a family contains genera and so on. Moving up through this hierarchy, the taxa contain larger and larger numbers of species that share fewer and fewer traits.

In practice, it is often difficult to classify organisms according to this hierarchy.

- It can be unclear how populations should be grouped into species (see *Section A3.1.5*).

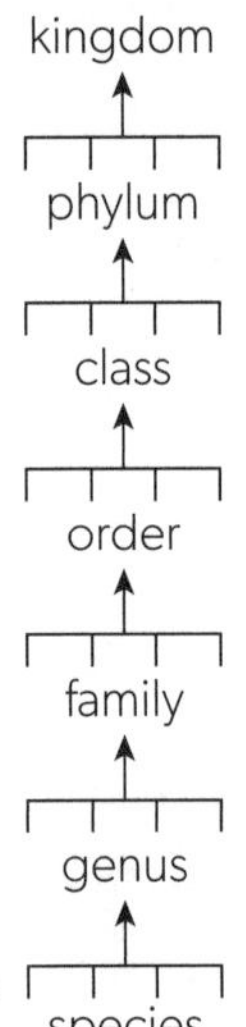

- There can then be disagreement about how species should be grouped into genera or larger groups.
- Even when taxonomists agree on which species should be classified in the same group, they often disagree over what taxonomic rank the grouping should have. One taxonomist might think the traits in a group of species are similar enough to form a genus; another might think they are different enough to be a family.

These uncertainties are a result of the gradual divergence of species and larger groups over time. The instant in time when a group splits into two or more groups cannot be determined objectively so taxonomic rankings within the hierarchy from domain to genus are inevitably rather arbitrary.

3. Classifying using evolutionary relationships

Biologists agree that an ideal classification should follow evolutionary relationships, so all the members of a taxonomic group have evolved from a common ancestor. Two criteria can be used to judge whether a classification achieves this:

- Every organism that has evolved from a common ancestor is included in the same taxonomic group. In the example below, Group A fails this criterion.
- In each taxonomic group, all the species are evolved from the same common ancestor. Group B fails this criterion in the example below.

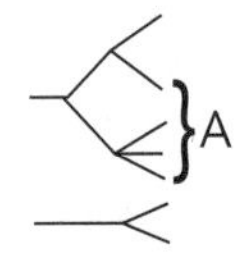

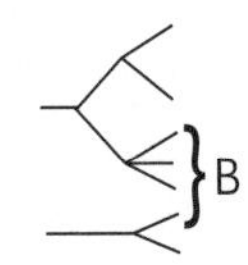

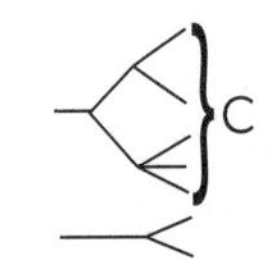

If these criteria are satisfied (as Group C in the example above), all members of a taxonomic group will share traits inherited from their common ancestor. Sharing of traits between members of a taxonomic group allows biologists to make predictions based on classification.

For example, new species of bat are sometimes discovered. Because bats are classified as mammals, predictions can be made with reasonable certainty: a new species of bat will have a four-chambered heart, hair, mammary glands, a placenta and therefore a navel (belly button), plus many other mammalian features.

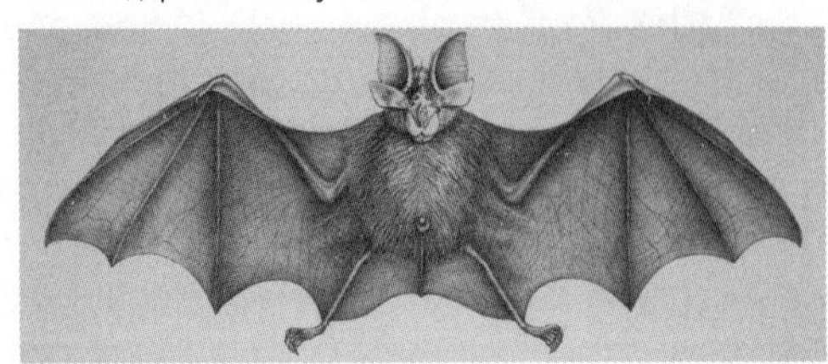

▲ *Rhinolophus pearsonii* (Pearson's horseshoe bat)

NOS

Theories

A paradigm is an ideal example for demonstrating a theory. Sometimes there are revolutions in science when a theory that has been widely accepted is abandoned and replaced by a new theory. When this happens, a shift takes place from old to new paradigms.

In the 1990s, when base sequence data became available for increasing numbers of species, it became obvious that a fixed ranking of taxa (kingdom, phylum and so on) is arbitrary because it does not reflect the gradual divergence of species. An alternative approach to classification that avoids this problem has therefore become widely accepted. This is **cladistics,** in which groups of species that have evolved from a common ancestor (clades) are identified, but they are not given a rank such as order or family. The new classifications produced by cladistics are examples of paradigm shift.

AHL

4. Organisms in a clade have common ancestry and shared characteristics

Due to the difficulties in classifying species according to the traditional hierarchy of taxa, an alternative approach is increasingly used, based on clades. A **clade** is a group of organisms that have evolved from a common ancestor. It includes the ancestral species and all species evolved from it, whether alive today or now extinct. Because of this common ancestry, species in a clade share characteristics.

Taxus baccata (yew)
Cephalotaxus fortunei
Cupressus sempervirens (cypress)
Araucaria araucana (monkey puzzle)
Podocarpus totara
Pinus radiata (Monterey pine)
Ephedra sinica
Welwitschia mirabilis
Gnetum africanum
Ginkgo biloba

▲ *Cladogram for non-seed plants (gymnosperms)*

It is not always obvious which species have evolved from a common ancestor and should therefore be included in a clade. The most objective evidence comes from base sequences of genes or amino acid sequences of proteins. The genomes of organisms contain a huge amount of information, from which their evolutionary history can be deduced. If sequence data are not available, morphological traits can be used to assign organisms to clades. This is particularly useful with species that have become extinct and for which sequence data are not available, so the only evidence comes from fossils.

Every species is in multiple clades, not just one. Smaller clades are "nested" within larger clades. For example, *Araucaria araucana* (in the cladogram above) is in a clade with *Podocarpus totara* because they share a common ancestor. That clade is nested in a larger clade with *Taxus baccata* and other species. That larger clade is nested in an even larger clade with *Pinus radiata* and other species. Finally, that clade is nested with *Ginkgo biloba* in a clade that includes all 10 of these species, plus all other gymnosperms (non-flowering seed plants).

Clades can include many living species, or just a few. For example, *Pinus radiata* is in a clade with 112 other species of pine, all evolved from a common ancestor. In contrast, *Ginkgo biloba* is the only living member of a clade that evolved about 270 million years ago. *Yimaia recurva* is an extinct member of this clade, that lived 170 million years ago.

▲ *Ginkgo biloba*

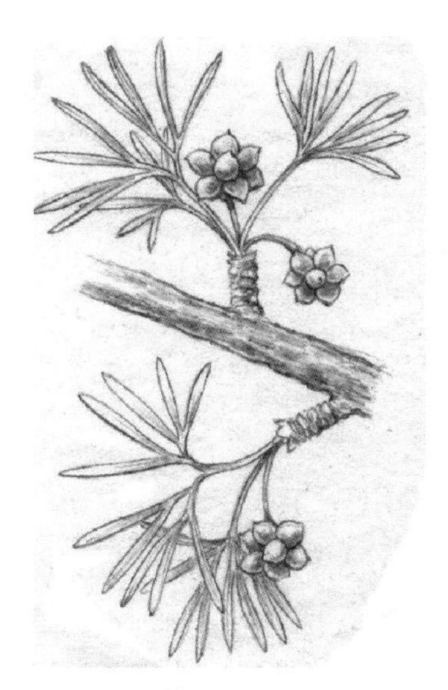

▲ *Yimaia recurva*

AHL

5. The "molecular clock"

Differences in the base sequence of DNA and therefore in the amino acid sequence of proteins, are the result of mutations. These differences accumulate gradually over long periods of time. If we assume that this happens at a roughly constant rate, we can use the number of differences to estimate the time since two species diverged from a common ancestor. This method of estimating time is known as the molecular clock. The larger the number of sequence differences between two species, the longer since they diverged from a common ancestor.

When considering timings based on the molecular clock, it is important to remember the assumption that has been made—that mutations accumulate at a constant rate. In fact, the mutation rate can vary. It is affected by length of the generation time, size of the population, intensity of selective pressure and other factors. Thus, the molecular clock can only give estimates.

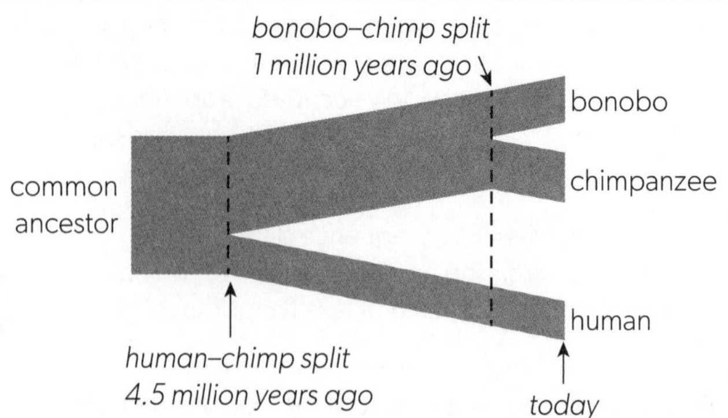

Base sequence differences have been used to estimate when humans, bonobos and chimpanzees diverged, assuming a mutation rate of 10^{-9} yr^{-1}. Using variations in the base sequence of mitochondrial DNA as a molecular clock, the most recent common ancestor of all humans is estimated to have lived 150,000 years ago.

6. Constructing cladograms

Sequence analysis is used to construct a **cladogram**.

A cladogram is a branching diagram that represents ancestor–descendant relationships. By comparing base sequences, it is possible to estimate when a pair of species diverged from a common ancestor. These estimates can then be used to suggest the sequence in which divergences occurred in a clade of several species. From this, a cladogram can be constructed.

Much more sophisticated analysis of large groups of species can be done using computer software. Sequences for all pairs of species in the clade are compared. The software then uses complex calculations to determine how the species could have evolved with the fewest sequence changes (maximum parsimony). The outcome does not prove how a clade evolved but it indicates the most probable pattern of divergence.

7. Analysing cladograms to deduce evolutionary relationships

These are the principles used when analysing cladograms:

- A cladogram is a tree diagram with a number of branches.
- The **terminal branches** are ends that represent individual clades. These may be species or groups of species that are not subdivided on the cladogram.
- The branching points on a cladogram are called **nodes**. Usually, two clades branch off at a node but sometimes there are three or more. A node represents the point at which a hypothetical ancestral species split to form two or more clades.
- Two clades that are linked at a node are relatively closely related. Clades that are only connected via a series of nodes are less closely related.
- The **root** is the base of the cladogram. It represents the hypothetical **common ancestor** of the entire clade.
- Some cladograms include numbers to indicate how many sequence differences there are.
- Some cladograms are drawn to scale, based on estimates of the time since each split occurred.
- The pattern of branching in a cladogram is assumed to match phylogeny (evolutionary origins).

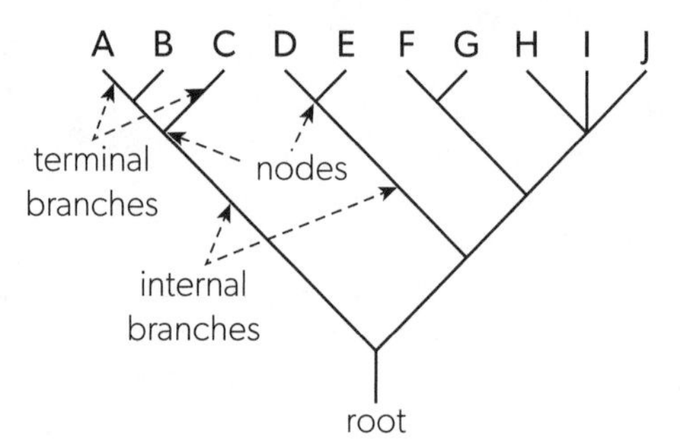

Cladograms are constructed to show how base or amino acid sequences could have evolved in a group with the fewest mutations. Sometimes the pathways of evolution were more convoluted and a cladogram does not mirror evolutionary history. Where possible, several cladograms should be produced independently using different genes. If they show the same pattern of branching, the evidence that this is how the clade evolved is strong, but it must still not be regarded as proof.

NOS

Hypotheses

A hypothesis is a provisional explanation for a pattern.

It may be possible to generate more than one hypothesis. Which hypothesis is then accepted will depend on the judgement criteria that are used.

A cladogram is a hypothesis for the evolutionary relationships between species in a clade, based on the variation between them. If alternative cladograms are constructed using differences in morphology, it may be difficult to decide which should be accepted. If the alternative cladograms are constructed using base sequence data, parsimony can be used as the criterion. The cladogram that accounts for all base sequence variation with the smallest number of sequence changes is the most probable.

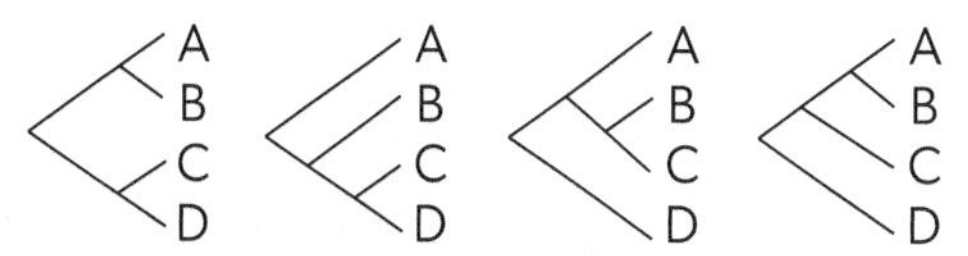

Four alternative hypotheses for evolutionary relationships between species A to D

AHL

8. Using cladistics to compare classifications

As base sequence data has been obtained for more and more species, cladistics has been used to check traditional classifications of plants and animals that were based on morphology.

- In many cases, cladistics has confirmed that traditional classifications correspond to evolutionary relationships.
- In some cases, cladistics indicates that the species in a taxonomic group do not all share a common ancestor.
- In other cases, cladistics indicates that species with a common ancestor have been placed in different groups.

Where classifications obtained by traditional methods and by cladistics are different, cladistics is usually trusted more because the evidence is more objective.

Cladistics has triggered changes in the classification of the figwort family and many other families of flowering plants. It has shown that the traditional classification of birds and reptiles as separate classes does not correspond to evolutionary relationships. Birds are a clade that is nested with several clades of reptile

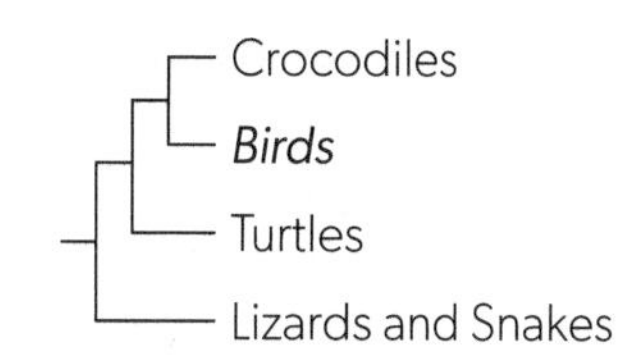

AHL

9. Three domains classification

Traditional classification systems recognize two major categories of organisms based on cell types: eukaryotes and prokaryotes. In the 1970s, base sequences of ribosomal RNA were determined in a wide range of organisms and differences were analysed. This revealed that there are two distinct groups of prokaryotes: eubacteria and archaea. There are therefore three major categories of organism, eubacteria, archaeans and eukaryotes. These categories are called domains and all organisms belong to one of them.

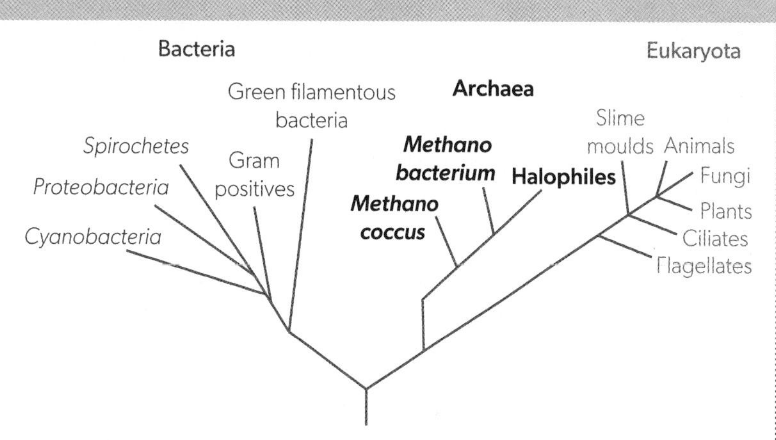

In 1977, the reclassification of life into three domains was proposed, based on this cladogram.

Falsification

Theories and other scientific knowledge claims may eventually be falsified. Some traditional classifications based on similarities in morphology have been falsified by cladistics. In these cases, morphological similarities were due to convergent evolution (described in *Section A4.1.5*) rather than common ancestry.

End of topic questions — A3 Questions

A3.1 Diversity of organisms

1. The micrograph shows a metaphase spread of chromosomes from a *Muntiacus muntjac* (muntjac deer) body cell.

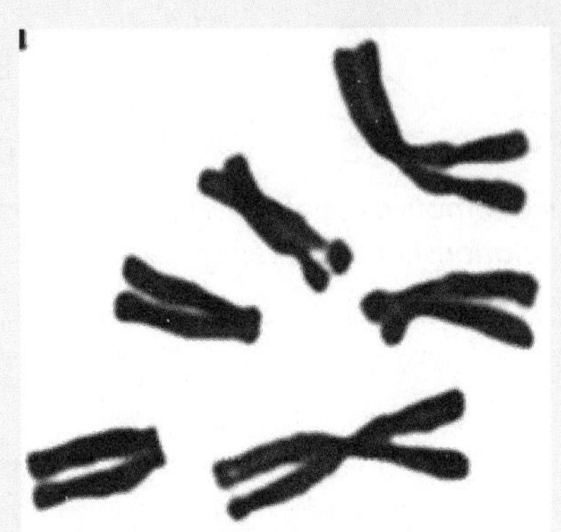

   a. Outline how metaphase spreads of chromosomes such as this are produced. (2)

   b. i. Identify two features of the chromosomes, visible in the micrograph, that allow them to be classified into types. (2)

   ii. Outline another method that can be used to distinguish between chromosome types. (2)

   c. Describe how a karyogram could be produced from the micrograph. (2)

   d. Deduce what chromosomes there would be in a sperm or egg of *Muntiacus muntjac*. (2)

2. State the biological term for these groups (5):

   a. all the genes of an organism

   b. organisms that share traits and a binomial

   c. all organisms of one species living together in an area

   d. a DNA molecule carrying a sequence of genes

   e. organisms that can interbreed and produce fertile offspring. (5)

3. (HL only) The diagram shows an example of hybridization between two species of duck that live in mixed flocks in some areas of Argentina.

   (n = chromosome number of body cells)

   Anas flavirostris (n=56) × *Anas georgica* (n=64)

   |

   interspecific hybrid

   a. Predict, with reasons, the chromosome number of the interspecific hybrid. (2)

   b. Only one hybrid was found by researchers. If more were discovered, predict whether they would be identical. (5)

   c. Explain, with reasons, whether the interspecific hybrid is likely to be able to produce gametes. (3)

A3.2 Classification and cladistics (HL)

1. The figure below shows the base sequence of part of a a hemoglobin gene in four species of mammal.

Human	TGACAAGAACA–GTTAGAG–TGTCCGA
Orang-utan	TCACGAGAACA–GTTAGAG–TGTCCGA
Lemur	TAACGATAACAGGATAGAG–TATCTGA
Rabbit	TGGTGATAACAAGACAGAGATATCCGA

   a. Determine the number of differences between the base sequences of:
   i. humans and orang-utans
   ii. humans and lemurs
   iii. humans and rabbits
   iv. orang-utans and lemurs
   v. orang-utans and rabbits
   vi. lemurs and rabbits. (6)

   b. Using the differences in base sequence, construct a cladogram for the four species. (4)

   c. From your cladogram, deduce the evolutionary relationships of these species. (2)

2. In the current system of classification, all living organisms are placed in one of three major groups.

   a. i. State which type of group this is in the hierarchy of taxa. (1)

   ii. Eukaryotes are one of the three major groups. State the names of the other two. (2)

   b. State the seven levels in the hierarchy of taxa used to classify eukaryotes. (7)

3. The cladogram shows seven species of plant. All are monocotyledons.

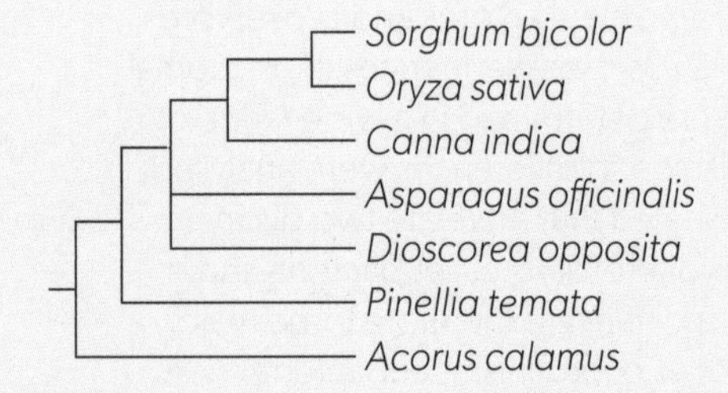

   a. Outline the conclusions that can be drawn from a cladogram such as this. (3)

   b. All but two of the species are traditionally classified in different orders. Deduce which two species are classified in the same order. (2)

   c. Explain whether *Dioscorea opposita* is more closely related to *Pinellia ternata* or *Sorghum bicolor*, giving reasons for your answer. (2)

   d. Monocotyledons are a clade that does not fit any of the levels in the traditional hierarchy of taxa. Discuss the reasons for difficulties such as this in classifying groups of organisms. (3)

B3.1 Gas exchange

1. Gas exchange

All organisms absorb one gas from the environment and release another one. This is gas exchange. Redwood trees absorb carbon dioxide for use in photosynthesis and release oxygen produced in the process. Humans absorb oxygen for cell respiration and release the carbon dioxide produced.

The relationship between surface area and volume (described in *Section B2.3.6*) has consequences for gas exchange.

Unicellular and other small organisms have a large surface area-to-volume ratio. They can therefore use their outer surface for gas exchange. *Amoeba* (described in *Section A2.2.7*) is an example.

In larger organisms, the surface area-to-volume ratio is smaller, so the outer surface of the organism cannot carry out gas exchange rapidly enough. A specialized gas exchange surface is required that is much larger than the outer surface, for example alveoli in lungs or the spongy mesophyll in a leaf.

2. Features of gas exchange surfaces

Gas exchange happens at a surface where the cells of the organism are exposed to the environment. In terrestrial organisms the **gas exchange surface** is where cells are exposed to air as in the lungs of a mammal. In aquatic organisms it is where cells are exposed to water as in the gills of a fish.

Gases are exchanged by diffusion across the surface. Because the molecules of oxygen and carbon dioxide move randomly, diffusion is a relatively slow process. To ensure that exchange is rapid enough for an organism's needs, its gas exchange surfaces must have these properties:

1. **permeable**—oxygen and carbon dioxide can diffuse across freely
2. **large**—the total surface area is large in relation to the volume of the organism
3. **moist**—the surface is covered by a film of moisture in terrestrial organisms so gases can dissolve
4. **thin**—the gases must diffuse only a short distance, in most cases through a single layer of cells.

3. Importance of concentration gradients at exchange surfaces

Gases and other substances diffuse if there is a concentration gradient. For example, carbon dioxide diffuses from the air into photosynthesizing leaf cells because the CO_2 concentration of the cells is lower. Diffusion tends to reduce concentration gradients, which could decrease the rate and eventually stop gas exchange if the concentrations become equal. For gases to continue to diffuse across exchange surfaces, concentration gradients must be maintained. In small, aerobically respiring organisms, cell respiration maintains concentration gradients. Oxygen is continuously used and carbon dioxide is produced, so the oxygen concentration within the organism remains lower than outside and the carbon dioxide concentration remains higher.

blood arriving with high $[CO_2]$ and low $[O_2]$

continuous blood flow through capillary

O_2

CO_2

air with high $[O_2]$ and low $[CO_2]$

VENTILATION

O_2

CO_2

air with higher $[CO_2]$ and lower $[O_2]$

alveolar duct

wall of alveolus

blood leaving with high $[O_2]$ and low $[CO_2]$

In large multicellular animals with a specialized organ for gas exchange (lungs or gills), pumping is required to maintain concentration gradients.

- Blood is pumped through **dense capillary networks** close to the gas exchange surface. Due to aerobic respiration in the animal, blood arriving at the surface has a low concentration of oxygen and a high concentration of carbon dioxide.
- Air or water adjacent to the gas exchange surface is replaced by the process of **ventilation**. Mammals pump air in and out of their lungs to maintain high enough concentrations of oxygen and low enough concentrations of carbon dioxide. Fish pump fresh water over their gills and then out through the gill slits. This one-way flow of water, combined with blood flow in the opposite direction, ensures that the oxygen concentration in the water adjacent to the gills remains high and the carbon dioxide concentration remains low.

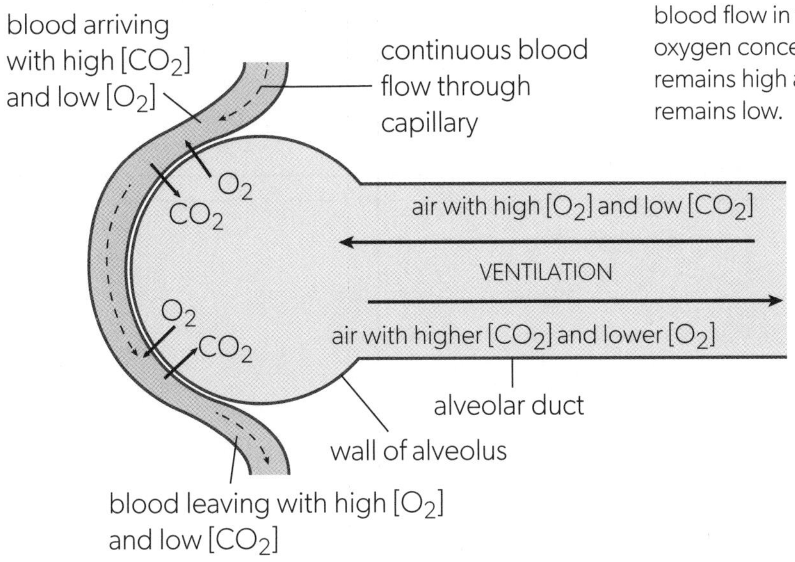

Key

$[CO_2]$ = concentration of carbon dioxide

$[O_2]$ = concentration of oxygen

5. Lung structure and ventilation

The lungs are in the thorax. Air can only get into or out of the thorax through the airways. The airways used to ventilate the lungs consist of the nose, mouth, trachea, bronchi and bronchioles.

If gas is free to move, it will always flow from regions of higher pressure to regions of lower pressure. During ventilation, muscle contractions cause pressure changes inside the thorax that pull extra air into the alveoli and then push it out again. The muscles causing this are:

- the diaphragm that divides the thorax and abdomen
- muscle in the front wall of the abdomen
- intercostal muscle between the ribs, in two layers (internal and external) that are antagonistic.

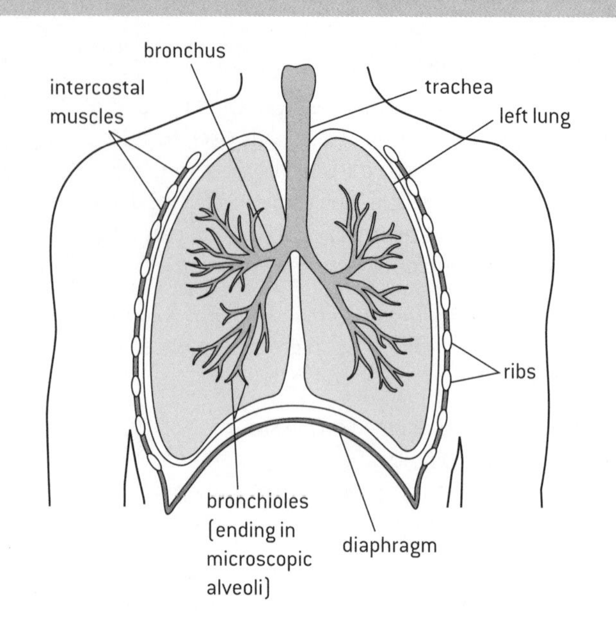

Inhaling (inspiration)	Exhaling (expiration)
The external intercostal muscles contract, moving the ribcage up and out	The internal intercostal muscles contract, moving the ribcage down and in
The diaphragm contracts, becoming flatter and moving down	The abdominal muscles contract, pushing the diaphragm up into a dome shape
These muscle movements increase the volume of the thorax	These muscle movements decrease the volume of the thorax
The pressure inside the thorax therefore drops below atmospheric pressure	The pressure inside the thorax therefore rises above atmospheric pressure
Air flows into the lungs from outside the body until the pressure inside the lungs rises to atmospheric pressure	Air flows out from the lungs to outside the body until the pressure inside the lungs falls to atmospheric pressure

air movement
ribcage movement
diaphragm movement

4. The lungs are adapted for efficient gas exchange

All mammals use lungs for gas exchange, which have these adaptations:

- **Airways** for ventilation of each lung, consisting of branching bronchioles, ending in alveolar ducts, each of which leads to a group of five or six alveoli (air sacs).
- **Large surface area** for gas exchange—provided by having about 300 million alveoli in a pair of adult lungs. One alveolus is only 0.2–0.5 mm in diameter so only provides a small surface area for gas exchange, but because there are so many of them, the total area is very large: about 40 times greater than the outer surface of the body.

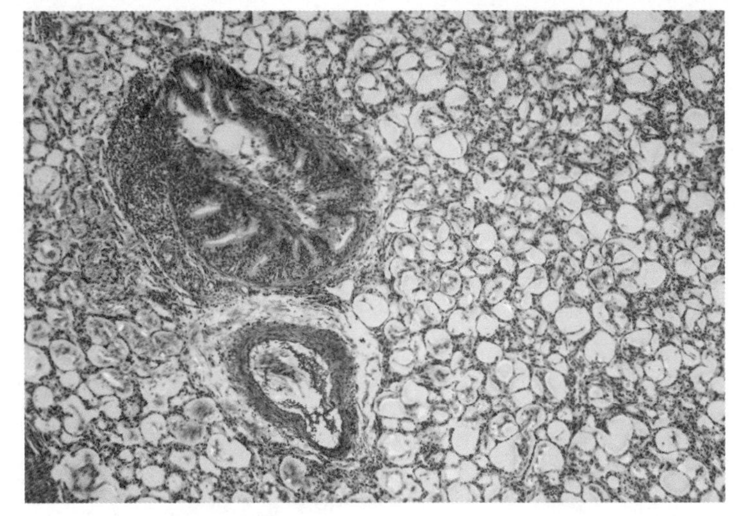
▲ human lung tissue

- **Extensive capillary beds**—the surface area of the basket-like networks of blood capillaries around the alveoli is almost as large as that of the alveoli.
- **Short distance for diffusion**—both the alveolus wall and adjacent capillary walls are single layers of extremely thin cells (HL see also *Section B2.3.8*). Air and blood are therefore a very short distance apart. The distance for diffusion of O_2 and CO_2 is less than a micrometre.
- **Moist surface with surfactant**—a fluid is secreted by cells in the alveolus wall that keeps the lining of the alveolus moist, allowing oxygen to dissolve. The fluid contains a pulmonary surfactant, that reduces the surface tension and prevents the water from causing the sides of the alveoli to stick together when air is exhaled from the lungs. This helps to prevent collapse of the lung.

6. Application of skills: measurement of lung volumes by spirometry

Lung volumes are measured as part of tests into general health and to help diagnose conditions such as asthma, COPD and cystic fibrosis.

- **Ventilation rate** is the number of times that air is drawn in or expelled per minute.
- **Tidal volume** is the volume of fresh air inhaled or the volume of stale air exhaled with each ventilation.
- **Vital capacity** is the total volume of air that can be exhaled after a maximum inhalation.
- **Inspiratory reserve volume** is the amount of air a person can inhale forcefully after normal tidal inhalation.
- **Expiratory reserve volume** is the amount of air a person can exhale forcefully after normal tidal exhalation.

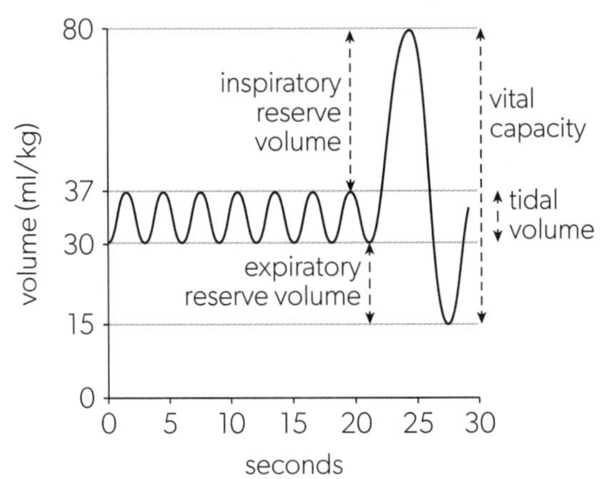

A spirometer is a device used to measure lung volumes. A simple version can be constructed using a bell jar and a tube. It is not safe to use this apparatus for repeatedly inhaling and exhaling air as the carbon dioxide concentration will rise too high.

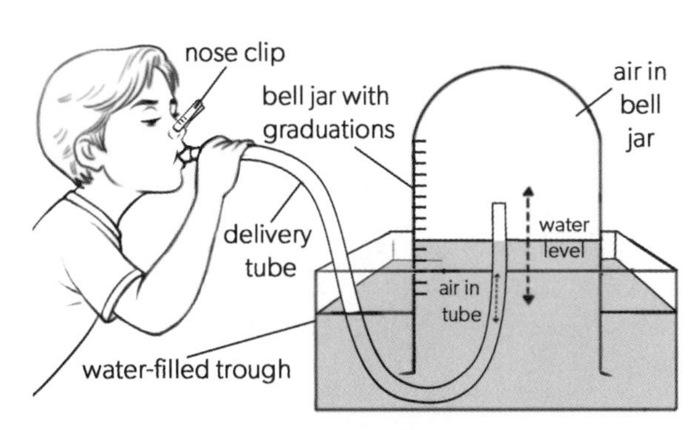

Doctors use specially designed electronic spirometers that measure flow rate into and out of the lungs and then use data logging software to deduce lung volumes. There are many different designs.

The patient has a clip placed on their nose and they breathe into and out of the spirometer through a mouthpiece.

Tidal volume is measured by breathing into the spirometer, three or more times, to check the readings are consistent.

Vital capacity is measured by breathing in as deeply and as fast as possible and then breathing out as fast and as forcefully as possible until the lungs are empty.

7. Leaves are adapted for gas exchange

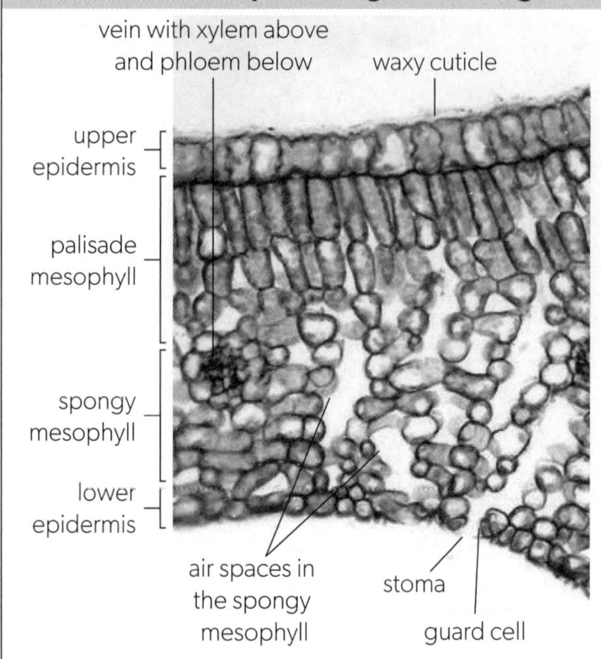

Chloroplasts need a supply of carbon dioxide for photosynthesis. The oxygen produced during the process of photosynthesis must be removed. A large area of moist surface is required over which carbon dioxide can be absorbed and oxygen excreted, without excessive water loss.

The following leaf adaptations provide this moist surface area:

- **Waxy cuticle**—the upper and lower surface of leaves is covered in a layer of waterproof wax, secreted by the epidermis cells. It reduces water loss but also prevents movement of carbon dioxide and oxygen.
- **Guard cells**—there are pairs of guard cells in the epidermis, which can change their shape either to open up a pore or close it. The pore is called a stoma (plural, stomata) and it allows carbon dioxide and oxygen to pass through. The guard cells usually close the stomata at night when photosynthesis is not occurring and gas exchange is not required. Stomata also close during water stress when plants might die from dehydration.
- **Air spaces**—the stomata connect the air outside to a network of air spaces in the spongy mesophyll of the leaf. Carbon dioxide and oxygen can diffuse through these air spaces.
- **Spongy mesophyll**—the inner tissue of the leaf with extensive air spaces is the spongy mesophyll. It provides a very large total surface area of permanently moist cell walls for gas exchange. Carbon dioxide in the air spaces dissolves and diffuses into the cells. Oxygen diffuses from the cells to the air. Photosynthesis maintains the concentration gradients.
- **Veins**—inevitably, there is some loss of water by evaporation from the moist spongy mesophyll cell walls and diffusion out through the stomata. This is replaced by water supplied by xylem vessels, located in the leaf veins.

8. Leaf tissues

Plan diagrams show the areas of tissues, but not individual cells. The lines indicate the junctions between tissues.

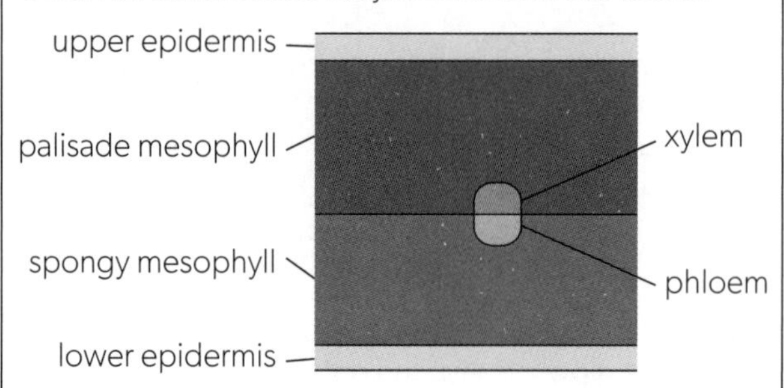

Measurements

NOS

Reliability of data is increased by repeating measurements. When measuring stomatal density (see *Section B3.1.10*), stomata should be counted repeatedly in randomly selected areas of leaf surface and the mean density can then be calculated. If a count is done in only one field of view, the stomatal density may not be representative of the whole leaf.

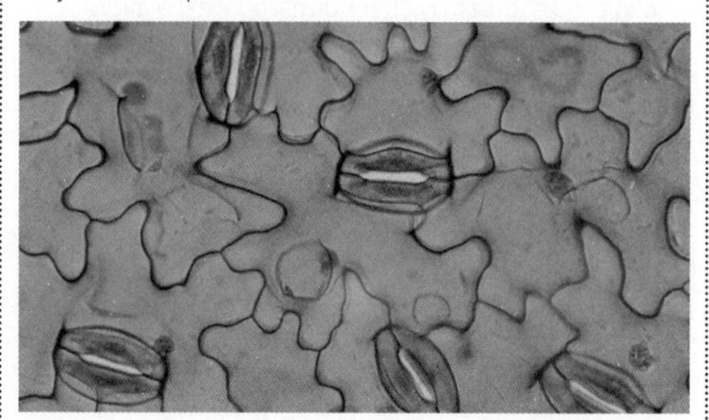

▲ Lower epidermis of *Vicia faba* leaf

9. Transpiration

Water molecules evaporate when hydrogen bonds between them break. The molecules separate from each other and become **water vapour** molecules in air. The opposite process is condensation, where water vapour molecules join others to become liquid water. If air is very humid and the number of water molecules evaporating is equal to the number condensing, the air is **saturated** with water vapour.

Air spaces inside the leaf are usually saturated (or nearly saturated). Water vapour molecules diffuse out of the leaf through the stomata unless the stomata are closed or the air outside the leaf is already saturated. This causes the humidity of the air spaces to drop below the saturation point, so more water evaporates from the permanently moist spongy mesophyll cell walls. Loss of water vapour from the leaves and stems of plants is **transpiration**. Transpiration rates are affected by environmental factors.

- Temperature (positive correlation): at higher temperatures there is more energy available to break hydrogen bonds between water molecules, so the evaporation rate is higher and air holds more water vapour molecules before becoming saturated.
- Humidity (negative correlation): the higher the humidity of the air, the smaller the concentration gradient of water vapour between the air spaces inside the leaf and the air outside, so the lower the rate of diffusion. There is no transpiration if the air outside the leaf is saturated with water vapour.
- Wind: in still conditions, transpiration is restricted by formation of pockets of saturated air near the stomata, even if the air further away is drier. Air movements prevent this, so increase transpiration, though stomata close in strong winds, so transpiration rate drops.

10. Measuring stomatal density

Stomatal density is the number of stomata per unit area of leaf surface. The number in a known area (field of view) is counted, by one of these three methods.

Application of skills: measuring stomatal density

1. A sample of epidermis is peeled off the leaf, mounted in water on a microscope slide and examined.
2. Colourless nail varnish is painted on small areas of epidermis. The varnish forms a cast of the leaf surface with stomata visible. When dry, it is peeled off, mounted on a microscope slide and examined.
3. The surface of the leaf is photographed, and the resulting micrograph used for stomatal counts.

$$\text{stomatal density (mm}^{-2}) = \frac{\text{mean number of stomata}}{\text{area of field of view (mm}^2)}$$

AHL

11. Haemoglobin is adapted for the transport of oxygen

Humans produce foetal haemoglobin before birth and adult haemoglobin afterwards. During pregnancy a foetus obtains oxygen via the placenta. Oxygen dissociates from haemoglobin in maternal blood in the placenta and binds to haemoglobin in foetal blood. This can only happen because foetal haemoglobin has a stronger affinity for oxygen than adult haemoglobin. At any partial pressure of oxygen, foetal haemoglobin is therefore more saturated with oxygen than adult haemoglobin. At birth, a baby still has red blood cells with foetal haemoglobin. It takes several months for all red blood cells carrying foetal haemoglobin to be replaced with cells carrying adult haemoglobin.

Oxygen dissociation curves show percentage oxygen saturation of haemoglobin over a range of oxygen concentrations, including those found in the body. The partial pressure of oxygen in the atmosphere is 21.2 kPa. In the alveoli it only reaches 13 kPa, but this is enough for haemoglobin to become 100% saturated. In respiring tissues, the partial pressure of oxygen can be 5 kPa or lower, so much of the oxygen carried by haemoglobin dissociates.

The graph below shows the dissociation curves for adult and foetal haemoglobin. Both are S-shaped (sigmoid) due to cooperative binding (see *Section B3.1.13*).

The curve for foetal haemoglobin is to the left of the adult curve, indicating increased affinity for oxygen. Foetal haemoglobin has a stronger affinity than adult haemoglobin, so percentage saturation is higher at every partial pressure of oxygen.

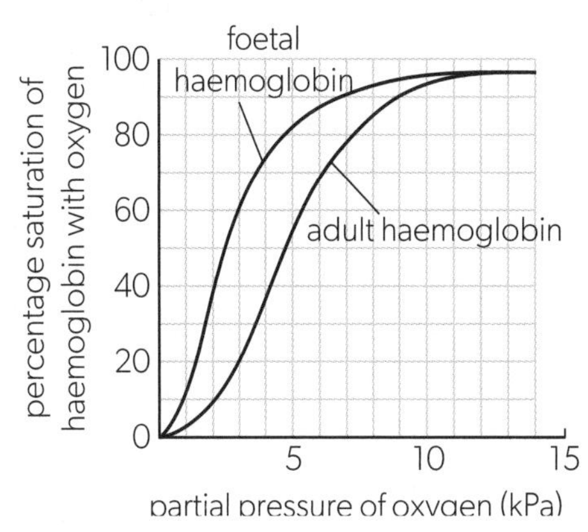

12. Bohr shift

Increases in carbon dioxide concentration reduce the affinity of haemoglobin for oxygen by two mechanisms:

1. There is a positive correlation between pH and affinity of haemoglobin for oxygen. CO_2 reduces pH ($CO_2 + H_2O \rightarrow H^+ + HCO_3^-$) so decreases affinity for oxygen.
2. CO_2 binds reversibly to the polypeptides in haemoglobin, producing carbaminohaemoglobin (haemoglobin + $4CO_2 \rightarrow$ carbaminohaemoglobin). Carbaminohaemoglobin has a lower affinity for oxygen than haemoglobin.

Reduced affinity of haemoglobin for oxygen in high CO_2 concentrations shifts the oxygen dissociation curve to the left—this is the **Bohr shift**.

The Bohr shift promotes release of oxygen in actively respiring tissues such as contracting muscle, where high blood CO_2 concentration causes low pH (≈7.2) and haemoglobin to be converted to carbaminohaemoglobin.

The Bohr shift allows blood to be fully oxygenated in the lungs where blood CO_2 concentration is low so pH is high (≈7.4) and carbaminohaemoglobin has been converted back to haemoglobin.

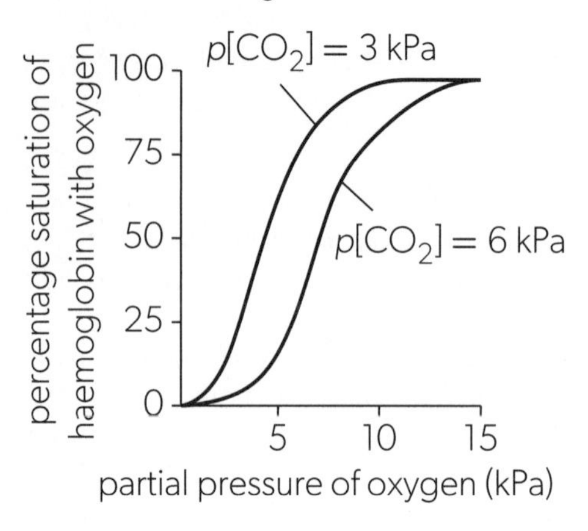

AHL

13. Oxygen dissociation curves

- Each subunit in haemoglobin (see *Section B1.2.11*) has a haem group to which one oxygen molecule can bind reversibly, so one haemoglobin molecule can transport up to four oxygens.
- Binding is cooperative, because binding of oxygen to any haem group causes conformational changes that increase affinity for oxygen in the other haem groups. Conversely, dissociation of oxygen reduces affinity in other haem groups. The two most probable states for haemoglobin are with four oxygen molecules bound or none.
- Blood in which all haemoglobin molecules are carrying four oxygens is 100% saturated. If no oxygen is bound to any of the haemoglobin molecules, it is 0% saturated. Any saturation level from 0 to 100% is possible.
- Oxygen concentration is measured in partial pressures, with kilopascals (kPa) as the pressure units. There is a positive correlation between partial pressure of oxygen and % saturation of haemoglobin. In human adults, haemoglobin reaches 100% saturation when partial pressure of oxygen reaches 10 kPa. This happens as blood flows through capillaries around the alveoli.
- 100% oxygenated blood leaving the lungs is carried to all other organs of the body, where due to aerobic respiration the partial pressure of oxygen is below 10 kPa, so oxygen dissociates (separates) from haemoglobin and diffuses into the tissues.

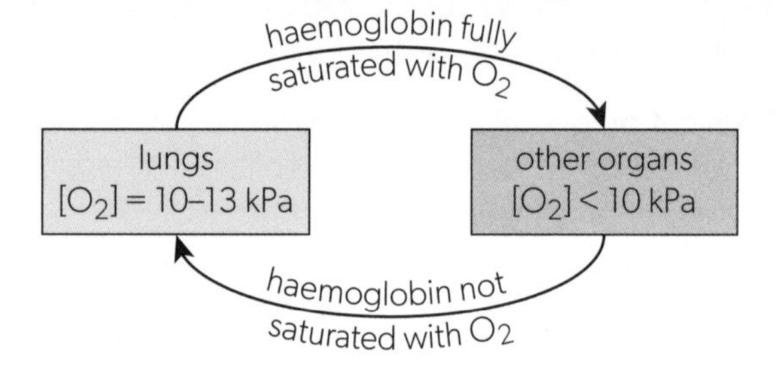

- Because of cooperative binding, oxygen saturation of haemoglobin is not directly proportional to oxygen concentration. Instead, it changes from fully saturated to unsaturated over a relatively narrow range of oxygen concentrations, ensuring rapid dissociation of oxygen in tissues where it is needed for aerobic respiration.

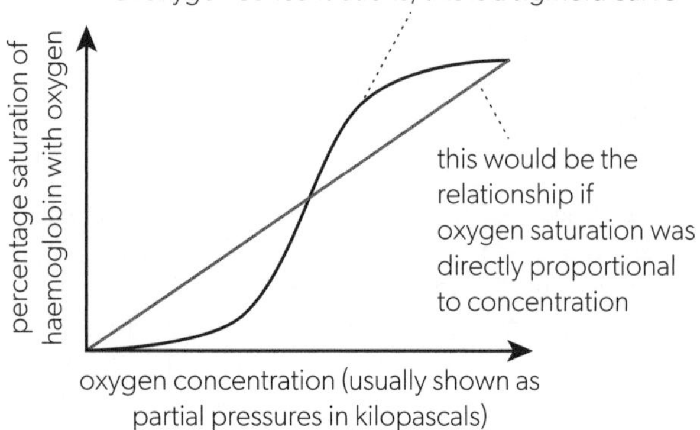

B3.2 Transport

1. Adaptations of capillaries

Capillaries are adapted for exchange processes, with some materials released from the capillary and other materials absorbed into it. There are capillaries in almost all tissues in the body. The density of capillary networks depends on the needs of the cells within a tissue, but all active cells in the body are close to a capillary. There are particularly dense capillary networks where capillaries exchange materials with the external environment, as in the lungs and the small intestine.

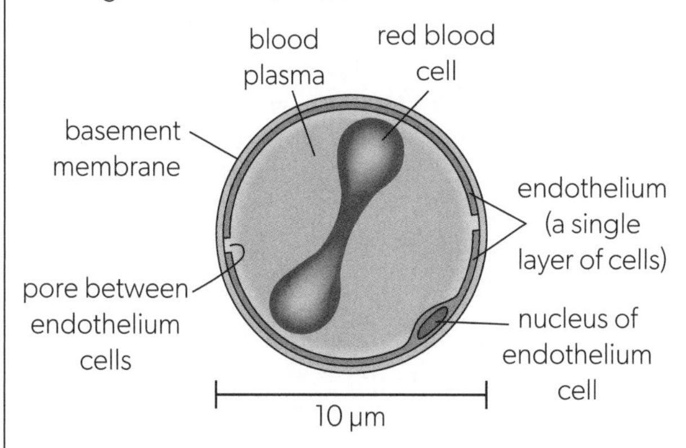

Capillaries have these three adaptations:

1. **Large surface area**

   Capillaries are the narrowest blood vessels with a diameter of about 10 μm, so blood cells have to pass through in single file. Capillaries branch and re-join repeatedly to form a capillary network with a huge total length. This gives a very large total surface area for exchange processes.

2. **Thin walls with pores**

   The capillary wall consists of one layer of endothelium cells which are a very thin and permeable layer. The layer of cells is supported by a coating of extracellular fibrous proteins. The basement membrane acts as a filter that allows small or medium-sized particles to pass through, but not macromolecules such as proteins. Fluid leaks out of capillaries through the basement membrane because blood pressure is higher than pressure in the surrounding tissue and because there are pores between the epithelium cells. The fluid passing out (tissue fluid) contains oxygen, glucose and other substances in blood plasma, but not plasma proteins. The tissue fluid flows between cells, allowing them to absorb useful substances and excrete waste products. The fluid then re-enters capillaries where pressure inside them has dropped, near where blood is transported out of the tissue in veins.

3. **Fenestrations**

   In some tissues, there are many particularly large pores (fenestrations) in the capillary walls. Fenestrated capillaries allow larger volumes of tissue fluid to be produced, which speeds up exchange between the tissue cells and the blood. Fenestrated capillaries in the kidney (described for HL in *Section D3.3.8*) allow production of large volumes of filtrate in the first stage of urine production.

2. Application of skills: distinguishing arteries and veins

- **Arteries** carry pulses of high-pressure blood away from the heart to every organ of the body.
- **Veins** carry a stream of low-pressure blood from the organs back to the heart.

Because of the difference in function, these two types of blood vessel have a different structure to their walls.

The table shows structural features that can be used to distinguish between arteries and veins. The micrographs in the table show an artery and a vein in transverse section. Clotted blood, with a grainy appearance, is visible inside both vessels.

Arteries	Veins
Thicker wall	Thinner wall
Narrower lumen	Wider lumen
Circular in section	Circular/flattened
Inner surface corrugated	Inner surface smooth
Fibres visible in the wall	No or few fibres visible
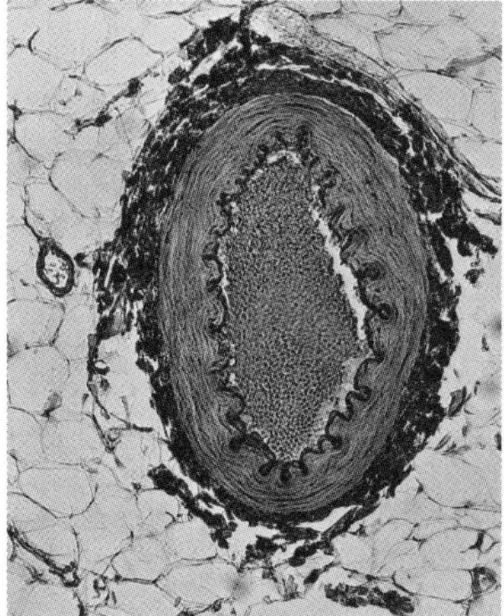	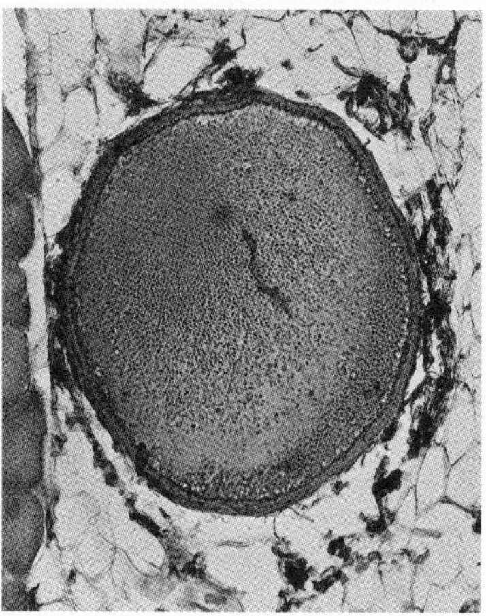

3. Arteries are adapted for carrying blood away from the heart

The wall of the artery is composed of several layers, shown below.

tunica externa—outer coat of connective tissues with tough collagen fibres to prevent swelling or bursting of the artery despite high blood pressures

tunica media—thick layer containing smooth muscle and elastic fibres (elastin) to helppump blood by transmitting the pulse

thick wall for overall strength

lumen—relatively narrow space through which blood flows to help maintain high blood pressure and velocity

tunica intima—smooth endothelium to line the artery and reduce resistance to flow, plus a layer of elastic fibres in some arteries

Collagen fibres are tough rope-like proteins with high tensile strength. They make arteries strong enough to withstand high and variable blood pressures without bulging outwards (aneurysm) or bursting. Each time the ventricles of the heart pump (systole), a burst of blood under high pressure enters the arteries and flows along them. The wall of the artery expands due to the high blood pressure and elastic fibres in the wall stretch and store potential energy. When the ventricles stop pumping (diastole) and blood pressure declines, the elastic fibres recoil, applying pressure on the lumen which helps pump blood on along the artery and makes flow more even. Artery walls also contain smooth muscle cells. They are circular (rather than radial or longitudinal), so they make the lumen narrower when they contract (vasoconstriction) and wider when they relax (vasodilation). There is a high density of smooth muscle fibres in branches of arteries (arterioles), so flow rate of blood to tissues in each organ can be adjusted, depending on availability and need.

4. Application of skills: measuring pulse rates

With each heartbeat, a wave of blood under high pressure passes along the arteries, stretching the artery wall, which then recoils. In arteries close to the body surface, this can be felt as a pulse. The carotid artery in the neck and the radial artery on the thumb side of the wrist both have pulses. There is one pulse per beat of the heart so the pulse rate allows heart rate to be deduced.

- Place your index and middle fingers on the side of the neck, in the soft hollow area just beside the windpipe.
- When you can reliably feel the pulse, use a timer to count the beats in a minute (or in 30 seconds and multiply by 2).

There are also digital methods of finding heart rate. For example, a pulse oximeter is clipped to a fingertip. It has LEDs that shine light into the finger and detectors to measure how much light is absorbed by the finger. This depends on the amount of blood in the tissues, so pulse rate and therefore heart rate can be calculated.

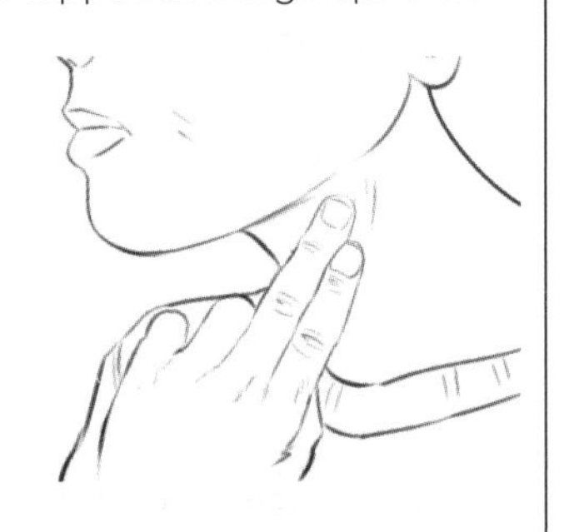

5. Veins are adapted for returning blood to the heart

Veins collect blood from all organs of the body and return it to the heart. Blood drains out of capillaries into veins continuously, so there is no pulse and blood pressure is low.

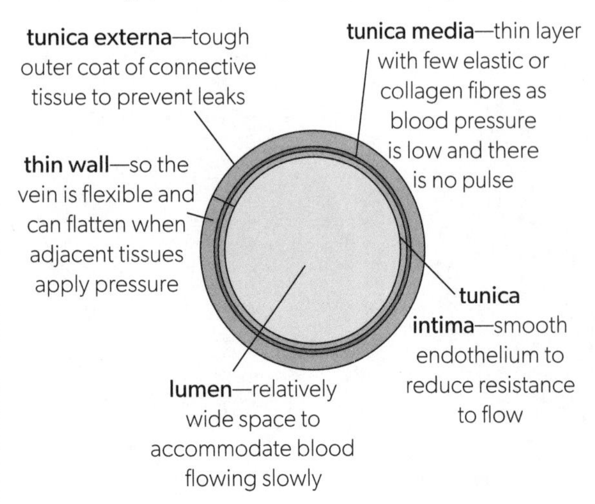
tunica externa—tough outer coat of connective tissue to prevent leaks
tunica media—thin layer with few elastic or collagen fibres as blood pressure is low and there is no pulse
thin wall—so the vein is flexible and can flatten when adjacent tissues apply pressure
tunica intima—smooth endothelium to reduce resistance to flow
lumen—relatively wide space to accommodate blood flowing slowly

Pressure in veins can drop so low that blood flow stops and there is a risk of backflow towards the capillaries. Valves in main veins prevent this. Each valve consists of three pocket-shaped flaps of tissue. If blood starts to flow backwards, it gets caught in the flaps, filling them and closing the valve. Blood flowing towards the heart pushes the valve open.

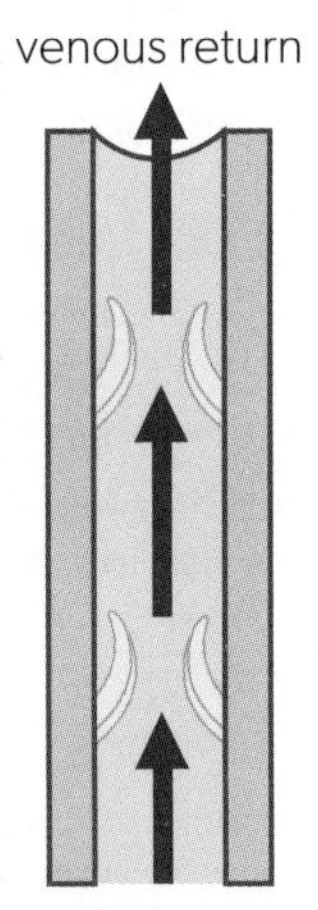
venous return
risk of backflow
valves open
valves closed

Venous blood flow is aided by skeletal muscles adjacent to veins that become wider when they contract, pressing the vein flatter and raising blood pressure. Valves ensure that the resulting flow of blood is towards the heart.

6. Application of skills: evaluating epidemiological data on coronary heart disease

All blood pumped out by the left ventricle enters the aorta. Branches of this artery carry oxygenated blood to every organ of the body apart from the lungs. The first two branches are coronary arteries that carry blood into the wall of the heart itself. One of these soon divides in two, so there are three main coronary arteries. Each of these branches repeatedly to provide oxygenated blood to all parts of the muscular wall of the heart.

Lipids, including fats and cholesterol, are sometimes deposited in the walls of arteries. These deposits are **atheroma** (plaque). They make the lumen of the artery narrower, restricting blood flow. If atheroma continues to build up, it may cause **occlusion** (total blockage of an artery).

When coronary arteries are narrowed or blocked, blood flow to a region of the heart wall is restricted, often causing pain in the chest (angina) or shortness of breath, especially during exercise. Medical conditions due to narrowed or blocked coronary arteries are collectively known as **coronary heart disease**.

Epidemiology is research into the nature and spread of diseases in the human population. It can identify risk factors, which are variables associated with increased incidence of a disease. Multiple risk factors for coronary heart disease (CHD) have been identified:

- High blood pressure (hypertension)
- Smoking
- Obesity (body mass index ≥30)
- Inactive lifestyle
- Family history of heart disease
- Old age
- High blood cholesterol concentration
- Diabetes

There is a positive correlation between each of these variables and the incidence of CHD.

Risk factors for CHD can be quantified using this 2x2 table, in which a to d are numbers of people:

		CHD?	
		Yes	No
Risk factor?	Yes	a	b
	No	c	d

$$\text{absolute risk} = \frac{a}{(a+b)}$$

$$\text{relative risk} = \frac{a/(a+b)}{c/(c+d)}$$

$$\text{odds ratio} = \frac{a/b}{c/d} = \frac{ad}{bc}$$

$$\text{excess risk} = (a/(a+b)) - (c/(c+d))$$

To show that a variable is a risk factor, variation in other factors should be reduced to a minimum in epidemiological research. For example, a study into the effects of smoking should be carried out on an even-aged group of people. However, as epidemiology is not based on controlled experiments, it is rarely possible to entirely avoid factors other than the variable being investigated having effects.

NOS

Patterns and trends

Associations and correlations are types of pattern in data. An important principle in science is that **correlation does not prove causation**. For example, a positive correlation has been found in some studies between saturated fat intake and coronary heart disease, but this does not prove saturated fats cause CHD. It is possible that foods high in saturated fats contain large amounts of another substance such as cholesterol that is the real cause.

7. Water is transported from roots to leaves during transpiration

Plants transport large volumes of water from roots, where it is absorbed, to leaves. In flowering plants, xylem vessels transport most of the water, as part of xylem sap which has low concentrations of K^+ and other dissolved ions.

In transpiring leaves, water evaporates from walls of spongy mesophyll cells and the water vapour molecules then diffuse out through stomata. This is transpiration (described in *Section B3.1.9*). Cell walls contain a mesh of cellulose molecules which are hydrophilic and form hydrogen bonds with water. Any water lost by evaporation from the surfaces of leaves is replaced by water drawn through pores between cellulose molecules in leaf cell walls, due to adhesion of water to cellulose and cohesion between water molecules. This is a type of **capillary action** (see *Section A1.1.4*).

The water drawn through interconnected leaf cell walls comes from xylem vessels in a leaf vein. Tensions (pulling forces) are generated inside xylem vessels when water is drawn out of them. This is described in more detail for HL in *Section D2.3.10*.

Because of cohesion between water molecules, tension generated in the leaf is transmitted down the continuous columns of water in xylem vessels to the roots. This is **transpiration pull**. It is remarkable because it can transport water passively against the force of gravity to the top of the tallest tree. The energy that drives it comes from the heat used in transpiration and the rope-like resistance to breaking of the column of water due to hydrogen bonding.

8. Xylem vessels are adapted for transport of water

Xylem vessels are the structures in xylem tissue that are adapted for transport of water inside plants. They develop from columns of cells, arranged end-to-end.

- **Wall thickening and lignification**
  Side walls of xylem vessels are thickened and the thickenings are impregnated with a polymer called lignin. This prevents the vessels from collapsing when pressure inside is very low because the plant is transpiring.
- **Lack of end walls and cell contents**
  End walls between adjacent cells are removed during development of a xylem vessel and the plasma membranes and contents of the cells break down. This creates long continuous tubes, in which flow of xylem sap is unimpeded. When mature, xylem vessels are non-living, so the flow of water along them must be a passive process.
- **Pits for entry and exit of water**
  Lignified wall thickenings are impermeable to water but there are always gaps in the thickening through which water can enter and exit. In the xylem vessels formed by young plants, the wall thickenings are in rings or helices with large gaps for water passage. In older plants, the wall thickenings are more extensive, with holes called pits through which water can pass.

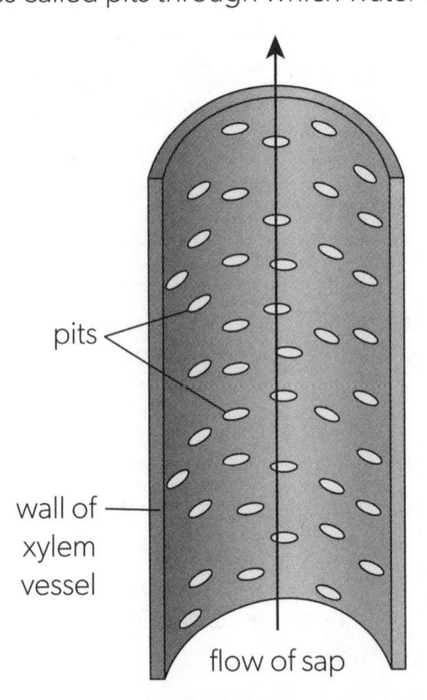
pits
wall of xylem vessel
flow of sap

9. Distribution of tissues in stems of dicotyledonous plants

There are many variations in stem structure. Dicotyledons (dicots) are plants with two embryo leaves in their seeds. Their stems are composed of epidermis, cortex and pith, with a ring of vascular bundles containing xylem and phloem. Some stems have a hollow centre.

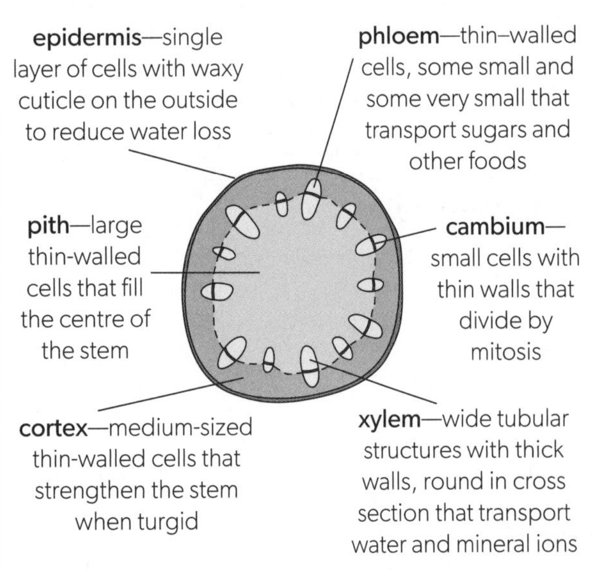
epidermis—single layer of cells with waxy cuticle on the outside to reduce water loss
phloem—thin-walled cells, some small and some very small that transport sugars and other foods
pith—large thin-walled cells that fill the centre of the stem
cambium—small cells with thin walls that divide by mitosis
cortex—medium-sized thin-walled cells that strengthen the stem when turgid
xylem—wide tubular structures with thick walls, round in cross section that transport water and mineral ions

10. Distribution of tissues in dicotyledonous roots

Vascular tissue is grouped in the centre of dicot roots, with xylem in a star-shaped area and phloem between the points of the star. The outer layer of cells is epidermis, with small cells that may have root hairs protruding. Between the vascular tissue and the epidermis there is cortex, with relatively large and thin-walled cells.

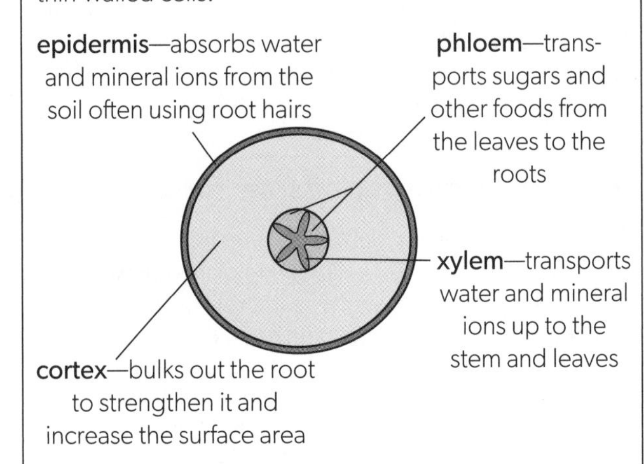
epidermis—absorbs water and mineral ions from the soil often using root hairs
phloem—transports sugars and other foods from the leaves to the roots
xylem—transports water and mineral ions up to the stem and leaves
cortex—bulks out the root to strengthen it and increase the surface area

Application of skills: plan diagrams to show tissue distribution in an organ

The arrangement of tissues in an organ can be shown by drawing a plan diagram, with areas of tissues indicated, but not individual cells. It is useful to show both names of tissues and their functions. The plan diagrams (above and left) are transverse sections (cross-sections) showing the distribution of tissues in a dicot stem and dicot root.

AHL

11. Tissue fluid

Oxygenated and nutrient-rich blood enters capillary networks from arterioles (branches of arteries). Capillary walls are permeable and the blood is initially at high pressure, so some of the blood plasma leaks out, forming **tissue fluid**. The process that produces tissue fluid is **pressure filtration** (see *Section B3.2.1*). At any time, there are about 14 litres of tissue fluid in the tissues of a 70 kg human, so it constitutes about 20% of body mass.

Blood drains out of capillary networks into venules (vessels that unite to form veins). This happens because of low blood pressure in venules. Drainage of blood from capillaries into venules lowers blood pressure in capillaries, which allows tissue fluid that is nutrient-depleted and deoxygenated to re-enter the capillaries.

12. Substances exchanged between tissue fluid and cells

Tissue fluid contains oxygen, glucose and all other substances in blood plasma apart from large protein molecules. As the fluid drains through the intercellular spaces in a tissue, there is an exchange of substances. Cells absorb oxygen, glucose and other useful substances from the tissue fluid around them and release carbon dioxide and other waste products of metabolism. Tissue re-entering capillaries is therefore depleted in oxygen and other useful substances and has raised concentrations of waste products. The capillaries merge to form venules, which carry the waste products out of the tissue. Carbon dioxide is excreted by the lungs and other waste products are detoxified by the liver or excreted by the kidneys.

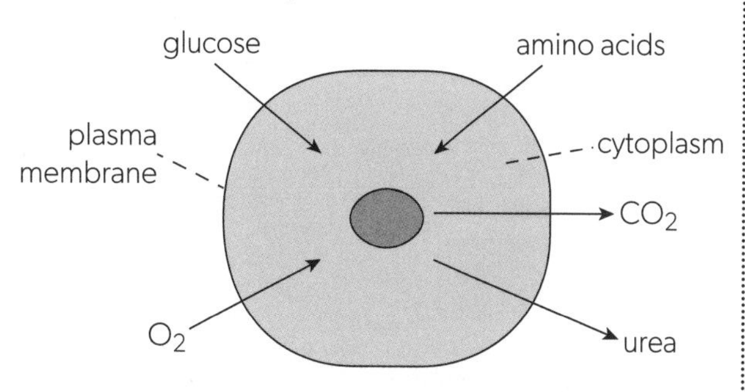

13. Excess tissue fluid drains into the lymphatic system

Most of the tissue fluid released by capillaries returns to them, but some does not. Of the 20 litres of tissue fluid produced per day in an average adult's body, 17 litres return to the capillaries. If the other 3 litres of fluid stayed in tissues it would cause swelling, called oedema. This is prevented by the drainage of tissue fluid into vessels of the lymphatic system.

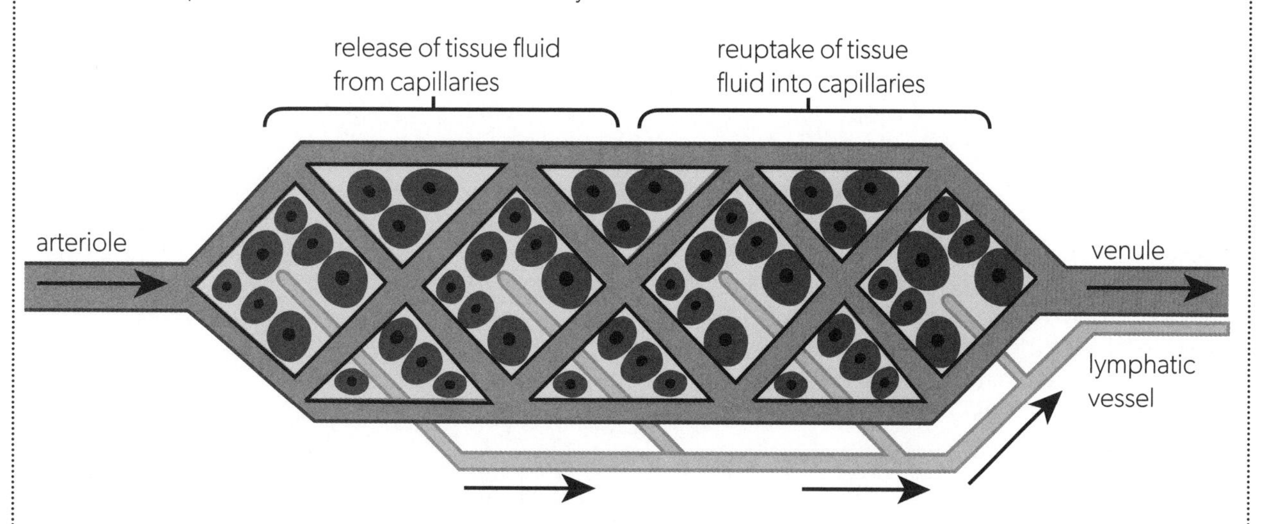

In all tissues, there are narrow blind-ended lymphatic vessels with permeable walls through which tissue fluid can pass. After entering the lymphatic vessels, the fluid is known as lymph rather than tissue fluid. The narrow vessels join up repeatedly to form wider lymphatic vessels, with valves to prevent backflow. All lymph from the left and right sides of the body is returned to the blood circulation through two large lymphatic ducts (left and right) which merge with the left and right subclavian veins. Blood in the subclavian veins flows into the vena cava and on to the right side of the heart.

AHL

14. Comparing single and double circulation systems

In fish, the heart only has one ventricle (pumping chamber), which pumps deoxygenated blood to the gills. The blood can be pumped at high pressure through the gills because the surrounding water provides support and prevents the capillaries bursting. After flowing through the gills, the blood is oxygenated and still has enough pressure to flow directly to another organ of the body. While passing through capillaries in an organ, the blood becomes deoxygenated and its pressure falls, so it must return to the heart to be repumped to the gills. Fish thus have a **single circulation**.

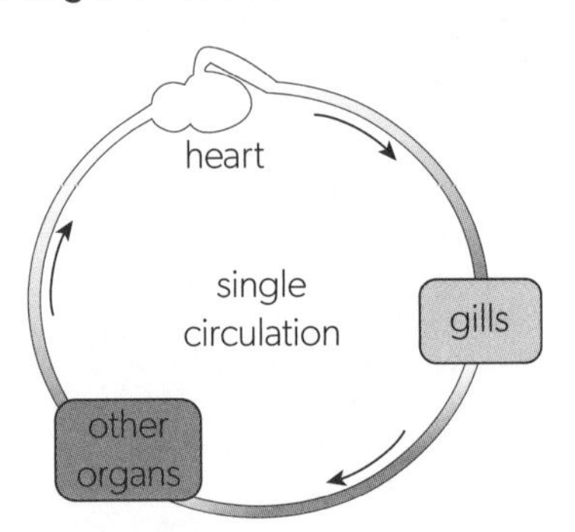

In mammals, the heart has two sides, right and left, each with a ventricle. The right ventricle pumps deoxygenated blood to the lungs via the pulmonary arteries. The blood must be at relatively low pressure to prevent capillaries in the alveoli from bursting.

After flowing through the alveolar capillaries, the pressure is too low for the blood to flow on to another organ of the body, so it returns to the left side of the heart via the pulmonary veins to be repumped. The left ventricle pumps oxygenated blood via the aorta to all organs of the body apart from the lungs. This requires relatively high blood pressure. The kidneys in particular carry out pressure filtration of blood, so need much higher blood pressure than the lungs. Oxygenated blood pumped by the left ventricle flows through capillaries in one organ of the body and is then deoxygenated and low pressure. It returns to the right side of the heart via the vena cavae (main veins), for repumping to the lungs. Mammals thus have a double circulation, with the blood passing twice through the heart to make a full circuit. The heart is a double pump, delivering blood under different pressures to different organs of the body. The two circulations are known as the pulmonary and systemic circulations.

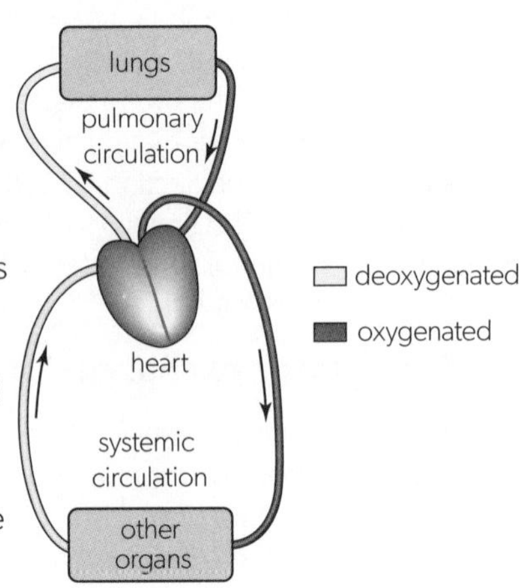

15. Adaptations of the heart

The structure of the heart and the unidirectional flow of blood through it are shown in the following diagram.

- **Atria**—collecting chambers with relatively thin muscular walls, which gradually fill with blood returning in veins to the heart, and then pump the blood into the ventricles.
- **Ventricles**—pumping chambers with thick muscular walls that pump blood out into the arteries. (Reasons for the left ventricle having a thicker wall than the right ventricle are explained in *Section B3.2.14*.)
- **Septum**—the wall between the left and right sides of the heart that ensures the heart acts as a double pump and that deoxygenated and oxygenated blood do not mix.
- **Valves**—atrioventricular valves between the atria and ventricles and semilunar valves between the ventricles and the arteries ensure that blood circulates by preventing backflow.
- **Cardiac muscle**—muscle tissue with the special property of contracting on its own without being stimulated by a nerve (myogenic contraction). Cardiac muscle cells are described in *Section B2.3.9*.
- **Coronary vessels**—the many capillaries in the muscular wall of the heart supply oxygen and glucose for aerobic respiration and remove waste products. The blood running through these capillaries is supplied by the **coronary arteries** (see *Section B3.2.6*) and removed by **coronary veins**.
- **Pacemaker**—a region of specialized cardiac muscle cells in the wall of the right atrium that initiates each contraction. The role of this region (the sinoatrial (SA) node) is described in *Section B3.2.16*.

AHL

16. The cardiac cycle

The cardiac cycle is the repeating sequence of actions in the heart that pump blood. The graph shows pressure changes in the left atrium, the left ventricle and the aorta during the cardiac cycle. The numbered brackets indicate the three phases of the cardiac cycle:

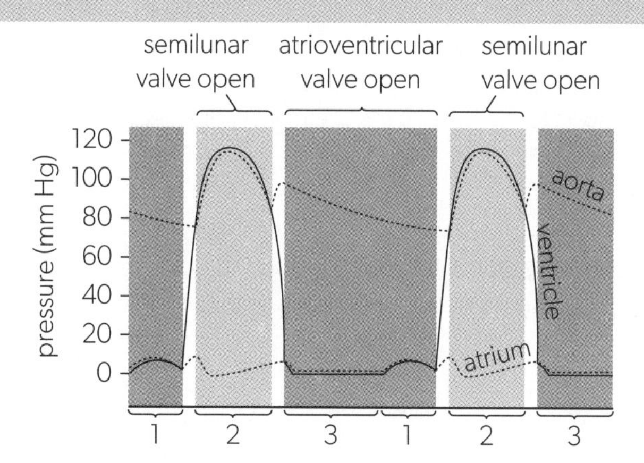

1. The walls of the atria contract, pushing blood from the atria into the ventricles through the atrio-ventricular valves, which are open. The semilunar valves are closed, so the ventricles fill with blood.
2. The walls of the ventricles contract powerfully and the blood pressure rapidly rises inside them. This first causes the atrioventricular valves to close, preventing back-flow to the atria and then causes the semilunar valves to open, allowing blood to be pumped out into the arteries. At the same time the atria start to refill by collecting blood from the veins.
3. The ventricles stop contracting so pressure falls inside them. The semilunar valves close, preventing back-flow from the arteries to the ventricles. When the ventricular pressure drops below the atrial pressure, the atrioventricular valves open. Blood entering the atrium from the veins then flows on to start filling the ventricles. The next cardiac cycle begins when the walls of the atria contract again.

Application of skills: interpreting blood pressure graphs

- The graph shows the maximum blood pressure reached in the left ventricle and aorta during a typical cardiac cycle (systolic pressure). This happens about half way through the period when the ventricles are contracting and the semilunar valve is open.
- The graph also shows the minimum pressures reached in the left ventricle and aorta (diastolic pressure). This happens at the end of the period when the ventricle is relaxing and the atrioventricular valve is open.

Each heartbeat is initiated by the sinoatrial node (SA node or pacemaker) which sends an electrical impulse that spreads out in all directions through the walls of the atria, causing atrial contraction. The impulses are prevented from spreading directly into the walls of the ventricles by a layer of fibrous tissue. Instead, they travel to the ventricles via a second node and a bundle of conducting fibres that lead down to the base of the ventricles. This gives the atria time to pump blood into the ventricles before the ventricles contract. Impulses spread out through the walls of the ventricles from the base upwards, causing contraction and pumping of blood into the arteries.

17. Root pressure in xylem vessels

The movement of water from a higher to a lower water potential is explained in *Section D2.3.9*. Root cells absorb water from the soil. The water can pass by capillary action through the walls of root cells until it has nearly reached the xylem in the centre of the root. It then enters an endodermis cell by osmosis—the endodermis cells have a higher solute concentration and therefore a lower water potential than the water in the soil. Water then passes from the endodermis cell into an adjacent xylem vessel—the water potential is lower in the xylem vessel than in the endodermis cell.

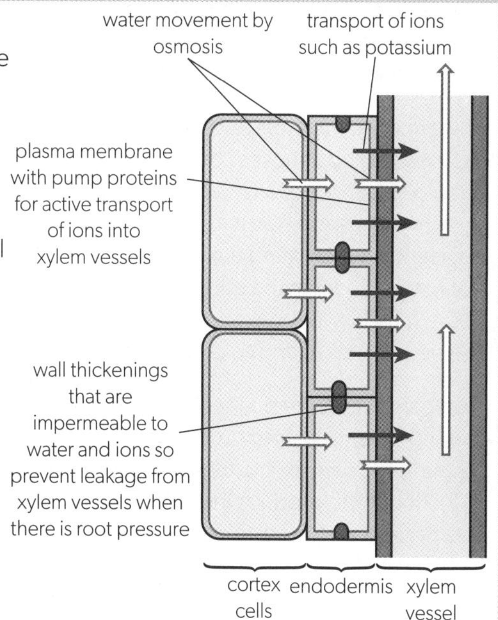

When a plant is transpiring, water xylem vessels are filled by sap under tension, which has a very low water potential (see *Section D2.3.10*). The tension draws water into xylem vessels even though the solute concentration is low. A different mechanism—**root pressure**—is used when a plant is not transpiring, but needs xylem sap to flow upwards. Endodermis cells load mineral ions into the adjacent xylem vessels by active transport, making the xylem sap hypertonic, so water moves from the endodermis cells to xylem vessels by osmosis. This raises the pressure inside the vessels and pushes the sap upwards, against the force of gravity. Unlike pumps that cause fluids to rise by creating a vacuum above them, root pressure is not dependent on atmospheric pressure so there is no limit to the height to which xylem sap can rise. Root pressure is used in spring to refill xylem vessels that have been air-filled in deciduous plants that become leafless in winter. It is also used when the atmosphere is saturated with water vapour, so transpiration is not occurring, but a plant needs to transport minerals up to the leaves.

AHL

18. Adaptations of phloem tissue for translocation

Plants use phloem tissue to translocate carbon compounds, such as sucrose, from sources to sinks. Sources are parts of the plant where photosynthesis is occurring (stems and leaves) and storage organs where the stores are being mobilized. Sinks are parts of a plant which need a supply of carbon compounds, such as roots and storage organs that are accumulating stores.

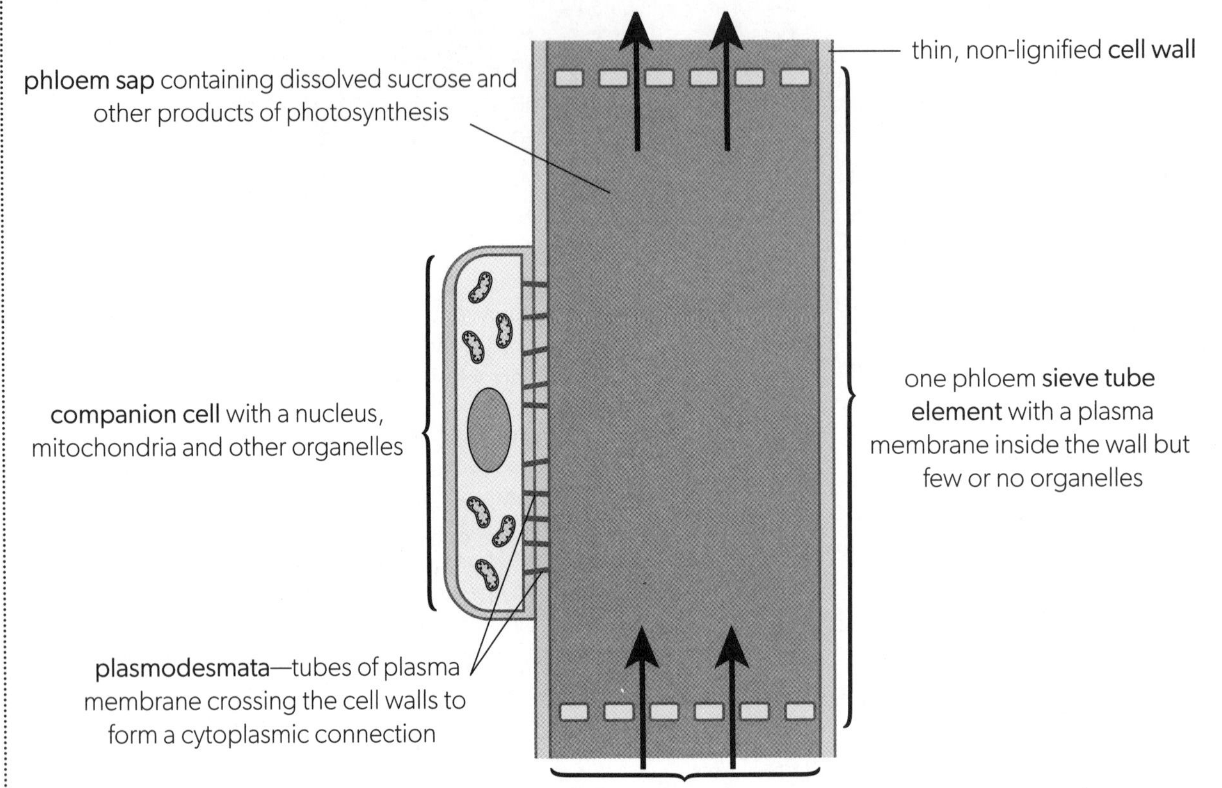
thin, non-lignified cell wall
phloem sap containing dissolved sucrose and other products of photosynthesis
companion cell with a nucleus, mitochondria and other organelles
one phloem sieve tube element with a plasma membrane inside the wall but few or no organelles
plasmodesmata—tubes of plasma membrane crossing the cell walls to form a cytoplasmic connection
sieve plate with pores through which phloem sap can flow (indicated by arrows); sap can move in either direction through a phloem sieve tube, but it cannot move in both directions simultaneously

Translocation from source to sink happens in phloem sieve tubes. Sucrose is loaded into the sieve tubes by active transport, using pump proteins in the plasma membrane. This increases the solute concentration inside the sieve tube and lowers the water potential. The hydrostatic pressure of sap in the sieve tube therefore increases (see *Section D2.3.10*). These processes are reversed in sieve tubes in the sink, reducing the pressure. There is therefore a pressure gradient which causes phloem sap containing sucrose to flow from source to sink.

Phloem sieve tubes develop from columns of cells that break down their nuclei and almost all of their cytoplasmic organelles, but remain alive, with a plasma membrane that can pump substances by active transport. Large pores develop in the end walls between adjacent cells, creating the sieve plates that allow sap to flow. By not breaking down the end walls completely, as happens in xylem vessels, the sieve tube is better able to resist high pressures, with the sieve plates acting as cross-braces.

Companion cells are small cells adjacent to sieve tubes that help with loading. They have many pump proteins in their plasma membranes for pumping sucrose into their cytoplasm. They also have many mitochondria to produce the ATP needed for active transport. Plasmodesmata (cytoplasmic connections) allow sucrose-rich sap to flow from the companion cell to the adjacent sieve tube.

▼ Vascular bundle in a wheat leaf

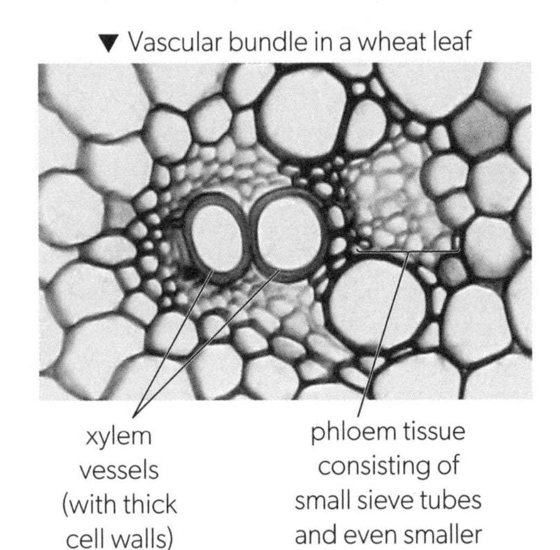
xylem vessels (with thick cell walls)
phloem tissue consisting of small sieve tubes and even smaller companion cells

B3.3 Muscle and motility

AHL

1. All living organisms are adapted for movement

Movement is one of the functions of life and all organisms have adaptations for it.

- In every organism there are **internal movements** such as peristalsis in the gut, or ventilation of the lungs. There are movements in the cytoplasm of unicellular organisms.
- **Motile** organisms move their entire body from one place to another. This is **locomotion**, with each motile organism adapted to its method of locomotion. For example, bar-tailed godwits (*Limosa lapponica*) have wings for flight. They migrate 10,400 km from Siberia to New Zealand in a week, doubling their body weight with fat reserves before the journey.
- **Sessile** organisms remain in a fixed position. Most plants are sessile, with roots growing into the soil. Most animals are motile, but some are sessile. For example, a coral consists of a colony of sessile polyps. In hard corals, the polyps construct a rigid skeleton around themselves. They can extend their tentacles into the water when they are filter-feeding, but cannot move to a new location.

2. Muscle contraction

The structure of muscle fibres is introduced in *Section A2.2.9*. Each fibre contains many parallel, cylindrical myofibrils.

Each myofibril consists of a series of sarcomeres linked end-to-end at Z-discs. There are light bands at either end of a sarcomere and a dark band in the centre.

one sarcomere
dark band
light band
part of one myofibril
Z-disc between sarcomeres

Two types of protein filament are arranged in a regular pattern within sarcomeres—thin actin filaments and thick myosin filaments. The dark band in the centre of a sarcomere contains many parallel myosin filaments. The ends of these myosin filaments overlap with six equidistant actin filaments. The light bands at the ends of sarcomeres contain actin filaments but not myosin. Each actin filament is attached to a Z-disc at one end and overlaps with myosin filaments at the other end.

light band
dark band
light band
z-disc
sarcomere relaxed
contraction is due to actin being pulled towards the centre of the sarcomere by myosin
dark band remains the same length during contraction (but light bands shorten)
sarcomere contracted
transverse section (TS) of sarcomere where actin and myosin filaments overlap

The contraction of sarcomeres is due to the sliding of actin and myosin filaments. Myosin has "heads" that can attach to binding sites on actin. These heads undergo a cycle of binding to form a cross-bridge, pulling the actin molecule towards the centre of the sarcomere by about 10 nm and then detaching and swivelling to the next binding site on actin. This is a molecular ratchet mechanism.

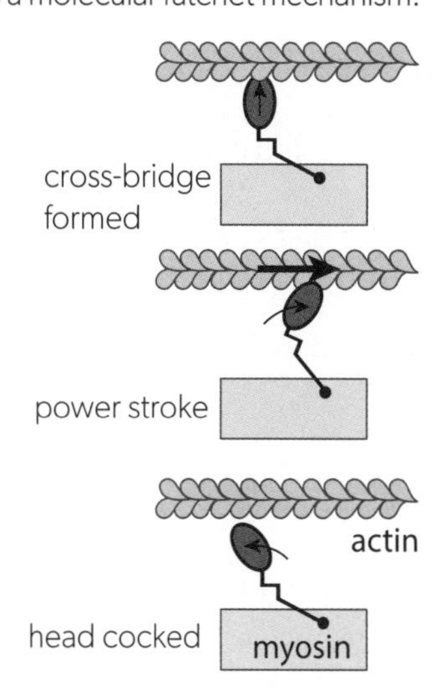

Because of the many heads per myosin and many myosin filaments, in many sarcomeres, in many myofibrils, in many muscle fibres, the small force exerted by each myosin head is multiplied up and muscles can exert very powerful forces.

AHL

3. Muscle relaxation

When muscles relax, potential energy is stored by titin, an elastic protein that has the largest polypeptides so far discovered (over 34,000 amino acids long in humans). Titin releases potential energy when it recoils during muscle contractions. This increases the amount of force that a muscle can exert. Titin has two other roles. It connects the end of myosin filaments in sarcomeres to the Z-disc and holds each myosin filament in the correct position in the centre of six parallel actin filaments. It also prevents overstretching of the sarcomere.

Energy is needed to stretch titin and therefore to lengthen a muscle. Lengthening of muscles happens when they relax. Muscles can only exert force when they contract, so a muscle cannot supply the energy it needs to lengthen. The energy has to be provided by another muscle that is known as the antagonist. Despite the name, an antagonistic pair of muscles work together, with the contraction of each member of the pair providing the energy needed to lengthen the titin molecules in the other as it relaxes.

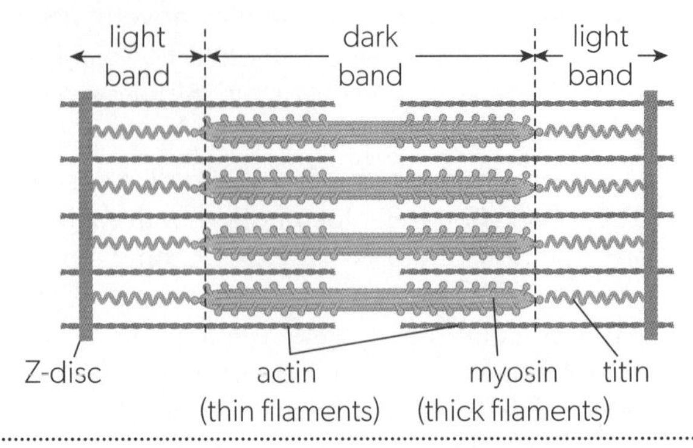

4. Motor units

Skeletal muscles are composed of striated muscle fibres, which contract when stimulated by a motor neuron. The synapse between a motor neuron and a muscle fibre is a **neuromuscular junction**. The neurotransmitter used is acetylcholine. Each motor neuron has branches that form neuromuscular junctions with different muscle fibres, usually hundreds. A nerve impulse conveyed by the motor neuron therefore stimulates simultaneous contraction in a group of muscle fibres. A **motor unit** is one motor neuron together with all the muscle fibres that it stimulates. This pattern helps to achieve coordinated contraction of a muscle with as few motor neurons as possible.

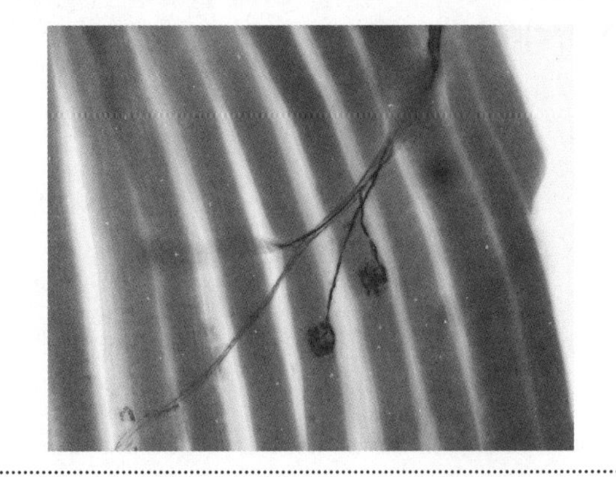

5. Skeletons facilitate movement

A skeleton is a hard framework that supports and protects an animal's body. Arthropods such as spiders, crustaceans and insects have **exoskeletons** consisting of tough plates of chitin that cover most of the body surface. Vertebrates have **endoskeletons** consisting of bones.

Skeletons facilitate movement by providing an **anchorage** for muscles and acting as **levers**. Typically, a muscle is attached to two parts of the skeleton. One attachment is the insertion, where muscle contraction causes movement. The other is the origin and is fixed, so contraction does not cause movement.

By acting as levers, bones can change the size and/or direction of a force. Levers have a fixed point called the fulcrum, which is the pivot point. The force applied to the lever is the effort. It is converted by the lever into a resultant force. The diagrams show how limb bones and muscles can be adapted either for maximum rapidity of movement (as in the limbs of gazelles), or for maximum force (e.g. a mole's front limb that it uses for digging).

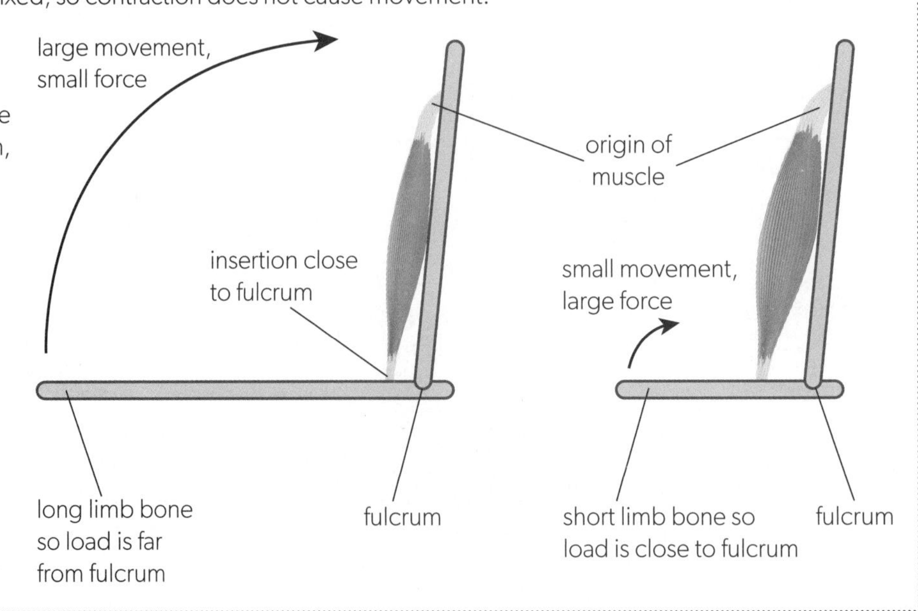

AHL

6. Synovial joints

Bones meet at joints. Most joints allow bones to move in relation to each other (articulation). Synovial joints are self-lubricating articular joints that have the following parts:

- **Bones**—an anchorage for muscles and ligaments, with the bones shaped to allow a specific range of movements
- **Muscles**—cause movement at a joint because the origin and insertion of a muscle are on opposite sides of the joint
- **Tendons**—tough collagen-rich cords of tissue that attach muscle to bone and transmit force from contractions
- **Cartilage**—tough, smooth tissue covering bone at joints to prevent friction and absorb shocks, preventing fractures
- **Synovial fluid**—fluid that fills the cavity between the cartilages on the ends of the bones, lubricating the joint
- **Ligaments**—tough cords of tissue with much collagen that prevent movements that would dislocate the joint
- **Joint capsule**—tough ligamentous covering that seals the joint, holds in the synovial fluid and prevents dislocation.

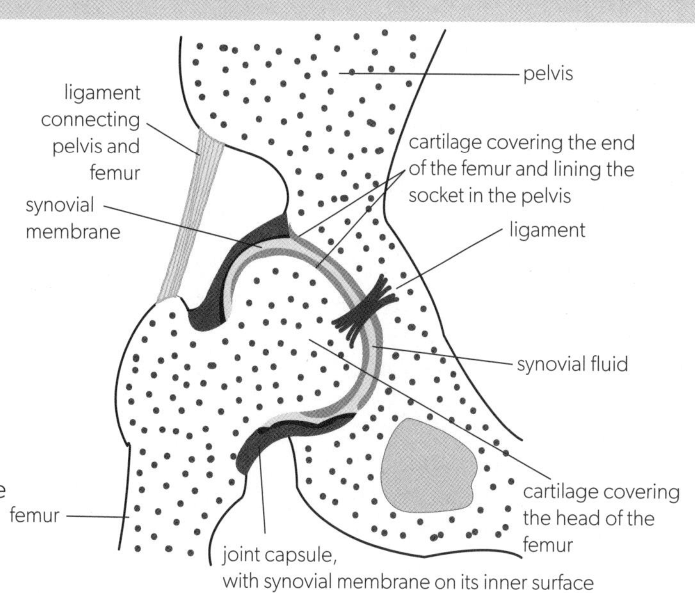

7. Application of skills: measuring the range of motion at a joint

The elbow and knee are hinge joints allowing movements in one plane: flexion (bending) and extension (straightening). The hip is a ball-and-socket joint that moves in three planes: protraction/retraction, abduction/adduction, and rotation.

The range of movement at a joint can be measured with a goniometer or by computer analysis of images.

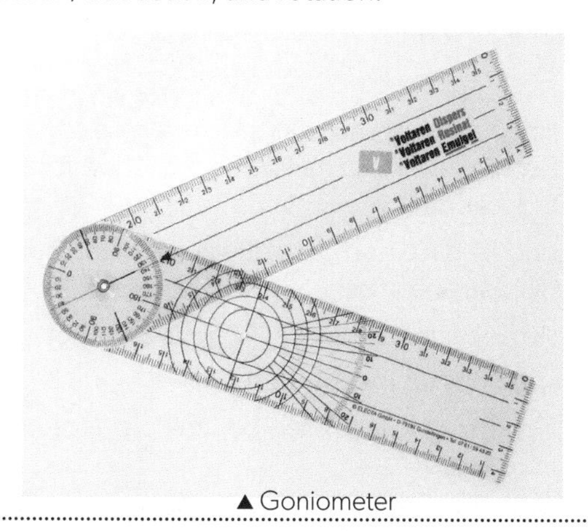

▲ Goniometer

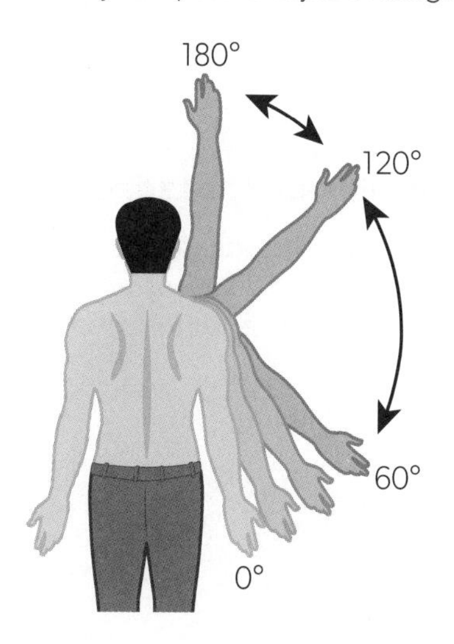

9. Importance of locomotion

Animals have many reasons for moving from place to place. The table shows four reasons with examples of each.

Reason	Examples in **honey bees**	Examples in **salmon**
Foraging for food	Bees fly from flower to flower searching for nectar and pollen	Salmon in the sea swim to catch their prey of smaller fish and large invertebrates
Escaping from danger	Bees fly back to their colony when a storm is approaching because heavy rain is a danger	Salmon in the sea swim to escape from predators such as bluefin tuna and swordfish
Searching for a mate	Male bees (drones) fly at a height of 10–40 m and mate with a virgin queen if they find one	Male salmon search for a female laying eggs in spawning grounds, then shed sperm on the eggs
Migration	A swarm of bees is a migrating colony containing a queen and many workers	Young salmon migrate from rivers to the sea and then as adults migrate back to the river to breed

AHL

8. Intercostal muscles

Ventilation of the lungs is explained in *Section B3.1.5*. It is an example of internal body movement and is due to the antagonistic action of two layers of intercostal muscle, external and internal. Muscle fibres in each layer are attached to adjacent ribs in the ribcage and cause the ribcage to move when they contract. The diagram shows the orientation of muscle fibres in the two layers (with only some of the fibres shown). External and internal intercostal muscle fibres are orientated differently so they cause the ribcage to move in different directions.

ribcage up and out with external intercostal muscles contracted and internal intercostals relaxed

vertebrae

sternum

rib

external intercostal muscle

internal intercostal muscle

ribcage down and in with internal intercostal muscles contracted and external intercostals relaxed

When the external intercostal muscles contract, the ribcage is moved up and out, increasing the volume of the thorax and drawing air into the lungs (inhalation). When the internal intercostal muscles contract the ribs are pulled down and in, decreasing the volume of the thorax and forcibly expelling air from the lungs (exhalation).

Contraction in either layer stretches muscle fibres in the other layer, which will be relaxing. Titin molecules in the sarcomeres of the relaxing muscle are elongated by forces from the contracting muscle, generating a store of potential energy. This energy is released when the relaxing muscle starts to contract and there is elastic recoil of the titin molecules.

10. Marine mammals are adapted for swimming

Water is about 1,000 times denser than air and much more viscous. Swimming therefore requires different adaptations from those needed for locomotion on land or in the air.

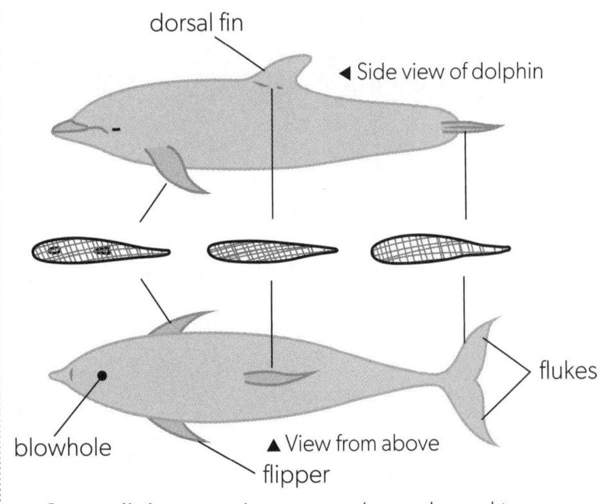

- **Streamlining**—marine mammals are shaped to minimize resistance to motion by these features:
  - shaped to be widest near the front and tapering towards the rear, which causes less drag than other shapes
  - flippers, flukes and dorsal fin have an elongated teardrop profile in transverse section which reduces drag
  - body surface is smooth due to even distribution of blubber and absence of hind limbs and ear flaps
  - skin is hairless, reducing friction.
- **Adaptations for locomotion:**
  - flippers, which are used for steering, instead of front legs
  - tail flukes, which are lobes to left and right that increase thrust when the tail is moved up and down
  - dorsal fin to provide stability by preventing rolling
  - blubber, which provides buoyancy.
- **Adaptations for periodic breathing between dives:**
  - airways can be closed during dives using the nostrils or blowhole
  - airways are reinforced with rings of cartilage or smooth muscle to ensure ventilation can restart quickly after a dive.

End of topic questions—B3 Questions

B3.1 Gas exchange

1. The micrograph shows cells in leaf epidermis of a lily plant, with a 0.1 mm scale bar.

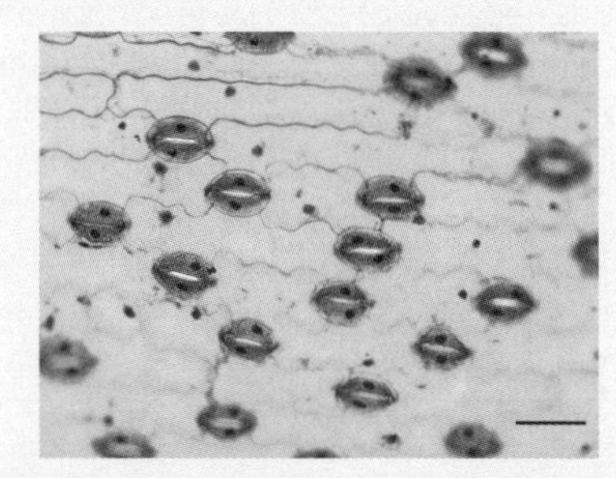

   a. Compare and contrast the two types of cell that are visible in the micrograph. (5)
   b. Calculate the stomatal density of the epidermis. (5)
   c. The epidermis was peeled off the lily leaf. Outline one other method of obtaining an image from which stomatal density can be measured. (3)
   d. Deduce, with a reason, whether the epidermis was peeled off in the day or in the night. (2)

2. The diagram shows the gas exchange system.

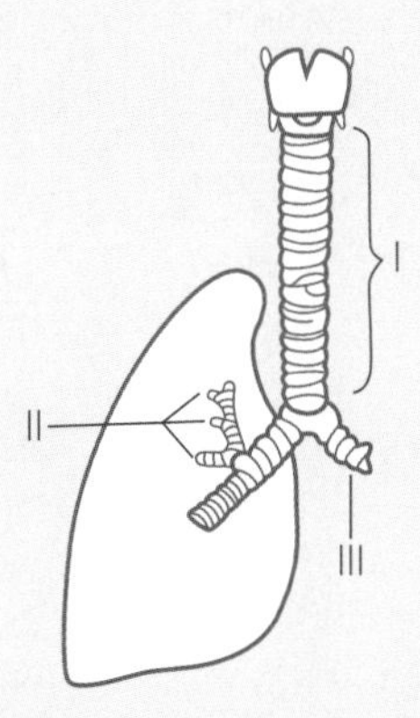

   a. State the name of structures I, II and III. (3)
   b. I, II and III allow the lungs to be ventilated. Briefly explain the need for ventilation. (2)
   c. Draw and label a diagram of an alveolus and adjacent blood capillaries. (5)

3. (HL only) Explain, using an annotated graph, the benefits of the Bohr shift in oxygen affinity of haemoglobin. (5)

B3.2 Transport

1. The light micrograph below shows the centre of a *Ranunculus* root in transverse section.

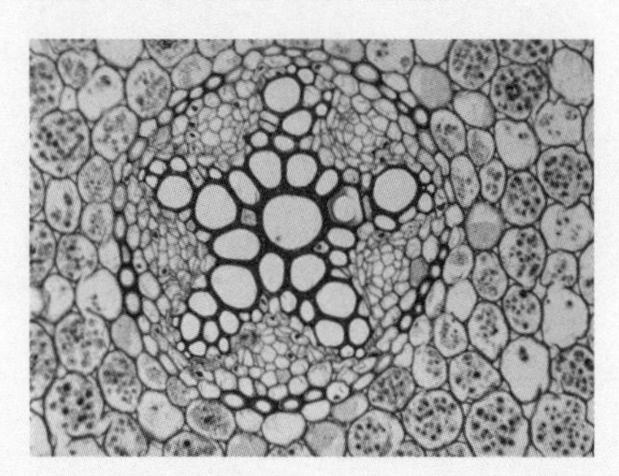

   a. Draw a labelled plan diagram to show the distribution of tissues in this part of the root. (5)
   b. Describe the adaptations of xylem vessels for water transport. (3)
   c. State the conditions that will cause most rapid transport of water in xylem. (2)

2. a. Compare and contrast the functions of arteries and veins. (3)
   b. Distinguish between the arteries and capillaries in the structure of their walls. (4)
   c. Outline, with reasons, how pulse rate is measured. (3)

3. (HL only) a. State where a heartbeat is initiated. (1)
   b. Explain this sequence of changes in ventricular blood pressure following initiation of a heartbeat:
      i. an initial small rise (2)
      ii. a rapid rise (2)
      iii. a further rise to a maximum and then gentle fall (2)
      iv. a steep fall (2)
      v. a very gentle rise. (2)
   c. Draw a sketch graph of the cardiac cycle to show these pressure changes and also pressure changes in the left atrium and aorta. (9)

B3.3 Muscle and motility (HL)

1. Explain two methods of measuring the range of movement at a joint. (5)

2. The micrograph shows part of a myofibril.

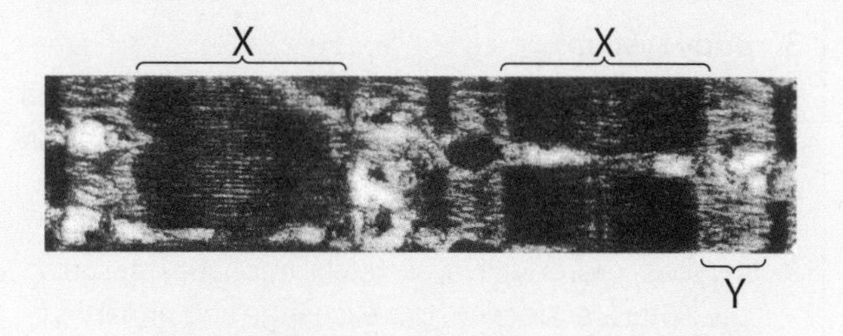

   a. State the type of filament present only in X. (1)
   b. State the other filament type in myofibrils. (1)
   c. The myofibril is semi-contracted. Deduce any changes in length of regions X and Y if the:
      i. myofibril contracted more (2)
      ii. myofibril relaxed and the antagonistic muscle contracted. (2)
   d. Draw a labelled diagram of the structure of a sarcomere in the semi-contracted myofibril. (4)

3. Describe adaptations for swimming in a named example of a marine mammal. (5)

C3.1 Integration of body systems

1. Coordination to integrate systems

All organisms use multiple systems to perform the various functions of life. Within these systems, there are interdependent subsystems that work together to perform an overall function.

At every level in the functioning of an organism, there must be coordination between and within systems. This is achieved by system integration. System integration depends on effective communication between components so they can interact. The interactions may be as simple as negative or positive feedback between two components. More commonly, however, they are complex and multifactorial, with many loops and branches.

Comparisons can be made with systems integration in engineering projects or software design, such as the control of wind turbines.

2. Cells, tissues, organs and body systems

The cells within a multicellular organism interact with each other at multiple levels in a hierarchy of organization, shown in the flow chart (right).

1. Tissues

   Cells within multicellular organisms are specialized to perform specific functions. One cell by itself cannot usually carry out its function on a large enough scale to meet the needs of the organism. Instead, cells are part of tissues. A tissue is a group of cells that carry out a function together. There may be only one cell type, or several cell types that are specialized for different aspects of the function of the tissue. Cells in a tissue adhere to each other and also communicate with each other using chemical or electrical signals.

2. Organs

   An organ is a group of tissues in an animal or plant that work together to carry out a specific function of life. For example, the kidney is an organ of excretion and the leaf is an organ of photosynthesis. The tissues within an organ are interdependent—unless each tissue carries out its function, the overall function of the organ is not achieved.

3. Body systems

   Groups of organs interact with each other to perform an overall function of life. These groups are known as body or organ systems. In humans, 11 body systems are recognized: the digestive, integumentary, nervous, reproductive, skeletal, lymphatic, muscular, circulatory, endocrine, gas exchange and urinary systems. In most cases, the organs in a body system are physically linked as for example in the digestive and nervous systems. In other cases, the organs are dispersed around the body, as in the endocrine system.

4. Organisms

   An organism is a living individual made up of interconnected parts—organ systems, composed of organs, made up of tissues with constituent cells. These parts are interdependent so failure of a single group of cells in a tissue can cause an organism to die.

Plant example		***Animal example***
Lamium album (dead-nettle)	organism	*Homo sapiens (human)*
	↑	
flower	body systems	*blood system*
	↑	
petal	organs	*heart*
	↑	
phloem	tissues	*cardiac muscle*
	↑	
sieve tube cell	cells	*cardiomyocyte*
	↑	
mitochondria	organelles	*mitochondria*

Interactions within and between all the levels of organization within an organism result in the integration of body systems and the development of **emergent properties**. For example, integration of body systems makes a cheetah an effective predator. This would be difficult to predict if each subsystem was studied separately. To understand the emergent properties of organisms, whole systems must be studied.

3. Comparing hormonal and nervous signalling

Integration of organs in an animal requires transport of materials and energy, and effective communication.

Materials and energy are transported between organs by the circulatory system (see *Topic B3.2*). Blood circulates through all organs and almost all tissues, transporting these things:

- energy in the form of substrates for respiration, such as glucose
- oxygen for aerobic respiration
- water and carbon compounds needed for growth or repair
- waste products of metabolism.

Communication between organs is carried out by both the nervous system (see *Topic C2.2*) and the endocrine system, which consists of glands that secrete hormones. The roles of these two methods of communication are compared in the table.

	Hormonal signalling	Nervous signalling
Type of signal	Chemical	Electrical (nerve impulses)
Transmission route	In the blood	In neurons
Destination of signal	Widespread, but only certain target cells respond	Signal passes only to specific cells via synapses
Effectors	Target cells in any tissue	Muscles or glands
Types of response	• growth • development (e.g. puberty) • reproduction (e.g. gamete production and pregnancy) • changes to metabolic rate • changes to solute concentration in the blood • mood (e.g. thirst and sleep)	• contraction of striated muscles used in locomotion • contraction of smooth muscle (e.g. peristalsis in the gut) • change to the rate of cardiac muscle contraction • secretion by glands
Speed of response	Slower	Very rapid
Duration of response	Long duration—until the hormone has broken down	Short duration—unless nerve impulses are sent repeatedly

4. The brain integrates information

The brain is the central integrating organ of our body. It receives information, processes it, stores some of it and sends instructions to all parts of the body to coordinate life processes. Information is received from sensory receptors, both in specialized sense organs such as the eye and also from receptor cells in other organs, such as pressure receptors in blood vessels. The brain can store information, for the short term or longer term. The capacity to store information is called memory and it is essential for learning. Processing of information leads to decision making by the brain. This may result in signals being sent to muscles or glands, which cause these organs to carry out a response.

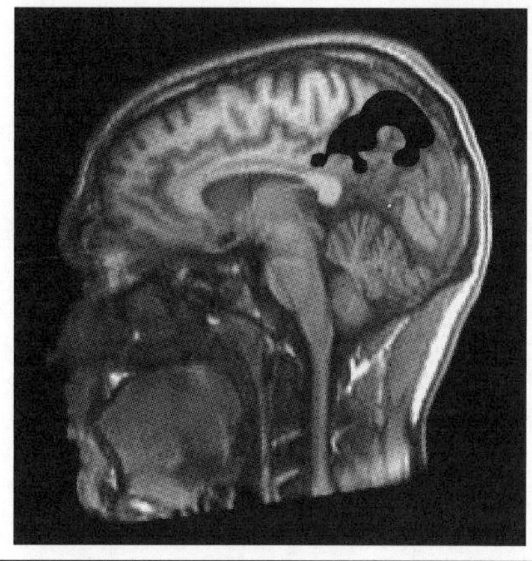

fMRI scan of a 24 year-old man showing activity in part of his brain

5. The spinal cord coordinates unconscious processes

The spinal cord is located inside the vertebral column (backbone). The area of tissue in the centre of the spinal cord is the grey matter. It acts as an integrating centre for unconscious processes.

Neurons bring information to the grey matter from the brain and the sense organs. Motor neurons convey signals from the grey matter to muscles and glands. Interneurons pass impulses via synapses between neurons in the grey matter. The pattern of neurons and synapses determines how information is processed in the grey matter and what decisions are made.

The spinal cord only coordinates unconscious processes, especially reflexes. It can do this more quickly than if signals were conveyed to and from the brain.

The table shows differences between unconscious and conscious processes.

Unconscious processes	Conscious processes
Can happen when asleep	Only happen when awake
Involuntary—no control through thought	Voluntary—controllable through thought
Controlled by brain and spinal cord	Controlled only by cerebral hemispheres of the brain
Glands and smooth muscle are controlled involuntarily	Striated muscle is controlled voluntarily
Examples: peristalsis in the intestine; saliva secretion	Example: putting food into the mouth, chewing

6. Sensory neurons convey messages from receptors to the CNS

Receptor cells, located in the skin and sense organs, detect changes in the external environment. For example, rod and cone cells in the retina of the eye detect light. Receptor cells then pass impulses to sensory neurons. Nerve endings of some sensory neurons act as receptors for touch and heat, without the need for a separate receptor cell. There are also receptor cells inside the body that monitor internal conditions. Stretch receptors in striated muscle sense the state of contraction, allowing the brain to deduce the posture of the body. Stretch receptors in the walls of arteries give a measure of blood pressure. Chemoreceptors in the walls of blood vessels monitor concentrations of oxygen, carbon dioxide and glucose.

Signals from all receptor cells are conveyed to the central nervous system (brain and spinal cord) as nerve impulses in sensory neurons. The axons of sensory neurons enter either the spinal cord through one of 31 pairs of spinal nerves, or the brain by one of the 12 pairs of cranial nerves.

- The spinal cord receives signals from other organs of the body including skin and muscles. The structure of a section of spinal cord is shown in the diagram.
- The brain receives all the signals from the main sense organs located in the head: the eyes, ears, nose and tongue. Sensory inputs to the brain are received by specialized areas in the cerebral hemispheres. For example, the visual cortex that receives signals from rod and cone cells is in the posterior part of the cerebrum.

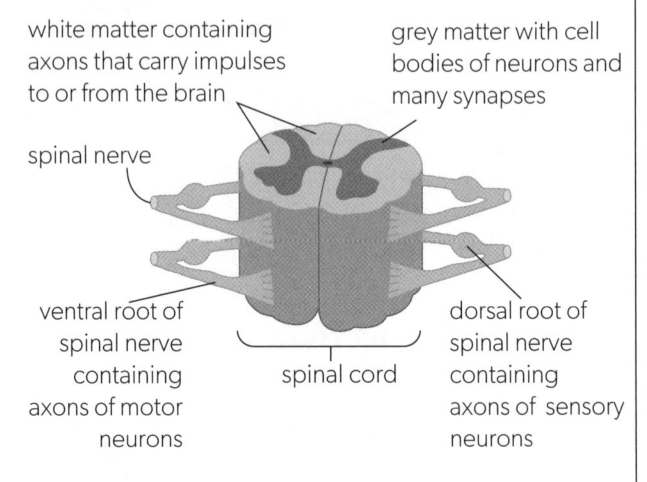

7. Motor neurons convey messages from the CNS to muscles

The cerebral hemispheres of the brain play a major role in the conscious (voluntary) control of striated muscles. The motor cortex can send nerve impulses to any striated muscle in the body. Striated muscle is attached to bone. It maintains posture and is used for locomotion. For example, to stand up from a sitting position, impulses are sent from the motor cortex via motor neurons to muscles in the legs.

Grey matter in the cerebral hemispheres contains many motor neurons. Each motor neuron has many dendrites that receive signals from interneurons. One axon leads from the cell body of the motor neuron out of the brain and down the spinal cord. There it forms a synapse with a second motor neuron, whose axon leads to one specific striated muscle. When a nerve impulse reaches the end of the axon, it stimulates contraction.

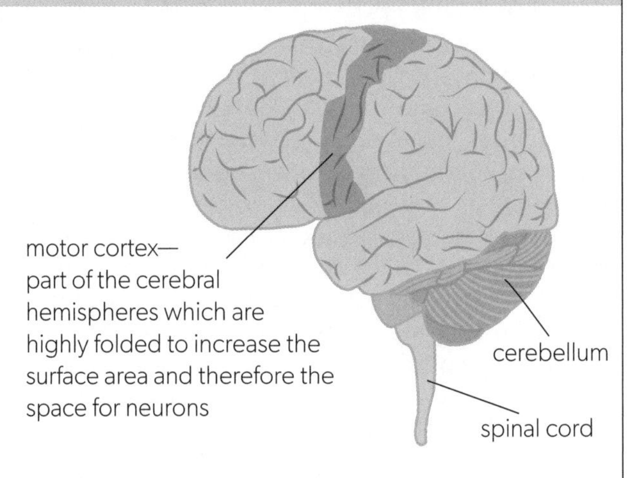

8. Nerves are bundles of nerve fibres

A nerve is a bundle of nerve fibres enclosed in a protective sheath. Nerves vary in size depending on the number of nerve fibres and how many of them are myelinated.

- The widest is the sciatic nerve (20 mm across).
- The optic nerve contains up to 1.7 million nerve fibres.
- Small nerves may contain fewer than a hundred fibres.

Most nerves contain nerve fibres of both sensory and motor neurons. However, some contain only sensory neurons (e.g. the optic nerve) and some contain only motor neurons (e.g. the oculomotor nerve).

All organs of the body are served by one or more nerves.

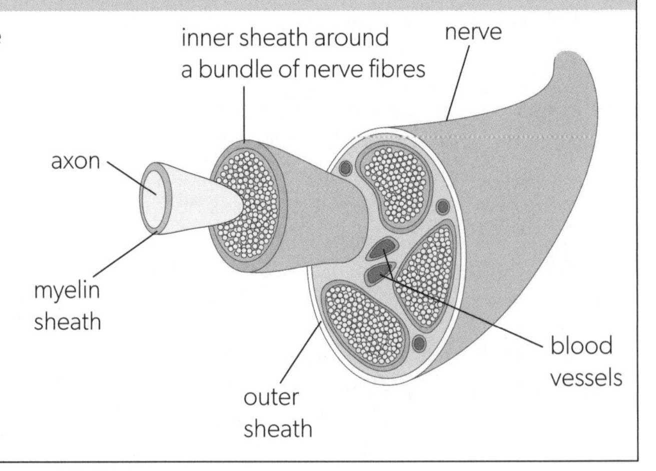

9. The reflex arc

A reflex action is a rapid, involuntary response to a specific stimulus. Reflexes are the simplest type of coordination by the nervous system, as the signals pass through the smallest number of neurons. This helps to speed up reflexes, which is an advantage if the response prevents harm to the body. A reflex action is carried out by a series of neurons that link receptor cells that perceive a stimulus to effector cells that make a response. Synapses between the neurons in a reflex arc are either in the spinal cord or the brain. Synapses for the photo-pupillary reflex that constricts the pupil of the eye in response to bright light are in the brain. Synapses for the **pain reflex** (e.g. when we pull our hand away after touching a hot object) are in the spinal cord. The elements of a reflex arc used in such a spinal reflex are shown in the diagram and described in 1–5 below.

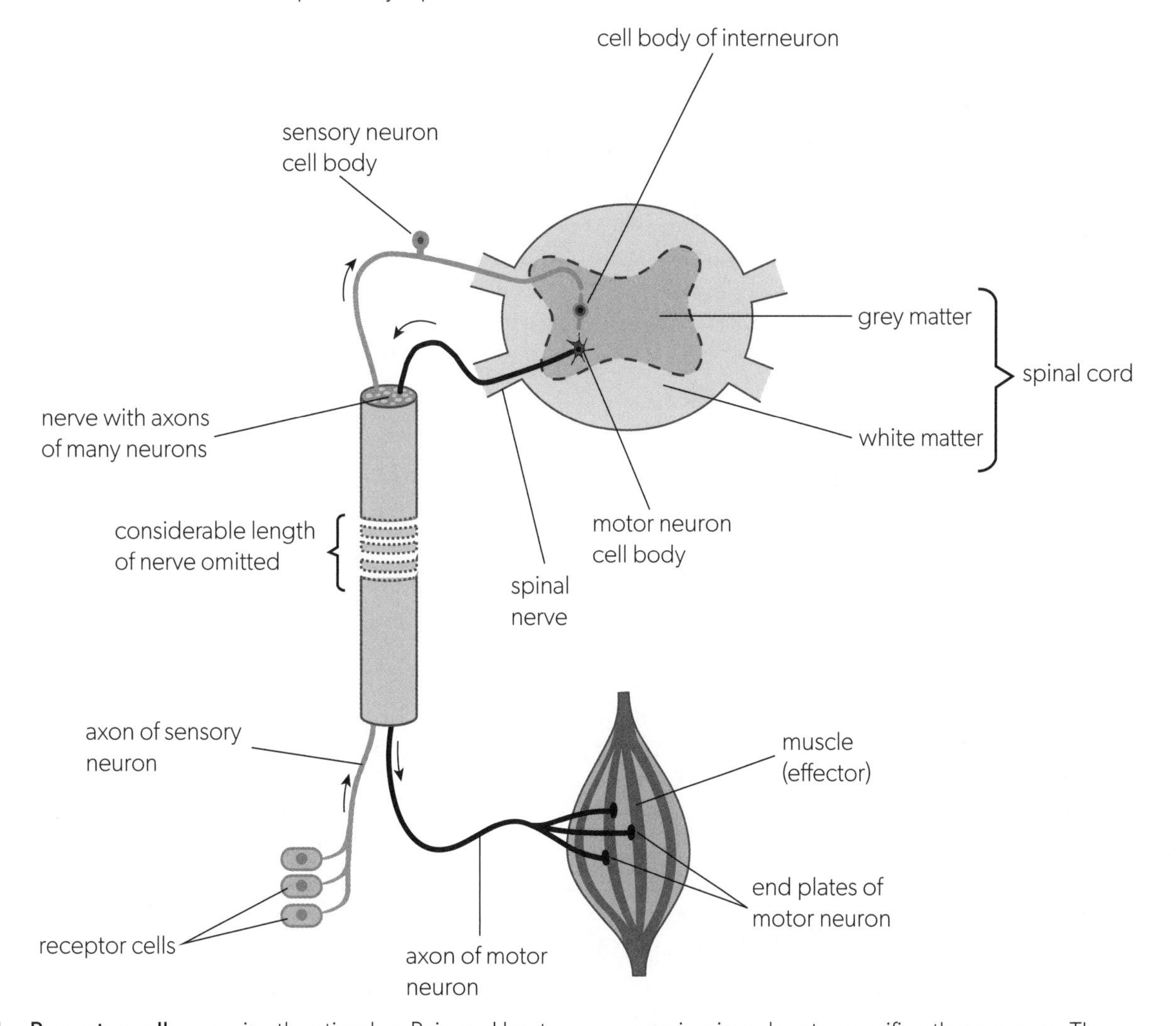

1. **Receptor cells** perceive the stimulus. Pain and heat are perceived directly by nerve endings of sensory neurons in the skin, so there is no need for a separate receptor cell. This is how the stimulus is perceived when the hand touches a hot object.
2. **Sensory neurons** receive signals, either from receptor cells or from their own sensory nerve endings and pass them as nerve impulses to the brain or spinal cord, via long axons. These axons end at synapses with interneurons in the grey matter of the spinal cord or brain (see *Section C3.1.6*).
3. **Interneurons** are located in the grey matter of the brain and spinal cord. They have many branched fibres called dendrites, along which nerve impulses travel. Interneurons process signals brought by sensory neurons and make decisions about appropriate responses. They do this by combining impulses from multiple inputs and then passing impulses to specific other neurons. The decision-making process in a reflex action is very simple because there may be only one interneuron connecting a specific sensory neuron to the motor neuron that can cause an appropriate response.
4. **Motor neurons** (described in *Section C2.2.1*) receive signals via synapses with interneurons. If a threshold potential is achieved in a motor neuron, an impulse is passed along the axon which leads out of the central nervous system (CNS) to an effector. The axon does not change its position or connections, so the impulse always travels to the same effector cells.
5. **Effectors** carry out the response to a stimulus when they receive the signal from a motor neuron. The two types of effector are muscles and glands. When the hand has touched a hot object, the effectors are muscles which flex the arm at the elbow, pulling it away.

10. The cerebellum coordinates skeletal muscle contraction and balance

The cerebellum is a part of the brain. Its position is shown in the diagram. The cerebellum has important roles in the control of skeletal muscle contraction and balance. It does not make decisions about which muscles will contract, but it fine-tunes the timing of contractions. It allows very precise coordination of movements and helps us to maintain posture, for example when we are standing. It also helps us with activities requiring motor memory, such as riding a bike or typing on a keyboard.

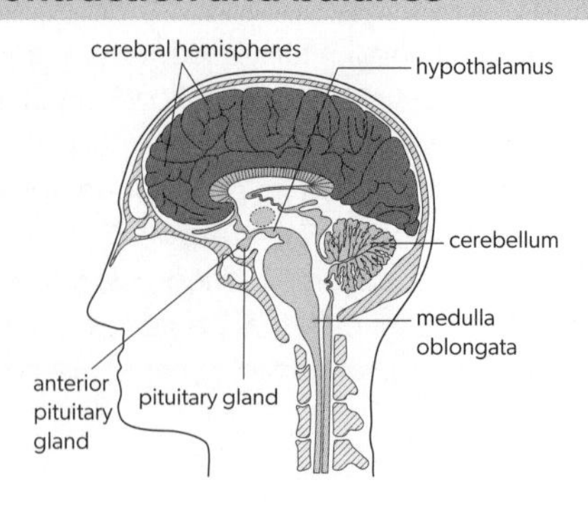

11. Role of melatonin in modulating sleep patterns

In a circadian rhythm, something happens once per 24 hours. There is a circadian rhythm in human behaviour with diurnal and nocturnal phases. The rhythm is set by groups of cells in the hypothalamus called the suprachiasmatic nuclei (SCN). They control the secretion of the hormone melatonin by the pineal gland. Melatonin secretion increases in the evening and drops to a low level at dawn. The hormone is rapidly removed from the blood by the liver, so blood concentrations rise and fall rapidly in response to rate of secretion. The graph shows melatonin concentrations at different ages, with the period in which it is dark shown in grey.

The most obvious effect of melatonin is the sleep–wake cycle. High melatonin levels cause feelings of drowsiness and promote sleep through the night. Falling melatonin levels encourage waking at the end of the night.

A special type of ganglion cell in the retina of the eye detects light of wavelength 460–480 nm and passes impulses to cells in the SCN. This signals to the SCN the timing of dusk and dawn and allows it to adjust melatonin secretion so that it corresponds to the day–night cycle.

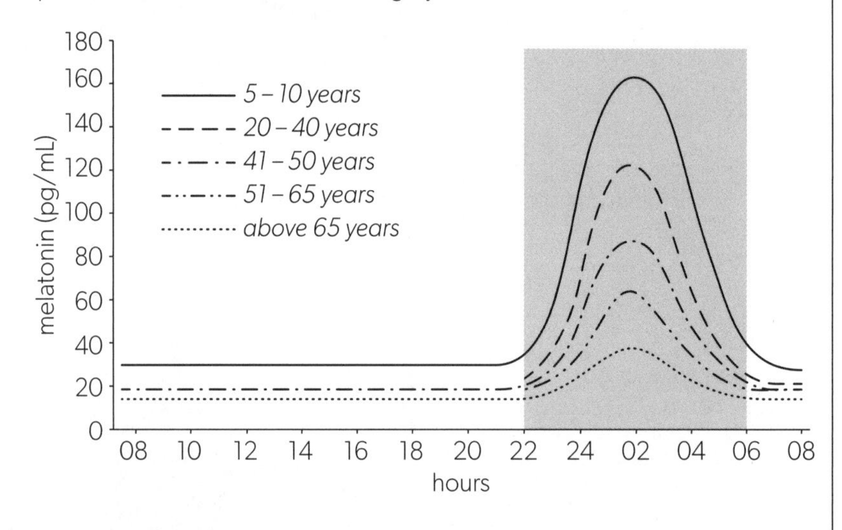

12. Epinephrine prepares the body for vigorous activity

Epinephrine (adrenaline), is secreted by the adrenal glands and triggers responses in a wide range of cells, which collectively prepare the body for vigorous physical activity. (Epinephrine receptors are described for HL in *Section C2.1.10*.)

These are specific effects of epinephrine on target cells:

- striated muscle fibres convert stored glycogen to glucose, increasing supplies for aerobic or anaerobic respiration
- liver cells also convert glycogen to glucose and release it into the blood for transport to muscles
- bronchioles in the lungs dilate (widen) due to relaxation of smooth muscle cells, making ventilation easier
- cells in the brainstem that control ventilation stimulate intercostal muscles and diaphragm to contract at a faster rate and more forcefully, so a larger total volume of air is breathed in and out per minute, increasing gas exchange
- the sinoatrial node (pacemaker) speeds up the heart rate, so cardiac output increases
- arterioles carrying blood to muscles and liver widen (vasodilate) due to relaxation of smooth muscle cells in their walls, so more blood flows to them
- arterioles carrying blood to the gut, kidneys and skin narrow (vasoconstrict) due to contraction of smooth muscle cells, so less blood flows to them.

As a result of these responses, striated muscles receive a greater volume of blood per minute. This blood carries more glucose and oxygen, allowing increased production of ATP by aerobic or anaerobic respiration and therefore more frequent and/or powerful muscle contractions.

Epinephrine secretion is controlled by the brain. It increases when vigorous physical activity may be necessary because of a threat or an opportunity. For this reason, epinephrine is known as the "fight or flight" hormone.

13. The hypothalamus and pituitary gland

The hypothalamus is a small region of the brain that has major roles in the integration of body systems. It links the nervous system to the endocrine system via the pituitary gland.

Within the hypothalamus there are specialized areas called nuclei. Each nucleus operates one or more specific control systems, using information from a variety of sources. Some nuclei have sensors for blood temperature, blood glucose concentration, osmolarity and the concentrations of various hormones. Many nuclei receive signals from sense organs, either directly or indirectly via the cerebral hemispheres. There are also inputs from other parts of the brain, such as the medulla oblongata.

There are close relationships between the hypothalamus and the pituitary gland, which is located directly below it and connected to the hypothalmus by a narrow stalk. The pituitary gland has two distinct parts: the anterior and posterior lobes. They both secrete hormones into blood capillaries with the hypothalamus controlling this. The table shows examples of hormones secreted.

Osmoregulation and puberty are two processes based on system integration by the hypothalamus and pituitary gland.

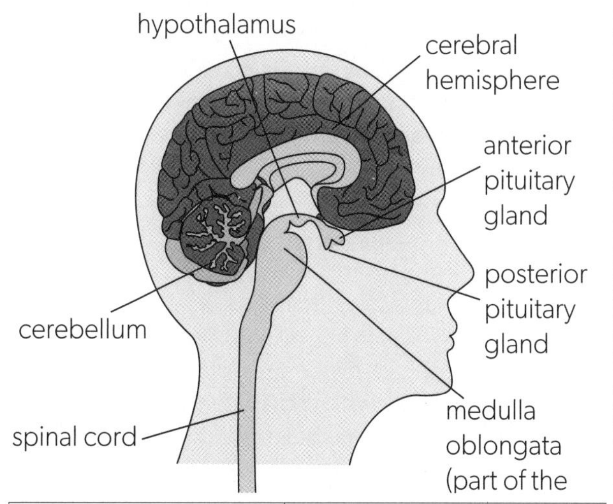

Posterior pituitary	Anterior pituitary
Antidiuretic hormone (ADH)	Luteinizing hormone (LH)
Oxytocin	Follicle-stimulating hormone (FSH)

(Details of the hormonal control of puberty and osmoregulation for HL are given in *Sections D3.1.13* and *D3.3.10*.)

14. Control of heart rate

Negative feedback control causes the heart rate to rise if the blood pressure, pH or O_2 concentration is low, or if CO_2 concentration is high. It causes heart rate to drop if blood pressure, pH or O_2 concentration is high, or if CO_2 is low.

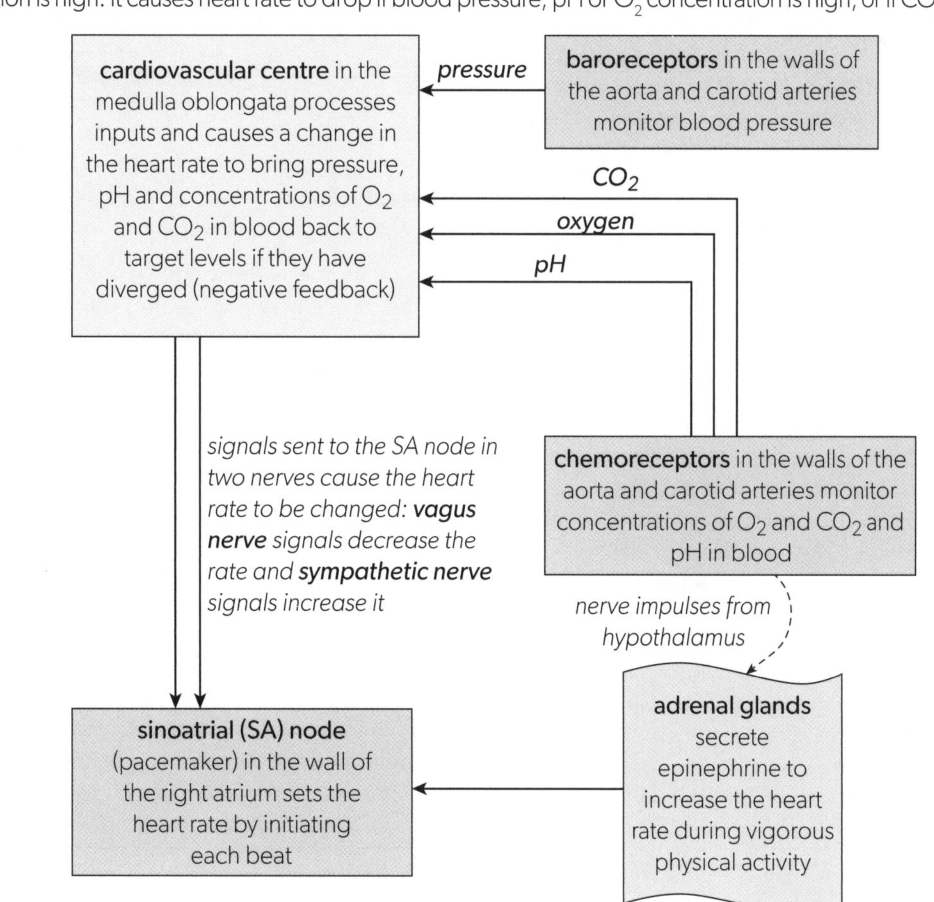

15. Control of ventilation rate

The normal range for blood pH is 7.35–7.45. It is kept within this range by negative feedback. If cell respiration rates in the body increase, for example during vigorous physical exercise, the CO_2 concentration of the blood rises and therefore blood pH falls. Levels below 6.8 (acidosis) can be life-threatening. To prevent this, the ventilation rate is increased, so CO_2 is removed from the blood more rapidly and blood pH rises. If cell respiration rates in the body are low, so blood CO_2 concentration falls and pH rises, the ventilation rate is decreased (see also *Sections B3.1.5* and *B3.1.6*).

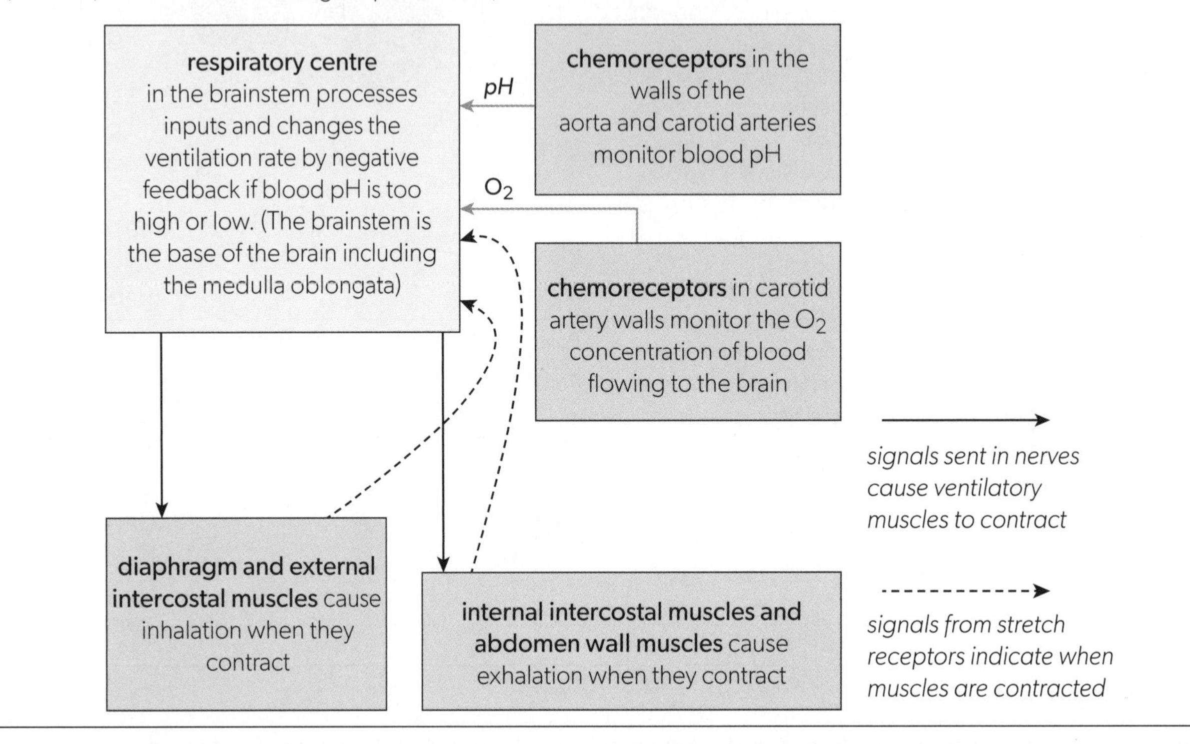
respiratory centre
in the brainstem processes inputs and changes the ventilation rate by negative feedback if blood pH is too high or low. (The brainstem is the base of the brain including the medulla oblongata)
pH
chemoreceptors in the walls of the aorta and carotid arteries monitor blood pH
O2
chemoreceptors in carotid artery walls monitor the O2 concentration of blood flowing to the brain
signals sent in nerves cause ventilatory muscles to contract
diaphragm and external intercostal muscles cause inhalation when they contract
internal intercostal muscles and abdomen wall muscles cause exhalation when they contract
signals from stretch receptors indicate when muscles are contracted

16. Control of peristalsis

Peristalsis is the wave of contraction and relaxation in the wall of the gut that moves food from the mouth to the stomach and then on through the intestines to the anus. Two layers of smooth muscle cause the movement, circular and longitudinal. They relax in front of a bolus of food, widening and lengthening the gut, and contract behind the food to shorten the gut and make the lumen narrower, pushing food on along the gut.

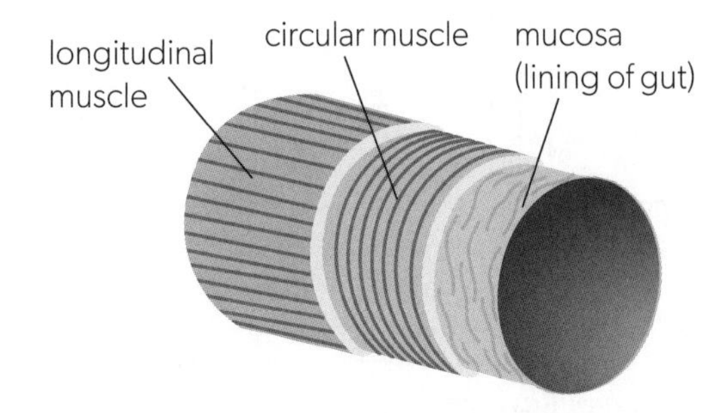
longitudinal muscle
circular muscle
mucosa (lining of gut)

Peristaltic muscle contractions in the gut are controlled by the enteric nervous system (ENS) which is extensive and complex. This control happens without inputs from the CNS and is involuntary.

There is voluntary control, by parts of the CNS, of swallowing and defecation:

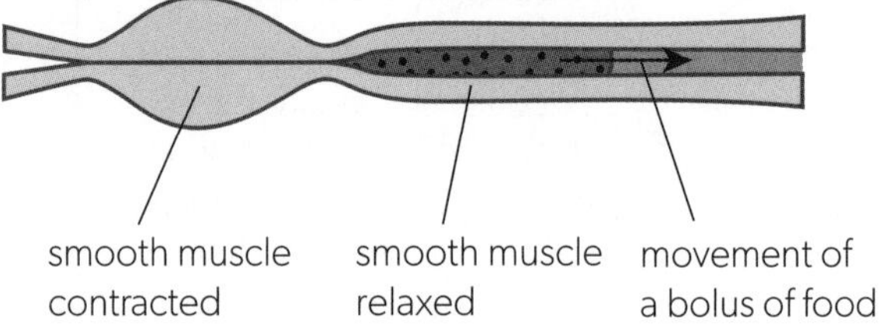
smooth muscle contracted
smooth muscle relaxed
movement of a bolus of food

- Striated muscle in the tongue is under voluntary control by the brain. To initiate swallowing, the tongue pushes food to the back of the mouth cavity. The food stimulates touch receptors in the pharynx. Signals from these receptors pass to the brainstem, which stimulates muscle contractions that push the food into the oesophagus. Once food reaches the oesophagus, peristalsis is controlled by the ENS and is entirely involuntary.
- Defecation is the removal of faeces from the rectum via the anus. The anus contains a ring of smooth muscle (a sphincter). The wall of the rectum contains layers of circular and longitudinal smooth muscle. During defecation, the anus relaxes and widens and the wall of the rectum contracts. In babies this is controlled involuntarily, but during the early years of life humans achieve voluntary control of the process.

AHL

17. Application of skills: investigating tropic responses in seedlings

Plants control the direction of growth of their roots and shoots. These parts of the plant have meristems at their tips where cell division and enlargement occur (see *Section D2.1.12*).

Roots and shoots become curved if one side grows more quickly than the other side. This type of unequal growth happens in response to external stimuli perceived by the plant, such as the direction of gravity or sunlight.

Differential growth responses to directional stimuli are called **tropic responses** or tropisms.

- Positive tropism is growth towards the stimulus.
- Negative tropism is growth away from the stimulus.

Most roots are positively gravitropic (geotropic). This means they grow downwards, in the same direction as gravity. Most shoots are positively phototropic and negatively gravitropic. This means they grow towards the source of light and, in darkness, they grow upwards in the opposite direction to gravity.

The roots and shoots of plants do not all show the same tropic responses. You can investigate these responses qualitatively—by recording observations in drawings or photos—or quantitatively. The angle of curvature of a root or shoot that has carried out a tropic response is an example of a quantitative measure.

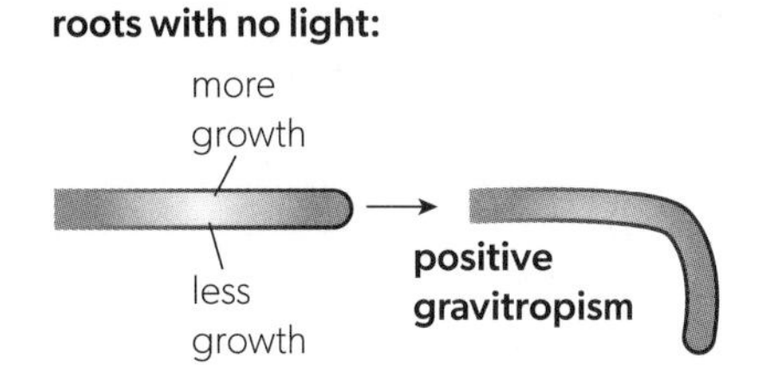

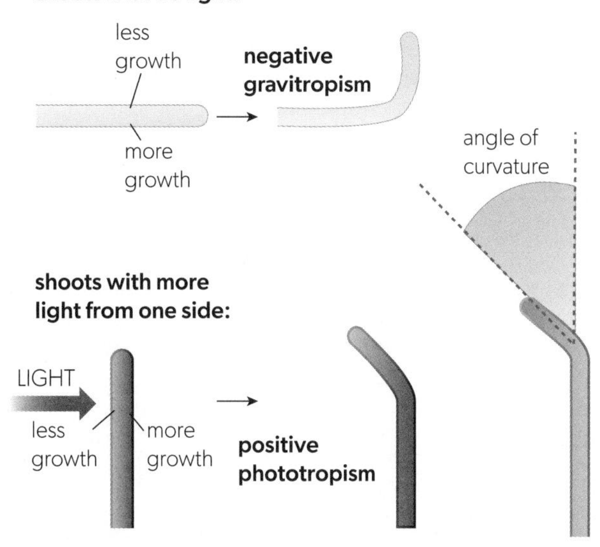

NOS

Measurements

Qualitative observations are made directly with the senses and do not involve measurements. For example, stating that a shoot has grown towards the light is a qualitative observation.

Quantitative measurements are made by counting or using measuring devices, for example measuring the angle of curvature of a shoot that has grown towards the light. They are more objective than qualitative observations.

Accuracy is how close a measurement is to the true value.

Precision is the smallest difference in size that can with certainty be distinguished. Angles can be measured to the nearest degree with a protractor, but digital inclinometers can measure to the nearest hundredth of a degree.

Reliability is achieved if measurements are both accurate and precise.

18. Positive phototropism

If one side of a shoot receives a higher intensity of light than the opposite side, the shoot responds with positive phototropism. The response to lateral light is differential growth, with the sunnier side growing more slowly than the shadier side. When the shoot has curved towards the direction of maximum light intensity, growth becomes equal on all sides, so the shoot carries on growing in that direction.

The benefit of positive phototropism is obvious: it increases the amount of light absorbed by a shoot's leaves for use in photosynthesis. This is particularly important where there is competition with other plants for light and where the brightest light is to one side rather than directly above.

A pigment detects light intensities in the shoot tip and auxin (a growth-promoting phytohormone) is then redistributed in the shoot, causing differential growth.

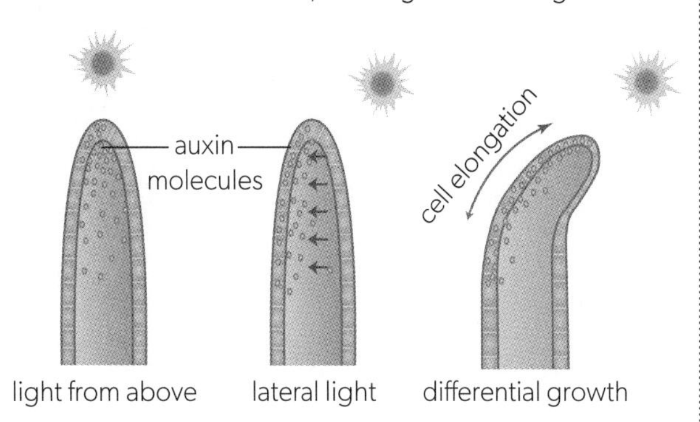

AHL

19. Phytohormones

A hormone is a chemical message that is produced and released in one part of an organism to have an effect in another part of the organism. Plants and animals produce, transport and use hormones in different ways, so plant hormones are called phytohormones. A variety of chemicals are used as phytohormones by plants, with roles in the control of growth, development and responses to stimuli.

1. **Growth**

   Phytohormones can promote or inhibit growth, by affecting rates of cell division and cell enlargement. For example, gibberellin promotes stem growth. Wheat and other crop plants have been bred with short stems by introducing alleles that make the plant less responsive to gibberellin.

2. **Development**

   Phytohormones can promote or inhibit aspects of development—for example, whether a bud starts to grow to produce a side shoot, or whether the apex of a stem produces more leaves or changes to produce flowers. Fruit ripening is promoted by the phytohormone ethylene in many plants.

3. **Responses to stimuli**

   Tropic responses are controlled by phytohormones. Tendrils of climbing plants respond to touch stimuli by coiling around a potential support. Communication using electrical signals is used for rapid responses, such as the capture of an insect by a Venus flytrap plant. However, a phytohormone called jasmonic acid triggers the subsequent secretion of enzymes to digest the fly.

20. Auxin efflux carriers

Auxin is the phytohormone that promotes differential stem growth in phototropic responses.

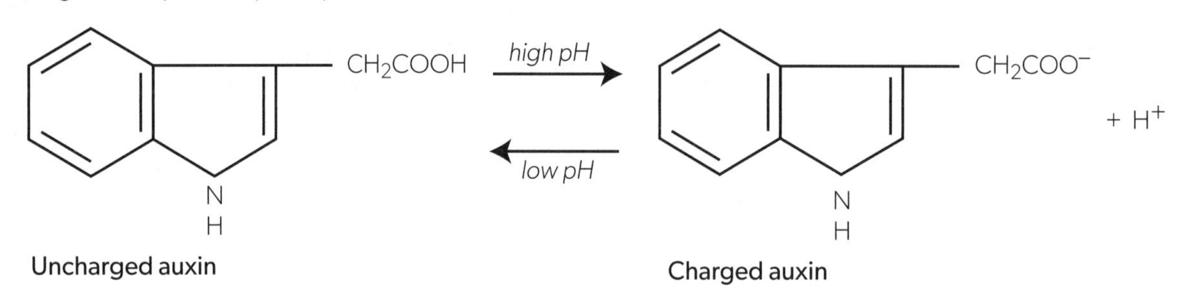

Auxin can enter cells by passive diffusion if its carboxyl group (COOH) is uncharged. The cytoplasm of plant cells is alkaline, so auxin loses a proton (H^+) from its carboxyl group and becomes negatively charged (COO^-). This traps the auxin inside the cell. However, auxin efflux carriers can pump negatively charged auxin molecules across the plasma membrane into the surrounding cell wall. The cell wall is acidic, so the auxin reverts to its uncharged state. It can then diffuse into an adjacent cell.

To transport auxin across a tissue, efflux carriers are moved to the same end of each cell. Auxin is therefore pumped in the same direction by all the cells in the tissue, generating a concentration gradient.

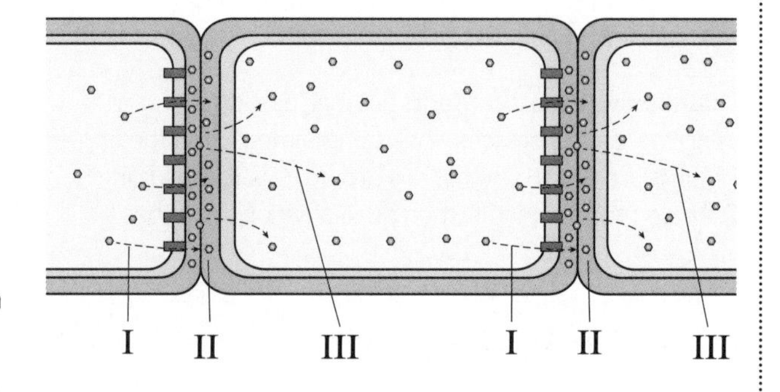

Key to diagram:

I = pumping of charge auxin by efflux carriers

II = high concentration of uncharged auxin in cell walls

III = diffusion of uncharged auxin into cells

AHL

21. Auxins and the promotion of fruit growth

Bundles of cellulose molecules (microfibrils) are the main structural components of plant cell walls.

Cellulose molecules (see *Section B1.1.6*) are inelastic, so a microfibril cannot stretch or extend in length. Extension of walls during cell growth therefore involves microfibrils moving further apart or sliding past each other. Cellulose microfibrils are crosslinked in cell walls by a variety of other carbohydrates, including pectin. The strength of these crosslinks is influenced by pH. Decreases in pH weaken the links, allowing the wall to extend.

Auxin promotes the synthesis of proton pumps by a cell and their insertion into the plasma membrane. These pumps transport H^+ ions from inside the cell (the protoplast) to the cell wall outside (the apoplast), acidifying the apoplast. This allows the wall to expand so the cell can grow.

Concentration gradients of auxin cause gradients of apoplastic pH and therefore differences in cell growth—as in phototropism.

22. Interactions between auxin and cytokinin

- Auxin is produced in shoot tips and transported in phloem down stems and into roots.
- Cytokinin, another type of phytohormone, is produced in root tips and transported in xylem up roots and into stems. The amounts of auxin and cytokinin produced in a plant provide a means of balancing root and stem growth. They work together to stimulate some processes (synergism) and have opposite effects in other cases (antagonism).

Key: ↑ promotes ↓ inhibits	Auxin	Cytokinin
Cell division in root and shoot tip meristems (synergism)	↑	↑
Cell growth in root and shoot tip meristems (synergism)	↑	↑
Development of new roots and branching of roots (antagonism)	↑	↓
Branching of stems by growth of axillary buds (antagonism)	↓	↑

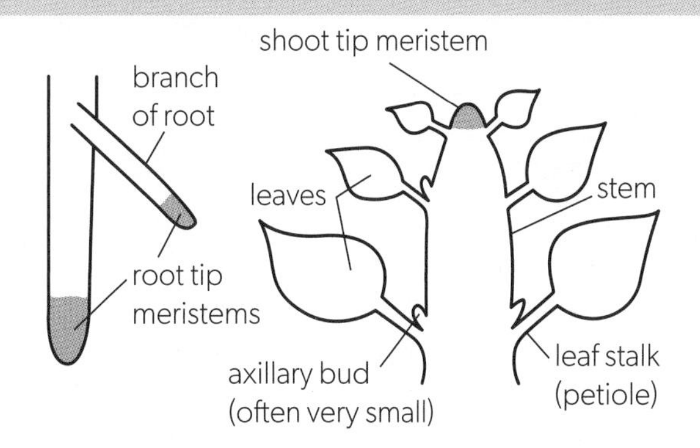

Auxin produced by the shoot tip inhibits growth of axillary buds nearby, so the main shoot grows strongly, without competition from side branches. If the main shoot of a plant is eaten by an animal, auxin concentrations decrease, which allows one or more nearby axillary buds to develop into branches of the stem, replacing the lost main shoot. These side shoots produce auxin, which stimulates the root growth needed to supply water and nutrients and inhibits development of more axillary buds.

23. Ethylene and fruit ripening

Succulent fruits such as peaches ripen when the seeds inside are fully developed. Animals are then attracted to eat the fruits and disperse the seeds.

During ripening, the flesh becomes softer, acids and starch are converted to sugar and the skin colour changes and volatile scents are produced to advertise the fruit to animals.

Many fruits are stimulated to ripen by ethylene (ethene) and produce this phytohormone as they ripen, so there is a positive feedback mechanism that promotes rapid ripening. Ethylene is volatile so can diffuse through the air from ripening fruits to other fruits, initiating their ripening. This helps synchronize the ripening of fruits, increasing the attractiveness of a plant with fruits to animals and encouraging dispersal of the seeds.

$H_2C=CH_2$

ethylene

pericarp (flesh) that ripens

seed

protective endocarp (stays hard)

C3.2 Defence against disease

1. Pathogens

- Pathogens are organisms that cause infectious diseases.
- The organism that is infected and develops the disease is the host.
- A broad range of pathogens can cause diseases in humans. The main groups are viruses, bacteria, fungi and protists. The bacteria that cause diseases in humans are all eubacteria.
- Archaea, which are the other domain of bacteria, are not known to cause infectious diseases in humans. Further information on archaea is given in *Section B4.2.7*.

NOS

Observations

Important progress has been made in finding the causes of diseases by careful observation. Two famous 19th century examples are described here:

1. **Childbed (puerperal) fever**—infections of the mother's reproductive system after childbirth were once common and often fatal. In Vienna, Ignaz Semmelweis observed that childbed fever was less frequent in woman giving birth at home than in a maternity ward and concluded that doctors were spreading the disease from mother to mother. He also observed that if doctors washed their hands in antiseptic before delivering a baby, the incidence of the disease was 90% lower.
2. **Cholera**—a bacterial disease that causes severe diarrhoea, dehydration and sometimes death. John Snow produced a map of cases during an epidemic of cholera in London. This led him to the observation that everyone who contracted the disease had drunk water from one particular street pump and those who used other sources of water did not become infected.

2. Primary defence against pathogens

The skin and mucous membranes are the primary defence against infection by pathogens. They form physical and chemical barriers that few microorganisms can penetrate.

- The outer layers of the skin are tough and form a physical barrier. Sebaceous glands in the skin secrete lactic acid and fatty acids, which make the surface acidic. This prevents the growth of most pathogenic bacteria and therefore acts as a chemical barrier.
- Mucous membranes are soft areas of skin that are kept moist with mucus. There are mucous membranes in the nose, trachea, penis, vagina and urethra. Although they do not form a strong physical barrier, mucus secreted by these membranes contains lysozyme, an enzyme that kills many bacteria, so it acts as a chemical barrier.

3. Blood clotting

When the skin is cut and blood leaks from blood vessels, the cut is quickly sealed by a blood clot.

At the start of the clotting process, platelets (small cell fragments in blood plasma) are attracted to the wounded tissues, where they release clotting factors. These clotting factors initiate a cascade of reactions in which the product of each reaction is the catalyst of the next reaction. This system helps to ensure that blood only clots when necessary and also that it is a very rapid process. The penultimate reaction in the cascade produces thrombin. In the last reaction thrombin converts fibrinogen, a soluble plasma protein, into long protein fibres called fibrin.

Fibrin forms a mesh of fibres across wounds. Blood cells are caught in the mesh and soon form a semi-solid clot to seal the cut and prevent the entry of pathogens. If exposed to air, the clot dries to form a protective scab, which remains until the wound has healed.

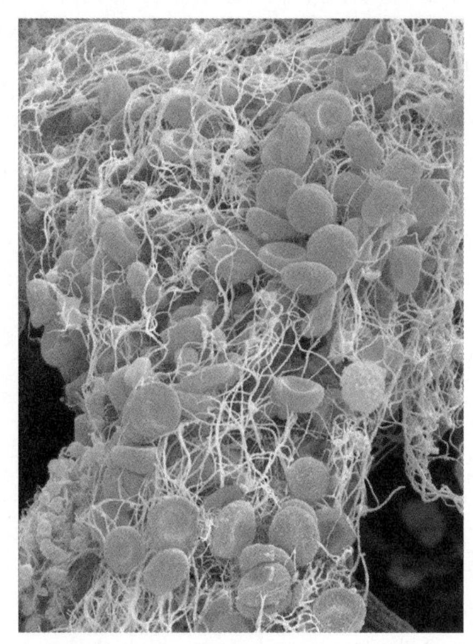

▲ Blood cells trapped in fibrin

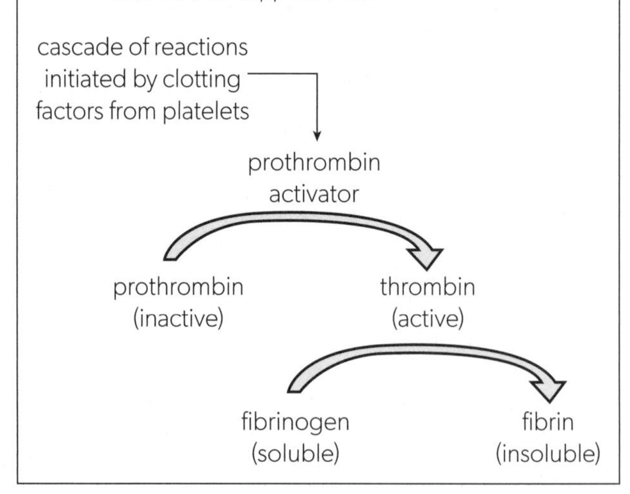

4. Comparing the innate with the adaptive immune system

The immune system has two main parts:

Innate immune system: non-specific, as different pathogens are all responded to in the same way and the responses do not change during an organism's life. Phagocytes are part of the innate immune system.

Adaptive immune system: specific, as each pathogen encountered elicits a new and different response and immune responses develop during an organism's life. Lymphocytes are part of the adaptive immune system.

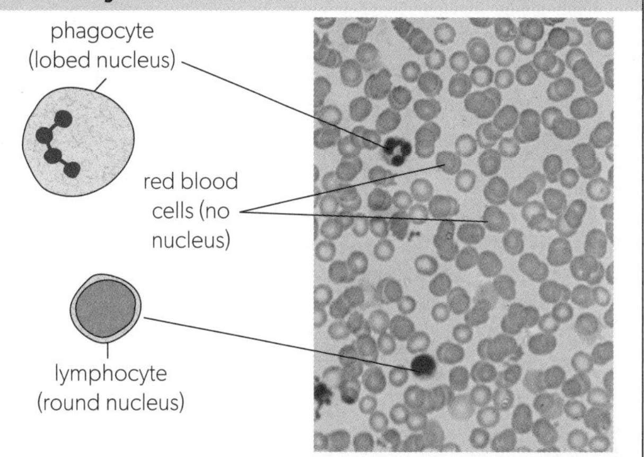

5. Phagocytosis

Phagocytes engulf (ingest) all pathogens that they encounter in the body. This happens by endocytosis (HL—see *Section B2.1.13*). Once the pathogen is inside a vacuole in the cytoplasm of the phagocyte, lysosomes fuse with the vacuole, to add enzymes which digest and kill the pathogen. Phagocytes can ingest pathogens in the blood. They can also squeeze out through the walls of blood capillaries and move through tissues to sites of infection. Their movement is amoeboid (like an amoeba). Pus that forms at sites of infection consists of large numbers of phagocytes.

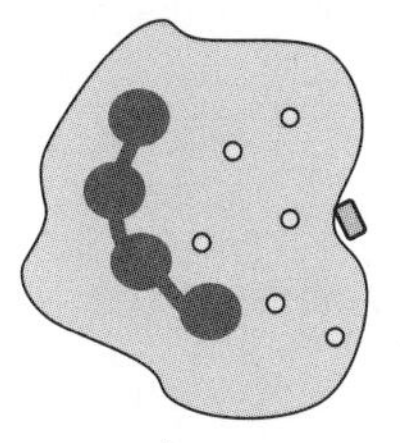
pathogen encountered

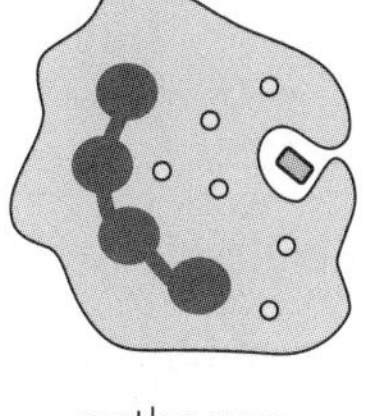
pathogen engulfed

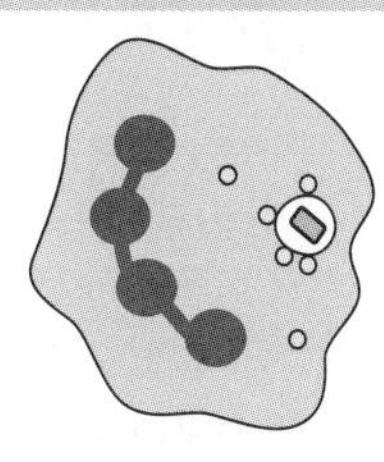
lysosomes add enzymes

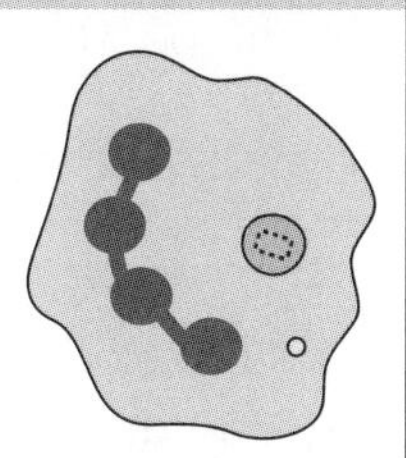
pathogen digested

6. Lymphocytes produce antibodies

- Lymphocytes have a rounded nucleus and until activated they only have a small amount of cytoplasm.
- Lymphocytes circulate in the blood. There are also large numbers of them in lymph nodes of the lymphatic system. This system consists of vessels that drain excess fluid from body tissues. Lymph nodes are small bean-shaped structures that develop at intervals along lymph vessels.
- Lymphocytes of different types cooperate to produce antibodies. The specific roles of B-lymphocytes and helper T-lymphocytes are described in *Sections C3.2.8* and *C3.2.9*. These cells are often referred to as B-cells and helper T-cells.
- Antibodies are large Y-shaped proteins. The two arms are variable, with hypervariable parts that recognize and bind to a specific molecule on a pathogen. The stem of the Y helps the body to destroy the pathogen, for example, by making it more recognizable to phagocytes that then engulf it.
- Humans can be infected by many different pathogens, including new strains that have recently evolved.
- The immune system as a whole can produce a vast array of different antibodies, but each individual B-lymphocyte can produce only one type of antibody.
- Only a small number of B-lymphocytes for producing each type of antibody exist in the body. When a new pathogen infects the body, the cells that can produce the appropriate antibody divide to form a large clone of antibody-producing cells.

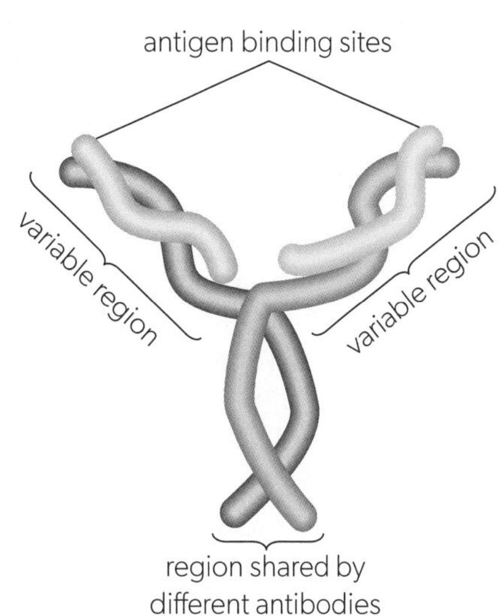

7. Antigens trigger antibody production

Lymphocytes have to distinguish between body cells ("self" cells) and "non-self" cells such as invading pathogens. Lymphocytes recognize pathogens by differences between their molecules and those of body cells. The molecules used for recognition are called antigens. They are mostly proteins, glycoproteins or large polysaccharides and are usually located on the surface of the pathogen.

The immune response to an antigen is the production of specific antibodies. Any molecule that causes this response is an antigen. There are antigens on the surface of bacteria, viruses, parasites and cancer cells. They also occur on the surface of cells from another human with a different tissue type. This explains the need to match tissue types for organ transplants. If the wrong blood type is transfused into a patient, molecules on the surface of red blood cells act as antigens and trigger antibody production.

Lymphocytes produce antibodies that bind specifically to the antigen. This is dependent on matching shapes and chemical properties, so it is similar to the binding of a ligand to a receptor, or the binding of a substrate to the active site of an enzyme. However, unlike the binding of ligands to receptors, antibody to antigen binding is irreversible. Unlike the binding of substrates to enzymes, the antigen is not changed chemically.

The part of an antibody that binds to the antigen is the hypervariable region. As the name suggests, there is immense variation in the hypervariable regions of antibodies and the immune system can generate new versions—perhaps up to a quintillion different versions. However, one lymphocyte only produces antibodies with one type of hypervariable region.

8. B-lymphocytes are activated by helper T-lymphocytes

There are many types of lymphocytes in the immune system. Each type has antibody-like receptor proteins in their plasma membrane, to which one type of antigen can bind. Helper T-lymphocytes and B-lymphocytes have essential roles in ensuring that large amounts of required antibody are produced during an infection, and no other types.

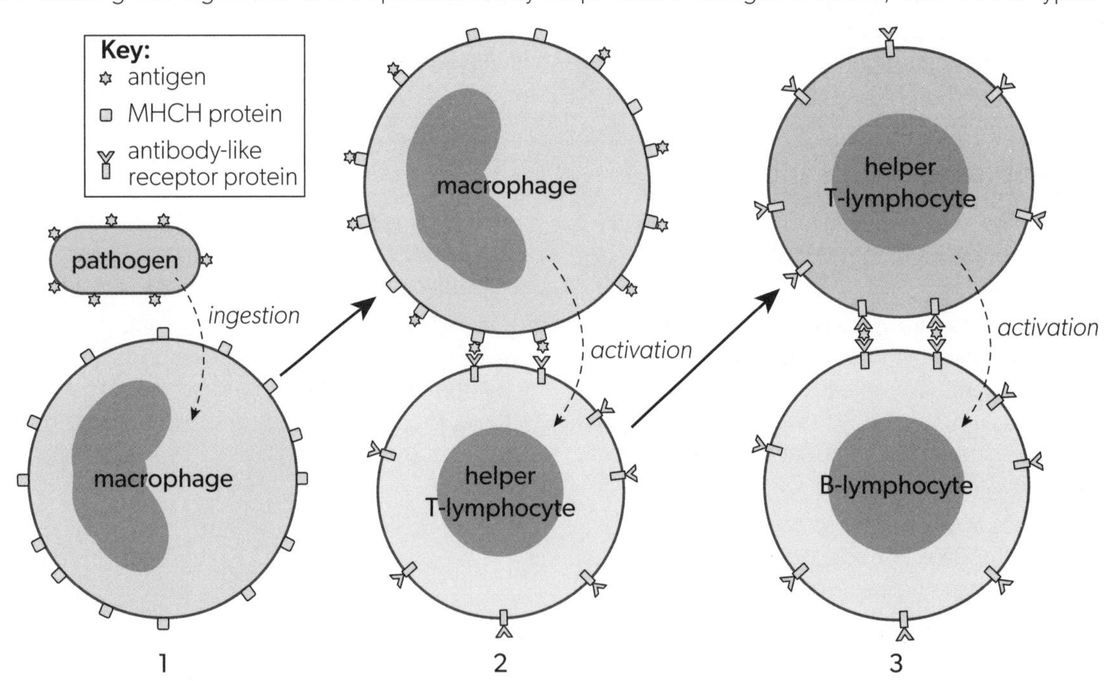

1. The pathogen that has infected the body is ingested by macrophages (a type of phagocyte). Antigens from the pathogens are then displayed by MHCH proteins in the plasma membrane of the macrophages, so the macrophages resemble the antigenic nature of pathogen.
2. Specific helper T-lymphocytes that have antibody-like receptors that match the displayed antigens bind to the macrophages. These bound helper T-cells are then activated by the macrophage.
3. The activated helper T-lymphocytes bind to B-lymphocytes that have the same antibody-like receptor. The helper T-lymphocytes activate these B-lymphocytes, both by means of the binding and by release of a signalling protein.

Only activated B-lymphocytes carry out the next stages in antibody production, which are described in *Section C3.2.9*.

9. Clonal expansion of activated B-cells

After activation, B-lymphocytes do not immediately start to produce antibodies. This is because there are too few of them to make significant quantities. Instead, the activated B-lymphocytes divide repeatedly by mitosis to form a clone of cells that all produce the same type of antibody. These B-lymphocytes grow in size and develop an extensive endoplasmic reticulum with many ribosomes attached to it, along with a large Golgi apparatus. This allows rapid production of antibodies by protein synthesis. The cells that have grown and differentiated for antibody production are plasma B-cells.

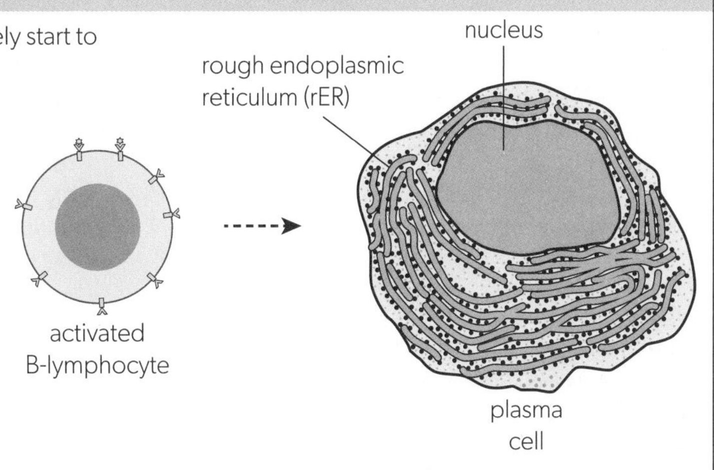

10. Memory cells

Immunity is the ability to eliminate an infectious disease from the body.

- Antibodies can give us immunity to a disease but they only persist in the body for a few weeks or months.
- The plasma B-lymphocytes that secrete antibodies are also gradually lost after an infection has been overcome.
- However, immunity can last for much longer and in many cases for the rest of our lives. This is due to memory B-lymphocytes.

Most B-lymphocytes in a clone become active plasma B-cells. A smaller number of the cells do not actively secrete antibodies but persist for a long time after the infection. These memory B-lymphocytes remain inactive unless the same pathogen reinfects the body. They then are activated and respond very rapidly. Immunity to an infectious disease is thus due to having either antibodies against the pathogen or memory cells that allow rapid production of the antibody.

11. HIV is transmitted in body fluids

Human immunodeficiency virus (HIV) is the cause of acquired immunodeficiency syndrome (AIDS). The virus cannot usually survive for long outside the body and infection with HIV only occurs if blood or other body fluids pass from an infected to an uninfected person. In a person infected with HIV, there may be viruses in blood, semen, vaginal fluids, rectal secretions and breast milk. Cross-infection may therefore happen during these actions:

- sex without a condom
- sharing of hypodermic needles by intravenous drug users
- transfusion of infected blood or blood products
- childbirth and breastfeeding.

12. AIDS as a consequence of HIV infection

The human immunodeficiency virus (HIV) invades and destroys helper T-lymphocytes. This leads to a progressive loss of the capacity to produce antibodies, because helper T-lymphocytes have an essential role in antibody production.

In the early stages of infection with HIV, the immune system can still make antibodies against the virus. If these are detected, a person is said to be HIV-positive. Helper T-lymphocytes are gradually destroyed by the virus. The rate at which this happens varies greatly, but in most HIV-positive patients who do not receive anti-retroviral drugs, antibody production eventually becomes so ineffective that a group of opportunistic infections can strike. These are caused by pathogens which would be eliminated easily by a healthy immune system. Several of the opportunistic infections are otherwise so rare that they can be used as markers for the latter stages of HIV infection, such as Kaposi's sarcoma.

Acquired immunodeficiency syndrome (AIDS) is the combination of diseases that occur in a person infected with HIV. A syndrome is a group of diseases or conditions that occur together. If HIV infection is untreated, AIDS usually leads to the death of the patient.

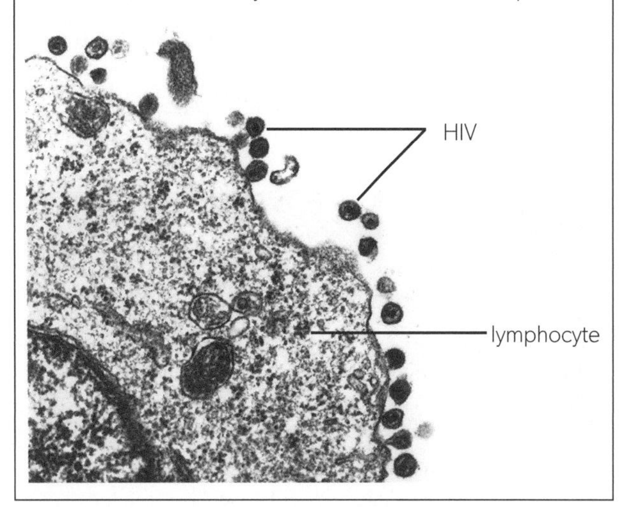

13. Antibiotics treat bacterial infections

An antibiotic is a chemical that inhibits the growth of microorganisms. Most antibiotics are antibacterial. They block processes that occur in prokaryotes but not in eukaryotes. They can therefore be used to kill bacteria inside the body without causing harm to human cells. Antibiotics target vital bacterial processes such as DNA replication, protein synthesis and cell wall formation.

Many antibacterial antibiotics were discovered in saprotrophic fungi. These fungi compete with saprotrophic bacteria for the dead organic matter on which they both feed. By secreting antibacterial antibiotics, saprotrophic fungi inhibit the growth of their bacterial competitors. An example is penicillin. It is produced by some strains of the *Penicillium* fungus at times when nutrients are scarce and competition with bacteria would be harmful.

Viruses are non-living and can only reproduce when they are inside living cells. They use the chemical processes of a living host cell, instead of having a metabolism of their own. They do not have their own means of transcription or protein synthesis and they rely on the host cell's enzymes for ATP synthesis and other metabolic pathways. These processes cannot be targeted by drugs as the host cell would also be damaged.

All the commonly used antibiotics such as penicillin, streptomycin, chloramphenicol and tetracycline control bacterial infections but are not effective against viruses. It is inappropriate for doctors to prescribe antibiotics to treat viral infections and it contributes to the overuse of antibiotics and increases in antibiotic resistance in bacteria.

14. Antibiotic resistance

Strains of bacteria with resistance are usually discovered soon after the introduction of an antibiotic. It happens because resistant strains are not killed by the antibiotic and so multiply and spread. This is not of huge concern as long as an alternative antibiotic is available that kills the bacteria, but strains of pathogenic bacteria with multiple resistance are now widespread. For example, MRSA (methicillin-resistant *Staphylococcus aureus*) can infect the blood or surgical wounds of hospital patients and resists all commonly used antibiotics.

Evolution of multiple antibiotic resistance happens rapidly because genes can be passed from one species of bacteria to another. (This process is described for HL in *Section A3.1.12*.) Also, antibiotic-resistance genes (ARGs) can remain in the genomes of pathogenic bacteria even if an antibiotic is no longer used.

Multiple antibiotic resistance is an avoidable problem.

- Doctors must prescribe antibiotics only for serious bacterial infections and for the minimum period.
- Hospital staff must maintain high standards of hygiene to prevent cross-infection.
- Farmers must avoid the use of antibiotics in animal feeds as growth stimulants.
- Pharmaceutical companies must develop new classes of antibiotic—none have been introduced since the 1980s.

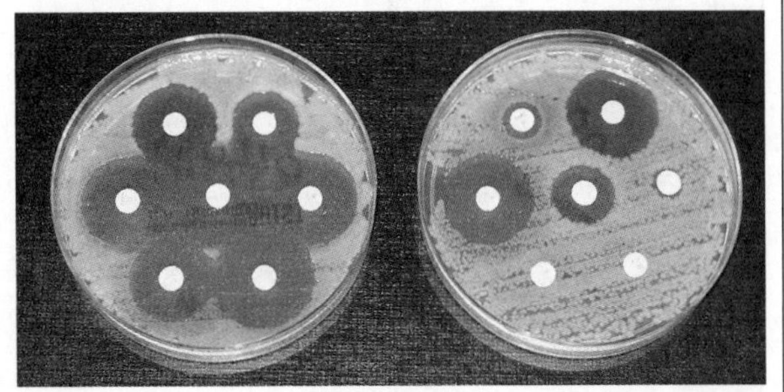

▲ Clear areas on the plates show where antibiotic in the disc has killed bacteria

Experiments

NOS

Computers have made it easy to store data and then retrieve and analyse it. Compound libraries have been developed that contain the structures of vast numbers of molecules. Researchers are using computer software to screen such libraries to identify molecules with the potential to act as antibiotics. Compounds with potential can then be tested experimentally for effectiveness as antibiotics. This is an example of a new technique leading to new avenues of research in science.

15. Zoonosis

Pathogens are often highly specialized, with a narrow range of hosts. For example, humans are the only known organism susceptible to the pathogens that cause syphilis, polio and measles. However, some pathogens can use more than one species as a host.

Mycobacterium bovis causes tuberculosis in cattle but can also infect a wide variety of other animal species. Milk produced by infected cattle may contain live cells of the bacterium which transmit the tuberculosis to humans if the milk is drunk. This is an example of a zoonosis—a disease that can be transmitted to humans from other animals in natural circumstances.

Rabies is also a zoonosis. The lyssavirus that causes it can be transmitted from infected dogs to humans by a bite or scratch or if saliva from the dog comes into contact with the eye, mouth or nose of a human.

Japanese encephalitis is a zoonosis that can be transmitted from infected pigs or birds by mosquito bites.

COVID-19 infection is a disease that has recently transferred from another species, with profound consequences for humans.

16. Vaccinations

Immunization is the use of a vaccine to trigger immunity. Most vaccines are given by intramuscular injection (into the muscle); they can also be given by subcutaneous injection (under the skin) or by mouth (orally).

All vaccines contain either antigens or nucleic acids from which antigens can be made by human cells. Three types of material can be used in a vaccine:

- pathogens that are either killed, or live but attenuated so they carry the antigens but do not cause the disease
- antigens from the pathogen (usually proteins)
- mRNA or DNA coding for a protein that acts as an antigen

The antigens stimulate a primary immune response, by activation of helper T-lymphocytes and B-lymphocytes and production of plasma cells and then specific antibodies. If memory cells are also produced, long-lasting immunity develops. If a vaccine successfully triggers such immunity, the pathogen will be destroyed by a secondary immune response if it ever enters the body.

17. Herd immunity

Herd immunity is achieved when a significant proportion of a population has already contracted a disease or been vaccinated. As a result, the spread of a virus or other pathogen is impeded, because it repeatedly encounters people who are already immune. With herd immunity, any new outbreak of the disease will decline and disappear.

Not everyone in the population has to be immune for herd immunity to develop. The following formula can be used to estimate the percentage of people who must be immune for the population as a whole to be protected.

$$\left(1 - \frac{1}{R}\right) \times 100\%$$

R is the average number of people that an infected person infects. Measles is highly infectious and has an *R*-value of 15, so $(1 - 1/15) \times 100\% = 93\%$ of the population must be vaccinated to reach herd immunity.

NOS

Global impacts of science

Vaccines are tested rigorously and the risks of side effects are minimal but not nil. Scientists have a responsibility to communicate their findings to the public with honesty and clarity, but some media reports have misrepresented research findings. The distinction between pragmatic truths and certainty is widely misunderstood. This has fuelled anti-vaccination campaigns that risk human health.

18. Application of skills: evaluating data related to the COVID-19 pandemic

During the COVID-19 pandemic, huge amounts of data were collected. This data is being analysed and evaluated by epidemiologists to find out how to prevent or control future pandemics.

1. The World Health Organization has published data for individual countries and for six regions. The data shows a series of waves of infection. The table below gives the numbers of cases and deaths in each week that was the peak of a wave in the Americas region.

Week starting:	Cases	Deaths
July 20 2020	1,018,106	30,292
Jan 12 2021	2,481,490	47,310
April 12 2021	1,514,719	41,495
Aug 23 2021	1,622,515	24,936
Jan 10 2022	8,462,254	21,532
July 11 2022	1,887,544	6216
Dec 12 2022	1,044,173	4737

Calculate deaths as a percentage of cases for each of the peak weeks, to identify trends in mortality

Suggest reasons for the waves of infection and for changes in mortality rate.

2. The table shows the number of deaths attributed to COVID-19 in the UK between April 2021 and May 2023 by vaccination status.

Period	Death rate/100,000 person years	
	Ever vaccinated	Unvaccinated
Apr-Jun 2021	8.7	78.7
Jul-Sep 2021	45.3	358.0
Oct-Dec 2021	63.7	481.2
Jan-Mar 2022	86.3	376.4
Apr-Jun 2022	40.7	122.9
Jul-Sep 2022	29.3	103.5
Oct-Dec 2022	27.0	100.9
Jan-Mar 2023	27.6	100.3

Calculate the percentage difference in mortality rate between vaccinated and unvaccinated people for each time period. Suggest reasons for the trends.

Calculate the percentage change in mortality rate for unvaccinated people between each period and the next. Suggest reasons for the trends.

$$\text{percentage change} = \frac{\text{final number} - \text{initial number}}{\text{initial number}} \times 100\%$$

To calculate percentage difference, use this formula:

$$\text{percentage difference} = \frac{\text{number A} - \text{number B}}{\text{number A}} \times 100\%$$

End of topic questions — C3 Questions

C3.1 Integration of body systems

1. V_E is the total volume of air expired from the lungs per minute. The graph below shows the relationship between V_E and the carbon dioxide content of the inspired air.

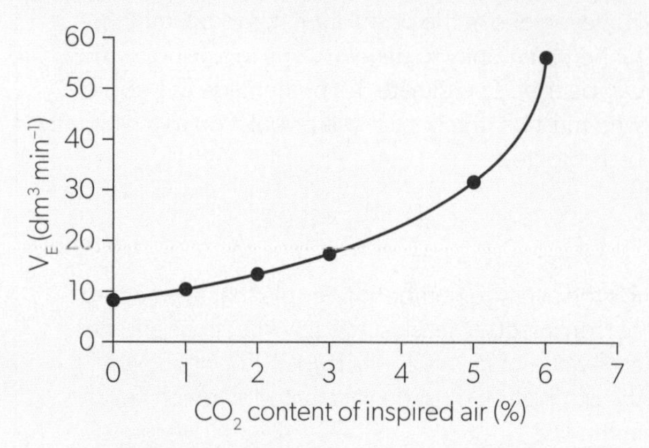

   a. Outline the relationship between the CO_2 content of inspired air and V_E. (2)
   b. Explain the effect of increasing CO_2 content of air on V_E. (4)
   c. Predict the effect on V_E of increasing the CO_2 concentration of inspired air above 7%. (4)
   d. Suggest one other change that increases V_E. (1)
   e. Identify another feedback control system in the body that will be affected by changes in the CO_2 content of inspired air. Explain how it will respond. (2)
   f. (HL only) Outline the effect of increasing blood CO_2 concentration on the affinity of hemoglobin for oxygen. (2)

2. The diagram shows part of the central nervous system (CNS).

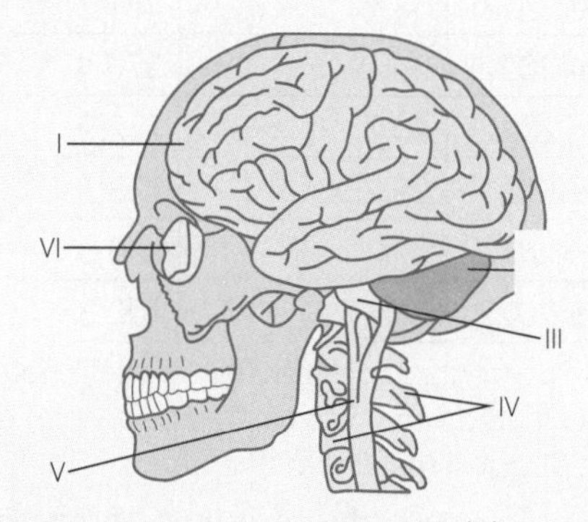

   a. State the name of structures I–V. (5)
   b. Outline two functions for each structure. (10)

3. (HL only)
   a. Outline how auxin promotes growth in plant cells. (2)
   b. i. Outline how concentration gradients of auxin are established in a shoot apex. (4)
      ii. Explain the role of these auxin gradients. (4)

C3.2 Defence against disease

1. The table shows WHO data for COVID-19 in the United States of America from 2020 to 2022.

Ages	Cases (×1000)		Deaths (×1000)	
	Females	Males	Females	Males
80+	1227	838	89	82
60–79	409	445	20	37
40–59	10,279	8746	16	30
20–39	12,995	10,666	3	5
<20	306	300	0.06	0.09

   a. Comment on the relationship between age and numbers of cases. (3)
   b. i. Distinguish between males and females in the numbers of cases and numbers of deaths. (3)
      ii. Suggest reasons for the differences. (3)
   c. Calculate the percentage death rate in females aged 20–39 who became infected. (3)
   d. Analyse the data to identify which group had the highest percentage death rate if infected. (3)

2. The graph shows cases of polio in Brazil. On the dates with arrows in the graph, all children aged 0–4 were vaccinated.

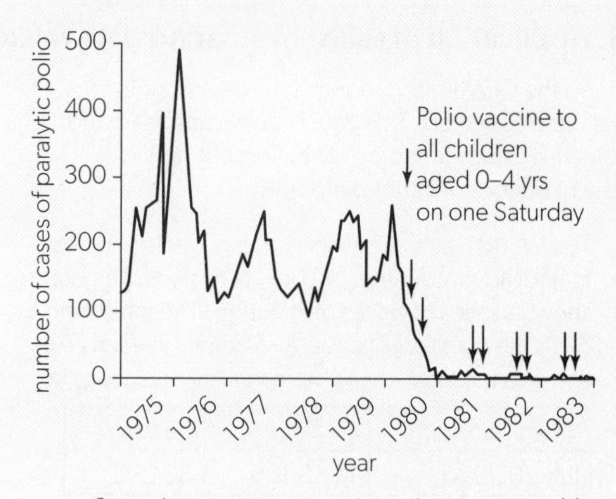

   a. State the maximum number of polio cases. (1)
   b. Evaluate the success of the vaccination programme using the data in the graph. (3)
   c. Describe the response of the immune system to a polio vaccination. (5)
   d. Suggest reasons for:
      i. a second vaccination soon after the first (2)
      ii. unvaccinated children continuing to be identified each year. (2)
   e. Explain reasons for the polio vaccination program me continuing in Brazil despite no cases in North or South America since 1991. (2)

3. a. Distinguish between HIV and AIDS. (4)
   b. Compare lymphocytes and phagocytes. (3)
   c. Compare and contrast antibiotics and antibodies. (3)

D3.1 Reproduction

1. Comparing sexual and asexual reproduction

Reproduction is production of offspring by parents. It can be either sexual or asexual. Sexual reproduction brings about change whereas asexual reproduction brings about continuity.

Asexual reproduction	Sexual reproduction
One parent	Two parents (♀ + ♂)
No meiosis—only mitosis in an asexual life cycle	Meiosis is part of every sexual life cycle
Offspring are genetically identical to each other and to the parent	Offspring are genetically different from each other and from their parents
No genetic variation is generated as existing gene combinations pass unchanged from generation to generation	Genetic variation is generated as new gene combinations are produced in every generation
Advantage: in an unchanging environment, well-adapted parents produce offspring that are also well-adapted	Advantage: species can evolve in a changing environment, as offspring can be better-adapted than their parents

2. Role of meiosis in sexual reproduction

Meiosis and fusion of gametes have different roles.

Fusion of gametes: a male and female gamete join together to form a new individual. This brings alleles (versions of genes) together in new combinations. Fusion of gametes is also referred to as fertilization. It doubles the number of chromosomes each time it occurs.

Meiosis: one diploid nucleus divides to form four haploid nuclei. This breaks up parental combinations of genes, allowing new combinations to form when gametes fuse. The terms haploid and diploid are explained in *Section D2.1.9*. By halving the number of chromosomes, meiosis reverses the doubling that is caused by fusion of gametes, so there is no overall change in the number of chromosomes over a sexual life cycle.

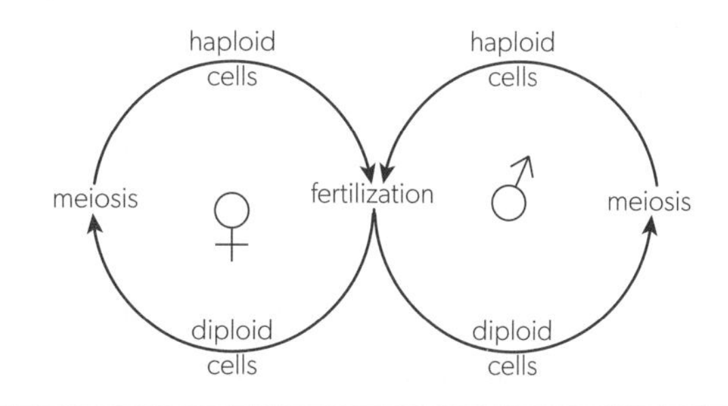
haploid cells
haploid cells
meiosis
♀
fertilization
♂
meiosis
diploid cells
diploid cells

3. Comparing male and female gametes

All plants and animals have different types of male and female gametes. The table shows the differences.

	Male	Female
Motility of gamete	Male gametes travel to the female	Female gametes are non-motile
Size of gamete	Smaller, allowing faster movement	Larger due to stores of food reserves
Food reserves	Less—only enough for the gamete	More—for embryo development
Numbers produced	More—often very large numbers	Few—sometimes only one

4. Structure of the reproductive systems

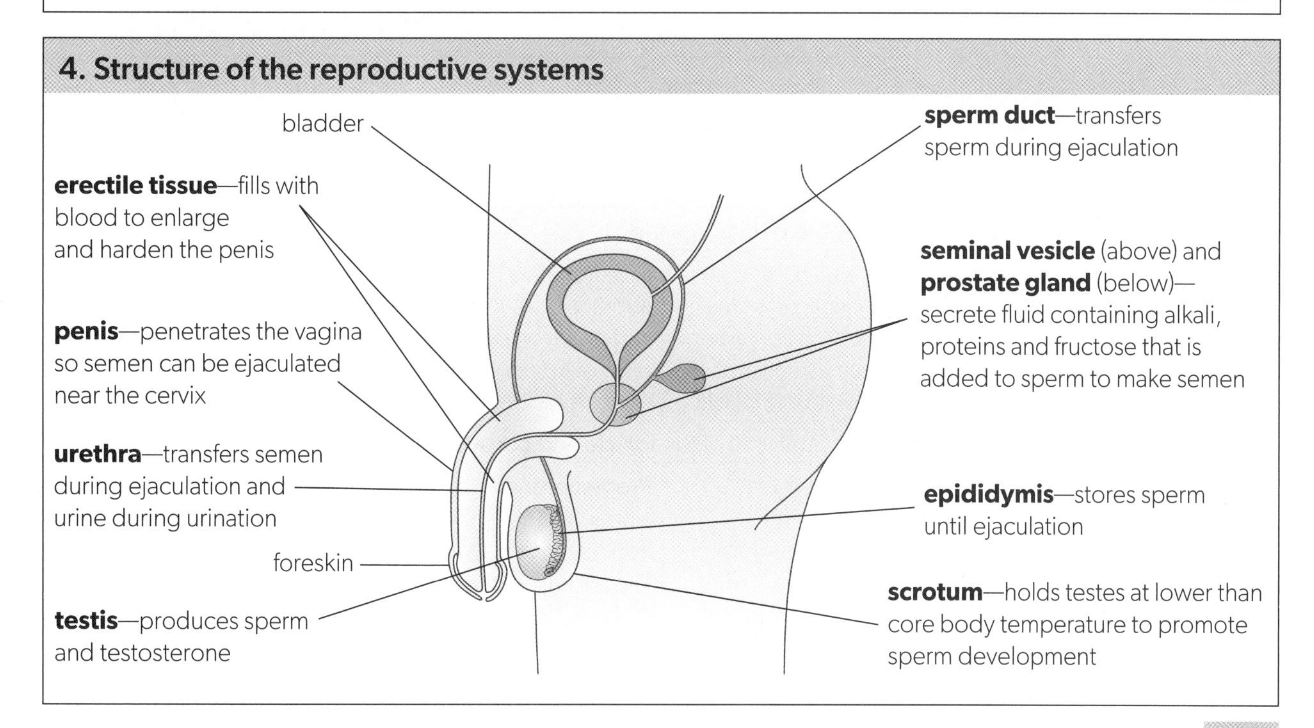
bladder
erectile tissue—fills with blood to enlarge and harden the penis
penis—penetrates the vagina so semen can be ejaculated near the cervix
urethra—transfers semen during ejaculation and urine during urination
foreskin
testis—produces sperm and testosterone
sperm duct—transfers sperm during ejaculation
seminal vesicle (above) and **prostate gland** (below)—secrete fluid containing alkali, proteins and fructose that is added to sperm to make semen
epididymis—stores sperm until ejaculation
scrotum—holds testes at lower than core body temperature to promote sperm development

4. Structure of the reproductive systems (continued)

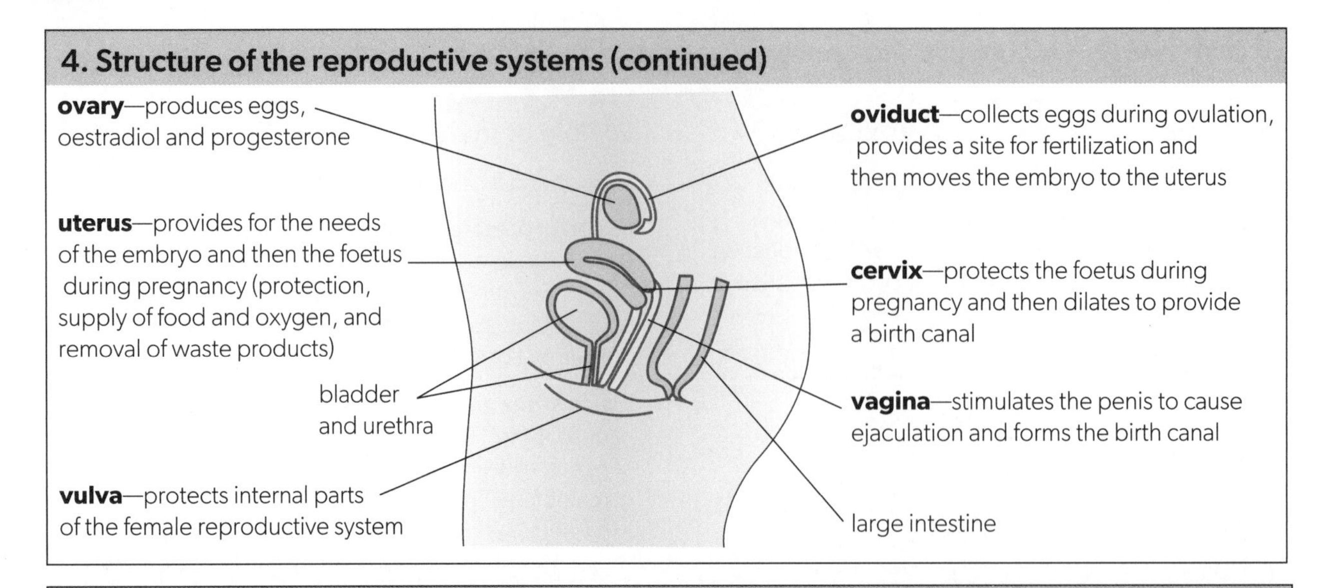
ovary—produces eggs, oestradiol and progesterone
uterus—provides for the needs of the embryo and then the foetus during pregnancy (protection, supply of food and oxygen, and removal of waste products)
bladder and urethra
vulva—protects internal parts of the female reproductive system
oviduct—collects eggs during ovulation, provides a site for fertilization and then moves the embryo to the uterus
cervix—protects the foetus during pregnancy and then dilates to provide a birth canal
vagina—stimulates the penis to cause ejaculation and forms the birth canal
large intestine

5. Hormonal control of the menstrual cycle

The menstrual cycle takes about 28 days and is composed of cycles that happen in the ovaries and uterus.

In the **ovarian cycle**, follicles start to develop in the ovary, but usually only one completes development and releases its egg (ovulation) on about Day 14. After ovulation, the wall of the follicle enlarges and becomes the corpus luteum. If an embryo is not present, the corpus luteum breaks down towards the end of the menstrual cycle.

In the **uterine cycle**, the endometrium (inner layer of the uterus) becomes thickened, with an enhanced blood supply, in preparation for implantation of an embryo. If no embryo is present, the thickening breaks down and passes out of the body. This is menstruation (known as a "period"). As the start of menstruation is an obvious event, it is used to define Day 1 of each cycle.

Four hormones regulate the menstrual cycle by negative and positive feedback. FSH and LH bind to receptors in the membranes of follicle cells. Oestradiol and progesterone affect gene expression and therefore development in the uterus and other parts of the female body.

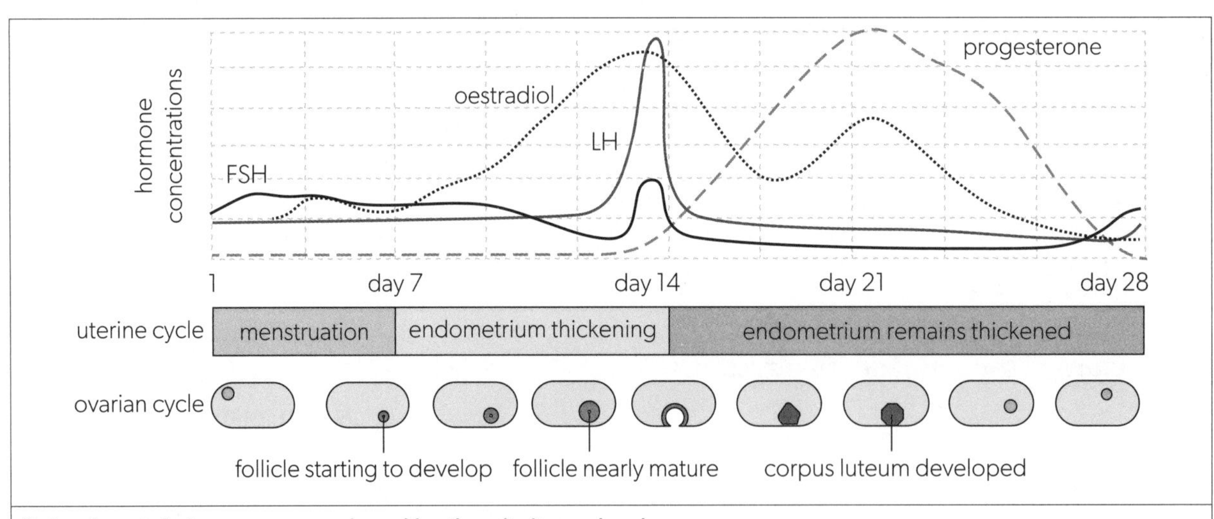
hormone concentrations
FSH
oestradiol
LH
progesterone
1
day 7
day 14
day 21
day 28
uterine cycle
menstruation
endometrium thickening
endometrium remains thickened
ovarian cycle
follicle starting to develop
follicle nearly mature
corpus luteum developed

Role of protein hormones produced by the pituitary gland	
FSH (follicle-stimulating hormone) rises to high levels in the first ten days of the menstrual cycle. During this time, it stimulates the development of follicles, each containing an oocyte (egg) and follicular fluid. FSH also stimulates oestradiol secretion by the wall of the developing follicle.	**LH** (luteinizing hormone) rises to a sudden sharp peak on about Day 14. It stimulates the maturation of the oocyte and ovulation by bursting of the follicle wall. LH then promotes the development of the corpus luteum, which secretes oestradiol (positive feedback) and progesterone.

Roles of steroid hormones, produced by the wall of the follicle and corpus luteum	
Oestradiol rises to a peak in the second week of the cycle. It stimulates repair and thickening of the endometrium after menstruation and an increase in FSH receptors to make the follicles more receptive to FSH, which boosts oestradiol production (positive feedback). When it reaches high levels, oestradiol inhibits FSH secretion (negative feedback) and stimulates LH secretion.	**Progesterone** levels rise following ovulation, reaching a peak and then dropping back to a low level by the end of the menstrual cycle if no embryo is present. Progesterone promotes the thickening and maintenance of the endometrium. It also inhibits FSH and LH secretion by the pituitary gland (negative feedback).

6. Fusion of a sperm and egg cell—fertilization

Fertilization is the fusion of a sperm with an egg to form a zygote. Sperm have receptors in their plasma membranes that detect chemicals released by the egg. This enables the sperm to swim towards the egg. Around the egg is a cloud of follicle cells and a layer of glycoproteins (zona pellucida).

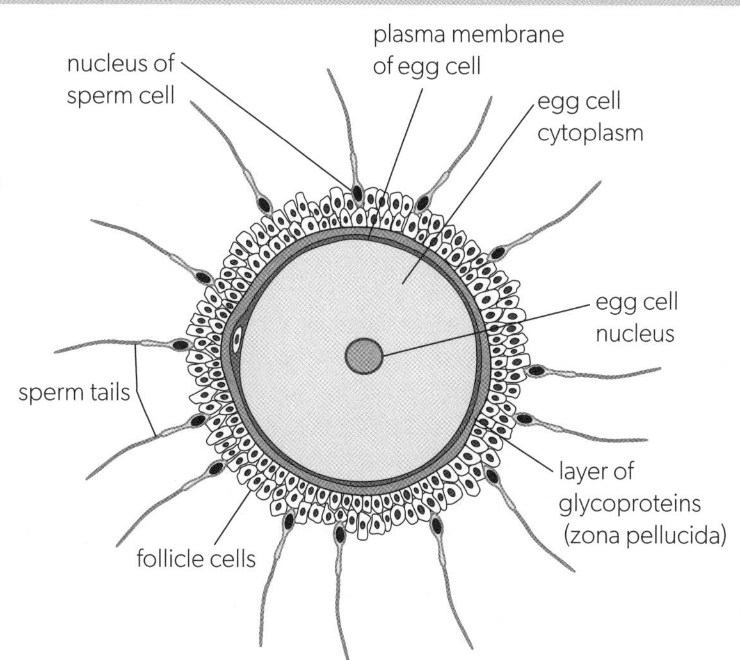

The sperm push between the cells and digest a route through the glycoproteins to reach the plasma membrane of the egg cell. The sperm's plasma membrane has proteins that bind to the egg cell's plasma membrane. The first sperm that manages to reach the egg binds to it and the membranes of the sperm and egg fuse together. The sperm nucleus then enters the egg cell. This is the moment of fertilization. Immediately afterwards the layer of glycoprotein hardens to prevent entry of more sperm.

The sperm tail either does not penetrate the egg during fertilization or is broken down inside the zygote. Sperm mitochondria may also penetrate, but they are destroyed by the egg cell.

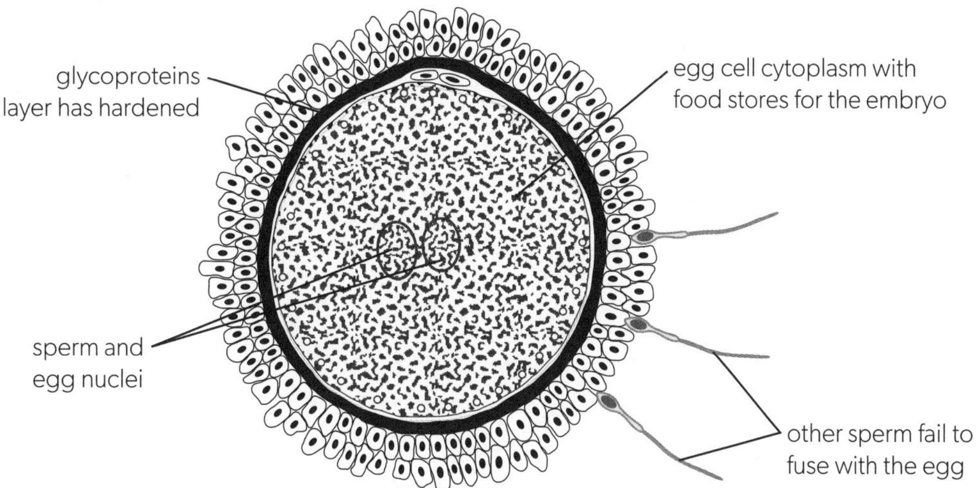

The nuclei from the sperm and egg remain separate until the zygote's first mitosis. Then both nuclear membranes break down, releasing 23 chromosomes from each nucleus. These chromosomes, half from the mother and half from the father, participate jointly in mitosis, using the same spindle of microtubules. Two genetically identical nuclei are produced, each with 46 chromosomes.

AHL

15. Preventing polyspermy

Fusion of more than one sperm with an egg is polyspermy. Structures in the sperm and the egg (see *Section B2.3.10*), make polyspermy very infrequent. A coat of glycoproteins (zona pellucida) surrounds and protects the egg. When sperm make contact with the zona pellucida, they release the contents of their **acrosome**. This is the **acrosome reaction**. Enzymes from the acrosome digest a small region of zona pellucida, allowing the sperm to penetrate and reach the egg.

When the first sperm has fused with the egg, the many cortical granules (vesicles) near the egg's plasma membrane release their contents by exocytosis. This is the **cortical reaction**. The enzymes that are released toughen the zona pellucida making it very difficult for any more sperm to penetrate it. The enzymes also change specific glycoproteins in the zona pellucida to which sperm bind, so this can no longer happen.

7. *In vitro* fertilization (IVF) treatment

Natural fertilization is *in vivo*, as it occurs inside the body. Fertilization can also happen outside the body in dishes in a laboratory. This is *in vitro* fertilization, usually abbreviated to IVF. The procedure has been used extensively to overcome male or female fertility problems. There are various protocols for IVF. These are the main stages:

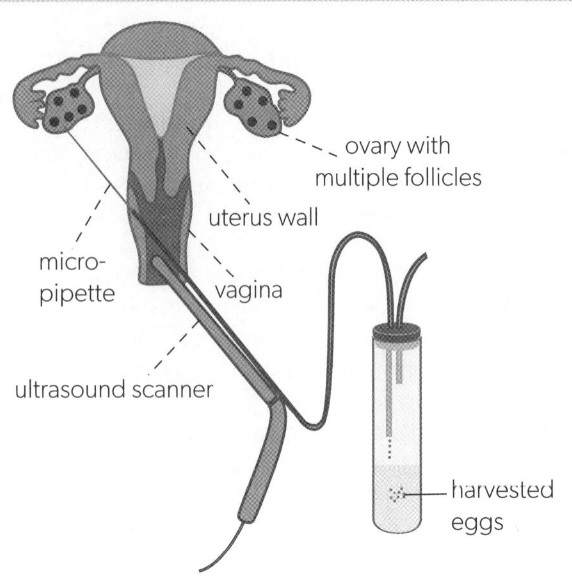

1. **Down-regulation**—every day for about two weeks, the woman has an injection or nasal spray containing a drug to stop the pituitary gland secreting FSH or LH. Secretion of oestradiol and progesterone therefore also stops, pausing the woman's normal menstrual cycle and allowing doctors to control the timing and amount of egg production.
2. **FSH injections**—intramuscular injections of FSH are given daily for 7–12 days, to stimulate follicles to develop. The aim is to generate a very high FSH concentration, resulting in far more follicles than normal (superovulation). The aim is 8–15 follicles, each containing an egg.
3. **hCG injection**—when the follicles are 18 mm in diameter, they are stimulated to mature by an injection of human chorionic gonadotropin (hCG). This is the hormone embryos secrete to signal to their mother that they are present.
4. **Egg collection**—this is a minor surgical procedure taking about 20 minutes. A micropipette mounted on an ultrasound scanner is used to draw the eggs out of the follicles. Egg collection is done about a day and a half after the hCG injection.
5. **Fertilization**—each egg is mixed with 50,000–100,000 sperm cells in sterile conditions in a shallow dish, which is then incubated at 37°C until the next day.
6. **Embryo transfer**—one or more embryos are placed in the uterus when they are about 48 hours old. Progesterone is given as a tablet placed in the vagina, to ensure that the uterus lining is maintained. If the embryos implant and continue to grow, the pregnancy that follows is no different from a pregnancy that began by natural conception.

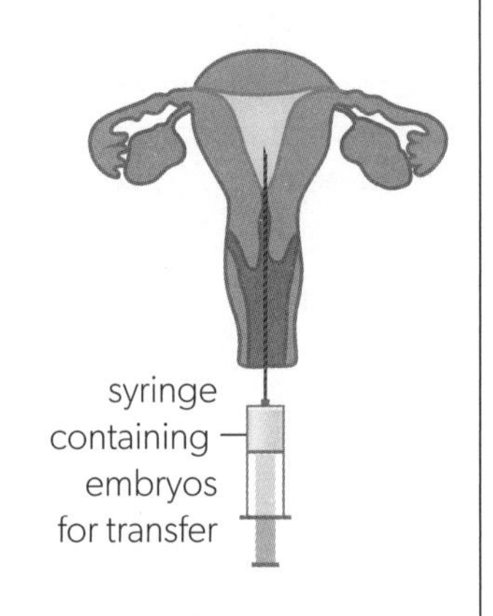

AHL

17. Pregnancy testing

The hormone human chorionic gonadotropin (hCG) is a medium-sized protein. hCG is produced by the trophoblast cells in the blastocyst and subsequent embryonic stages, so it is an early indicator of the presence of an embryo. Later in pregnancy, cells in the placenta continue the secretion of hCG.

Tests for pregnancy are based on detection of hCG in a woman's urine. A test stick has an absorbent strip inside a plastic casing. There are three types of monoclonal antibody in the strip.

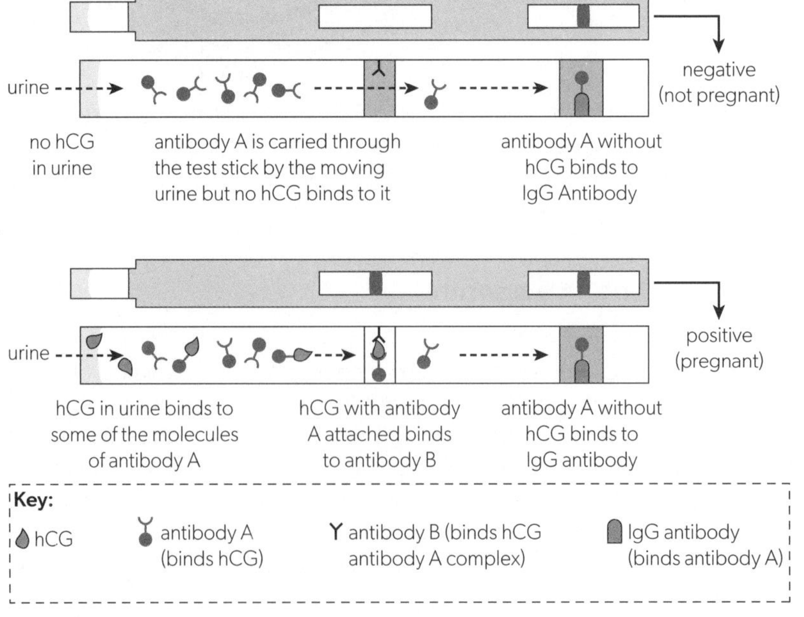

A urine sample is placed on the strip where it sticks out at one end. The urine is drawn through the strip by capillary action. It first meets antibody A and has a molecule of blue dye attached. Any hCG molecules in the urine bind to this antibody. Antibody A, with or without bound hCG, moves on with the urine along the strip. Next is a band of immobilized antibody B, which binds to antibody A molecules that have hCG bound, creating a blue band that indicates pregnancy. Molecules of antibody A without hCG bound move on along the strip and reach a band of IgG antibody, to which they bind, creating a blue band that indicates the test has worked.

AHL

14. Production of gametes

Gametogenesis is the production of gametes. Male gametes are sperm (spermatozoa) and female gametes are eggs (oocytes). Spermatogenesis happens in the testes and oogenesis in the ovaries. The four stages in both types of gametogenesis are mitosis, cell growth, two divisions of meiosis and then differentiation.

Spermatogenesis happens in the testes, which are a coiled mass of seminiferous tubules. The outer layer of cells in the walls of these tubules (shown right) is germinal epithelium, where **mitosis** occurs continuously, generating vast numbers of cells that are gradually displaced inwards towards the fluid-filled centre of the seminiferous tubule. The cells **grow** as they migrate inwards and then each cell divides by **meiosis** to produce four haploid cells. Each of these haploid cells **differentiates** into a sperm by growing a tail and reducing its cytoplasm to a minimum.

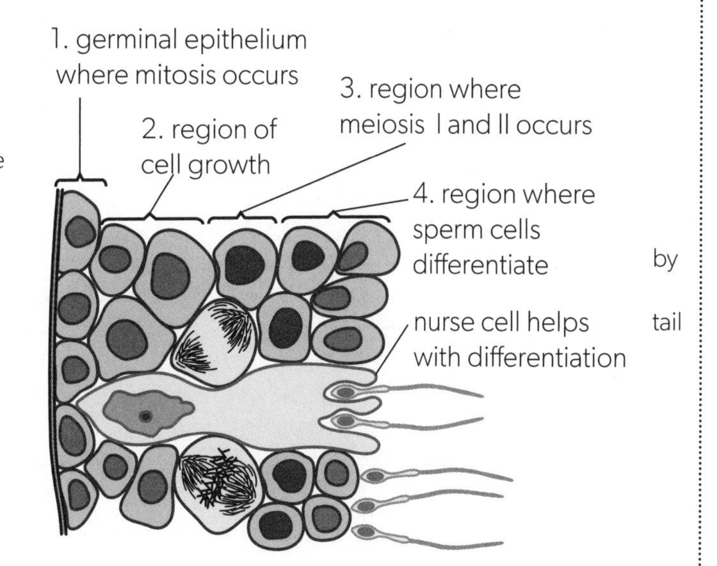

Oogenesis happens in the ovaries (shown right). The outer layer of cells is germinal epithelium. These cells divide by **mitosis** during foetal development. The cells produced migrate inwards to distribute themselves through the cortex of the ovary. When a foetus is 4 or 5 months old, these cells **grow** and start to divide by **meiosis**, pausing while still in the first division of meiosis. At birth, a baby girl has large numbers of primary follicles in her ovaries, each consisting of the cell that has started meiosis, together with surrounding follicle cells. The primary follicles do not undergo further development until after puberty. At the start of each menstrual cycle a small batch of primary follicles starts to develop, but usually only one completes development and releases an egg. The egg is produced by completion of the first division of meiosis, to produce one large cell and one very small cell, which does not develop further. The larger cell carries out the second division of meiosis and again one large and one small cell is produced. The large cell differentiates into the egg and the smaller cell does not develop further.

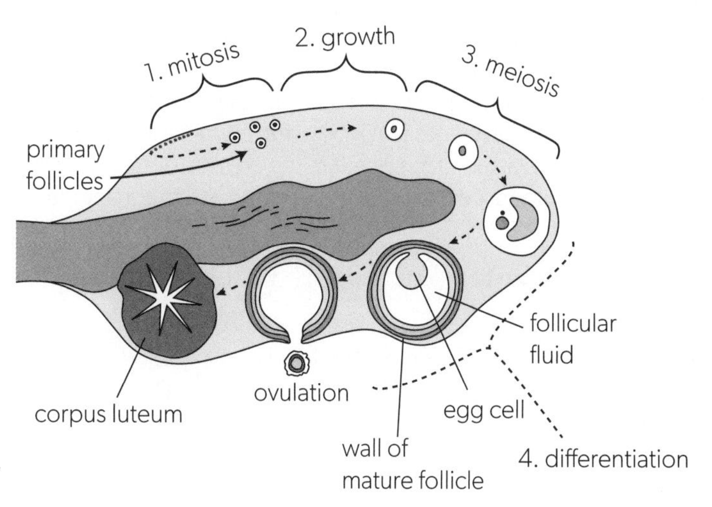

The table contrasts spermatogenesis and oogenesis.

	Gametes per meiosis	Production rate	Timing of production	When released?	Amount of cytoplasm after differentiation
♂	4 sperm	Millions of sperm per day	From puberty onwards, taking about 75 days to produce a sperm	During ejaculation in semen	Sperm have little cytoplasm, helping them to swim faster
♀	1 egg	1 egg per month usually	Eggs released from puberty until menopause; early stages of production in the foetus	At ovulation, on about Day 14 of the menstrual cycle	Eggs have more cytoplasm than any other human cell, to provide food reserves for the embryo

AHL

16. Development of a blastocyst

The zygote produced by fertilization in the oviduct divides by mitosis to form a 2-cell embryo. Further rounds of the cell cycle double the number of cells about every 18 hours. Because the egg has a large amount of cytoplasm, these early rounds of division can happen without any cell growth, so cell size decreases. Initially the embryo is a solid ball of cells. When it is 6 or 7 days old it has changed into a hollow ball, due to unequal cell divisions and cell migration. This embryonic stage is the blastocyst. It has about 250 cells and is approximately 200 μm in diameter. The diagrams show some embryonic stages. The structure of a human zygote is shown in *Section D3.1.6*.

2-cell embryo

4-cell embryo

inner cell mass (develops into the embryo)

fluid inside blastocyst

trophoblast (helps with implantation)

blastocyst

While the embryo is developing, it is wafted down to the oviduct by cilia in the oviduct wall. The embryo arrives in the uterus when it is about 7 days old and has become a blastocyst. The embryo has used up the food reserves of the egg by this stage, so it must obtain supplies from its mother. Cells in the outer layer (trophoblast) of the blastocyst secrete enzymes that loosen the connections between cells in the lining of the uterus wall (endometrium). This allows the blastocyst to penetrate the uterus wall and become implanted. If implantation does not occur, the embryo is not supplied with enough food and the pregnancy fails.

18. The placenta

The placenta is a disc-shaped structure, embedded in the uterus wall. Its development begins about 4 weeks after conception in humans. The basic functional unit is a finger-like piece of foetal tissue called a placental villus. The size of the placenta and the number of villi grow larger during pregnancy, so that the surface area matches the increasing demands of the foetus for exchange of materials with the mother. Maternal blood flows in spaces around the villi (intervillous spaces). This is a very unusual type of circulation as elsewhere blood is almost always retained in blood vessels. Foetal blood is pumped to the placenta though arteries in the umbilical cord by the foetal heart and then passes through a dense network of blood capillaries close to the surface of each villus.

The distance between foetal and maternal blood is very small—as little as 5 μm. The cells that separate maternal and foetal blood form the placental barrier. This must be selectively permeable, allowing some substances to pass, but not others. Glucose, amino acids, oxygen and all other substances required by the foetus pass from maternal to foetal blood. Carbon dioxide, urea and other waste products pass from foetal to maternal blood. Diffusion, facilitated diffusion, osmosis and endocytosis are all used in these exchanges for specific substances. The blood passes from the placenta to the body of the foetus in the umbilical vein.

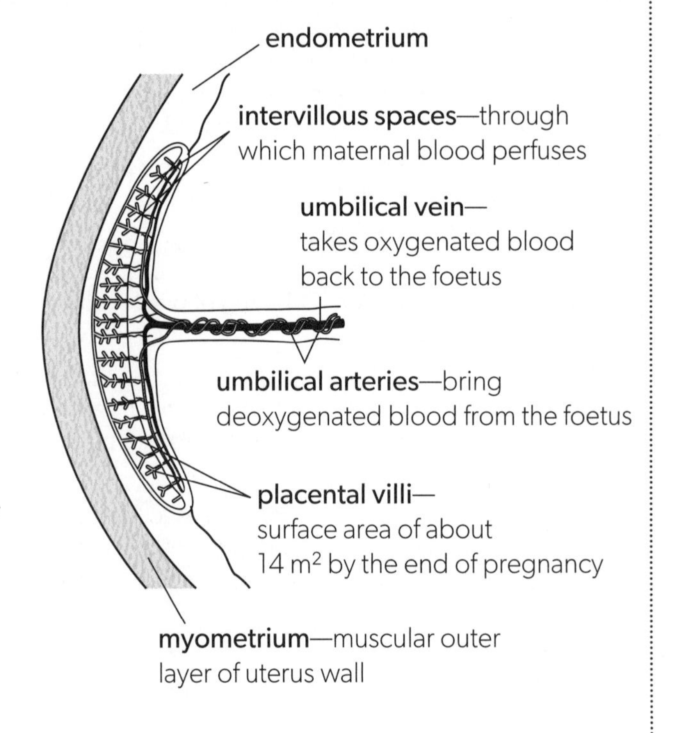
endometrium
intervillous spaces—through which maternal blood perfuses
umbilical vein—takes oxygenated blood back to the foetus
umbilical arteries—bring deoxygenated blood from the foetus
placental villi—surface area of about 14 m² by the end of pregnancy
myometrium—muscular outer layer of uterus wall

The foetus can be retained in the uterus to a much later stage of development in placental mammals than in mammals such as kangaroos that do not develop a placenta.

AHL

13. Hormonal control of puberty

Puberty is development from childhood to sexual maturity. When the brain determines that the time for puberty has arrived, the peptide hormone GnRH (gonadotropin-releasing hormone), is synthesized by neurons in the hypothalamus and transported to the pituitary gland where it is secreted into the bloodstream. Secretion continues through puberty and adulthood. GnRH stimulates secretion of FSH and LH by the pituitary gland. These two hormones are gonadotropins because they cause changes in the gonads—the testes and ovaries.

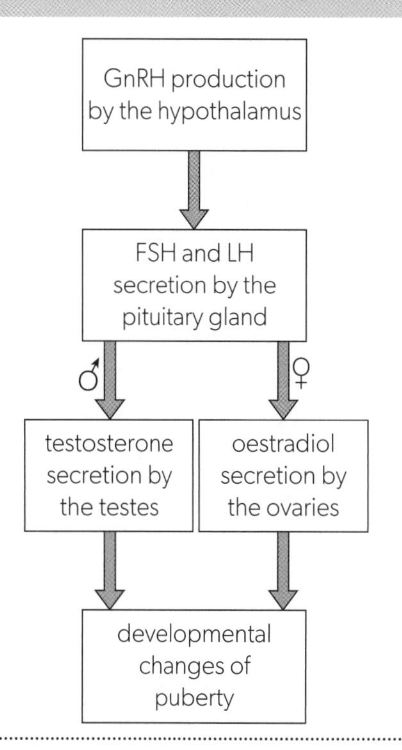

In boys, FSH stimulates testis growth and LH stimulates secretion of the steroid hormone testosterone by the testes. Testosterone causes the development of secondary sexual characteristics in boys during puberty such as enlargement of the penis, growth of pubic hair and deepening of the voice due to growth of the larynx.

In girls, FSH stimulates the development of follicles in the ovary. The follicle wall secretes the steroid hormone oestradiol. LH causes the development of the follicle wall into the corpus luteum after ovulation, which continues the secretion of oestradiol. Oestradiol causes the development of secondary sexual characteristics in females during puberty such as enlargement of the uterus, development of the breasts and growth of pubic and underarm hair.

19. Hormones of pregnancy and childbirth

Secretion of hCG throughout pregnancy stimulates continuing secretion of oestradiol and progesterone. These two steroid hormones are initially secreted by the corpus luteum, but after about 10 weeks of pregnancy the placenta takes over. They are essential to prevent miscarriage and allow the pregnancy to continue. Oestradiol and progesterone prevent degeneration of the uterus lining. Progesterone prevents contractions of the muscular outer wall of the uterus (myometrium) by inhibiting oxytocin secretion in the pituitary gland.

Concentrations of both steroid hormones gradually rise, but near the end of a pregnancy the foetus signals to the placenta to stop secreting progesterone, so the concentration starts to decline. This allows the pituitary gland to start secreting oxytocin. Oxytocin stimulates contractions of the muscle in the myometrium. The contractions are detected by stretch receptors, which signal to the pituitary gland to increase oxytocin secretion. Increased oxytocin concentration makes the contractions more frequent and more vigorous, causing more oxytocin secretion.

This is an example of positive feedback. In this case, it has the advantage of causing a gradual increase in the myometrial contractions, allowing the baby to be born with the minimum intensity of contraction. The baby is pushed out through the cervix and vagina. The umbilical cord is broken and the baby takes its first breath and achieves physiological independence from its mother.

20. HRT

Hormone replacement therapy (HRT) is used to relieve menopausal symptoms. It supplements levels of the oestradiol and progesterone that naturally decrease as a woman approaches the menopause. HRT can relieve symptoms such as hot flushes, night sweats, mood swings, vaginal dryness and reduced sex drive. Many of these symptoms pass after a few years, but they can be unpleasant and HRT offers relief to many women. It can also reduce osteoporosis (loss of bone density) which is more common after the menopause.

Patterns and trends

NOS

Correlation does not prove causation. Epidemiological research revealed that women taking HRT had a lower-than-average risk of coronary heart disease (CHD). This was assumed to be a cause-and-effect relationship. Randomized, controlled, double-blind trials were then carried out which showed that use of HRT actually caused a small increase in risk of CHD. The lower risk of CHD in HRT patients is due to the patients having a higher-than-average socioeconomic status, and this status is correlated with a lower risk of CHD. (The causes and consequences of CHD are explained in *Section B3.2.6*.)

8. Sexual reproduction in flowering plants

The three key stages in sexual reproduction in flowering plants all happen inside flowers: meiosis, gamete production and fertilization. The zygote produced by fertilization grows and develops into an embryo inside a seed, which is then dispersed. The parts of a flower are shown below in a half-view drawing.

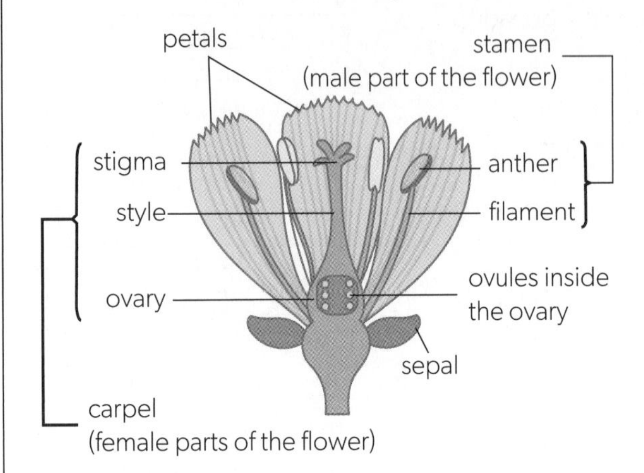

Anthers produce pollen, containing male gametes. Diploid cells inside the anther divide by meiosis to produce four haploid cells, each of which develops into a pollen grain. The nucleus inside a pollen grain divides by mitosis, to produce the male gametes. Pollen grains develop a thickened wall for protection during pollination.

Ovules are ovoid structures inside the ovary. One cell in the centre of the ovule grows particularly large and then divides by meiosis. One of the haploid nuclei produced divides three times by mitosis to produce eight haploid nuclei, one of which becomes the female gamete (egg nucleus).

Successful sexual reproduction in flowering plants depends on pollination, fertilization and embryo development.

- **Pollination** is the transfer of pollen from an anther to a stigma. The pollen is usually moved by wind or by animals.
- **Fertilization** happens inside an ovule. Each pollen grain that lands on the stigma grows a tube down the style to the ovary, to transport the male gametes from the pollen grain. Once inside the ovary, the pollen tube grows to one ovule and digests a route into it. When the tube reaches the centre of the ovule where the female gamete (egg) is located, the male gametes are released and fertilization occurs, resulting in the production of a zygote.
- **Embryo development**—the zygote divides repeatedly by mitosis and the cells produced develop into an embryo, with an embryo root, embryo shoot and either one or two embryo leaves (cotyledons). The outer layers of the ovule develop into the seed coat.

The type of reproduction that happens inside flowers is sexual. Many flowers are hermaphrodite because they have both male and female parts, so can act as both a male parent and a female parent. In some cases, hermaphrodite flowering plants act as both the male and female parent, by self-pollination and self-fertilization. Even so, this is not asexual reproduction as all the key events of sexual reproduction happen: meiosis, gamete production and fertilization.

10. Increasing cross-pollination

Cross-pollination is transfer of pollen from the anther of a flower to the stigma of a flower on a different plant. An outside agent is needed to transfer the pollen, usually an animal or the wind. Cross-pollination leads to fusion of male and female gametes from different plants, so promotes genetic variation and therefore evolution, which is essential when there is environmental change.

Many plants are hermaphrodite: they produce both pollen with male gametes and ovules with female gametes. This makes self-pollination possible (transfer of pollen from anther to stigma on the same plant), causing inbreeding. In most human societies there are taboos or laws against closely related individuals reproducing. This is because of high rates of miscarriage and genetic disease in offspring in such cases. Inbreeding increases the chance of a rare recessive allele in one ancestor being inherited twice by an individual, thus causing a genetic disorder. The offspring of two genetically different plants tend to be healthy and grow strongly (hybrid vigour). Natural selection therefore tends to favour plants that reproduce by cross-pollination, and mechanisms have evolved to promote it and reduce the chance of inbreeding from self-pollination. The table shows strategies for promoting cross-pollination:

Method	Example
separate male and female plants so anthers and carpels (stigma, styles and ovary) are on different plants	*Ginkgo biloba* (ginkgo tree) *Urtica dioica* (stinging nettle)
separate male and female flowers on the same plant so anthers and carpels are not in the same flower	*Zea mays* (corn/maize) *Betula papyrifera* (paper birch)
stigmas and pollen on anthers mature at different times (protandry = pollen first, protogyny = stigma first)	*Nelumbo nucifera* (lotus)—protogynous *Digitalis purpurea* (foxglove)—protandrous

9. Insect-pollinated flowers

Pollen grains cannot move themselves, so an agent is needed for pollination (transfer from anther to stigma). Insects are the commonest agents of pollination. Bees and other insects are attracted to flowers that secrete nectar because the nectar is an energy source as it contains sugars. Insects are attracted by the pollen, which is rich in protein.

The structure of insect-pollinated flowers varies depending on the species of insect used as pollinator and the strategy for pollination, but there are some common features.

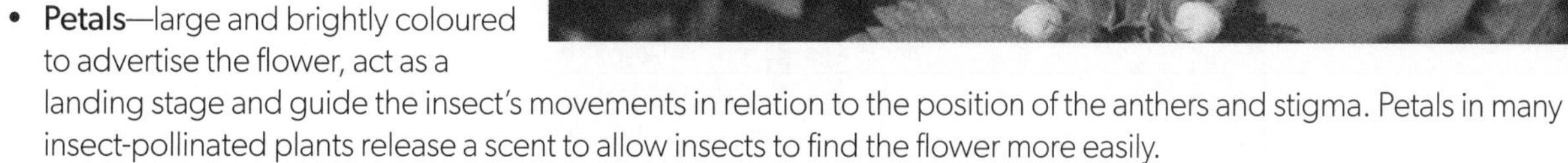

- **Petals**—large and brightly coloured to advertise the flower, act as a landing stage and guide the insect's movements in relation to the position of the anthers and stigma. Petals in many insect-pollinated plants release a scent to allow insects to find the flower more easily.
- **Pollen grains**—spiky so they stick to the anther initially and then to the visiting insect. The grains can be relatively large as they do not need to be light to be blown by wind.
- **Anther**—positioned to deposit pollen on the insect.
- **Stigma**—positioned where a visiting insect will brush past it and sticky so pollen from it adheres.
- **Nectaries**—glands that secrete nectar; nectaries are positioned deep inside the flower so insects can only reach them by brushing past the anthers and stigma.

The photo shows a bee visiting a white dead-nettle flower (*Lamium album*). The drawing below shows the structure and adaptations of a white dead nettle flower.

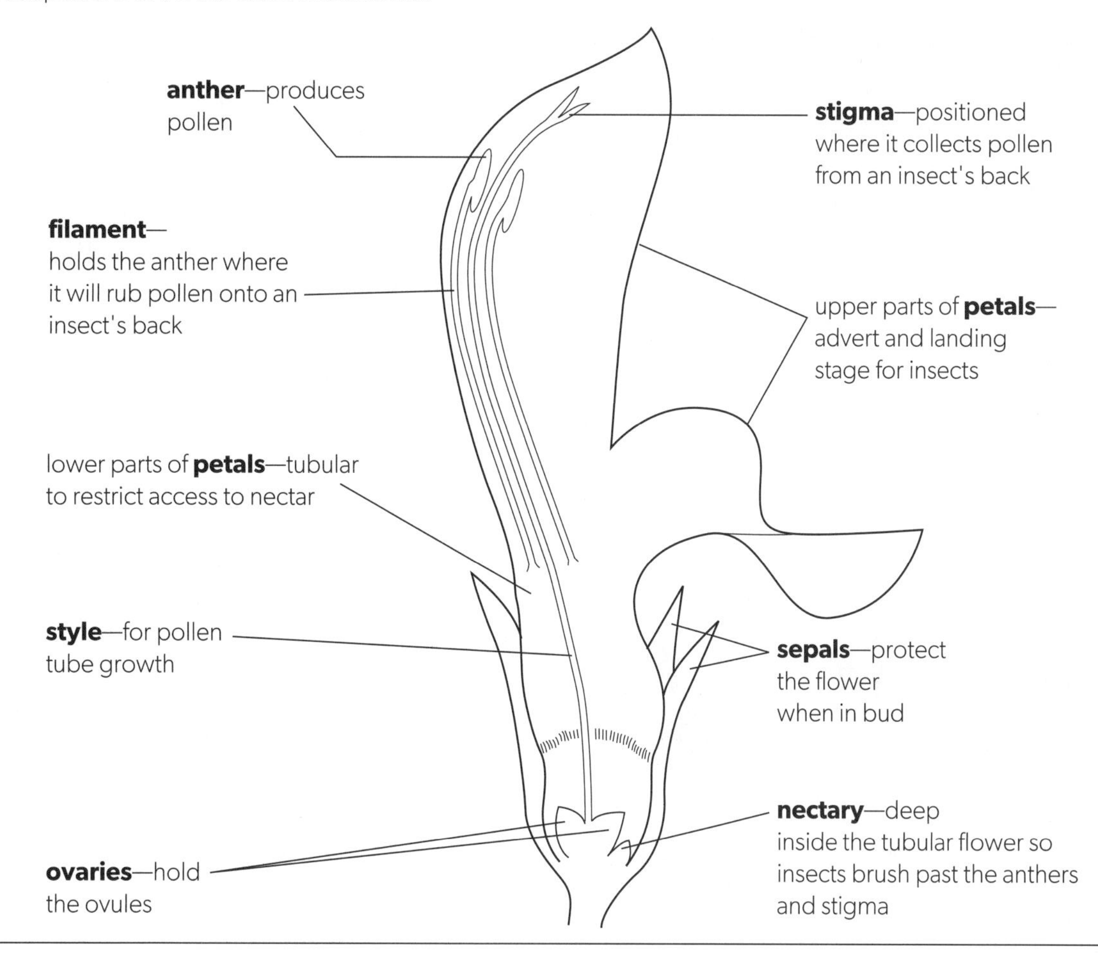
anther—produces pollen
stigma—positioned where it collects pollen from an insect's back
filament—holds the anther where it will rub pollen onto an insect's back
upper parts of petals—advert and landing stage for insects
lower parts of petals—tubular to restrict access to nectar
style—for pollen tube growth
sepals—protect the flower when in bud
nectary—deep inside the tubular flower so insects brush past the anthers and stigma
ovaries—hold the ovules

11. Self-incompatibility mechanisms

Despite adaptations that reduce the chance of self-pollination, the stigma of a hermaphrodite plant may receive pollen from that plant's own anthers. In many plants this pollen fails to germinate, or the pollen tube stops growing before it reaches the ovary. This protection against inbreeding due to a single plant acting as both male and female parent is **self-incompatibility**. It has evolved more than once and there are different mechanisms, but there is always a genetic basis, with alternative alleles of one or more genes. Plants with the same self-incompatibility alleles cannot produce offspring together.

In the following diagrams, the genotype of the female parent (which is diploid) is shown in the style. The genotype of the pollen (which are haploid) is shown in each pollen grain. The diagram shows what happens if pollen grains from a plant land on a stigma of the same plant.

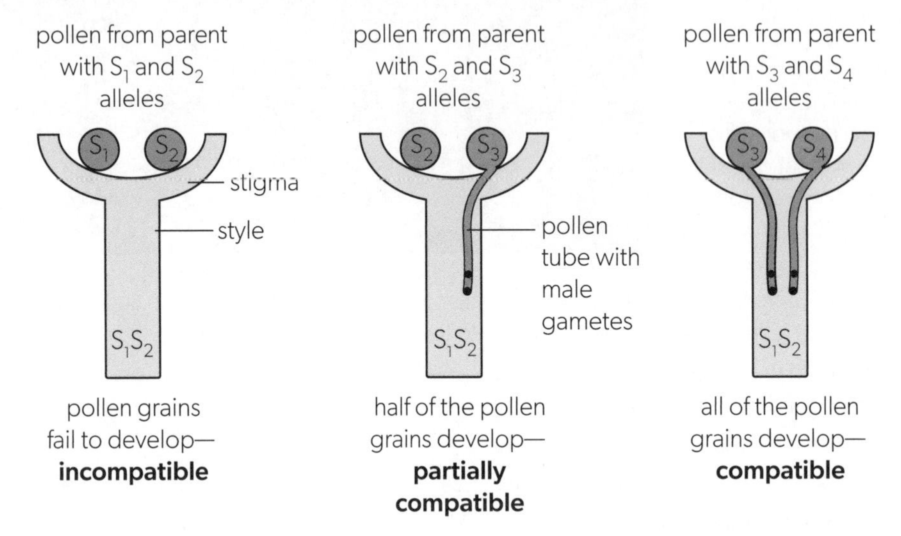

Apple trees are an example of self-incompatibility. Fruit growers know that planting a single variety in an orchard may result in little or no fruit, but if there are two varieties of apple tree in an orchard with different alleles of self-incompatibility genes, abundant crops can be produced.

12. Seed dispersal and germination

Seeds are often transported long distances from the parent plant. This is seed dispersal. It helps to spread the species and reduces competition between offspring and parent. Seed dispersal and pollination are separate processes in the sexual life cycle of plants. They are compared and contrasted in the table (right). Seed dispersal is the function of the fruit, which develops from the ovary of the flower. The structure of fruits is very variable and corresponds to the seed dispersal strategy:

- fleshy and attractive for animals to eat
- feathery or winged to catch the wind
- covered in hooks that catch onto the coats of animals
- explosive.

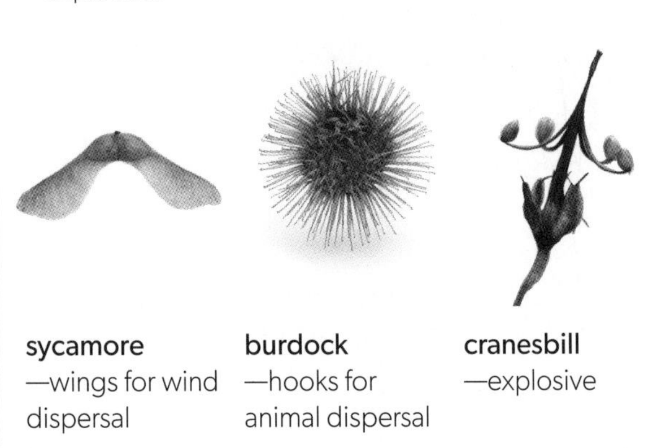

sycamore —wings for wind dispersal
burdock —hooks for animal dispersal
cranesbill —explosive

	Pollination	Seed dispersal
What is transferred?	Pollen	Seeds
From where to where?	Anther to stigma	From female parent to the site of germination
What are the agents?	Wind or animals	Wind, animals or explosion

- Seed germination follows dispersal.
- It happens when conditions are suitable. There must be water, oxygen and warmth.
- Food reserves inside the seed are mobilized by being digested and transferred to the growing embryo.
- The diagram below shows a germinating rice seed.

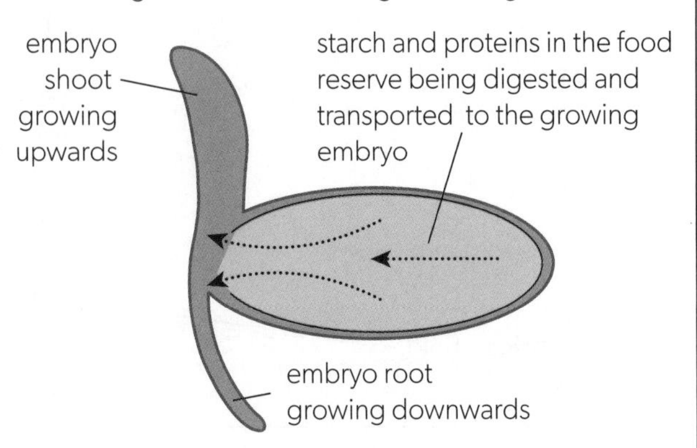

D3.2 Inheritance

1. Inheritance as the fusion of haploid gametes to give a diploid zygote

- Plants, animals and other eukaryotes that reproduce sexually pass genes to offspring in gametes. This is the basis of inheritance.
- Male and female gametes have the same haploid number of chromosomes so male and female parents make an equal genetic contribution to their offspring.
- As gametes are produced from diploid body cells, meiosis is required to halve the chromosome number.
- Diploid body cells have two copies of each autosomal gene (genes located on a non-sex chromosome). Only one of each gene is passed on to offspring in the gamete.
- Fusion of male and female gametes doubles the chromosome number, so the zygote is diploid, as are all body cells subsequently produced by mitosis.

2. Carrying out genetic crosses in flowering plants

Patterns of inheritance can be investigated by crossing different varieties of flowering plants such as peas. Pea plants produce both male and female gametes so can self-pollinate and therefore self-fertilize. The following method (1–4) ensures cross-pollination:

1. Cut off all the anthers from a flower on the plant that is intended to be the female parent. The anthers must be removed before they start to shed pollen, so the flower cannot self-pollinate.
2. Enclose the flower in a paper bag to prevent insects or wind from transferring pollen to it.
3. When the stigma of the flower is mature, transfer pollen to it from anthers on the intended male parent.
4. Wait for the pollen to germinate and the male gametes to be carried down to the ovary in a pollen tube, where they will fertilize egg cells inside the ovules, resulting eventually in seeds which can be harvested.

The parents are known to geneticists as the **P generation** and the offspring inside the seeds as the **F1 generation**. Offspring of the F1 are the **F2 generation**.

The procedure for crossing two plants together has been widely used to produce new varieties of crop plant and ornamental plant.

The results of genetic crosses are analysed using a table called a Punnett grid. There are examples on the following pages.

***Flower of Filipendula* (meadowsweet)**

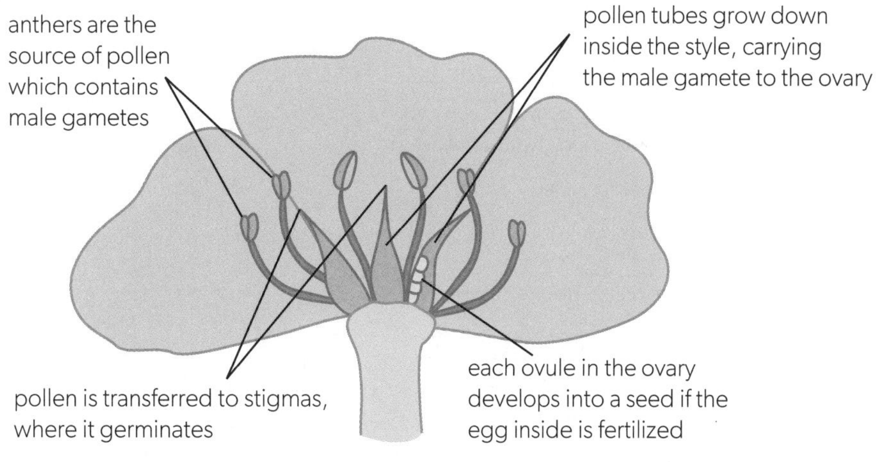
anthers are the source of pollen which contains male gametes
pollen tubes grow down inside the style, carrying the male gamete to the ovary
pollen is transferred to stigmas, where it germinates
each ovule in the ovary develops into a seed if the egg inside is fertilized

3. Genotype

Alleles are different versions of the same gene. Humans and other diploid organisms have two alleles of autosomal genes, one inherited from each parent. There could be two copies of one allele, or two different alleles. For example, for a gene with the alleles D and d, an individual could have DD, dd or Dd. Combinations of alleles such as these are known as **genotypes**.

If a parent's genotype is DD, all gametes produced by them will contain a single copy of allele D. Similarly, all the gametes produced by a parent with the genotype dd will have one allele d. Individuals with the genotypes DD and dd are **homozygous** because all the gametes they produce have the same allele of this gene.

If a parent's genotype is Dd, 50% of their gametes will have allele D and 50% will have allele d. Individuals with the genotype Dd are **heterozygous**, because they produce gametes with different alleles of the gene.

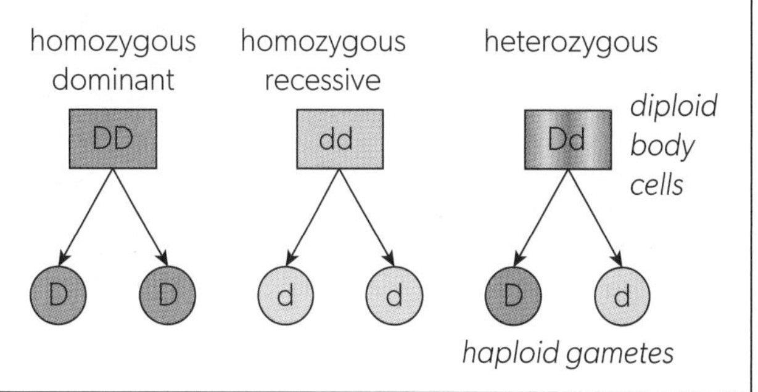
homozygous dominant
homozygous recessive
heterozygous
DD
dd
Dd
diploid body cells
D
D
d
d
D
d
haploid gametes

4. Phenotype

The phenotype of an organism is its observable traits (characteristics). Phenotype includes structural traits such as whether hair is curly or straight and functional traits such as the ability to distinguish red and green colours.

Most phenotypic traits are due to the interaction between the genotype of an organism and the environment in which it exists, but there are some determined solely by genotype and some solely by environmental factors.

Traits determined by **genotype only**:
- eye colour—brown or blue/grey
- haemophilia—blood slow to clot
- ability to smell β-ionone—an odorant in violets.

Traits determined by **genotype and environment**:
- height in humans
- autism—a personality trait
- diabetes—failure to regulate blood glucose concentration.

Traits determined by **environment only**:
- scars due to surgery or wounds
- river blindness—due to parasitic worms in the eye
- body art such as tattoos and piercings.

5. Dominant and recessive alleles

Pure-breeding varieties of plant develop the same phenotype, generation after generation, if they are self-pollinated. This is because they are homozygous for all their genes. Using pure-breeding varieties of pea plant, Gregor Mendel discovered a pattern of inheritance in which one allele of a gene is dominant and another allele is recessive.

- **Dominant alleles** determine the phenotype in both individuals that are homozygous for the dominant allele (DD, for example) and in individuals that are heterozygous with one dominant and one recessive allele (Dd, for example).
- **Recessive alleles** only determine the phenotype if an individual is homozygous with two recessive alleles (dd, for example). Mendel crossed two pure-breeding varieties together that differed in a clear trait such as height (tall or dwarf). With each of the traits that Mendel tested, the F1 offspring all had the same phenotype as one of the two parents. For example, offspring of a cross between tall and dwarf pea plants were all tall. When Mendel self-pollinated these F1 pea plants, the phenotype that was not seen in the F1 generation reappeared in 25% of the F2 pea plants. The following chart shows a typical example of a cross.

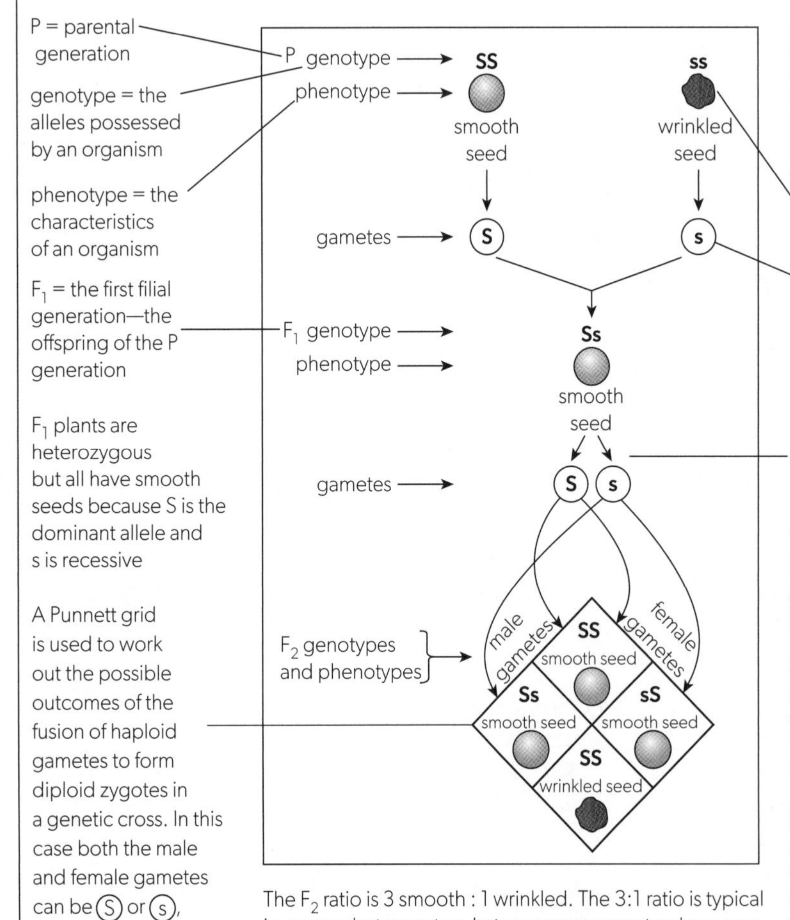
P = parental generation
genotype = the alleles possessed by an organism
phenotype = the characteristics of an organism
F_1 = the first filial generation—the offspring of the P generation
F_1 plants are heterozygous but all have smooth seeds because S is the dominant allele and s is recessive
A Punnett grid is used to work out the possible outcomes of the fusion of haploid gametes to form diploid zygotes in a genetic cross. In this case both the male and female gametes can be (S) or (s), giving four possible F_2 genotypes.
P genotype
phenotype
SS
smooth seed
ss
wrinkled seed
gametes
S
s
F_1 genotype
phenotype
Ss
smooth seed
gametes
S
s
male gametes
female gametes
F_2 genotypes and phenotypes
SS
smooth seed
Ss
smooth seed
sS
smooth seed
ss
wrinkled seed
The F_2 ratio is 3 smooth : 1 wrinkled. The 3:1 ratio is typical in crosses between two heterozygous parents where one allele is dominant and the other is recessive.

Key: S = allele for smooth seed
s = allele for wrinkled seed
(The letter used as a symbol for a gene should be upper case for the dominant and lower case for the recessive allele)

pea plants are diploid so they have two copies of the gene; the parental varieties are homozygous

gametes are produced by meiosis so are haploid and only have one copy of each gene

the two alleles of each gene separate into different haploid daughter nuclei during meiosis—this is **segregation**. In this case each daughter nucleus and therefore each gamete receives either S or s

The S gene codes for a starch-branching enzyme. The full name for the gene is SBE1. The enzyme makes 1–6 glycosidic bonds in starch (see *Section B1.1.5*).

The recessive s allele codes for a non-functional version of this enzyme, resulting in unbranched starch molecules, a higher sugar content and a wrinkled shape when the seed dries out.

As long as one copy of the dominant S allele is present, enough of the functional version of the enzyme is produced to catalyse the starch-branching reaction, which is the reason for the recessive s allele not affecting the phenotype in a heterozygous individual.

6. Phenotypic plasticity

Organisms can respond to their environment by varying their patterns of gene expression and therefore their traits. This is a form of adaptation, but it is reversible because genes have only been switched on or off, not changed into new alleles. It is known as phenotypic plasticity and is particularly useful if the environment a population inhabits is variable. For example, a person with pale skin may become darker-skinned if there is an increase in exposure to sunlight. A change in gene expression results in increased synthesis of the black pigment melanin in the skin. If the sunlight stimulus diminishes, gene expression reverts to its former pattern and the skin gradually becomes paler again, as the melanin concentration reduces. In some cases, phenotypic changes in traits cannot be reversed during the lifetime of the individual, but can when offspring are produced.

7. Phenylketonuria

- Most genetic diseases are caused by a recessive allele.
- A person with one recessive allele and one dominant allele does not have symptoms of the disease but is a carrier, because they can pass on the disease-causing recessive allele to offspring.
- If two parents are carriers of the same recessive allele, the chance of their child inheriting the allele from both of them and therefore developing the disease is 1 in 4, or 25%.

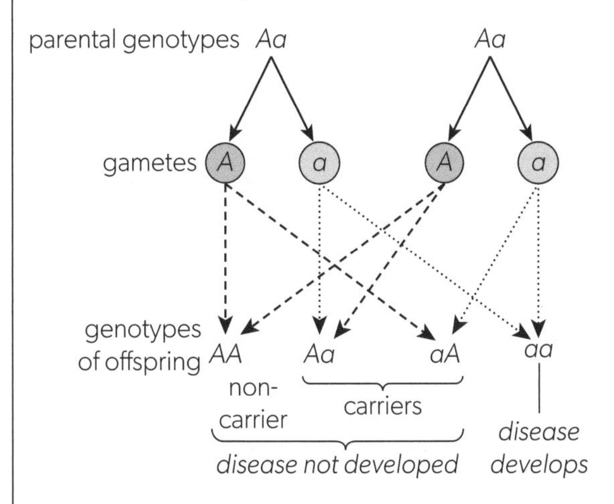

The genetic disease phenylketonuria (PKU) is due to a recessive allele of the gene that codes for the enzyme phenylalanine hydroxylase. This enzyme converts phenylalanine into tyrosine.

The PKU allele is recessive because a carrier with one PKU allele can still produce functioning enzymes by expressing their normal allele. A person with two recessive PKU alleles does not produce functioning enzyme so phenylalanine accumulates in the body and there is tyrosine deficiency.

In excess, phenylalanine impairs brain development, leading to intellectual disability and mental disorders. This can be prevented by screening for PKU at birth and giving affected children a diet low in phenylalanine.

8. Gene pools contain multiple alleles

- A gene pool is all genes of all individuals in a sexually reproducing population.
- Every new individual inherits a selection of genes from the gene pool.
- Evolution is changes in the gene pool over time.
- A gene is a length of DNA, with a base sequence that can be hundreds or thousands of bases long.
- Alleles are different versions of a gene, that were originally generated by mutation.
- The alleles of a gene differ in their base sequence. Usually only one or a very small number of bases are different. For example, adenine might be present at a particular position in one allele and cytosine at that position in another allele.
- Positions in a gene where different bases can be present are called **single nucleotide polymorphisms** (abbreviated to **SNPs** and pronounced snips).
- Even within one gene, there can be many different positions with SNPs. There can therefore be many different alleles of a gene in the gene pool. This is known as multiple alleles.
- The S-gene in apples is an example of multiple alleles. More than 30 different S-alleles have been discovered in the apple gene pool, numbered S1, S2, S3 and so on. The role of the S-gene is described in *Section D3.1.11*.

Unambiguous communication: naming alleles

NOS

To avoid confusion, biologists must all use the same names for alleles of genes. A simple method is to use an upper case letter for the dominant allele and a lower case letter for the recessive allele, for example *A* and *a*. However, there are too many genes and alleles for all genes to be named in this way. Any new gene is therefore given a name consisting of 3 to 5 characters, beginning with an upper case letter, for example BRCA2. Alleles of the gene are named using superscript characters after the gene name. Dominant alleles start with an upper case letter and recessive alleles with a lower case letter. For example Wnt3a^{vt} is a recessive allele of the Wnt3a gene in mice.

9. ABO blood groups

The ABO blood group system in humans is an example of multiple alleles. One gene determines the ABO blood group of a person. There are three alleles of the gene: I^A, I^B and i. There are four different blood groups: A, B, AB and O.

I^A is dominant over i, so people with either genotype I^AI^A or I^Ai are in Blood Group A	I^B is dominant over i, so people with either genotype I^BI^B or I^Bi are in Blood Group B	i is recessive to I^A and I^B, so only people with genotype ii are in Blood Group O
I^A and I^B are codominant, so people with the genotype I^AI^B are in Blood Group AB		

The grid shows how two parents with Blood Group A and B can produce children with any of the four ABO blood groups.

P phenotype → Group A　　Group B
genotype → I^Ai　　I^Bi
gametes → I^A, i　　I^B, i
F_1 genotypes and phenotypes shown on a Punnett grid →
I^AI^B Group AB
I^Bi Group B
I^Ai Group A
ii Group O

The cross below shows how ABO blood groups are an example of codominance, which is explained in *Section D3.2.10*.

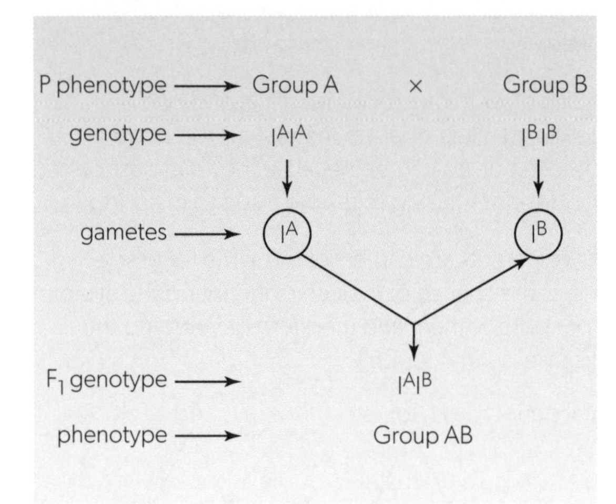

10. Codominance and incomplete dominance

In each of Mendel's crosses between varieties of pea plant, there was one dominant and one recessive allele. There are also genes where neither allele is fully dominant over the other.

P phenotype: red flowers　white flowers
genotype: C_RC_R　C_WC_R
F1 phenotype: pink flowers
genotype: C_RC_W
male gametes: C_R　C_W
female gametes: C_R　C_W

	C_R	C_W
C_R	C_RC_R red	C_RC_W pink
C_W	C_WC_R pink	C_WC_W white

Some pairs of alleles show **incomplete dominance**. The phenotype of a heterozygous individual is intermediate between the phenotypes of the two types of homozygotes. For example, if homozygous red-flowered plants of *Mirabilis jalapa* (four o'clock plant) are crossed with homozygous white-flowered plants, the heterozygous offspring all have pink flowers.

White flowers contain no red pigment. Pink flowers are intermediate because they contain some red pigment but less than in a red flower. If two pink flowered plants are crossed together, the ratio of flower colours in the offspring is 1 red : 2 pink : 1 white.

Some pairs of alleles show codominance. Heterozygous individuals have a dual phenotype that is different to those of either of the two types of homozygotes.

The I^A and I^B alleles in the ABO blood group system are an example, because blood group AB is a dual phenotype and is not intermediate between group A and group B.

- I^A causes production of a specific glycoprotein in the plasma membrane of red blood cells that acts as an antigen.
- I^B causes production of another glycoprotein in the plasma membrane that acts as a different antigen.

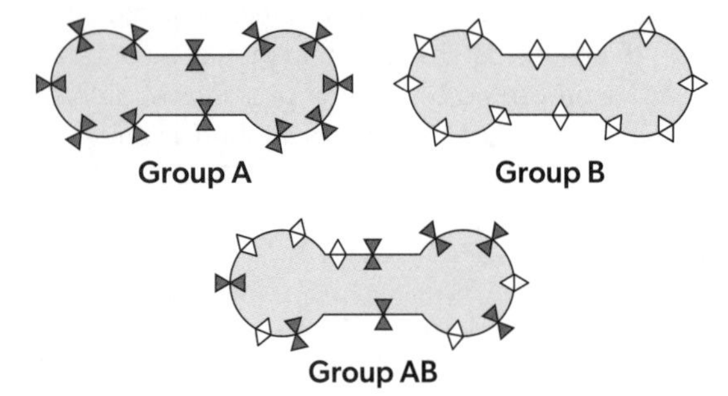

11. Sex chromosomes

Humans have 23 pairs of chromosomes in their body cells (shown in a karyogram in *Section A3.1.7*). Sex is determined by the 23rd pair of chromosomes. There are two types of sex chromosome, X and Y.

- Females typically have two X chromosomes, so all female gametes (eggs) have one X chromosome and all offspring inherit an X chromosome from their mother.
- Males typically have one X and one Y chromosome, so male gametes (sperm) either contain an X or a Y chromosome.
- The sex of offspring is therefore determined by the sperm that fertilizes the egg. A sperm with a Y chromosome makes the resulting child male, whereas an X-bearing sperm makes the child female.

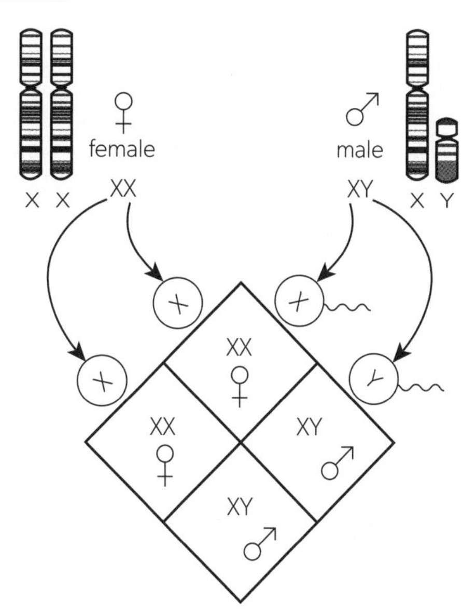

1 female : 1 male

The Y chromosome is small with only about 55 genes, many of which are unique to the Y chromosome and not needed in females. One key gene on the Y chromosome causes gonads in a human embryo to develop into testes. This gene is the testis-determining factor (TDF). The developing testes in an embryo start to secrete testosterone, which causes development of other organs of a male reproductive system.

The gonads develop into ovaries in an embryo without a Y chromosome and therefore no TDF gene. The embryonic ovaries start to secrete oestradiol, causing development of a female reproductive system.

The X chromosome is relatively large and has about 900 genes, many of which are essential in both males and females. All humans must therefore have at least one X chromosome. Because females have two copies of genes on the X chromosome and males only have one, the inheritance pattern differs in males and females. This is described in the following section.

12. Haemophilia

Sex-linked genetic disorders are due to genes located on the X chromosome. Most sex-linked disorders are due to a recessive allele of the gene. Males only have one copy of genes on the X chromosome, so they have the disorder if this one copy is the recessive allele. Females are much less likely to be affected because as long as one of their two X chromosomes carries the dominant allele, they are unaffected.

Haemophilia is an example of this pattern of sex-linked inheritance. People with this disorder, usually males, either lack or have a defective form of Factor VIII. This protein is a clotting factor that normally circulates in the blood. Cuts and other wounds bleed for much longer than normal in people with haemophilia.

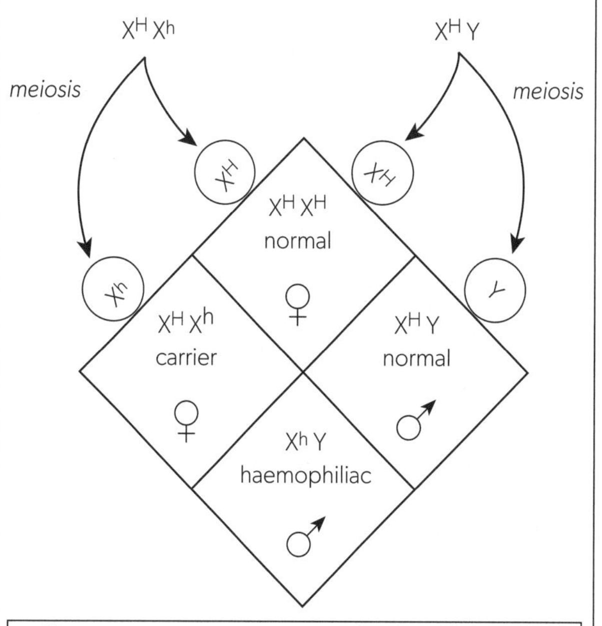

X^H = X chromosome carrying allele for normal clotting
X^h = X chromosome carrying allele for haemophilia

The gene for Factor VIII is located on the X chromosome. The allele that causes haemophilia is recessive. The frequency of the allele is about 1 in 10,000. This is therefore the frequency of the disease in boys. Females only develop haemophilia in the very rare cases where both of their X chromosomes carry the recessive allele, but much more frequently they are carriers of the haemophilia allele.

The pattern of sex-linked inheritance can be shown using Punnett grids. The alleles should always be shown as a superscript letter on a letter X to represent the X chromosome. The Y chromosome should also be shown although it does not carry an allele of the gene.

It is important not to confuse sex linkage and gene linkage. Gene linkage is due to two or more genes being located close together on a chromosome, so alleles of them tend to be inherited together rather than independently.

13. Pedigree charts

Pedigree charts (family tree diagrams) can be used to deduce how genetic disorders are inherited.

- males are shown as squares and females are shown as circles
- horizontal lines link parents and also siblings
- vertical lines link parents and offspring
- a key is used to show how phenotypes are indicated
- generations and individuals are sometimes numbered.

The two real pedigrees shown here are analysed in the following NOS section.

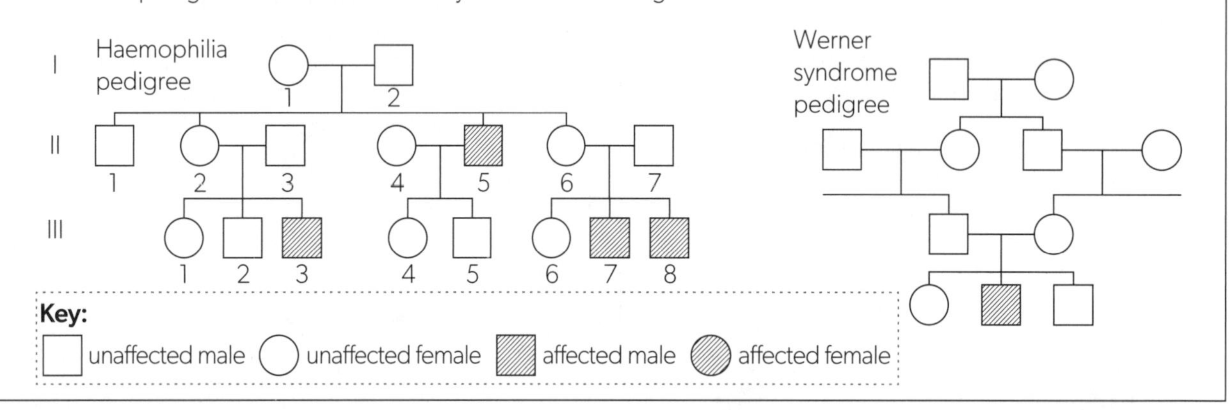

NOS

Patterns and trends

Scientists make observations and look for patterns or trends. They can only make observations on a limited number of particular examples or cases, but then develop a general hypothesis or theory that is intended to apply to all cases. This is **inductive reasoning**. Scientists use their general theories to explain particular cases. This is **deductive reasoning**. This process can be used to test the general hypothesis or theory to see if it is false.

Inductive reasoning can be used to develop a hypothesis for the inheritance of a genetic disorder, using observations from pedigree charts. Deductive reasoning based on the hypothesis can then be used to predict the genotypes of specific individuals in pedigree charts for the disease. For example, in the haemophilia pedigree in *Section D3.2.13*, we observe that only males are affected, and inductive reasoning leads to the hypothesis that the condition is sex-linked. Using this hypothesis, we can deduce all the genotypes of males in the pedigree chart and some of the females.

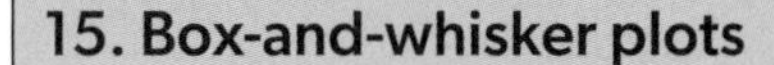

In the pedigree for Werner syndrome, the affected male's parents do not show the condition, leading to the hypothesis that it is due to a recessive allele. Based on the observation that Werner syndrome is very rare, it is possible to decide whether it is more likely that the allele is sex-linked or autosomal.

The pedigree for Werner syndrome indicates the harm that can be caused by inbreeding. The parents of the affected individual were first cousins, making it possible for the same recessive allele to be inherited twice from the same grandparent. In most societies there is a law or taboo against marriages between close relatives, which would have prevented this.

15. Box-and-whisker plots

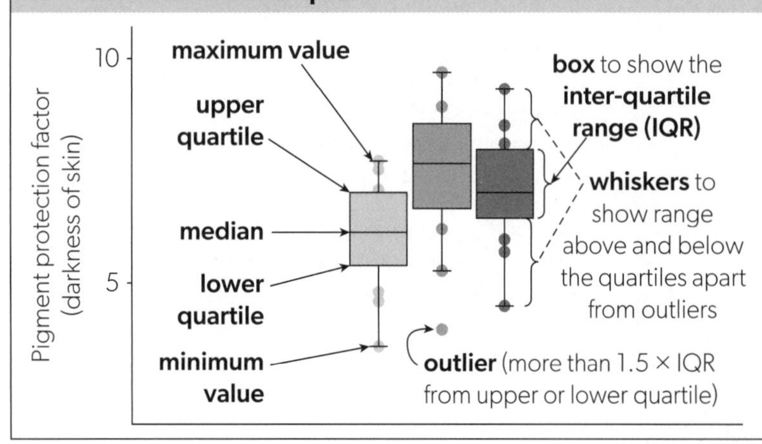

Box-and-whisker plots are used to represent continuously variable data such as human height.

The box plots show the skin pigmentation of the buttocks (left), arm (centre) and forehead (right) of a group of 12 Brazilian people.

One value for arm pigmentation is an outlier as it is more than 1.5 times the interquartile range (IQR) below the lower quartile.

14. Polygenic inheritance

Variation is one of the defining features of life. There are two types of variation: discrete and continuous.

- With **discrete variation**, every individual fits into one of a number of non-overlapping categories. For example, all humans are in blood group A, B, AB or O. In most cases discrete variation is due to one or at most a few genes, without the environment having any influence.
- With **continuous variation** any level of a variable is possible, between the extremes. Continuous variation is due to the environment only in most cases, or to genes in combination with the environment.

Skin colour depends on the amount of the black pigment melanin synthesized by skin cells. Multiple genes affect this process (polygenic inheritance), with some alleles for darker skin and some for paler and many different possible combinations of alleles. Also, sunlight stimulates the production of melanin, so pale skin becomes darker in the days following increased exposure to sunlight. This is not an all-or-nothing effect. The combined effects of genes and environment result in continuous variation in melanin concentration, from little in the palest skin to much larger amounts in the darkest.

Application of skills: measures of central tendency—mean, median and mode

Three different measures of central tendency are used:

Mean—also known as the average

$$\text{mean} = \frac{\text{sum of all values}}{\text{total number of values}}$$

Median—the middle value if numerical data are placed in order of increasing value. If there is an even number of values, then the median is the average of the two values in the middle. The median may be a better choice than the mean if there are outliers.

Mode—the most common value. The mode is useful when the data are non-numerical, such as blood type, so a mean or a median cannot be calculated.

Example: Clutch size (numbers of eggs per nest) in grey partridge (*Perdix perdix*). The range was 4–29 eggs. Data in biology often follow the normal distribution. Mean, median and mode are then all very similar.

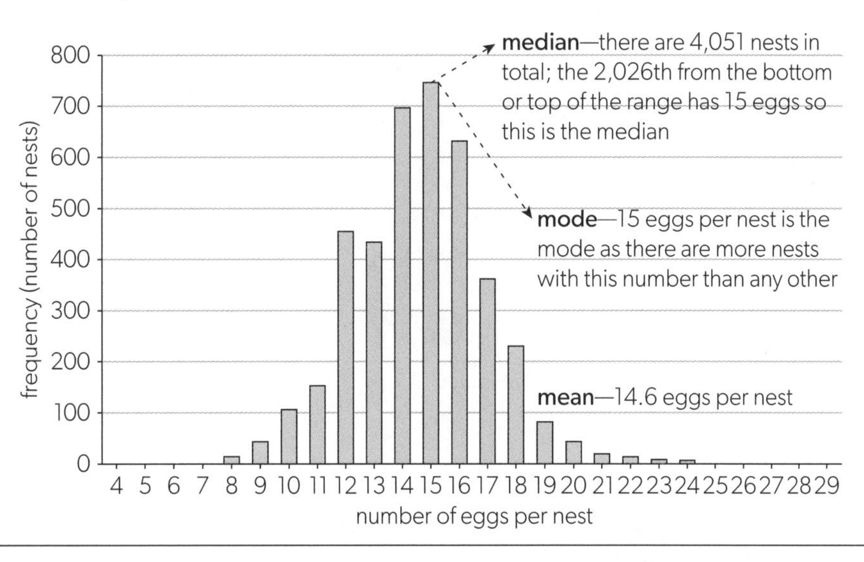

AHL

16. Meiosis—segregation and independent assortment of unlinked genes

Segregation in genetics is the separation of chromosomes and the genes that they carry, during meiosis. For example, in an individual with the genotype Dd, the alleles D and d will segregate. If the individual has the genotype Ee for a second gene, segregation could result in any of the combinations DE, De, dE and de. Which combinations are produced depends on the movements of chromosomes in meiosis. Assuming that the genes are on different chromosomes, this will depend on which way homologous pairs of chromosomes (bivalents) are oriented in Metaphase I or Metaphase II of meiosis. The orientation of each bivalent is random and is unaffected by how other bivalents are oriented. The probability of each combination of alleles is therefore equal. This is **independent assortment**.

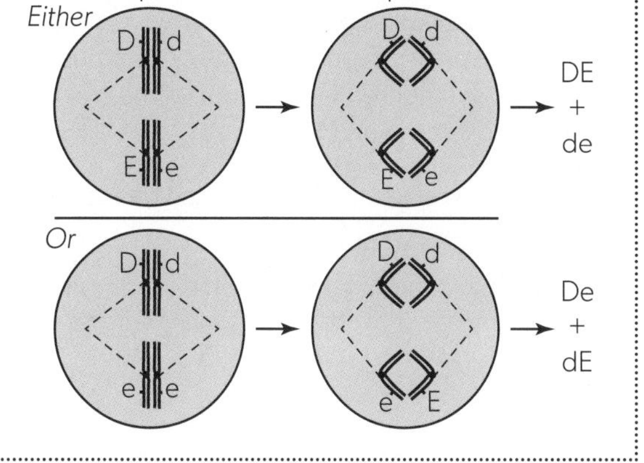

Genes that assort independently, because they are on different chromosomes, are **unlinked**. Segregation and independent assortment were discovered by Gregor Mendel, who performed careful dihybrid crosses and recorded the results meticulously. An example of Mendel's crosses is shown in *Section D3.2.17*.

AHL

17. Predicting genotypic and phenotypic ratios

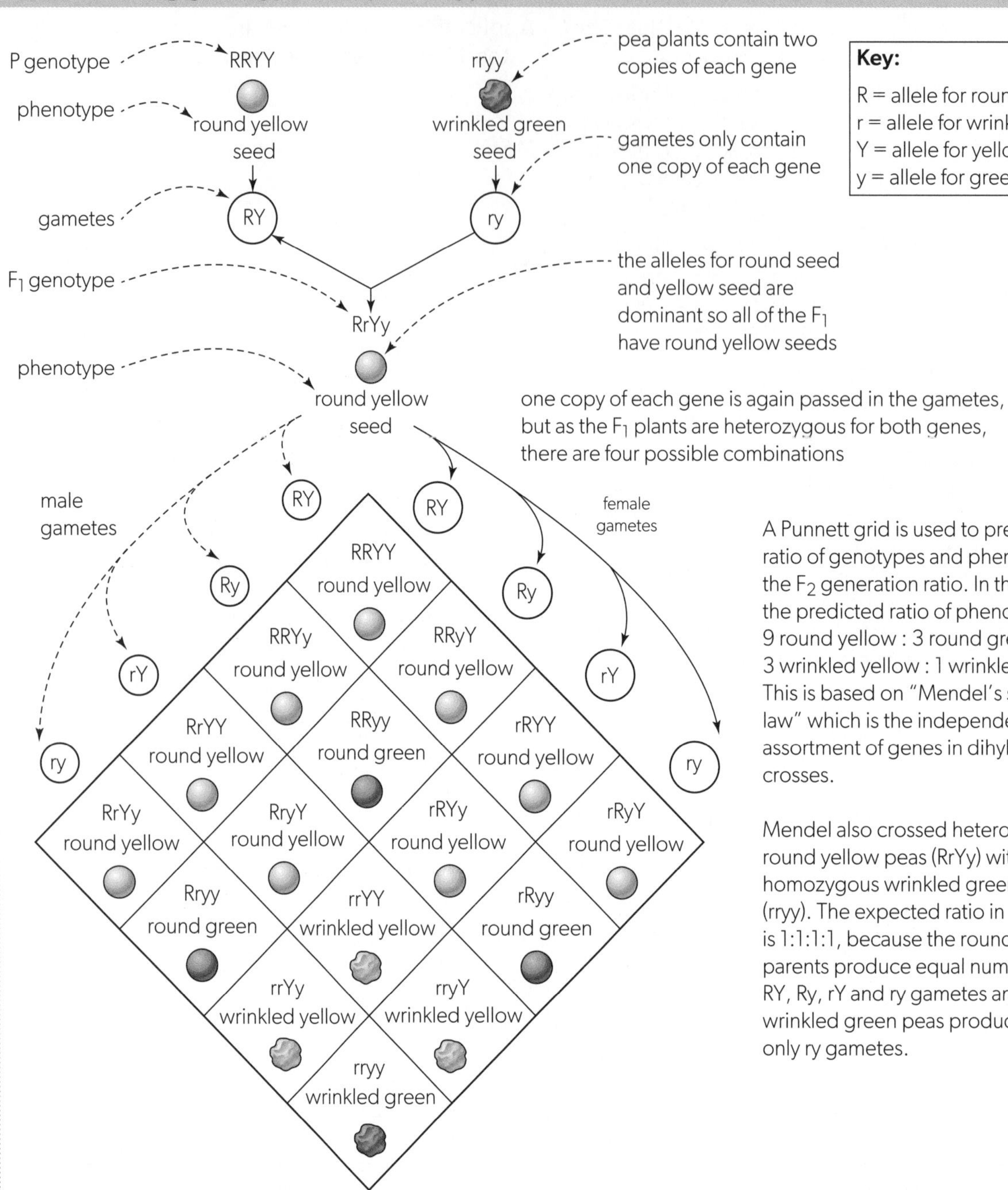

A Punnett grid is used to predict the ratio of genotypes and phenotypes in the F_2 generation ratio. In this case, the predicted ratio of phenotypes is 9 round yellow : 3 round green : 3 wrinkled yellow : 1 wrinkled green. This is based on "Mendel's second law" which is the independent assortment of genes in dihybrid crosses.

Mendel also crossed heterozygous round yellow peas (RrYy) with homozygous wrinkled green peas (rryy). The expected ratio in this case is 1:1:1:1, because the round yellow parents produce equal numbers of RY, Ry, rY and ry gametes and the wrinkled green peas produce only ry gametes.

18. Using databases to find positions of genes

There are about 20,000 genes in the human genome that code for the amino acid sequence of a polypeptide. Each gene has a characteristic base sequence, varying somewhat between alleles. Each gene has a locus, which is its specific position on one of 22 types of autosomes (numbered 1–22) or one of the two types of sex chromosome (X and Y).

The databases Ensembl and NCBI can be used to find

- the locus of any human gene
- how many genes are located on each chromosome
- whether pairs of genes are linked or unlinked depending on whether they are on the same or different chromosomes
- how close the loci of linked genes are and therefore how high the recombination frequency between them will be
- the protein products of protein-coding genes.

Databases are periodically redesigned so detailed instructions for their use are not given here, but usually methods of navigation are quickly learned.

AHL

19. Autosomal gene linkage

Some pairs of genes do not follow Mendel's second law (independent assortment) and the expected 9:3:3:1 or 1:1:1:1 ratio is not found in dihybrid crosses. Instead, the parental combinations of alleles tend to be inherited together. This is called **gene linkage**. It is due to a pair of genes being located on the same chromosome. In most cases this is an autosome (non-sex chromosome) so the inheritance pattern is **autosomal gene linkage**.

Linkage is rarely 100% because crossing over during meiosis between the linked genes can generate new combinations of alleles. Crossing over results in an exchange of DNA between chromatids. The generation of new combinations of alleles is **recombination**. Individuals that have a different combination of alleles or phenotypic traits from parents, due to crossing over, are **recombinants**.

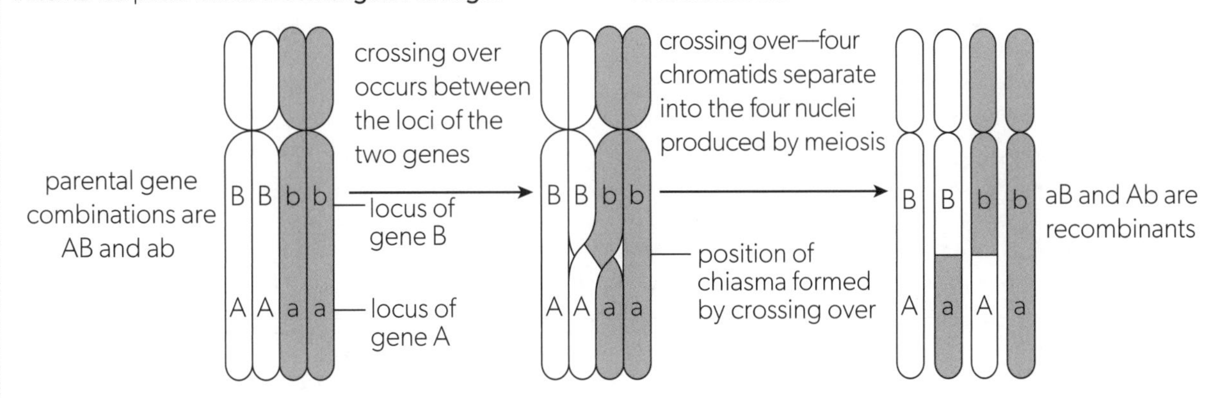

The diagrams below show the effect of alleles being located on the same chromosome, when meiosis takes place and gametes are produced. Linked genes are indicated with a line to represent the chromosome and letters alongside it for the alleles.

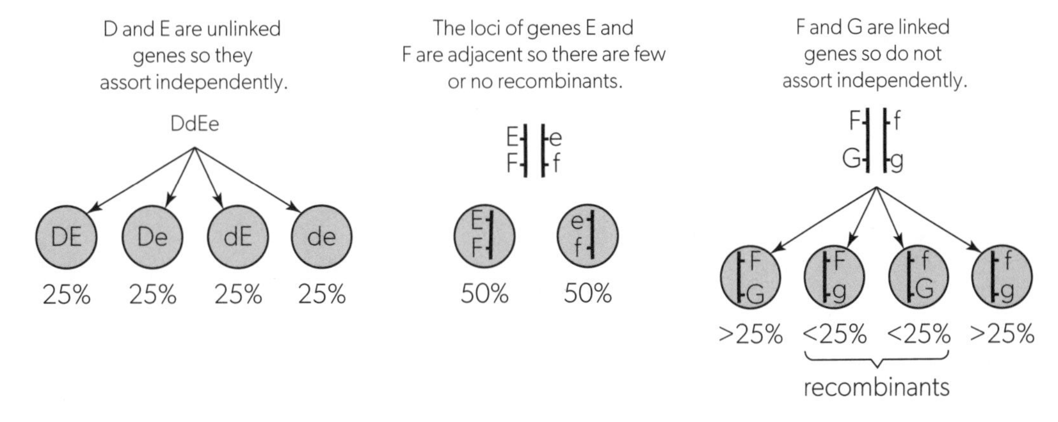

The first case of autosomal gene linkage to be discovered was in the plant *Lathyrus odoratus*. A variety with purple flowers and long pollen grains was crossed with a variety with red flowers and round pollen grains. All the F1 hybrids had purple flowers and long pollen grains. When these F1 plants were self-pollinated, four phenotypes were observed as expected in the F2 generation, but not in the familiar 9:3:3:1 ratio.

The results of the cross are shown. There were more of the purple long and red round plants than expected. Purple round and red long individuals were recombinants because they had a new combination of traits that neither of the original pure-breeding parents had. The recombinants were the result of crossing over between the loci of the genes for flower colour and pollen shape.

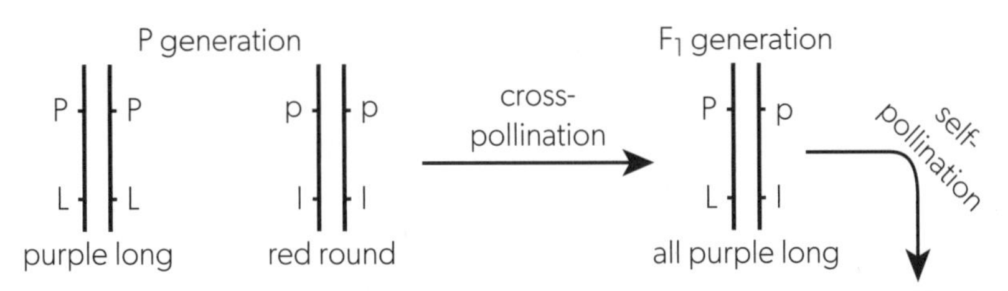

Expected F_2 ratio	9 purple long	3 purple round	3 red long	1 red round
Expected results (total of 6,952 plants)	3,910.5	1,303.5	1,303.5	434.5
Observed results	4,831	390	393	1,338

AHL

20. Identifying recombinants in crosses

A recombinant is an individual with a different combination of alleles (and therefore traits) from either parent. To find the recombination frequency between two genes, an individual heterozygous for both genes is crossed with an individual homozygous recessive for both genes.

1. Outcome with unlinked genes

The Punnett grid predicts the outcome of a cross between pea plants with round yellow seeds that were heterozygous and plants with wrinkled green seeds that were homozygous recessive.

Details of the alleles are shown in *Section D3.2.17*.

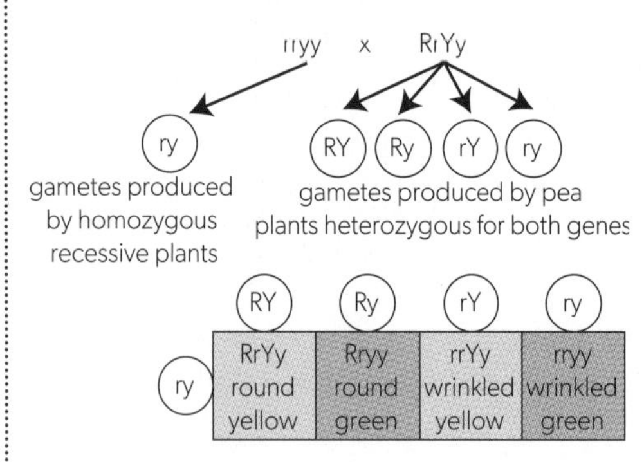

	RY	Ry	rY	ry
ry	RrYy round yellow	Rryy round green	rrYy wrinkled yellow	rryy wrinkled green

When Mendel performed this cross his results were 55 round yellow, 51 round green, 49 wrinkled yellow and 52 wrinkled green. This is close to a 1:1:1:1 ratio. The round green and wrinkled yellow offspring are recombinants because they have a new combination of traits. The expected recombination frequency due to independent assortment of unlinked genes is 50%.

2. Outcome with linked genes

The following diagram shows a cross between pure-breeding spotted short-haired and unspotted long-haired rabbits. The F_1 hybrid offspring were back-crossed to unspotted long-haired rabbits. The observed results in the F_2 generation are far from a 1:1:1:1 ratio. There are more offspring with the parental combinations of alleles and traits, and fewer recombinants with new combinations of alleles and traits. This shows that the genes are linked.

recombination frequency

$$= \frac{26 + 23}{157 + 26 + 23 + 144} \times 100\% = 14\%$$

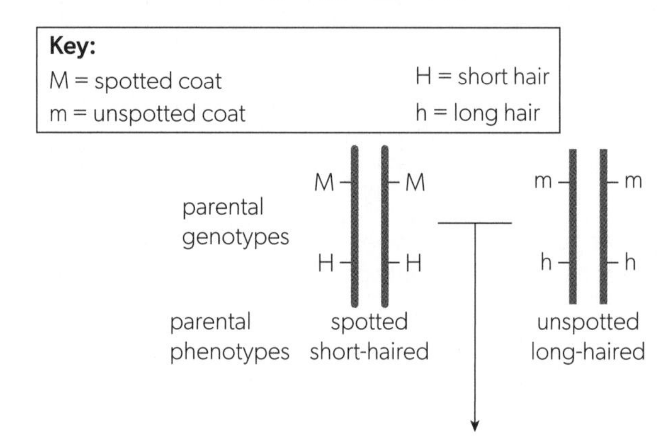

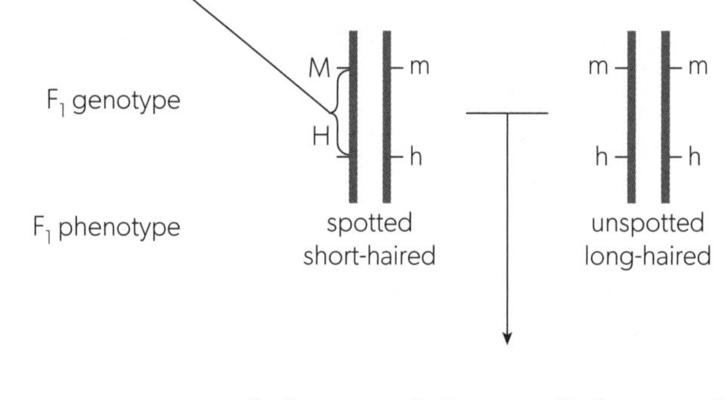

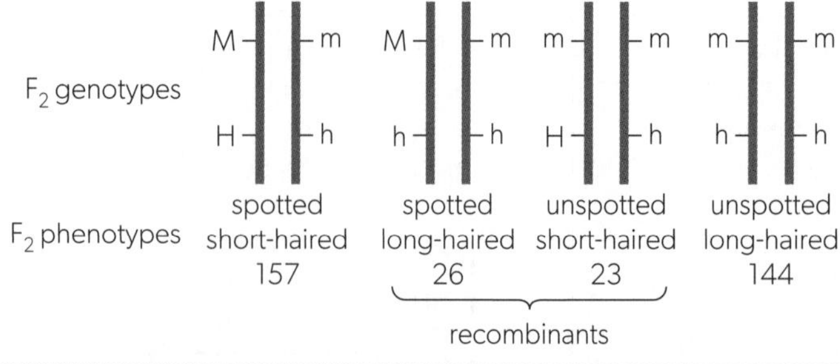

NOS

Theories

Theories provide predictions and explanations. A law represents a prediction of what will reliably happen under a narrow set of conditions. 9:3:3:1 and 1:1:1:1 are predicted ratios for dihybrid crosses based on what has been called Mendel's Second Law. This states that alleles of a gene sort into gametes independently of the alleles of another gene. The law only operates if genes are on different chromosomes, or are far enough apart on one chromosome for recombination to reach 50%. Laws operate best under a narrow range of conditions. There are exceptions to all laws in biology, especially if they are applied to a greater range of conditions.

21. Chi-squared test

The chi-squared test is used in genetics to test whether a predicted ratio fits observed results. The null hypothesis (H_0) is that there is no difference between predicted and observed results. The alternative hypothesis (H_1) is that there is a difference.

Method for chi-squared test

1. Draw up a table of observed frequencies (the numbers of individuals of each phenotype resulting from the cross).
2. Calculate the expected frequencies, based on a Mendelian ratio and the total number of offspring.
3. Determine the number of degrees of freedom (df), which is one less than the total number of possible phenotypes. In a dihybrid cross there are four phenotypes so df = 3.
4. Find the critical region for chi-squared from a table of chi-squared values, using df and a significance level (p) of 0.05 (5%). The critical region is any value of chi-squared larger than the value in the table.
5. Calculate chi-squared using this equation:

$$X^2 = \sum \frac{(\text{obs} - \text{exp})^2}{\text{exp}}$$

6. Compare the calculated value of chi-squared with the critical region. If the calculated value is in the critical region, the differences between the observed and the expected results are statistically significant and we reject the null hypothesis. There is significant evidence that the ratio is not 1:1:1:1. If the calculated value is outside the critical region, the differences between the observed and the expected results are not statistically significant and there is no evidence to reject the Mendelian ratio.

Example: rabbit coat colour and spotting (from *Section D3.2.20*)

	Spotted short	Spotted long	Unspotted short	Unspotted long
Observed	157	26	23	144
Expected	87.5	87.5	87.5	87.5

Degrees of freedom = 4 − 1 = 3

Critical values of the χ^2 distribution

df	p = 0.5	0.1	0.05	0.025	0.01	0.005	df
1	0.455	2.706	3.841	5.024	6.635	7.879	1
2	1.386	4.605	5.991	7.378	9.210	10.597	2
3	2.366	6.251	7.815	9.348	11.345	12.838	3

$$\text{Chi-squared} = \frac{(69.5)^2}{87.5} + \frac{(-61.5)^2}{87.5} + \frac{(-64.5)^2}{87.5} + \frac{(56.5)^2}{87.5}$$

$$= 182.5$$

At the 0.05 level of significance, the critical value is 7.815.

The calculated value for chi-squared is in the critical region so the null hypothesis is rejected. The results do not fit the 1:1:1:1 ratio, so we conclude that the genes for coat colour and spotting do not assort independently and are linked.

NOS

Measurement

Measurements are repeated to strengthen the reliability of data. A larger sample gives greater reliability. In statistical testing, a sample is used to represent a population. In this case, the sample is the F_2 generation, with a total of 350 offspring. A larger sample could have been obtained, but is not needed here, given that chi-squared greatly exceeds the 5% significance level. Genetic ratios from a small number of offspring are not reliable, for example the children of two parents.

NOS

Hypotheses

Scientists routinely use statistical tests in their research. Research is unlikely to be accepted for publication unless such tests have been done using accepted procedures. A **null hypothesis** is set up; for example, the null hypothesis could be that there is no difference between the mean heights of two populations, or it could be that features of the population occur in specified ratios, such as in Mendel's research which predicted that numbers of peas with particular characteristics would occur according to genetic ratios such as 3:1 or 1:1:1:1. Measurable predictions are made on the assumption that the null hypothesis is true. Observed data are collected and a calculation made to see how closely the predictions fit what was actually observed.

The observations, of course, are based on a sample, not on the whole population. If the whole population were available, there would be no need for a hypothesis, as everything could be known about the population! As each sample is different, the observed results depend on which sample was observed. Some samples will be more representative of the population than others. Some unrepresentative samples lead to the conclusion that the null hypothesis is false, even when it is true. Before carrying out the hypothesis test, the scientist must decide what level of risk is acceptable for rejecting the null hypothesis when in fact it is true. This level of risk is called the **significance level** of the hypothesis test.

D3.3 Homeostasis

1. Homeostasis

The environment for a cell inside a multicellular organism is the immediate surroundings outside its plasma membrane. For a plant cell, this is the cell wall and the fluid held in it. For an animal cell, it is tissue fluid between cells, which may be in spaces or in an extracellular matrix made of collagen and elastin. Blood is an unusual tissue as it is liquid, with the cells suspended in tissue fluid (plasma).

An advantage of multicellularity is that internal environments between cells can be regulated, with variables kept as close to optimal as possible. This process is **homeostasis**. Blood glucose concentration, blood osmotic concentration, blood pH and core body temperature are key variables that are kept relatively constant as a part of homeostasis in humans, despite any fluctuations in the external environment.

2. Negative feedback

Feedback control uses information about the outcome of a process to make decisions about the future of that process. There are two types of feedback control: positive and negative.

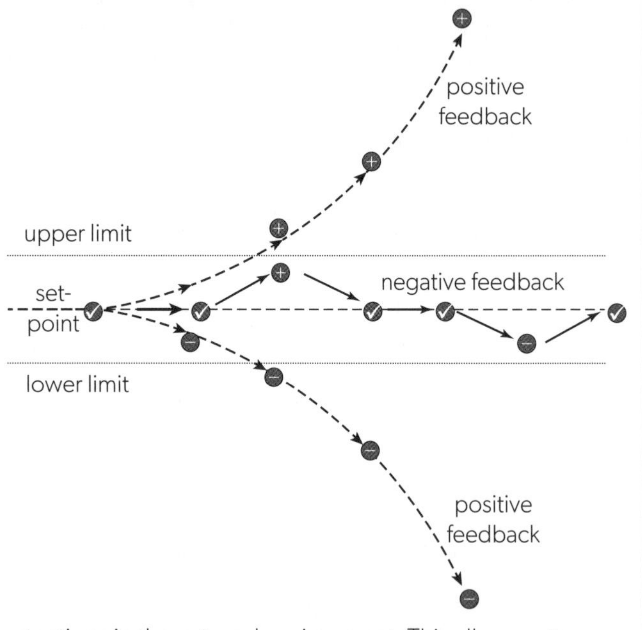

- **Positive feedback** increases the gap between an original level and a new level. Specific positive feedback mechanisms are described in *Section D3.1.5* and for HL in *Sections C3.1.23* and *D3.1.19*. Positive feedback promotes change rather than stability so it is unsuitable for homeostasis.
- **Negative feedback** decreases the gap between an original level and a new level, so the original level is restored. A set-point can be chosen and any deviations from it can be reversed, keeping the variable close to the set-point. Negative feedback mechanisms therefore promote balance and they form the basis of homeostasis in the body. Large amounts of energy have to be used, but for many multicellular organisms this is worthwhile so body cells are kept in ideal and stable conditions, despite fluctuations in the external environment. This allows extreme and hostile environments to be inhabited so there are very few parts of Earth where life is totally absent.

3. Regulation of blood glucose

Blood glucose concentration is kept within limits, by balancing the amount of glucose removed from and added to the blood. Cells in the pancreas monitor blood glucose concentration and secrete insulin or glucagon when the level is too high or too low. The hormones are secreted directly into the bloodstream and convey signals to target cells.

Responses to high blood glucose levels

Insulin is secreted by β (beta) cells in the pancreas. Insulin stimulates the liver and muscle cells to absorb glucose and convert it to glycogen. Granules of glycogen are stored in these cells. Other body cells are stimulated to absorb glucose and use it in cell respiration instead of fat. These processes lower the blood glucose level.

Responses to low blood glucose levels

Glucagon is secreted by α (alpha) cells in the pancreas. It stimulates liver cells to break glycogen down into glucose and release the glucose. This raises the blood glucose level.

These negative feedback control systems usually keep blood glucose concentration between 4 and 8 millimoles per litre of blood. Alpha and beta cells are in the islets of Langerhans, which are small regions of endocrine (hormone-secreting) tissue dotted through the pancreas.

4. Type 1 and type 2 diabetes

Diabetes is consistently elevated blood glucose levels, leading to the presence of glucose in the urine. There are two types.

	Causes (physiological changes)	Risk factors	Prevention or treatment
Type 1	The body's own immune system destroys β cells in the pancreas, so insulin secretion becomes insufficient. This can happen over a short period, with severe and obvious symptoms of the disease starting rather suddenly. The causes are still being researched.	• Youth—type 1 diabetes usually develops in children, teenagers or young adults • Family history of type 1 diabetes or another autoimmune disease	Blood glucose concentration is tested regularly and insulin is injected, often before a meal, to prevent peaks of blood glucose as food is digested and absorbed. Implanted devices can release insulin into the blood when necessary. In the future, stem cells may be used to replace the lost beta cells.
Type 2	Target cells become insensitive to insulin because of a deficiency of insulin receptors or glucose transporters. Onset is gradual and may go unnoticed for many years. It usually happens in older adults but earlier onset now sometimes occurs.	• Diets rich in fat and low in fibre • Obesity due to over-eating and lack of exercise • Genetic factors that affect fat metabolism	Diet can reduce the peaks and troughs of blood glucose. Sugar should be avoided and also starchy foods unless they have a low glycaemic index indicating slow digestion. High-fibre foods help to slow digestion. Strenuous exercise and weight loss are beneficial because they improve insulin uptake and action.

5. Thermoregulation through negative feedback control

Thermoregulation is control of core body temperature, to keep it close to a set-point despite fluctuations in external temperature. Humans have a set-point close to 37°C. Thermoregulation is achieved through negative feedback.

Body temperature is monitored by nerve endings of sensory neurons in the skin that act as peripheral thermoreceptors. They anticipate rates of heat loss from the body and therefore changes in core temperature. Central thermoreceptors are located in the core of the body, including the hypothalamus.

The hypothalamus (see *Section C3.1.13*) is the integrating centre for thermoregulation.

Heat is generated by metabolism in cells. The metabolic rate can be increased or decreased to raise or lower the amount of heat generated. Thyroxin increases the metabolic rate of cells. All cells respond, but the most metabolically active such as liver, muscle and brain are the main targets.

Muscle and adipose tissue have special roles as effectors of temperature change which are described in the next section.

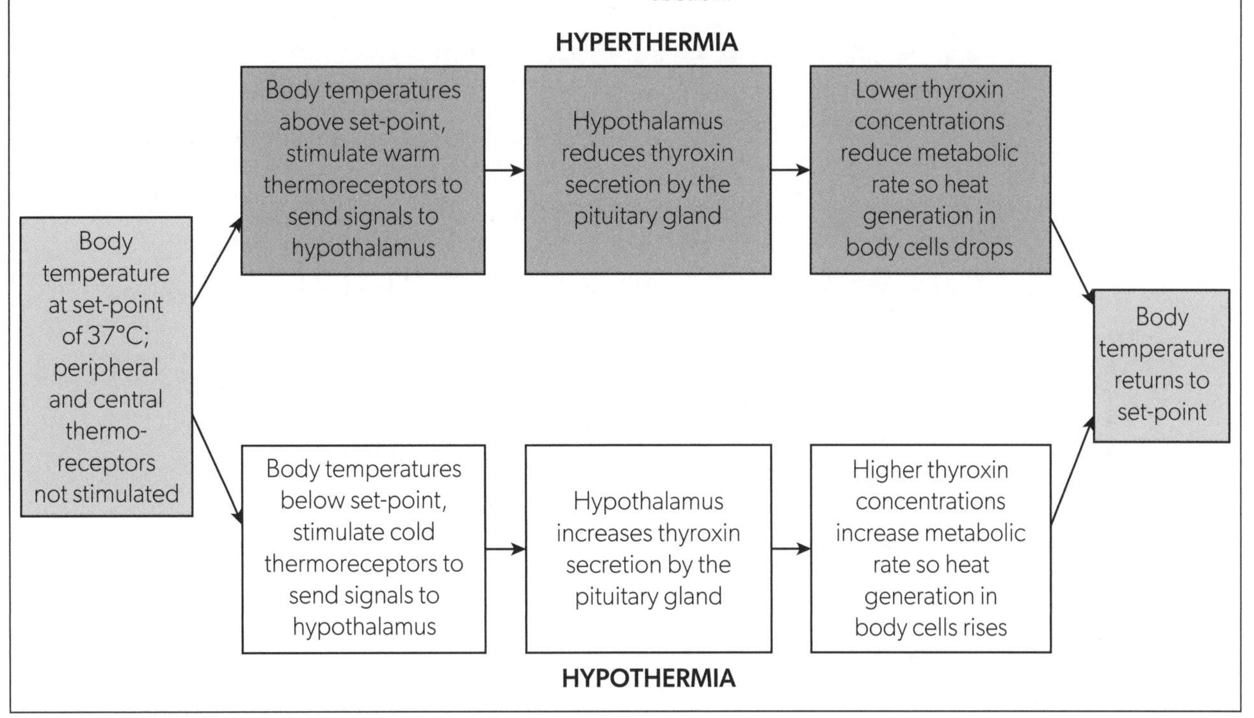

6. Mechanism of thermoregulation

Both birds and mammals regulate their body temperature using both physiological and behavioural methods.

Responses to cold in humans

Vasoconstriction

Arterioles are branches of arteries. Contraction of circular muscle in an arteriole wall lumen narrows the lumen (vasoconstriction), so less blood flows to the tissues served by the arteriole. Vasoconstriction of arterioles supplying the skin reduces blood flow so the skin cools below core body temperature and less heat is lost to the environment.

Shivering

Muscle contraction generates heat. Sometimes many small, involuntary muscle contractions and relaxations are carried out at a rapid rate solely to generate heat. This is shivering.

Uncoupled respiration

Brown adipose tissue is a modified version of the white adipose tissue that is used for fat storage. The brown colour is due to the cells containing less fat and more mitochondria. These mitochondria oxidize fat by normal metabolic pathways but whereas the oxidation reactions are normally coupled to ATP production, in brown adipose tissue all the energy released by the oxidation is transformed into heat and no ATP is produced. This is known as uncoupled respiration. During childhood, the amount of brown adipose tissue decreases, but even in adulthood some is retained to generate heat and help prevent hypothermia.

Hair erection

In mammals with a thick coat, the air between the hairs acts as a thermal insulator. Erector muscles can move the hairs to make the coat thicker and the insulating effect greater. During human evolution, the amount of hair over most of the body has been reduced to a few short hairs. The erector muscles can still make the hairs stand up, but they do not trap air well enough to insulate the body. This ineffectual response to cold is also known as goosebumps.

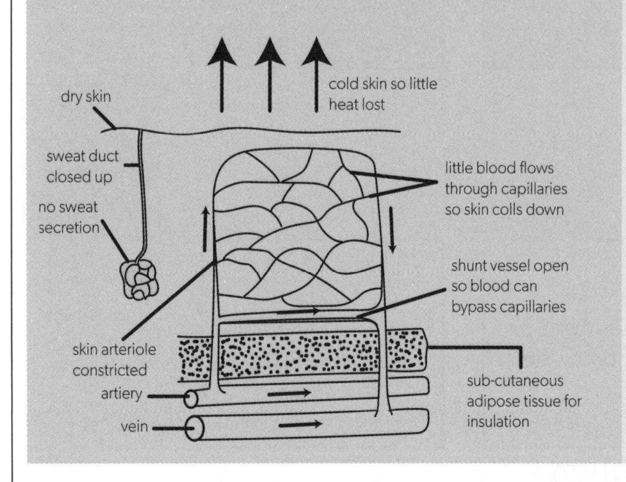

Responses to heat in humans

Vasodilation

Relaxation of circular muscle cells in the walls of arterioles supplying the skin causes widening (vasodilation), increasing blood flow. This warms the skin to core temperature, so more heat is lost to the environment. Important: Capillaries do not move closer to the skin surface—it is the rate of blood flow through them that changes.

Sweating

Sweat is secreted by glands in the skin and then passes through narrow ducts to the skin surface, where water in the sweat evaporates. Solutes in the sweat, especially ions such as sodium, are left on the skin surface and can sometimes be detected by their salty taste. Water has a high latent heat of vaporization as hydrogen bonds have to be broken for water molecules to separate (see *Section A1.1.2*). Evaporation of water from sweat therefore causes significant cooling of the skin. Blood flowing through the skin loses heat and can then cool other parts of the body.

Sweat secretion is controlled by the hypothalamus. If the body is overheated, the hypothalamus stimulates the sweat glands to secrete up to two litres of sweat per hour. Usually, no sweat is secreted if body temperature is below the set-point, but epinephrine can cause sweat secretion in anticipation of a period of intense activity that will cause overheating.

Behavioural responses

Humans respond to overheating by a variety of behavioural responses:

- removing layers of clothing
- moving from an area of sunshine to the shade
- reducing physical activity so less heat is generated by muscle contraction.

The converse of these actions are responses to feeling cold.

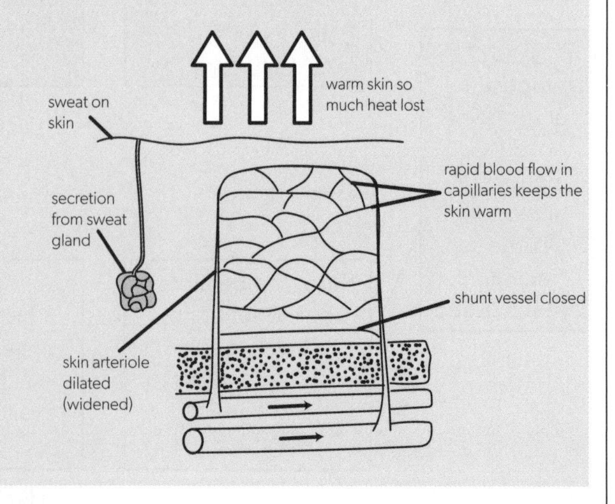

AHL

11. Blood supply to organs changes depending on activities

The aorta divides repeatedly to supply all the organs of the body apart from the lungs. The cardiac output is not enough to supply every organ at a maximal rate. Rings of circular muscle in the walls of the arterioles relax to increase blood flow to an organ (vasodilation) or contract to restrict it (vasoconstriction). In some organs, shunt vessels are used to direct blood directly from arterioles to venules. Three contrasting patterns of blood distribution are shown in the following table, with total cardiac output per minute.

Intense physical activity (up to 25 dm^3)	During wakeful rest (about 5 dm^3)	During sleep (about 4 dm^3)
Greatly increased supply to skeletal muscles and to the brain to supply more O_2 and glucose for muscle contraction. Increased supply to the brain as mental activity is heightened. Reduced supply to the gut and kidneys as digestion and excretion can be temporarily suspended.	Maximal supply to the kidney to remove waste products rapidly. Moderate supplies to the brain for mental activity and to skeletal muscles for maintaining posture while standing or sitting. Variable supplies to the digestive system—less after fasting and more with food in the gut after feeding.	Increased supply to the brain to remove toxins. Reduced supply to skeletal muscles as muscle contractions are limited while lying prone (lying flat on stomach). Reduced supply to kidneys so avoiding waking to urinate. Variable supply to the digestive system depending on whether food was recently eaten.

7. Osmoregulation and excretion

The kidney (shown right) has the twin roles of osmoregulation and excretion. It achieves these roles by filtering out about 20% of the water and solutes from the blood plasma and then selectively reabsorbing the substances in the filtrate that the body requires.

Osmoregulation is keeping the osmotic concentration of body fluids within narrow limits as a part of homeostasis. Osmotic concentration (measured in osmoles per litre) is the overall concentration of the solutes that can affect movement of water by osmosis. The kidney carries out osmoregulation by varying the relative amounts of water and salts that pass out of the body in urine.

Excretion is removal of the toxic waste products of metabolism from the body. An example is removal of nitrogen compounds from the breakdown of excess amino acids such as urea. They would become toxic if they accumulated.

The kidneys also remove substances passively absorbed from food in the gut that are not used by the body—for example, many drugs and pigments from food.

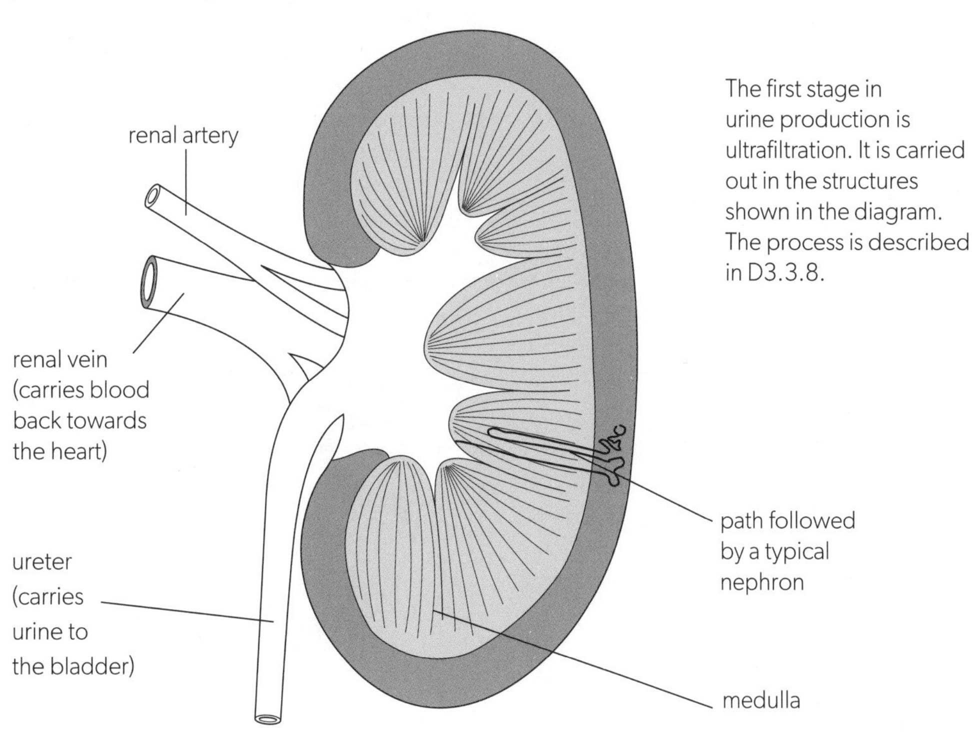

The first stage in urine production is ultrafiltration. It is carried out in the structures shown in the diagram. The process is described in D3.3.8.

AHL

8. Role of the kidney in excretion

Ultrafiltration is the first stage in the production of urine. It happens in many small structures in the cortex of the kidney that each consist of a glomerulus surrounded by a Bowman's capsule. The **glomerulus** is a ball-shaped network of blood capillaries. Blood flows into it through an afferent arteriole and away in an efferent arteriole to other capillaries in the kidney.

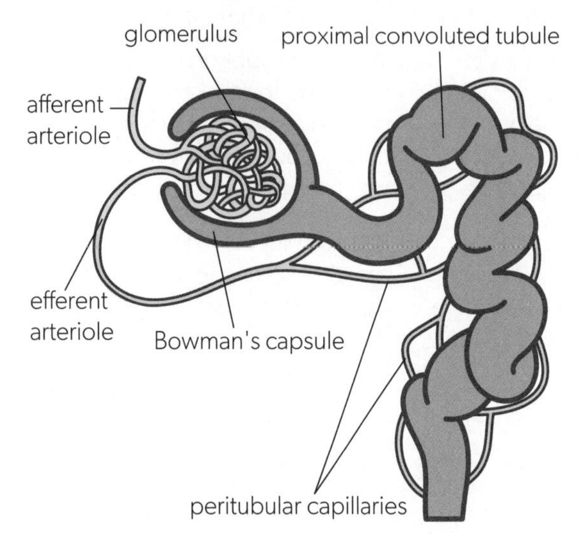

Fluid is filtered out through the walls of all capillaries to produce tissue fluid (see *Section B3.2.1*). A much larger proportion of the blood plasma is filtered out in glomerular capillaries. This is because of high blood pressure and very permeable capillary walls. Two factors cause high blood pressure:

- the efferent arteriole being narrower than the afferent arteriole
- the contorted route that blood must follow to pass through the glomerulus.

High permeability is due to the presence of fenestrations, which are pores between capillary wall cells that are unusually wide (100 nm diameter) and numerous. The fluid forced out of the blood plasma is called **glomerular filtrate**.

Ultrafiltration is carried out by two layers:

1. The basement membrane that covers and supports the wall of the glomerular capillaries. It is a non-cellular gel, made of negatively charged glycoproteins that are cross-linked to form a mesh. Most plasma proteins cannot pass through, due to their size and negative charges.
2. The inner wall of Bowman's capsule consists of cells with branching outgrowths that wrap around the glomerular capillaries. The cells are podocytes and the branches are foot processes. Very narrow gaps between adjacent foot processes help prevent proteins from being filtered out of blood in the glomerulus.

The glomerular filtrate is collected by the cup-shaped Bowman's capsule and then flows on into the nephron. This is a tubular structure with associated peritubular blood capillaries. A large total volume of glomerular

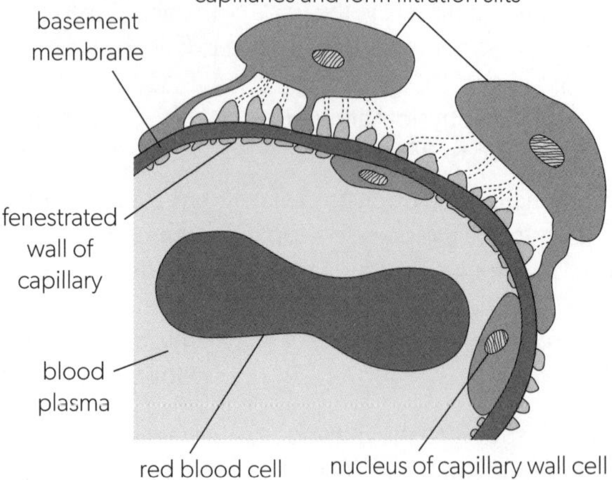

filtrate containing many useful substances is produced per day (about 180 litres). Most of these useful substances are selectively reabsorbed from the filtrate to the blood as the filtrate flows through the nephrons. Water products such as urea and excess water and salts are not reabsorbed, leaving about 1.5 litres of urine to be excreted per day.

Much of the selective reabsorption happens in the proximal convoluted tubule at the start of the nephron. The convolutions increase the length of this part of the nephron, so the filtrate takes longer to flow through and there can be more reabsorption. Adaptations of the wall cells are described in *Section B2.3.7*.

- Sodium ions (Na^+) are reabsorbed by active transport.
- Chloride ions (Cl^-) follow N^+ ions passively due to their negative charge.
- Glucose is reabsorbed by sodium cotransport (see *Section B2.1.16*).
- Amino acids are also reabsorbed by cotransport.
- Water is reabsorbed by osmosis because reabsorption of solutes lowers the osmotic concentration of the filtrate inside the proximal convoluted tubule.

By the end of the proximal tubule, all glucose and amino acids and 80% of the water, sodium and other mineral ions have been reabsorbed and the filtrate flows into the loop of Henlé.

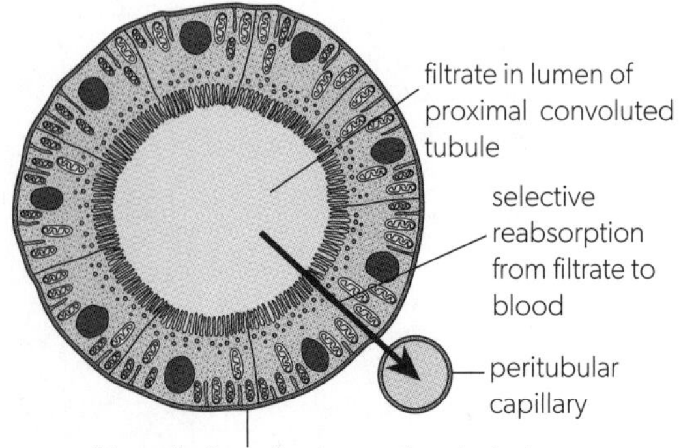

AHL

9. The loop of Henle

The kidney has two main regions—an outer cortex and an inner medulla. The cortex contains the glomeruli and Bowman's capsules and also the proximal and distal convoluted tubules. The medulla contains loops of Henle and collecting ducts. (A whole nephron is shown on page 175). The role of the loop of Henle is to maintain an osmotic concentration gradient from a normal 300 mOsm near the cortex to a much higher concentration near the centre of the kidney. Filtrate enters the loop of Henle from the proximal convoluted tubule and first flows towards the centre of the kidney in the descending limb. It then does a U-turn and flows back to the cortex in the ascending limb.

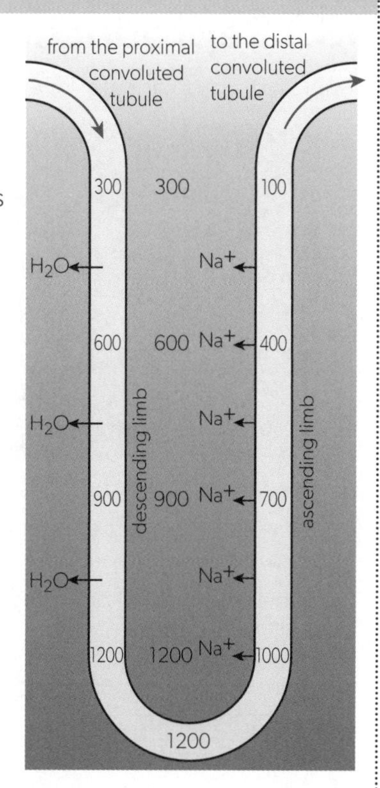

The ascending and descending limbs of the loop of Henle act as a countercurrent mechanism that works due to differences in permeability. The descending limb is permeable to water but impermeable to Na^+ ions and the ascending limb is permeable to Na^+ ions but impermeable to water. As filtrate flows down the descending limb, the osmotic concentrations of the interstitial fluid are increasingly high, so water is continually reabsorbed from the filtrate by osmosis, making it hypertonic to normal body fluids. As the filtrate then flows up the ascending limb, Na^+ ions are transferred out of the filtrate into the interstitial fluid by active transport. The Na^+ pump proteins can increase the Na^+ of the interstitial fluid by 200 mOsm, but because of the countercurrent mechanism, the loop of Henle can increase the concentration in the deepest parts of the medulla by much more than this. The longer the loops of Henle in the kidneys, the greater the concentration that can be achieved. In humans, the concentration can reach 1,200 mOsm (4 × hypertonic to normal body fluids). The diagram shows movements of water and Na^+ ions in the loop of Henle, with solute concentrations inside and outside in mOsm.

10. The collecting ducts

After the loop of Henle, filtrate passes through the distal convoluted tubule, where K^+ and other ions can be exchanged between the filtrate and the blood to adjust blood concentrations. The filtrate then passes though the collecting duct, with increasing osmotic concentrations of interstitial fluid generated by the loop of Henle. The collecting duct carries out osmoregulatory functions of the kidney. Osmoreceptors in the hypothalamus monitor the osmotic concentration of the blood and adjust the amount of the hormone ADH secreted by the pituitary gland (see *Section C3.1.13*). ADH concentrations determine the permeability to water of cells in the wall of the collecting duct. Aquaporins (water pores) can be added to the plasma membranes of wall cells by fusion of vesicles or they can be removed from the membrane by formation of vesicles from plasma membrane containing aquaporins. The table shows responses to high or low blood concentrations. The diagram (right) shows solute concentrations in the collecting duct.

Osmotic concentration of blood plasma	Too low	Too high
Amount of ADH secreted by the pituitary gland	Less	More
Movement of aquaporins in cells in the wall of the collecting duct	Plasma membrane to vesicles	Vesicles to plasma membrane
Permeability of collecting duct wall to water	Decreased	Increased
Amount of water reabsorbed from the filtrate	Less	More
Flow rate of filtrate through the collecting duct	High	Low
Volume of urine produced	Large	Small
Urine concentration compared to blood plasma	Hypotonic	Hypertonic
Effect on the osmotic concentration of blood	Increased	Decreased

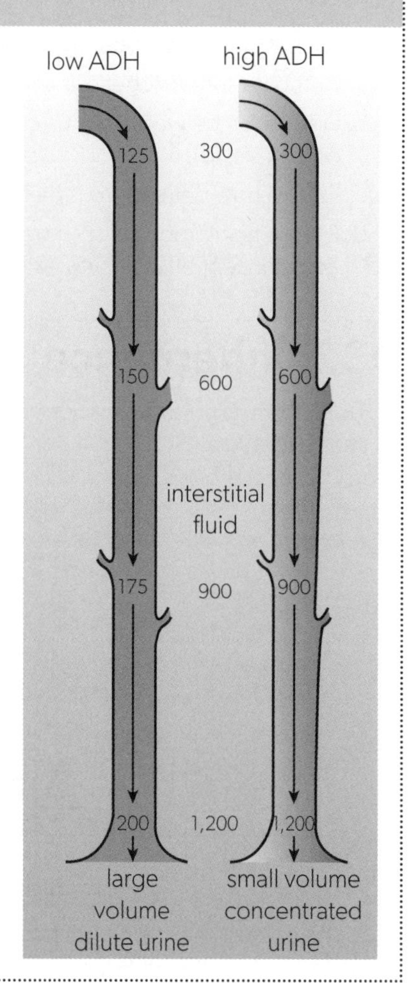

End of topic questions — D3 Questions

D3.1 Reproduction

1. The photograph shows a flower of *Erythronium*.

   a. State the names of structures V–Z. (5)
   b. Draw a diagram of the flower with annotations to show the functions of each structure. (10)
   c. Explain the adaptations of the flower for insect pollination. (5)

2. Explain whether reproduction by these methods is sexual or asexual by:
   a. flowering
   b. IVF
   c. mitosis in Amoeba
   d. taking cuttings of plants
   e. artificial insemination in cattle.

3. (HL only) Humans reproduce sexually.
   a. Compare spermatogenesis and oogenesis. (3)
   b. Distinguish between spermatogenesis and oogenesis. (3)
   c. Explain how polyspermy is prevented. (2)
   d. Explain how progesterone levels are maintained from conception until birth. (2)

D3.3 Homeostasis

1. a. Compare insulin and glucagon. (2)
   b. Distinguish between Type I and Type II diabetes. (4)
   c. Outline the roles of adipose tissue in regulation of body temperature. (4)

2. Identify the costs and benefits of homeostasis. (5)

3. (HL only) The diagram shows two nephrons and a collecting duct in the kidney.

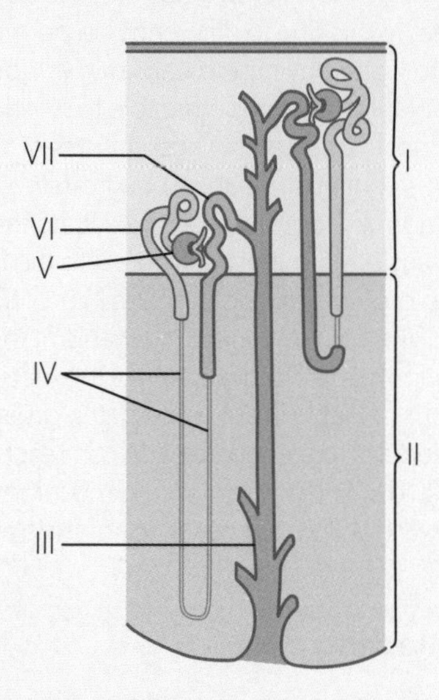

   a. State the names of tissues I and II. (2)
   b. i. List structures III–VII in the sequence that glomerular filtrate flows through them. (2)
      ii. State the name and role of each structure in this sequence in the production of urine. (10)
   c. State the name of the hormone that makes III more permeable to water.

D3.2 Inheritance

1. The bar chart shows the menopause age of women in central Portugal.

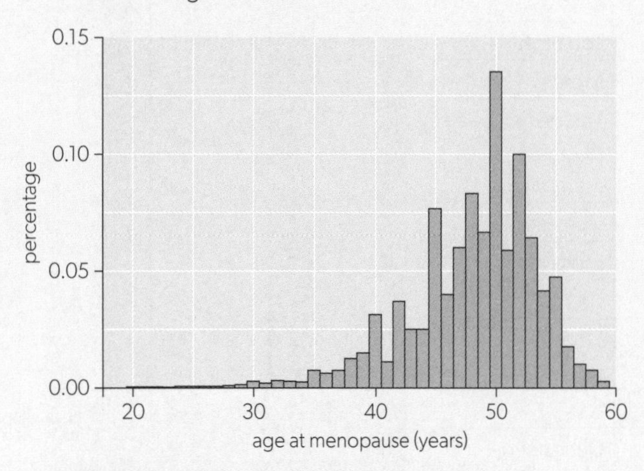

   a. State the mode age for menopause. (1)
   b. Define mean, median and mode. (5)
   c. Discuss the types of factor that could affect age at menopause. (4)

2. Compare and contrast phenylketonuria and haemophilia. (5)

3. (HL only) Two genes affect flower colour in a plant:

   A_B_ has blue flowers   A_bb has red flowers

   aa_ has white flowers   _ represents any allele.

   Homozygous blue-flowered plants are crossed with homozygous white-flowered plants.
   a. Predict the outcome of this cross. (2)
   b. Predict, using a Punnett grid, the ratio of flower colours in an F2 generation produced by self-pollination of the F1 plants. (5)
   c. The two genes code for enzymes used to convert a white substance into a red pigment and the red pigment into a blue pigment.
      Deduce the effect of the enzymes coded for by alleles A, a, B and b. (3)

A4.1 Evolution and speciation

1. Evolution by natural selection

There is strong evidence for the characteristics of populations changing over time. Biologists call this process evolution. It is how the diversity of life developed. Evolution concerns **heritable characteristics** (traits inherited by offspring from parents). This is emphasized in the definition: **Evolution is change in the heritable characteristics of a population**. The mechanism of evolution is natural selection (explained in *Topic D4.1*). Evolution by natural selection is Darwinism.

The characteristics of individual organisms can change during their lifetimes. For example, tennis players develop stronger muscles and bones in the arm used to hold the racket. These are **acquired characteristics**. Before the discovery of natural selection, the most widely accepted theory for evolution was based on inheritance of acquired characteristics. This is Lamarckism. No mechanism has been discovered for inheritance of acquired characteristics. It would require specific changes to be made to genes, whereas random mutations are the only types of change that are known. All claims of the discovery of cases of Lamarckism have been falsified. It seems obvious that a tennis player's children will not develop stronger bones in one arm than the other, unless they use that arm more.

Trees develop an asymmetric form if exposed to wind but seeds from such trees do not grow asymmetrically unless exposed to the same environment as the parent.

NOS

Theories

Scientists use their observations to form generalizations that are then tested. If the generalizations are supported, a theory emerges. A theory that predicts and explains observations is a pragmatic truth (a truth that works). The theory of evolution by natural selection is accepted as a pragmatic truth because it predicts and explains a broad range of observations, such as antibiotic and pesticide resistance and also the existence of homologous and analogous structures.

The nature of science makes it impossible to prove that the theory of evolution by natural selection corresponds to reality (that it is "true"). This contrasts with mathematics, where formal proof for theories can be obtained. The impossibility of formal proof does not, however, make us doubt that evolution happens and that it is driven by natural selection. There is a huge weight of supporting evidence, so it is extremely unlikely to ever be falsified and it is this theory that underpins the whole of biology.

In 1828, Darwin as a young man was struggling to learn enough mathematics to pass a university exam. The extract is from a letter that he wrote to Charles Whiteley, a friend and eminent mathematician. 'I am as idle as idle can be: one of the causes you have hit on, viz irresolution and the other being made fully aware that my noddle is not capacious enough to retain or comprehend Mathematics. Beetle hunting & such things I grieve to say is my proper sphere.'

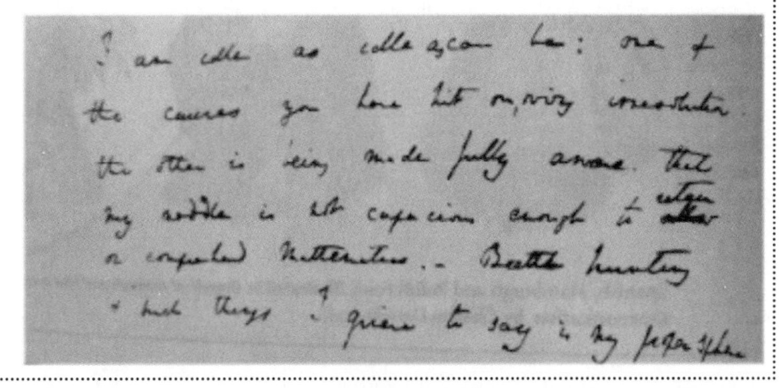

I am idle as idle can be: one of
the causes you have hit on, viz irresolution
the other is being made fully aware that
my noddle is not capacious enough to retain
or comprehend Mathematics.– Beetle hunting
& such things I grieve to say is my proper sphere

2. Evidence for evolution—comparing sequences

Evidence for evolution comes from comparing base sequences of the same gene in different species. Base sequences of RNA or amino acid sequences of proteins can also be compared. A clear relationship is seen: the more closely related two species are in their morphology and other traits, the fewer differences in sequence there are. This trend is convincingly explained by the theory that species develop over time, gradually diverging from a **common ancestor** as a result of differences in natural selection. In addition, observed combinations of differences are only easily accounted for by repeated splitting of ancestral species by evolution.

The gradual accumulation of differences in base or amino acid sequence allows cladograms (tree diagrams) to be constructed that usually match accepted theories for patterns of speciation in a group. (Cladograms are described in more detail for HL in *Topic A3.2*.)

3. Evidence for evolution—selective breeding

The breeds of animal and varieties of crop plant that are grown for human use are clearly related to wild species and in many cases can still interbreed with them. Domesticated animals and crop plants have been developed from wild species by selecting individuals with desirable traits for breeding. This selective breeding is referred to as artificial selection.

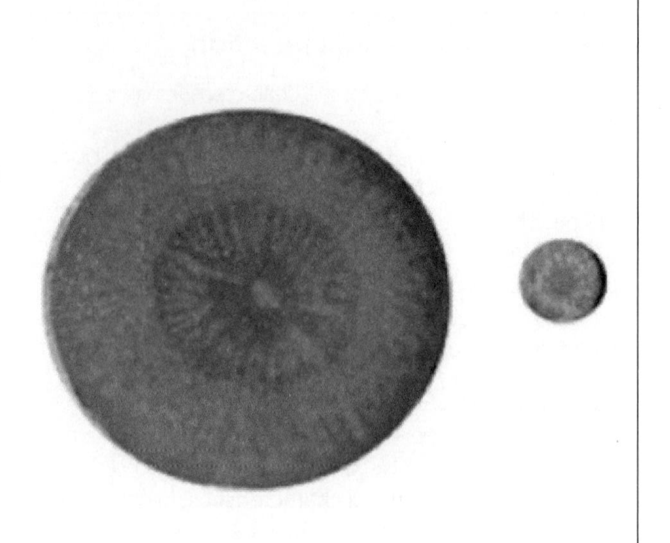

The considerable changes that have occurred in domesticated animals and crop plants over relatively short periods of time show that artificial selection can cause rapid evolution. If artificial selection can achieve this, it seems reasonable to assume that natural selection could have caused major evolutionary changes over the billions of years of life on Earth. The photo shows sections through a wild carrot and a modern variety of cultivated carrot. The wild carrot root is a cream colour and the cultivated carrot is bright orange due to the high carotene (vitamin A) content.

4. Evidence for evolution—homologous structures

Four groups of vertebrates have limbs: amphibians, reptiles, birds and mammals. These vertebrates use their limbs in a wide variety of ways, for example walking, jumping, swimming, climbing and digging. Despite this, the basic bone structure is the same in all of them. The structure is known as the pentadactyl limb.

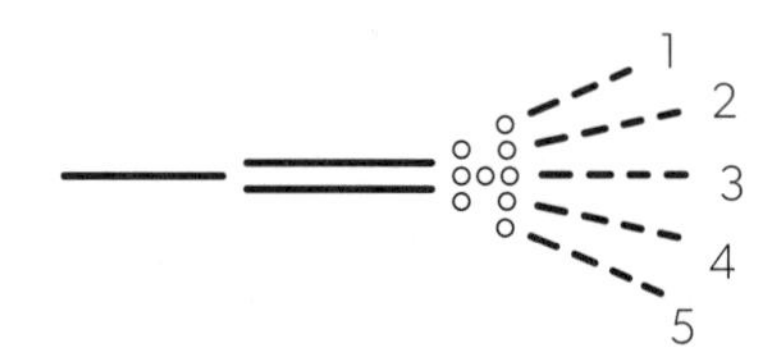

Bone structure	Forelimb bones
Single bone in proximal part	Humerus
Two bones in distal part	Radius and ulna
Group of wrist bones	Carpals
Series of bones in each of five digits	Metacarpals and phalanges

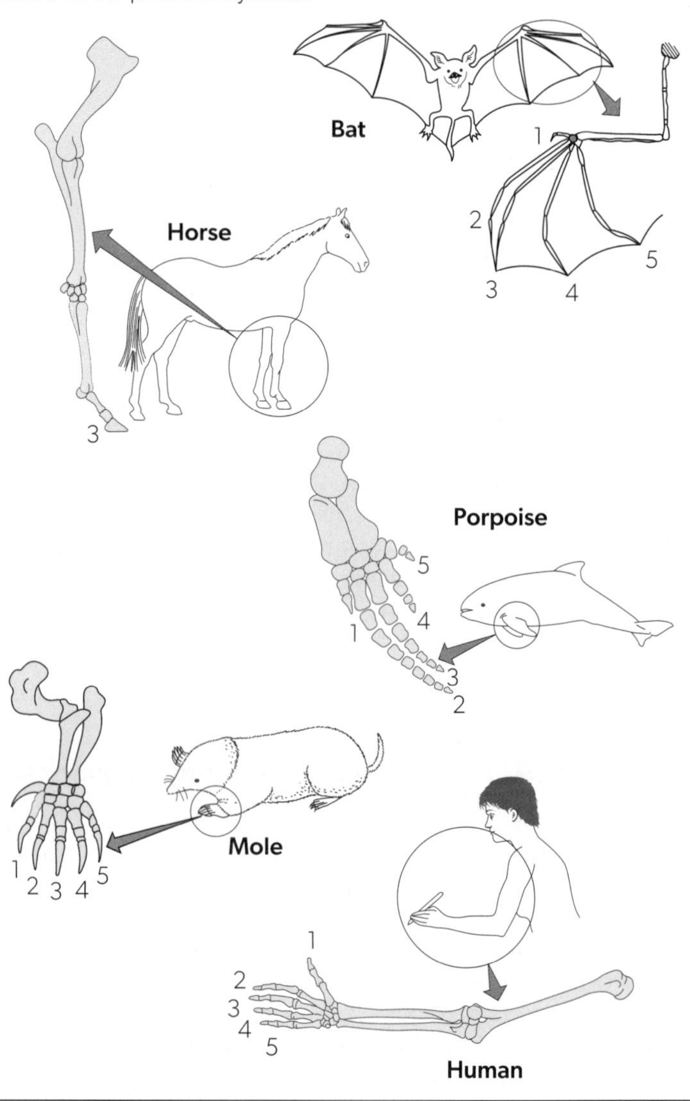

The most plausible explanation is that all these vertebrates share an ancestor that had pentadactyl limbs. Many different groups have evolved from the common ancestor, but because they adopted different types of locomotion, the limbs developed in widely different ways, to suit the type of locomotion. This type of evolution is called **adaptive radiation**.

Parts of the body like the pentadactyl limb that have evolved from the same part of a common ancestor are **homologous structures**. They have structural similarities despite the differences in their function, which would be difficult to explain in any way apart from evolution.

5. Convergent evolution

There are similarities between the tails of fishes and the tail fins of whales. However, when we study these structures, we find that they are very different. The wings of birds and insects are also similar in some respects but close examination reveals that the similarities are superficial. Such features are known as **analogous structures**.

The evolutionary explanation of analogous structures is that they had different origins but became similar because they perform the same or a similar function. This is called **convergent evolution**. It can be difficult to determine whether similar structures in different organisms are homologous or analogous.

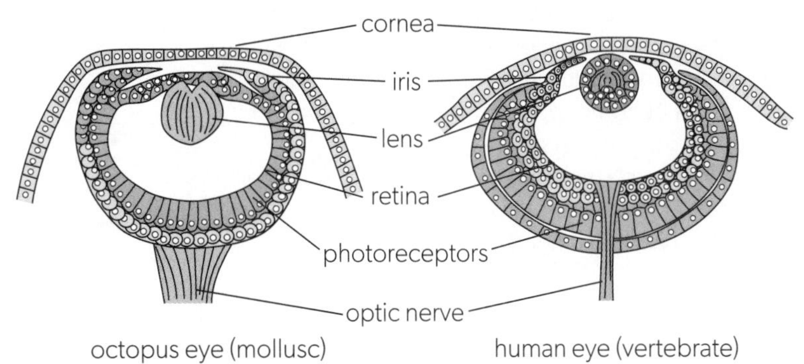

▲ The diagrams show an early stage of eye development in octopus and human embryos. There are striking similarities, but also significant structural differences. From cladograms constructed using base sequence data, we can conclude that the last common ancestor of molluscs and vertebrates existed more than 500 million years ago and was eyeless, indicating that human and octopus eyes are analogous structures. The similarities are due to convergent evolution with some genes from the common ancestor used in the evolution of an eye in both groups.

6. Speciation

If two populations of a species become separated so they cannot interbreed and natural selection then acts differently on the two populations, then they will evolve in different ways. The characteristics of the two populations will gradually diverge and after a time, they will be noticeably different. If the two populations subsequently have the opportunity of interbreeding but fail to do so, it is clear that they have evolved into separate species. The process of one species separating into two by evolution is **speciation**.

- Speciation adds to the total number of species on Earth and therefore its biodiversity.
- Gradual evolutionary change in a single species does not add to the number of species so is not speciation.
- Extinction is the converse of speciation in that it reduces the number of species on Earth.

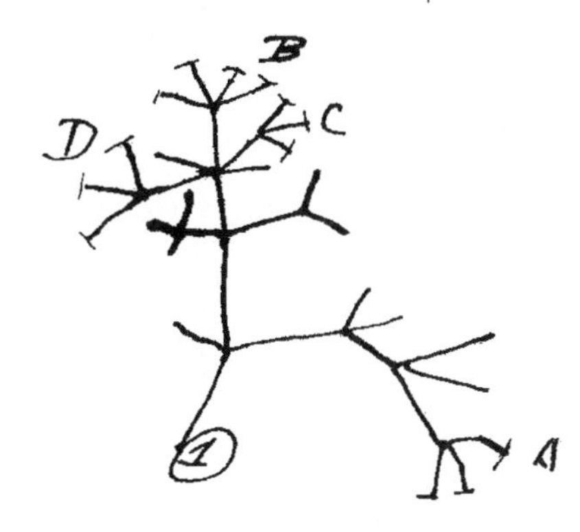

◄ Darwin's famous 1837 evolutionary tree diagram, with species splitting and diverging. Darwin calls the tree's root (numbered 1) "an ancient" and comments on the immense "gap of relation" between A and B

7. Reproductive isolation and differential selection

Two processes are required for speciation to occur:

1. Reproductive isolation

Before two populations can split into separate species, they must stop interbreeding with each other. Interbreeding mixes genes and therefore blends traits, whereas speciation depends on separation and divergence. Biologists refer to the genes of a population as a gene pool. Speciation requires barriers preventing gene flow between the gene pools of the two populations. This can be achieved by any method of reproductive isolation.

Geographical separation is the most obvious cause of reproductive isolation. The separation can be due to mountain ranges, wide rivers or stretches of ocean between islands. For example, both lava lizards and finches on the Galápagos archipelago have migrated from island to island, becoming reproductively isolated and splitting into different species.

▲ An adult female bonobo. In comparison with chimps, bonobos are more slender, with longer limbs, narrower chests, rounder heads and less protruding faces. There are many behavioural differences, with bonobos living in more egalitarian and peaceful social groups.

2. Differential selection

Natural selection can cause the traits of a population to change, but if it operates in the same way in two populations, their traits will tend to remain the same and they will not become separate species. Differences in selection cause the traits of the populations to gradually become more and more different. Any or all of these three factors might be different from the other parts of the species' range:

- climate—temperatures, rainfall and other aspects
- predation—there might be different predators or even no predators in some areas
- competition—there might be more or less competition for resources.

When the divergence between two populations is judged by taxonomists to be significant, the populations are classified as separate species. (Difficulties in discerning this are discussed in *Section A3.1.5*.)

Bonobos and chimpanzees—an example of speciation

Bonobos (*Pan paniscus*) and chimpanzees (*Pan troglodytes*) are closely related. Their ranges do not overlap as they are geographically separated by the Congo River which is both wide and deep. Neither species is thought to be able to swim.

It is probable that at one point in history, the water level fell drastically for a time allowing chimpanzees to cross the river and spread to rainforests to the south. When the water level of the Congo rose again, the migrants became geographically isolated from the other populations of their species. This founder population, being subject to different selection pressures, including more abundant supplies of food, diverged from chimpanzees to become bonobos. (The timing of this divergence is discussed for HL in *Section A3.2.5*.)

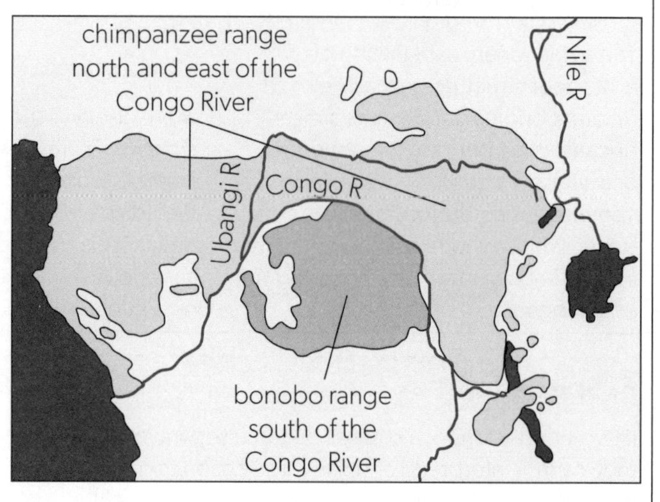

AHL

8. Comparing sympatric and allopatric speciation

Speciation is the divergence of populations into separate species. Speciation is **allopatric** if the populations live in different areas. Speciation is **sympatric** if the populations live in the same area.

With both allopatric and sympatric speciation, the populations must be reproductively isolated and natural selection must be different so there is divergence in the traits of the populations.

With allopatric speciation, the reproductive isolation is **geographical** (see *Section A4.1.7* for examples). With sympatric speciation, reproductive isolation can be either **temporal** or **behavioural**.

Examples of reproductive isolation due to temporal and behavioural separation are given here.

Temporal—populations of a species breed at different times. For example, the cicada *Magicicada septendecim* only breeds every 17th year. A switch to breeding every 13th year took place in some individuals within the range of this species, causing reproductive isolation and generating a new species, named *Magicicada neotredecim*.

▲ *M. septendecim*

Behavioural—populations of a species have differences in behaviour that prevent interbreeding. For example, the fruit fly *Rhagoletis pomonella* is attracted by volatile compounds emitted from hawthorn fruits, where it lays its eggs and the larvae that hatch from the eggs feed.

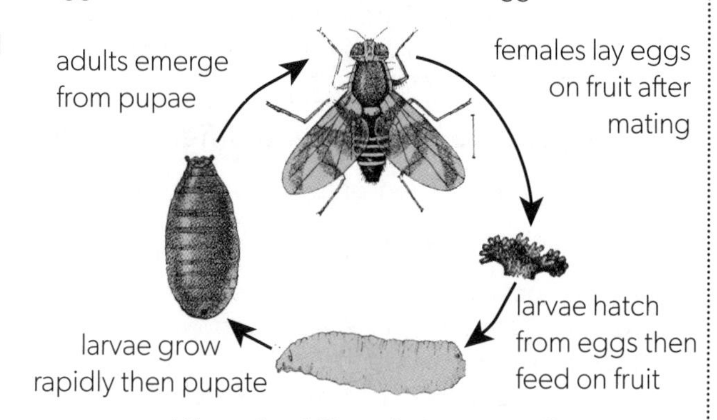

Life cycle of *Rhagoletis pomonella*

Some fruit flies of this species are attracted instead to volatile compounds from apple and dogwood fruits. These fruits are therefore used as the larval food source. Hybrids between the flies attracted to hawthorn, apple and dogwood fruits fail to respond to any of the volatile compounds. Differences in the times when the three types of fruit ripen will also promote reproductive isolation and, over time, sympatric speciation.

AHL

9. Adaptive radiation leads to biodiversity

Characteristics that make an individual suited to its environment or way of life are **adaptations**. The process of adaptation happens as structures evolve over time to fit their functions more and more closely.

If some members of a species become a separate, reproductively isolated population, a period of adaptation is likely to follow. This could be in response to differences in the environment encountered by the new population, or to a change of ecological niche. Vacant ecological niches are sometimes available, to which a population can become adapted. This can reduce or eliminate competition between the new population and original populations of the species. (The concept of ecological niches is explained in *Topic B4.2*.) The new population will eventually be different enough to be considered a separate species.

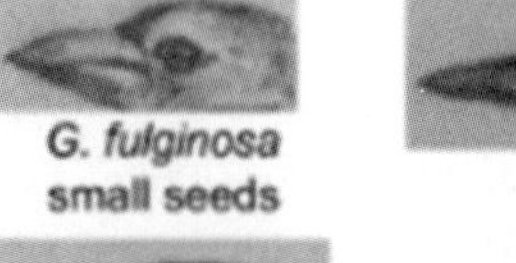

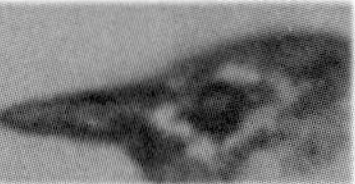

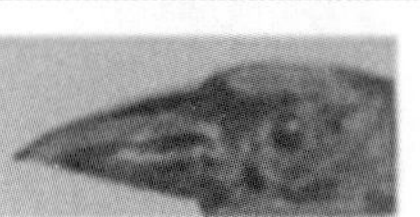

Speciation and adaptation to new niches has happened repeatedly in some groups. This is **adaptive radiation**. It is defined as a pattern of diversification in which species that have evolved from a common ancestor occupy a range of ecological roles. Adaptive radiation is a source of considerable biodiversity.

Galápagos finches are the best-known example of adaptive radiation. Over the past 2.3 million years, 14 species of finch have evolved from a common ancestor on the islands of the Galápagos archipelago. These finches have become adapted to different food sources: leaves, fruits, pollen, nectar, small soft seeds, large hard seeds, insects on leaves and insects under bark. The beaks of the finches show particularly clear adaptations.

Up to 10 species of Galápagos finch have been found living together in one locality. It is unlikely that this would be possible without adaptive radiation as there would be too much competition.

10. Barriers to hybridization

Interspecific hybrids are produced by cross-breeding members of different species. The hybrids combine traits of the species that were crossed. Hybridization is often done deliberately by plant or animal breeders. The mule was probably the first hybrid, produced by cross-breeding a horse with a donkey (*Equus caballus* × *Equus asinus*). Horses have 64 chromosomes and donkeys have 62 so a mule has 63. This causes problems in meiosis. For that reason and other genetic incompatibilities, mules are nearly always sterile.

▲ Mules are used for transport and plowing

Interspecific hybridization sometimes happens naturally if the ranges of closely related species overlap in an ecosystem. Like artificial hybrids, natural interspecific hybrids are often totally or partially sterile so they cause little or no permanent mixing of alleles between the parent species. In evolutionary terms, the resources that a parent expends on producing a sterile hybrid are wasted. Many species have evolved barriers to prevent the development of hybrid offspring. The barriers can be molecular. For example, when a host is infected with more than one species of Plasmodium (the malarial parasite), proteins in the membrane of female gametes prevent fertilization by sperm of a different species.

Courtship behaviour is used by a bird to check whether a potential partner is a member of its own species. There are often several stages in courtship, with rejection at any stage if the characteristic behaviour pattern of the species is not displayed. To prevent interspecific hybridization, courtship behaviour needs to be distinctive. This explains the immense diversity among birds of paradise in Papua New Guinea, for example.

▲ Red-crowned cranes (*Grus japonensis*) have an elaborate courtship dance

AHL

11. Hybridization and polyploidy

A polyploid organism has more than two sets of homologous chromosomes. Polyploidy is whole-genome duplication. It happens when the chromosomes in a cell are duplicated, but the cell does not then divide. If whole-genome duplication happens in diploid cells, the result is autotetraploid (non-hybrid tetraploid) cells. The diagram below shows that an autotetraploid individual cannot produce fertile offspring with diploid individuals of their species.

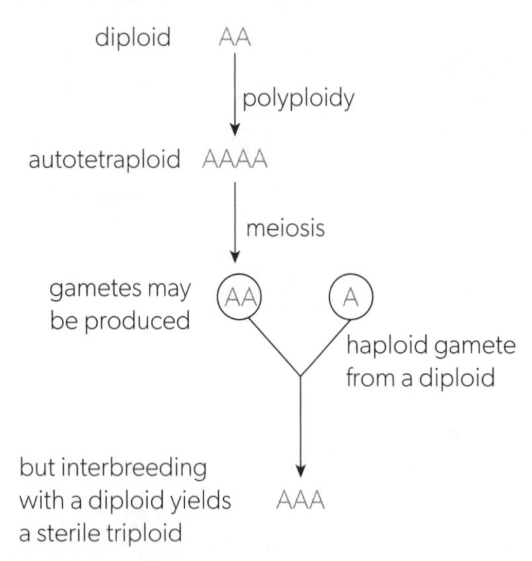

▲ Brown trout *(Salmo trutta)* are native to rivers in Europe. To increase stocks, young trout are raised in fish-farms and released into rivers. By interbreeding, the released trout can reduce the genetic diversity and capacity for evolution of the native populations. In the UK it is now illegal to release diploid trout, but triploid fish can still be released because they are sterile and do not therefore interbreed with native trout populations.

Despite barriers to hybridization in many species, interspecific hybrids are sometimes produced. They have two sets of chromosomes, with one set from each of the two different parent species. Unless these two species are very closely related, chromosomes will not form homologous pairs during meiosis, so the hybrids are sterile.

If whole-genome duplication happens in a cell in a sterile interspecific hybrid, the resulting cell will have four sets of chromosomes. It is an allotetraploid because the four sets of chromosomes are from two different species.

More of these allotetraploid cells can be produced by mitosis. The diagram (top right) shows that these allotetraploid cells will be able to divide by meiosis because there are two homologous chromosomes of each type, which can reliably form pairs. By becoming allopolyploid, the interspecific hybrid overcomes its fertility problems.

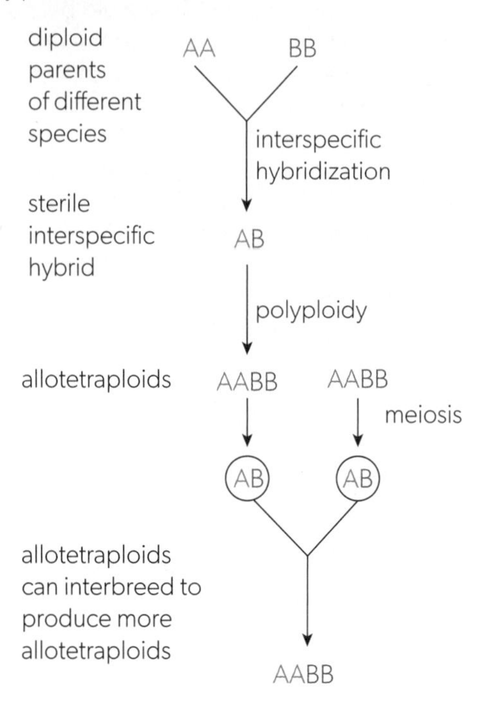

Allotetraploids can interbreed with other allotetraploids, but not with either of the diploid parent species. They are therefore a new species, with a mixture of traits from both parent species. Many species have been produced by this abrupt process of hybridization followed by polyploidy, especially in the plant kingdom. The genus *Persicaria* is an example. There are over 100 species in this genus, with species occurring in most parts of the world. There is evidence for at least 15 species in the genus having originated by allopolyploidy. One of these is *P. maculosa* ($2n = 44$ chromosomes), which is native to Europe and Asia. This species arose by hybridization between *P. foliosa* ($2n = 22$) and *P. lapathifolia* ($2n = 22$), followed by a doubling of the chromosome number.

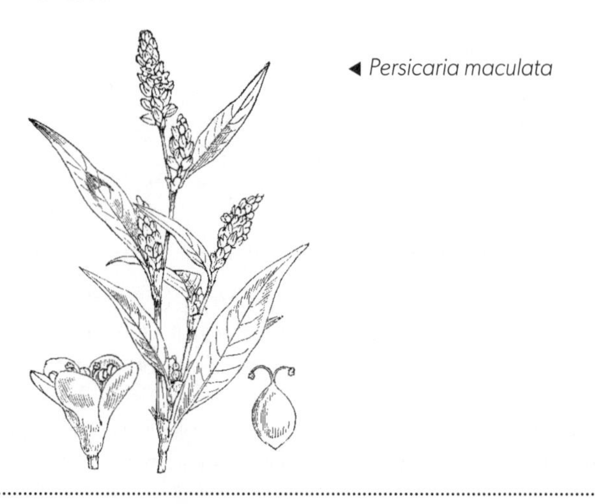

◀ *Persicaria maculata*

A4.2 Conservation of biodiversity

1. Types of biodiversity

The word biodiversity (biological diversity) is the variety of life in all its forms, levels and combinations.

- **Ecosystem diversity**—variety in the combinations of species living together in communities. This diversity is partly due to the very varied environments on Earth and the geographical ranges of organisms.
- **Species diversity**—the many different species on the evolutionary tree of life. These species have varied body plans, internal structure, life cycles and modes of nutrition.
- **Genetic diversity** within species—variety in the gene pool of each species. There is variation between geographically separated populations and within populations.

3. Anthropogenic causes of the sixth mass extinction

A sixth mass extinction of species is underway. The causes are all anthropogenic (due to human activities). Three case studies of extinction are described here. Local case studies should also be studied:

1. **Caribbean monk seal—a marine mammal**

   Neomonachus tropicalis was native to the warm temperate and tropical waters of the Caribbean Sea and western Atlantic, but has not been sighted for over 70 years. It was hunted for its oil through the 18th and 19th centuries. The Caribbean monk seal was an easy target because of its need to breed on beaches, where it was slow-moving and lacking in fear of humans. A second factor was overfishing of the coral reefs where the seals fed, leading to starvation.

2. **Giant moa—part of terrestrial megafauna**

   Dinornis novaezealandiae, had a height of up to 3.6 m and mass of 230 kg. It was native to the north island of New Zealand, which remained uninhabited by humans until the 13th century, when Polynesian settlers became the Māori iwi. It then took less than 200 years for the giant moa to be hunted to extinction, for meat.

   Rothschild, R.L.W. (1907) Extinct birds. London: Hutchinson.

3. **Silphium—an early plant extinction**

   This plant grew in Libya and probably became extinct within a few hundred years of the arrival of ancient Greeks, who harvested it for use as a birth control agent. Overgrazing and desertification may have also contributed.

Overharvesting was the main cause of extinction in these three case studies—the species was exploited at a faster rate than it could replace lost individuals by reproduction. There are other common causes of extinction:

Habitat destruction

Natural habitats (such as forests or grasslands) have been destroyed, leading to species extinctions. Agriculture is the main cause, with over 13 billion hectares of land now cultivated or used for rearing livestock. Natural habitats have also been destroyed to build towns and cities.

Invasive species

When alien species are introduced to ecosystems, they can drive native species to extinction by predation, spreading of pests and diseases, or competition for resources. Endemic species become extinct if they hybridize with alien species.

Pollution

Chemical industries produce a vast range of substances that are used and then discarded in the environment. Burning of fossil fuels, agriculture, mining, oil extraction and pharmaceuticals are all major sources of pollutants.

Global climate change

Human activities are currently causing very rapid changes in temperature, rainfall and other climatic variables. Species that fail to adapt quickly enough or cannot migrate face extinction.

4. Ecosystem loss due to anthropogenic causes

If environmental conditions change, the replacement of one ecosystem by another is natural. This has happened repeatedly over the past 2.6 million years due to alternation between glacials and interglacials (warmer and colder periods). However, there has been an unprecedentedly rapid loss of ecosystems during the past few centuries and the causes are anthropogenic. Two case studies of ecosystem loss are described here but local examples will also be worthy of study.

1. Mixed dipterocarp forest of southeast Asia

Dipterocarps are a family of about 700 species of tropical hardwood tree. They used to dominate large areas of rainforest in southeast Asia. Mixed dipterocarp forest (MDF) has an extremely high diversity of dipterocarp and other tree species. On the island of Brunei, for example, there are 20 native dipterocarp species. Small areas of MDF often contain 10 or more of these. The highest diversity of tree species tends to occur on nutrient-poor sandy soils.

MDF typically has particularly high quantities of merchantable timber per hectare so it has been widely targeted for **logging**, both legal and illegal. Since the 1970s, most areas of MDF have been lost; undisturbed areas are now largely found in upland sites where access is more difficult. Areas of MDF that have suffered the greatest losses are on lowland sites, especially where nutrient-rich soils overlie deep peat. Large areas have been lost due to **land conversion** to palm oil plantations. This is particularly unfortunate as the peat in these areas, formed over the past 4,000–5,000 years, can be up to 15 m deep. This peat can store 250 tonnes of carbon per hectare. Drainage during conversion to palm oil plantations causes the peat to decompose, releasing CO_2 into the atmosphere. This contributes to another threat: rising sea levels caused by **global warming** will flood deep-peat lowland areas with seawater, destroying what little MDF remains there.

2. Loss of the Aral Sea—an ecological disaster

The Aral Sea, between Kazakhstan and Uzbekistan, was the fourth largest lake in the world. It was fed by rivers but had no outflows, with water only removed by evaporation. As a result, the salinity was higher than in a freshwater lake.

In the 1960s, a major **water management** scheme diverted two major rivers that fed the Aral Sea in order to irrigate an area of desert. This led to falling water levels and much of the former lake is now desert.

Apart from the reduction in the area and depth of the lake, the increase in the water salinity was a major contributor to ecosystem collapse. In some of the remaining parts of the lake, salinity has risen from 1% to more than 22%, compared with about 3.5% for normal seawater. A total of 24 species of fish were endemic to the Aral Sea, all of which are now extinct. Most invertebrate species have also disappeared. The NASA satellite images show the extent of the Aral Sea in 1989 (left) and 2014 right.

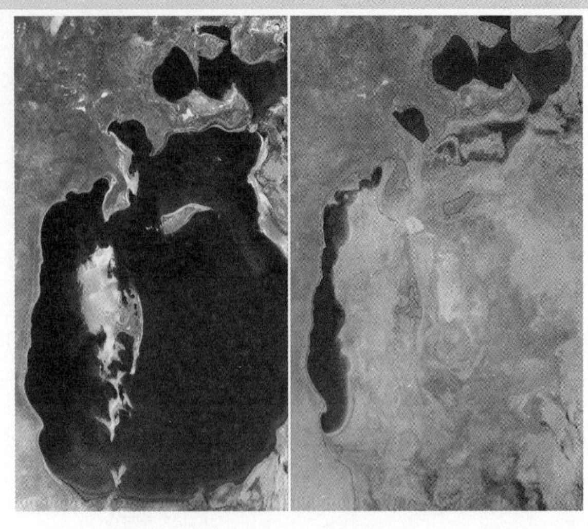

Eight categories of direct or indirect cause of ecosystem loss are outlined here:

1. **Agriculture**—the main cause of ecosystem loss. Most temperate forests and grasslands (such as the prairies of North America) were cleared before the 1970s. Since then, much tropical forest has been lost.
2. **Urbanization**—building of homes, offices and factories, together with associated infrastructure of roads and railways. This has been inevitable given the rapid and continued rise in the human population.
3. **Overexploitation of natural resources**—such as gathering of fuel wood, hunting of animals for bushmeat and fishing. Loss of a single keystone species can threaten whole ecosystems. Overfishing on the Canadian Grand Banks is explored in *Section D4.2.6*.
4. **Mining and smelting**—opencast mines destroy areas of natural ecosystem entirely. Smelting and disposal of waste from mining can cause pollution and more widespread damage. Much tropical rainforest has been lost due to mining.
5. **Water management**—reservoirs created by building dams can flood natural ecosystems. Extraction of water for irrigation and for industrial or domestic use can greatly reduce river flows. For example, the Colorado River no longer reaches the sea.
6. **Drying of wetlands**—swamps and other wetlands are drained for conversion to agriculture. This is explored for HL in *Section D4.2.15*. Wetlands are also destroyed by diverting the water that flowed into them for human use.
7. **Leaching**—washing of fertilizers into rivers and lakes causes eutrophication and algal blooms. Oligotrophic ecosystems, in which organisms are adapted to low nutrient concentrations, have been lost. This is explored in *Section D4.2.8*.
8. **Climate change**—anthropogenic climate change is the most common cause of loss. Relationships between ecosystem types and climate are further explored in Theme B and the likely future effects of climate change are considered in Theme D.

2. Comparing current number of species on Earth with past numbers

Estimates of the number of species currently inhabiting the Earth vary widely. Most are between 2 and 10 million. It is even more difficult to estimate how many species lived on Earth in the past, but relative levels of biodiversity can be deduced from fossil evidence. This shows much variation. The graph shows an example of such data.

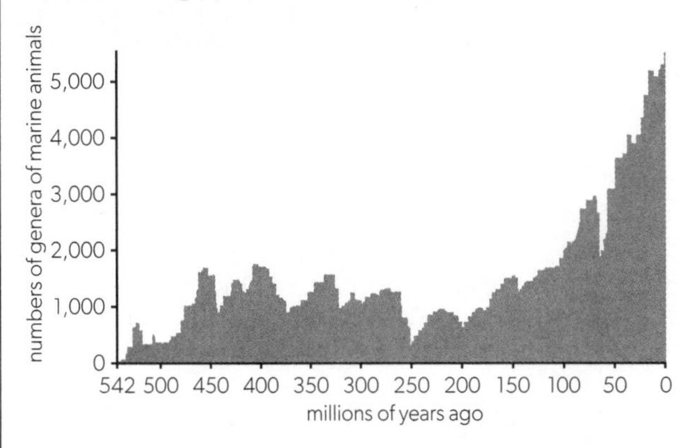

The effects of speciation and extinction on biodiversity are explained in *Section A4.1.6*. There have been five mass extinctions when many species disappeared. The most recent was 66 million years ago at the end of the Cretaceous period, when a huge asteroid collided with the Earth. The consequent environmental disruption caused many species to die out, including all non-avian dinosaurs. The previous four mass extinctions were due to volcanic activity and major changes to the atmosphere and global climate. Biodiversity tends to rise gradually between mass extinction events, with new forms of life evolving. For example, the extinction of the non-avian dinosaurs and other groups at the end of the Cretaceous period was followed by the evolution of many new species of birds and mammals.

There have been no mass extinction events for 66 million years. As a result, biodiversity is probably higher now than it has ever been.

5. The biodiversity crisis

Journalists use the term "biodiversity crisis" to describe the unprecedented losses of ecosystems and species occurring today. As scientists, we must always look for evidence before making a claim.

In this case we need evidence of losses before declaring that there is indeed a biodiversity crisis. One of many sources of evidence is IPBES (Intergovernmental Science-Policy Platform on Biodiversity and Ecosystem Services).

Evidence can be gathered directly by carrying out reliable surveys. If repeated, surveys can provide evidence of change in these variables in a species:

- numbers in populations of the species
- genetic diversity
- range of the species.

Surveys can also give evidence of change in an ecosystem for these variables:

- species diversity
- richness and evenness of biodiversity
- area occupied
- extent of ecosystem degradation.

Surveys can also provide evidence for a taxonomic group:

- number of threatened species within the group.

Although expert scientists play a key role in monitoring biodiversity and identifying the most serious threats, there are opportunities for all citizens to contribute. This is an example of what is often called "citizen science". Some of the most useful data has been collected by individuals who have monitored a population or an ecosystem regularly over many years.

NOS

Patterns and trends

Scientists analyse their observations, looking for patterns or trends. Classification is an example of pattern recognition but the same observations can be classified in different ways. For example, "splitters" recognize more species than "lumpers" in any taxonomic group. This makes it impossible to be sure how many species of living organism there are on Earth today. In 1857, after analysing the numbers of species and varieties per genus in different taxonomic groups, Charles Darwin referred to "hair-splitters & lumpers". His conclusion was that "varieties are only small species—or species only strongly marked varieties". Do you agree?

NOS

Evidence

It is now easy to generate fake text using AI, so it is more important than ever to have evidence for claims. In science it is essential.

- The evidence must be verifiable, so it must usually come from a trusted published source and have been peer-reviewed (checked by other scientists).
- It must be clear how the evidence was obtained (methodology). Data recorded by citizens rather than scientists is often very valuable, but the methodology must be rigorous.

6. The biodiversity crisis—causes

Species extinction is a natural process but current rates are 100–1,000 times higher than normal and are rising. A biodiversity crisis has been developing since about 1970. The causes (also discussed in *Sections A4.2.3* and *A4.2.4*) are:

- **hunting** and other forms of **over-exploitation**
- **urbanization**, with towns and cities growing ever larger
- **deforestation** and clearance of land for **agriculture**, leading to loss of natural habitats
- **pollution** of land and sea throughout the world
- **alien invasive species** spread by global transport / movement or deliberate introductions. Such species may be pests, cause disease or compete with native species.

▲ Dipterocarp forest—rich in biodiversity but much has been lost.

Humans have been causing species extinctions for thousands of years, and none of these causes are new, but their intensity has increased significantly over the last 100 years. This is a consequence of the enormous rise in the number of people on Earth. Between 1920 and 2020 the human population more than quadrupled, from less than two billion to almost eight billion. Overpopulation is the overarching issue that makes human activities a threat to most other species and risks widespread ecosystem collapse.

7. Conservation of biodiversity

No single approach to tackling the biodiversity crisis will be enough. Measures must be selected according to the target species or ecosystems and the causes of biodiversity loss.

In situ conservation leaves species in their natural habitats. Ideally, large areas of the Earth's surface remain as pristine wilderness, but partially degraded areas can still become valuable nature reserves or national parks. With in situ conservation, species live in the abiotic environment to which they are adapted, interacting with other wild species, so they remain adapted to their ecological niches and the integrity of whole ecosystems is conserved.

There is often a need for **management of nature reserves**. This could involve the removal of alien species, reintroduction of locally extinct species, control of population sizes, control of access by humans and prevention of poaching.

Pangolins are being poached in huge numbers from forests in Africa and Asia

Some ecosystems are so damaged that major intervention is needed. The process of **rewilding** is the return of degraded ecosystems to as natural a state as possible. Recovery can be remarkably rapid and balance is then maintained by natural ecological processes instead of human intervention.

Ex situ conservation is preservation of species outside their natural habitats. The initial step is removal of individuals from the wild. Traditionally, plant species are then grown and propagated in **botanic gardens** and animals are kept and bred in **zoos** with the ultimate aim of releasing captive-bred individuals in their native habitats. Ecosanctuaries are now being set up on islands or in large fenced areas with semi-natural conditions but predator control.

A more radical approach to ex situ conservation is the long-term **storage of germ plasm** (living material that could be used for propagation in the future). Seeds of plants are stored dry in seed banks at low temperatures (around −20°C), so they can maintain viability for long periods. Animal germ plasm (samples of tissue, eggs or sperm) is stored at temperatures of between −20 and −200°C, in tissue banks.

8. The EDGE of Existence programme

The EDGE of Existence project uses two criteria to identify animal species that are most deserving of conservation.

- **E**volutionarily **D**istinct: does the species have few or no close relatives, so it is a member of a very small clade?
- **G**lobally **E**ndangered: Is the species likely to become extinct because all remaining populations are threatened?

Species that fit both criteria (EDGE species) are listed and targeted for intense conservation efforts. Some species are the last members of a clade that has existed for tens or hundreds of millions of years and it would be tragic for them to become extinct as a result of human activities.

Global impacts of science

NOS

Prioritization of one species for conservation efforts and not another has consequences, with complex ethical, environmental, political, social, cultural and economic implications. Scientists therefore have an obligation to ensure that such issues are debated. The preparation of lists of EDGE species is part of the debate.

A4.1 Evolution and speciation

1. The map shows the distribution of *Microlophus* species (lava lizards) on the Galápagos islands.

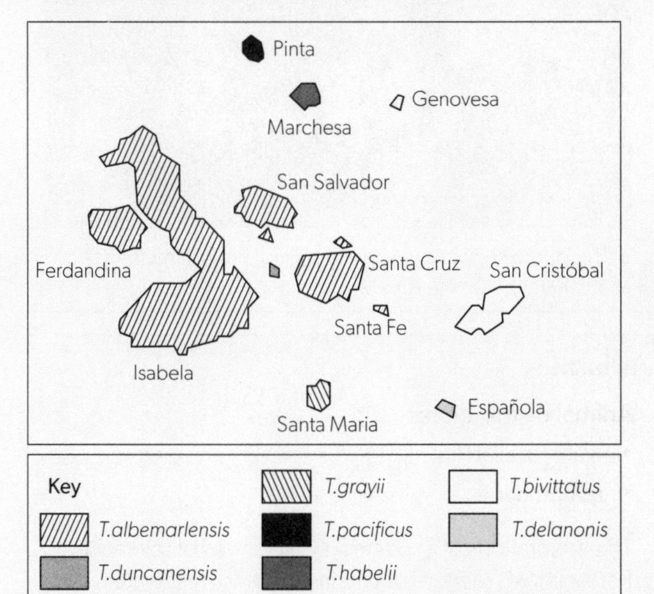

   a. Analyse the distribution of *Microlophus* species on the islands of the Galápagos archipelago. (3)

   b. These species of *Microlophus* do not occur elsewhere. Explain the origins, by named biological processes, of the Galápagos lava lizards. (7)

2. a. Distinguish between these biological terms: evolution, natural selection and speciation. (5)

   b. Identify whether the following pairs of structures are analogous or homologous:

      i. wing of hoverfly and wing of hummingbird

      ii. leg of ostrich and leg of orang-utan

      iii. wing of ostrich and arm of orang-utan

      iv. stings in *Urtica dioica* and *Phacelia malvifolia*. (4)

   c. Outline how evidence for evolution is provided by:

      i. base sequences in DNA (3)

      ii. selective breeding of domesticated animals. (3)

3. *Brassica napus* (rapeseed or canola) is a widely grown crop. The diagram shows how it arose by natural processes 5–10,000 years ago. $2n$ is diploid number of chromosomes.

Brassica rapa	×	*Brassica oleracea*
$2n = 20$		$2n = 18$

Brassica napus
$2n = 38$

   a. Explain how *B. napus* was formed. (4)

   b. Justify *B. napus* being named a separate species. (3)

   c. If the natural processes that gave rise to *B. napus* are repeated, the resulting plants yield much smaller quantities of oil, with a different ratio of fatty acids from modern crop varieties. Suggest reasons for this. (3)

A4.2 Conservation of biodiversity

1. The pie charts show the percentage of land area in New Zealand that was forested on three dates. Māori arrived in New Zealand between 1200 and 1300 and Europeans from 1769 onwards.

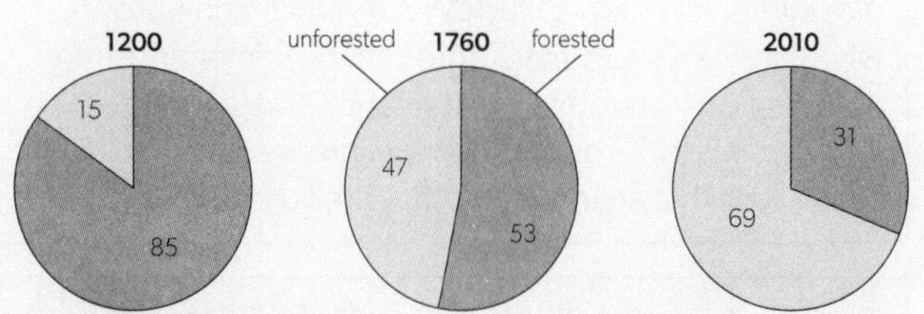

   a. Calculate the amounts of deforestation before and after the arrival of European colonists. (2)

   b. Suggest the consequences of deforestation. (3)

   c. There are 158 surviving native bird species in New Zealand. 16 species have become extinct since 1760 and 35 between 1200 and 1760.

      Calculate the percentage decrease since 1200. (1)

   d. A high proportion of New Zealand bird species in 1200 were flightless. Suggest reasons for this and for flightless birds being particularly vulnerable to anthropogenic species extinction. (4)

2. Explain the reasons for considering that there is a biodiversity crisis, despite there being more species of living organism currently living on Earth than ever before. (5)

3. The Wollemi pine (*Wollemia nobilis*) was discovered in 1994 after they were thought to be extinct. There is only one population with a few hundred trees located in a remote valley in the Blue Mountains of Australia.

   The cladogram shows relationships between *W. nobilis* and three other genera of conifer tree. Only one species of both *Wairarapaia* and *Emwadea* are known from 100 million year-old fossils.

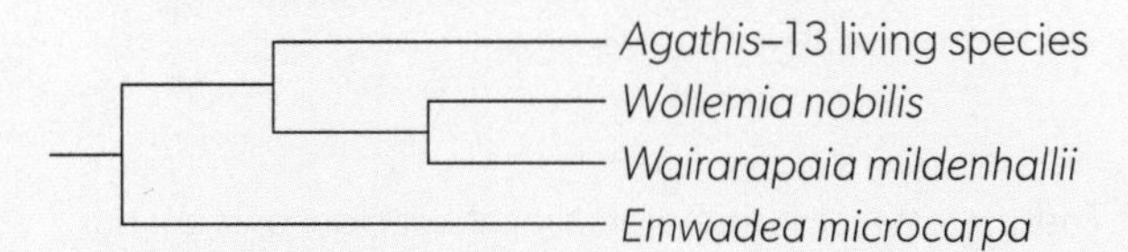

   a. Discuss whether *Wollemia nobilis* should be a priority species for conservation efforts. (3)

   b. Outline two approaches to conservation that could be used for a species such as *Wollemia nobilis*. (4)

   c. Bush fires in 2019–2020 killed some juvenile trees in the Blue Mountains habitat of *Wollemia nobilis*. Suggest global measures that should be taken to protect species such as this. (3)

B4.1 Adaptation to the environment

1. Habitats

Habitat is the place where an organism lives. It is a description of the geographical location, the type of ecosystem, the physical location within the ecosystem and both the physical and chemical conditions. It usually refers to one species but the habitat of one organism, a population or a whole community can also be described.

As an example, the habitat of the species *Ranunculus glacialis* is very high altitudes on mountains in Europe, where there is snow cover through the winter and little competition from other plants in the short summer growing season. These sites have intense sunlight and acidic soils that are moist but also well drained.

▲ This photo shows *R. glacialis* growing through melting snow at 3,000 metres in the Alps.

3. Species distribution is affected by abiotic variables

The distribution of a species is where it lives in the world, so it can be shown on a map. An example is shown below. Distribution is limited by abiotic factors. The adaptations of plants and animals suit them for living in some physical environments but not others.

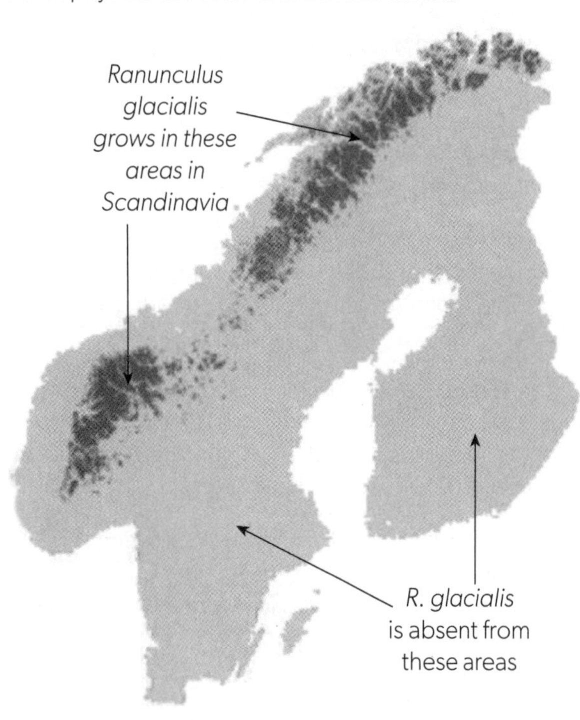
Ranunculus glacialis grows in these areas in Scandinavia
R. glacialis is absent from these areas

These are the abiotic factors that affect plant and animal distributions:

Plant distribution:

- temperature
- water availability
- light intensity
- soil pH
- soil salinity
- availability of mineral nutrients.

Animal distribution:

- water availability
- temperature.

The adaptations of a species give it ranges of tolerance. For example, salmon require fast-flowing freshwater streams no more than 3 m deep for spawning. They must have gravel substrates with particle size between 10 mm and 100 mm and a water pH of between 5.5 and 8.0.

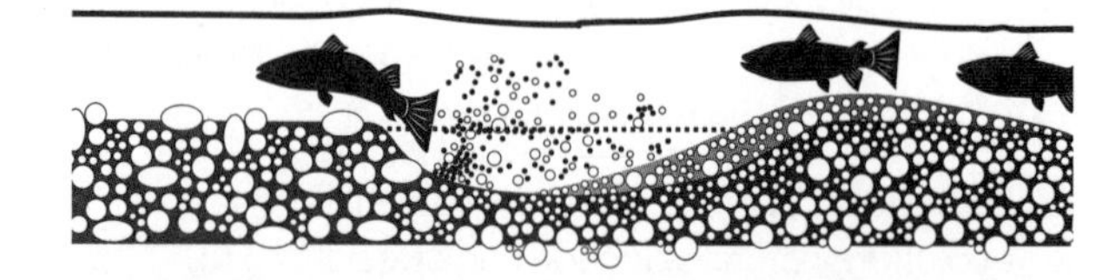

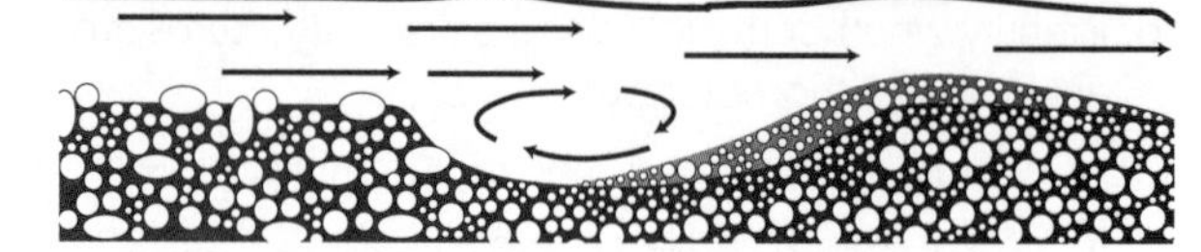

▲ Salmon spawn in fast-flowing streams with high oxygen concentrations. They dig a shallow depression in gravel, so there is shelter from the currents and their eggs and sperm are not washed away.

▲ Salmon jumping falls on a river in Alaska to reach their spawning grounds

2. Organisms are adapted to their abiotic environment

The environment of an organism is everything that is around it. This includes other living organisms and non-living materials such as air, water and rock. Living things are referred to as **biotic factors** and non-living things are called **abiotic factors**. Biotic factors dominate in ecosystems where there are dense communities of organisms, for example, in tropical rainforests. Abiotic factors have more influence in extreme habitats where population densities are low, for example, desert or taiga. All organisms are adapted to their abiotic environment. This is clearly seen in plants that live in extreme habitats such as sand dunes and mangrove swamps.

Adaptations of grasses to sand dunes

Sand dunes are accumulations of wind-blown sand at the top of beaches. Sand retains little water after rainfall and newly formed dunes contain little water-retaining organic matter. Sand on beach dunes may contain high salt concentrations, hindering water uptake by osmosis. These are the challenges for plants on beach dunes:

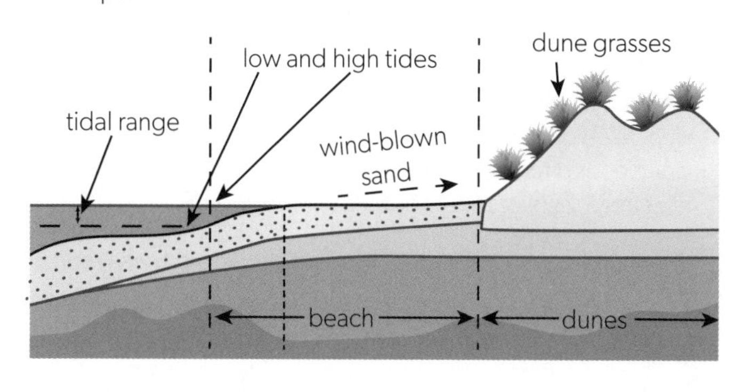
low and high tides
dune grasses
tidal range
wind-blown sand
beach
dunes

- tolerance of sand accumulation
- tolerance of high salt concentrations
- water conservation.

Special adaptations are required to meet these challenges. Grasses are the dominant plant in this habitat in many parts of the world. Lyme grass (*Leymus mollis*) occurs where sand is accumulating at the seaward edge of dunes in North America. It has rhizomes (underground stems) that grow upwards as sand accumulates and extend deep into the dune to obtain water. The leaf section (right) shows other adaptations:

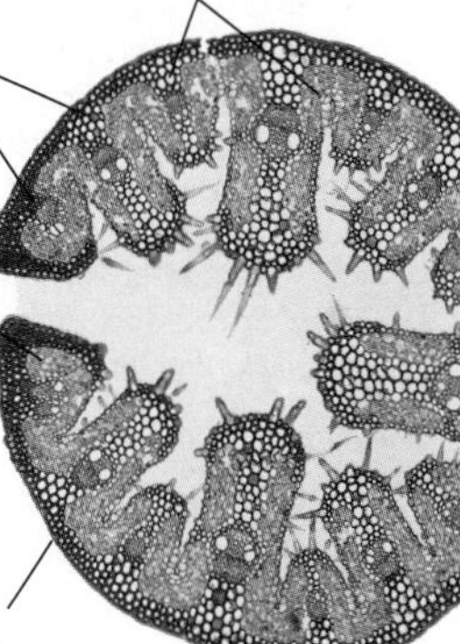
during droughts tough sclerenchyma tissue near one leaf surface prevents wilting and causes the leaf to roll up, creating a humid chamber that is less exposed to wind
stomata at the base of hairy furrows, where humid air remains even in windy conditions
fructans (a carbohydrate) accumulates in leaf and root cells, which increases osmotic potential and thus water uptake
thick waxy cuticle reduces transpiration

Adaptations of trees to mangrove swamps

Mangrove swamps develop on the coast in the tropics and subtropics where there are sheltered conditions and mud accumulates. These swamps are flooded with seawater at high tide. The dominant species are trees.

These are the environmental challenges of mangrove swamps:

- waterlogged anaerobic soils which make it difficult for tree roots to obtain the oxygen they need for cell respiration
- high salt concentrations which tend to draw water out of cells by osmosis and prevent water uptake. The salt concentration of the mud can be twice as high as that of seawater. This is due to the daily flooding with seawater and evaporation concentrating the salt in the mud.

This section shows adaptations of mangrove trees that allow them to thrive in their habitat:

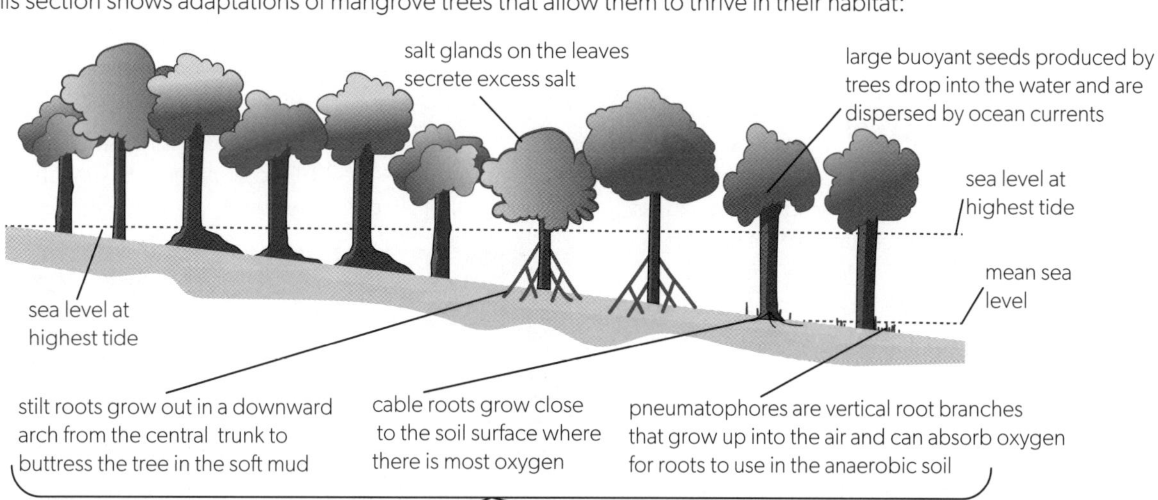
salt glands on the leaves secrete excess salt
large buoyant seeds produced by trees drop into the water and are dispersed by ocean currents
sea level at highest tide
mean sea level
sea level at highest tide
stilt roots grow out in a downward arch from the central trunk to buttress the tree in the soft mud
cable roots grow close to the soil surface where there is most oxygen
pneumatophores are vertical root branches that grow up into the air and can absorb oxygen for roots to use in the anaerobic soil
root epidermis is coated in suberin (cork) which reduces permeability to salt so prevents excessive uptake
root and leaf cells contain mineral ions and carbon compounds such as mannitol, which increase osmotic potential, enabling water absorption from the very saline environment

4. Range of tolerance of an abiotic factor

Plant and animal species have ranges of tolerance for abiotic variables. Some of these variables are listed in *Section B4.1.3*. If a species is unable to grow in an area because of the level of a variable being outside the range of tolerance, that variable is acting as a limiting factor. Ranges of tolerance can be investigated by carrying out experiments, or by collecting data from natural or semi-natural habitats, to look for correlations. Transects can be used. A transect is a line, or a belt between two lines, along which data are collected.

Application of skills: collecting ecological data on a transect

Two types of data are needed to investigate tolerance of a limiting factor:

1. **Measurements of the abiotic variable:** The transect should span different levels of the variable. For example, a line taken down a slope from woodland to peat bog might reveal correlations between the distribution of plant species and temperature, light intensity and soil pH. These and other abiotic variables can be measured using electronic sensors and portable data loggers.
2. **Measurements of species distribution:** There are several possible methods.
   - numbers of individuals touching a line transect are recorded (line intercept sampling)
   - abundance is measured using quadrats at regular intervals along a belt (belt transect)
   - sightings are tallied by an observer walking along a line (observational transect).

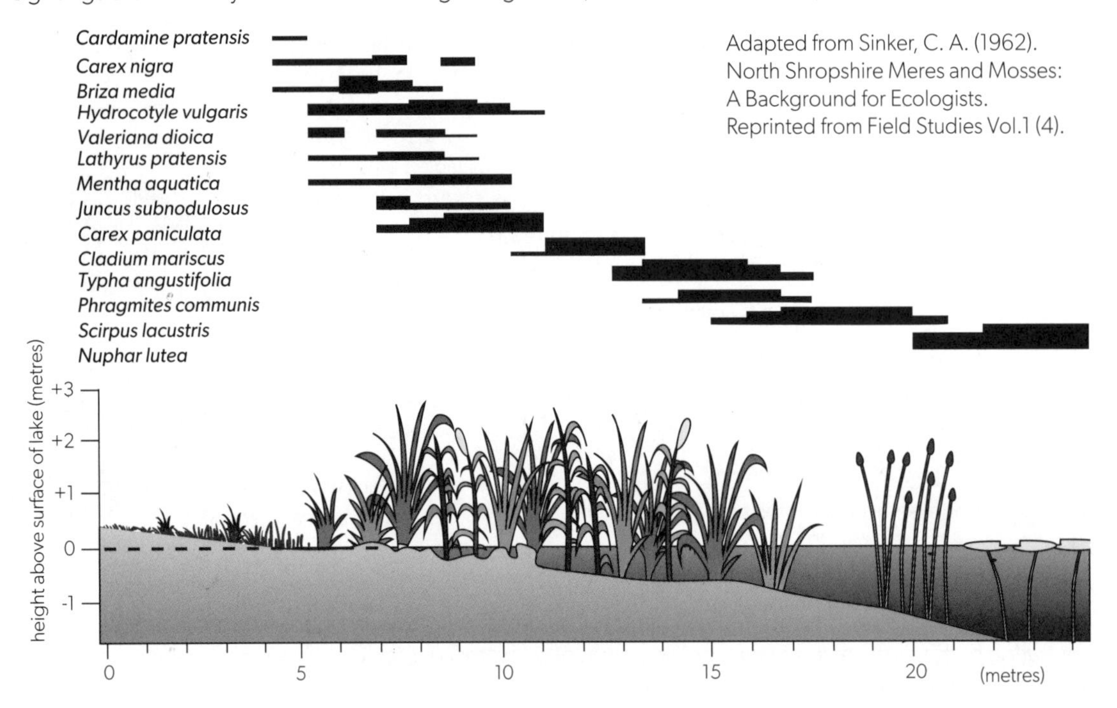

The diagram above shows a belt transect at right angles to the shore of Crose Mere in Shropshire, with plants adapted to increasing depths of water in the lake.

5. Formation of coral reef

Coral reefs are biodiverse marine ecosystems that can only develop where conditions are suitable for hard corals, as their skeletons form the rocky structure of the reef. Hard corals contain mutualistic zooxanthellae (described in *Section C4.1.12*), which need light for photosynthesis.

- **Depth**—water less than 50 m, so enough light penetrates.
- **pH**—above 7.8 so $CaCO_3$ can be deposited in the skeleton.
- **Salinity**—between 32 and 42 parts per thousand of dissolved ions to avoid osmotic problems.
- **Clarity**—turbidity would prevent penetration of light so the water must be clear.
- **Temperature**—23–29°C so both the coral and its zooxanthellae remain healthy.

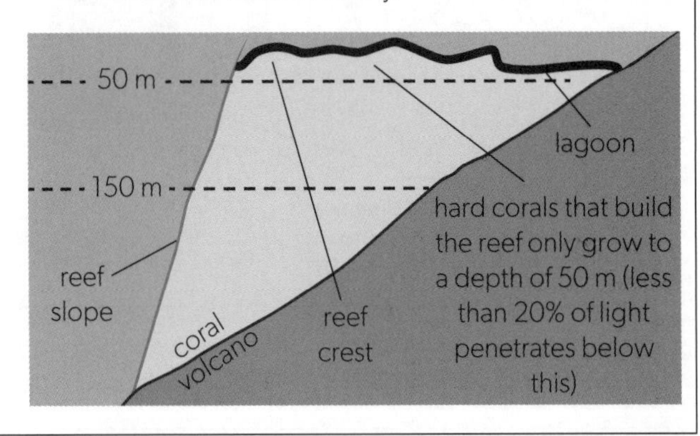

6. Terrestrial biome distribution

- With any combination of abiotic factors, one particular type of ecosystem is likely to develop.
- For example, taiga (boreal forest) develops in subarctic regions, with spruces and other conifers as the dominant trees.
- Species composition will vary depending on the geographical location, but the adaptations of the species are likely to be similar.
- All ecosystems of a specific type are a **biome**.
- Temperature and rainfall are the principal determinants of biome distribution on Earth.
- The most likely ecosystem with any particular combination of these factors can be shown using a graph.

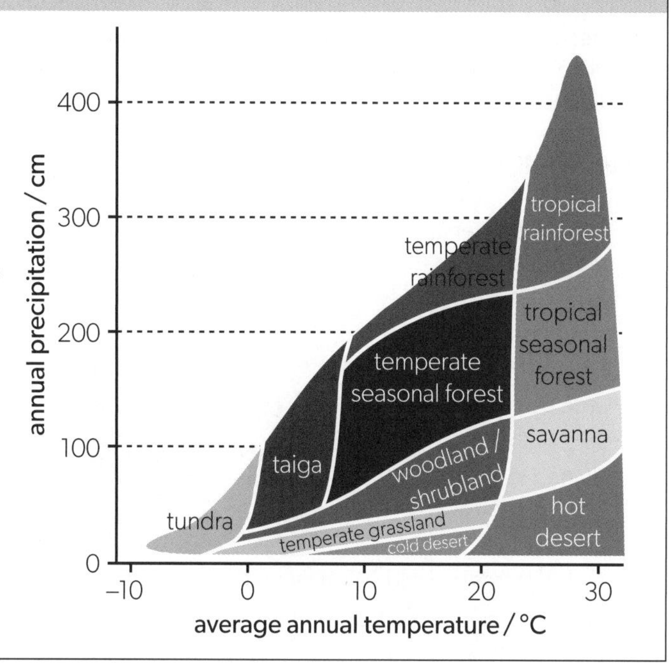

7. Biomes

Biomes are groups of ecosystems that resemble each other, even though they may be widely separated in the world. The resemblance is due to the similar abiotic conditions, with organisms evolving similar adaptations. The origin of analogous structures by convergent evolution is described in *Section A4.1.5*.

Climatic conditions in major biomes:

Temperate forest: temperatures moderate with summers warm and winters cold, rainfall medium to high, light intensity moderate

Grassland: temperatures medium to high in summer but may be cold in winter, rainfall moderate with a dry season, light intensity medium/high

Taiga (boreal forest): temperatures low with short summers, precipitation medium to high, light intensity low to medium

▲ Cacti (left) and Euphorbias (right) have adapted in similar ways to deserts in Africa and America.

Tundra: temperatures very low with very short summer, precipitation low to medium mostly as snow, light intensity low

Hot deserts and **tropical rainforest** are described in *Section B4.1.8*.

NOS

Observations

Scientists can make observations directly using human senses, or with the aid of electronic sensors. A sensor is a device that records the level of a parameter. Electronic sensors are now available for many parameters that are of interest in ecological research. A log is a permanent record of measurements taken at regular intervals. Data logging is digital storage of measurements from electronic sensors. Compact, portable data loggers have been designed with sensors to monitor an environmental condition such as temperature, light intensity or pH, together with an internal memory to record and store the digital data.

Data loggers have many advantages:

- inexpensive
- can be operated with limited technical expertise
- available for measuring hundreds of different parameters
- can take repeated measurements very rapidly
- can be left to take measurements automatically over long periods
- stored data can be transferred easily to a computer for analysis or long-term storage.

8. Adaptating to life in hot deserts and tropical rainforest

Hot deserts have very high daytime temperatures and much colder nights. There is little rainfall and long droughts. Soil development is very limited, with little soil organic matter. The saguaro and fennec fox are adapted to these conditions.

saguaro cactus (*Carnegia gigantea*)

- wide-spreading roots to collect water from a wide area
- tap roots to collect water from deep in the subsoil
- wide stems with water storage tissue
- pleated stems that shrink in droughts and swell after rain

- vertical stems to avoid overheating by hot midday sun
- thick waxy cuticle on stem epidermis—less transpiration
- leaves reduced to spines—less surface area so less transpiration
- CAM metabolism so stomata open only at night and close during the heat of the day, reducing transpiration.

fennec fox (*Vulpes zerda*)

- nocturnal so it avoids high daytime temperatures
- builds an underground den where it stays cool in the day
- long thick hair, heat insulation in cold nights and hot days
- hairs cover the pads of the feet to provide insulation when walking on very hot sand
- pale-coloured coat reflects sunlight (a darker coat would absorb it)
- large ears radiate heat—keeps body temperature down
- ventilation rate rises very high (panting) to cause heat loss by evaporation.

Tropical rainforests have high light intensity, high temperatures, no cold season and much rainfall. Soils tend to be thin and nutrient-poor due to leaching. Yellow meranti (second largest living tree) and the spider monkey are adapted to these conditions.

yellow meranti (*Shorea faguetiana*)

Shenkin, A. et al. (2019a). The world's tallest tropical tree in three dimensions. Frontiers in Forests and Global Change, 2. doi:10.3389/ffgc.2019.00032

- grows to over 100 m tall so avoids competition for light
- trunk of hard dense wood for support against wind stress
- trunk buttressed at base for support in shallow soil
- smooth trunk to shed rainwater rapidly
- oval leaves with pointed tips to shed rainwater rapidly
- evergreen leaves to carry out photosynthesis all year
- leaf enzymes work in temperatures as high as 35°C
- flowers and seeds produced in large quantities only about one year in five, to deter animals that eat the seeds.

spider monkey(*Ateles geoffroyi*)

- long arms and legs for climbing and reaching for fruit
- flexible shoulders allowing swinging from tree to tree
- large hook-like thumbless hands to grasp branches and lianas (woody vines) and pick fruit
- feet can grasp branches so arms can be used for feeding
- long tail to grip branches
- highly developed larynx for communication in the dense rainforest canopy
- only awake in the daytime—vision is better so movement between branches is safer
- breeding in any season, as food always available.

B4.2 Ecological niches

1. Ecological niche

A key concept in ecology is that each species in an ecosystem fulfils a unique role, called its ecological niche. Niches have both biotic and abiotic elements.

- Zones of tolerance for abiotic variables determine the habitat of a species—where it lives in the ecosystem.
- Food supply is a biotic element and can be autotrophic (synthesis using an energy source, water and carbon dioxide), or heterotrophic (taking food from other organisms). To minimize competition, species become specialists in sourcing food. To compete effectively with any specialized mode of nutrition, adaptations are required.
- Other biotic elements of ecological niches are utilization of other species to provide a diverse range of services, such as pollination of flowers or nesting sites in tree holes.

The ecological niche of a species is made up of many factors—it is multidimensional. Unless all the dimensions of the niche are satisfied in an ecosystem, a species will not be able to survive, grow or reproduce.

2. Comparing obligate anaerobes, facultative anaerobes and obligate aerobes

Animals and plants require oxygen for aerobic cell respiration, but some microorganisms do not. This allows them to live in anoxic habitats where molecular oxygen (O_2) is sometimes, or always, lacking. Such conditions occur in swamps, water-logged soil or mud, intestinal tracts (guts) of animals, and deep in lakes or seas.

All organisms are in one of three categories according to oxygen requirements:

Category	Requirements	Examples
Obligate aerobes	Oxygen must be continuously available for aerobic respiration	• All plants and animals • *Micrococcus luteus* (a bacterium)
Obligate anaerobes	Conditions must be anoxic as oxygen kills or inhibits the organism	• *Clostridium tetani* (tetanus bacterium) • Methanogenic archaea
Facultative anaerobes	Oxygen is used if available but anoxic conditions are tolerated	• *Escherichia coli* (a gut bacterium) • *Saccharomyces* (yeast—a fungus)

3. Photosynthesis

In photosynthesis, energy from sunlight is used for fixing carbon dioxide and making the carbon compounds such as sugars and amino acids on which life is based. Three groups of organisms use photosynthesis:

- **plants**—mosses, ferns, conifers and flowering plants
- **eukaryotic algae** including seaweeds that grow on rocky shores and unicellular algae such as *Chlorella*
- **cyanobacteria** (blue–green bacteria) and several other groups of bacteria, but many are not photosynthetic.

Photosynthesis therefore occurs in two of the three domains of life (in eukaryotes and bacteria). It does not occur in the other domain (archaea) as explained in *Section B4.2.7*.

4. Holozoic nutrition

Animals obtain supplies of carbohydrates, amino acids, and other carbon compounds by consuming food. They are **heterotrophic** because the carbon compounds come from other organisms. Molecules such as polysaccharides and proteins must be digested before they can be absorbed. Digestion in most animals happens internally, after the food has been ingested. This is **holozoic nutrition**—whole pieces of food are swallowed and are then fully digested.

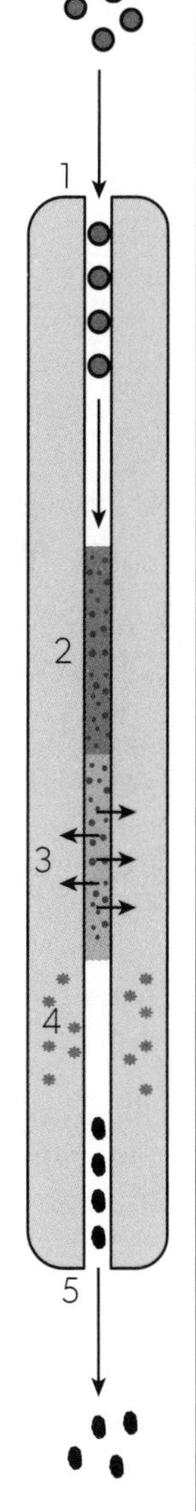

These are the five stages:

1. **ingestion**—taking the food into the gut
2. **digestion**—breaking large food molecules into smaller molecules
3. **absorption**—transport of digested food across the plasma membrane of epidermis cells and thus into the blood and tissues of the body
4. **assimilation**—using digested foods to synthesize proteins and other macromolecules; this makes them part of the body's tissues
5. **egestion**—voiding undigested material from the end of the gut.

Some animals digest their food externally so they are not holozoic. Spiders, for example, inject digestive enzymes into their prey and suck out the liquids produced. They absorb the products of digestion in their gut and then assimilate them.

5. Mixotrophic nutrition

Some protists (unicellular eukaryotes) can obtain carbon compounds from other organisms or can make them themselves. Organisms that are not exclusively autotrophic or heterotrophic are **mixotrophic**.

Facultative mixotrophs can be entirely autotrophic, entirely heterotrophic, or use both modes. *Euglena gracilis*, for example has chloroplasts and carries out photosynthesis when there is sufficient light, but it can also feed on detritus or smaller organisms by endocytosis.

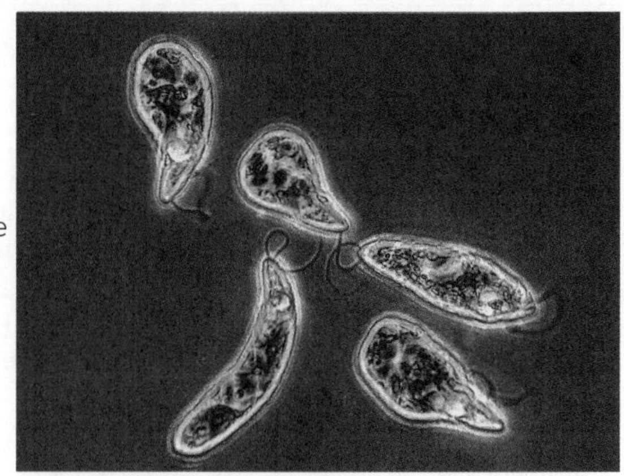
▲ *Euglena gracilis*

Obligate mixotrophs cannot grow unless they utilize both autotrophic and heterotrophic modes of nutrition. This may be because the food that they consume supplies them with a carbon compound that they cannot themselves synthesize. In other cases, a protist that does not have its own chloroplasts obtains them by consuming algae. It uses the "klepto-chloroplasts" obtained in this way for photosynthesis until they degrade and have to be replaced.

7. Archaea—diverse nutrition

There are three domains of life: archaea, bacteria, and eukaryotes. (This system of classification is described for HL in *Section A3.2.9*.) The archaea are unicellular and have no nucleus, which is a similarity with bacteria. In other respects, archaea are closer to eukaryotes. Some types of archaea are adapted to extreme environments such as hot springs, salt lakes and soda lakes. Many are difficult to culture in the laboratory, so they are less well researched than the other domains of life. Archaea are extremely diverse in their sources of energy for ATP production and carbon. The table shows the sources for the three main categories of archaea.

	Energy for ATP production	Carbon compounds
Chemoheterotrophs	Oxidation of carbon compounds obtained from other organisms	Obtained from other organisms—not photosynthesis
Photoheterotrophs	Absorption of light using pigments (not chlorophyll in archaea)	Obtained from other organisms—not photosynthesis
Chemoautotrophs	Oxidation of inorganic chemicals, for example Fe^{2+} ions oxidized to Fe^{3+}	Synthesized from carbon dioxide by anabolic reactions

6. Saprotrophic nutrition

Saprotrophs feed on dead organic matter, but have cell walls so cannot take it in by endocytosis. Instead, they secrete digestive enzymes into the dead organic matter around them and digest it externally. They secrete proteases to digest proteins into amino acids and other enzymes depending on the composition of the dead organic matter, for example cellulase to digest cellulose into glucose.

If the small, soluble products of digestion diffuse to the saprotroph's plasma membrane, they are absorbed and used. Many types of bacteria and fungi are saprotrophic.

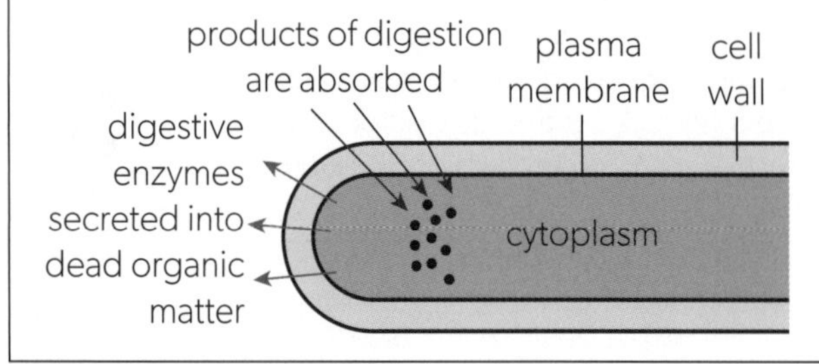

Theories

NOS

A theory in science is a general explanation, based on observed patterns or tested hypotheses, that is widely applicable. Predictions can be generated from theories by deductive reasoning.

If observations are made of dentition in animals with known diets, including herbivores, carnivores and omnivores, theories can be developed about the structure–function relationships of teeth.

These theories can be tested by predicting the diet of living animals from the characteristics of their teeth and then checking whether the actual diet matches the prediction. This may corroborate the theories or show that they are false and should be rejected.

Theories about dentition can also be used to infer the diet of extinct species of hominid. However, it is not possible to verify these predictions as we cannot be sure what the diet of an extinct hominid was. We might therefore consider these predictions to be non-scientific.

8. Dentition and diet in the family Hominidae

The family Hominidae includes the genera that contain humans (*Homo*), orang-utans (*Pongo*), gorillas (*Gorilla*), and chimpanzees (*Pan*). Some members of the Hominidae have an exclusively herbivorous diet and others are omnivorous as animal prey are sometimes eaten to supplement their plant-based diet.

Living members of the Hominidae show a relationship between diet and dentition. The teeth of herbivores tend to be large and flat to grind down fibrous plant tissues. Omnivores tend to have a mix of different types of teeth to break down both meat and plants in their diet. Humans have flat molars in the back of their mouth to crush and grind food, and sharper canines and incisors than herbivores to tear tougher food, like meat.

Application of skills: observations on dentition

Hypotheses about the diet of extinct species in the Hominidae can be developed from their dentition and the structure of the jaw bone and skull, to which muscles used for chewing are attached.

The photos below show the mandibles (lower jaws) of *Paranthropus robustus* (left), *Homo floresiensis* (centre) and, for comparison, modern *Homo sapiens* (right). *P. robustus* lived 1.0–2.6 million years ago and probably ate tough plant foods including grasses. *H. floresiensis* lived between 50,000 and 200,000 years ago and probably ate uncooked plant foods and meat.

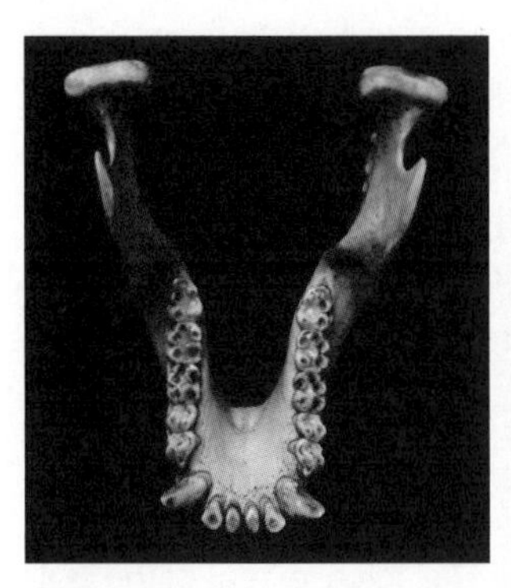

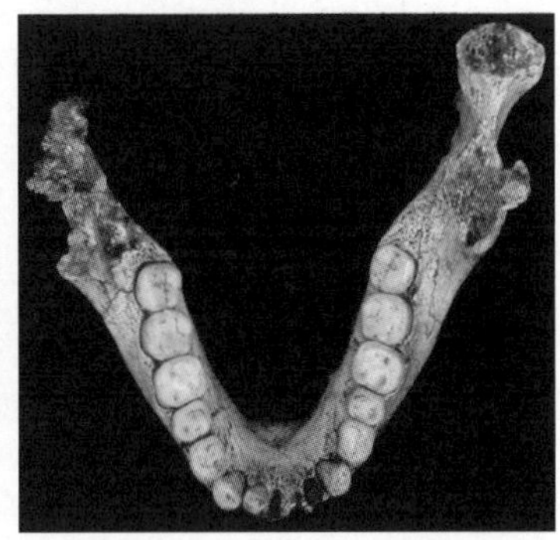

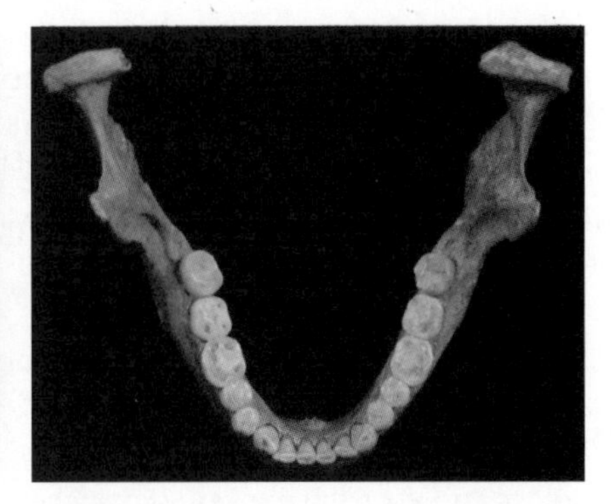

9. Adaptations of herbivores for feeding and of plants for resisting herbivory

Animals that feed only on plants are herbivores. They have structural features that adapt them to their diet. Insect mouthparts show great diversity, but are all homologous—they have been derived by evolution from the same ancestral mouthparts.

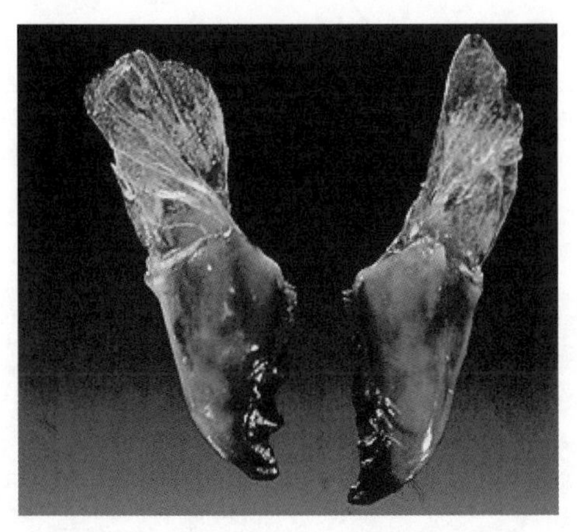

- beetles and other insects that feed on leaves have jaw-like mouthparts with tough mandibles for biting off, chewing, and ingesting leaves (above)
- aphids and other insects that feed on phloem sap have sharp, tubular mouthparts for piercing leaves or stems to reach phloem sieve tubes
- butterflies and other insects that feed on nectar have tubular mouthparts long enough to reach the nectary in flowers (right).

Plants have varied adaptations for deterring herbivore attacks:

- sharp spines (e.g. the thorns of a rose)
- stings to cause pain (e.g. stinging nettle)
- synthesis and storage of secondary metabolites that are toxic to herbivores. They may be stored in any part of a plant, particularly seeds, which are attractive to herbivores because of their high concentrations of protein and starch or oil. Primary metabolites are substances that are part of the basic metabolic pathways of a cell.

In some cases, herbivores have responded to toxic compounds in plants by developing metabolic adaptations for detoxifying them. This has resulted in plant–herbivore specificity, with only a few species of herbivore adapted to feed on a particular plant.

10. Adaptations of predators and prey

Predators are adapted to find, catch, kill and digest other animals. The prey may be killed before it is ingested, or it may die inside the predator's digestive system. Prey species are adapted to resist predation. The table shows examples of structural, chemical or behavioural adaptation.

Adaptations	Predators	Prey
Structural	Large pointed upper front teeth in **vampire bats** for piercing prey to suck blood	Shells of **limpets** on rocky shores to protect soft parts of the mollusc's body
Chemical	Venom containing toxins produced by **black mambas** to paralyse and kill prey	In **cinnabar moth larvae** toxins are accumulated from ragwort plants eaten
Behavioural	Waving of a modified luminescent fin ray in **anglerfish** to lure prey	Swimming in tight groups (schooling) in **blue-striped snappers** and other fish

11. Adaptations of plants for harvesting light

In ecosystems where light intensity is the limiting factor for photosynthesis, especially forests, plants compete for light. Plants use a variety of strategies in forests for obtaining light, so they show great diversity of form.

- Trees have a dominant leading shoot, allowing rapid growth in height up to the forest canopy so other trees do not cast shade.
- Lianas climb other trees, using them for support, so they need less xylem tissue (wood) than free-standing trees.
- Epiphytes grow on the trunks and branches of trees, so they receive higher light intensity than if they grew on the forest floor, but there is minimal soil for their roots.
- Strangler epiphytes climb up the trunks of trees, encircle them and outgrow the tree's branches, shading out its leaves. Eventually the tree dies leaving only the epiphyte.
- Shade-tolerant shrubs and herbs absorb the small amounts of light that reach the forest floor.

12. Fundamental and realized niches

Each species tolerates a range of abiotic conditions and their adaptations do not allow them to survive outside this range. This is described in *Section B4.1.4*. There are also biotic factors that a species needs. The **fundamental niche** of a species is the range of abiotic conditions tolerated together with the requirements for biotic factors. If a species was living without any competitors, it would occupy the entire fundamental niche.

In natural ecosystems, there is competition and typically a species is excluded from parts of its fundamental niche by competitors. The actual extent of the potential range that a species occupies is its **realized niche**.

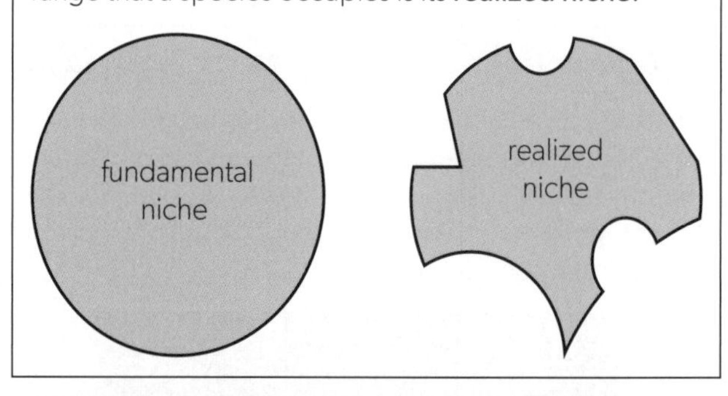

13. Competitive exclusion

Where the fundamental niches of two species overlap, one species is expected to exclude the other from that part of its range by competition. This was demonstrated experimentally with the flour beetles *Tribolium castaneum* and *Tribolium confusum*. These species both thrived when put individually into flour at varying combinations of temperature and humidity. However, when they were both introduced to the flour, *T. castaneum* was excluded by *T. confusum* in some combinations of temperature and humidity, but *T. confusum* was excluded by *T. castaneum* in other combinations, so they had different realized niches.

If two species in an ecosystem have overlapping fundamental niches and one species outcompetes the other in all parts of the fundamental niche, the outcompeted species does not have a realized niche and will be competitively excluded from the whole ecosystem. According to ecological theory, every species must have a realized niche that differs from the realized niches of all other species if it is to survive in an ecosystem.

▲ Limpets (larger) and barnacles (smaller) are co-existing here on a rocky shore on the island of Eriskay. This suggests that there are differences between their fundamental niches.

End of topic questions — B4 Questions

B4.1 Adaptation to the environment

1. *Typha latifolia* and *Typha angustifolia* are plants that grow on the margins of ponds and lakes.

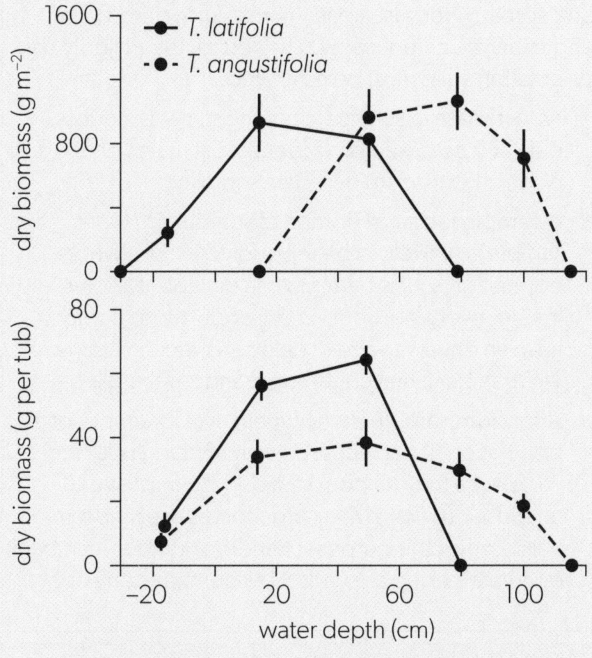

   a. The upper graph shows the natural distribution of *T. latifolia* and *T. angustifolia* in a lake. Compare and contrast the two distributions. (3)

   b. The lower graph shows the results of an experiment in which the species were planted separately in tubs, and placed at different depths in water to assess their growth. Deduce the depths that are within the limits of tolerance and zones of stress of each species. (3)

   c. Explain the differences between the realized and fundamental of *T. angustifolia*. (4)

   d. State one sampling technique that is used to investigate the distribution of plants at increasing depths of water from the shore of a lake. (1)

2. a. Outline what the habitat of a species is. (3)

   b. Distinguish between *ecosystem* and *biome*. (2)

   c. Plants are adapted to specific types of habitat.

      i. Suggest one reason for tropical rainforest plants not surviving in hot deserts. (1)

      ii. Suggest one reason for hot desert plants not surviving in tropical rainforests. (1)

   d. State three biomes other than hot deserts and tropical rainforests. (3)

3. Explain how coral reefs are threatened by:

   a. melting of ice and thermal expansion of ocean water (3)

   b. increases in CO_2 concentration in the oceans (3)

   c. warming of the oceans (2)

   d. turbidity from algal blooms or soil erosion. (2)

B4.2 Ecological niches

1. The photograph shows the lower jaws of a 25-year old Neanderthal (above) and a human of similar age (below). On both the left and right sides, the Neanderthal has two incisors and one canine but the pre-molar next to the canine is missing.

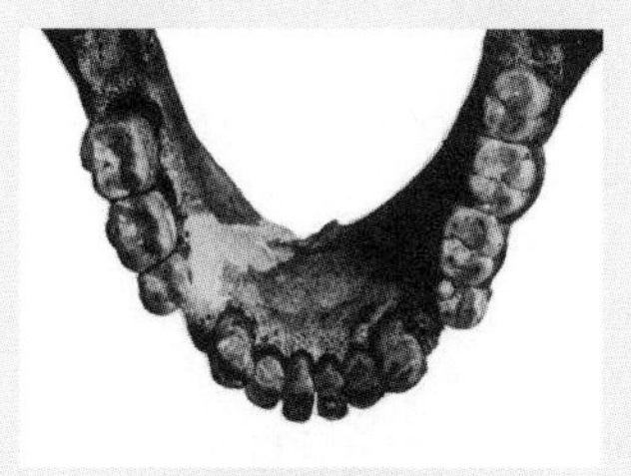
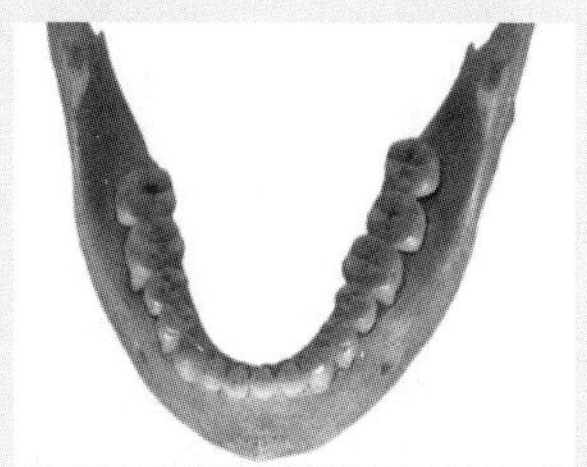

   a. Compare and contrast the teeth of the Neanderthal and the human. (5)

   b. Human dentition is adapted to an omnivorous diet. Deduce whether Neanderthal dentition is adapted to an omnivorous or herbivorous diet. (5)

2. Distinguish between:

   a. habitat and niche (3)

   b. photosynthetic and photoheterotrophic (2)

   c. chemoheterotrophic and chemoautotrophic. (2)

3. *Faecalibacterium prausnitzii* is an abundant bacterium in human intestines. It ferments dietary fibre and produces butyrate ($CH_3CH_2CH_2COO^-$) and other short-chain fatty acids as waste products.

   a. Identify, with a reason, whether *F. prausnitzii* is:

      i. autotrophic, heterotrophic or mixotrophic (2)

      ii. holozoic or saprotrophic. (2)

   b. *F. prausnitzii* is difficult to culture in the laboratory because it is intolerant of very low concentrations of oxygen. Explain two conclusions that can be drawn from this. (4)

   c. Gut epithelium cells absorb butyrate. Suggest how they might use this substance. (2)

C4.1 Populations and communities

1. Populations

A population is a group of individual organisms of the same species living in an area. Members of a population interact in various ways. They normally interbreed with each other and interbreed less often or not at all with individuals in other populations (reproductive isolation; see *Section A4.1.7*). There are usually many non-breeding interactions between individuals in a population, such as competition for food or cooperation to avoid predation. The number of individuals in a population can be anything from a few up to billions. There may be one population of a species or many. Populations of a species are often separated by a geographical barrier, for example the sea that separates two islands.

NOS

Measurement

Measurements are repeated to increase the reliability of data. Repeats are essential in random sampling to estimate population size, but however large the sample size, there will be a difference between the estimate and the true population size. This is the **sampling error**. Random sampling reduces sampling error, but cannot eliminate it.

2. Random sampling is used to estimate population size

The size of a population is the total number of individuals. It is rarely possible to count every individual in a population reliably. Populations may be very large and spread over vast areas. Animals move around and many are camouflaged. Therefore, the majority of population sizes must be estimated.

- An **estimate** in science is not the same as a guess. It should be based on evidence. Estimates of population size are based on sampling.
- A **sample** is a small portion of something. One sample is unlikely to be representative of a whole population so it is better to use multiple samples. Ideally, every individual in the population should have an equal chance of being included in a sample. This can be achieved through random sampling.
- A **random sample** is one where every member of a population has an equal chance of being selected. To select a truly random sample, you must avoid unconscious bias. Many procedures use random numbers for this purpose. Random numbers can be generated using a computer or a smartphone app.

3. Estimating population size with quadrats

Quadrats are square sample areas, usually marked out using a quadrat frame. Quadrat sampling involves repeatedly placing a quadrat frame at random positions in a habitat and recording the numbers of organisms present each time. This is the procedure for positioning the quadrat:

- Random coordinates are generated (x and y), using either a table or a random number generator.
- The coordinates are used to place a quadrat in the area being sampled. This could be done using measuring tapes or a GPS device. Each part of the area must have an equal chance of being sampled.

e.g. if we use the coordinates 14, 7, the quadrat would be positioned here

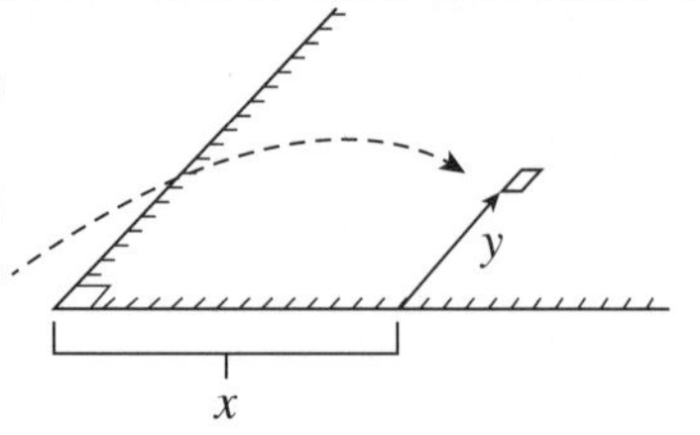

A population estimate can then be calculated:

$$\text{population estimate} = \frac{\text{mean count per quadrat} \times \text{area of whole site (m}^2\text{)}}{\text{area of one quadrat (m}^2\text{)}}$$

Quadrat sampling is only suitable for plants and other organisms that are sessile (organisms with a fixed position that do not move).

Application of skills: standard deviation

Standard deviation is a statistic that is used to give a measure of the variability of data. A low standard deviation shows that there is little variation between the values in a sample and a high standard deviation shows that there is much variation.

Using a calculator or computer, it is easy to find the mean and the standard deviation for a sample of observations. The observations must be quantitative, for example, the number of individuals per quadrat in quadrat sampling of a population. The lower the standard deviation, the more confidence you can have in any estimates based on the data. With quadrat sampling, a low standard deviation indicates that the sampling error is likely to be small and the estimate closer to the true population size than for a high standard deviation.

The standard deviation also indicates how evenly distributed a population is. A low standard deviation shows that the population is evenly spread, with a similar number of individuals in each quadrat, whereas a high standard deviation shows that the population is clumped and there are more individuals in some parts of the habitat than others.

Three types of distribution are shown in the squares: even (left), random (centre) and clumped (right).

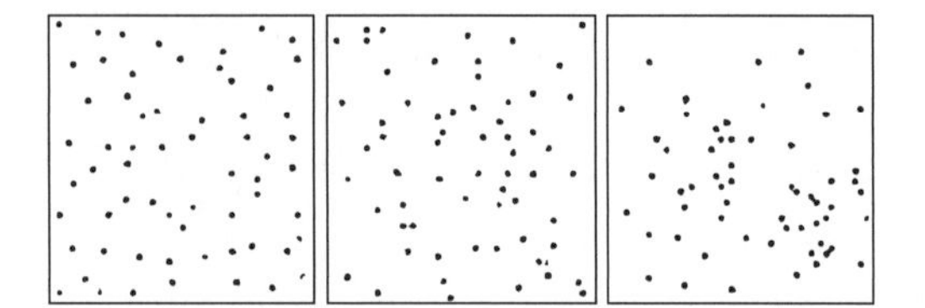

4. Application of skills: estimating population sizes of motile organisms by capture–mark–release–recapture

1 Capture as many individuals as possible in the area occupied by the animal population, using netting, trapping or careful searching, for example careful searching for banded snails *(Cepaea nemoralis)*.

2 Mark each captured individual, without making them more visible to predators, for example, marking the inside of the snail shell with a dot of non-toxic paint.

The following two assumptions are made about the period of time between capture and recapture:

- no migration into or out of the population
- no deaths or births.
- marked individuals mix back into the population and have the same chance of being captured on the second occasion as unmarked individuals
- the marks remain visible.

3 Release all the marked individuals and allow them to settle back into their habitat.

4 After a day (or two), recapture as many individuals as possible and count how many are marked and how many unmarked.

5 Calculate the estimated population size by using the Lincoln index:

$$\text{population size} = \frac{M \times N}{R}$$

where: M is the number of individuals caught and marked initially
N is the total number of individuals recaptured
R is the total number of individuals recaptured with marks.

Example: 248 snails were caught in a pond and marked. 168 were recaptured, with 42 marked.

$$\text{estimated population size} = \frac{248 \times 168}{42} = 992 \text{ snails}$$

5. Carrying capacity

Resources needed by populations, such as water and food, vary in abundance but all are limited. Resource limitation determines maximum population size.

Carrying capacity is the maximum population size that an environment can support.

If a resource becomes scarce, the members of a population will compete for it. If a population grows too large, some individuals will be unable to obtain enough of the resource. These individuals are likely to die, reducing the population size to the carrying capacity of the environment.

In practice, one resource (or a small number of resources) is likely to limit population size and so determine carrying capacity. Examples of resources that may limit carrying capacity in plants and animals are shown in the table (right).

Animals:	Plants:
• water	• water
• space for breeding	• light
• food or territory for obtaining food	• soil nitrogen (NO_3^- or NH_4^+) soil phosphorus (PO_4^{3-})
• dissolved oxygen in water	

▲ Carrying capacity of gannets may be determined by availability of suitable nest sites on rocky islands that are close enough to feeding grounds in the sea

6. Controlling population size by density-dependent factors

Two types of factor can cause populations to increase or decrease.

Density-independent factors have the same effect whatever the population size. For example, in a population of plants that are not adapted to low temperatures, a frost kills all the plants, whether the population is large or small. Forest fires kill plants and animals. Density-independent factors cause populations to fluctuate.

Density-dependent factors have an increasing effect as a population becomes larger. They are the basis for negative feedback mechanisms because they reduce larger populations and allow smaller populations to increase. Density-dependent factors tend to bring population size back to carrying capacity.

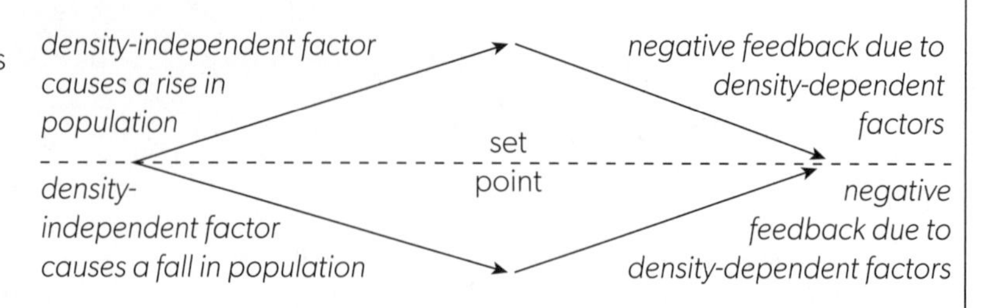

There are three groups of density-dependent factors:

- **Competition** for limited resources such as water and food in animals and light in plants.
- **Predation**—this becomes more intense if a population of prey becomes denser and therefore easier to find, and less intense if the prey become scarcer. There are similar interactions between plants and herbivores.
- **Infectious disease, parasitism and pest infestation**—these increase with population density because the transfer of pathogens, parasites and pests from host to host is easier if the hosts are closer together.

7. Sigmoid population growth curves

Four factors contribute to a change in the number of individuals in a population:

natality—offspring produced and added to the population

mortality—individuals die and are lost from the population

immigration—individuals move into the area from elsewhere

emigration—individuals move from the area to live elsewhere.

The overall change in the size of a population can be calculated using this equation:

population change = (natality + immigration) − (mortality + emigration)

The graph is a sigmoid (S-shaped) population growth curve. There are three key phases:

1. Exponential phase

If a population is established in an ideal unlimited environment, it follows an exponential growth pattern, with the population increasing more and more rapidly. This is because the natality rate is higher than the mortality rate. The resources needed by the population (e.g. food) are abundant, and diseases and predators are rare. With abundant resources, immigration to the area is more likely than emigration.

2. Transitional phase

Population growth slows as the carrying capacity of the environment is reached—the maximum population size that can be supported by the environment. The natality rate starts to fall and/or the mortality rate starts to rise. Natality is still higher than mortality, but by a decreasing amount.

3. Plateau phase

Something has limited the population such as:

- shortage of food or other resources
- more predators
- more disease or parasites.

All of these factors limit population increase because they become more intense as the population rises and becomes more crowded. They either reduce the natality rate or increase the mortality rate. Emigration is now more likely than immigration. If the population is limited by a shortage of resources, it has reached the carrying capacity of the environment.

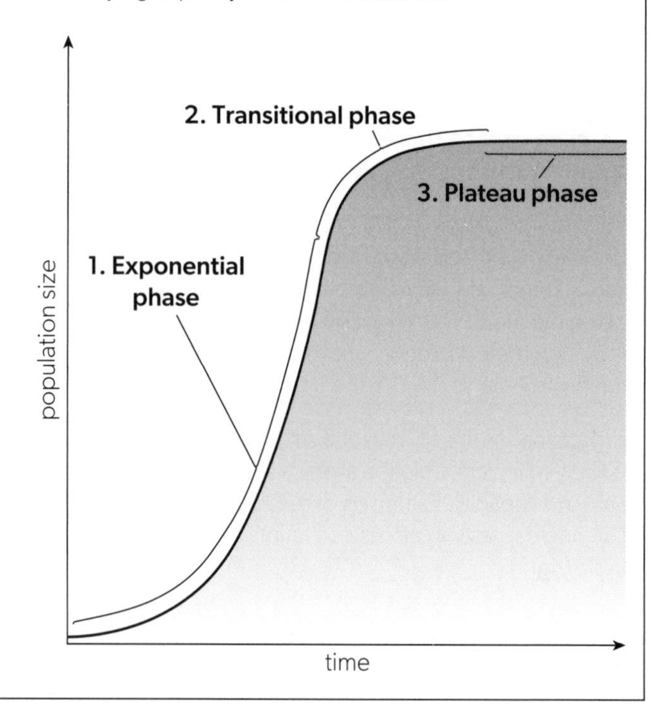

Application of skills: logarithmic scales

The spread of the collared dove in Europe is an interesting population growth case study. The upper graph shows the population of this species in the Netherlands during the 1950s and 1960s.

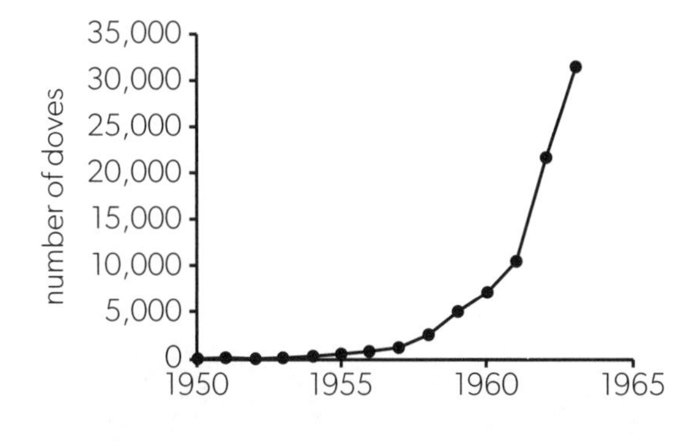

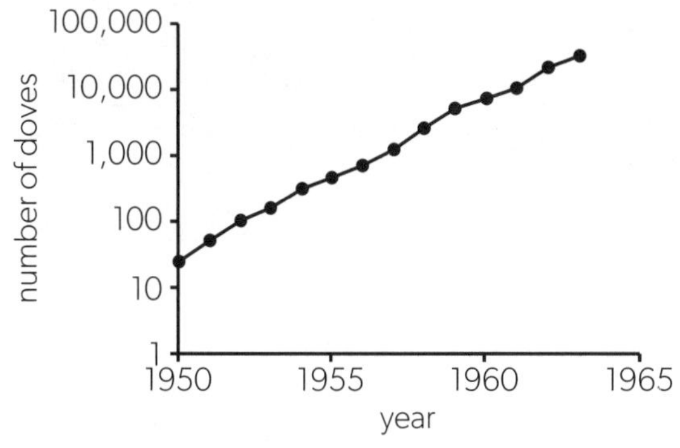

The lower graph shows the same data plotted with a logarithmic scale on the y-axis. With this type of graph, an exponential increase forms a straight line. The data points are close to this, which indicates that numbers of the collared dove did increase exponentially, so resources must have been unlimited.

NOS Models

Models are simplifications of complex systems. The sigmoid population growth curve is an idealized graphical model of how populations exploiting new environments can increase by positive feedback mechanisms and then be regulated by negative feedback. Natural populations are unlikely to conform precisely to this model, but it allows dynamic processes in a population to be analysed.

9. Communities

All species depend on relationships with other species for their long-term survival. A population of one species can never live in isolation. Instead, groups of populations live together. In ecology, a group of populations living together in an area and interacting with each other is known as a community. A typical community consists of hundreds or even thousands of species, including all the plants, animals, fungi and bacteria, that live together in an ecosystem.

8. Application of skills: modelling sigmoid population growth curves

Experiments can be performed to test whether the model of a sigmoid curve fits the growth of a real population. Any organism that proliferates under experimental conditions can be used, provided there are no ethical concerns.

A small number of individuals is given abundant resources and the numbers in the population are counted at regular intervals. There should be repeats so that reliability can be tested.

Floating plants such as *Lemna* (duckweed, above) can be grown on water in beakers. The water should contain supplies of nitrate, phosphate and other mineral ions needed by the plants. The beakers should be placed in bright light and warm temperatures, so conditions are initially suitable for rapid growth. The numbers of *Lemna* can easily be counted on the water surface. The experiment should be continued until one of the resources needed by the *Lemna* becomes limiting.

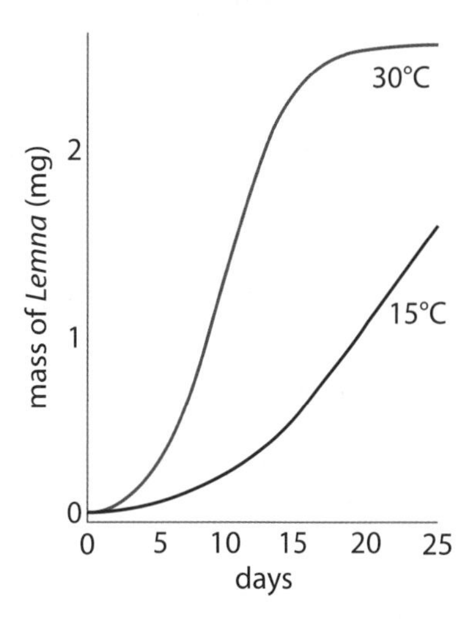

The graph shows population growth curves for *Lemna* at 30°C and 15°C.

▲ A simple experiment with Lemna growing in yoghurt pots (5 replicates)

10. Intraspecific competition and cooperation

An **intraspecific** relationship is one that exists between individuals **of the same species** and usually also within the same population. Competition and cooperation are categories of intraspecific relationship.

1. Competition

Members of a population have the same ecological niche so require the same resources. Unless a resource is abundant, there will be competition for it. Some individuals will be more successful and gain more of the resource, helping them to survive and reproduce. As a result, there is natural selection over the generations for traits that allow individuals to compete more effectively.

Examples:

- duckweed competes for light when crowded
- gannets compete for nest sites on sea cliffs (below)

- creosote bushes compete for water in their desert habitat
- waxwings compete for berries on trees in northern forests in winter.

2. Cooperation

Individuals in a population may cooperate in a variety of ways. The extent of cooperation varies, with most in social animals such as termites.

Examples:

- emperor penguin males huddle together (below) in winter on Antarctic ice to conserve body heat

- chimpanzees hunt in groups, increasing the chance of catching monkeys or other prey
- mackerel swim in tightly packed, fast-moving "bait balls" making it harder for predators to catch them
- eider duck parents take turns to care for groups of offspring of multiple parents (crèches).

Cooperative relationships have strong advantages because all individuals benefit, whereas in competitive relationships all individuals tend to be harmed to some degree.

11. Categories of interspecific relationship within communities

An **interspecific** relationship is one that exists between individuals **of different species**. Six categories of interspecific relationship are outlined below, divided into two groups.

Relationships between species not living in close association	Relationships between species living in close association
Herbivory Primary consumers feed on producers. The producer may or may not be killed. *Example*: bison feeding on grasses	**Mutualism** Two species live in a close association, with both species benefiting from the association. *Example*: zooxanthellae in hard corals
Predation One consumer species (the predator) kills and eats another consumer species (the prey). *Example*: anteaters feeding on ants	**Pathogenicity** One species (the pathogen) lives inside another species (the host) and causes a disease in the host. *Example*: anthrax bacteria in kudu (African antelope)
Interspecific competition Two or more species use the same resource, with the amount taken by one species reducing the amount available to the other species. *Example*: ivy competing with oaks	**Parasitism** One species (the parasite) lives in or on another species (the host) and obtains food from them. The host is harmed and the parasite benefits. *Example*: black-legged ticks on white-tailed deer

12. Mutualism

Mutualisms are close associations between species, where both species benefit. In many cases, the two species are from different taxonomic kingdoms so they have different capabilities and supply different services. Three examples are described here.

Root nodules in Fabaceae (legumes)	Mycorrhizae in orchids (Orchidaceae)	Zooxanthellae in hard corals
Many plants in the pea and bean family form a mutualistic relationship with *Rhizobium* bacteria. The plant grows a root nodule in which the bacteria can safely live. The plant provides sugars and a low oxygen environment which allows *Rhizobium* to convert nitrogen gas into ammonium ions (NH_4^+), some of which are supplied to the plant, promoting growth in low-nitrogen soils.	The hyphae of *Russula* and other mycorrhizal fungi grow into the roots of orchids and penetrate root cell walls but not the plasma membrane. The fungus acts like an extension to the root system, absorbing water and mineral nutrients and passing them to the orchid. The orchid supplies the fungus with sugars and other carbon compounds made by photosynthesis.	The cells of most reef-building hard corals contain zooxanthellae, which are algae that were absorbed from the seawater. The zooxanthellae are in a safe environment and gain CO_2 from aerobic respiration of the coral cells. They use this in photosynthesis. The coral cells gain oxygen and carbon compounds such as glucose and amino acids produced by this photosynthesis.

13. Invasive species compete with endemic species

Species that occur naturally in an area are **endemic**. Species that were introduced by humans, deliberately or accidentally, are **alien**. Density-dependent factors (see *Section C4.1.6*) usually regulate the population size of endemic species. However, many alien species are not effectively regulated, because the pests or predators that would control them in their native habitat are absent in their new habitat. If an alien species increases in number and spreads rapidly, it is **invasive**.

Invasive species can have devastating impacts on communities. The competitive exclusion principle (see *Section B4.2.13*) predicts that two species cannot occupy the same ecological niche indefinitely. Alien species compete for resources with endemic species that have the same or overlapping ecological niches. To become invasive, an alien species must be successful in the competition for resources with endemic species. As a result, the endemic species may occupy a smaller realized niche, causing a decline in population, or lose its niche entirely and become extinct in an area. This is currently a widespread phenomenon because humans transport high numbers of species to new areas, where there are no limiting factors (or not enough) to control the populations of alien species.

▲ Red lionfish are endemic to coastal seas in parts of the Indo-Pacific. Because of their spectacular appearance they are kept in aquariums. Small numbers escaped from an aquarium during Hurricane Andrew in 1992 and have since multiplied and spread on coral reefs in Florida and the Caribbean, helped by a lack of predators adapted to avoid the venomous spines. Red lionfish compete for prey with endemic fish species by establishing territories from which the other fish are aggressively excluded.

14. Investigating interspecific competition

A range of approaches can be used to test for interspecific competition between species in a community that require the same resource.

1. Field manipulation can be used. For example, one of two species could be removed from quadrats in grassland. There is evidence of interspecific competition if the other species then increases in number or biomass.
2. Laboratory experiments can be performed, under controlled conditions. Species can be grown together and apart to investigate whether they compete for resources.
3. Tests for association between species can be carried out by random sampling. The procedures are described in *Section C4.1.15*.

NOS

Observations and experiments

Hypotheses can be tested by both experiments and observations. A key difference is that in experiments, the scientist intervenes to change or control conditions. With observational approaches, the scientist avoids changing conditions and instead looks at natural phenomena.

15. Application of skills: chi-squared tests for association between species

Quadrat sampling (described in *Section C4.1.3*) is used to investigate species distributions. The chi-squared test is used to test for association—are two species found in the same quadrats, different quadrats or are they randomly distributed?

1. Define the two alternative hypotheses:

   H_0: two species are distributed independently (This is the null hypothesis)

   H_1: two species are associated.

2. Draw up a contingency table of observed frequencies (the numbers of quadrats containing and not containing the species).

	Species A present	Species A absent	Row totals
Species B present			
Species B absent			
Column totals			

   Calculate row and column totals. Adding the row or column totals should give the same grand total in the lower right cell of the table.

3. Calculate the expected frequencies for the four species combinations, assuming independent distribution.

$$\text{expected frequency} = \frac{\text{row total} \times \text{column total}}{\text{grand total}}$$

4. Calculate the number of degrees of freedom (df):

   df = $(m-1)(n-1)$, where m and n are the number of rows and number of columns in the contingency table.

5. Find the critical region, using a table of chi-squared values and $p = 0.05$ (5%).

   If df = 1, the critical region is 3.83 or larger.

6. Calculate chi-squared using this equation:

$$X^2 = \sum \frac{(f_o - f_e)^2}{f_e}$$

   where f_o is the observed frequency, f_e is the expected frequency and $\sum$ is "the sum of".

7. If the calculated value of chi-squared is in the critical region, there is evidence at the 5% level for an association between the two species and we can reject the null hypothesis H_0. The species are either found together more frequently or less frequently than if they were randomly distributed. Species that tend to occur together in quadrats may have the same habitat requirements or have an interspecific relationship that encourages co-location. Species that tend to occur in different quadrats may be competing for resources or may have different habitat requirements.

Skill in applying the chi-squared test for association can be developed by answering question 2 on page 214.

16. Density-dependent control of animal populations by predator–prey relationships

Predators kill and consume prey, but in many communities, the population of prey does not change much overall, because new prey individuals are born at about the same rate as they are lost due to predation. Similarly, the birth and death rates of the predator are approximately equal, so the predator population remains stable. Some communities do not show this dynamic equilibrium and instead there are cyclical oscillations in numbers of prey and predators, due to four types of density-dependent interaction:

A rise in prey numbers increases prey availability, so predator numbers rise.	A rise in predator numbers increases predation, so prey numbers fall.
A fall in prey numbers decreases prey availability, so predator numbers fall.	A fall in predator numbers decreases predation, so prey numbers rise.

Case study—red fox (predator) and mountain hare (prey)

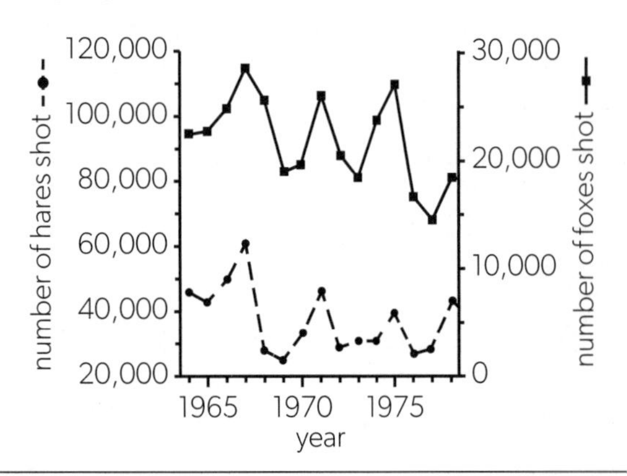

The graph shows numbers of red foxes and mountain hares shot by hunters in Sweden. The values give a measure of the relative size of the populations, because hunters' success depends on the abundance of their target species. Four cycles of population rises and falls occurred between 1964 and 1980. Cyclical oscillations in predator and prey populations are mostly seen in habitats where weather conditions vary from year to year. In northern zones, a warmer than average spring and summer causes more plant growth than normal. This provides extra food for herbivores such as mountain hares, so their numbers rise. This triggers a cycle of rising and falling predator and prey numbers in the following years.

17. Control of populations in communities

Interactions between trophic levels in a food chain are the basis for population control in many communities. There are direct interactions, for example, when predators feed on prey or herbivores feed on producers. There are also indirect interactions. For example, if a herbivore population decreases due to a population increase of its predator, there may be a population increase in the producer the herbivore eats. Within a food chain, these interactions can operate in two directions:

- Top-down control acts from a higher trophic level to a lower one. For example, an increase in predator numbers will decrease the numbers of prey in lower trophic levels.
- Bottom-up control acts from a lower trophic level to a higher one. For example, a population of producers may be limited by the availability of mineral nutrients in the soil or in water.

Communities vary in whether more populations are controlled by top-down or bottom-up interactions.

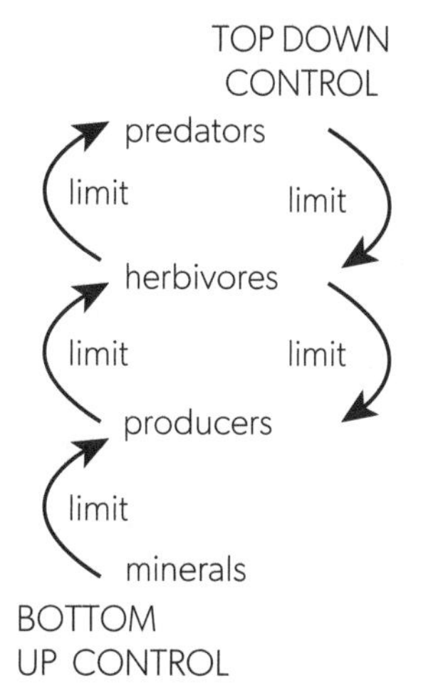

18. Antibiotics and allelopathic agents

Antibiotics and allelopathic agents are secondary metabolites. A secondary metabolite is a substance produced by a pathway that only exists in some taxonomic groups. Such substances are not essential for cell growth and instead have a wide range of other functions. Antibiotics and allelopathic agents are two functional groups of secondary metabolites. Another functional group is described in *Section B4.2.9*, together with the distinction between primary and secondary metabolites. Both antibiotics and allelopathic agents are released into the environment, where they are toxic to other organisms and deter potential competitors.

Antibiotics are secreted by microorganisms to kill, inhibit or prevent the growth of other species of microorganism.

Penicillium is a genus of fungi that inhabit natural habitats such as soil, but also fruit, bread, cheese and other foods. *Penicillium* fungi are saprotrophic (see *Section B4.2.6*). A risk for saprotrophic fungi is that the foods they digest may be absorbed by bacteria living in the same habitat. Some species of *Penicillium* secrete the antibiotic penicillin to reduce this competition. Penicillin interferes with cross-linking of peptidoglycan molecules in the cell walls of Gram-positive bacteria. This causes the walls to become weak so the bacteria eventually burst and die. Production of penicillin requires resources so *Penicillium* only secretes it when supplies of food are scarce.

Allelopathic agents are secreted into the soil by plants to kill or deter the growth of neighbouring plants. This can result in bare areas of soil near the secreting plant, reducing competition for water or mineral ions.

Ailanthus altissima (tree of heaven), is native to China, but has become an invasive species across North America. It releases the secondary metabolite ailanthone into the soil, which inhibits the germination, growth and survival of other tree species for up to 5 m from the trunk of the *Ailanthus*.

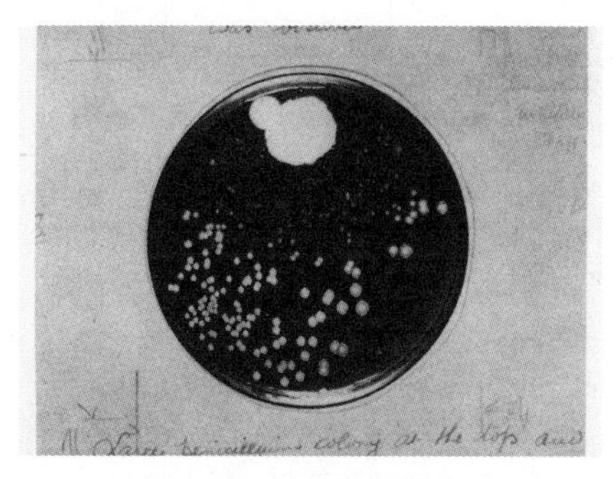

▲ This is the original Petri dish on which Alexander Fleming first observed inhibition of bacteria by the antibiotic penicillin. Fleming inoculated the dish with *Staphylococcus aureus* bacteria, which formed colonies on the surface of the gel in the dish. When he left the dish open, spores of *Penicillium* fungus entered and grew to form a large fungal mycelium (visible at the top). Over the following hours, bacterial colonies near to the fungus degenerated due to the release of penicillin and its diffusion through the gel in the dish.

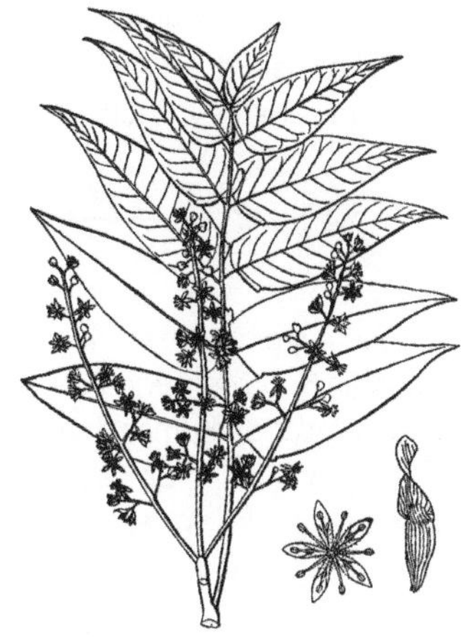

▲ Leaves and flower of *Ailanthus altissima*

C4.2 Transfers of energy and matter

1. Energy and matter can enter and exit ecosystems

Living organisms cannot live alone. They depend on interactions with other organisms for supplies of energy and chemical resources. They also depend on their abiotic surroundings of air, water, soil and rock.

Biologists have developed the concept of **ecosystems**, which are ecological systems such as a lake or a forest. An ecosystem is composed of all the organisms in an area together with their abiotic environment.

Systems are an important concept in biology. A system is a set of interacting or interdependent components. There are two main types of system:

- open systems where resources can enter or exit, including both chemical substances and energy
- closed systems where energy can enter or exit, but chemical resources cannot be removed or replaced.

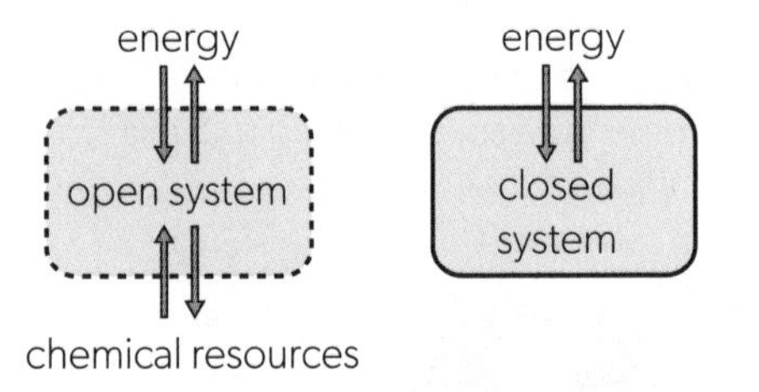

2. Sunlight sustains most ecosystems

Organisms that use an external energy source to make carbon compounds are **producers**. Energy fixed by producers in carbon compounds is available to other organisms, so sustains the whole ecosystem.

The principal source of energy in most ecosystems is sunlight and the process used by producers to make carbon compounds is photosynthesis. Three groups of organism that carry out photosynthesis are described in *Section B4.2.3*.

There are ecosystems where little or no light penetrates, for example caves and in oceans at depths greater than 200 m. Some energy may pass to these ecosystems in dead organic matter transferred from other ecosystems, which can be digested by saprotrophs. Another source of energy is inorganic chemical reactions, which chemoautotrophs use. This mode of nutrition is described in *Section B4.2.7*. In sealed caves, this is the only energy source for an ecosystem.

NOS Theories

The term **law** is sometimes used in science for statements that describe natural phenomena and allow predictions to be made about them without offering an explanation. In contrast, a theory provides an explanation. Both laws and theories can be used to make predictions.

Laws are rare in biology because statements usually explain aspects of the living world. For example, the statement that sunlight is the principal source of energy for ecosystems is a theory rather than a law.

3. Chemical energy flows through food chains

A food chain is a sequence of organisms (usually between two and five), each of which feeds on the previous organism. Producers are the first organisms in a typical food chain because they do not need to feed on another organism; they use an external energy source instead to make all the carbon compounds they require from simple inorganic substances such as CO_2. The other organisms in a food chain are **consumers**. They obtain chemical energy from carbon compounds in the organisms on which they feed. Primary consumers feed on producers; secondary consumers feed on primary consumers; tertiary consumers feed on secondary consumers, and so on. The last organism in a food chain is not fed on. Chemical energy thus flows along a food chain from organism to organism. Arrows are used to indicate the direction of energy flow.

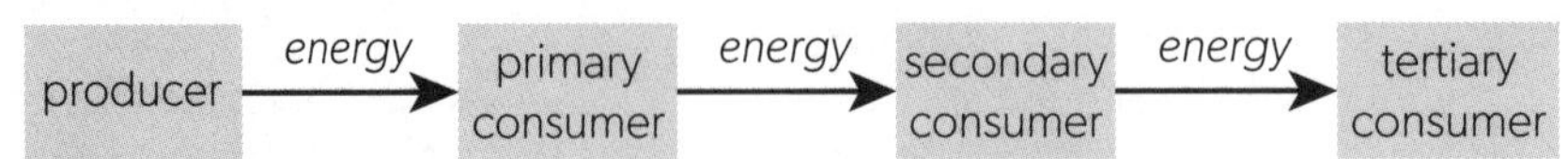

In any ecosystem, there are many specific food chains that provide organisms with a supply of energy. For example, in the Monte Desert (in South America), leaves of a shrub with the local name of tara (*Senna arnottiana*) are eaten by guanaco (*Lama guanicoe*). Pumas (*Puma concolor*) are predators of the guanaco. They are regarded as apex predators because nothing kills or eats them, though fleas and other parasites can obtain energy from them by feeding on their blood.

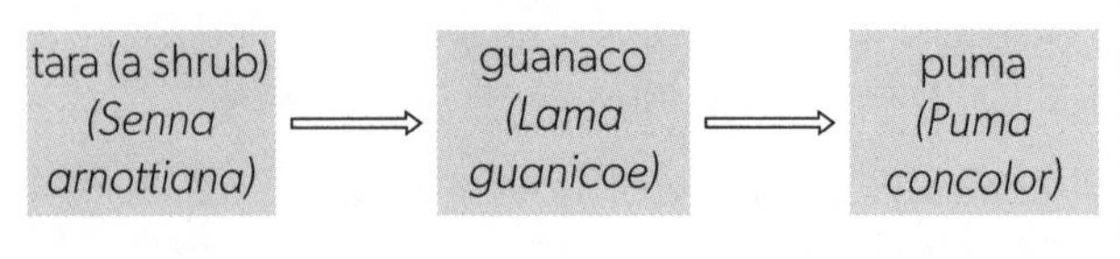

4. Food chains and food webs

Feeding relationships within ecological communities tend to be complex and web-like. This is because many consumers feed on more than one species and are fed upon by more than one species. A food web is a model that summarizes all of the possible food chains in a community. Arrows indicate the direction of transfer of energy and biomass.

When a food web is constructed, organisms at the same trophic level are often shown at the same level in the web. However, this is not always possible because some organisms feed at more than one trophic level. A generalized food web is shown right. Real food webs are far more complicated with many more organisms and links.

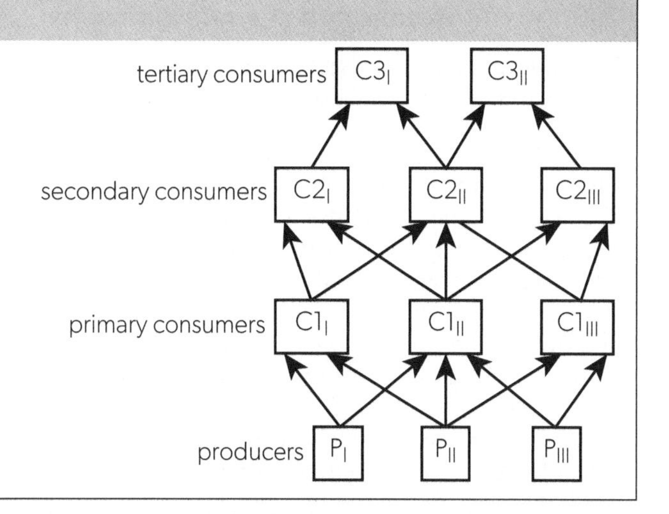

5. Decomposers

Dead organic matter is generated by these processes:

- death of whole organisms
- defecation (removal of faeces from the gut)
- shedding of leaves, skin cells, hairs, arthropod exoskeletons (moulting) and other unwanted body parts.

Dead organic matter contains chemical energy in carbon compounds.

Some dead organic matter is eaten by animals such as earthworms and vultures, but large amounts are digested by **saprotrophs**. This process is described in *Section B4.2.6*. Dead organic matter supplies saprotrophs with amino acids, glucose and other carbon compounds, which are used for growth and also as a source of energy, which is released by cell respiration.

Saprotrophic bacteria and fungi are **decomposers** because they break down insoluble macromolecules in dead organic matter into small, soluble molecules and ions. By doing this, they cause the gradual breakdown of solid structures. For example, a tree trunk on the forest floor will gradually soften and crumble away and fallen leaves disappear.

Without extracellular digestion carried out by decomposers, dead organic matter would build up year by year. Also ions such as ammonium (NH_4^+) would not be released into the abiotic environment, so other organisms that absorb them would lose their supply. Decomposers are the waste disposers and recyclers of ecosystems.

6. Autotrophs

All organisms need a variety of carbon compounds. Some organisms make all of these carbon compounds themselves, using carbon dioxide (CO_2) or hydrogen carbonate (HCO_3^-) as a carbon source. Organisms that do this are called **autotrophs**, meaning self-feeding. A reduction reaction inside autotrophic cells converts the simple inorganic carbon sources into an initial carbon compound. This process is carbon fixation (HL see *Section C1.3.15*). The initial carbon compound produced by carbon fixation is then built up into a wide variety of other carbon compounds by **anabolic reactions** (see *Section C1.1.3*).

Carbon fixation and anabolic reactions in autotrophs require an external energy source. The two possible sources of external energy are inorganic chemical reactions and light.

21. Interdependence of photosynthesis and respiration

The diagram shows how autotrophs and heterotrophs are dependent on each other for supplies of oxygen and carbon dioxide. Autotrophs split water molecules during photosynthesis and release oxygen from them into the atmosphere. This process is described for HL in *Section C1.3.11*. Heterotrophs absorb oxygen produced in photosynthesis and use it to oxidize carbon compounds, producing carbon dioxide and releasing it into the atmosphere. Autotrophs absorb the carbon dioxide and use it in photosynthesis.

Global carbon fluxes are extremely large so estimates are in gigatonnes (10^{15} grams). In terrestrial ecosystems approximately 120 gigatonnes of carbon are fixed by photosynthesis per year and nearly 120 gigatonnes are released by respiration.

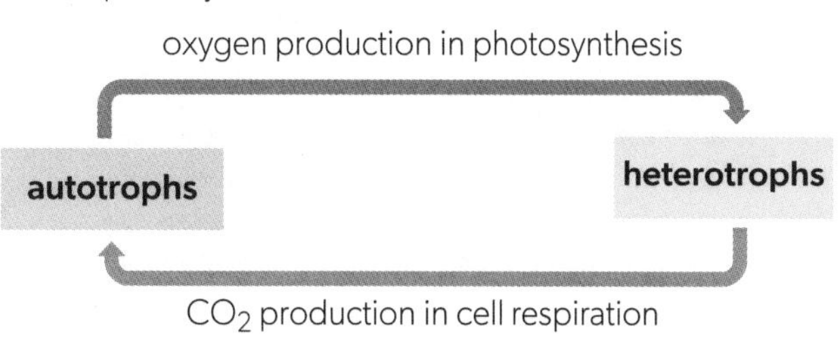

7. Photoautotrophs and chemoautotrophs

Photoautotrophs use sunlight to make carbon compounds by photosynthesis. This is described in *Section B4.2.3* and *Topic C1.3*.

Chemoautotrophs use exothermic inorganic chemical reactions. A substrate in a reduced state, such as sulfur, hydrogen sulfide, iron, hydrogen or ammonia, is absorbed and then oxidized. Oxidation reactions release energy. Chemoautotrophs use the energy from the oxidation reaction to synthesize carbon compounds, such as sugars and amino acids. Two of the three domains contain chemoautotrophs: bacteria and archaea. Iron-oxidizing bacteria are an example, such as *Acidithiobacillus ferrooxidans*.

Iron-oxidizing bacteria absorb Fe^{2+} ions from the environment and remove an electron from them. Because this is an oxidation reaction, the electron is excited (carries extra energy).

$$Fe^{2+} \rightarrow Fe^{3+} + \text{electron (excited)}$$

The excited electrons are accepted by chains of electron carriers in the plasma membrane of the iron-oxidizing bacterium. Energy is released as the electrons flow along these chains. Some electrons flow to proton pumps and their energy is used to build a proton gradient that is then used for ATP production by chemiosmosis. Other excited electrons are passed to NAD, converting it to reduced NAD.

Reduced NAD and ATP can then be used to fix carbon dioxide and produce carbon compounds by reactions similar to those of photosynthesis.

8. Heterotrophs

Many organisms obtain carbon compounds from other organisms. These organisms are **heterotrophic**, which means they feed on others. They digest carbon compounds that were part of another organism and then use the products of digestion to build the large complex carbon compounds they need. For example, guanacos digest proteins in the leaves of tara bushes (see *Section C4.2.3*), breaking them down into amino acids. Then they use these amino acids to synthesize the proteins they (the guanacos) need. The process of absorbing carbon compounds and making them part of the body is called assimilation. Assimilation requires absorption of carbon compounds into cells, so the molecules must be small and soluble enough to pass across cell membranes. Proteins, polysaccharides, nucleic acids and other large compounds must be digested before they can be absorbed.

Heterotrophs are subdivided according to whether they digest food internally or externally.

- **Saprotrophs** grow into or across the surface of food and secrete hydrolytic enzymes to digest the food externally.
- **Consumers** ingest their food.
  - Multicellular consumers take food into their gut by swallowing it (see *Section B4.2.4*). Then they mix the food with enzymes from digestive glands. This is regarded as internal digestion although the food has not yet entered any cells.
  - Unicellular consumers such as *Paramecium* take the food into their cells by endocytosis, then digest it inside phagocytic vacuoles. They absorb products of digestion from the vacuoles into their cytoplasm.

9. Release of energy by cell respiration

All organisms require supplies of energy in the form of ATP in their cells. They use the energy for the following four processes:

- anabolic reactions to synthesize molecules such as proteins, polysaccharides, triglycerides and nucleic acids
- active transport to generate concentration gradients
- movement of vesicles and other structures inside cells; movement of whole organisms (locomotion) and of blood and other fluids in organisms due to muscle contraction.
- maintaining constant body temperature (birds and mammals).

In both autotrophs and heterotrophs, ATP is produced by cell respiration. Carbon compounds such as carbohydrates and lipids are oxidized to release energy and this energy is used to phosphorylate ADP, producing ATP.

10. Grouping organisms into trophic levels

Ecologists classify organisms into groups according to how they obtain energy and carbon compounds and therefore where they are positioned in food chains. These groups are called trophic levels.

Trophic level	Food	Food chain
Producers	(autotrophic)	1st place
Primary consumers	producers	2nd place
Secondary consumers	1st consumers	3rd place
Tertiary consumers	2nd consumers	4th place

Many consumers have a varied diet and occupy different trophic levels in different food chains. For example, red foxes (*Vulpes vulpes*) mostly eat primary consumers, making them secondary consumers. However, they also eat some leaves and other plant organs, making them primary consumers.

11. Application of skills: constructing energy pyramids

A pyramid of energy is a type of bar chart with a horizontal bar for each trophic level. It shows the amount of energy gained per year by each trophic level in an ecosystem. Differences between the length of bars show the amount of energy lost between one trophic level and the next.

- Amounts of energy are measured per unit area and per year. The units are often kilojoules per metre squared per year (kJ m^{-2} yr^{-1}).
- Pyramids of energy should be stepped, not triangular, with producers in the lowest bar.
- Bars should be labelled producer, primary consumer, secondary consumer, and so on.
- If a suitable scale is used, the length of each bar can be proportional to the amount of energy that it shows.

Energy pyramid for grassland, drawn to scale:

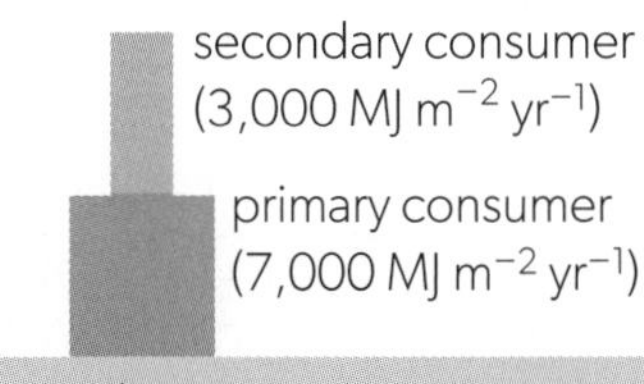

12. Energy is lost between trophic levels

In any ecosystem, there are large energy losses between trophic levels. The losses vary and are not always 90%. There are three main forms of energy loss from food chains.

1. **Incomplete consumption**

   Some organisms are never consumed and instead they eventually die. Energy in dead organisms, or dead parts of organisms, passes to saprotrophs or detritus-feeders (e.g. earthworms), which are not part of food chains.

2. **Incomplete digestion**

   Not all substances in food are digested. For example, some animals cannot digest cellulose. Indigestible material is egested in faeces and the energy passes to saprotrophs.

3. **Cell respiration**

   Substrates are oxidized to carbon dioxide and water to release energy from them, which is used by the respiring organism. Carbon compounds that have been oxidized in respiration cannot pass to the next trophic level and the energy that they contained is lost from the food chain.

Biomass is also lost between trophic levels so organisms in higher trophic levels do not need to eat a greater mass of food to gain enough energy.

13. Heat loss to the environment

Energy transfers are never 100% efficient, so when energy is released by oxidizing substrates in cell respiration, some of the energy is converted to heat. When the ATP is used within cells, more of the energy is converted to heat. Both autotrophs and heterotrophs generate heat in this way. Ultimately all of the energy that enters food chains is transformed into heat and lost to the abiotic environment. For this reason, energy flows through food chains and cannot be recycled (unlike chemical elements).

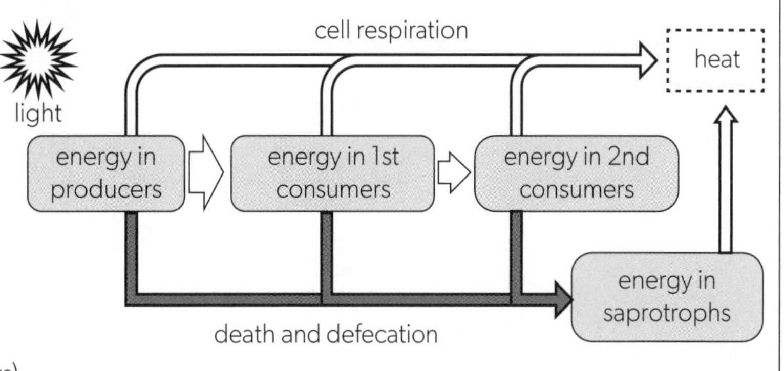

14. Limited length of food chains

Food chains are limited in length because so much energy is lost between each trophic level and the next. After only a few stages, not enough energy remains to support another trophic level. For this reason the number of trophic levels in ecosystems is restricted to a maximum of four or five.

Animals in higher trophic levels do not have to eat more food to gain enough energy. Their prey contains large amounts of energy per unit mass—there just is not much prey available. A condor for example is mainly a tertiary consumer and may need a territory of more than 10,000 km^2 to find enough to eat.

▲ California condor *(Gymnogyps californianus)* with an identification tag on its wing

15. Primary production

Production in ecosystems is the accumulation of carbon compounds in biomass. Both autotrophs and heterotrophs produce biomass by growth and reproduction.

- **Primary production** is mass of carbon compounds synthesized from CO_2 and other simple substances by autotrophs (producers). The units of measurement are usually grams of carbon accumulated per square metre of ecosystem per year (g C m^{-2} yr^{-1}).
- **Gross primary production** (GPP) is the total biomass of carbon compounds made by plants (and other autotrophs).
- **Net primary production** is GPP minus the biomass lost due to respiration of the plant. It is the amount of biomass available to consumers.

Biomes vary in their capacity to accumulate biomass, depending mainly on rates of photosynthesis.

16. Secondary production

Animals and other heterotrophs (consumers) obtain carbon compounds such as sugars and amino acids from organisms in a lower trophic level and use them in growth and reproduction. This results in an increase in biomass.

Secondary production is accumulation of carbon compounds in biomass by consumers.

Carbon compounds are used as respiratory substrates by all organisms. Cell respiration results in a loss of carbon compounds and therefore biomass in every trophic level.

These are the consequences for ecosystems:

- secondary production is lower than primary production
- net secondary production is lower than gross secondary production in every trophic level of consumers
- secondary production declines with each successive trophic level from primary consumers onwards.

17. The carbon cycle

The arrows in this carbon cycle diagram are **fluxes** which are transfers of the element from one pool to another. Three types of carbon flux are due to living organisms.

1. Photosynthesis—absorption of CO_2 from air or water and its conversion to carbon compounds
2. Feeding—gaining carbon compounds from other organisms
3. Respiration—release to the atmosphere of CO_2 produced by respiring cells.

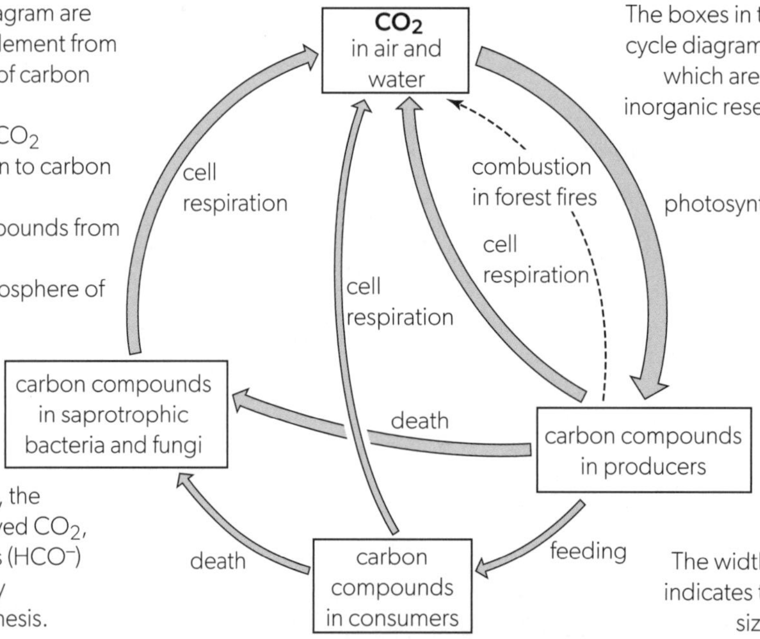

The boxes in this carbon cycle diagram are **pools** which are organic or inorganic reserves of the element.

CO_2 in air and water

cell respiration

combustion in forest fires

photosynthesis

cell respiration

cell respiration

carbon compounds in saprotrophic bacteria and fungi

death

carbon compounds in producers

death

carbon compounds in consumers

feeding

In marine and aquatic ecosystems, the inorganic pool of carbon is dissolved CO_2, and also hydrogen carbonate ions (HCO^{-}) both of which can be absorbed by producers and used in photosynthesis.

The width of arrows indicates the relative size of fluxes.

18. Carbon sinks and carbon sources

Ecosystems are open systems because both matter and energy can enter or exit.
Carbon enters and exits in the form of carbon dioxide, through photosynthesis and respiration.
The rates of these processes for an ecosystem as a whole are not always equal.

If photosynthesis exceeds respiration, there is net uptake of carbon. The ecosystem is acting as a **carbon sink**. This happens in growing forests and also in waterlogged habitats (bogs or swamps) where anaerobic and acidic conditions prevent decomposition of dead organic matter by saprotrophs, so peat containing carbon accumulates.

If respiration exceeds photosynthesis, there is net release. The ecosystem is acting as a **carbon source**. This happens if peatlands are drained and the peat decomposes. Fires in forests and other ecosystems cause release of CO_2 by combustion of carbon compounds in living organisms and dead organic matter. The ecosystem therefore becomes a carbon source.

19. Release of carbon dioxide from combustion

Ecosystems can act as carbon sinks by accumulating biomass. Forests can store over 5,000 tonnes of biomass per hectare. Carbon atoms may remain sequestered in the wood of trees for hundreds of years. Peat formed in wetland ecosystems can store carbon for thousands of years. Dead organic matter has been converted to coal, oil and natural gas at different times in the Earth's history and the carbon in these sinks can remain sequestered for many millions of years.

When carbon compounds burn in air, carbon dioxide is produced and released into the atmosphere. Fires are natural and frequent in some ecosystems, ignited by lightning strikes.

In recent years, there have been increasingly frequent fires in areas of tundra located inside the Arctic Circle. Combustion of peat, accumulated over thousands of years, has released large quantities of carbon dioxide. Most coal, oil and natural gas is deeply buried and so cannot burn due to a lack of oxygen. Humans have developed methods of extracting these materials and burning them as an energy source. Since the start of the Industrial Revolution (late 18th century onwards), the rate of extraction and combustion of fossil fuels has risen rapidly and huge quantities of carbon dioxide have been released into the atmosphere.

20. The Keeling Curve

Since 1959, atmospheric carbon dioxide concentrations have been measured at Mauna Loa Observatory in Hawaii. Graphs of the results (Keeling Curve) show two trends:

1. **Annual fluctuations**

   CO_2 concentration increases between October and May and then falls from May to October, due to global imbalances in rates of CO_2 fixation by photosynthesis and release due to respiration. There is relatively more photosynthesis during summer in the northern hemisphere, when plants over most of the Earth's land surface are in their growth season, and relatively more respiration during the northern hemisphere winter.

2. **Long-term trend**

   The graph of carbon dioxide concentrations for one year shows that the increase is not completely reversed by the decrease, so the concentration at the end of the year is higher. This is also shown by the full Keeling curve, from 1959 onwards. This trend is largely due to burning of fossil fuels by humans, together with other anthropogenic factors such as deforestation.

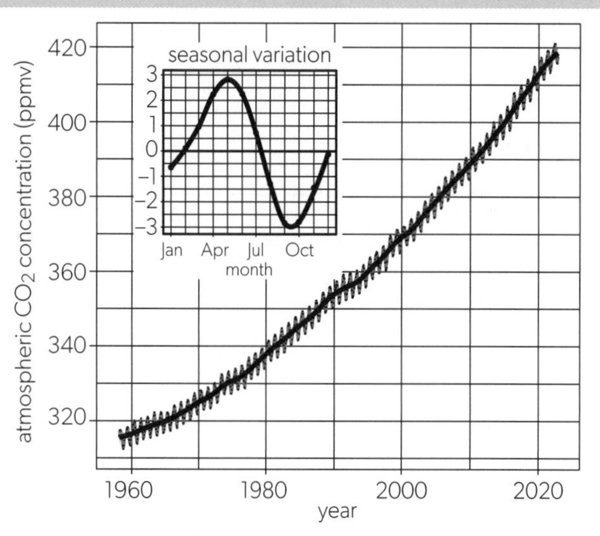

▲ The Keeling Curve is named after US scientist Charles Keeling, who developed a system for accurately measuring carbon dioxide concentrations in air. In 1958 he started a monitoring project at Mauna Loa observatory on Hawaii, which continues to this day. The smoother curve on the graph shows annual mean atmospheric CO_2 concentration and the fluctuating curve shows monthly means.

22. Recycling in ecosystems

Living organisms contain large amounts of C, H, O, N and P in their molecules. About 15 other elements have roles in living organisms. The quantities of each element are finite on Earth, but despite living organisms using them for three billion years, no element has run out. This is because all elements can be endlessly recycled. They are absorbed from the abiotic environment as inorganic ions or molecules, used within living organisms and then returned to the abiotic environment with the atomic structure unchanged. Autotrophs obtain all elements they need as inorganic nutrients from the abiotic environment, including C and N. Heterotrophs obtain these two elements and several others as part of the carbon compounds in their food. They obtain some other elements as inorganic nutrients from the abiotic environment, including Na^+, K^+ and Ca^{2+}. Decomposers play a key role in recycling because as a consequence of their saprotrophic nutrition (see *Sections B4.2.6* and *C4.2.5*) they digest carbon compounds and return elements from them to the abiotic environment. All elements needed by plants are in the first four periods of the periodic table.

H																	
												B	C	N	O		
Na	Mg												Si	P	S	Cl	
K	Ca					Mn	Fe	Co	Ni	Cu	Zn				Se		
					Mo												

End of topic questions — C4 Questions

C4.1 Populations and communities

1. The following graph shows the growth of a population of ring-necked pheasants (*Phasianus colchicus*) on Protection Island off the north-west coast of the United States of America. The original population released by the scientists consisted of two male and eight female birds, but two females died before breeding.

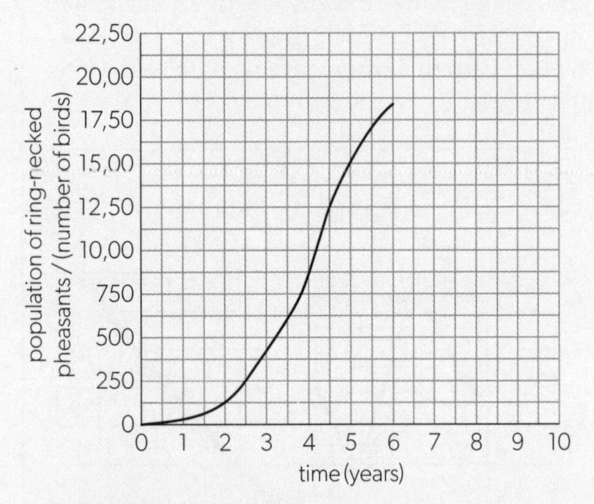

a. State the term used to describe the shape of a growth curve of this type. (1)

b. i. Distinguish between the phases of the growth curve before and after 4.5 years. (2)

ii. Explain the difference between these two phases in terms of the processes that can increase or decrease the size of a population. (4)

c. Explain how to replot the graph to test whether population increase is exponential. (2)

d. i. The scientists predicted that the population would reach its carrying capacity of 2,000 by Year 8. Draw a line on the graph to show the population growth between Years 6 and 10. (1)

ii. Suggest factors that could cause the plateau. (3)

e. Discuss whether the outcomes would have been different if all of the eight females released had survived. (2)

2. The table shows the presence or absence of two plants in 20 quadrats in a lawn.

		Lotus corniculatus	
		✓	×
Hypochoeris radicata	✓	11	2
	×	1	6

Deduce whether there is an association between the two species using the chi-squared test. (10)

3. Compare and contrast:

a. populations and communities (3)

b. mutualism and parasitism (3)

c. predators and pathogens (4)

d. allelopathic compounds and antibiotics. (5)

C4.2 Transfers of energy and matter

1. The diagram below shows (in simplified form) the transfers of energy in a generalized ecosystem. A box represents a category of organisms, grouped together by their trophic level in the ecosystem.

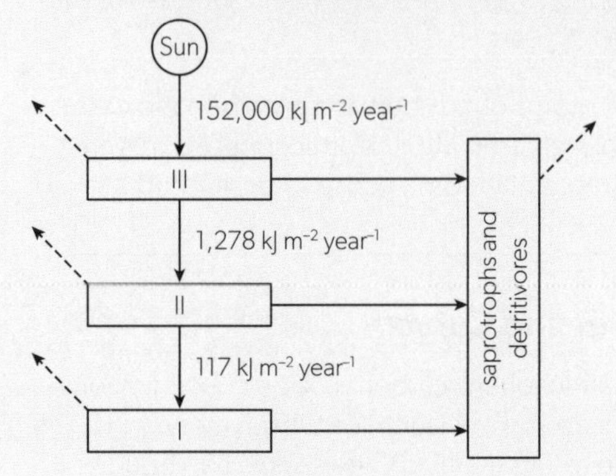

a. Deduce trophic levels I, II and III. (3)

b. State the form of energy entering box I. (1)

c. Explain what the dotted arrows indicate. (3)

d. The amount of energy flowing to each trophic level in a salt marsh ecosystem is indicated. Construct an energy pyramid for the salt marsh using these values. (4)

e. Calculate the percentage of energy received by 1st consumers that flows on to 2nd consumers. (2)

2. The graph shows the Keeling Curve for 2019–23.

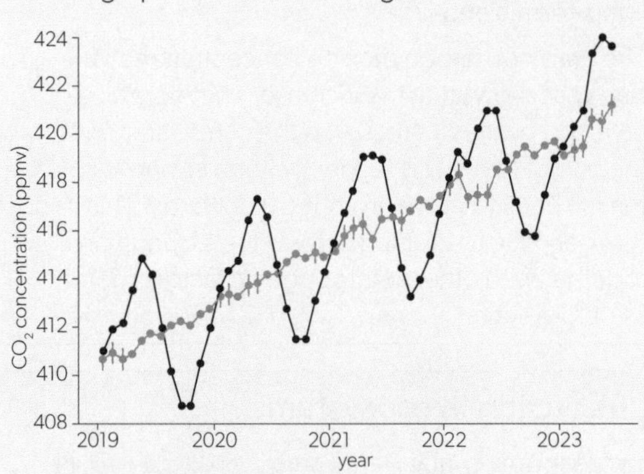

a. Estimate the seasonal variation in CO_2. (1)

b. Explain the falls in CO_2 concentration from May to October and rises from November to April. (4)

c. CO_2 concentration is higher every year.

i. Calculate the mean annual increase. (2)

ii. Predict the level in 2050 if the rate of increase remains the same. (3)

iii. Explain the increases in CO_2 concentration. (3)

3. a. Suggest processes which show that ecosystems are open systems. (3)

b. Explain reasons for recycling of elements being possible in ecosystems but not energy. (4)

c. Outline the reasons for food chains having a limited number of stages. (3)

D4.1 Natural selection

1. Natural selection

The theory of evolution by natural selection can be explained using the following series of statements.

- Organisms produce more offspring than the environment can support.
- Among these offspring, there is variation.
- Some variants are better suited to the environment and have a higher chance of surviving to reproductive age. Less fit (less well-adapted) variants have a higher risk of mortality from predation or other factors. This is sometimes called survival of the fittest.
- The features that aid survival are disproportionately inherited by successful offspring. These features therefore increase in frequency in the population. The heritable features of the population have changed, so it has evolved.

Evolution by natural selection, over the billions of years that life has existed, has resulted in the immense biodiversity now present on Earth.

NOS

Theories

Charles Darwin's grandfather Erasmus understood that species evolve, so this idea was not new when Darwin published *On the Origin of Species* in 1859. Instead, the revolution in understanding was natural selection as a mechanism for evolution. It is an example of a paradigm shift, with a new theory replacing an older one. The older theory was Lamarckism (explained in *Section A4.1.1*).

▲ Charles Darwin, aged 51, when he published *On the Origin of Species*

2. Variation is driven by mutation and sexual reproduction

Natural selection can only occur if there is variation within a population, so some variants decrease in frequency and others increase. The origins of variation in populations are well understood.

1. **Mutation** is the original source of variation. New alleles are produced by mutation, which enlarges the gene pool of a population.
2. **Sexual reproduction** generates variation in two stages:
   (a) **Meiosis** produces new combinations of alleles, by breaking up the existing combination in the diploid cells of a parent to produce haploid cells with only one allele of each gene. Because of crossing over and the independent orientation of bivalents, every cell produced by meiosis in an individual is likely to carry a different combination of alleles.
   (b) **Fertilization** (the fusion of male and female gametes) brings together gametes that usually come from different parents, so offspring have a combination of alleles from two individuals. This allows mutations that occurred in different individuals to be brought together.

3. Factors that promote natural selection

Living organisms vary in the number of offspring they produce but there is an overall trend for more offspring to be produced than can be supported by the available resources.

The population size that can be supported is the carrying capacity of the environment (described in *Sections C4.1.5* and *C4.1.6*). It is determined by the limiting resource that is in shortest supply. This is likely to be water for a plant species in a desert, for example, or light in a rainforest. For an animal species it is often food.

Darwin pointed out that overproduction of offspring results in a struggle for existence within a population. There is competition for resources and not every individual will obtain enough to allow them to survive and reproduce.

6. Evolutionary change relies on heritable traits

Traits of fitter individuals can only be passed on to offspring if they are coded for in the base sequences of genes and are therefore heritable.

Living organisms acquire characteristics during their lifetimes in response to environmental factors. As these acquired characteristics are not due to changes in the base sequence of genes, they are not inherited by offspring and they cannot contribute to the evolution of a species. The requirement for traits to be heritable for evolutionary change to occur is further explored in *Section A4.1.1*.

4. Selection pressures

- Selection pressures are factors that cause some individuals in a population to have higher chances of survival and reproductive success than others.
- Selection pressures can be **biotic** or **abiotic** (see *Section B4.1.2* for the differences).
- Selection pressures can be **density-dependent** or **density-independent** (see *Section C4.1.6* for the differences).

Examples of abiotic selection pressures:

- Availability of dissolved nitrogen (NO_3^- or NH_4^+) can act as a density-dependent abiotic factor in some aquatic ecosystems. It results in bottom-up control of populations of producers (see *Section C4.1.17*). Individuals best-adapted to absorb nitrogen are able to reproduce and others die from nitrogen deficiency or fail to grow and reproduce.
- Temperature can act as a density-independent abiotic factor in some terrestrial ecosystems. For example, the chance of an individual being killed by freezing temperatures is the same whether the population density is high or low. Differences in tolerance to cold rather than competition between individuals are the basis of the selection. Similarly, deaths due to high temperature during a heat-wave or a forest fire are density independent.

▲ Shoots growing on the blackened trunk of this Eucalyptus tree shows that it survived a forest fire on Tasmania in 2019, when many trees were killed

5. The basis for natural selection

- An adaptation is a change that makes an organism better-suited to its ecological niche in an ecosystem.
- Fitness is how well-adapted an individual is. It influences whether or not an individual survives and then reproduces.
- When there is intraspecific competition (see *Section C4.1.10*), the fittest individuals tend to survive longest and have the most offspring. The traits of the fittest individuals are thus passed on to the next generation, rather than those of less fit individuals who produce fewer offspring.
- Differences in survival and reproduction due to differences in fitness are thus the basis of natural selection.

7. Sexual selection

A well-adapted individual can increase the chance of their offspring also being well-adapted and successful by choosing a mate who is also well-adapted. Mate selection is not possible in plants which do not control the movement of male gametes. It is possible in animal species with internal fertilization after copulation, such as birds and mammals. The fitness of a potential mate can be assessed during a process known as **sexual selection**.

In some species, the criteria for sexual selection are obvious, for example the ability of a male to overpower other males by fighting. In other species, the rationale is less obvious. Some animals, such as birds of paradise have physical and behavioural traits that seem bizarre, but can be explained.

Sexual selection in birds of paradise

The ribbon-tailed astrapia is one of about 40 species of bird of paradise. It lives in rainforests in Papua New Guinea. Females have drab (dull) brown and black plumage. They invest time, energy, and food in building a nest, incubating eggs, and rearing young. Males copulate with females but do not assist with rearing offspring in any other way. Males have iridescent green and bronze plumage with two white tail feathers that can be over a metre long. To try to attract a mate, they gather at a site (called a lek) and jump back and forth between perches on branches, with their tail feathers arched. Females select a mate from the males displaying.

▲ Male ribbon-tailed astrapia (*Astrapia mayeri*)

During the evolution of this species, females must have selected males with brighter plumage, longer tail feathers and more vigorous courtship dances. These qualities do not obviously aid survival in the rainforest. However, males that evade predators despite bright plumage and inconveniently long tail feathers and have enough energy for vigorous courtship displays must be healthy and well-adapted to their niche in the rainforest. Females favour them in sexual selection and the plumage evolves to become brighter, the tail feathers longer and the courtship displays more showy.

8. Application of skills: modelling sexual and natural selection

Guppies (*Poecilia reticulata*) are small fish that are native to freshwater habitats in the northeast of South America. Males have a wide variety of coloured markings that evolve by sexual selection. John Endler and his colleagues investigated this in controlled experiments.

Application of skills: Endler's guppy experiments

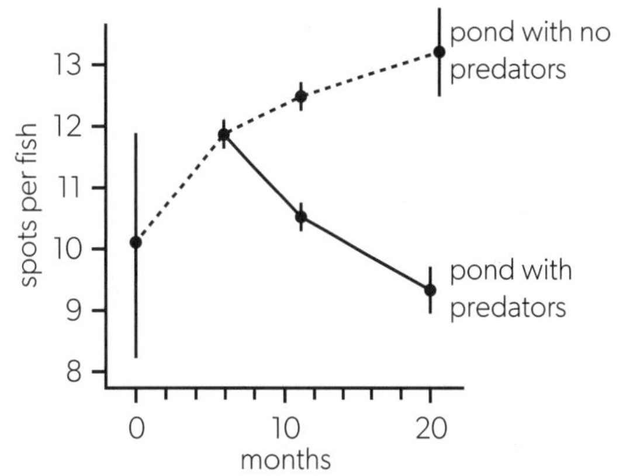

Endler transferred guppies from a natural population to a pond with no predators. The males initially had an average of 10 blue and iridescent black spots. After six months he transferred some of the fish into a pond that contained pike-cichlid fish, a strong predator of guppies. The graph shows the results.

In the pond with no predators, the average number of spots per male increased, especially the blue spots due to sexual selection by females. In the pond with predators, the number of spots decreased due to males with more spots being more visible to the predators.

In another experiment, Endler transferred a population of males from a stream where pike-cichlid fish were the predators (stream A) to a stream where there were killifish instead (stream B). Killifish are weaker predators of guppies than pike-cichlids. After two years, he measured the area of spots on the male guppies in stream B. The bar chart shows the mean results. The mean area of brightly coloured spots increased in the stream with a weaker predator.

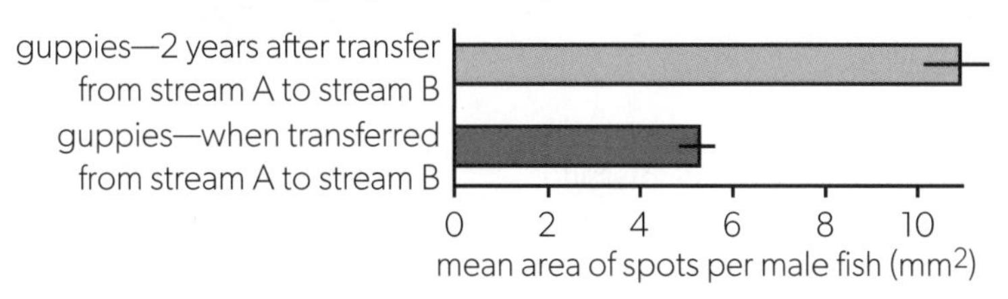

Endler's experiments show that there are two selection pressures acting on male guppies:

- sexual selection by females for males with bright coloration
- natural selection for dull coloration to reduce the chance of a male being seen and predated.

This helps to explain the variation in male coloration in natural populations of guppies. In parts of streams where there are fewer or weaker predators, males are more colourful. In locations where there are more predators and also in shallow water with good visibility, males tend to be less colourful. Evolution in the coloration of males can happen remarkably rapidly in response to changes in selection pressures.

AHL

9. Gene pools

- A gene pool is all the genes and their different alleles that are present in a population.
- A population is a group of individual organisms of the same species living in an area. Populations are described more fully in *Section C4.1.1.*
- When an individual dies, its alleles are lost from the gene pool.
- Individuals increase the gene pool when they reproduce, with the alleles of their offspring added to it.
- Natural selection results in some individuals reproducing more than others, so they contribute more of their alleles to the gene pool.
- The fitness of an individual can be measured in terms of their contribution to the gene pool.
- Small populations with small gene pools are less likely to be able to evolve and are more vulnerable to extinction.

10. Application of skills: using databases to search for allele frequencies of populations

If a geographical barrier prevents interbreeding between two populations of a species, their gene pools are separate. A common allele in the gene pool of one population may be much rarer in another. Reasons for this are explained in *Sections A4.1.6* and *A4.1.7*. Geographically separated groups of humans develop differences in allele frequencies, which can be studied using online databases.

Databases of human allele frequency can be found online. An example is the Allele Frequency Net Database (**www.allelefrequencies.net**). It has data on genes that can cause tissue rejection after stem cell or organ transplants. These genes can vary considerably between ethnic groups. The database allows populations to be browsed by geographical region, so allele frequencies in local populations can be investigated. Databases such as this are frequently updated and improved, so they are increasingly easy to navigate. The best way to learn how to do this is by having a go!

AHL

11. Allele frequency changes in gene pools

Evolution by natural selection is a change in heritable traits. Despite discovering this, Charles Darwin did not find out how inheritance works and it was Gregor Mendel who demonstrated that discrete units (genes) are inherited. August Weismann showed that genes are passed on to offspring in gametes (the germ plasm theory), so genetic changes in body cells cannot be inherited and Lamarckism (see *Section A4.1.1*) is impossible.

Neo-Darwinism is the combination of natural selection with the principles of inheritance discovered by Mendel and Weismann. It explains the basis of variation between individuals, how natural selection acts on it and how it is inherited. According to Neo-Darwinism, evolution is a change in the frequency of alleles in the gene pool. Individuals who are better adapted tend to have more offspring, so their alleles increase in frequency in the gene pool and more individuals in future generations inherit them.

12. Comparing stabilizing, directional and disruptive selection

Allele frequencies change in response to natural selection. If allele frequencies do not change, either there are no selection pressures acting on a population, or opposing selection pressures are balanced.

There are three patterns of natural selection, each of which causes a change in allele frequencies.

1. **Stabilizing selection**

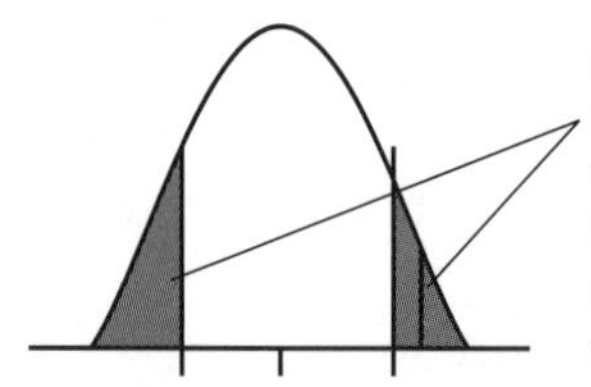

Examples:

- Mortality is higher with human babies of low birth weight or high birth weight.
- Blackbirds (*Turdus merula*) usually lay between three and five eggs. Fewer offspring are reared with higher or lower numbers of eggs than this.

2. **Directional selection**

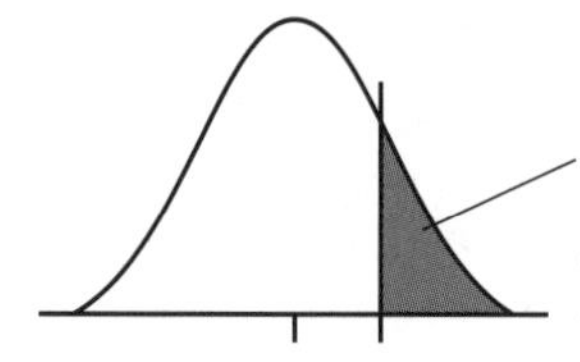

selection pressures remove variants from the upper (or lower) part of the range, so the average for the trait changes

Examples:

- The body size of house mice (*Mus musculus*) introduced to Gough Island in the South Atlantic rose to twice that of mainland populations. Larger mice were more successful at biting ground birds and feeding on their blood.
- In the bird species *Parus major* (great tit), more offspring have been reared by birds that breed early in the spring than by those that breed later, because the peak availability of prey is now earlier in the year due to climate change.

3. **Disruptive selection**

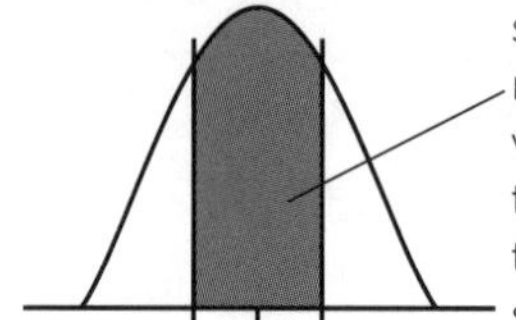

Examples:

- In coho salmon (*Oncorhynchus kisutch*), small and large males can both be successful in gaining access to females and fertilizing their eggs. Small, early maturing males (jacks) sneak in unnoticed and shed their sperm over eggs that a female has laid. Large, late maturing males can successfully fight other males, coerce females to spawn, and then shed their sperm over the eggs. Intermediate-sized males are at a competitive disadvantage to both jacks and large males because they are more targeted for fights which they lose and are less successful at the sneaking strategy.
- In the bird species *Passerina amoena* (lazuli bunting), one-year-old males with the dullest and brightest plumage are more successful than males with intermediate plumage at obtaining high-quality territories, pairing with females and siring offspring. There is less aggression towards dull males from older males so they are more likely to establish a territory but females prefer to mate with brighter coloured males.

15. Comparing natural and artificial selection

Natural selection and artificial selection can both change allele frequencies in a gene pool.

Artificial selection is the deliberate choice of traits and the use of individuals showing those traits to breed the next generation. It is the method that has been used to develop varieties of crop plant and breeds of domesticated animal. The process of artificial selection and how it provides evidence of evolution is described in *Section A4.1.3*.

Natural selection can be due to human actions as long as there is no deliberate choice of traits. For example, medical use of antibiotics to treat bacterial infections has had the unintended consequence of the evolution of antibiotic resistance in bacteria. This is natural selection rather than artificial selection because humans did not deliberately breed bacteria with antibiotic resistance.

AHL

13. Hardy–Weinberg equation

If there are two alleles of a gene in a population, there are three possible genotypes: homozygous for each of the two alleles and heterozygous. If the frequency of these genotypes in a population is known, the probability of inheriting each of the two alleles can be calculated. The probabilities are usually represented by the letters p and q. So $p + q = 1$. Assuming that mating in the population is random, the probabilities of inheriting two copies of either the p or the q allele are $p \times p$ and $q \times q$. The probability of inheriting two different alleles is $2pq$.

The sum of all genotype probabilities is 1.0, so:

$$p^2 + 2pq + q^2 = 1$$

This is the Hardy–Weinberg equation. It can be used to predict allele frequencies in a population from phenotype frequencies and also genotype frequencies from allele frequencies.

Example: Albinism (lack of skin and hair pigmentation)
Albinism is caused by a recessive allele, so a person must be homozygous recessive to be albino. Albinism occurs in North America in approximately one in 20,000 people.

Let q represent the probability of inheriting the allele for albinism and p represent the probability of inheriting the allele for pigmentation in skin and hair.

Probability of having two alleles for albinism = $q \times q$ or q^2.
Thus: $1/20{,}000 = q^2$ so $q = \underline{0.007}$.

Probability of p plus q must equal 1.
Thus: $p + 0.007 = 1$ and $p = \underline{0.993}$.

The probability of being a carrier or non-carrier of the allele for albinism can now be deduced:

female gametes \ male gametes	p	q
p	$0.993 \times 0.993 = 0.9860$	$0.007 \times 0.993 = 0.007$
q	$0.993 \times 0.007 = 0.007$	$0.007 \times 0.007 = 0.00005$

The probability of being a carrier is 0.014 or 1.4%

The probability of being a non-carrier is 0.986 or 98.60%

14. Hardy–Weinberg conditions required for genetic equilibrium

According to the Hardy–Weinberg equation, if a gene has two alleles and their frequencies are p and q, the frequencies of the two homozygous genotypes will be p^2 and q^2 and the frequency of the heterozygous genotype will be $2pq$. These frequencies are only expected if the following series of conditions is met in a population:

- There is no mutation of the gene, so the alleles are not changed, and new alleles are not being generated.
- Mating is random, so no phenotype preferentially mates with another particular phenotype.
- There is no immigration or emigration that is likely to change allele frequencies.
- The population is large enough to prevent allele frequencies changing due to chance. This is called genetic drift.
- Natural selection does not favour one phenotype over another.

If the genotypic frequencies in a population do fit the predictions from the Hardy–Weinberg equation, we conclude that all the conditions are being met. In particular, natural selection is not causing allele frequencies to change, so evolution is not occurring. The population is said to be in **genetic equilibrium**.

If the genotypic frequencies diverge from the Hardy–Weinberg predictions, one or more of the conditions is not being met. If we can be sure that the first four conditions are being met, then natural selection must be favouring one phenotype over another, causing allele frequencies to change—evolution is occurring within the population.

Example: MN blood groups

MN blood groups were surveyed in a Japanese town. The frequencies of the three blood groups were

M = 0.274,
MN = 0.502,
N = 0.224.

The two alleles of the gene are codominant, so the probability of inheriting each allele can be determined:

Probability of M allele (p) = $0.274 + 0.502/2 = 0.525$

Probability of N allele (q) = $0.224 + 0.502/2 = 0.475$

These allele probabilities can be used to predict genotype frequencies, using the Hardy–Weinberg equation:

	Predicted genotype probability	Actual blood group frequency
MM	$p^2 = 0.276$	0.274
MN	$2pq = 0.499$	0.502
NN	$q^2 = 0.226$	0.224

The actual probabilities fit the predicted probabilities very closely. From this, we conclude that all the Hardy–Weinberg conditions are being maintained in the population. Natural selection is not favouring one blood group over any other and the allele frequencies are not expected to change in the population. The population is in genetic equilibrium.

D4.2 Sustainability and change

1. Sustainability

Systems are sustainable if they can continue for an unlimited period of time. Ecosystems have the potential to be sustainable. This is demonstrated by examples that have existed for very long periods of time, such as the Daintree rainforest. It is a 1,200 km^2 remnant of the tropical forest that once covered much of Australia. The climate of a landmass usually changes radically over geological time, due to movement of tectonic plates, but by chance conditions where the Daintree rainforest is located have remained warm and wet for over 100 million years, allowing the forest to endure. This ecosystem is now very biodiverse, with plants and animals found nowhere else, including many species from ancient plant families that dominated the world before the evolution of flowering plants.

The mechanisms that sustain ecosystems are fragile and easily disrupted, so ecosystems are not always stable. Even minor perturbations (disturbances) can cause change.

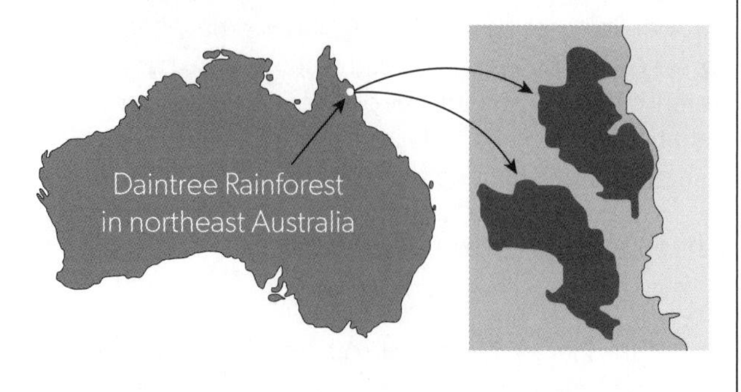

2. Maintaining sustainability in ecosystems

- There must be a steady supply of energy, as it cannot be recycled. Sunlight is the energy source in most ecosystems. Very rarely this has been blocked by dust from volcanic activity, causing ecosystem collapse and mass extinctions.
- Nutrient cycles should replenish abiotic reserves of all chemical elements needed by organisms. Any losses from the ecosystem should be balanced by gains.
- Climatic variables, especially temperature and rainfall, must remain within ranges of tolerance of organisms in the ecosystem.
- Individual species, especially keystone species, must have high genetic diversity, so there is variation for natural selection to work on. This allows adaptation in response to environmental change, so new conditions can be endured.

3. Tipping points in ecosystem sustainability

The Amazon rainforest is so vast that it has major effects on climate. Evaporation of water from leaves (transpiration) has a cooling effect. Water vapour that has transpired from leaves condenses in the atmosphere above the forest, lowering air pressure and causing air flow (wind). The condensed water falls as rainfall, so it can be absorbed by trees and transpired again.

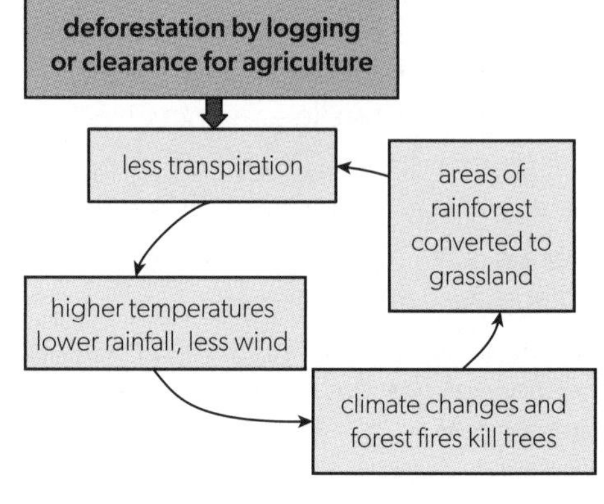

Ecosystems show resilience, but this is not unlimited
Above a certain level of disturbance, a tipping point may be reached, beyond which positive feedback mechanisms cause rapid changes that are difficult or impossible to reverse. In the Amazon rainforest there is disturbance due to deforestation (by logging or clearance for agriculture). If a tipping point is reached, a positive feedback cycle (shown above right) will cause unstoppable changes. Even without further deforestation, all remaining parts of the Amazon rainforest would then change to another ecosystem type, probably grassland. It is uncertain what area of the Amazon rainforest is needed to prevent the tipping point being reached.

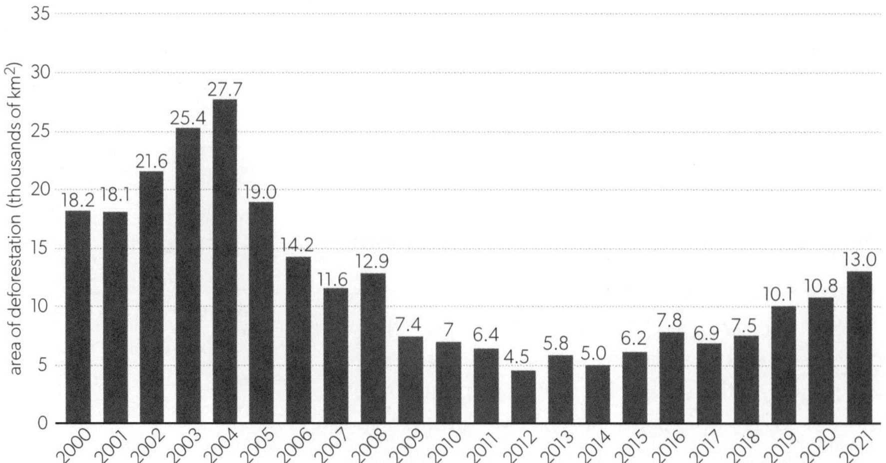

▲ The bar chart shows the area of deforestation in the Amazon rainforest for each year from 2000 to 2021.

Application of skills: calculating percentage change

To calculate percentage change, use this formula:

$$\frac{\text{final amount} - \text{initial amount}}{\text{initial amount}} \times 100\%$$

In 1970, there was an estimated 4,100,000 km^2 of Amazon rainforest in Brazil, with 3,268,000 km^2 remaining in 2022.

$$\text{percentage change} = \frac{3{,}268{,}000 - 4{,}100{,}000\ \text{km}^2}{4{,}100{,}000\ \text{km}^2} \times 100\%$$
$$= -20.3\%$$

Between 1970 and 2022, there was a 20.3% reduction in the area of Amazon rainforest in Brazil.

4,600 km^2 of Amazon rainforest in Brazil was lost in 2012; 11,600 km^2 was lost in 2022.

$$\text{percentage change} = \frac{11{,}600 - 4{,}600\ \text{km}^2}{4{,}600\ \text{km}^2} \times 100\%$$
$$= 152\%$$

In 2022, the loss of Amazon rainforest in Brazil was 152% higher than in 2012.

4. Modelling ecosystem sustainability

Ecosystems have the potential to be sustainable over long periods of time. As long as nutrients are recycled and there is a supply of energy, usually in the form of light, ecosystems have the potential to persist endlessly. This can be investigated using mesocosms.

A mesocosm is a small experimental enclosure, set up for ecological research. Fenced-off enclosures in grassland or a forest model terrestrial mesocosms. Open tanks or sealed glass vessels model aquatic ecosystems. Sealed vessels allow entry and exit of matter to be controlled, with energy transfer happening freely. The diagram below shows one design of mesocosm.

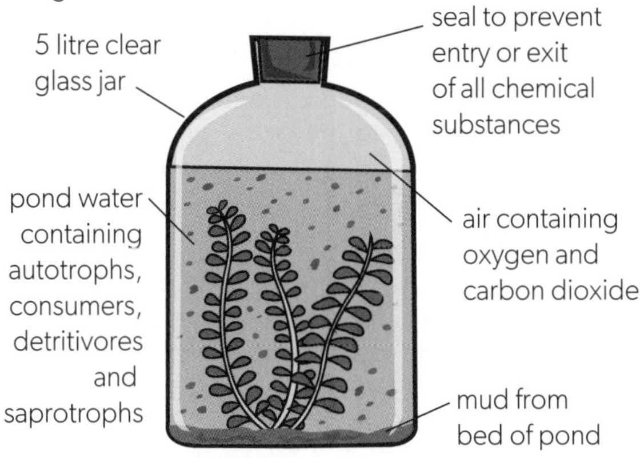

For sustainability, autotrophs and saprotrophs are essential components, but consumers and detritivores may not be essential. It is unethical to include large animals in mesocosms that cannot obtain enough food or oxygen.

5. Keystone species

A keystone species has a disproportionate effect on the structure of an ecological community. Species diversity decreases if the keystone species is lost and there may be a collapse of the entire ecosystem.

Example: *Pisaster ochraceus*

This species of sea star is a keystone species on rocky shores along the Pacific coast of North America. An experiment was done by removing *Pisaster* from one area of the shore and leaving it in an adjacent area. The community remained biodiverse where *Pisaster* was still present with many species of animals and seaweeds (algae).

Where *Pisaster* was removed, *Mytilus californianus*, a bivalve mollusc, became overwhelmingly dominant. All seaweeds disappeared apart from one species that grows on mollusc shells. Other animal species were crowded out or lost their food source so they died or migrated.

Pisaster is acting as a keystone species on the rocky shore by predation of *Mytilus*.

Global impacts of science

NOS

Scientists must aim to do no harm. Research scientists must submit their proposals for scrutiny by ethics boards.

IB has published ethical experiment guidelines and these must be followed when setting up mesocosms. In particular, organisms in the mesocosms must not endure more than minimal suffering as a consequence of the experiment.

6. Maintaining balance in sustainability

Before agriculture was developed, all foods and other resources needed by humans were harvested from natural ecosystems. This is sustainable if the rate of harvesting is lower than the rate of replacement. There is a long history of unsustainable harvesting and it has resulted in many species extinctions. Outside Africa, the megafauna was driven to extinction long ago by overharvesting, following the arrival of the first human migrants. Because the human population has risen above 8 billion, there is more pressure than ever on plants and animals harvested from natural ecosystems.

Brazil nuts—a harvest from plants

About 40,000 tonnes of nuts are harvested each year from *Bertholletia excelsa* trees in the Amazon rainforest. The trees can grow to 50 m and live for a thousand years. The trees are being lost due to logging in some areas, reducing the maximum sustainable yield. Sustainable harvesting depends on leaving some nuts to germinate and grow into new trees. Agoutis (large rodents) living in the forest feed on the nuts but bury some of them, so help to establish new trees. In areas of intense harvesting, there are few or no young trees, so harvesting is unsustainable. Planting monocultures of Brazil nut trees has been attempted, and planting of individual trees in degraded or deforested areas, but almost all harvesting is still from trees in intact forest.

Atlantic cod fishing—harvest of an animal species

Over a million tonnes of cod (*Gadus morhua*) is harvested per year from the north Atlantic. There was once a very high density on the Grand Banks off Newfoundland, but overfishing led to a total collapse of this population in the early 1990s. The cod population has still not recovered, demonstrating the importance of sustainability in fish harvesting. Outside territorial waters of individual countries, fish are an open-access resource so conservation depends on international cooperation. The aim is not to exceed the maximum sustainable yield, which is point M on the sigmoid growth curve shown for a fish population. At this point population growth is at its maximum.

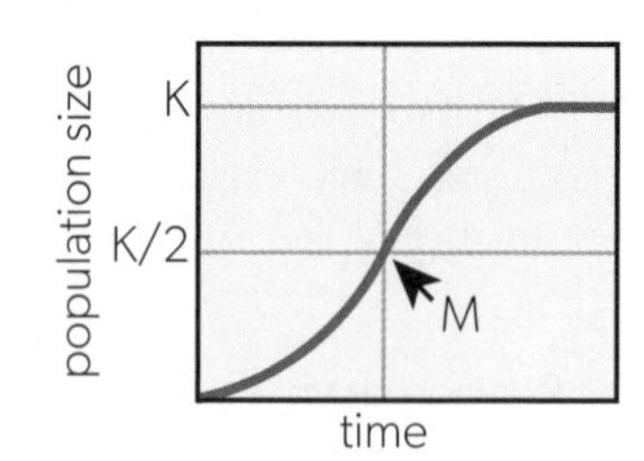

Cod stocks in the North Sea between Britain and Norway dropped by more than 80% in the latter part of the 20th century. The measures agreed internationally to reverse this trend were:

- exclusion zones in nursery areas to allow undisturbed breeding
- increasing the size of holes in nets so smaller cod escape
- reducing the fishing fleet by decommissioning some boats
- monitoring the numbers and ages of cod in the North Sea population and setting quotas for each boat based on this information, to limit the overall catch per year.

Since 2005, the biomass of adult cod in the North Sea has tripled. Current quantities of cod caught per year are allowing continued increases, so cod fishing in the North Sea is sustainable.

7. The sustainability of agriculture

The human population depends on foods produced by agriculture and it is essential that this is done using sustainable methods. Yields can be increased by using more intensive methods, but these may reduce sustainability, either by overuse of finite resources or by damage to ecosystems.

- Tillage is preparing soil for a crop. Soils are loosened by plowing, harrowing and other cultivations. Soil structure can become degraded and both wind and water can cause soil erosion at a much faster rate than new soil is being generated. Tropical forests that are cleared for agriculture often have soils which quickly degrade and cannot sustain high-yield agriculture for long.

- Nutrient depletion of soils is caused by removal of harvested crops and by leaching (see *Section D4.2.8*). Repeated applications of chemical fertilizer are required because of depletion. Phosphate and most other minerals are mined from non-renewable rock deposits. The manufacture of nitrogen fertilizer from fossil fuels requires energy.
- Cultivating large areas of a single variety of crop plant (monoculture) and growing the same crop year after year encourages pests and weeds to become increasingly problematic. Intensive agriculture responds to this with applications of pesticide and herbicide. This can cause pollution problems, especially with persistent chemicals such as DDT. Resistance to an agrochemical tends to evolve in the pest or weed if the chemical is repeatedly used. Manufacture of agrochemicals requires an energy source, which currently is supplied by fossil fuels.
- Mechanical tillage requires power, most of which comes from diesel oil used in tractors. Energy is also required for heating glasshouses and animal housing. The carbon footprint of agriculture is high. It makes a significant contribution to climate change.

8. Eutrophication as a result of leaching

When rainwater falls on terrestrial ecosystems, soluble nutrients such as phosphates and nitrates dissolve and are washed out of the soil as the water drains through it. This process is **leaching**. The nutrients enter river catchments and are eventually carried out to the sea. Intensive crop production increases leaching, because of the use of artificial fertilizers. Intensive livestock production also increases the transfer of nutrients into river systems, especially if manure and urine are not stored correctly or are spread on land before rainfall. Intensive agriculture therefore tends to cause nutrient enrichment of ponds and lakes and also flowing water in streams and rivers and in estuaries and shallow seas. Nutrient enrichment of aquatic and marine ecosystems is **eutrophication**.

The water in some ecosystems is naturally eutrophic but agriculture has caused eutrophication of many lakes and rivers, with harmful consequences, as shown in the diagram.

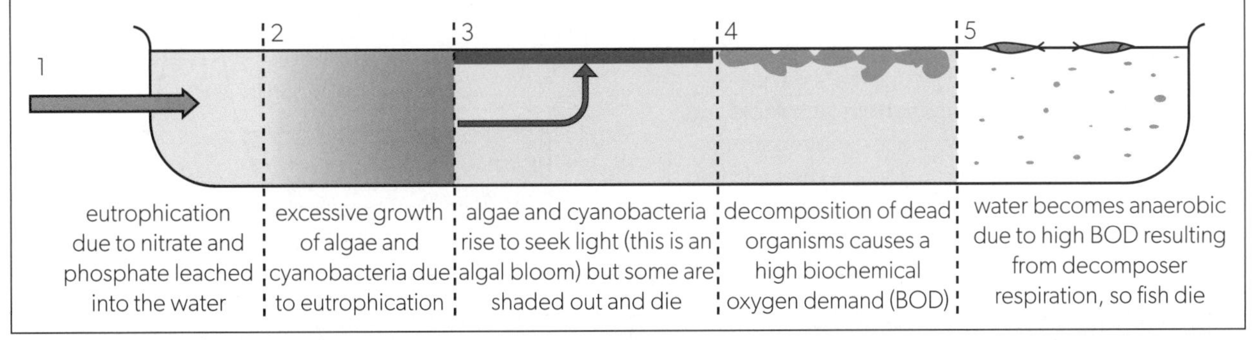
1
2
3
4
5
eutrophication due to nitrate and phosphate leached into the water
excessive growth of algae and cyanobacteria due to eutrophication
algae and cyanobacteria rise to seek light (this is an algal bloom) but some are shaded out and die
decomposition of dead organisms causes a high biochemical oxygen demand (BOD)
water becomes anaerobic due to high BOD resulting from decomposer respiration, so fish die

10. Effects of plastic pollution of the oceans

Plastic is a broad term that describes a range of polymers widely used in human manufacturing. Packaging and other items made from plastic are single-use in many cases and although some plastic is recycled, much is discarded every year (over 350 million tonnes in 2020). The oceans now contain huge quantities of plastic. It is accumulating because it is either **non-biodegradable**, or degrades (breaks down) very slowly.

Macroplastics are large visible items, such as fishing nets, ropes, drink bottles and grocery bags. Marine wildlife such as seabirds and turtles can become entangled in nets and ropes and ingest plastic bags and other debris because they are mistaken for prey. Albatrosses confuse floating plastic bags with jellyfish or squid and give them to their chicks resulting in gut blockages and high mortality.

Microplastics are fragments of plastic that measure between 5 mm and 1 μm in diameter. They are in many products, for example microbeads in skin cleansers. They are also produced by fragmentation of textiles in clothing, vehicle tyres and macroplastic wastes. They have been found in every marine ecosystem investigated. Filter-feeders ingest microplastics together with carbon compounds that accumulate on the surface of the plastic, some of which are toxic.

Nanoplastics are less than 1 μm in diameter and are formed by fragmentation of microplastics. They can pass through plasma membranes and enter cells. They accumulate in the organs of fish and other animals, including humans. They almost certainly have harmful effects on cells but these are not yet fully researched.

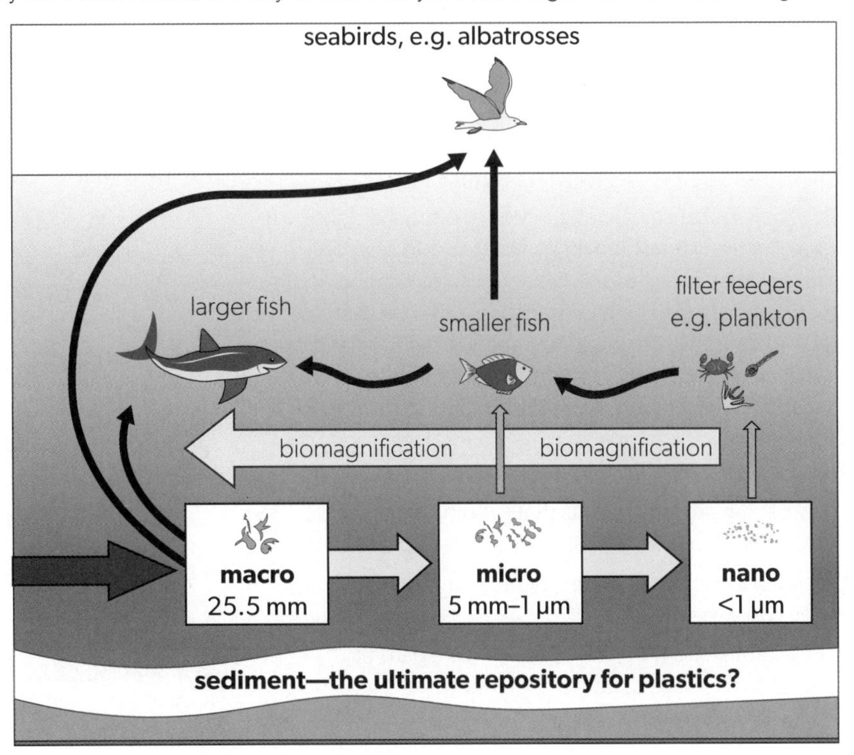
seabirds, e.g. albatrosses
larger fish
smaller fish
filter feeders e.g. plankton
biomagnification
biomagnification
macro
25.5 mm
micro
5 mm–1 μm
nano
<1 μm
sediment—the ultimate repository for plastics?

9. Biomagnification

Natural ecosystems in many parts of the world have been polluted with human-made chemicals. Concentrations of these chemicals in the environment may be very low, yet some organisms, particularly at the ends of food chains, contain concentrations great enough to be lethal. This can be explained by the twin processes of bioaccumulation and biomagnification. DDT (dichlorodiphenyltrichloroethane) caused catastrophic falls in the populations of peregrine falcons, ospreys and otters in the 1950s and 1960s.

Bioaccumulation is an increase in concentration of a toxin in body tissues during an animal's life. It is a particular problem with toxins that are fat-soluble and therefore not easily excreted. For example, carbon compounds containing mercury such as methyl mercury are more likely to accumulate in droplets of fat in adipose tissue than metallic mercury.

Biomagnification is an increase in concentration of a chemical substance at each successive trophic level in a food chain. Predators tend to accumulate higher concentrations of a toxin than their prey. This is because the predator consumes large quantities of prey during its lifetime and bioaccumulates the toxins that they contain.

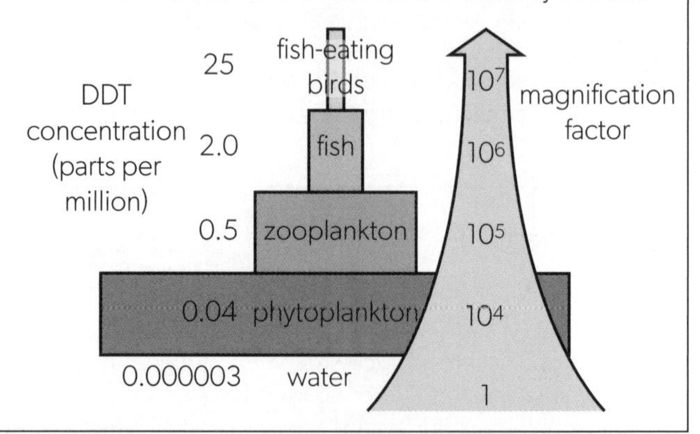

NOS Global impacts of science

Scientists have a responsibility to communicate their research findings to the public with honesty and clarity. If they do this effectively, they can influence the actions of citizens. Popular media coverage of the effects of plastic pollution on marine life changed public perception globally, which has driven measures to address this problem.

11. Rewilding

Natural ecosystems have been degraded by human actions and relatively little of the Earth's surface remains as pristine natural habitat. Among the consequences are:

- loss of biodiversity
- rapid rates of species extinction
- loss of ecosystem services, e.g. carbon sequestration and climate regulation, flood protection, prevention of soil erosion and purification of air and water.

In many parts of the world, efforts are being made to encourage natural ecosystems to return. One approach to this is rewilding. The essential principle of rewilding is that there should be as little intervention by humans as possible because natural processes restore habitats more effectively than humans. A first step is to stop or reduce human activities such as agriculture, logging and other forms of resource harvesting. That may be all that is required for forests to recolonize abandoned farmland or for marine ecosystems to re-establish in fishing exclusion zones. More commonly, there is a need for specific interventions to undo past human actions. Here are some examples of interventions that can speed up rewilding:

- spreading seeds of plants that should be part of the ecosystem but no natural seed source is present
- reintroduction of apex predators and other keystone species
- re-establishment of connectivity where natural ecosystems have become fragmented
- control of invasive alien species.

The **Hinewai Reserve** on the Banks Peninsula in New Zealand is an example of successful ecological restoration. A total of 1,250 hectares of farmland has been allowed to return to native forest. Alien mammals such as goats, brushtail possums and deer are rigorously controlled but apart from that there has been minimal interference. Alien plants are mostly tolerated because over time they are mostly eliminated by competition from better-adapted native species. Gorse (*Ulex europaeus*) is invasive on pasture land in much of New Zealand but in Hinewai, it provides nurse canopies for saplings of native trees, and then dies out because of shading from the native trees that it helped to establish.

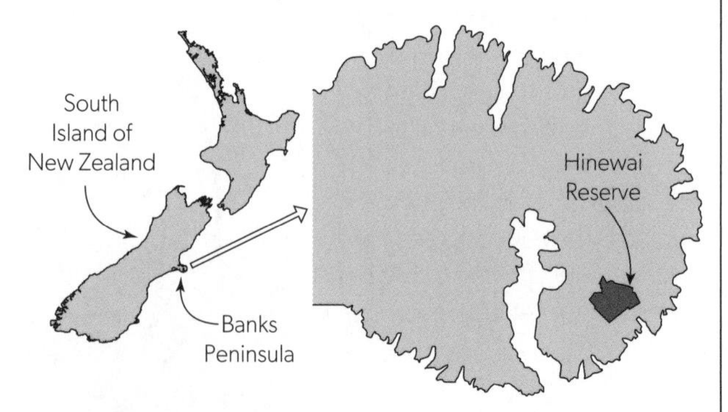

The speed of regeneration of natural ecosystems at Hinewai has been remarkable, but threats remain with increasing incidence of both droughts and floods after extreme rainfall. This can be attributed to climate change due to human activities, which threatens natural ecosystems throughout the world.

AHL

12. Ecological succession and its triggers

Ecological successions are sequences of changes that progressively transform ecosystems. Species composition of the community and abiotic factors both change over time.

Consider an area of grassland that is being colonized by shrubs or trees. As the trees grow, light intensity at ground level diminishes and lower temperatures and higher humidity result. Leaf litter from the trees increases nutrient concentration, water infiltration and capacity for water retention of the soil. This means plant species adapted to conditions in grassland will be lost from the community and others adapted to conditions in the forest will join it. There will also be changes in the animal species because of interdependency between specific species of animals and plants.

Changes in an ecosystem often trigger other changes, so one ecosystem replaces another in a series. This is an ecological succession. A stable and persistent ecosystem may then develop that does not undergo further significant change. This is the climax community.

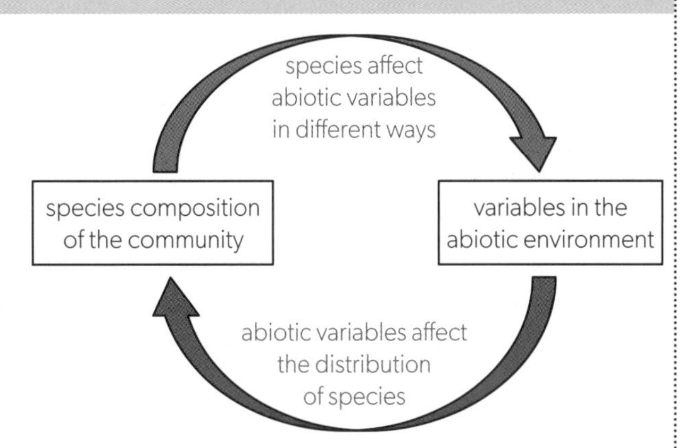

This raises the question of what initiates an ecological succession. In some cases, the trigger is abiotic. An avalanche in mountains may sweep away forest and underlying soil, creating a bare substratum on which a new succession begins. In other cases, the trigger is biotic. For example, beavers may colonize a river and cause areas of flooding, leading to a series of successional changes that change open water into a swamp.

13. Principles of primary succession

Succession is either primary or secondary. **Primary succession** begins in environments where living organisms are largely or completely absent. On land this could be bare rock or deposits of silt, sand, or larger rock fragments, but not soil. Only organisms such as bacteria, lichens and mosses can colonize these inorganic substrata. Early colonizers generate small amounts of soil, allowing herbs with roots to start to colonize. As deeper soil develops, successively larger plants colonize, for example tall herbs, shrubs and then trees in most areas. Animal populations change with the plant populations, as do populations of decomposers.

These are the general principles of primary succession:

- species diversity increases as more species join the community than are eliminated
- primary production increases as larger plants colonize and there is more photosynthesis per unit area
- food webs become more complex
- nutrient cycling increases as animals and plants generate more dead organic matter.

The diagram below shows changes occurring during primary succession on sand dunes.

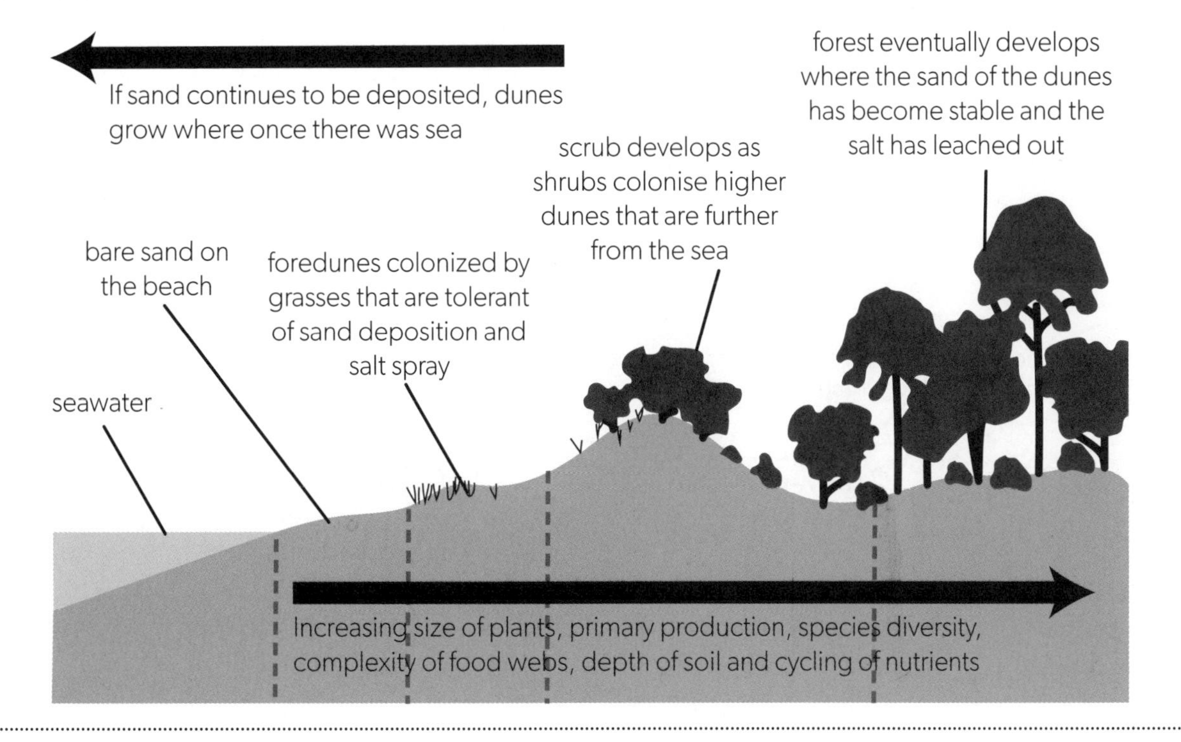

AHL

14. Cyclical succession

Some ecosystems are characterized by cycles of change rather than a stable climax. In cyclical succession, species replace each other over time repeatedly, even without the stimulus of large-scale disturbance. Wood-pasture in northwest Europe is an example (right).

Cyclical succession also occurs when a community is changed by recurring events. An example of this is the repeated fire cycles of the coastal chaparral ecosystem of California. The climax community in this type of ecosystem is dominated by deciduous shrubs and evergreen trees. Fires are the major source of disturbance and typically happen every 10–15 years.

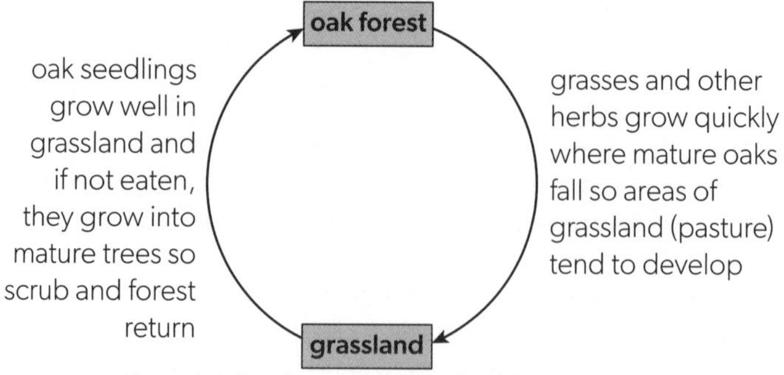
oak seedlings do not grow in the shade of larger trees so oak woodland tends not to regenerate
oak forest
grasses and other herbs grow quickly where mature oaks fall so areas of grassland (pasture) tend to develop
grassland
if grazing by deer and other herbivores is intense, grassland may persist for some time
oak seedlings grow well in grassland and if not eaten, they grow into mature trees so scrub and forest return

15. Human influences can block climax communities from developing

As succession proceeds, a stable climax community may develop that is not superseded. The type of climax community that develops depends on climate and other environmental conditions, as explained in *Section B4.1.6*. Human influences can cause a deflected or arrested succession, so a plagioclimax develops (an alternative stable community). Grazing by farm livestock and drainage of wetlands both result in a plagioclimax, instead of the climatic climax community.

Grazing is the method of feeding farm livestock such as cattle and sheep. The livestock are kept at high stocking densities so grazing is more intense than in natural ecosystems. Grasses and many herbs can tolerate grazing, but tree and shrub seedlings are killed, so grassland persists as a plagioclimax where it would naturally be replaced by scrub and then forest.

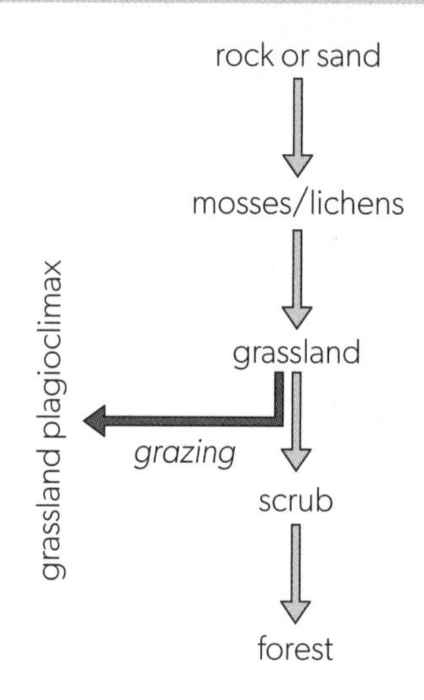
rock or sand
mosses/lichens
grassland
grazing
grassland plagioclimax
scrub
forest

Drainage of wetlands removes water from swamps and other waterlogged sites and increases soil aeration. Plants and animals adapted to wetlands migrate or die and saprotrophic fungi, which were inhibited by the lack of oxygen, can decompose any peat that had developed in the swamp. If the land is not cultivated, shrubs and trees may be able to colonize areas that were previously waterlogged.

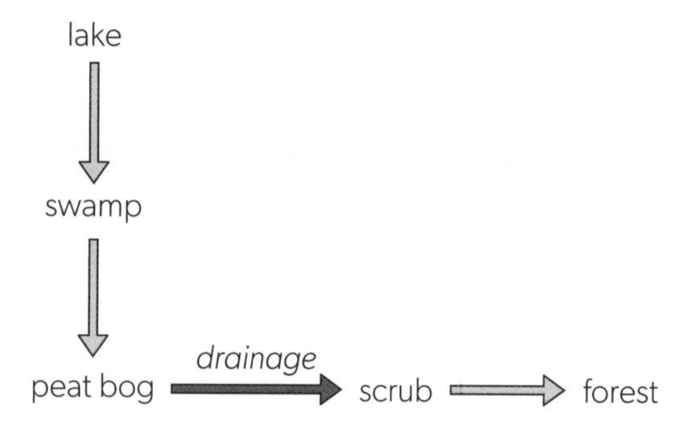
lake
swamp
peat bog
drainage
scrub
forest

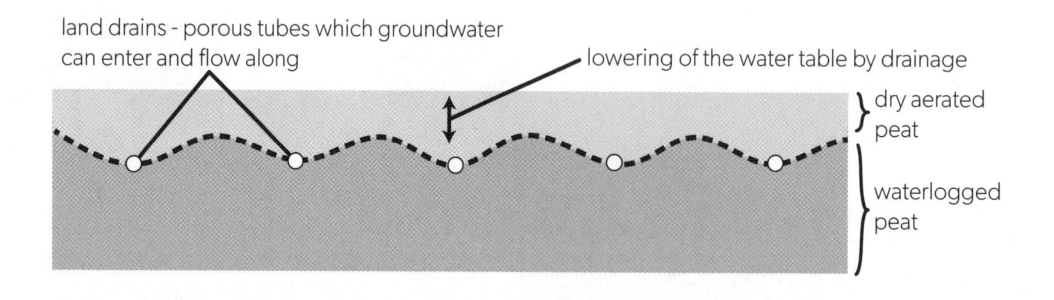
land drains - porous tubes which groundwater can enter and flow along
lowering of the water table by drainage
dry aerated peat
waterlogged peat

D4.3 Climate change

1. Climate change

The "greenhouse effect" keeps the Earth much warmer than it would otherwise be. Greenhouse gases absorb long-wave thermal radiation (heat). Without any greenhouse gases in the atmosphere, the average temperature on Earth would be below 0°C. The higher the concentrations of greenhouse gases, the warmer the Earth becomes.

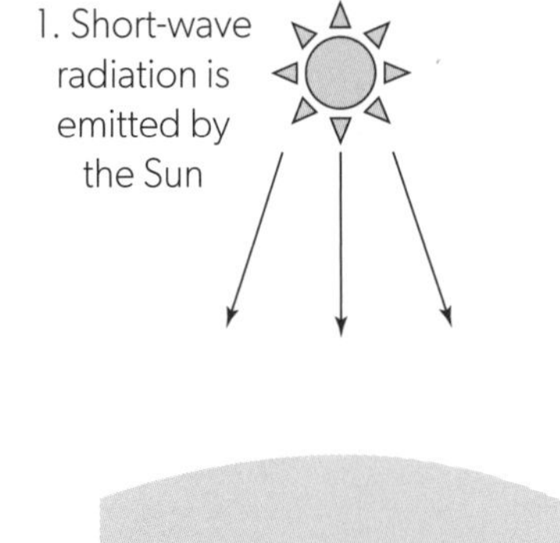

2. Short-wave radiation can pass through the atmosphere

5. Greenhouse gases absorb longwave radiation emitted by the Earth, making the atmosphere warmer

atmosphere

Earth

3. The Earth's surface is warmed by absorbing sunlight

4. Long-wave radiation is emitted by the warmed Earth

Methane and carbon dioxide are the most significant greenhouse gases. Humans are increasing the amounts of both that are released into the atmosphere, resulting in anthropogenic (human-caused) climate change.

Carbon dioxide is released by respiration (shown in the carbon cycle diagram in *Section C4.2.17*) and removed by photosynthesis. These natural processes would normally be in balance, but humans are causing the carbon dioxide concentration to increase (shown in the graph in *Section C4.2.20*).

Methane is naturally emitted by methanogenic organisms (*Section B4.2.2*) in marshes and other waterlogged habitats. It is gradually oxidized in the atmosphere so the atmospheric concentration would naturally remain stable.

So, rises in atmospheric CO_2 and methane increase the greenhouse effect, causing global warming. Heat causes water to evaporate from the oceans and plant leaves (transpiration), subsequently condensing and falling as rain. Heat also provides the energy for winds in the atmosphere and currents in the oceans. Rises in temperature therefore cause many changes to climate.

Anthropogenic emissions of carbon dioxide:

- combustion of fossil fuels (coal, oil and natural gas)
- burning or decomposition of biomass during deforestation
- increases in frequency and severity of forest fires
- drainage and decomposition or burning of peat.

Anthropogenic sources of methane:

- anaerobic decomposition of organic matter in landfill sites
- leaks during fossil fuel extraction and processing
- digestive systems of ruminants (cattle and sheep)
- bubbles of methane released from melting permafrost.

Changes in climate due to global warming:

- changes in prevailing wind direction
- increased cloud cover
- increased rainfall overall, but some areas are drier with longer and more severe droughts
- increased average wind speeds with more frequent and intense cyclones, hurricanes and typhoons.

◀ Satellite image of northern parts of the Earth, where warming has been particularly rapid

NOS

Patterns and trends

The graph shows the results of a study of ice cores drilled in the Antarctic. The upper curve shows the CO_2 concentration in bubbles of air trapped in the ice. The lower curve shows trends in temperature, which can be deduced from hydrogen isotope ratios in the water. The lower curve shows an alternation between shorter periods of rapid warming and longer periods of gradual cooling, which have caused repeated glaciations on Earth.

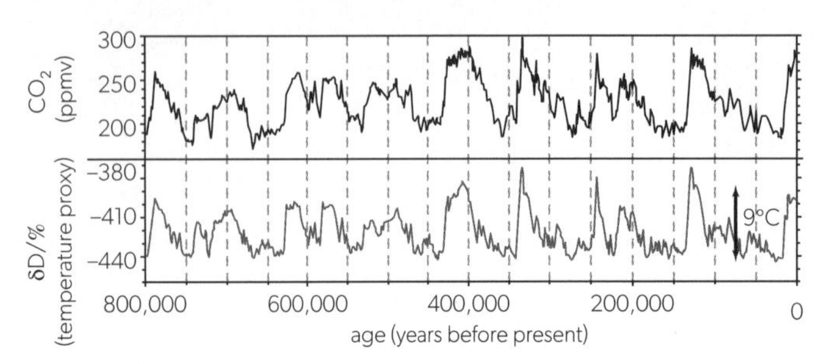

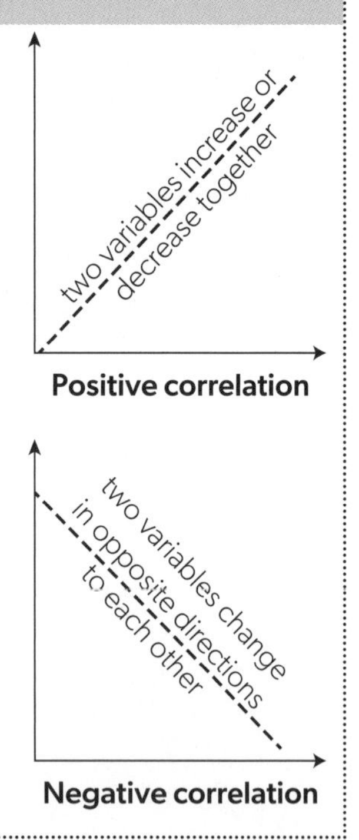

There is a clear correlation between the upper and lower curves: rises in atmospheric CO_2 concentration correspond to rises in temperature and falls in CO_2 concentration correspond to falls in temperature. This is a **positive correlation**. The correlation does not itself prove that increases in CO_2 concentration cause global warming, but the strong evidence for CO_2 acting as a greenhouse gas makes it reasonable to conclude that there is indeed a causal link.

2. Cycles of positive feedback in global warming

Positive feedback is the amplification of a process by its end product. Global warming is amplified by positive feedback cycles, because an increase in the Earth's temperature causes increases in factors that cause warming.

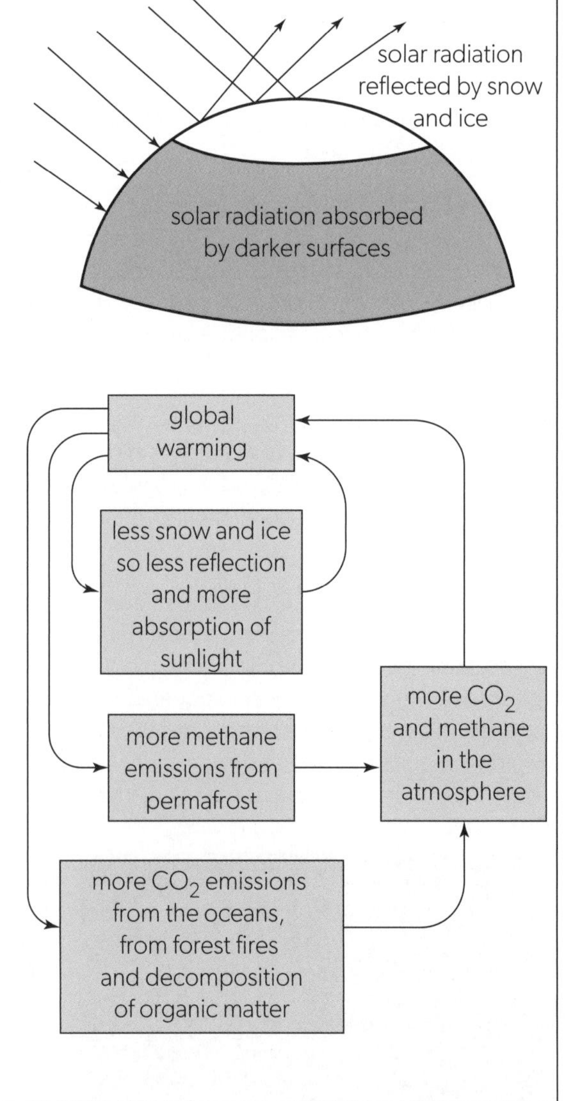

Proportion of sunlight that is reflected (albedo)

- Snow and ice are white so they reflect solar radiation back out into space. With global warming, snow and ice are melting and being replaced by open ocean, rock, or vegetation, all of which are darker in colour so they tend to absorb solar radiation rather than reflect it, causing further warming.

Atmospheric CO_2 concentration

- Decomposition of peat and other dead organic matter by saprotrophs speeds up as temperature rises. Cell respiration in saprotrophs releases carbon dioxide.
- Global warming causes the temperature of the oceans to rise, which reduces the solubility of carbon dioxide in the water. Carbon dioxide is therefore released from deep in the oceans into the atmosphere. This carbon dioxide then contributes to the greenhouse effect, whereas dissolved carbon dioxide in the oceans does not.
- Increased temperatures lead to drier, more fire-prone conditions, so forest fires are more frequent and severe. Carbon dioxide emissions from combustion are increased. Also there is less absorption of carbon dioxide by photosynthesis in the ecosystems that replace forest.

Atmospheric methane concentration

- Permafrost is soil that remains frozen throughout the year. Any dead organic matter in permafrost (such as peat) remains undecomposed because saprotrophic bacteria and fungi are inactive. When global warming causes melting, frozen soils become waterlogged and anaerobic. This encourages methanogenic microbes to break down dead organic matter and release methane into the atmosphere.

3. Effects of climate change on boreal forests

Boreal forest (also known as taiga; see *Section B4.1.7*) covers huge areas of the northern hemisphere, with tundra further north and temperate forests to the south.

Ecosystems can be carbon sources or sinks (see *Section C4.2.18*). Boreal forests are typically sinks because carbon is stored in the biomass of conifer trees and because dead wood, leaf litter and peat accumulate. It is in the cold conditions that it is digested by saprotrophs more slowly than it is produced. With climate change, summers in the boreal forests have become warmer and drier, resulting in widespread fires and huge emissions of CO_2 from combustion of the legacy carbon.

The concept of a tipping point is explained in *Section D4.2.3*. As global temperatures continue to rise, a tipping point could be reached beyond which boreal forests as a whole change from being carbon sinks to sources. Instead of helping to keep the Earth cooler by removing carbon dioxide from the atmosphere, they would contribute to warming by releasing it instead and, further hastening the loss of this biome.

5. Changes in ocean currents affecting nutrient upwelling

The ocean is stratified. Warmer, less salty water is less dense and floats on top of denser, colder, saltier water. There is some mixing of the upper and lower layers, but transfers of heat and chemicals are restricted by the stratification.

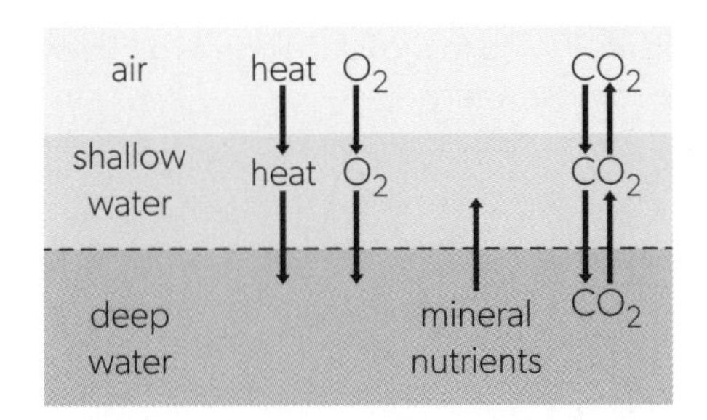

Atmospheric warming increases ocean stratification. This happens because the upper warmer water becomes less dense as it is heated and less saline as freshwater from melting ice flows into the ocean. As a result, there is less mixing.

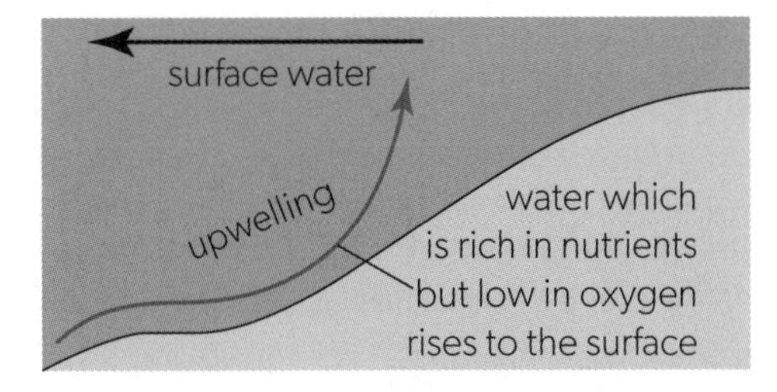

Rotation of the Earth and prevailing winds cause currents that bring the colder, deeper water towards the coast in some parts of the oceans. This water is forced up to the surface, displacing warmer water. It causes an upwelling of mineral nutrients, increasing the growth of producers and therefore availability of food for consumers (above). Areas where upwelling occurs have very productive biological communities. If surface water becomes warmer, there tends to be less upwelling, reducing availability of mineral nutrients and therefore productivity. Areas of upwelling cover about 1% of the ocean surface but provide about 50% of the fish harvested for human consumption.

The map (below) shows chlorophyll concentrations in the Pacific Ocean to the west of parts of Central and South America. There is upwelling in the darker areas, increasing the growth of phytoplankton and therefore the concentration of chlorophyll in the water. The main areas of upwelling are off Peru and the Galápagos archipelago. During El Niño events, there is a reversal in ocean currents and areas of upwelling move elsewhere, with profound effects for marine ecosystems. Because of global warming, El Niño events are becoming more frequent and severe. As the Earth becomes hotter, there will be other significant changes to ocean currents and therefore the timing and extent of nutrient upwelling.

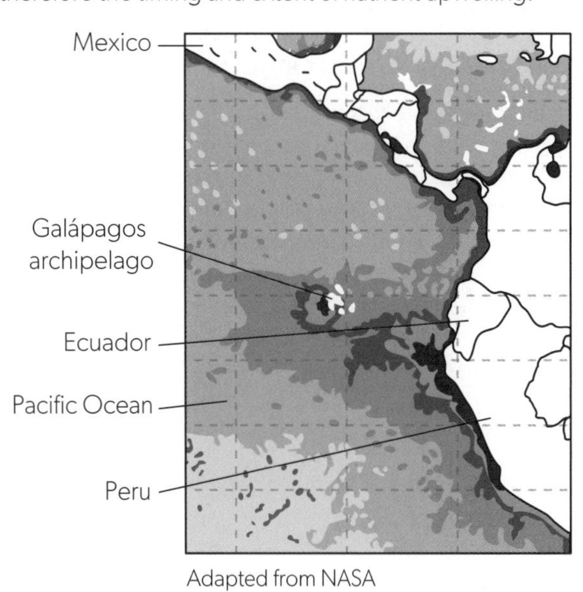

Adapted from NASA

4. Melting of the polar ice caps

Ice floats on the surface of seawater, so it forms a solid surface. Sea ice moves, due to the wind and ocean currents, whereas landfast ice remains attached to a shore. The extent of landfast and sea ice is reducing due to global warming, with consequences for animals that use it as a habitat in both the Arctic and Antarctic.

Emperor penguins breed on landfast ice in the Antarctic. It provides a relatively flat surface and the penguins are too large and unagile to climb over rocks or broken sea ice. To avoid predation, communal breeding sites are chosen at least 5 km from the landfast ice edge; however, breeding success drops as distance from the ice edge increases beyond this, due to the difficulty of returning to the open ocean to feed. Climate change is making the extent of landfast ice very variable and unpredictable, making it difficult for emperor penguins to choose where they can successfully breed.

Walruses use sea ice to rest between feeding sessions, shelter from rough seas and evade predators. They also use sea ice for breeding, giving birth and nursing their young. They can also use areas of coastal land for these purposes but they are limited in area and females prefer sea ice, so as to avoid the risk of their pups being trampled by the larger males. Sea ice also expands access to a broader range of feeding sites. Global warming is reducing sea ice so land-based walruses are having to make more feeding trips from coastal haul-outs to areas of high prey abundance that are far from shore. Walruses lose more heat in the water than when out of the water, so they expend more energy on these trips on thermoregulation.

6. Global warming is shifting climate zones

The world can be divided into climate zones, as shown in the diagram below. In both the northern and southern hemispheres, there is a belt with temperate and continental climates. Continental climates are not influenced much by the oceans and tend to be hot in summer and very cold in winter. Temperate climates have intermediate temperatures throughout the year with nearby oceans making the summers cooler and the winters warmer.

polar climates
temperate and continental climates
dry climates
tropical climates
dry climates
temperate and continental climates
polar climates

Climate change is making many parts of the world warmer, so temperate zones are moving further towards the poles.

Plant and animal species that are adapted to temperate zones are therefore having to move their ranges towards the poles. Animal species may be able to achieve this by migration. Plant species are sessile, so range changes are due to deaths at the hotter end of the range nearer the equator and colonization of cooler areas nearer the poles.

On mountains, the climate becomes colder as altitude increases. There is therefore a series of altitudinal climate zones. Species adapted to the temperate zone on a mountain are having to move upslope as global warming shifts the zones upwards.

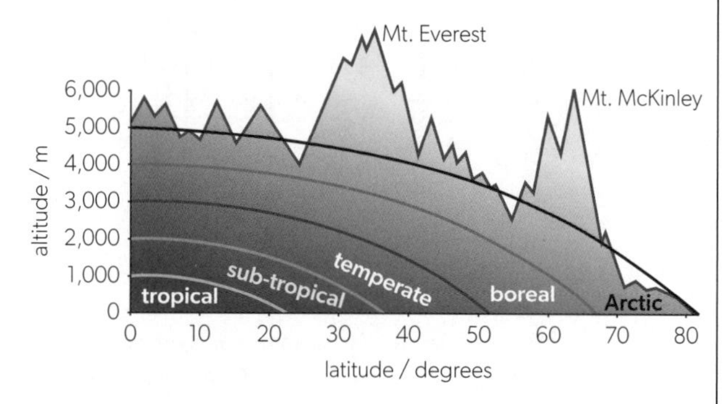

Example of poleward range shift

There is evidence that the ranges of temperate tree species in North America are shifting northwards. A large study of seed production and seedling survival rates in tree species showed that many species are indeed shifting northwards, with the shift happening faster in western species. Another study suggested that conifers are moving north but trees that are flowering plants are tending to shift westwards.

Example of upslope range shift

There is evidence that temperate-zone montane bird species in New Guinea are shifting their range upslope. The upper altitude limit of the ranges of 20 species were measured in 1969 and again in 2013. The limit in all but four of the species had shifted upslope by up to 650 metres. In the other four species, the upper limit had not changed or had reduced a little.

7. Threats to coral reefs

In addition to its contribution to global warming, emissions of carbon dioxide are affecting the oceans. Over 500 billion tonnes of carbon dioxide released by humans since the start of the industrial revolution have dissolved, reducing the pH of the Earth's oceans. In the late 18th century, when there had been little industrialization, the average surface pH was 8.18. The graph shows measurements in an area of the Pacific to the north of Hawaii. The average pH is now below 8.06. The seemingly small drop from pre-industrial levels is in fact 30% acidification.

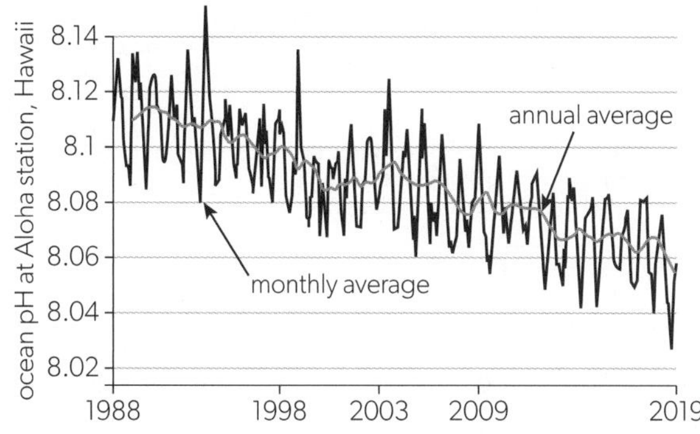

Marine animals (e.g. reef-building corals) that deposit calcium carbonate in their skeletons need to absorb carbonate ions from seawater. The concentration of these ions in seawater is low, because they are not very soluble. Dissolved carbon dioxide makes the carbonate concentration even lower as a result of two chemical reactions. Carbon dioxide reacts with water to form carbonic acid, which dissociates into hydrogen and hydrogencarbonate ions. Hydrogen ions react with dissolved carbonate ions, reducing their concentration.

$$CO_2 + H_2O \rightarrow H_2CO_3 \rightarrow H^+ + HCO_3^-$$
$$H^+ + CO_3^{2-} \rightarrow HCO_3^-$$

The conditions required for coral reef formation are described in *Section B4.1.5*. Reduced carbonate ion concentrations make it more difficult for reef-building corals to absorb carbonate and use it to calcify their skeletons. Also, if seawater ceases to be saturated with carbonate ions, calcium carbonate tends to dissolve, so existing skeletons of reef-building corals are eroded.

Hard corals live in a mutualistic association with photosynthetic algae called zooxanthellae (see *Section C4.1.12*). The algae benefit by being kept safe from organisms that would feed on them and close to the ocean surface where they can access the sunlight penetrating the water. The corals get the benefit of carbohydrates and oxygen produced by the algae. When the ocean water surrounding corals becomes too warm, the zooxanthellae are ejected leading to a loss of colour, hence the term "coral bleaching" which is happening more frequently due to global warming.

The concept of keystone species is described in *Section D4.2.5*. Coral species with calcium carbonate skeletons are collectively the keystones of the reef. Many other species depend on them and their loss due to ocean acidification and warming would cause the collapse of reef ecosystems globally.

8. Approaches to carbon sequestration

Carbon sequestration is capture and storage of carbon dioxide from the atmosphere. Two biological processes sequester carbon.

- Accumulation of biomass, produced in ecosystems by photosynthesis, especially the long-lasting wood of trees.
- Accumulation of undecomposed or partially decomposed organic matter, especially peat in wetlands.

There is an urgent need for carbon sequestration, to bring atmospheric carbon dioxide concentrations back down to levels that will avoid catastrophic changes for wildlife and humans. The biological approach is to enhance natural processes that sequester carbon:

1. **Afforestation** is planting trees in areas where they currently do not exist. This should only be done where forests are the natural ecosystems (shown on the map). There is ample opportunity for afforestation. For example, it is estimated that in the 8,000 years since the end of the last glaciation, the forests that grew in the upper Midwest of the US stored nearly a billion tonnes of carbon. This carbon was released into the atmosphere as forests were cleared, to extract timber and convert land to agriculture, over about 150 years. If such areas were reforested, large amounts of carbon could be sequestered.

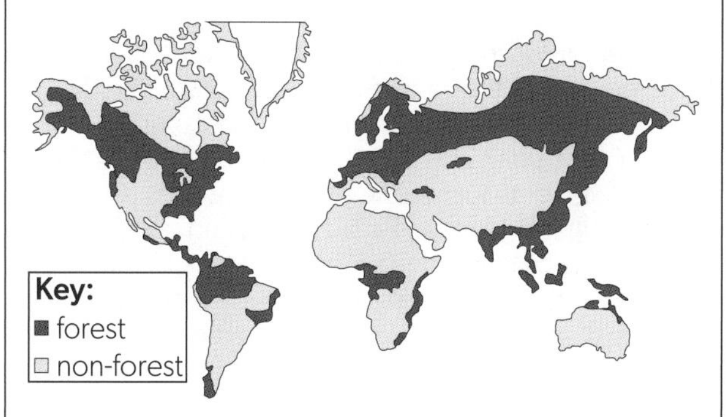

   There is active scientific debate over whether non-native or native species offer the best approach to carbon sequestration. Native species have evolved to be adapted to the conditions in an area so they should grow rapidly, but climate change may result in non-native species being better adapted than native species.

2. **Restoration of wetlands:** Peat is partially decayed organic matter that forms in waterlogged ecosystems in both temperate and boreal zones and also very rapidly in some tropical ecosystems. Peatlands are a huge carbon sink, but in many areas they have been drained to convert the land to plantation forestry or agriculture. After the soils have dried out, saprotrophs can decompose the peat and may also be lost through fire. It can be difficult to rewet former peatlands so that carbon sequestration restarts, but it can be done by blocking drains, restoring high water levels and re-establishing native species such as sphagnum moss.

AHL

9. Phenology

Living organisms are adapted to carry out stages in their life cycles at the most appropriate time of year. Photoperiod and temperature are used as cues by living organisms to determine when the appropriate time of year has arrived. There is much variation between species in how these cues are used.

Photoperiod is the length of daylight during a 24-hour period. Each year it follows the same cycle of change, with minimum and maximum daylength at the winter and summer solstices. Towards the poles there is greater variation in daylength through the year. Plants can measure the length of the night to an accuracy of five minutes and many species use it to time flowering. In most birds, the timing of migration and of egg-laying are determined mainly by daylength.

Temperature follows an annual cycle of warming and cooling in many parts of the world, though there is variation from year to year in how quickly temperatures rise in spring and drop in the fall. Warm temperatures in spring advance the dates of egg-laying in some bird species and bud-burst in many deciduous trees. Warm temperatures in the fall delay leaf abscission (leaf-drop) in many trees.

Phenology is studying the timing of seasonal events. Data obtained each year for as many years as possible can provide evidence of global warming and other climate changes. For example, the date of opening of the first bud on a tree in Geneva has been recorded each year since 1810 (see graph). It varies considerably from year to year but there is a clear trend for the date becoming earlier.

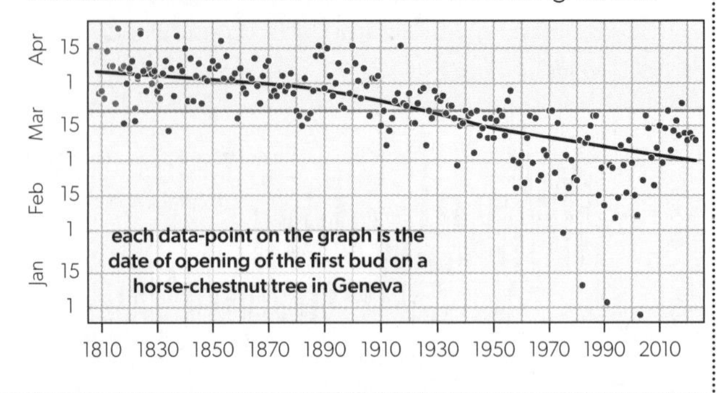

10. Climate change and phenology

Some events in life cycles are timed according to day length, which is not affected by climate change. Other events are timed according to temperature, so they are affected by global warming. Because of this, there is a mismatch between some events that were formerly synchronized.

Examples:

1. ***Rangifer tarandus*** is native to tundra ecosystems in the Arctic. They are known as caribou in North America and reindeer in Europe. Their spring migration coincides with the emergence and growth of food plants such as the Arctic mouse-ear (*Cerastium arcticum*). This allows females secreting milk for their calves to obtain enough food. Evidence suggests that climate change has led to a mismatch between plant growth and caribou migration patterns so caribou and reindeer are less able to meet their nutritional needs.

2 ***Parus major*** (great tit) feeds its young on caterpillars. The dates of egg-laying and peak caterpillar biomass have been studied for over 50 years in a population of *Parus major* in the Netherlands. Caterpillar biomass now peaks much earlier in spring. The mean date of egg-laying has also become earlier, but not by as much. The graph shows how many days earlier peak caterpillar availability is than egg-laying (positive values on the graph). In most but not all years natural selection is still favouring birds laying eggs earlier.

Visser, M.E. et al. (2021) 'Recent natural variability in global warming weakened phenological mismatch and selection on seasonal timing in great tits (parus major)', Proceedings of the Royal Society B: Biological Sciences, 288(1963). doi:10.1098/rspb.2021.1337.

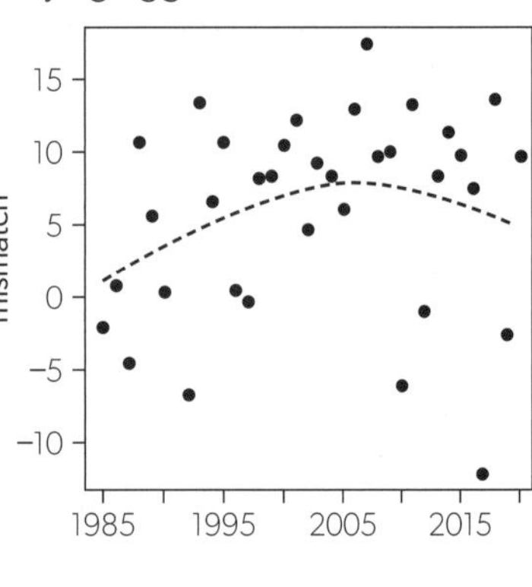

AHL

11. Climate change is increasing the number of insect life cycles

Insects vary in how long their life cycle takes. Some species complete several cycles per year. Others take one or more years for a single cycle. In some species the time taken per cycle has become shorter due to global warming. An example is the spruce bark beetle, *Dendroctonus rufipennis,* which is native to forests in North America. Its larvae feed on the inner bark of older and weaker spruce trees and also deadwood and stumps. It takes between one and three years to complete a life cycle, but warmer temperatures have reduced the average time, increasing the potential population growth rate. The health of older spruce trees has declined due to reduced rainfall and droughts, together with warmer temperatures, so more trees are succumbing to beetle attacks. As a result, there have been major outbreaks in Alaska and other areas of boreal forest with hundreds of millions of spruce trees killed.

12. Climate change is leading to evolution

Global warming and other climate changes on Earth are changing the adaptations that living organisms need to thrive. Many traits are now subject to directional selection (see *Section D4.1.12*). For example, *Strix aluco* (tawny owl) varies in colour, with its feathers ranging from brown to pale grey. This is a heritable trait. A single gene has a dominant allele for brown and a recessive allele for pale grey feathers. The pale grey variant is better-camouflaged against snow. Winters have become milder in Finland, reducing snow cover. Between 1985 and 2010, the percentage of brown owls in the Finnish population of tawny owls more than doubled.

End of topic questions — D4 Questions

D4.1 Natural selection

1. Trophy hunting of *Ovis canadensis* (bighorn sheep) on Ram Mountain, Alberta, was allowed from 1973 to 2011. Permits were only granted for shooting males with horns above a minimum size.

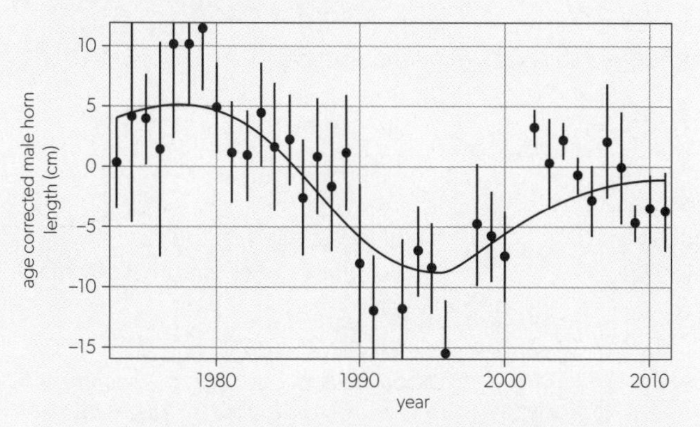

   a. Trophy hunting was intense between 1973 and 1995. Explain the effects on horn length. (5)

   b. Hunting decreased by 88% from 1995. Suggest reasons for the increase in horn size after 1995. (3)

   c. Outline what conclusions can be drawn from the error bars on the graph. (2)

2. a. Distinguish between density-dependent and density-independent factors. (3)

   b. Suggest one example of selection pressure due to each type of factor. (2)

3. (HL only) Explain how the Hardy–Weinberg equation is used to test for genetic equilibrium. (5)

D4.2 Stability and change

1. The graph shows the concentrations of methyl mercury in feathers from museum specimens of the black-footed albatross (*Phoebastria nigripes*).

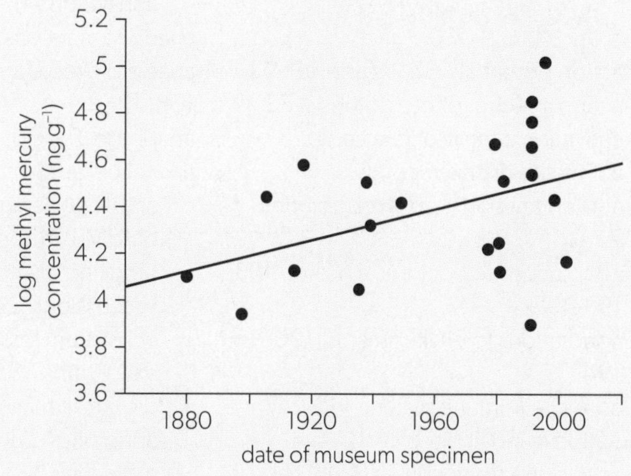

   a. Explain how methyl mercury can be more concentrated in the feathers than in the seawater. (4)

   b. i. Outline the trend shown in the graph. (2)

      ii. Suggest reasons for the trend. (2)

   c. Outline one other threat to albatross populations due to the pollution of oceans. (2)

2. Outline how ecosystems can be destabilized by:

   a. removal of keystone species (5)

   b. eutrophication. (5)

3. Describe one example of how rewilding of an area has been carried out and its benefits. (5)

D3.3 Climate change

1. The graph shows NASA estimates of global mean temperature, compared with the mean for 1951–80, based on records from meteorological stations and satellite monitoring.

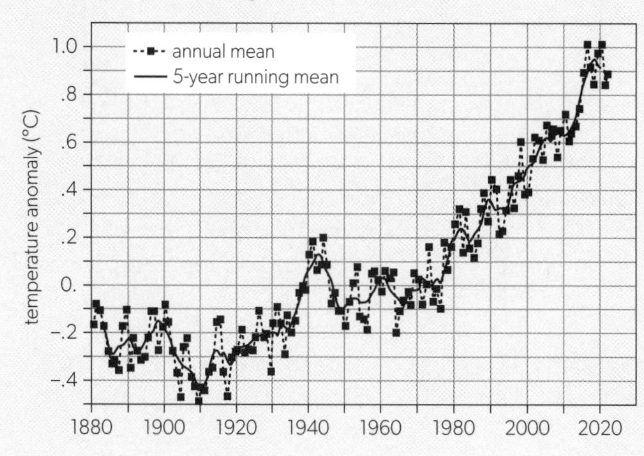

   a. Suggest reasons for fluctuations from year to year. (2)

   b. Discuss the long-term trends shown in the graph. (3)

   c. List the anthropogenic causes of global warming. (3)

   d. Discuss where there is evidence of tipping points having been reached by 2020. (2)

2. Describe the changes that rising temperatures will cause:

   a. in the oceans (5)

   b. on land. (5)

3. Explain what you can do to help prevent climate change. (10)

Index